GREAT IS THE LORD

GREAT IS THE LORD

Theology for the Praise of God

Ron Highfield

WILLIAM B. EERDMANS PUBLISHING COMPANY

GRAND RAPIDS, MICHIGAN / CAMBRIDGE, U.K.

Published 2008 by
Wm. B. Eerdmans Publishing Co.
2140 Oak Industrial Drive N.E., Grand Rapids, Michigan 49505 /
P.O. Box 163, Cambridge CB3 9PU U.K.
www.eerdmans.com

Library of Congress Cataloging-in-Publication Data

Highfield, Ron, 1951-
Great is the Lord: theology for the praise of God / Ron
Highfield.
p.   cm.
Includes bibliographical references.
ISBN 978-0-8028-3300-6 (pbk.: alk. paper)
1. Praise of God.   2. Theology, Doctrinal.   I. Title.

BV4817.H54   2008
230 — dc22

2008010808

In gratitude to all my teachers,
especially my first teachers:

Thornton Curtis Highfield (1915-1968)

Beulah Josephine Highfield (1926-2003)

Contents

Contents

PART II: THE DIVINE ATTRIBUTES

PART III: ETHICS

Preface

Every book begins with an introduction; every good book begins with passion and pain. Whether this book is good is for you to judge. But I'd like you to know from the start that the passion at the heart of this book is for knowing God. The pain is about the widespread indifference toward this passion. Some things make little difference, while others tower in importance. God matters supremely. For God is the beginning and end, the support and guide for all things. Whatever our successes or failures otherwise, God is the "the one thing" we must have, the "pearl of great price" worth everything. To have this "one thing" frees us to give up everything else without genuine loss. Augustine's words express the conviction animating this book: "'Happy is the person who loves you' (Tobit 13:18) and his friend in you, and his enemy because of you (Matt. 5:44). Though left alone, he loses none dear to him; for all are dear in the one who cannot be lost."[1]

From the oceanside slopes of the Santa Monica Mountains on the campus of Pepperdine University, I look over the moonlit bay to the giant city of Los Angeles and feel a stab of pain. The word "God" finds a place, in some language, in the vocabulary of every resident of that city of nations. But do they know what it really means? I fear that many do not. If they did, every street corner would echo with thanksgiving and every courtyard would ring with praise. I feel that same stab, if to a lesser extent, when I enter my general studies classes the first day of a given semester. I see beautiful, intelligent, and privileged young people, and I love them. In that poignant moment I feel the weight of my responsibility: How can I help them see why their joy must come from loving above all things "the one who cannot be lost"?

---

1. Augustine, *Confessions*, trans. Henry Chadwick (New York: Oxford, 1991), p. 61.

Then there is the annoyance. Passion and pain resonate with nobility and romance, and that's why I began with them. But I have to admit that I am a little frustrated by some theology written today. First of all, one would think that the subject of most theology books would be God. But that's not quite true. Every year, as I look for textbooks about God or Christ or the Spirit, I find many good books about books about God, that is, books on method or politics or humanity. But I find few that keep the reader focused on God. Second, many theology books adopt an "academic" style — cold, analytical, and objective — that projects a mood foreign to the divine subject. Sometimes this academic style even degenerates into the skeptical or dark or cynically playful. (There comes that stab of pain again.)

The great Franciscan theologian Bonaventure (1217-1274) warned that the deadliest enemies of theology are the pride and curiosity of theologians. The purpose of theology, he urged, is to "become virtuous and attain salvation." Theologians, he cautioned, should not fool themselves into thinking that "reading is sufficient without unction, speculation without devotion, investigation without wonder, observation without rejoicing, work without piety, knowledge without love, understanding without humility or endeavor without divine grace."[2] The academic style that is dominant today leaves little room for a Bonaventure-style theology. And it is not easy to swim against this current. Geoffrey Wainwright laments that "to mention the praise of God as the theologian's motivation runs the risk of provoking dissent from colleagues anxious for academic neutrality."[3] Wainwright, I am sure, speaks from experience; nonetheless, I believe writing a theology that praises God is worth the risk of such "dissent."

The Aim

The aims of this book are educational, apologetic, and religious. I designed it to introduce students, teachers, ministers, and others to the "traditional" doctrine of God, its past and current defenders, and its contemporary critics. I endeavor to set out Christian teaching about God from Scripture, tradition, and widely esteemed theologians in a way that corrects common misunderstandings and superficial criticisms. I address especially the charge that the traditional doctrine views God as uncaring, uninvolved, and threatening to human freedom. I engage

2. Bonaventure, *Itinerarium mentis in Deum,* quoted in Michael Robson, "Saint Bonaventure," in *The Medieval Theologians,* ed. G. R. Evans (Malden, MA: Blackwell, 2001), pp. 190-92.

3. Wainwright, "The Praise of God in the Theological Reflection of the Church," *Interpretation* 39 (1985): 42.

certain contemporary critics in debate, namely, representatives of process theology and open theism. These schools of thought argue that unless God is temporal, suffering, changeable, and limited in power and knowledge, he cannot be loving and responsive — and we cannot be free. I have tried to be fair, to refrain from caricature and overheated rhetoric, and to learn from those with whom I disagree. This book also aims at a religious goal. I reject the rigid dichotomies that rule the contemporary theological landscape: the dichotomies between theology and spirituality, between the academic and the religious, and between doctrine and ethics. Here I will challenge those separations. My hope is that this book, while holding to the highest intellectual principles, will facilitate the seeking, the following, and the praising of God. God is inherently praiseworthy, and no work about God that neglects this fact is worthy of the name "theology."

The Argument

I think it will help the reader better evaluate this book if I point, ahead of time, to where I think the crux of my argument lies. In each section I document the "traditional" doctrine of God from Scripture and tradition. I do not offer the Scripture section as *proof* that Scripture teaches the traditional doctrine. At a minimum, I wish to show that the traditional doctrine can plausibly be argued from Scripture. However, I think that a case can be made that the traditional view finds much more support in Scripture than do the main alternatives. Concerning my use of tradition, again my claims are modest: I am not arguing that the traditional doctrine is true because tradition teaches it; rather, I am attempting to show that the position I am defending at least approximates the long-term and widely held teaching of the church. The heart of the argument comes in the theology subsections. There I argue not only that the traditional doctrine is not guilty of making God uncaring, aloof, and threatening to human freedom, but that it actually preserves our confidence in God's love, intimate presence, and liberating action better than its opponents do. Far from effacing our humanity, the traditional doctrine grounds our dignity and freedom in the center of reality, the Trinitarian life of God. Here is the heart and soul and passion and pain of the book. Whether in praise or blame, make your judgment here.

The "Traditional" Doctrine of God

I have already indicated that I shall defend the "traditional" doctrine of God. Perhaps, then, I should explain briefly what I mean by this term. I mean by it the teachings about God that were held by almost the whole church from the second to the twentieth century, those teachings that are still held by most believers: God is triune, loving, merciful, gracious, patient, wise, one, simple, omnipotent, omniscient, eternal, omnipresent, immutable, impassible, and glorious. The church understood these characteristics as scriptural teachings, not as philosophical theories. They were explained and defended by such fourth-century theologian/bishops as Athanasius, Basil the Great, Gregory of Nyssa, and Gregory of Nazianzus. They were enshrined in the ecumenical creeds and the denominational confessions of faith. These teachings were explained and defended by Augustine of Hippo, who became the theologian to the Western world. They were summarized by the Eastern theologian John of Damascus (c. 675–c. 749) in his *Orthodox Faith*. During the Middle Ages, such theologians as Anselm of Canterbury, Thomas Aquinas, Duns Scotus, and Bonaventure wrote treatises expounding and defending the traditional divine attributes. These teachings were held by the Protestant Reformers and their descendants in almost all Protestant churches. And they were cherished by Alexander Campbell, the leading light of my own tradition, the Stone-Campbell Movement.

This doctrine of God went almost unchallenged within the church until the eighteenth century, and then it was challenged by only a few writers on the periphery. Only in the twentieth century did it come under widespread criticism. Today, even among many evangelical and otherwise conservative writers, rehearsing the shortcomings of the "traditional" or "classical" teachings has become a standard way to introduce one's own (presumably better) doctrine of God. Unfortunately, many of these writers show little real knowledge of the traditional doctrine and offer such a caricature of that teaching that the reader has to wonder how the church's most saintly and brilliant teachers could have been so deceived for so long. I have written this book to correct this caricature and show why the traditional doctrine of God dominated the church's thinking for so long. My answer is intimated in the title of this book: *Great Is the Lord: Theology for the Praise of God*. I believe the traditional doctrine of God focuses our attention on the unsurpassable greatness of God and urges us to praise him according to his infinite worth. I am overjoyed to add my little "Amen" to the great chorus of angels, psalmists, apostles, saints, martyrs, doctors, and teachers who have said to us through the ages: "Great is the Lord and most worthy of praise!"

In Appreciation

I would like to express my appreciation to everyone who helped me complete this work. My thanks go to Pepperdine University, which granted me a sabbatical leave in the spring semester of 2003, two release-time grants, and two summer research grants. These gifts of time and money enabled me to bring this book to press sooner than I could otherwise have done. I am grateful for the encouragement and support I received from the chair of my division, Randall Chesnutt, from all my colleagues in the Religion Division, and from Assistant Dean for Research Lee Kats, Seaver College Dean David Baird, and University Provost Darryl Tippens. I want to thank my students who listened to this material in lectures or read the manuscript in its earlier forms and gave invaluable feedback. I owe a special debt of gratitude to Richard Hughes, whose encouragement at a decisive point made all the difference. Finally, I want to thank my family, who put up with my "obsession" with this project for four years.

Abbreviations

ANF	*Ante-Nicene Fathers*
CD	Karl Barth, *Church Dogmatics*
NPNF	*Nicene and Post-Nicene Fathers,* Series 1 and 2
PRRD	Richard A. Muller, *Post-Reformation Reformed Dogmatics*
SCG	Thomas Aquinas, *Summa Contra Gentiles*
SumTh	Thomas Aquinas, *Summa Theologica*
TPRL	Robert D. Preus, *The Theology of Post-Reformation Lutheranism*

· I ·

KNOWING GOD

The Word Is Near You: Revelation,
Scripture, and Tradition

Revelation

Tradition calls him "the theologian." Gregory Nazianzus (c. A.D. 330-390) earned this title with his single-minded passion for knowing God. In the Chapel of the Resurrection in Constantinople, somewhere around A.D. 378, Gregory preached his most famous series of sermons. The introductory oration signaled the mood of what would follow: "It is more important that we should remember God than that we should breathe: indeed, if one may say so, we should do nothing else besides."[1] I have written this book in the belief that Gregory's affirmation sets the right tone for the study of God. We can aim no higher than to know God, who is the source and substance of every good we can hope to enjoy. God is worthy of our mind's passion, our heart's devotion, and our body's strength. To know God is life itself.

Paradoxically, however, God's surpassing greatness, which makes it so important to know him, also stands as the greatest barrier to achieving this goal. If we had to rely on our own powers, our quest for God would be futile. We cannot lay hold of God. But God can lay hold of us and enable us to know him. The doctrine of God thus begins on a joyous note: God wills to be known by us. He has revealed himself and promises to show himself again and again to those who seek him. Therefore, in this first section I take up the theme of revelation. Standing securely on the foundation of faith, I shall ask about the divine ground, means, nature, and goal of our knowledge of God.

---

1. Gregory Nazianzus, *Oration 27,* 4, in *On God and Christ: The Five Theological Orations and Two Letters to Cledonius,* trans. Frederick Williams and Lionel Wickham (Crestwood, NY: St. Vladimir's, 2002), pp. 27-28.

3

Can We Know God?

We worship God and pray to him. We read Scripture and hear the gospel proclaimed. We are baptized into the name of the Father, Son, and Holy Spirit, and we eat at the table of the Lord. We celebrate the resurrection of Christ. We confess our sins and rejoice in God's forgiveness. We invoke the Holy Spirit to come, assure us of our salvation, and transform us into the image of the Son of God.

These churchly activities presuppose that we know God. Apart from such faith, they are meaningless. Our study of God will also be pointless unless we know something of God. Hence, I will not approach the study of God as if our faith were doubtful and in need of verification. Rather, I will set out from faith and seek to understand the means by which the church knows God.

What about God's nature makes God knowable? One might think that this question is too esoteric to be practical, but history has produced many philosophers and theologians who argue that thinking of God as knowing and knowable ascribes imperfections to him. Plotinus (A.D. 204-270), the most famous advocate of the philosophy known as Neo-Platonism, taught that we can attain an adequate concept of the divine only by negating all imperfect qualities of beings. The perfect reality must be free of all change and composition, since such attributes are signs of imperfection. Accordingly, Plotinus named the divine reality "One." The One cannot know anything because all thinking and knowing assumes a distinction between the thinking subject and the object of thought and thus indicates composition. Therefore, thought is a sign of imperfection and incompleteness. Plotinus criticizes Aristotle because he understands the highest divine principle as self-thinking thought. Plotinus puts the "Intellectual-Principle" second on the ladder of being. It is deficient because "it needs an object" in order to be itself. Moreover, since the One is beyond thought and thinking, we cannot know what it *is;* we can only know what it is not.[2]

In contrast to Plotinus's book *The Enneads,* the Bible overflows with references to God's knowing, thinking, seeing, and hearing. God "looks down from heaven on the sons of men" (Ps. 53:2) and hears the groans of the oppressed (Exod. 3:7). God created the organs of human perception, and thus it makes sense that he perceives everything they tell us and more: "Does he who implanted the ear not hear? Does he who formed the eye not see?" (Ps. 94:9).

---

2. Plotinus, *The Enneads,* 5.1.9 and 5.4.2 (trans. Stephen Mackenna, abr. John Dillon [London: Penguin Books, 1991], pp. 358 and 389). For further study on "the One" in Plotinus, see Lloyd P. Gerson, ed., *The Cambridge Companion to Plotinus* (New York: Cambridge University Press, 1996), pp. 38-65.

Even apart from the world and "before" creation, God knows himself. In the creation narrative, God speaks before creation exists: "Let there be light, and there was light" (Gen. 1:3). According to 1 Peter, Christ was "foreordained before the foundation of the world" (1 Pet. 1:20). God thought about us before creation, for "he chose us in him before the creation of the world" (Eph. 1:4). Foreordination and choosing are acts of deliberation. And to anticipate the doctrine of the Trinity, Jesus prayed to the Father, who loved his Son "before the foundation of the world" (John 17:24).

Karl Barth discusses this issue under the heading "the readiness of God."[3] He contends that God is knowable because he knows himself perfectly and is willing and able to make himself known to us. Barth stands in the tradition of the post-Reformation Reformed and Lutheran theologians — and the medieval theologians before them — who argue that our confidence that we know God presupposes that God knows himself completely from all eternity. Traditional theologians designate God's primal self-knowledge as "archetypical" theology, whereas they describe *our* knowledge of God as "ectypical" theology. Archetypical theology, according to the Reformed theologian Amandus Polanus (1561-1610), is "the wisdom of divine things that is resident in God, essential to him and uncreated."[4] Put another way by the Lutheran John Gerhard (1582-1637), it is "the theology according to which God knows Himself in Himself and also knows everything that is outside Him by an indivisible and immutable act of knowing."[5] Ectypical theology, on the other hand, according to Franciscus Junius (1545-1602), is the "wisdom of divine things given conceptual form by God, on the basis of the archetypical image of himself through the communication of Grace for his own glory."[6] Our imperfect theology is possible only on the supposition of God's perfect theology, his willingness to be known by us, and his ability to make himself known. Therefore, the existence of Christian theology presupposes God's self-knowledge and his good will toward us.

How shall we understand the possibility of God's self-knowledge? Shall we think of it as analogous to human self-knowledge, which presupposes the existence of objects distinct from our minds? Or shall we follow Plotinus in placing

---

3. *Church Dogmatics*, vol. 2, part 1, eds. G. W. Bromiley and T. F. Torrance, trans. T. H. L. Parker et al. (Edinburgh: T&T Clark, 1957), pp. 65-128 (hereafter *CD*).

4. Polanus, *Syntagma*, 2.3, quoted in Richard A. Muller, *Post-Reformation Reformed Dogmatics: The Rise and Development of Reformed Orthodoxy*, vol. 1, *Prolegomena to Theology* (Grand Rapids: Baker Academic, 2003), p. 231 (hereafter *PRRD*).

5. Quoted in Robert D. Preus, *The Theology of Post-Reformation Lutheranism*, vol. 1, *A Study of Theological Prolegomena* (St. Louis: Concordia Publishing House, 1970), p. 113 (hereafter *TPRL*).

6. Junius, *De vera theologia*, 5 (quoted in Muller, *PRRD*, 1, p. 235).

the divine being above thought? We can hope that these are not the only alternatives. For how could we worship a God who needs the world in order to be self-conscious, and why would we pray to a God who cannot hear our prayers? Christian theology finds the answer to this problem in the doctrine of the Trinity. Karl Barth says: "We know God in consequence of God knowing himself — the Father knowing the Son and the Son the Father by the Holy Spirit of the Father and the Son. Because He is first and foremost knowable in Himself as the triune God, He is knowable to us as well."[7] From all eternity, the Father knows the Son in the Spirit; and through the Spirit the Father knows himself in the Son, and the Son knows himself in the Father. God is never without thought and life, for the Father is never without the Word and the Spirit (John 1:1). Nor is God a human-like consciousness that depends on the objects of the world for its ability to know itself. God lives eternally as a perfect communion of loving persons — Father, Son, and Spirit.

Unlike the absolute "One" of Plotinus, the three-in-one God knows himself fully, and consequently he can know the world and make himself known to others. According to Scripture, not only is God able to reveal himself; he is eager to be known by us. Just as the Father loves the Son and reveals himself to him, God loves the world and reveals himself to the world through the Word and the Spirit. The church knows God at God's initiative, and in that knowledge finds that God is able and ready to reveal himself.

I shall return to the doctrine of the Trinity for a fuller treatment below; but I must observe here that God's self-knowledge is personal. Though we must use abstractions, concepts, and negations to speak of God, these are not the reality of God. God is Father, Son, and Holy Spirit. To know God is to know the Father through the Son in the power of the Spirit.

What Is Revelation?

Revelation as Showing

In the Bible, to "reveal" means to uncover something hidden. The book of Revelation contains a series of revelations of "what must soon take place" (Rev. 1:1). A revelation is a prevision of future divine actions: "The glory of the Lord will be revealed and all flesh shall see it together" (Isa. 40:5). Only the visionary sees the events, and he sees them only spiritually. Typical are the visions of Daniel (Dan. 10) and the revelations of Paul, which he describes in 2 Corinthians 12.

---

7. *CD*, 2/1, p. 66.

For the prophet and his hearers, those events exist only as previsions. However, these private revelations anticipate revelation in another sense: God's future enactment of these events in a way that will uncover his character, judgment, and power for all to see.

The concept of revelation is most often associated with sight as a way of knowing: that is, revealing is showing. At least in the Western world, sight is the dominant metaphor for knowing. We want *light* shed on the matter; then we become *enlightened,* and we *see* the connection. Receiving a revelation involves seeing something previously hidden. But we create problems for the study of God when we confine the concept of revelation to the visual sense. Wolfhart Pannenberg restricts revelation in history to public, historical events that are subject to historical-critical investigation. Private visions, inspired communications, and the proclamation of these to others do not count as revelation in the strict sense. They have only provisional character and must await verification in public historical events and ultimately in the eschatological consummation of all things.[8] Pannenberg criticizes Karl Barth and other "dialectical" theologians, who view revelation as God's speech or the Word of God. In contrast, Pannenberg subordinates the "word" of God to God's indirect manifestation in "historical action," which will be complete only "at the end of history."[9] Responding to Pannenberg, I do not deny that our knowledge of God is incomplete and provisional in this life (cf. 1 Cor. 13:9-12); but his rationalizing approach jeopardizes faith's certainty and projects a mood different from the confident and joyful way we speak about God in the church.

Revelation as Hearing

Not all knowing is seeing. We also know by touching, and the sense of touch can become a metaphor for knowing in general: we "grasp" a concept; we "feel" something; we "take hold" of an idea. In Scripture, however, the most important way of knowing God is hearing. However much the visionary may see, it is through words that the prophet understands and communicates this knowledge to others. Signs and wonders, such as God's deliverance of the Israelites from Egypt, the giving of the law, his judgments on Israel and Judah, and the cross and resurrection of Jesus occur in a linguistic context that makes their meaning clear. Who God is, what God is like, and what God wills become clear

8. Pannenberg, *Systematic Theology,* vol. 1, trans. Geoffrey W. Bromiley (Grand Rapids: Eerdmans, 1991), pp. 189-257. In this long chapter on revelation, the older Pannenberg defends the theses on revelation that he and his young colleagues advanced in 1961 in their *Revelation as History,* ed. Wolfhart Pannenberg, trans. David Granskou (London: Macmillan, 1968).

9. Pannenberg, *Systematic Theology,* 1, p. 257.

in these events only through the word. In a sense, then, these visible events *are* words.

Faith is knowledge awakened by the word. According to Paul, "faith comes by hearing the message, and the message is heard through the word of Christ" (Rom. 10:17). In another place, Paul contrasts faith with sight: sight is an eschatological way of knowing God, but faith is the present mode (2 Cor. 5:7). We can believe firmly even though we "see darkly" (1 Cor. 13:12). The First Epistle of John brings all these ways of knowing together in a striking way:

> That which was from the beginning, which we have heard, which we have seen with our eyes, which we have looked at and our hands have touched — this we proclaim concerning the Word of life. The life appeared; we have seen it and testify to it, and we proclaim to you the eternal life, which was with the Father and has appeared to us. We proclaim to you what we have seen and heard, so that you also may have fellowship with us. And our fellowship is with the Father and with his Son, Jesus Christ (1 John 1:1-4).

In the incarnation, the Word of life became flesh, visible, and touchable. The apostolic witnesses experienced him firsthand and now tell us what they saw and touched and heard. Their words create "fellowship" between them and us, a relationship that is at the same time "fellowship with the Father and his Son." Sight, touch, and hearing serve personal knowing: the giving, receiving, and sharing that Scripture calls fellowship. The Christian doctrine of revelation, I conclude, is rooted in the fellowship of the triune persons. The Father reveals himself to the world through his Word (the Son) in the power of the Spirit. The prologue to the Gospel of John declares: "The Word became flesh and made his dwelling among us. We have seen his glory, the glory of the One and Only, who came from the Father, full of grace and truth. . . . No one has ever seen God, but God the One and Only, who is at the Father's side, has made him known" (John 1:14, 18). God's acts of creation, revelation, and salvation are often called the administration or economy (Greek: *oikonomía* [Eph 3:9]), that is, the ordered activity of God in ushering the world to its goal. It becomes clear in the New Testament that the economic activity of God always takes a Trinitarian form. God creates and sustains the world through the Word (John 1:10; Col. 1:17; Heb. 1:2, 3). Through the incarnate Word, God saves sinners and reconciles the world to himself (Rom. 3:25; 5:17, 19; 2 Cor. 5:18). In the power of the Spirit, God raised Jesus, and he "will give life to your mortal bodies through his Spirit, who lives in you" (Rom. 8:11). It is through Christ that we may offer praise to God (1 Pet. 4:11; 2 Cor. 1:20). These texts are only a few of hundreds one could cite in support of the economic Trinity. I will examine some of them in the chapter on the Trinity.

Revelation as a Trinitarian Event

Early in the twentieth century, Karl Barth retrieved the doctrine of the Trinity from the obscurity into which it had fallen in Protestant theology. Rather than appealing to an analogy with something in nature, as Augustine had appealed to a threefold structure of the human mind, Barth derived his doctrine of the Trinity from the pattern of revelation. Since God has in fact revealed himself in Christ and through the Spirit, we can reflect on its possibility. Barth's examination shows that the idea of revelation requires three components: something revealed, a revealer, and the revealedness. In other words, revelation must have an objective content, a means by which this content is communicated, and a principle by which it is appropriated. However, unless the revealer (the Son) and the revealedness (the Spirit) are also of the same nature as the revealed (the Father), true self-revelation cannot occur. Therefore, the doctrine of the Trinity is established: one nature, three persons or "modes of being."[10]

By linking the doctrine of revelation to the doctrine of the Trinity, Barth illuminates both doctrines and highlights the Trinitarian character of all Christian theology. The *reality* of the triune God is disclosed in revelation, and the *possibility* of revelation is grounded in the triune life and economic activity of God. Only by developing our understanding of revelation in the light of the inner Trinitarian knowing among Father, Son, and Spirit can we understand why the goal of revelation is and must be establishing personal "fellowship" with "the Father and with his Son, Jesus Christ" (1 John 1:4). Revelation is not essentially a matter of revealing the will of God in laws or of anticipating future events in prophecy. A Trinitarian understanding treats revelation as the event that draws us into the eternal "fellowship" among Father, Son, and Spirit. The Father through the Son in the power of the Spirit invites us to join the eternal movement of divine love. Through the Son we know the Father and love him with the love placed in our hearts by his Spirit (Rom. 5:5; John 17:3, 25, 26).

A Trinitarian understanding of revelation also helps us understand why the biblical theme of revelation centers on the word, hearing, and faith rather than on vision, seeing, and reason. Looking on a body does not reveal the person; nor can we know persons adequately by thinking such concepts as humanity, deity, and oneness. Rather, we know persons through their words and symbolic actions. Only in honest conversation, symbolic gestures, and shared experiences can two persons come to know each other. The word is the medium of personal knowledge and fellowship. The prophetic and apostolic word proclaimed to us in the church is a fully adequate means for the triune God to es-

10. Barth, *CD*, 1/1, pp. 304-33, prefers to call the persons "modes of being."

tablish the fellowship with us he desires. Understandably, we long to *see* and *feel* the personal reality we know through the word of revelation. That longing will be fully satisfied in the resurrection to eternal life when we shall see "face to face" (1 Cor. 13:12). In the meantime, it finds expression in preaching, worship, theology, and Christian living. Theology is the activity of faith longing and endeavoring to understand itself, to see its truth. The disciplines of Christian living are ways that we practice listening to and obeying the indwelling Spirit's prompting.

Revelation as Feeling?

Before leaving the concept of revelation, I must deal with an important contemporary issue, which will occasion a final distinction. The liberal tradition of theology, which began with Friedrich Schleiermacher (1768-1834), reacted against the dogmatism of traditional Protestant theology and the rationalism of the Enlightenment. Liberal theology draws on the resources of the Romantic movement, which rejected the rationalist goal of comprehending reality in thought. Reality is not a "concept," the Romantics rhapsodized, but a bubbling, chaotic caldron of nature's vital forces. One cannot think it; to know it, one must feel it and join its reverie. Applying this perspective to theology, Schleiermacher and his liberal heirs considered revelation the experience of a mysterious Reality. Though only a few people experience it intensely (most notably, Jesus), while others hardly notice it, this experience is universal and intrinsic to our humanity. Revelation, then, is not a cognitive experience and does not touch us first in conceptual form. We contact it in feeling. When Schleiermacher says "feeling," he does not mean feeling *something;* he means feeling *itself.* Revelation enters language only on the human side, through our powers of cognition. Revelation itself supplies no cognitive norms for determining the adequacy of the words in which it is expressed. The measure of its success is whether or not it preserves and enhances the original feeling. Theology is, in effect, religious poetry: it allows for no orthodoxy or heresy, no true or false religion.

Schleiermacher saw little value in the doctrine of the Trinity, which he placed in the back of his systematic theology, *The Christian Faith.*[11] He could

---

11. See Schleiermacher, *The Christian Faith,* trans. D. M. Baillie et al., ed. H. R. Mackintosh and J. S. Stewart (Philadelphia: Fortress Press, 1976). For a more positive reading of Schleiermacher's view of the Trinity, see Stanley Grenz, *Rediscovering the Triune God: The Trinity in Contemporary Theology* (Minneapolis: Fortress Press, 2004), pp. 21-22.

find nothing in Christian experience that called for the doctrine of the Trinity. The Trinity, he explains, "is not an immediate utterance concerning the Christian self-consciousness, but only a combination of several such utterances" (p. 738). Indeed, Schleiermacher denied that we know anything about God in himself. In revelation we neither see nor hear God; we *feel* our "absolute dependence" on something we name God. The word "God" means "the *Whence* of our receptive and active existence, as implied in this self-consciousness" (p. 16). The Christian church has articulated a web of language about God, but the words that the church speaks are human words, not God's Word. We can know God only in his effects on us, felt in our feelings; theology is the study of these effects. According to Schleiermacher's much-quoted definition, "Christian doctrines are accounts of Christian religious affections set forth in speech" (p. 76).

In contrast to the liberal tradition and in agreement with theologians such as Karl Barth and Thomas Torrance, I am arguing that the doctrine of the Trinity *determines* the concept of revelation. God speaks his Word eternally, and that Word became flesh without ceasing to be the eternal Word. Faith is not blind feeling, and theology is not poetry. God's eternal Word crosses over to the human side and takes form as words that, through the Spirit's power, make themselves heard and create faith in the hearer. Torrance maps out the course for us concisely when he says, in praise of the Trinitarian faith clarified by the Council of Nicea:

> It represents the radical shift in people's understanding in the Church as they were grasped by the enlightening reality of the living God and were freed from imprisonment in the darkness of their own prejudices, baseless conjectures and fantasies, that is, a shift away from a centre of thinking in the in-turned human reason . . . alienated from its intelligible ground in God, to a centre in God's revealing and reconciling activity in the incarnation of his Mind and Word *(logos)* in Jesus Christ within the temporal and spatial structures of our creaturely world.[12]

Natural Revelation

Does God reveal himself in nature as well as in Scripture? Thomas Aquinas (c. 1225-74) argued that the existence of God and certain divine attributes can be established by reason. We can reason from the world as the effect to God as

---

12. Torrance, *The Trinitarian Faith: The Evangelical Theology of the Ancient Catholic Church* (Edinburgh: T&T Clark, 1988), p. 19.

its cause.[13] After the Reformation, Lutheran and Reformed theologians distinguished between general revelation and special revelation. God gives general revelation in the natural structures and activities of the world. He gives special revelation to restricted audiences at certain times. God reveals himself in three ways, says Wolfgang Musculus (1497-1563): "The first and most general is that which arises from his works. The second is more special, declared by his own speech. The third is most special of all, which is his secret inspiration."[14] Stephen Charnock (1628-1680) explains: "The creatures tell us that there is a God, and Christ tells us who and what that God is."[15] The Westminster Confession of Faith (1646) refers to natural revelation somewhat cautiously: "Although the light of nature, and the works of creation and providence, do so far manifest the goodness, wisdom, and power of God, as to leave men inexcusable; yet they are not sufficient to give that knowledge of God, and of his will, which is necessary unto Salvation" (1.1).[16] In the dogmatic decrees of the First Vatican Council (1870), however, the Roman Catholic Church declares confidently that "[t]he same Holy Mother Church holds and teaches that God, the beginning and end of all things, may be certainly known by the natural light of human reason by means of created things."[17] Roman Catholic and Protestant theology agree that natural revelation cannot provide knowledge of God adequate for salvation.[18]

According to the Romanian Orthodox theologian Dumitru Staniloae, Orthodox theology recognizes natural revelation, but "makes no separation between natural and supernatural revelation."[19] Yet, because of sin, "only through supernatural revelation do we fully know what nature, and the revelation it represents, are. Natural revelation appears to us in its full meaning only through supernatural revelation."[20]

13. Aquinas, *Summa Theologica*, 1.2.1-3, in *Basic Writings of Saint Thomas Aquinas*, vol. 1, ed. Anton C. Pegis (New York: Random House, 1945), pp. 18-24 (hereafter *SumTh*).

14. Musculus, *Loci communes*, 1, quoted in Muller, *PRRD*, 1, p. 292.

15. Charnock, *Discourse of the knowledge of God in Christ*, quoted in Muller, *PRRD*, 1, p. 296.

16. Philip Schaff, ed. *The Creeds of Christendom*, vol. 3, rev. David S. Schaff (1931; reprint, Grand Rapids: Baker Book House, 1990), p. 600.

17. Schaff, *Creeds of Christendom*, 2, p. 240.

18. Muller, *PRRD*, 1, pp. 270-310; Preus, *TPRL*, 1, p. 178.

19. Staniloae, *The Experience of God*, vol. 1, *Revelation and Knowledge of the Triune God*, trans. and ed. Ioan Ionita and Robert Barringer (Brookline, MA: Holy Cross Orthodox Press, 1994), p. 1.

20. Staniloae, *Experience of God*, 1, p. 16.

Natural Theology and Deism

Christian theology should proceed with greater caution on this issue today than it did before the modern era. In the early seventeenth century, some theologians began to catalog lists of truths that could be known about God from natural revelation.[21] In the late seventeenth and early eighteenth centuries, rationalists used the church's belief in natural revelation to justify an independent natural theology. Amid the political strife that followed the division of the European church into Protestants and Roman Catholics, politically minded thinkers began searching for a rational basis for political life to replace Christendom. All rational individuals, they asserted, can know most important truths about God and morality from reason alone, that is, apart from Scripture and tradition, and these truths constitute clear, certain, and adequate foundations for political life. Thus these thinkers secularized European political life and safely isolated theology. The church and its theologians could continue their interminable controversies about words and interpretations, they said in effect. Just keep it out of politics![22]

Some thinkers were not content with constructing a merely rational foundation for politics. They asserted not only independent validity for natural theology but also its superiority to the church's Scripture-based theology. In opposition to the church, these deists (as they are called) championed a religion of nature, which expresses itself in a life based on belief in God, the moral law, and an afterlife in which good is rewarded and evil punished. The liberal religion and theology of the nineteenth century internalized the basic principle of natural theology by accepting its assumption of the autonomy of reason. Refusing submission to Scripture, liberal theology forced Scripture into harmony with the autonomous activity of human reason and experience, which function as ultimate norms.

For these reasons Karl Barth attacked natural theology in all its forms. He rejected the natural theology of Protestant orthodoxy as well as that of Thomas Aquinas and the First Vatican Council. Even the natural theology of an otherwise orthodox theologian, according to Barth, undermines our reliance on

21. See Otto Weber, *Foundations of Dogmatics*, vol. 1, trans. Darrell L. Guder (Grand Rapids: Eerdmans, 1981), p. 200. Richard Muller, *PRRD*, 1, pp. 270-310, argues persuasively against Weber and Barth that natural theology was never accorded independent status by the Reformed orthodox and was carefully qualified to prevent it from attaining such independence.

22. See Leo Strauss, *Natural Right and History* (Chicago: University of Chicago Press, 1950), for the story of the political shift from a religious to a secular foundation in the work of such thinkers as Niccolo Machiavelli (1469-1527), Thomas Hobbes (1588-1679), and John Locke (1632-1704).

God's grace and inexorably leads to the autonomous natural theology of the Enlightenment.[23] We should take Barth's opposition seriously, for the idea of natural revelation has been greatly abused. Yet Christians should not deny natural revelation, because Scripture proclaims that God created, sustains, and governs the world. It tells us that "the heavens declare the glory of God" and that all his works praise him and reflect his wisdom, glory, and power (Ps. 19:1). Denying natural revelation would darken the world and defame the Creator. We could not look at a sunset, a rose, or the face of a child and think, "If his works are this beautiful, how beautiful God must be!" We could not look at the heavens and wonder at God's power. From gazing on the towering mountains, we could not legitimately turn our minds toward God's immensity. We could not even thank God for our daily bread. This would be intolerable. We need to find a way to incorporate natural revelation into our faith without creating the possibility of an independent natural religion and theology.

Romans 1:18-32: No Excuses

As a step in this direction, let us distinguish among natural revelation, natural religion, and natural theology. The classic text around which many discussions of natural revelation revolve is Romans 1:18-32:

> The wrath of God is being revealed from heaven against all the godlessness and wickedness of men who suppress the truth by their wickedness, since what may be known about God is plain to them, because God has made it plain to them. For since the creation of the world God's invisible qualities — his eternal power and divine nature — have been clearly seen, being understood from what has been made, so that men are without excuse. For although they knew God, they neither glorified him as God nor gave thanks to him, but their thinking became futile and their foolish hearts were darkened. Although they claimed to be wise, they became fools and exchanged the glory of the immortal God for images made to look like mortal man and birds and animals and reptiles (vv. 18-23).

Paul's argument, I believe, turns on the distinctions among these three concepts: revelation, religion, and theology. God's wrath, Paul tells us, is now being revealed against wicked and godless people (v. 18). But why is God angry with these gentiles, ones who have never heard of the Lord and his law? Paul anticipates this objection and replies that ignorance of biblical revelation is no excuse, because God's "eternal power and divine nature" are "plain" and "clearly

23. *CD*, 2/1, pp. 78-128.

seen" (vv. 19-20). The gentiles know enough. No one can say, "I didn't know I should thank God and seek him. I didn't know that I wasn't free to do as I please." So, according to Paul, there is a natural revelation. And this revelation is not obscure, subject to many possible interpretations. It is plain.

Although nature reveals God's "power and deity" clearly and undeniably, many people deny God and live in opposition to him. Paul accounts for this strange situation by maintaining that natural revelation is both clear *and* obscure, but in different senses. It is objectively clear but obscured for us by sin. As interpreters we are tempted to cling to one side of the argument or the other. Since many people do not find God's "power and deity" obvious, we may wish to deny natural revelation altogether. Or, focusing only on Paul's affirmation of natural revelation, we may dream of building a system of natural religion and theology independent of the biblical revelation. Paul admits no tension between these two aspects of his argument: human beings see God's revelation in nature clearly; but at the same time they deny it by suppressing "the truth by their wickedness" and exchanging "the truth of God for a lie" (1:18, 25). The pagans saw God's deity and power; they still see, but they do not like it, and they do not will its truth. In their rebellion, therefore, they neither think (theology), nor worship (religion), nor live (ethics) in harmony with the obvious. For Paul, then, God reveals himself clearly in nature, but the human response in theology and religion suppresses and distorts the truth of that revelation. We are like people walking in darkness until lightning flashes. For one split second all is clear; but then we are darkened again and continue to stumble on. The lightning does not provide the light we need to walk safely, but it makes it impossible to say we never saw.[24]

Following Paul, then, I will distinguish among natural revelation, natural religion, and natural theology. The church has always recognized that God reveals himself in creation and providence. It has been nearly as unanimously affirmed that, apart from Scripture, natural revelation serves only to render humanity without excuse. According to Paul, natural religion is not a sincere response to natural revelation. It is idolatry, a knowing attempt to evade worshiping God and to substitute a piety and ethics more congenial to the desires of the sinful heart. Nor is natural theology a sincere effort to think about God on the basis of natural revelation. Rather, it attempts to justify the practice of natural religion.

---

24. John Calvin uses this metaphor.

Four Uses of Natural Revelation

Our wariness of natural religion and theology should not prevent us from making cautious use of natural revelation. By faith we believe that the God of Abraham, Isaac, and Jacob is God and that only by loving the Father through the Son in the power of the Holy Spirit can we enjoy fellowship with God. We know the God that created us, and we know that we should worship and thank him. Everything is for the "praise of his glory" (Eph. 1:12). We know that God created the world, sustains it, and guides it. We know that every good gift comes from the "Father of lights" (James 1:17; Acts 17:24-28). Every created thing receives its being, goodness, and beauty from its Creator. The Psalms of Israel emphasize that the glory, longevity, immensity, and power of creation all witness to the greater glory and power of the Creator (8:3; 19:1; 33:6; 50:6; 97:5, 6; 102:24-26; 104:1-3; 113:3-6; 148:1-14). I can discern four important roles natural revelation continues to play.

NATURAL REVELATION LEAVES HUMANITY WITHOUT EXCUSE   I have already discussed the first function in the treatment of Romans 1:18-32. Creation's display of God's wisdom, glory, and power renders human beings without excuse for their false religion and theology and their moral corruption. We act as though our wills were the law of being, as though the universe were our creation and subject only to the law of our desire. In short, we act as though we were gods. Creation itself contradicts this mad dream. It cries out loudly: "Who do you think you are? Did you create yourself, and can you sustain yourself? You know the answer: you received yourself and everything you enjoy from another. Apart from that gracious reality, you are nothing. Think about it: you cannot be the highest being in the universe. What of the glories of the heavens and the mysteries of the ocean depths? You did not create them. Their maker must be greater than you are. Even the work of his hands strikes wonder and terror in your soul. Yet, you do not thank and honor your Creator. Rather, you pretend to worship created powers and glories. In reality, you seek only to satisfy your own lusts. Liar! Fool! God's wrath rests on you justly."

NATURAL REVELATION PROVIDES LANGUAGE FOR EXPRESSING GOD'S GREATNESS   The words and concepts we use to speak about God derive from creation. Scripture, as we saw earlier, leads the way in using the language of nature to praise God. Behold the glories of the heavens, the sun, moon, and stars. Gaze in wonder. But know that God is more glorious! Feel the power of the pounding surf and the thundering waterfall. Let their deafening voices awaken in you awe for the Creator who spoke them into action.

16

He is greater! At the base of Half Dome or El Capitan in Yosemite National Park, I stand dumbfounded at their immensity and my insignificance. As I begin to praise them, they say to me (as the angel said to the apostle John in Rev. 19:10), "Do not worship us. We are creatures just as you are. Worship God! He is greater." It is impossible to grasp eternity, but on a hike to the bottom of the Grand Canyon, descending past layer after layer, representing ancient oceans, deserts, and rainforests, I am overwhelmed with the feeling that we are but "flies of the summer," to use Edmond Burke's poignant phrase.[25] Then I think of Psalm 102:25-27: "In the beginning you laid the foundations of the earth, and the heavens are the work of your hands. They will perish, but you remain; they will all wear out like a garment. Like clothing you will change them and they will be discarded. But you remain the same, and your years will never end."

A sunset over the Pacific, a dew-laden rose in dawn's first light, a snowcapped peak rising, lone, above the cloud cover. These are beauties too sublime to take in, much less render into speech. According to our faith, these magnificent things are tiny cracks, pinholes in nature through which God's beauty shines. No wonder none can look on God and live (Exod. 33:20). If our bodies respond to beauty in created things by ceasing to breathe and increasing our heart rates, if we cannot help crying and feeling intense longing, how could we function at all in the unfiltered light of infinite beauty?

The First Epistle of John exclaims, "God is love" (1 John 4:8). John goes on to tell us that God demonstrated his love for us by sending his "Son into the world that we might live through him" (4:9). Jesus compares our "heavenly Father's" love to the love of an earthly father: if earthly fathers, who are sinners, can love their children, "how much more" will God love his children (Luke 11:11-13)? Isaiah compares God's love for his people to a mother's love for her child (Isa. 49:15). Though the love I feel for my two sons is no doubt imperfect, at times I have wept at the joy they have brought into my life and at my inability to express it. Without experiencing love at some level, how could we get an inkling of God's love for us? Romans 5 builds on the analogy of human love. It is rare for a person to give his life for even the best of people, though one can imagine it. "But God demonstrates his own love for us in this: While we were still sinners, Christ died for us" (Rom. 5:8). God's love is greater, infinitely greater. Yet how could the story of God's love move us unless we had experienced something of human love?

25. Burke, *Reflections on the Revolution in France,* in *Works,* 2, pp. 366-67, quoted in Russell Kirk, *The Conservative Mind: From Burke to Eliot,* 7th rev. ed. (Washington, DC: Regnery, 1985), p. 44.

NATURAL REVELATION STIRS OUR FEELINGS DIRECTLY We see, touch, hear, taste, and smell the creation. We experience it directly, and it moves us deeply. Calvin, no friend to natural theology, looked to creation as a "theater" displaying God's glory.[26] Immanuel Kant, the fierce critic of natural theology, could not help but rhapsodize about creation: "[T]wo things fill the mind with new and ever increasing awe the oftener and more steadily we reflect on them: the starry heavens above me and the moral law within me."[27] God will not leave us alone. He presses in from every angle, within and without, and through every sense. Perceiving this pressure requires no metaphysical or scientific reasoning about causes, natural or supernatural. It requires no faith in the testimony of others. In creation, God touches us whether we like it or not, whether we know it or not. Keep in mind, however, that without special revelation we would not know who is touching us, and to what end. Nevertheless, we are being touched, and it affects us profoundly. We are moved, inspired, shaken, and awed — even the atheists among us — by God's creation. We laugh, weep with joy, grieve, love, fear, long, and hope. Our faith teaches us to refer all these feelings to God, to look beyond the finite and fading joys of creation toward the infinite rest and joy found only in the Creator. Augustine of Hippo (A.D. 354-430) observed long ago:

> Man is one of your creatures, Lord, and his instinct is to praise you . . . since he is part of your creation, he wishes to praise you. The thought of you stirs him so deeply that he cannot be content unless he praises you, because you made us for yourself and our hearts find no peace until they rest in you.[28]

NATURAL REVELATION PROVIDES OCCASION FOR THANKSGIVING AND PRAISE Natural revelation affords constant opportunities for thanksgiving and praise. The objects of God's wrath, chided by Paul in Romans 1, would not give thanks and glory to God in response to his natural revelation. In contrast, God's special revelation liberates us to thank God for his good creation and praise him for the wisdom, power, and glory manifest in his works. We live. Thank God! The sun rose this morning to give us light and warmth. Thank God! The earth is solid beneath our feet. We have air to breathe, water to drink, and food to eat. Thank God! We should cultivate the frame of mind

---

26. For a study of Calvin's subtle position on natural knowledge of God, see Michael Czapkay Sudduth, "The Prospects for 'Mediate' Natural Theology in John Calvin," *Religious Studies* 31 (1995): 53-68.

27. Kant, *Critique of Practical Reason*, trans. Lewis White Beck (New York: Macmillan, 1956), pp. 289.

28. Augustine, *Confessions*, trans. R. S. Pine-Coffin (London: Penguin Books, 1961), p. 21.

in which we see the continued existence of the universe as God's constant act and thus the revelation of God's glory and grace. Recognizing God's glory in creation inspires us to live a ceaseless prayer of thanksgiving and hymn of praise. With the psalmist we can say, "Great is the Lord and most worthy of praise; his greatness no one can fathom" (Ps. 145:3).

Holy Scripture

Our ability to speak rightly about God depends on God's speech about himself. We look to God's history with Israel, to Jesus Christ, and to the apostolic church for this speaking. We remember, tell, live, and anticipate this story. The church can point to natural revelation as a witness to God's existence and power, but it possesses no commission to teach on this basis. Relevant here are the pointed words Karl Barth directed toward Paul Tillich in his criticism of the latter's attempt to speak of God based on general experience:

> If the question what God can do forces theology to be humble, the question of what is commissioned of us forces it to concrete obedience. God may speak to us through Russian Communism, a flute concerto, a blossoming shrub, or a dead dog. We do well to listen to Him if He really does. But, unless we regard ourselves as the prophets and founders of a new Church, we cannot say that we are commissioned to pass on what we have heard as independent proclamation.[29]

The Christian message does not derive from natural science, critical history, metaphysics, psychology, or sociology; nor does it allow itself to be judged by these. It derives from God's own incarnate Word. Jesus Christ commissioned his church to preach the gospel of the kingdom of God, to baptize the believers, and to instruct them to live as he taught. We receive and proclaim this gospel — none other — as the word of God.

God's word meets us today as Holy Scripture. Even in discussing the concept of revelation I have relied on Scripture. In this book I will quote Scripture as the authority by which to judge all theological statements, including my own. I write expecting the church to listen to Scripture and reject other authorities. The sheep know the voice of the good shepherd, but "they do not recognize a stranger's voice" (John 10:4-6).

---

29. *CD*, 1/1, p. 55.

Scripture and the Apostolic Tradition

Jesus and the Old Testament

The church began as the continuation and fulfillment of Israel's hope. From the beginning, the church regarded Hebrew Scripture as canonical. Jesus quoted Scripture as authoritative and interpreted it for his contemporaries. After his resurrection, as he broke bread with the Emmaus travelers, "he explained to them what was said in all the Scriptures concerning himself" (Luke 24:27). When he appeared to the eleven disciples, "he opened their minds so they could understand the Scriptures" (Luke 24:45). Jesus gave no indication that Israel's Scriptures need to be revised or reinterpreted according to the dictates of human reason and experience. He expressed full confidence that we can meet the one he called "Father" in Israel's Scriptures. Jesus accomplished a new work of God and heralded a new message. However, he made clear that he came "not to abolish" the law and the prophets, but "to fulfill them" (Matt. 5:17).

The apostolic church saw Scripture "fulfilled" in Jesus Christ (Acts 1:16); it "reasoned" from Scripture (Acts 17:2); and it "examined the Scriptures" (Acts 17:7). Scripture "teaches us" and gives us "encouragement" (Rom. 15:4). The servant of God should be devoted to "public reading of Scripture" (1 Tim. 4:13), and we must not forget that Scripture is "able to make [us] wise for salvation through faith in Christ Jesus" (2 Tim. 3:15). Indeed, "all Scripture is God-breathed and is useful for teaching, rebuking, correcting and training in righteousness, so that the man of God may be complete, thoroughly equipped for every good work" (2 Tim. 3:16-17).

However, the church did not begin as a Jewish sect, set apart from others by its distinctive interpretation of Hebrew Scripture. Jesus had taught as "one who has authority" and not as the scribes (Matt. 7:29). He proclaimed that something new was on the horizon. In his miracles, teaching, death, and resurrection he embodied the coming kingdom, thus becoming the good news he preached. He gave his followers new sacraments, and he commanded them to be baptized into his name and to remember him in the bread and wine of the supper (Matt. 26:26-29; Mark 14:22-25; Luke 22:14-22; cf. 1 Cor. 11:23-26). After his resurrection, he commissioned his disciples as apostles to the world: "All authority in heaven and on earth has been given to me. Therefore go and make disciples of all nations, baptizing them in the name of the Father and of the Son and of the Holy Spirit, and teaching them to obey everything I have commanded you" (Matt. 28:18-20).

The Church Is Inherently Apostolic

In the Acts of the Apostles, we learn that the apostolic office required the oc-
cupant to have been a witness to Jesus' life, death, and resurrection (Acts
1:22). Peter stands before the crowd at Pentecost and proclaims: "God has
raised this Jesus to life, and we are all witnesses of the fact" (Acts 2:32; cf.
1 Cor. 9:1). Given the commission and unique calling of the apostles, we are
not surprised that Pentecost converts "devoted themselves to the apostles'
teaching and to the fellowship, and to the breaking of bread" (Acts 2:42).
From the beginning, the apostles' remembrance of Jesus' words and their witness to his resurrection were authoritative for the church: this unique apostolic role became part of the gospel itself. Integral to the things of "first importance" that Paul had "passed on" to the Corinthians was not only the
death, burial, and resurrection of Christ. Paul clearly considers the apostolic
witness itself foundational, for he completes his list of "first things" in this
way: ". . . that he appeared to Peter, and then to the Twelve . . . to James, then
to all the apostles, and last of all he appeared to me also, as to one abnormally
born" (1 Cor. 15:3-7). Apostolicity was and is an essential mark of the Christian church.

How can the church preserve its apostolic character and maintain the
faith "once for all entrusted to the saints" (Jude 3)? Already within the apostolic era we can see three ways in which the church sought to discharge this responsibility: office, tradition, and Scripture. Those holding the office of elder
or bishop were assigned the work of guarding the church from error and passing on the faith unchanged. At the Jerusalem Conference, the "apostles and elders" met to discuss questions raised by the mission to the gentiles (Acts 15:6).
The resulting decree was sent out under the name of "the apostles and elders,
your brothers" (Acts 15:22). Paul's instructions to the Ephesian elders makes
clear that the office of elder focused on protecting the community's doctrine
and life: "Keep watch over yourselves and all the flock of which the Holy Spirit
has made you overseers. Be shepherds of the church of God, which he bought
with his own blood" (Acts 20:28; see also 1 Tim. 3:1, 2; Titus 1:5-7; 1 Pet. 5:2). We
receive a hint of the interconnection between tradition and office in 2 Timothy
2:2: "And the things you have heard me say in the presence of many witnesses
entrust to reliable men who will also be qualified to teach others." The apostles
established a succession of officials commissioned with the sacred duty of reli-
ably passing on the faith. These officers discharged this duty in a variety of
ways: by remembering and teaching, by writing down their remembrances, by
keeping old institutions and liturgies unchanged, and by preserving the apostolic writings.

The Christian Canon

In the early postapostolic era, office, tradition, and the apostolic writings stood closely intertwined and mutually supportive in the goal of preserving the original faith for future generations. Late first-century and early second-century writings (by the so-called apostolic fathers) appealed to the apostolic writings and to the traditions and established practices of the church. They did not view the apostolic writings as the sole reliable sources for the faith. This generation took for granted the harmony of the apostolic writings and the unwritten tradition it had received. "Christians just 'know' the original truth; no one refers in support to texts and documents, regarded as an acknowledged and established norm."[30] However, they were aware that certain heretics had departed from the "catholic" church and had created false traditions. Some Gnostics, for example, charged that the catholic tradition had been corrupted and that the truth had been preserved only in their secret traditions. The Alexandrian Gnostic Valentinus quoted the church's scriptures as authoritative but interpreted them in keeping with a secret tradition opposed to the church's public tradition.[31] This challenge forced the church to assert the authenticity of the catholic tradition.[32]

Toward the middle of the second century, the church faced a significant challenge to its sense of continuity. The heretic Marcion published a canon of scriptures that excluded many of the church's revered writings. He rejected the Old Testament completely, and he edited ten letters of Paul and the Gospel of Luke to remove all positive references to the God of the Old Testament. He did not merely pit a secret tradition against the public tradition of the church; rather, Marcion appealed to his new canon to support his views and demonstrate that the public tradition was corrupt. According to von Campenhausen (following Harnack), Marcion was the first theologian to set Scripture against the tradition and to call for a reform of the tradition based on Scripture alone.[33] Marcion thus forced the church to address "the question of the 'au-

30. Hans von Campenhausen, *The Formation of the Christian Bible*, trans. J. A. Baker (Philadelphia: Fortress Press, 1972), p. 147.

31. See Irenaeus, *Against Heresies*, 3.12.12 (*ANF*, 1, pp. 434-35). See also Tertullian, *The Prescription Against Heretics*, 38 (*ANF*, 3, p. 262), where the latter contrasts Valentinus's reinterpretation of the church's Scripture with Marcion's reduction.

32. Von Campenhausen, *Formation of the Christian Bible*, p. 134.

33. Von Campenhausen, *Formation of the Christian Bible*, pp. 148-53, 162. See also Harry Y. Gamble, "The New Testament Canon: Recent Research and the *Status Quaestionis*," in *The Canon Debate*, ed. Lee Martin McDonald and James A. Sanders (Peabody, MA: Hendrickson, 2002), pp. 267-94, which sets out briefly the historic debate between Adolf von Harnack and Theodor Zahn concerning the development of the New Testament canon, a debate that still sets the agenda for the discussion of canon.

thentic' witnesses to the original gospel, which were to provide the standard of all later tradition and the norm for the preaching of the Church."[34] Not all historians agree with von Campenhausen that Marcion had such a dramatic impact on the formation of the Christian canon.[35] Nevertheless, it is undeniable that the church responded to Marcion, Valentinus, and other heretics with deeper reflection on its sources of authority: Scripture, tradition, and office.

Irenaeus, bishop of Lyon (c. A.D. 130–c. 200), saw clearly the inadequacy of merely asserting the truth and purity of the public tradition against the Marcionite and Gnostic heresies. He realized that Marcion's challenge had made it necessary for the church to defend the authenticity of its ancient authorities. Combining office, tradition, and Scripture, he developed an effective argument against these heresies. A false and truncated canon calls for a true and full canon.[36] Irenaeus, in his treatise *Against All Heresies* (hereafter *AH*), defends a canon that includes the Old Testament, the four Gospels and Acts, as well as the letters of Paul. The bishop of Lyon does not simply oppose his list of scriptures to Marcion's. Confident that the public tradition of the church stands in harmony with the Scriptures, he appeals to the apostolic tradition preserved in the oldest churches — above all, to the church at Rome. This truth, he argues, has been faithfully passed down since the time of the apostles Paul and Peter by an unbroken line of bishops. The teaching of heretics, in contrast, is unknown in the churches founded by the apostles. The apostolic writings preserved by these churches mention none of their heretical speculation (*AH*, 3.2-5). For Irenaeus, the church's memory of the original gospel, embodied in its tradition and passed on by the bishops of its oldest congregations, enables it to judge between writings that contain the authentic faith and those that do not. In addition, it serves to guarantee that wild speculations masquerading as "interpretations" cannot easily replace the authentic meaning of the apostolic writings. In the face of these heresies, the believer should "retain unchangeable in his heart the rule of the truth which he received by means of baptism" (*AH*, 1.9.4; *ANF*, 1, p. 330).

The core of the New Testament canon was fixed by at least the early second century; the edges took longer. Some churches included several extra books, and many churches left out some that were eventually accepted as canonical.[37]

---

34. Von Campenhausen, *Formation of the Christian Bible*, pp. 164-65.

35. See John Barton, "Marcion Revisited," in *The Canon Debate*, pp. 340-54; see also Everett Ferguson, "Factors Leading to the Selection and Closure of the New Testament Canon: A Survey of Some Recent Studies," in *The Canon Debate*, pp. 295-320.

36. Von Campenhausen, *Formation of the Christian Bible*, p. 186.

37. For a full history of the New Testament canon, several resources are available in addition to von Campenhausen: Bruce M. Metzger, *The Canon of the New Testament: Its Origin, De-*

The history of the New Testament canon came to an end in the late fourth century: in A.D. 367, Athanasius, bishop of Alexandria, wrote a letter in which he listed the books held to be canonical by the church in Alexandria. This was the first list to include all twenty-seven books — and only those — that are in our New Testament today.[38]

The Doctrine of Scripture

It is beyond the scope of this study to develop a comprehensive doctrine of the origin, nature, and characteristics of Scripture, so I will leave that discussion to others.[39] I will remain focused on the issue with which I began this section: How can the church preserve God's revelation in Jesus Christ for future generations? What role does Scripture play in accomplishing this task? In seeking to answer this question, I shall argue that Scripture gives us perennial access to the authentic Christian gospel.

I Believe the Apostolic Church

Christianity is inherently apostolic: without the apostles there would be no church and no Christianity. If those witnesses were mistaken or were lying, our faith is "useless" (1 Cor. 15:14, 15). Yet we can have no independent proof that they were not mistaken. The apostolic witnesses testified to what they saw and heard. They staked their lives and their souls on this message. We can believe or disbelieve; there is no middle ground. But first we must hear their witness.

If the Christian church is to survive, it must have continued access to the authentic apostolic witness. What can we say to Gnostics, Manicheans, Muslims, and since their time a host of others who assert that the authentic faith was lost or perverted? Historical study provides important assistance, and the

velopment and Significance (Oxford: Clarendon, 1987); Harry Y. Gamble, The New Testament Canon: Its Making and Meaning (Minneapolis: Augsburg/Fortress, 1985); Lee Martin McDonald, The Formation of the Christian Biblical Canon, rev. and enl. ed. (Peabody, MA: Hendrickson, 1995); John Barton, Holy Writings, Sacred Text: The Canon in Early Christianity (Louisville: Westminster John Knox, 1997); and F. F. Bruce, The Canon of Scripture (Downers Grove, IL: InterVarsity, 1988).

38. Festal Letter 39 (NPNF, 2nd ser., 4, pp. 551-52).

39. For a recent survey of theologies of Scripture, ancient and modern, see Justin S. Holcomb, Christian Theologies of Scripture: A Comparative Introduction (New York: New York University Press, 2006). For the Lutheran doctrine, see Robert D. Preus, TPRL, 1, pp. 255-378; for the Reformed doctrine, see Richard A. Muller, PRRD, 2.

witness of the Holy Spirit is the ultimate ground of our faith. But between those two stands the witness of the church. To conspiracy mongers, ancient or contemporary, we can say: "I trust the church to have preserved the apostolic faith. I trust Clement, Ignatius, Papias, Polycarp, Justin Martyr, Theophilus, and Irenaeus. I trust the elders and bishops of Jerusalem, Rome, Alexandria, Antioch, and other ancient churches. I do not believe Marcion, the Gnostics, Mani, or Mohammed. I do not believe the Gospel of Thomas or the Gospel of Judas. I do not trust modern revisionists. I believe the gospel. And I believe that the teaching preserved by the church's public tradition is the authentic apostolic gospel." In response to the Manicheans, who claimed to represent authentic Christianity, Augustine said: "For my part, I should not believe the gospel except as moved by the authority of the Catholic Church."[40] Even if we do not wish to express ourselves in Augustine's exact words, we should not dismiss his point. Trusting Scripture implies that we trust the church to have recognized and protected those writings that preserved apostolic witness uncorrupted.

Scripture as Authority

By canonizing the New Testament as Scripture, the patristic church certified that it embodies the apostolic tradition, "the faith once delivered to the saints" (Jude 3). It attested that these documents contain the rule of faith, the heart of the public tradition that the church received from the Lord and his apostles. Therefore, these writings serve as a canon or rule by which the church can measure its teaching concerning faith and doctrine.

We must keep in mind that the church's decisions about canon were not directed to outsiders. The church defined the canon to protect the faithful from *heresy,* that is, from teachers that "go bad" and attempt to draw away part of the church to follow them. To make their alien doctrines plausible, for example, Marcion and his followers had to dispute the church's traditional authorities. Settling the issue of canon within the church made success unlikely for any sect that appealed to other scriptures or traditions. For it inoculated the faithful with holy suspicion against such claims. After the limits of the canon were clearly recognized, the chief disputes within the church turned on the interpretation of canonical Scripture. Tradition was invoked to authenticate or dispute a reading of Scripture.

Canonization, then, is the process of concentrating the church's sources of authority into a single focus. Tradition and office still play a crucial role as au-

---

40. Augustine, *Against the Epistle of Manichaeus Called Fundamental,* 5 (*NPNF,* 1st ser., 4, p. 131).

thoritative interpreters of the canon. However, they are no longer independent sources of authority. As I explained earlier, tradition and office functioned all along as preservers of the original apostolic faith. Once a written canon containing the original faith from its authenticated sources had been established, tradition and office could assume a different role: aids to interpretation.

Since canonization was completed, the church has expected all its teachers to root their teaching in canonical Scripture. Teachers who want to be recognized as "Christian" should expect to have their theology judged by Scripture. The church rightly rejects doctrines that contradict Scripture. And it submits gladly to Scripture as the norm of all other norms. Therefore, since the patristic period, the church has asserted the "infallibility" or "inerrancy" of Holy Scripture. With respect to God and the things of God, Scripture's teaching is the standard by which all other teaching must be measured. This assertion is based not on philosophical or historical-critical investigation but on the discernment of faith. The church receives Scripture by faith, and it cannot reject it except by departing from faith. From the beginning, the church of Christ has lived under the apostolic rule of faith preserved in Scripture. It is the norm that judges all other norms. And to acknowledge Scripture as the norm of other norms entails treating it as infallible, since we acknowledge no other norms by which it may be judged.

I am aware that my understanding of Scripture's authority will be considered in many circles, even relatively orthodox ones, as antiquated or at least contrarian. For many contemporary theologians and biblical scholars, such a view became indefensible long ago, and those who continue to hold it are burying their heads in the sand. But are things really that simple? I think not. The real issue cannot be articulated adequately, let alone be settled, by posing easy dichotomies, such as whether the Scriptures are infallible or fallible, inerrant or errant? We need some deeper analysis.

Let's suppose someone wishes to deny the infallibility of Scripture. How could such an allegation be established? First, we must note a common misunderstanding. The church preserved Scripture, treasured it, and held it to be authoritative for what it teaches about God, his saving actions on our behalf, and the response he wants from us. The church did not canonize Scripture because of what it says about chemistry, physics, botany, geology, biology, ancient geography, or secular history. Scripture touches on these subjects only incidentally; it does not *teach* anything about them. The church is not an antiquarian society or a museum of natural history. It is the harbinger of the kingdom of God, and Scripture is the sole source and norm of this gospel. Believe the gospel or not — that is the decisive challenge. Calling a news conference with great fanfare to charge Scripture with error because it does not teach modern science is like a romantic throwing the phonebook into the trash because it contains no poetry or the logician's criticism of the verse of Keats and Shelly for its lack of precision. Such fanfare is as boring as it is irrelevant.

Other accusations of error are more sinister, because they deny Scripture's infallibility as a *source for the true faith*. Such denials are usually based on one of two alien foundations. The first rejects the apostolic faith itself as false: everyone knows that writings that assert falsehoods cannot be infallible. Now Christians should not be surprised to discover that some people do not believe the gospel. The church has faced challenges from unbelievers, learned and ignorant, in every generation. Such revelations should not cause the church to revise its doctrine of Scripture, for, as I have observed above, this doctrine was not developed to address objections from external critics but from heretics within. The church developed other, more effective, apologetic strategies for outsiders. The doctrine of Scripture is a set of hermeneutical rules for insiders, and thus we need not revise it to meet objections from the outside.

More common than direct charges of falsehood are the claims of religious thinkers who profess to have better access to the original faith than the church does. They invoke an independent source of religious knowledge. One school of thought revives the Marcionite project and, on the basis of secret *gnosis,* logical analysis, philosophical speculation, psychology, ethical insights based on cultural consensus, ideologies based on race or gender, common sense, or historical-critical reason, claims to see Scripture's defects. Those who bow to one of these other authorities do not acknowledge Scripture as the norm of all norms (or they do so in word only); rather, they judge Scripture by their own self-chosen norm.

Others use Valentinus's strategy: they attempt to take shelter under the banner of interpretation. The Valentinian approach also judges and "corrects" Scripture by an alien norm, but it hides the stranger beneath the veil of interpretation. It co-opts the respect Scripture has accrued among Christian or quasi-Christian people and uses it to gain a hearing for its alien views. It somehow "discovers" or "rediscovers" its own thoughts in Scripture. The Valentians of today, consciously or unconsciously, practice deception. Unfortunately, the way philosopher John M. Rist describes the state of modern ethics also applies to contemporary theology: "The perception in many academic and professional circles . . . of the theoretical crisis, combined with the ignorance of ordinary people, makes way for deceptions, equivocations and outright lying and humbug in public debate."[41]

41. Rist, *Real Ethics: Reconsidering the Foundations of Morality* (Cambridge, UK: Cambridge University Press, 2002), pp. 1-2.

The church has always recognized that Scripture must be interpreted properly and that there can be legitimate differences in interpretation; but it has never recognized the *rejection* of its plain meaning as a valid interpretation. Good Christian theology gladly submits to Scripture as the norm of all other norms. It seeks knowledge of the triune God within Scripture and joyously gives its mind to be formed spiritually by it in the company of the whole church. I have tried to follow this rule in this book.

Tradition

I have already observed how Scripture, tradition, and office support each other in preserving the apostolic faith for the postapostolic age, considering this mutuality from the perspective of Scripture in the preceding section. Now let us view it from the perspective of tradition.

Recent efforts at retrieving the idea of tradition for "suspicious Protestants" have met with mixed results.[42] For Bible-loving, low-church Protestants, the word "tradition" calls to mind Jesus' strictures against those who use their traditions to trump the word of God (Mark 7:9). It conjures up the image of the hidebound traditionalists who refuse to adapt to cultural changes — even in nonessentials. It hints at the stubborn authoritarianism of the Roman Catholic Church on the eve of the Reformation. These images, I believe, represent abuses of tradition and do not argue for excluding it from Christian thought and life. In fact, tradition plays a vital role in the life of the church and receives its biblical warrant in the Fifth Commandment: "Honor your father and your mother" (Exod. 20:12). But no one would conclude from this text that we should honor father and mother above God; the command assumes that our fathers and mothers are usually means through which we learn to honor God. In the same way, we can honor tradition as a means through which we receive the faith, and we can do so without replacing the faith itself or usurping the normative role of Scripture.

---

42. Daniel H. Williams, "Reflections on Retrieving the Tradition and Renewing Evangelicalism: A Response," *Scottish Journal of Theology* 55 (2002): 105-12. Williams, the author of *Retrieving the Tradition and Renewing Evangelicalism: A Primer for Suspicious Protestants* (Grand Rapids: Eerdmans, 1999), tells of a review of his book in the *Fort Worth Star-Telegram*, in which the reviewer acknowledged that, for conservative Protestants, the words *tradition* and *creed* are "fightin' words" (p. 106).

The Roman Catholic View

The Council of Trent

Defining tradition and clarifying its relationship to Scripture occasioned controversy in the history of the church. Is tradition a second source for the apostolic faith in that it contains revelation not included in Scripture? This is the impression we get from the Fourth Session of the Council of Trent (1545-1564), where the Roman Catholic Church responded to the Reformers' contention that Scripture alone is the source of revelation. The Council asserts that the apostolic faith has been preserved by canonical Scripture

> and the unwritten traditions which, received by the Apostles from the mouth of Christ himself, or from the Apostles themselves, the Holy Ghost dictating, have come down even unto us, transmitted as it were from hand to hand; [the Synod] following the examples of the orthodox Fathers, receives and venerates with an equal affection of piety, and reverence, all the books both of the Old and of the New Testament — seeing that one God is the author of both — as also the said traditions, as well those appertaining to faith as to morals, as having been dictated, either by Christ's own word of mouth, or by the Holy Ghost, and preserved in the Catholic Church by a continuous succession. . . .
>
> Furthermore, in order to restrain petulant spirits, It decrees, that no one, relying on his own skill, shall — in matters of faith, and of morals pertaining to the edification of Christian doctrine — wresting the sacred Scripture to his own senses, presume to interpret the said sacred Scripture contrary to that sense which holy mother Church — whose it is to judge of the true sense and interpretation of the holy Scriptures — hath held and doth hold. . . .[43]

The twentieth-century Roman Catholic theologian Yves Congar, in his massive study *Tradition and Traditions,* admits that theologians working in the wake of the Council of Trent understood that the council taught two partial sources of the faith.[44] In the view of Robert Bellarmine (1542-1621), for example, the catholic and apostolic faith derives "partly" from tradition and "partly" from Scripture. Without disparaging such previous interpreters of the Council, Congar argues that the Council decree's "and" *(et),* which joins tradition to Scripture, should not be taken to mean "partly . . . partly" but that one and the same apostolic faith

---

43. Schaff, *Creeds of Christendom,* 2, pp. 79-83.
44. Yves M. Congar, *Tradition and Traditions: An Historical and a Theological Essay* (New York: Macmillan, 1967).

comes to us through Scripture *and* tradition (pp. 166-69). Congar argues that the church fathers and medieval theologians taught that Scripture "includes in itself the whole of saving truth" (p. 381). Congar justifies his interpretation of the Council in this way: "It is undoubtedly true that a text of the magisterium ought to be interpreted according to the intentions of its authors, but it is also true that we are bound by the divine intention of the Holy Spirit, and not the human intention of men. The latter can in fact be transcended by the former, whose instrument it is and which, on the whole, it expresses" (pp. 168-69).

The Second Vatican Council

As one might suspect from reading Congar, the Roman Catholic Church does not seem to hold the same position today on tradition and Scripture that it did at the time of the Council of Trent. Accordingly, the Second Vatican Council (1962-1965) declared:

> The words of the holy fathers witness to the presence of this living tradition, whose wealth is poured into the practice and life of the believing and praying Church. Through the same tradition the Church's full canon of the sacred books is known, and the sacred writings themselves are more profoundly understood and unceasingly made active in her; and thus God, who spoke of old, uninterruptedly converses with the bride of His beloved Son; and the Holy Spirit, through whom the living voice of the Gospel resounds in the Church, and through her, in the world, leads unto all truth those who believe and makes the word of Christ dwell abundantly in them (see Col. 3:16).
>
> Hence there exists a close connection and communication between sacred tradition and Sacred Scripture. For both of them, flowing from the same divine wellspring, in a certain way merge into a unity and tend toward the same end. For Sacred Scripture is the word of God inasmuch as it is consigned to writing under the inspiration of the divine Spirit, while sacred tradition takes the word of God entrusted by Christ the Lord and the Holy Spirit to the Apostles, and hands it on to their successors in its full purity, so that led by the light of the Spirit of truth, they may in proclaiming it preserve this word of God faithfully, explain it, and make it more widely known. Consequently it is not from Sacred Scripture alone that the Church draws her certainty about everything which has been revealed. Therefore both sacred tradition and Sacred Scripture are to be accepted and venerated with the same sense of loyalty and reverence (*Dei Verbum*, 2.8.9).[45]

45. Vatican website available at http://www.vatican.va/archive/hist_councils/ii_vatican _council/documents/vat-ii_const_19651118_dei-verbum_en.html (accessed Feb. 6, 2003).

An influential post–Vatican II dictionary of theology concludes from the above statements that the notion of "two materially different 'sources' for Christian Tradition rests on a misunderstanding."[46] On the contrary, argue Karl Rahner and Herbert Vorgrimler, "[t]radition occurs always and everywhere in harkening to Scripture, subject to Scripture as the critical norm which is always and everywhere necessary in order to distinguish 'divine' Tradition . . . from human traditions."[47] Karl-Heinz Weger, in another post–Vatican II dictionary of theology, says that *Dei Verbum* teaches that tradition "is not a certain amount of matter . . . handed on in propositions and practices. . . . The tradition of the Church is rather faith as lived."[48] Therefore, Weger concludes, "the magisterium of the Church functions merely as a hearer and servant of the tradition of the primitive Church, as inspired by God and committed to writing in Scripture."[49] In the sections on tradition and its relationship to Scripture, the *Catechism of the Catholic Church* is made up almost entirely of quotations from *Dei Verbum*. The Catechism speaks of tradition and Scripture as being "two distinct modes of transmission" of one apostolic faith (1.2.2.2).[50] However, it adds two paragraphs that distinguish the apostolic traditions from ecclesial traditions:

> The Tradition here in question comes from the apostles and hands on what they received from Jesus' teaching and example and what they learned from the Holy Spirit. The first generation of Christians did not yet have a written New Testament, and the New Testament itself demonstrates the process of living Tradition.
>
> Tradition is to be distinguished from the various theological, disciplinary, liturgical or devotional traditions, born in the local churches over time. These are the particular forms, adapted to different places and times, in which the great Tradition is expressed. In the light of Tradition, these traditions can be retained, modified or even abandoned under the guidance of the Church's Magisterium (1.2.2.2).

According to contemporary Roman Catholic teaching, as we can see in the *Catechism,* for a doctrine to be considered part of the authoritative Tradition (with a capital *T*) it must have originated within the apostolic era and be de-

46. Karl Rahner and Herbert Vorgrimler, eds., *Dictionary of Theology,* 2nd ed. (New York: Crossroad, 1985), s.v. "Tradition."

47. "Tradition," *Dictionary of Theology.*

48. Karl-Heinz Weger, "Tradition," in *Encyclopedia of Theology: The Concise Sacramentum Mundi,* ed. Karl Rahner (New York: Crossroad, 1975).

49. Weger, "Tradition."

50. Available at http://www.vatican.va/archive/catechism/ccc_toc.htm (accessed Feb. 6, 2006).

rived from Jesus or his inspired apostles. Theoretically, some of these teachings could have been (and probably were) preserved into the postapostolic era through oral transmission. However, for all practical purposes today, tradition is materially contained in canonical Scripture. The *Catechism* carefully distinguishes "Tradition" from mere traditions: the former is unchangeable, while the latter can be reformed under the guidance of the teaching office of the church.[51]

The Protestant View

Protestant theology has entertained a different view of tradition. Martin Luther (1483-1546) found his efforts at reform frustrated by his opponents' assertion that everything the church in fact teaches and practices goes back to the apostles. Even if those traditions cannot be found in Scripture, they are still binding, for they were passed on orally within the church's unbroken succession of bishops. Luther's opponents thus insulated the church from the possibility of reform. In the face of this obstinacy, Luther declared that Scripture alone is the final court of appeal for determining what the church teaches. Luther's famous response to the Holy Roman Emperor at the Diet of Worms (1520) is often quoted as exemplifying his view of Scripture and tradition:

> Unless I am convinced by the testimony of the Scriptures or by clear reason (for I do not trust either in the pope or in councils alone, since it is well known that they have often erred and contradicted themselves), I am bound by the Scriptures I have quoted and my conscience is captive to the Word of God. I cannot and I will not retract anything, since it is neither safe nor right to go against conscience.[52]

It is doubtful, however, that Luther meant to reject altogether the usefulness of tradition in determining church teaching.[53] Though he did not believe that they were infallible, Luther held a positive view of the church fathers and

51. See Hans Küng, *Justification: The Doctrine of Karl Barth and a Catholic Reflection,* trans. Thomas Collins, Edmund E. Tolk, and David Granskou (1964; reprint, Philadelphia: Westminster Press, n.d.), pp. 111-19.

52. *Luther's Works,* American ed., vol. 32, ed. Jaroslav Pelikan and Helmut Lemann (Philadelphia/St. Louis: Concordia Publishing House, 1955-1986), p. 112.

53. See Williams, *Retrieving the Tradition,* pp. 173-204. Williams argues that the Reformers held a much more positive view of tradition than we usually think. For a similar reading focused on Luther alone, see Mickey L. Maddox, "Martin Luther," in Holcomb, ed., *Christian Theologies of Scripture,* pp. 94-113.

called on them in his critique of the Roman church of his time. He characterized his early research as work in hope that "the pure study of the Bible and of
the Holy Fathers might be returned to honor."[54] According to Richard Muller,
"It is . . . entirely anachronistic to view the *sola scriptura* of Luther and his contemporaries as a declaration that all of theology ought to be constructed anew,
without reference to the church's tradition of interpretation, by the lonely exe-
gete confronting the naked text."[55]

However, there have always been a number of Protestants who seem to affirm this "anachronism," that is, that tradition and office should play no role in
establishing the teaching of the church. Since Scripture contains the whole apostolic faith and functions as the norm of other norms, it needs no help from
tradition. It does not need a succession of bishops or tradition to guarantee its
truth and authenticity. The Holy Spirit vouches to the individual believer for
Scripture's authority. Nor does Scripture need tradition to preserve its true interpretation. Scripture interprets itself: that is, it is clear by itself and of itself.

These assertions raised questions that Roman Catholic polemicists were
(and are) quick to ask.[56] How do you explain, in that view, the history of the
canonization of Scripture? Does the Holy Spirit tell each believer which books
of the Bible are canonical? Are all interpretations equally valid? If not, who will
distinguish between those we should accept and those we should not? If there is
no church office with authority to interpret Scripture and judge between orthodoxy and heresy, who can declare to the world what the church believes and
teaches? Indeed, how can we identify even the most radical deviation as heresy?
If the Holy Spirit gives each believer the power and the right to interpret Scripture, won't the church's unity be shattered into fragments, into thousands of little sects? Valerianus Magni, in his polemical work *De acatholicorum credendi
regula iudicium* (1628), exploited vulnerabilities in the Protestant position with
particular skill. According to Magni, "the question is therefore whether the
Holy Spirit infallibly distinguishes true from false teaching in Scripture
through the pastors of the church assembled for a general council or through
individual Christians who each call on the Holy Spirit for themselves and ask
his council from the Holy Scriptures."[57]

Post-Reformation Protestant theologians gave sophisticated answers to

54. *Luther's Works*, 1, p. 170.
55. Muller, *PRRD*, 2, p. 63.
56. See Richard J. Blackwell, *Galileo, Bellarmine, and the Bible* (Notre Dame, IN: University of Notre Dame Press, 1991), pp. 15-18.
57. Quoted by Klaus Scholder, *The Birth of Modern Critical Theology: The Origins and Problems of Biblical Criticism in the Seventeenth Century,* trans. John Bowden (Philadelphia: Trinity Press International, 1990), pp. 14-15.

these questions.[58] Martin Chemnitz (1522-1586), the Lutheran author of a massive response to the Council of Trent *(Examination of the Council of Trent)*, argued that "as much as the Holy Spirit judged necessary and sufficient for us for dogmas and morals to be consigned to writing . . . it will be clear that sacred Scripture is the canon, norm, rule, foundation, and pillar of our whole faith, so that whatever is to be accepted under this title and name that it is the doctrine of Christ and of the apostles must be proved and confirmed from the Scripture."[59] Viewing tradition as an alternative source of dogma and as an authoritative interpreter of Scripture would undercut Scripture altogether by depriving it of its status as the final norm.[60] The Geneva theologian Francis Turretin (1623-1687) acknowledged that the church and its tradition are the means through which we believe in the authority of Scripture; but they are not the material cause of that belief. Scripture itself, which has the marks of divine authority, convinces us of its truth. Nor are the church and its tradition the efficient causes of our belief in the authority of Scripture. The Holy Spirit is the efficient cause. Therefore, using his scheme of a threefold causality, Turretin grants an important role to tradition without yielding to the Roman Catholic arguments that render traditions immune to criticism.[61] According to Turretin, then, tradition is the process God uses to preserve Scripture, which has its own self-authenticating power.

A Continuing Role for Tradition?

The history of Christian theology since the Reformation demonstrates that extreme views of tradition, whether Catholic or Protestant, cannot provide satisfactory answers to the questions raised by the Protestant Reformation and the Catholic Counter-Reformation. An adequate view of tradition must take into account the history of the church and its teaching and must preserve the following theological principles that one or the other of the extremes violates: (1) canonical Scripture contains the whole of the apostolic faith and serves as the norm of all other norms; (2) the church can, and sometimes must, be reformed; (3) it is the task and right of the whole church to interpret Scripture under the guidance of the Spirit.

58. For an extensive survey of the post-Reformation Reformed approach to Scripture and tradition, see Muller, *PRRD*, 2, pp. 345-62.

59. Martin Chemnitz, *Examination of the Council of Trent*, trans. Fred Kramer (St. Louis: Concordia, 1971), p. 101.

60. For further information on the Lutheran view, see Preus, *TPRL*, 1, pp. 258-60.

61. Francis Turretin, *Institutes of Elenctic Theology*, trans. George Musgrave Giger, ed. James T. Dennison, Jr., vol. 1 (Phillipsburg, NJ: Presbyterian and Reformed, 1992), p. 87.

Asserting the radical "Scripture alone" position during the second-century battle against Marcion and the Gnostics would not have protected the church from heresy. As I noted in the section on Scripture, the extent of the canon was disputed in the early second century. Marcion published his own version of the canon of Scripture and called for reform of the church's public tradition. Irenaeus adopted the brilliant strategy of appealing to the public tradition in which the authentic apostolic faith had been passed down by a succession of bishops in the oldest churches. Thus tradition and office came to the defense of Scripture. By the early second century the apostolic writings had been copied, collected, and treasured by the church for some time. Tradition and office vouched for the authenticity and purity of these writings. With the core of the New Testament canon (the four Gospels and Paul's writings) preserved in authentic form and universally recognized, the church could meet the innovations of the Gnostics with ancient writings that clearly refuted them. Tradition, office, and Scripture together consequently provided a stronger defense against heresy than any one of them alone could have provided.[62]

Tradition Continues to Support the Authenticity of Scripture

Though tradition can no longer function as a witness to the apostolic faith independent of Scripture, theology must not forget that it once did. If the apostolic faith is now synonymous with "Scripture alone," it is significant that it was not always so. For our confidence that the canon of Scripture preserves the whole apostolic faith still depends on the trustworthiness of the early tradition and the faithfulness of the church that passed it on. The challenge of contemporary conspiracy theories, which deny that Scripture preserves the original faith, make evident our continued need of tradition. These philosophies exercise influence at the margins of the church and hence require an approach analogous to Irenaeus's refutation of the original Gnostics.

When I assert that "Scripture alone" is the norm, I do not mean that Scripture has ever been alone, that is, without tradition and officers; it could not have been a doctrinal principle until the closing of the canon. The "Scripture alone" rule could make sense only after the church concentrated the apostolic tradition in the canon of Scripture. In this process, Scripture, tradition, and office joined forces to authenticate a written canon by which to measure the apos-

---

62. According to Williams, the "three-legged stool" of tradition, office, and Scripture "acted as a foundation for determining orthodox doctrine, and it was a platform for faith not at all unique to Irenaeus" (*Retrieving the Tradition*, p. 90).

tolicity of the future church. When I speak of the apostolic tradition, then, I mean the faith preserved in Scripture.

Tradition Helps Interpret Scripture

With the canon set, further theological controversies within the church centered primarily on interpretation of Scripture. Heretics could no longer hope to convince the church of their innovations apart from Scripture. But how does the church discriminate between legitimate interpretations and illegitimate ones? Tradition retains an important role as a guardian of the true meaning, or "scope," of Scripture. Richard P. C. Hanson explains this principle: "The rule of faith interprets and detects the drift or burden or main body of truth, the 'scope' of Scripture. This is as important a truth today as it was in the second and third centuries."[63] The church has been slow to accept interpretations of Scripture that overthrow its traditional confession, its received interpretation, and its settled practices. It requires its teachers to root their theology and biblical exposition in the church's tradition and in the right use of reason. Trusting the consensus achieved in the life of the church over private opinions seems to be a reasonable venture.

However, the church has more important reasons for preferring tradition over private opinion. It cannot lightly overthrow its tradition for new interpretations because this would render its identity doubtful. For how can the church be sure that it grasps the faith completely now when it failed to do so previously? Furthermore, according to the New Testament, the Spirit has been given to the whole church. The Spirit accomplishes its work in diverse ways, bestowing gifts widely among the church's many members and officers. Hence, the church's faith cannot be grasped by one individual member in isolation from the whole. Tradition represents the church's time-tested grasp of the faith and manifests itself in the church's creeds, worship, ethics, and in its inexpressible, tacit sense of the faith. As such, it provides the appropriate and inevitable context for Scripture interpretation within the church.

This does not mean that tradition is infallible and above reform. Giving tradition such status would confer on the church's understanding of the apostolic faith higher authority than the faith itself. This view defines apostolicity by what the church believes rather than defining what the church believes by the apostolic rule. Reversing the order in this way deprives the church of any principle of reform. Here we should declare the Reformation's "Scripture alone"

---

63. Richard P. C. Hanson, *Tradition in the Early Church* (Philadelphia: Westminster, 1962), p. 253.

forcefully, for it embodies and protects the truth that God's word itself stands in judgment over our human understanding of God's word. We should treat tradition as a servant and a means of revelation, not as its master and content. The church's reverence for tradition should help it remain faithful and facilitate stability but not encourage intransigency and arrogance. Nevertheless, even in its servant role, tradition is the home of reservoirs of wisdom and inspired insight into the apostolic faith. Those who keep it alive and give it voice bring great blessing to the church.

2

With All Your Heart and Mind:
Reason, Experience, and Theology

Anselm of Canterbury (c. 1033–c. 1109) joined mind and heart in a passionate intellectual quest to know God: his *Proslogium* is as much a prayer as a theological treatise, as stirring as it is profound. He begins by lamenting the blindness of his fallen state: "It is thou that has made me . . . and not yet do I know thee. . . . I was created to see thee, and not yet have I done that for which I was made. O wretched lot of man, when he hath lost that for which he was made!" Apart from God's gracious revelation, Anselm acknowledges, our search for God will be in vain. Thus he confesses: "I strove toward God, and I stumbled on myself. . . . I wished to smile in the joy of my mind, and I am compelled to frown by the sorrow of my heart." Knowing that we cannot find God unless God wishes to be found, Anselm prays for enlightenment: "Be it mine to look up to thy light. . . . Teach me to seek thee, and reveal thyself to me, when I seek thee, for I cannot seek thee, except thou teach me, nor find thee, except thou reveal thyself."[1]

At the end of chapter 1, Anselm gives his justly famous "definition" of theology, a statement that combines heart and mind, humility and boldness, human ability and human limits, divine condescension and divine transcendence, as well as does any statement in the history of theology:

> I do not endeavor, O Lord, to penetrate thy sublimity, for in no wise do I compare my understanding with that; but I long to understand in some degree thy truth, which my heart believes and loves. For I do not seek to understand that I may believe, but I believe in order to understand. For this also I believe — that unless I believed, I should not understand.

1. Anselm, *Proslogium* 1, in *Saint Anselm: Basic Writings*, 2nd ed. and trans. S. N. Deane (LaSalle, IL: Open Court, 1969), pp. 4-7.

In the preceding chapter I focused on God's initiative toward us in revelation and his continued speaking to us through Scripture. In this chapter I will consider the prospects and limits of our comprehension and appropriation of this revelation through reason and experience. Anselm's passionate intellect and intellectual passion will be our inspiration; his prayerful theologizing and theological praying will serve as our guide.

Reason

The church has always affirmed that the right use of reason is necessary for the proper interpretation of Scripture and for theological argumentation. Theology's positive attitude toward rationality is not difficult to explain. Reason is operative in all our conscious life. We use reason in everything we do, including reading the Bible, praying to God, and living a good life.

Reason's Uses

As intimate as we are with reason, however, we seem unable to define it satisfactorily. Perhaps it would be wiser to clarify the different senses in which we use the term reason and to describe the different ways we use it. This exercise will help us understand why the church and her theologians have sometimes praised reason and sometimes denounced it, sometimes welcomed it as an ally and sometimes fought it as an enemy.

We use the term *reason* in at least three senses: reason is the capacity (1) to "see" logical and mathematical relationships among conceptual objects; (2) to intuit or see the conceptual objects themselves; and (3) to see causal patterns among contingent, empirical events and objects.[2] Theologians have rarely questioned the use of logical reasoning in biblical interpretation. Our experience of the world would be chaotic apart from our capacity to see logical relationships. What if we could not grasp the relationship, for example, between the first two clauses — "if it rains, the streets will be wet" — of a syllogism? Moreover, what if, after asserting the fact that "it is raining," we could not perceive that the conclu-

---

2. In *Essay Concerning Human Understanding* (ed. Maurice Cranston [London: Collier-Macmillan, 1965]), ch. 17, John Locke discusses these three functions of reason. However, he reserves the term "reason" for my first and third categories. He speaks of the second as "intuitive knowledge" (p. 386). See also John Macquarrie, *Principles of Christian Theology*, 2nd ed. (New York: Scribner's, 1976), pp. 15-17, and Paul Tillich, *Systematic Theology*, vol. 1 (Chicago: University of Chicago Press, 1967), p. 71.

sion "the streets are wet" follows? How could we interpret Scripture or construct a theological argument if we could not see the difference between statements that contradict each other and those that are consistent with each other? What if we had no comprehension of the relationship between generic and specific, class and individual, or whole and part? And what if we denied the validity of these relationships in biblical interpretation and theology? Confusion would reign.

Traditional theology viewed reason as instrumental to understanding the revelation of God. Let Benedict Pictet (1655-1724) speak for the post-Reformation Reformed view of reason as an instrument: "Reason is as it were the eye of the mind, but scripture is the standard, by which this eye measures the objects proposed. Reason is the instrument which the believer uses in examining the objects of faith by the scripture, as by the infallible norm of truth, but is not the rule itself of these objects of faith. Yet this does not prevent us from acknowledging that reason has many uses."[3] Most theologians assume that we are permitted to read Jesus' teaching in view of ordinary logic, grammar, and syntax. How could we understand, for example, Jesus' teaching on forgiveness without seeing logical relationships? "For if you forgive men when they sin against you, your heavenly Father will also forgive you" (Matt. 6:14). Or prayer? "If you, then, though you are evil, know how to give good gifts to your children, how much more will your Father in heaven give good gifts to those who ask him!" (Matt. 7:11). Understanding Paul's argument for justification by faith in Romans 4 requires careful attention to logic, rhetoric, and grammar. If logical reasoning were not binding on interpreters, one interpretation would be as good as another. Incoherent interpretations would assume as much authority as those that honor the logic of the text.

However, traditional theology insisted that logical reasoning must not undermine the teaching of Scripture. Interpreters should not deny a scriptural doctrine or pit one doctrine against another. Perhaps the most notorious violator of this rule was the second-century heretic Marcion (mentioned in the discussion of canon in chapter 1). In his book *Contradictions* he argued that the God of the Old Testament and the God of the New Testament are completely contradictory characters, the Old Testament God being wrathful and the New Testament God being benevolent.[4] This principle held sway within Christian

3. Benedict Pictet, *Christian Theology,* trans. Frederick Reyroux (London: Seeley and Burnside, 1834), 1.9, p. 53. See also Heinrich Heppe, *Reformed Dogmatics,* rev. and ed. Ernst Bizer, trans. G. T. Thomson (1950; reprint, London: Wakeman Great Reprints, n.d.), pp. 9-11, for similar statements by Heidegger, Rijssen, and Turretin. For Lutheran views of the proper use and abuse of reason, see Robert D. Preus, *The Theology of Post-Reformation Lutheranism,* vol. 2, *God and His Creation* (St. Louis: Concordia, 1972), pp. 260-61 (hereafter *TPRL*).

4. Irenaeus *(Against Heresies)* and Tertullian *(Prescription Against Heretics)* tell us most of what we know about Marcion.

theology until the eighteenth century. The Socinians of the sixteenth and seventeenth centuries became the first wave of a modern movement to revise traditional doctrine to conform to the dictates of reason. They based their objections to the doctrines of the Trinity, the incarnation, and the vicarious atonement in part on logic: God cannot be both one and three, for these exclude each other; Christ cannot be fully divine and fully human; and one person's moral responsibility cannot, by definition, be transferred to another.[5] Orthodox theologians responded that alleged contradictions can be resolved for someone sympathetic to the faith; or, they said, those contradictions point beyond themselves to a mystery transcending reason. The Christian faith does not ask us to believe genuine contradictions.

The term "reason" has been applied to a second kind of cognitive activity, *intuition*. Whereas discursive or logical reason sees relationships among mental objects whose presence is presupposed, intuitive reason is the power to see the objects themselves. Think of it as a light that makes an object appear. In empirical intuition we intuit empirical objects through the senses; in intellectual intuition we grasp conceptual objects. Without some intuition, our minds would be completely empty of objects, and logical reason would have nothing to think about. Theology presupposes that we have ideas in our minds: trees, sky, father, mother, sheep, space, time, numbers, causality, logical relationships. Believing in supernatural revelation does not require believing that revelation inserts into our minds new objects and concepts over and above those we naturally intuit. Revelation makes use of the natural to reveal the supernatural.

Third, we use the term reason to indicate our power to see empirical relationships among the phenomena of the natural world. Reason in this form manifests itself in the natural and human sciences, as well as their common-sense counterparts. In this sense, reason studies not logical and rhetorical relationships among words and concepts but causal and quantitative connections among natural phenomena. By expressing their theories mathematically, physics and chemistry give the impression of completeness and necessity. But such an impression misleads because mathematical formulations abstract quantitative aspects of the physical world and leave the rest. Unless the world is con-

---

5. According to Richard Muller, *Post-Reformation Reformed Dogmatics: The Rise and Development of Reformed Orthodoxy*, vol. 1, *Prolegomena to Theology* (Grand Rapids: Baker Academic, 2003), p. 394 (hereafter *PRRD*), the earlier Socinians "held to the necessity of revelation." However, as Socinianism developed, it "tended to press the rationality of Christian doctrine to the point that revelation was little more than a divinely sanctioned reiteration of natural theology." See also Jaroslav Pelikan, *The Christian Tradition: A History of the Development of Doctrine*, vol. 4, *Reformation of the Church and Dogma 1300-1700* (Chicago: University of Chicago Press, 1984), pp. 322-31.

structed entirely of numbers, mathematical formulas cannot explain what a thing is; nor can they account for real, nonquantitative relationships — such as causality — among entities.

The nonmathematical natural sciences study other kinds of relationships. Biology, for example, studies the roles that organs, limbs, and genes play within an organism, as well as the organism's relationship to its environment. Psychology studies the relationships internal to the mind/brain and nervous system and the relationship of that complex to the external world. The empirical sciences study connections among the phenomena of nature perceptible to the senses: a behavior, a feeling, an image on a screen, or an increase in temperature.

Bernard Lonergan distinguishes between science and common sense in a way that helps us distinguish between science and theology: "Where the scientist seeks the relation of things to one another, common sense is concerned with the relations of things to us. Where the scientist's correlations serve to define the things that he relates to one another, common sense not merely relates objects to a subject but also constitutes relations of the subject to objects."[6] In contrast, theology thinks about things in relationship to God. Empirical science is not the science of everything, and a great many conflicts between science and theology are rooted in the neglect of this fact. Empirical science studies the surfaces of things and cannot get to the reality of them, which would involve studying their relationships to God. Likewise, theology is not the science of everything; it does not use empirical reasoning. It does not study quantitative, causal, or other kinds of relationships among things in the world. Theology studies God, the things of God, and God's relationship to the world.

Reason Abused

As I have noted above, traditional theology valued reason as an instrument but rejected it as a material source or critical norm. For the Reformers and Protestant orthodoxy, Scripture was the starting point (the "principle") of theology, and the work of the Word and the Spirit were sufficient grounds for the knowledge of faith.[7] Enlightenment thinkers challenged the traditional view of reason in theology. I will briefly examine the thought of John Locke, who subverted the Protestant understanding of faith and substituted a rationalist theory, and of David Hume, who rejected the traditional view with skeptical cynicism.

6. Lonergan, *Insight: A Study of Human Understanding* (New York: Harper and Row, 1978), p. 181.
7. See Muller, *PRRD*, 1, pp. 430-45.

John Locke (1632-1704) was taken by many in his day — and most certainly understood himself — to be a pious and orthodox Christian. Indeed, he thought of himself as an apologist for the faith. He defended the idea that some truths are above reason's power to discover and that God can reveal these super-rational truths, if he chooses. However, Locke declared that reason has the power, and must assert the prerogative, to judge whether a particular claimant is an authentic revelation from God. In his *Essay Concerning Human Understanding,* he explains:

> Whatever God hath revealed is certainly true: no doubt can be made of it. This is the proper object of faith: but whether it be a *divine* revelation or no, reason must judge; which can never permit the mind to reject a greater evidence to embrace what is less evident, nor allow it to entertain probability in opposition to knowledge and certainty. There can be no evidence that any traditional revelation is of divine origin, in the words we receive it, so clear and certain as that of the principles of reason. And therefore *nothing that is contrary to, and inconsistent with, the clear and self-evident dictates of reason, has a right to be urged or assented to as a matter of faith, wherein reason hath nothing to do* (4.18).[8]

Is Locke simply saying what theologians had said for centuries, namely, that we should not interpret Scripture to teach contradictions? Unfortunately, further reading shows that Locke adopts a much more radical stance. His main targets are the "enthusiasts," who say they believe their "fancies" because they were revealed and know they were revealed because they believe them so strongly. To undercut this sort of credulity, Locke proposes a definition of responsible faith:

> Faith is nothing but a firm assent of the mind: which, if it be regulated, as is our duty, cannot be afforded to anything but upon good reason; and so cannot be opposite to it. He that believes without having any reason for believing, may be in love with his own fancies; but neither seeks truth as he ought, nor pays the obedience due to his Maker, who would have him use those discerning faculties he has given him, to keep him out of mistake and error (4.17.24).[9]

Locke insists that rational assent to a reported revelation requires more than the words of the report. It requires external signs ("good reasons") that can au-

8. Locke, *Essay Concerning Human Understanding,* ed. Maurice Cranston (London: Collier-Macmillan, 1965), p. 397 (italics in original).

9. Available at http://humanum.arts.cuhk.edu.hk/Philosophy/Locke/echu/ (accessed June 15, 2006).

thenticate the claimed revelation. The "enthusiasts" fail this test, but Christianity can be shown reasonable by fulfilled prophecy and miracles.[10] Locke thus vindicates Christianity's "reasonableness." However, we should not celebrate Locke's apologetic for Christianity too exuberantly until we consider the price that must be paid for it; for what he gives with one hand he takes away with the other. Reason's support for faith asks in return faith's admission that it needs reason's support. What is the difference between judging the authenticity of a revelation and determining its truth? In both cases reason claims to anticipate revelation with knowledge of the possibilities to which it must conform: it knows in advance what sorts of signs could confirm a revelation. But Locke overlooks something: any sign that can confirm a supernatural revelation needs also to be a supernatural revelation and hence needs confirmation from another sign, and so forth into infinity. Thus Locke's theory traps him in an infinite regression and makes withholding assent to revelation the most reasonable option, which is a kind of neutral, or default, position. Clearly, Locke's theory is but an inference away from Deism and thus a complete rejection of revelation.[11]

In David Hume (1711-1776), Locke's definition of rational faith works itself out into skepticism toward the very faith Locke intended to defend. Hume's discussion of miracles, in *An Enquiry Concerning Human Understanding*, lays down a very Lockean rule: "The wise man, therefore, proportions his belief to the evidence."[12] According to Hume, no event counts as a miracle unless it violates the laws of nature, and the laws of nature are established by our "firm and unalterable experience" (p. 79). Thus reason tells us: if it happens, it's not a miracle, and if it's a miracle, it doesn't happen. What kind of proof can overcome this strong presumption against miracles? Hume concludes that "no testimony is sufficient to establish a miracle, unless the testimony be of such a kind, that its falsehood would be more miraculous, than the fact, which it endeavours to establish" (p. 80). Nevertheless, if someone insists that he believes, he is declaring "a continued miracle in his own person which subverts all the principles of understanding and gives him a determination to believe what is most contrary to custom and experience" (p. 91). In Hume's ironic wit, then, Locke's demand for "good reason" for faith transmutes into an excuse for unbelief and a justification for skepticism. One can always say, "Not enough evidence."

10. Locke, *The Reasonableness of Christianity*, ed. Ian T. Ramsey (Stanford: Stanford University Press, 1958), pp. 32-34, 37.

11. For a study of the fourth book of Locke's *Essay Concerning Human Understanding*, see Nicholas Wolterstorff, *John Locke and the Ethics of Belief* (Cambridge, UK: Cambridge University Press, 1996).

12. Hume, *An Enquiry Concerning Human Understanding* (Kitchener, Ont.: Batoche Books, 2000), p. 77.

In summary, a sound Christian theology need not view reason as an enemy. While it opposes the abuse of reason, Christian theology values its correct use. Reason functions as an instrument through which we see logical connections and analogies among the data of revelation. It intuits the empirical and conceptual objects that constitute the grammar of our experience, and hence it provides the matrix within which we experience revelation. However, Christian theology insists that reason remain a servant. It must not be allowed to determine the content of revelation, judge its truth, or limit God's power to reveal himself.

Experience

Experience has been called — along with Scripture, tradition, and reason — a "source" of theology.[13] Although there is an element of truth in this suggestion, we can consider experience a source of theology, strictly speaking, only if we have in mind God's self-experience. Just as God's self-knowledge grounds revelation's possibility and theology's truth, God's experience of himself grounds the possibility of our experience of God. With the exception of prophets, apostles, and the incarnate Son of God, we should not look to human experience of God for theological truth. For us, experience is not the origin of theology but its goal. Indeed, experience is the goal of the history of revelation. God speaks to us that we might experience him. Scripture, tradition, and reason cooperate to facilitate our experience of God. Of what use are the means of revelation if they do not achieve the end they serve? What is Scripture without experience? Words. What is tradition? A graveyard. What is reason? An iceberg.

Experience Used

The concept of experience, like that of reason, requires some analysis. But we must appreciate from the beginning that any concept of experience Christian theology can acknowledge must be drawn from Scripture and based on faith. Whereas common sense, experimental psychology, and philosophy may stimulate our imaginations and provide helpful concepts, faithful theology asserts

---

13. See W. Stephen Gunter and others, *Wesley and the Quadrilateral: Renewing the Conversation* (Nashville: Abingdon, 1997), for a discussion of the so-called Wesleyan quadrilateral (Scripture, tradition, experience, and reason); see also Thomas Oden, *Systematic Theology,* vol. 1 (San Francisco: Harper and Row, 1987), pp. 330-35.

the freedom to select whatever ideas from these fields it finds useful. God remains God, sovereign and free, even in our experience of him. Therefore, in the analysis that follows I will be working with a concept of experience that I find in the Christian doctrines of the Trinity, the Holy Spirit, the union of the believer with Christ, and the resurrection of the dead. Here we find a concept of the ultimate experience that awaits us: union with the triune God. This concept provides the norm for the role that experience should play in Christian theology and life.

Experience is self-authenticating. We cannot doubt the presence of our feelings and emotions. Most often experience points to something external that causes or occasions it. When we experience something, we "feel" its presence: it makes itself known by causing something in us that corresponds to it. In contrast, we cannot experience something completely outside us. Sheer objectivity is not experience at all. On the other hand, sheer subjectivity is not an experience of anything in particular. If we absorb the thing we are experiencing completely, there will be nothing left to experience. I conclude that the ideal experience of something involves feeling that thing directly without losing a sense of its objectivity, of its being other than us. The perfect experience is the union of subject and object.

The desire to understand what we are experiencing accompanies every experience. Indeed, it is difficult to imagine becoming aware of our experience without already thinking of it as an experience of a certain character that is elicited by something in particular. Can pain, fear, disgust, anger, and joy, for example, be experienced without being named and associated with something that occasions them? We can distinguish feeling from thinking and experience from knowledge; but, if we were to separate them completely, we would diminish the quality of each. On the other hand, as the quality of knowledge and the quality of experience increase, they approach each other, so that perfect knowledge and perfect experience coincide.[14] For Christian theology, perfect knowledge and perfect experience overlap in the mutual indwelling of the Father, Son, and Holy Spirit.

We recognize that experiences differ, and the way we experience them differs accordingly. Three kinds of experience come to mind: sensual, aesthetic, and personal. In order to illustrate sense experience, let us consider taste. I believe that there is a substance named salt; I have studied its constituents and properties in my college chemistry classes. But it is only by tasting it that I get the dis-

---

14. See Caroline Franks Davis, *The Evidential Force of Religious Experience* (Oxford: Clarendon Press, 1989), pp. 19-22. Davis points out that we "undergo" experience, whereas thinking is something we "do."

tinctive sense of knowing a substance *as salt.* We do not so much experience salt itself, however, as we experience its effects. These effects are internal and undeniable; nevertheless, we know salt only as the thing that causes these particular sensations. The same analysis applies to the other senses. Do we feel, see, hear, and smell other things, or do we experience the sensations that are occasioned in us by external things? Sensual experience thus falls short of the ideal experience, that is, of perfect union with the other without loss of distinction.

Aesthetic experience displays likenesses and differences with sensual experience. I shall limit my analysis to experiences of the beautiful.[15] The most common aesthetic experiences come through the senses, though mathematics and other systems of ideas can also create a sense of the beautiful. Seeing an orange sunset over the blue Pacific, a red rose among green leaves and brown thorns, or a snow-capped peak towering above the green or gray horizon evokes a sense of wonder, serenity, and joy. Like the sensual experience of a physical thing, the beautiful thing sets in motion something in us that we know directly because it *is* us. Aesthetic experience, however, differs in many ways from sensual experience. In aesthetic experience, even though we meet the object through the senses, the object itself is not physical. A beautiful object is a harmonious constellation of relationships among other objects or properties. The beauty of music is the set of complementary relationships among different sounds. The beauty of an ocean sunset (in contrast to the noonday sun) is the set of contrasting yet complementary relationships among the orange circle, the light blue sky, and the straight dark blue line of the ocean horizon.

Since the object of aesthetic experience is not a material thing but an intelligible and spiritual reality, it can enter into us without ceasing to be itself. In sensual experience we focus on the feelings caused by the object, whereas in aesthetic experience we focus on the object and tend to forget ourselves and our feelings. The beautiful object is not reducible to the emotions it causes in us. Somehow we know that we cannot merely absorb beautiful objects into ourselves; they engender emotions within us and through them affect even our bodies. They do this, however, internally and spiritually and not externally and mechanically. In the aesthetic we approach the ideal experience: we know directly and subjectively something that remains, despite its closeness, other than us. Nevertheless, aesthetic experience falls short of the ideal. In the experience of beauty, though we remain conscious of the otherness of the object, we do not experience its otherness from the inside. There is still an unknown aspect. We

---

15. See Wladyslaw Tatarkicwicz, "The Great Theory of Beauty and Its Decline," *The Journal of Aesthetics and Art Criticism* 31 (1972): 165-80. For the history of aesthetics, see *The Encyclopedia of Philosophy,* ed. Paul Edwards (New York: Macmillan, 1967), s.v. "Beauty."

have not yet achieved the ideal union of subject and object, of knower and known, that retains the otherness of each even in the intimacy of union.

But what if the object of our appreciation were also a subject, able to reveal itself to us without giving up its difference from us? This addition moves us closer to the ideal experience, which we can achieve only in personal knowledge. Our experience of other persons, though having some things in common with sensual experience and even more with aesthetic experience, moves us into a new dimension of experience. In experiencing a physical object through the senses, we virtually absorb it into ourselves and lose sight of its objectivity. In aesthetic experience, we remain conscious of the object's otherness but at the price of our intimate knowledge of it. Ideally, we transcend these limitations in knowing other persons. In knowing another person, I express my self-knowledge in words and intentional actions that are understood by the other. That person then uses words and symbols to show understanding, which adds to my knowledge of myself: now I know myself as known by another. Building on the trust established so far, the other person reciprocates with self-revelation, and the dialogue continues to go deeper into mutual knowledge. At some point, when trust and mutual knowledge reach a certain threshold, a friendship is established. A friend is another person in whom I can see myself. She or he is a second me, an alter ego with whom I share interests, loves, and experiences.

Experiencing fully the reality of another person requires mutual love. In love, two persons unite so that each sees himself or herself only in and with the beloved. In the mutuality of love, we approach the ideal experience. The object we experience does not have to be absorbed into us to become an experience for us; nor does it have to continue outside of us to remain other than us. We experience our beloved ones as internal to us because they freely *give* themselves to us. Our beloved ones remain other than us because they give themselves to us *freely*. In knowing our beloved ones, we participate in their free self-revelation. But they are more than their self-revelation, infinitely more, and thus they always remain a mystery.

Personal knowledge, the union of two persons in love, is the best analogy I know for the experience of God. The goal of revelation is experiencing God, person to person, feeling God's love for us and loving God in return. And the center of God's personal self-communication, according to Paul, is the love for us revealed in Jesus Christ: "But God demonstrates his own love for us in this: While we were still sinners, Christ died for us" (Rom. 5:8). "But because of his great love for us, God, who is rich in mercy, made us alive with Christ even when we were dead in transgressions" (Eph. 2:4, 5; cf. Titus 3:4, 5). John also points to God's love for us: "This is love: not that we loved God, but that he loved us and sent his Son as an atoning sacrifice for our sins" (1 John 4:10).

God's love for us frees us to love in return. Jesus affirmed that the greatest commandment is to love God with our whole being (Matt. 22:37). We can know love only by loving; hence, apart from loving him, we cannot "know God" (1 John 4:7-8). Paul's hymn to love in 1 Corinthians speaks eloquently to this subject: "If I speak in the tongues of men and of angels, but have not love, I am only a resounding gong or a clanging cymbal. If I have the gift of prophecy and can fathom all mysteries and all knowledge, and if I have a faith that can move mountains, but have not love, I am nothing. If I give all I possess to the poor and surrender my body to the flames, but have not love, I gain nothing" (1 Cor. 13:1-3).

Great displays of religious activity, miracles, vast knowledge, eloquence, and even martyrdom, if done without love, are worthless. Tomes of erudite theology, endowed institutions, beautiful cathedrals, religious symbols, pilgrimages, and works of charity, bereft of love, are meaningless. Only if these acts express our self-emptying love for God and our neighbor do they rise above self-righteous display. Only in love can we know God; only in love does the self-revelation of God achieve its goal.

Paul recognizes that we will not achieve perfect love in this life. There will come a time, though, when "we shall see face to face" (1 Cor. 13:12). Loving, seeing face to face, and knowing as we are known point toward the ideal experience of God, a person-to-person knowledge. Though we can experience something of God now, we will have the fullness of that experience only in the future. The church fathers and modern orthodox theologians speak of this experience as "deification": deification will be achieved in the definitive union of the Christian with God in the resurrection.[16] That union bears similarities to the incarnation, where the human nature of Christ was united to the divine nature in the person of the Son of God. Thus united, the human nature shared in the eternal life of the divine nature, without ceasing to be human. On the other hand, the Western church and its theologians spoke about the vision of God: the saints in heaven see God "face to face" and are thereby united completely to God. They share in the eternal, personal life of the blessed Trinity.

Faith, hope, and love remain, concludes Paul (1 Cor. 13:13). We live by faith in this life: in faith we experience something of God through the words of Scripture, and in the power of the Spirit we trust that a fuller experience of God awaits us in God's future. In faith we are moved through the words to trust the hidden person who speaks them. In hope we anticipate the full reality of what

16. See Panayiotis Nellas, *Deification in Christ: Orthodox Perspectives on the Nature of the Human Person,* trans. Norman Russell (Crestwood, NY: St. Vladimir's, 1997); see also Dumitru Staniloae, *The Experience of God,* vol. 2, *The World: Creation and Deification* (Brookline, MA: Holy Cross Orthodox Press, 2000).

faith believes and love experiences. But love is the fulfillment of faith and the goal of hope (1 Cor. 13:13). In love we experience what faith believes and hope anticipates, that is, personal fellowship with God.

Our experience of God occurs within the Trinitarian life of the Father, Son, and Spirit. The Son reveals the Father in the power of the Spirit and draws us into the event of love among the persons of the Trinity. Responding to Philip's request ("show us the Father"), Jesus says: "If you really knew me, you would know my Father as well. From now on, you do know him and have seen him. . . . Anyone who has seen me has seen the Father. How can you say, 'Show us the Father'?" (John 14:7-9; cf. John 16:14, 15; 17:26). The Father shows his love for us as he becomes palpable and visible in the Son; the Son reveals the Father by loving us with the Father's love, and thus we see and know the love of the Father. The Son loves the Father by emptying himself in obedience to the Father. In this he shows us how to love the Father and how to love our neighbor with the love of the Father. The Spirit "pours" God's love into our hearts and creates fellowship between us and the Father and the Son (cf. Rom. 5:5).

Experience Abused

Like tradition and reason, human experience can be used as an excuse to overturn, ignore, or distort the apostolic tradition preserved in Scripture. According to many contemporary theologians, human experience is the source of revelation and the origin of theology. I shall call this viewpoint "liberal" because it considers scriptural doctrine and ethics revisable in view of experience. Experiential criteria for evaluating theologies differ from theologian to theologian. Schleiermacher judges doctrines by their effectiveness in preserving and enhancing the original *religious* experience, the "feeling of absolute dependence." In Schleiermacher, the normative experience has a religious character. "Christian doctrines," Schleiermacher says, "are accounts of Christian religious affections set forth in speech."[17]

Karl Rahner, one of the twentieth century's most influential Roman Catholic theologians, attempts to combine the liberal thesis that doctrine "expresses" religious experience with adherence to Roman Catholic teaching.[18] He argues that God is always present to every human being as a "supernatural existential."

17. Schleiermacher, *The Christian Faith,* trans. D. M. Baillie et al., ed. H. R. Mackintosh and J. S. Stewart (Philadelphia: Fortress, 1976), p. 76.

18. See George A. Lindbeck, *The Nature of Doctrine: Religion and Theology in a Postliberal Age* (Philadelphia: Westminster Press, 1984), pp. 31-32. Lindbeck criticizes the "experiential/expressive" view of doctrine and advocates a "cultural/linguistic" understanding.

This supernatural presence affects our consciousness at a deep level and constitutes a primitive experience and consciousness of God. Rahner interprets Christian teaching in view of this theory; doctrines can be traced back to this universal religious experience. However, in contrast to some theologians with a similar view of religious experience, Rahner does not use religious experience to criticize and revise the church's teaching. He assumes rather that church dogma infallibly articulates the experience of God. Theology serves the church by showing the existential and experiential vitality of its teaching.[19]

Other contemporary liberal theologians, though they do not discount *religious* experience, focus more on cultural experience: race, gender, and class consciousness. They develop pragmatic criteria to evaluate and revise doctrine. For example, Sallie McFague argues that, since God is radically mysterious, theologies can be judged only by such criteria as "fruitfulness" and "helpfulness."[20] Theologies that support illiberal (sexist, anti-environmental, and homophobic) values are "not appropriate *for our time*." McFague also suggests that we drop such offensive metaphors as "king, ruler, lord, master" and generate other metaphors for God and God's relationship to the world. She suggests the images of mother, lover, and friend.[21] Peter Hodgson broadens the list of experiential "sources" of theology to include other religions, cultural history, and social location. He proposes "liberation" as the "material norm" for theology so that whatever does not aid the "liberation of life" should be criticized. Hodgson rejects the appeal to Scripture and the other sources as "authorities" in the classic sense. Instead, the sources of theology must "win" authority with their "disclosive, life-giving power."[22] In other words — not to put too fine a point on it — Scripture is authoritative when it tells us to feel what we feel already, think what we thought previously, and do what we wanted to do anyway.

Gordon Kaufmann relies on nonreligious experience as his source of theology and expresses a radically agnostic position. According to Kaufmann, our experience of the world enables us to postulate God as the basis of unity in the world process: "God, I am proposing, should be understood as the underlying reality — the ultimate creativity, ultimate mystery — that manifests itself

19. Rahner, "Concerning the Relationship Between Nature and Grace," in *Theological Investigations I: God, Christ, and Mary* (New York: Crossroad, 1961), pp. 297-317. See also Rahner, ed., *Encyclopedia of Theology* (New York: Crossroad, 1975), s.v. "Man, Anthropology III: Theological," where Rahner uses the idea of "supernatural existential" to interpret the incarnation.

20. McFague, *Models of God: Theology for an Ecological, Nuclear Age* (Philadelphia: Fortress, 1987), p. 34.

21. McFague, *Models of God*, pp. 13-19.

22. Hodgson, *Winds of the Spirit: A Constructive Christian Theology* (Louisville: Westminster John Knox, 1994), pp. 24-29.

throughout the universe."[23] In a later work, *In the Beginning Creativity*, Kaufmann identifies God with the "serendipitous creativity" operative in the world.[24] Religious experience plays no part in his thought. He explains his lack of interest in religious experience autobiographically: "I seem to be 'tone deaf' with respect to so-called religious experience. When others speak of their 'experience of God' or of 'God's presence,' or the profound experience of 'the holy' or of 'sacredness,' I simply do not know what they are talking about" (pp. 109-10). To those who know God as Father, Son, and Spirit, Kaufmann's "God" seems rather distant and aloof, if not completely irrelevant. A God so submerged in nature and explained by a writer who is "tone deaf" to the experience of God seems hardly worth thinking about, much less seeking passionately to see face to face.

Experience in Retrospect

Let me summarize my thoughts on experience. Though I have rejected experience as a *source* of theology, I consider it an important *factor* in theology.[25] In faith and hope we anticipate the full experience of our union with the triune God. In love inspired by the Holy Spirit we experience the "first fruits" of that union even now. This imperfect experience, along with the promise of the full experience, gives Christian doctrine an experiential content and goal. This understanding of experience enables the theologian to show the experiential vitality of Christian doctrine without the drawbacks found in liberal theology.

Theology

Expanded Definition and Brief Justification

Aristotle used the word "theology" to differentiate metaphysics from other sciences.[26] Although the New Testament does not use the word "theology," the idea and the activity are clearly present.[27] The word of God became flesh and

---

23. Kaufmann, *God-Mystery-Diversity: Christian Theology in a Pluralistic World* (Minneapolis: Fortress, 1996), p. 107.

24. Kaufmann, *In the Beginning Creativity* (Minneapolis: Fortress, 2004), p. 53.

25. Randy L. Maddox, "The Enriching Role of Experience," in Gunter et al., *Wesley and the Quadrilateral*, pp. 125-27.

26. Aristotle, *Metaphysics*, 6.1 and 10.7, in *The Basic Works of Aristotle*, ed. with Intro. by Richard McKeon (New York: Random House, 1941), pp. 778-79; 860-62. According to Aristotle, there are three kinds of theoretical science: physics, mathematics, and theology.

has "made him known" (John 1:18). Paul instructed the Ephesian elders to guard the flock against those who would "distort the truth in order to draw away disciples after them" (Acts 20:30). Jesus sent his disciples to make "disciples of all nations . . . and teach them" (Matt. 28:19-20). Apollos debated the Jews of the Corinthian synagogue, "proving from the Scriptures that Jesus was the Christ" (Acts 18:28). Paul dismissed the pagan "scholar" and "philosopher" of this world; but he affirmed "Christ crucified" as the "power" and "wisdom" of God (1 Cor. 1:20-24). He differentiated his approach from the "theology" of the age by reminding his readers of the "Spirit's power" (1 Cor. 2:4-5). Nevertheless, he affirmed a Christian wisdom revealed "by God's Spirit," who knows "even the deep things of God" (1 Cor. 2:6-12).

Terminology aside, the church has always considered the knowledge and activity of theology essential to her life. In its theology the church seeks a deeper understanding of its faith. It reflects on God, the things of God, God's actions, and God's relationship to all things. The church is motivated by a desire to know God so that it might enjoy him, praise him, speak rightly of him, and obey him. A medieval saying sums up the traditional understanding of theology: "Theology is taught by God, teaches of God and leads to God."[28] The post-Reformation Reformed theologians defined theology variously as "the science of living blessedly forever" (Perkins), "the doctrine of living unto God" (Ames), "the teaching concerning God and divine things" (Spanheim), or "the true wisdom of divine things, divinely revealed unto us to live well and blessedly" (Leigh).[29]

What kind of knowledge and activity is theology? Medieval and post-Reformation theologians debated whether theology should be considered as theoretical or practical in character. Thomas Aquinas argued that theology is a science in the Aristotelian sense of that term. Aristotle had argued that an intellectual activity is a science if it reasons to its conclusions from intuitively certain first principles. Aquinas argued that Christian theology is a science in a derived sense. It receives its first principles not from intuition but from divine revelation and draws out its conclusions from these revealed princi-

---

27. Francis Turretin, *Institutes of Elenctic Theology,* vol. 1, trans. George Musgrave Giger, ed. James T. Dennison, Jr. (Phillipsburg, NJ: Presbyterian and Reformed, 1992), 1.1.2, p. 1, makes this point.

28. Turretin, *Institutes of Elenctic Theology,* 1.1.6, p. 2.

29. *A Golden Chaine or the Description of Theology,* 2, in *The Works of William Perkins,* ed. Ian Breward (Berkshire, UK: Sutton Courtenay Press, 1970), p. 177; William Ames, *The Marrow of Sacred Divinitie,* quoted in Muller, *PRRD,* 1, p. 155; Spanheim, *Disputationum theologicarum syntagma,* 1.1.9, quoted in Muller, *PRRD,* 1, p. 155; Leigh, *Body of Divinity,* quoted in Muller, *PRRD,* 1, p. 156. The Lutheran definition of theology parallels the Reformed; see Robert Preus, *TPRL,* 1, pp. 162-82.

ples.[30] Post-Reformation Lutheran theologians argued that theology is a "practical aptitude" rather than a science. Theology, according to Abraham Calov (1612-1686), aims not to "demonstrate something" but to "achieve something," namely, the salvation of humankind and the glory of God. "Whatever is considered by theology," Calov contends, "is either purely practical, or else it is considered primarily and properly for no other reason than that it has to do with action."[31] The majority of Reformed theologians argue that theology contains speculative elements and practical elements, with the emphasis falling on the practical.[32] I shall follow the Reformed view in this study. Though the speculative aspect should not predominate, theology must be concerned with knowing God: contemplating what God has revealed of himself and reasoning from it to extend and clarify our knowledge. In theology we set God's self-revelation before our minds, so that we may seek him as our good, imitate him as our righteousness, and praise him for his greatness — an eminently practical endeavor.

In the broad sense discussed above, theology is of vital concern to every Christian. In a narrower sense, theology is the church's activity of self-examination and can be practiced fruitfully only by a few. Pastors, teachers, and local church leaders carry on aspects of this work in the daily life of the church, in teaching, preaching, conducting worship, and spiritual counseling. Scholars and academic theologians conduct their work in schools — colleges, universities, research institutes, and seminaries — to prepare teachers, preachers, and pastors for the church. Academic theology addresses the vital question of whether the church is proclaiming, teaching, and living consistently with the Word of God. It exemplifies the virtues of other academic disciplines: rigor, precision, clarity, and comprehensiveness.[33] In the company of those in the historic church, living and dead, the academic theologian, acting in service to the church, compares the contemporary proclamation of the church with Scripture, so that we might know and love God truly. Theology does not function merely to uncritically defend the church's teaching. In theology, the church subjects itself to criticism by the Word of God. Karl Barth articulates the view of theology I am advocating in this book: theology is the "self-examination of the Christian Church with respect to the content of its distinctive talk about God."[34]

---

30. Aquinas, *Summa Theologica*, 1.1.2, in *Basic Writings of Saint Thomas Aquinas*, vol. 1, ed. Anton C. Pegis (New York: Random House, 1945), pp. 6-7.

31. Preus, *TPRL*, 1, p. 197.

32. For the Reformed discussion, see Muller, *PRRD*, 1, pp. 324-59.

33. See Muller, *PRRD*, 1, pp. 197-204, for the orthodox Reformed distinction between the two types of theology.

34. Barth, *Church Dogmatics*, trans. T. H. L. Parker et al., ed. G. W. Bromiley and T. F. Torrance (Edinburgh: T&T Clark, 1957), vol. 1, pt. 1, p. 3 (hereafter *CD*).

The Method of Theology

To increase our understanding of the faith, theologians select the subjects to be discussed, arrange their work in order, and use methods of analysis and synthesis. Traditionally, summaries of Christian doctrine treated the subjects and followed the order of the Apostles' Creed and the Nicene Creed, which themselves go back to the early church's teaching in preparation for baptism and the New Testament summaries of the apostles' preaching. This pattern is evident in the Eastern theologian John of Damascus and in the Western theologians Peter Lombard (1100-1160) and Thomas Aquinas. The first Protestant theology, *Loci Communes* (1521), written by Philip Melanchthon (1497-1560), began as a series of lectures on the book of Romans and followed the order of that book.[35] According to Richard Muller, the Reformed theologian Andreas Hyperius (1511-1564), suggested that Christian theology should be treated under six major topics: "God, creatures and man, the church, the doctrine of Law and gospel, signs or sacraments, and the consummation."[36] Though tradition and Scripture determined the major topics, theologians exercised much flexibility in choosing the subtopics to be discussed under the major headings — according to the needs and controversies of their day. The order of treatment was flexible, though there was a great deal of conformity as a matter of practice.

We must distinguish between the subjects and their order of treatment, on the one hand, and the method of argumentation used, on the other. Theologians gain insight by finding relationships among aspects of the faith and by answering certain questions commonly posed in our quest for understanding. In much traditional theology, the relationships sought were either logical or causal. If we think of theology as the principles, axioms, and propositions asserted in Scripture along with the conclusions that can be drawn from them, we will use a logical method. Every statement of fact or proposition has a subject and a predicate: the predicate defines the subject. In the statement "Rex is a ten-pound brown dog," the three predicates that follow the verb define the name "Rex." Aristotle, whose logic had an enormous impact on theology from the thirteenth century to the eighteenth century, proposed ten kinds of predicates we can use to understand *what* a thing is. According to Aristotle, if we can discover something's substance, quantity, quality, relation, place, time, position,

---

35. Clyde L. Manschreck, preface to *Melanchthon on Christian Doctrine,* trans. and ed. Clyde L. Manschreck (Grand Rapids: Baker Books, 1965), p. xxiii. The 1555 edition treats thirty-four topics.

36. Muller, *PRRD,* 1, p. 179. In this quote Muller summarizes the subjects in Hyperius's book *Methodus theologiae.*

state, action, and affection, we will know everything there is to know about what the thing is.[37]

If, on the other hand, we view theology as dealing with realities rather than propositions, we may approach the task of understanding causally. In this area, too, Aristotle's impact on traditional theology was pervasive. Aristotle proposed to explain *why* a thing is by discovering its four causes or explanatory principles: material causality (the stuff out of which a thing is made), formal causality (the design plan that makes it what it is), efficient causality (the power that brought together the matter and design plan), and final causality (the end for which it was brought into being).[38] Everything other than God exists because of something else. Discovering a particular thing's four causes explains why it exists.

The history of logic from the eighteenth century to the present is replete with new developments.[39] But modern theologians have been influenced by it only indirectly. Rarely have they adjusted their understanding of definition, proof, evidence, argumentation, and explanation to take into account the continuing developments in logic. Most theologians today write in a way that resembles ordinary conversation, storytelling, and commonsense reasoning. Rarely do they formalize their arguments in strictly logical terms, must less in the abstract symbols used in modern analytic philosophy.[40] Even in their theological criticism, the ideal place for logical analysis, contemporary theologians rarely use the formal tools of logic. This is not because they are lazy or fuzzy thinkers; rather, it arises from their conviction that theological meaning cannot be captured in a formal system of logic. They have given up on indubitable proofs, comprehensive explanations, and unimpeachable evidence. Michael Polanyi's words, originally expressed concerning scientific knowledge, apply to theology as well: "We know more than we can tell."[41] I would add that we can say more than we can account for logically. Few theologians today write "to whom it may concern" or to a disembodied intellect; instead, most theologians write for a target audience with whom they share certain presuppositions, concerns, and commitments, that is, for a community that shares a tradition.[42]

37. Aristotle, *Categories*, 4, in *Basic Works*, p. 3.

38. Aristotle, *Physics*, 2.3, in *Basic Works*, pp. 240-42.

39. This story is too complicated to rehearse here, even if I were competent to do so. See the 58-page, double-columned article "Logic, History of" in the *Encyclopedia of Philosophy* (1965).

40. See *The Cambridge Dictionary of Philosophy*, 2nd ed., ed. Robert Audi (New York: Cambridge University Press, 1991), s.v. "Analytic Philosophy."

41. Polanyi is quoted in Thomas F. Torrance, *Transformation and Convergence in the Frame of Knowledge: Explorations in the Interrelations of Scientific and Theological Enterprise* (Grand Rapids: Eerdmans, 1984), p. 112.

42. Alasdair MacIntyre speaks of the incommensurability of traditions. See *Whose Justice?*

My approach to theology falls into this latter category. I do not expect my expositions to convince someone outside my target audience: Christians who are genuinely committed to the apostolic tradition as it is passed on by the church and preserved in Scripture. My aim is to clarify the faith of this community rather than to convince outsiders. I shall seek to understand and explain what we confess rather than discover something previously unknown. I hope to enlighten our understanding of each aspect of the faith by placing it alongside others, which is an ancient method called the "analogy of faith." Since I understand the object of theology to be the being and activity of the triune God, I will attempt to relate all theological statements to this reality.

Objections to Theology from Ordinary Believers

Believers often view theology and theologians with caution and more than a little suspicion. They think professional theologians are likely to be heretics or arrogant snobs or cold rationalists — or all of the above. An acquaintance of mine habitually refers to theological seminaries as "theological cemeteries." He views ecumenical divinity schools and seminaries and most denominational seminaries as subversive to the faith of their students. They are places where, he believes, warm piety is transformed into heartless cynicism, and simple trust in the Bible and the church is debunked and replaced by suspicion and smugness. According to this friend, the "cemeteries" train a faithless clergy who do not preach the gospel or teach Scripture and who are likely to hijack the church and turn it into a social or political tool for advancing whatever agenda is current in elite circles.

Sadly, this common perception among those outside seminaries is not wholly unfounded. Individual theologians and theological schools share much of the blame. Many contemporary theologians do not share the church's faith and do not participate in the church's life. Few well-known seminaries and divinity schools can engage fully in the church's theological work, for they do not respect Scripture's authority and have little sympathy for the church's tradition. Rather than standing within the church and helping it submit to the norm of Scripture, they stand outside and subject Scripture and tradition to withering criticism.

As a teacher of theology, I feel obligated to expose my students to the whole range of theology. Thus, in studying modern theology we read theologians who

---

Which Rationality? (Notre Dame, IN: University of Notre Dame Press, 1988); see also MacIntyre, *Three Rival Versions of Moral Enquiry: Encyclopedia, Genealogy, and Tradition* (Notre Dame, IN: University of Notre Dame Press, 1990).

are representative of the eighteenth and nineteenth centuries, and in considering contemporary theology, we read theologians from the twentieth and twenty-first centuries. Many students find this experience excruciating. They feel as though they have moved from a faith-affirming environment of home and church into a world of criticism, suspicion, and unbelief. Before sending them in to be "sheep among wolves" (Matt. 10:16), I give them this rule: "Good theology makes you want to praise God, and bad theology makes you want to jump off a bridge." Good theology begins in faith, acts in love, proceeds with hope, and ends in praise. Good theology speaks confidently about God on the basis of God's own speech about himself. Good theology "walks humbly before its God" (Mic. 6:8) and seeks to "build up the body of Christ" (Eph. 4:12). In good theology, we meditate on our God and what he has done for us. Something is wrong with theology that is foreign to the mood of 1 Peter 1:8-9: "Though you have not seen him, you love him; and even though you do not see him now, you believe in him and are filled with an inexpressible and glorious joy, for you are receiving the goal of your faith, the salvation of your souls." No wonder theology has been called a "joyful" endeavor! Karl Barth hits the mark when he says the following: "The theologian who has no joy in his work is not a theologian at all. Sulky faces, morose thoughts, and boring ways of speaking are intolerable in this science."[43]

Believers often object to theology for its coldness and rationalism. The Christian life, for them, centers in experiences of worship, devotional reading, fellowship with other believers, and feeling God's love and acceptance. By contrast, theology cools the warm heart with a flood of complicated formulas, technical terms, fine distinctions, and obscure dogmas. These pious believers have a point: they're correct that the experience of God is the goal of divine revelation; they are also correct to point out that theology rarely connects with their Christian experience. Preachers and teachers, on the few occasions when they refer to theology, draw perfunctorily on their seminary class notes or textbooks to make a point. Rarely are they able to explain doctrine in a way that engages the congregation in an encounter with the living God. In my experience, the only way to overcome the objection that theology is joyless and boring is to write theology in a different mood, a mood of joy and praise, humility and thanksgiving, and confidence and hope.

Another common objection to theology comes from biblicism. Biblicists argue that the church should teach, preach, and confess its faith exclusively in the words of Scripture. In this way the church can remain faithful to the apostolic faith. According to biblicism, you cannot go wrong by believing and con-

43. *CD*, 1/1, p. 656.

fessing in the language of Scripture. Heresy arises from a desire to say something more than or different from what Scripture says. Hence biblicism frowns on using philosophical terms to explain the gospel, and it is wary of using logic to make connections and draw implications from Scripture. For biblicists, Christian doctrine is synonymous with "Bible doctrine." It is not what the church teaches that is important but what Scripture says that matters.[44] Biblicists fear that using complicated logic in theology will distort biblical teaching and will make ordinary Christians dependent on theological experts for access to God.

Biblicism is not without its strengths: it honors Scripture as the norm of all other norms, and it desires to remain faithful to the apostolic faith. Time after time, its suspicions of philosophy have been confirmed when theologians substitute a philosophical system for the biblical faith or, in bad faith, interpret Scripture against its plain meaning. Biblicists are correct in their concern that we not overextend our logic. However, as true as this may be, even ordinary assertions, when combined, have logical implications, and they have broader associations that take us beyond the bare words. The statement "I am going to get my oil changed now" communicates more than it explicitly says. Someone would probably be safe in concluding that I have a car, and that (if you know me) I probably have driven it about 3,000 miles since its last oil change, and that I plan to drive it somewhere to have this procedure done.

We realize, however, that this way of getting information is limited: one cannot extend that process very far from my explicit statement. For example, one would be going out on a limb to conclude something about the nature of oil, about my love of cars, or my tendency to procrastinate in matters mechanical. This caution also applies to explicit biblical teaching, where we would do well to avoid crawling out on logical limbs. John declares that "God is love." Perhaps we might conclude that everything love is, God is; however, this does not settle the question of what love is. Paul declares that love "keeps no record of wrongs" (1 Cor. 13:5). If God is love and love "keeps no record of wrongs," may we conclude that God keeps no record of wrongs? As a contemporary example of such logical overextension, consider one of Richard Rice's arguments for open theism. According to Rice, the incarnation shows that God limits himself by choosing to become involved with creation. His argument goes this way: "Accordingly, from a Christian standpoint it is appropriate to say not only that *Jesus is God,* but that *God is Jesus.* . . . The fact that God chose to express himself

---

44. For a thorough study of hermeneutics in a tradition in which theology is distrusted and biblicism is dominant, see Michael Casey, *The Battle Over Hermeneutics in the Stone-Campbell Movement* (Pittsburgh: Edwin Mellen Press, 1998).

through the medium of a human life suggests that God's experience has something in common with certain aspects of human life. . . . God enjoys relationships, has feelings, makes decisions, formulates plans and acts to fulfill them."[45] This argument rests on a fundamental logical mistake, a mistake the church fathers avoided: that is, it is not always true to say that if A is B then B is A. All apples are fruits, but not all fruits are apples. Jesus is God because the divine Son of God, who is God of God with the Father, joined himself to a full human nature. But the name "Jesus" does not refer to the divine nature alone but to the person who is both God and man. Therefore, the affirmation that "Jesus is God" cannot be reversed. Rice's logic, if pressed further, would lead us to absurd conclusions: for example, since God is Jesus and Jesus is a Jewish male, God is Jewish and male. No wonder biblicists are wary!

However, biblicism's weaknesses are significant. The notion that confining our theology to the words of Scripture will protect us from heresy is false and dangerously naive. Over and over during the church's long history, heretics have been able to communicate their heresies in the language of Scripture. In the fourth century, for example, Arius insisted that he confessed the apostolic faith in Jesus as the Christ, Son of God, and the agent of creation. Indeed, he could affirm every biblical text concerning the Son. However, he interpreted them to teach that the Son of God was a creature rather than God of God. The theologians of the Nicene Council struggled to find a way to confess the apostolic faith that would exclude the Arian heresy without introducing nonbiblical words. They failed in this endeavor, for Arius had his own interpretation of every biblical text. Arius happily confessed the words of the Bible, but he always had his own meaning in mind; and the church fathers knew that he did not hold the same faith. The church reluctantly added a nonbiblical word, *homoousia* (same essence), to explicitly contradict Arius's teaching, and thus it showed that Arius did not hold the same faith it had always held, even though he used biblical terms.[46]

A friend of mine was considering applying for a position to teach theology at an evangelical college, an institution that requires its entire faculty to sign a statement of faith that is thoroughly evangelical. Since I knew that my friend did not believe all of what the statement affirmed, I asked him how he could sign a doctrinal statement he could not assent to. He quickly replied, "Give me that thing. I will sign those things all day long." Words on a piece of paper — es-

45. "Biblical Support for a New Perspective," in *The Openness of God: A Biblical Challenge to the Traditional Understanding of God*, ed. Clark Pinnock, Richard Rice, John Sanders, et al. (Downers Grove, IL: InterVarsity Press, 1994), p. 39.

46. For this story, see Thomas F. Torrance, *The Trinitarian Faith* (Edinburgh: T&T Clark, 1995), pp. 120-22.

pecially old familiar words — whether the words of Scripture or of the creeds, are easily interpreted away by those who are motivated by something other than their desire to be faithful to God. I have been in discussions in which everyone present was a representative of a church body whose confessions of faith included the Nicene Creed. I knew for certain, however, that very few of those participants believed that creed, at least, taken in anything close to its original meaning. I have known theologians who would recite "Christ is risen indeed" with a congregation on Easter Sunday, but who do not believe, I am certain, what the first disciples reported or what most of the congregation joyfully celebrated that day.

Legalistically adhering to the words of Scripture is not the same activity as holding to the reality to which the words give witness. Verbal agreement is not the same as material agreement. Theology is a continuing process of finding other words that bring the reality witnessed to in Scripture into full view. Theology's perennial challenge is to help us avoid reading our own meanings into the old familiar words of Scripture, the creeds, and liturgies. Therefore, theologizing is not a matter of collecting Scripture quotes on select topics, or repeating the creeds, or collecting the church's past pronouncements, or cataloging traditions. It involves reading Scripture and assimilating tradition; but, more importantly, it requires prayer, spiritual discernment, patience, love, faith, hope, humility, and a disciplined life.

Elements and Activities of Theology

Theology, as I have defined it, is the church's self-examination with respect to its speaking and living. Though some Christians receive special gifts and a calling to the office of teacher, and hence to the theological task of self-examination, the whole church must participate in this work to some degree. Any Christian who examines himself or herself in the light of Scripture, interpreted in faith, humbly, prayerfully, obediently, and in the company of the whole church, is acting as a theologian. Every Christian is obligated to do this. Paul called on all the Corinthian Christians to exercise self-examination (2 Cor. 13:5-6).

Since Holy Scripture is the norm for all Christian speech and life, theology must involve a study of Scripture. The church studies canonical Scripture because it accepts the canon as the inspired and infallible norm of all its speech and action. It expends great energy examining them because it believes that the words of these texts are the words of God. In studying Scripture, the church remains in touch with its origin and its essence, its message and its mission. No other group sustains this relationship to these writings. Just as no other entity can preach the gospel or baptize or ordain Christian clergy, no other entity can study Scripture as its canon. The church witnessed to these writings as authentic bearers of the apostolic tradition, preserved their true interpretation, and bound itself to continue faithful to the tradition they contain. The church has no obligation to listen to interpretations of Scripture that do not begin with these presuppositions.

Must the church, then, reject the critical study of Scripture? As we have seen already, Christian theology involves the use of reason in an instrumental but not a material sense. Reason is a necessary and very useful servant in the church's work of examining Scripture, and the church is interested in what Scripture says. Therefore, studying the original languages (Hebrew, Aramaic, and Greek) and learning about the ancient cultures, languages, literatures, and religions of Egypt, Canaan, Mesopotamia, Greece, Rome, and other cultures are very important instruments to aid us in understanding Scripture. A variety of methods of study shed valuable light on Scripture. The church does not object to the critical study of Scripture as long as the word "critical" refers to the instrumental use of reason and not the material use.

Unfortunately, much contemporary critical study of the Bible also uses reason as material criterion by which to judge the teaching of Scripture. Some literary approaches seek to discover the oral or literary history that preceded the canonical form of the texts. Other biblical scholars study the editorial activities of the hypothetical editors that combined earlier (equally hypothetical) documents to form the canonical texts. Other methods of study use the canonical texts as historical sources for an imaginative reconstruction of "what really happened" in history. Still other approaches seek the human origins of the religious ideas found in the canonical texts. Each of these methods — and many others that I have not mentioned — has its own presuppositions, criteria, and goals.

I do not argue that these ways of studying the Bible cannot be ingenious and intriguing, nor do I doubt the brilliance and learning of many engaged in them. Many people make a living, a career, and even a reputation by practicing them well. Furthermore, I do not dispute that these studies often shed light on the canonical text in a way that can be appropriated by the church. However, insofar as modern biblical studies point away from the canonical texts to hypothetical history (oral traditions, documents, and human origins), they are completely irrelevant to the church's theological task. The canon of Scripture is the norm of all the church's speech and life, even its speech and life of biblical study. Hypothetical oral traditions, documents, imaginative reconstructions of historical events, and human origins have no authority for the church's theology. The Christian preacher has no commission and no authority to preach from these sources. Teachers have no right to teach from them in the name of the church. Theologians have no right to use them as norms in theology. Moreover, whoever presents these noncanonical sources in the church's name engages in a heretical act just as certainly as did the Gnostics of the second century, the Muslims of the seventh century, and the Mormons of the nineteenth century, when they created their own canons.

Theology also involves the study of church history. Since tradition plays such an important role in the church's activity of self-examination, a theologian must become thoroughly immersed in the history of the church's teaching, worship, and life. Theology is interested in the entire history of the church. Of great importance are those official statements of the early church fathers: the Apostles' Creed, the ecumenical councils, and the writings of the church fathers of the undivided church. A theologian should also become well acquainted with the great summative theologians of the West during the Middle Ages: Thomas Aquinas, Bonaventure (A.D. 1217-1274), and Duns Scotus (A.D. 1265-1308), as well as the Byzantine theologians John of Damascus (A.D. 675-749), Maximus the Confessor (A.D. 580-662), St. Symeon the New Theologian (A.D. 949-1022), and Gregory Palamas (A.D. 1296-1359). The theologian should study the controversies between the Western and Eastern churches and the dispute within the Western church that resulted in the division between the Protestant churches and the Roman Catholic Church. Theology must reflect on the Council of Trent and the First and Second Vatican Councils, as well as all the Protestant confessions of faith and catechisms: the Augsburg Confession of Faith (Lutheran), the Heidelberg Catechism (Reformed), the Westminster Confession of Faith (Puritan Reformed), and others. In addition, theologians must read theologians who theologized at other times and places and whose work has proved to be of value to the church. We should read contemporary theologians, but we must take care: even a hundred years is not enough time for the church to winnow out the theological wheat from the chaff.

Important also are the lives of the church's saints, heroes, and missionaries. The church's ideals of the Christian life are embodied in those to whom it looks as models. The martyrs of the early years (Polycarp and Justin), the monks of the patristic era (St. Anthony and Evagrius of Ponticus), and the founders of various monastic orders during the Middle Ages — St. Dominic (1170-1221), St. Francis (1181-1226), and Ignatius Loyola (1491-1556) — are models of the life of discipleship.

Most important of all for grasping the tradition is the theologian's deep and long-term participation in the worship and life of the church, whose liturgies for worship and baptism, whose hymns and prayers, and whose art contain its deepest beliefs about the meaning of Scripture and the nature of the Christian life. In order to understand the tradition of history, we must enter the history of tradition. As Roman Catholic and Orthodox theologians observe, we cannot simply collect a library full of documents and point to it as the church's tradition. The church's tradition is a living faith that can be known intimately only by living in the community of Christ. It is embodied not just in words but in countless symbolic actions, images, metaphors, subtle relationships, and moods. Our grasp of it is tacit and not fully expressed in words.

A theological reading of church history differs in at least two fundamental ways from a secular or "academic" reading. It assumes first that the church, the body of Christ, is under the providential care of God and that the Holy Spirit indwells, enlivens, protects, and leads it. This assumption does not require us to defend everything the church has done. It certainly gives us no right to claim perfect insight into the ways of God's providence. Indeed, this assumption does not guarantee that we can interpret church history in terms of a story of providence at all, even if we believe firmly, as we must, that omniscience could write such a story. However, this necessary theological assumption does prevent us from being taken in by histories of the church that reduce everything to human motivations or historical or natural circumstances or to psychological, political, sociological, and economic factors. Theologians should reject such reductionism.

Theological readings of church history differ from secular readings in a second way. Theologians are interested in grasping the mind of the church, in understanding her tradition for the sake of the theological task of self-examination. Secular historians have various motives for studying the history of the church, some of which may be laudable from a human point of view, and some not. But church history is of importance to theologians for the sake of maintaining Christian identity, of conforming contemporary faith to the apostolic archetype.

Theology must also take into account the norms, traditions, beliefs, values, systems of thought, and life patterns of the cultures within which the church lives. In popular culture (film, popular music, television, and athletics) we find the images and values that animate people in their daily lives. And in its apologetic and missionary work, the church must listen to those outside before it speaks to them. Understanding outsiders' views of the world can help locate the most appropriate contexts within which to express the Christian faith and the best beginning points for communicating the gospel. Such study will also help avoid needless misunderstandings and unnecessary offenses. Therefore, would-be theologians should take an interest in philosophy, literature, art, science, and popular culture. In philosophy, a culture articulates its beliefs and values in their clearest, most precise, and most coherent form. Those same values will be given powerful poetic and artistic expression in literature and art. Theology must also study philosophy, not simply to facilitate the church's missionary efforts, but also for its own constructive task.

Christian doctrine must be expressed in some language. The New Testament teaching about Christ, for example, draws on language present in the contemporaneous culture rather than inventing a new language. Terms such as "messiah," "word," "fullness," "wisdom," and "Son of God" were already current when Jesus and the early church took them into the Christian vocabulary and infused them with new meaning. As the church moved into different ages and into different cultures, the old terms gradually became opaque and needed to be explained in terms meaningful to people of later generations and different cultural backgrounds. The most obvious example of this need arose during the transition from Palestinian-Jewish to Greco-Roman culture. The apologists and the church fathers found themselves faced with a different set of questions and cultural assumptions than did the first Palestinian Christians. For the most part, they carefully maintained the normative status of biblical texts and the primacy of the tradition of the church over cultural beliefs and values. But they listened carefully to Greek metaphysics, and they chose those concepts that they believed could express the original message faithfully.

The same process of appropriation and expression in theology continues today, and it faces the same dangers. The theological formulas of the fourth- and fifth-century Greco-Roman church, the thirteenth-century European church, and the sixteenth-century Protestant churches require extensive explanation for a contemporary audience. Explanation requires translating obscure terms into familiar ones, terms that are usually derived from philosophy, high culture, or popular culture. The great challenge is to remain faithful to the original meaning. Failing this challenge, some theologians simply adopt a modern philosophical system — from Leibniz, Kant, Schelling, Hegel, Heidegger, or Whitehead — and reinterpret the Christian faith in terms of the new system. Remaining faithful to the apostolic faith, while explaining this faith in contemporary terms, requires careful adherence to the process I have outlined already: careful study of Scripture, listening respectfully to tradition, and participation in the life of the church: worship, prayer, humility, faith, hope, and love. Finally, the theologian must humbly submit his or her theology to the church for its judgment and obediently give it to the providence of God.

We must clearly differentiate Christian theology, the church's work of self-examination on the basis of Scripture, from other endeavors that call themselves "theology." Two kinds of such theology call for comment: philosophical theology and world theology. Philosophical theology is a relatively new name for that aspect of the old discipline of metaphysics that dealt with the existence and attributes of a divine being. Beginning in Greece, it influenced Christian theology's concepts through a dialogue sustained throughout the patristic era.[47] However, rarely in the patristic era did Christian thinkers write a metaphysical treatment of God independent of Christian theology. Through Anselm, Albert the Great, Thomas Aquinas, and others in the Middle Ages, the idea of a relatively autonomous philosophy of God became thinkable. Thomas Aquinas wrote *Summa Contra Gentiles,* a treatise that could be taken for such philosophy; but he did not intend to give people license to pursue such a discipline. On the contrary, he contended that only with the help of faith could reason clearly grasp the truth that is available to it.

With the dawning of the modern era, however, reason was eager to cast off its ecclesiastical guide. Between the times of Descartes (1596-1650) and Leibniz (1646-1716), a completely autonomous metaphysics of God developed as the basis of something called theism. Theism is the rationally based belief in a divine being who has certain attributes in common with the triune God of the Christian revelation. So confident were the Enlightenment thinkers in this new philosophy that some of them sought to break free of the church and establish their own religion, Deism. Others understood themselves to be Christians and used this new philosophy as a preparatory stage, incomplete in itself, for the fuller knowledge of God found in the supernatural revelation contained in Scripture. It seemed useful as an apologetic to use toward those who denied the existence of a divine being, even if it was found wanting as a basis for the Christian life.

Only recently has the term "philosophical theology" come into vogue. It is practiced by conservative and liberal Christians, as well as by a variety of theists. Even though philosophical theologians cannot deny that God is a religious concept and that it would be difficult for them to separate their religious faith from their philosophical reasoning, they attempt to give rational grounds for believing in a divine being that has certain characteristics in common with the Christian God. The community of philosophical theologians is composed of philosophers from Roman Catholic, Reformed, various evangelical groups, and Anglican backgrounds. Many see themselves not just as Christians who happen to be philosophers but as Christian philosophers, philosophizing in a Christian way, albeit without making assumptions that are based on faith in the Christian revelation.

World theology attempts to construct a theology that articulates the religious experience found in all the world's religions. Wilfred Cantwell Smith, for

47. See Jaroslav Pelikan, *Christianity and Classical Culture: The Metamorphosis of Natural Theology in the Christian Encounter with Hellenism* (New Haven: Yale University Press, 1993).

example, develops a world theology that centers in the concept of the transcendent.[48] All religions point to a reality that transcends the ordinary world, can be experienced in some way, and requires certain kinds of responses. In contrast to philosophical theology, world theology attempts to remain within the religious sphere. It aims to construct a theology that the adherents of the world's religions can acknowledge as their own. Thinkers from a variety of perspectives have raised significant objections to this project. Clearly, world theology has little more than the name in common with Christian theology.

I must address one more distinction that has often proved confusing and sometimes insidious. In certain settings a given endeavor will be designated as "academic" theology, but that name does not refer to a particular branch of theology with its own subject matter. Nor does it mean simply theology taught in a university or written by a professor of theology for other professors of theology or for use as a textbook in college classrooms. Rather, it refers to a particular set of rules to which theology is supposed to adhere. The term "academic theology" is most often used to differentiate theology practiced according to the rules of modern higher education (which we call "the academy") from what is practiced according to the rules of the church. The modern academy, being heir to the Enlightenment's rationalism, requires all disciplines wishing to have its imprimatur to reject the authority of tradition and Scripture, base themselves on publicly available data, and use reason to draw conclusions from that data. According to many defenders of the current academic regime, Christian theology practiced according to the rules I have laid out does not qualify as academic. The academy looks with suspicion at disciplines that use Scripture as the highest authority, that value tradition, that serve a community other than the university, and that aim at a religious goal.

Those who contrast "academic" theology to "ecclesiastical" theology intend to cast the latter in a bad light and expect us to conclude that academic theology is rational, open-minded, and public, while ecclesiastical theology is irrational, dogmatic, and parochial. We will be intimidated by this caricature only if we concede that the current academy has the exclusive right to determine what counts as rational.[49] I do not intend to make this concession. The

48. Smith, *Towards a World Theology* (Philadelphia: Westminster, 1981).

49. For recent critiques of a dominant academic model of rationality, see Alvin Plantinga and Nicholas Wolterstorff, eds., *Faith and Rationality: Reason and Belief in God* (Notre Dame, IN: University of Notre Dame Press, 1983); Alvin Plantinga, *Warranted Christian Belief* (New York: Oxford, 2000). See also Roy Clouser, *The Myth of Religious Neutrality: An Essay on the Hidden Role of Religious Beliefs in Theories* (Notre Dame, IN: University of Notre Dame Press, 1991), and *Knowing with the Heart: Religious Experience and Belief in God* (Downers Grove, IL: InterVarsity Press, 1999).

academy can offer degrees, jobs, social approval, accolades, tenure, professor-ships, publications, and other worldly rewards that tempt us to play along with it, but it cannot acquire exclusive proprietary rights to rationality or a monop-oly on the use of reason. It cannot speak the word of salvation or ordain a min-istry or dispense the sacraments or make a theologian. If, for now, the academy denies that Christian theology can be an academically respectable discipline, we need not be surprised, intimidated, or discouraged. We stand in good company, for the academy's rules would also exclude Paul, Irenaeus, Athanasius, Augus-tine, Aquinas, Luther, Calvin, Edwards, and Barth. Respectability is relative to the community whose approval one craves. If I am forced to choose between the academy and the church, I have no hesitation in choosing the company of these great ecclesiastical theologians over the contemporary academy.

3

What Fools Don't Know:
The Existence of God

"The fool has said in his heart, 'There is no God.'" Reading these blunt words from Psalm 14 provided the occasion for Anselm of Canterbury's *Proslogium*, his profound reflections on the existence of God.[1] The psalm does not call the atheist a liar or an ignoramus, but a fool. Anselm ponders this accusation. Why is one a *fool* for asserting the nonexistence of God? A fool is one who speaks (or acts) confidently about something he does not understand. Thus denying God is a sure sign, for Anselm, that one does not understand what the word "God" means. God is "that than which nothing greater can be conceived" (p. 7). The greatest conceivable being cannot be dependent on anything else for its existence; it exists necessarily. Anselm concludes: "So, then, no one who understands what God is can conceive that God does not exist; although he says these words in his heart, either without any or with some foreign, signification" (p. 10).

I find Anselm's reflections surprisingly contemporary. There is no lack of talk about God today. But one does not need to listen to it very long to realize that most speakers do not know what they are saying. Some atheists speak as though they could negate what the word "God" signifies without losing anything important. Some believers, too, seem unaware of what they are saying when they affirm that God exists. In this chapter I shall argue that the affirmation "God exists" is the most revolutionary, existentially decisive, and joyous affirmation possible. In contrast, I shall contend that the assertion "God does not exist" is equally revolutionary and existentially decisive — but in the opposite direction. God matters! And whether one believes or not, blabbing on about God without understanding is the activity of a fool. Let us not play the fool. Let

---

1. The page numbers in the text refer to the translation in *Saint Anselm: Basic Writings,* 2nd ed., trans. S. N. Deane (La Salle, IL: Open Court, 1968).

us rather pray with Anselm: "And so, Lord, do thou, who dost give understanding to faith, give me, so far as thou knowest it to be profitable, to understand that thou *art* as we believe; and that thou art *that which* we believe" (p. 7; italics added).

Asking the Right Question

A Misleading Question

"Does God exist?" Perhaps you have participated in classroom discussions that opened with this question. Authors place it in their book titles, and hundreds of book chapters and published articles ask this question.[2] It seems like the perfect prompt to initiate a dialogue among open-minded people on the existence and significance of God. I do not discount its rhetorical effectiveness as a discussion starter or as a book title. And I admit that many inquirers ask it in all honesty and fervently seek an answer. However, Christian theology must not allow this question to set the agenda for its discussion of God's existence. For, as I have argued in the preceding two chapters, Christian theology begins in faith, not in doubt. The existence of God is not a problem for Christian theology; it is its presupposition.

The church assembles to praise and thank God and to rejoice in what he has done for us, not to discuss whether he exists. We come together to pray and to encourage one another to live lives worthy of the gospel. We gather to cast out doubt. Why, then, would we want to institutionalize it as an aspect of theology? Scripture never deals seriously with the possibility that "no God or anything like God" exists.[3] "The fool says in his heart, 'There is no God.' They are corrupt, and their ways are vile; there is no one who does good" (Ps. 14:1). The Bible views denial of God as arising from blindness and wickedness, hardly a basis for taking doubt seriously as a theological question. People living in the ancient world did not need to be convinced that there is a reality higher — with more power and knowledge and longer life — than human beings. They did not require arguments to believe that they depend on these higher powers and must deal with them in some fashion. This was obvious.[4]

2. Perhaps the best-known example is Hans Küng, *Does God Exist? An Answer for Today*, trans. Edward Quinn (New York: Vintage Books, 1981).

3. This phrase comes from Alvin Plantinga, *Warranted Christian Belief* (New York: Oxford University Press, 2000).

4. For a study of ancient "religious man," see Mircea Eliade, *The Sacred and the Profane* (New York: Harper Torchbooks, 1961).

There is an even more important problem with the question "Does God exist?" *Which* God exists or does not exist? Or, to put the question another way: What do we mean by the word "God"? It makes no sense to question the existence of a being of which we have no conception. If the question "Does God exist?" is to be meaningful, we must have a clear concept of who or what God is — but simply do not know whether God exists. Where do we get such a God-concept? It appears that we have two possible sources: philosophy or theology. We must bear in mind that adopting a philosophical concept will require us to abandon the presuppositions of theology that I laid out in the first two chapters. It may comfort us to conclude that a "highest, infinite, and most perfect being," a "first cause," or an "unmoved mover" exists. However, without a religious relationship to that being, it seems no more significant to declare that God exists than to declare that the universe exists. Understood in that way, God would be just another constant in our lives. As with gravity, we could adjust to it and then ignore it.

Adopting a theological concept of God also presents a problem for the project of demonstrating God's existence. Suppose that, in our discussion of the question "Does God exist?" we assume a Christian concept of God. Christian theology, we must remember, insists that we cannot have a clear concept of God apart from his personal revelation. For Christian theology, the word "God" means the Creator of this universe, the God of Abraham, Isaac, and Jacob, the living God, the one who spoke through the prophets, the one who raised Jesus from the dead, and the Father, Son, and Holy Spirit. However, if our concept of God comes from God's personal revelation, why do we need to ask the question of his existence?

Let us restate the question in a way that takes into account the identity of the God whose existence is in question: "Does God (the Father, Son, and Holy Spirit) exist?" Notice how the issue has been transformed: we are no longer discussing the existence of an impersonal constant, but of the one who acts and personally relates to his creatures. Clearly, this new question cannot be answered by reasoning from the external world to its cause or from internal ideas to a transcendent reality. The only reason to define God as Father, Son, and Holy Spirit is that God has revealed himself as such. In other words, we cannot know that this is the proper concept of God without also believing in the existence of this God. And, as I have shown previously, we cannot know God as a person apart from hearing and believing his word. Thus, when nonbelievers demand that the church show that God exists apart from God's self-revelation, they are asking us to abandon the only possible demonstration of God's existence, God's self-demonstration. The church lives by the word of God, and on this basis it joyously meets God and celebrates his eternal being and glorious works.

The Right Question

What is the point of writing a chapter entitled "The Existence of God" but refusing to answer the question "Does God exist?" If God demonstrates his own existence, what can theology do? In what follows I hope to show that theology has plenty of work to do even if it presupposes God's existence. I have already described God's self-demonstration in the section on revelation. I treated the issue of how we know God personally, and I have indirectly dealt with how we know that this personal God exists. In this chapter I will address the question of what it means to say, "God (Father, Son, and Holy Spirit) exists." In an important sense, of course, this is the question of the entire doctrine of God. For the doctrine of God explores the full range of meaning in the word "God" and the far-reaching implications of the proposition "God exists." But here I want to address this question directly.

First, let us consider the issue of existence. What are we asserting of God or attributing to him when we claim that God *exists?* When we declare the existence of something, we are presupposing a distinction between its idea and its existence; when we declare its existence, we are adding something to its idea. What is it? It is outside my aim and beyond my philosophical knowledge to explore this question in detail, but I think we can safely argue that we are attributing to the thing a mode of being actual, independent of our minds.[5] Some power outside us and independent of our minds is operating. An existing red ball is more than the idea of a red ball, which can be called up or annihilated as we will. As existing, it exerts a power to persist and make itself known; it is a factor we have to deal with.

We are greatly tempted to relate to God as if God did not really exist, as if God were not a real power we must face. We treat God as an idea safely locked within our minds. Perhaps believing in God is important to our identity and to our efforts to make sense of the world. Nevertheless, we treat God as a concept rather than an existing reality. God, like the speed of light, is a universal constant, setting a limit to things but otherwise irrelevant. Sometimes our belief in God seems to function as no more than a symbolic way to express our preference for optimism over pessimism. Believing in God helps us get through life. But, for the most part, we occupy ourselves with the things of the world. Their existence exercises such power over us that we lose a sense of God's real presence and action. This habit of mind poses a genuine problem that theology must address.

---

5. See *Encyclopedia of Philosophy,* ed. Paul Edwards (New York: Macmillan, 1967), s.v. "Existence" and s.v. "Essence and Existence."

The Christian faith asserts that God really *exists.* God is more than a mere possibility, an idea in our minds, such as a unicorn, that might exist but (we think) does not. It declares that God is an actual reality independent of our thought. God is more than the concept of an all-knowing, omnipresent, all-powerful, and loving being who helps us make sense of the universe. God actually does know all, really does exercise power in all things, truly is present, and genuinely does love us. God is a real factor, *the* real factor.

Opposing Options

God matters. It makes a difference whether the child-eating Molech is God, whether the Father, Son, and the Holy Spirit is God, or there is no God or anything like God. George MacDonald put it this way: "To say *Thou art God,* without knowing what the *Thou* means — of what use is it? God is a name only, except we know *God.*"[6] Let us, then, clarify the name "God" by opposing the biblical understanding to the living options: paganism, atheism, and agnosticism. Pagans view the powers of nature as divine. Atheists believe that there is no God or anything like God. Agnostics affirm that neither the arguments for belief in God nor those for atheism compel assent.

The Pagan Option

We might not think that the pagan view of divinity is a living option for most people in the contemporary Western world. It is true that not many people seriously believe in the existence of beings like the gods of ancient mythology. However, thinking of the divine in mythic fashion does not represent the central intuition of paganism. At its heart is the conviction that "nature is but the manifestation of the divine."[7] It treats nature as the ultimate power and only source of good. It matters little whether this intuition is articulated in myths or philosophical concepts or is merely thoughtlessly lived out.[8] Indeed, a person can profess atheism, skepticism, or belief in God as a matter of theory, and still

6. C. S. Lewis, ed., *George MacDonald: 365 Readings* (New York: Macmillan, 1986), p. 14.

7. Henri Frankford et al., *Before Philosophy: The Intellectual Adventure of Ancient Man* (Baltimore: Penguin Books, n.d.), p. 241.

8. For a study of the contrast between ancient paganism and Israelite religion, see Yehezkel Kaufmann, *The Religion of Israel: From Its Beginnings to the Babylonian Exile,* trans. Moshe Greenberg (New York: Schocken Books, 1960), which is an older book and also controversial, but still stimulating.

live wholly as a pagan. The pagan option is the most natural and immediately attractive view of the divine.[9] We feel immediately the natural forces within us: the drives for sexual gratification, food, drink, air, warmth, beauty, honor, and power; what we fear is pain, deprivation of our body's needs, shame, and death. Insofar as we live for these things and treat them as ultimate goods, we follow the pagan option.

Christian belief views paganism as enslavement to the powers of nature. God created these powers as his servants and gave them to human beings, and we are meant to receive them as God's gifts and use them to serve and glorify God according to his will. In this way we can remain free and sovereign over them. But when we treat these powers as the ultimate sources of good for us, we become enslaved to them. Unlike God, they are not persons to whom we can relate in mutual love, and thus we put our personhood at risk in the impersonal flux of nature.[10] When we allow our wills to come under the control of the chaotic appetites within us and the kaleidoscopic attractions swirling around us, we lose our integrity as persons. The New Testament theme of freedom returns again and again to the promise of liberty from these impersonal and irrational drives and forces. You will not find freedom in abandoning yourself to "do what you feel" but in abandoning yourself to the love of God. If you do what you feel, you will become a slave to the powers that make you feel what you feel.

The Atheist Option

Modern atheism is a complex phenomenon. Hans Küng identifies three forms of atheism: humanistic, political, and scientific. Humanist atheism understands belief in God to be antihuman. In Küng's words, "God seemed to be possible only at the expense of man — being a Christian only at the expense of being human."[11] God is set up as the competitor of our freedom and the main roadblock to our quest for happiness. No one articulated this view more bluntly than did Friedrich Nietzsche, who blurted out: "But that I may reveal myself entirely unto you, my friends: *if* there were gods, how could I endure it to be no

9. Robert Sokolowski, *The God of Faith and Reason: Foundations of Christian Theology* (Washington, DC: Catholic University of America Press, 1995), p. xi. See especially ch. 2, "Pagan Divinity," pp. 12-20.

10. On this point, see Dumitru Staniloae, *The Experience of God: Orthodox Dogmatic Theology,* vol. 1, *Revelation and Knowledge of the Triune God,* trans. and ed. Ioan Ionita and Robert Barringer (Brookline, MA: Holy Cross Orthodox Press, 1998), pp. 1-14.

11. Küng, *Does God Exist?* p. 83.

God! *Therefore* there are no gods."[12] Political atheism thinks belief in God stands in the way of political progress. Whether in the humanist rhetoric of the French Revolution or in the socialism of Karl Marx, God plays the role of spoiler. The one casts God as the conservative guardian of the ancient authorities' throne and altar; the other sees God as the opium that numbs the people and robs them of energy for political activity by promising them heavenly rewards for their earthy suffering. Scientific atheism argues that reason shows that belief in God is unwarranted or false. Materialists, from Democritus and Epicurus to La Mettrie and d'Holbach to Sagan and Dawkins, argue that everything within our experience can be explained by the laws of the material universe. Almost every form of science — from physics to biology to psychology to economics — has representatives who argue that their particular science makes belief in God impossible. In this sense there are as many kinds of atheism as there are areas of scientific study and kinds of human motivations.

In his book *Warranted Christian Belief,* Alvin Plantinga simplifies matters considerably, classifying arguments for nonbelief, not according to the specific realm of experience from which they are drawn, but according to their epistemic status.[13] The first class, which he designates as de facto arguments, contends that the statement "God exists" is false; the second class of objections, which he designates as de jure arguments, maintains that belief in God's existence is either unjustified or irrational or unwarranted — even if it is true. Because it is notoriously difficult to frame persuasive de facto arguments against belief in God, de jure arguments predominate in the history of atheism. Plantinga deals with three kinds of de jure arguments in his search for the question that articulates the crux of the de jure objection. He rejects the first two options, which are: (1) Is belief in God justified? (2) Is belief in God rational? Neither of these articulates the genuine de jure question, for it is too easy to show that a person can be justified in believing that God exists (pp. 67-100). There are many open-minded and conscientious people who do their best to find out the truth, yet nevertheless remain convinced of God's existence (pp. 108-134).

Plantinga finds the genuine de jure question in the third kind of objection, the question of warrant (pp. 135-63). Karl Marx argues that belief in God is unwarranted because it originates in an alienated self-consciousness and in "disordered cognitive processes." And Sigmund Freud argues that belief in God arises from cognitive "processes that are not aimed at the production of true

---

12. Nietzsche, *Thus Spake Zarathustra,* trans. Thomas Common (New York: Random House, n.d.), p. 91.

13. Plantinga, *Warranted Christian Belief* (New York: Oxford University Press, 2000). Page references will be given parenthetically in the text.

beliefs" but at "psychological well-being" (p. 142). According to Plantinga, for a belief to have warrant, it must be produced by cognitive faculties that (1) are "functioning properly" (2) in an appropriate "cognitive environment," and (3) "according to a design plan that is successfully aimed at truth" (p. 156).[14] As is evident, Marx denies that belief in God meets the first condition, and Freud denies that it meets the third. In response to Marx and Freud, Plantinga argues (convincingly, to my mind) that the de jure and de facto questions cannot be separated. In reality, Freud's and Marx's de jure arguments depend on their de facto atheism. Marx can know that the cognitive processes that produce belief are not working properly only because they tell us that there is a God when there is no God. And Freud knows that the believer's cognitive processes cannot be aimed at truth only because they produce belief in God, which is a false belief. I think that Plantinga concludes correctly that "the dispute as to whether theistic belief is rational (warranted) can't be settled just by attending to epistemological considerations; it is at bottom not merely an epistemological dispute, but an ontological or a theological dispute" (p. 190).

The way to atheism is broad, and many itineraries will get you there. But whether you travel the humanist, scientific, or political route, whether your driver is Marx, Freud, or Dawkins, and whether your vehicle is a de facto or a de jure model, the destination is the same. Nothing like God will meet you there. Everything that depends on God must be left behind at the border crossing. However, just as many believers do not take God's existence seriously, many nonbelievers do not take their denial of God seriously. They inevitably rely on systems of meaning, habits of mind, and moral principles that directly or indirectly depend on the existence of God. Atheism, the belief that there is no God or anything like God, has profound cosmic and existential implications that negate not only the Christian view of life but also the pagan view. As we shall see, the City of (No) God is not a very habitable place.

Atheism's Cosmic Implications

A denial of God leaves nothing untouched. To understand what is at stake in the atheist option, we must strip away every idea, belief, and value that depends on the existence of God or anything like God. First, if there is no God or anything like God, there is no reason for the existence of the universe. It just is. It has no origin, no direction, and no destiny. It has no meaning because there is no larger framework to bestow meaning on it.

---

14. Alvin Plantinga developed this definition in his earlier works: *Warrant: The Current Debate* (New York: Oxford, 1993) and *Warrant and Proper Function* (New York: Oxford, 1993).

Second, atheism, by definition, denies the existence of a cosmic mind that could give the world its being and intelligibility and know it thoroughly. The universe as a whole does not exist inside a mind; no one thinks it. Therefore, neither the cosmos as a whole nor its parts individually exist as intelligible modes of being — as ideas or forms or design plans. The apparent order within the universe is merely a temporary state of a mindless, ceaseless, and chaotic process that is viewed, as it were, in a very slow-motion video. There is no cosmic intelligibility and no truth that precedes and informs the human mind. Indeed, the human mind itself cannot escape the reductionist logic of atheism. It is just as much a part of the chaotic and mindless universe as rocks, stars, and atoms are. Belief in the mind's intelligence and intelligibility cannot be sustained if we deny a cosmic mind and intelligibility, which would reduce the mind to mindless processes. In short, if there is no divine mind, there is no human mind.

A third cosmic implication of atheism is that there is no cosmic order of value. Since the universe exists for no reason and has no purpose, it cannot succeed or fail. In the cosmic context, such terms as suitability, value, good, evil, fittingness, and perfection are without meaning. Scales of value carry meaning only to intelligent beings who can work toward ends. Since the universe moves toward no end, nothing can speed or impede its progress. Fourth, if there is no God or anything like God, there is no cosmic plan. The world process cannot accomplish anything because it has no end in view. The French atheist Baron d'Holbach had no hesitation in admitting this: "The whole cannot have a distinct end, because there is nothing out of itself to which it can have a tendency."[15] And any pattern or meaning we think we see is illusory, an imaginary order we impose on a directionless process. Fifth, the individual things we experience have no real or substantial existence. If there is no God or anything like God, we must view everything we experience as composed exclusively of material stuff brought together by random, mindless forces. There is no plan, form, or blueprint for a whole thing, such as a tree or a human being, since there is no cosmic mind to conceive it and put it together. The word "tree" and the name "Paul" designate merely our experience of a particular temporary coalescence of material stuff.

Atheism's Existential Implications

Now we get personal. It is one thing to speak of cosmic plans and processes; it is quite another to face the implications of atheism for our own existence. Serious

---

15. Baron d'Holbach, *The System of Nature*, vol. 1, trans. H. D. Robinson (Kitchener, Ont.: Batoche Books, 2001), p. 38.

atheists will have to look into this void. As the first existential implication, we must accept that we were not planned and do not exist for a reason. We were not sent here or expected. We have no commission and no mission to accomplish in this world. We are responsible to no higher order, for there is no such order. Indeed, there is no *real* order at all. Hence, we cannot succeed or fail as people. Second, the meanings we live by are not rooted in any real pattern of meaning. To earn a college degree, to marry and have a family, to facilitate world peace, or to live to be a hundred years old — none of those goals has the slightest relationship to any objective meaning. We cannot find our place in the cosmos, for the idea of place implies a plan or pattern; that implies a cosmic mind. And, according to atheism, there is no cosmic mind.

Third, the values we use to evaluate things and guide our actions are not valued by the universe. However much we love someone or crave a thing for its beauty, we are not in touch with a real characteristic of the universe. Our experience of the most horrible evil will not be condemned by an amoral universe. A heartless universe cannot value love or recoil from evil, and a blind and deaf universe does not care about beauty. The loveless universe does not know us or care about us.[16] Fourth, the humans we are and the other people we meet are merely temporary phenomena in an impersonal universe. We and those we love will dissolve into absolutely nothing, leaving no trace or memory. The matter and energy that constitute our bodies is the only thing about us that will last beyond our death. On its elementary level it is indistinguishable from other matter and energy. Fifth, since there is no divine mind to remember it and no divine power to preserve it, nothing we do will achieve anything lasting. Everything we live for, everything we accomplish will be destroyed. And if nothing lasts, nothing matters.

Fortunately, most atheists do not live by atheism's implications. Perhaps there are many happy atheists who display virtuous characteristics and have a sense of meaning in their lives. I would not deny this. But I am arguing that they can do so only by living in opposition to their own theory. Happiness implies a fit between what one is and the universe one experiences. Fittingness, however, can have no place in an unplanned and mindless world. Displays of virtue, while retaining a survival advantage, cannot be praiseworthy, for praiseworthiness implies a cosmic scale of value. Meaning is the relationship between a part and its whole; but, according to theoretical atheism, meaning is a human construction, for there is no meaningful whole in which we could

---

16. See John Rist, *Real Ethics: Reconsidering the Foundations of Ethics* (Cambridge, UK: Cambridge University Press, 2002). Rist argues that there are only two ways to think of values: Platonic/Augustinian realism or Hobbesian nihilism.

play a part. However, I do not see any difference between self-generated meaning and self-delusion.

Some Difficulties with Theoretical Atheism

An in-depth response to atheism would be out of place in this book. However, lest I leave the impression that there are no good responses to it, I will make a few comments. In a sense, the exposition of atheism is its refutation. Once one understands what it asserts and what it implies, it begins to look implausible and unappealing. Explorations of the cosmic and existential implications of atheism have brought this out into the open. Atheism is the ultimate *reductio ad absurdum,* because it implies that the final "explanation" for everything is chaotic and absurd. Let us briefly consider two more possible responses.

THE BURDEN-OF-PROOF ISSUE We have learned from Plantinga that modern atheism uses, for the most part, a default strategy to argue against belief in God. It presumes that belief in God is not prima facie obvious, for it goes beyond our experience.[17] Therefore, it requires evidence to move us beyond our secular experience to the conclusion that God exists. William K. Clifford, in his infamous 1877 essay "The Ethics of Belief," declares this position energetically: "It is wrong always, everywhere, and for anyone, to believe anything on insufficient evidence."[18] Atheists claim that they do not need any evidence to bestow on them a right *not* to believe, but they deny that believers have a right to believe without evidence. Atheism, they claim, is the natural position of a mind that is careful not to go beyond experience. On this reading, atheism does not need to make positive arguments for its own truth or propose metaphysical theories to explain what belief in God explains.

If it is amazing that an honest atheist could make such a shoddy argument, it is even more amazing that any thinking believer would agree to such manifestly biased rules for argumentation. Whatever evidence believers present, atheists can always say, with a sense of justification, "Not enough evidence." In truth, however, there is no such epistemic asymmetry. Atheism is no more modest or natural than belief in God, for atheism is a *belief* just as much as faith

17. Anthony Flew, "The Presumption of Atheism," in *Contemporary Perspectives on Religious Epistemology,* ed. R. Douglas Geivett and Brendan Sweetman (New York: Oxford University Press, 1992), pp. 19-32.

18. William K. Clifford, *The Ethics of Belief and Other Essays* (London: Watts and Co., 1947), p. 77. See also Bertrand Russell, *Why I Am Not a Christian* (New York: Simon and Schuster, 1957); Anthony Flew, *The Presumption of Atheism* (London: Pemberton, 1976); and John Mackie, *The Miracle of Theism* (Oxford: Oxford University Press, 1982).

in God is a belief. Atheism cannot exist as mere nonbelief, that is, as a bare refusal to believe in God.[19] It must necessarily affirm that something other than God is the ultimate explanation for the world and everything in it. Alert believers will ask immediately: "Does this 'something' really exist, what is its nature, and how does it explain everything else?" If theism is obligated to demonstrate the existence of God, give a coherent explanation of his nature, and show how the world derives from him, atheism is equally obligated to demonstrate the existence of the alternative to God, give a coherent explanation of its nature, and show how the world derives from it.

MOVING BEYOND EVIDENTIALISM   Advancing beyond the issue of who bears the burden of proof, Plantinga rejects the evidentialist approach to belief in God. *Evidentialism* contends that all our beliefs must be "basic" (that is, self-evident or immediately obvious) or supported by basic beliefs. Belief in God, evidentialists claim, is not properly basic; thus it must be supported directly or indirectly by truly basic beliefs, that is, by evidence. And, as I have shown above, atheistic evidentialists deny that nonbelief is a "belief" at all: in this way they attempt to escape the need for evidence. In many places over the years, Plantinga has developed an elaborate model of theological epistemology in which Christian belief in God is "properly basic."[20] Plantinga finds it particularly significant that Aquinas and Calvin agree that "to know in a general and confused way that God exists is implanted in us by nature."[21] Plantinga develops his elaborate model of religious knowledge in dialogue primarily with Calvin. He summarizes: "Calvin's basic claim is that there is a sort of instinct, a natural human tendency, a disposition, a nisus to form beliefs about God under a variety of conditions and in a variety of situations."[22] Human beings have a natural tendency, for example, to believe in God when they look at God's creation or when they feel the demands of the moral law. Belief in God in these circumstances is not the conclusion of an argument; it is a basic belief arising from something like perception.[23] I shall

19. For an incisive critique of the idea that atheism should be exempt from providing evidence for its beliefs, see Scott A. Shalkowski, "Atheological Apologetics," in Geivett and Sweetman, *Contemporary Perspectives on Religious Epistemology,* pp. 58-77.

20. Plantinga, "Reason and Belief in God," in *Faith and Rationality* (Notre Dame, IN: University of Notre Dame Press, 1983), pp. 16-93; *Warranted Christian Belief,* pp. 167-90; and "Is Belief in God Properly Basic?" in Geivett and Sweetman, pp. 133-41.

21. *Sum Th.* 1.2.1, quoted in Plantinga, *Warranted Christian Belief,* p. 170.

22. *Warranted Christian Belief,* p. 171.

23. For references to Calvin, see *Warranted Christian Belief,* pp. 171-74; for Plantinga's discussion of experience and perception, see *Warranted Christian Belief,* pp. 180-84.

conclude something very much like this in my discussion of the traditional arguments for the existence of God.

THE POSSIBILITY OF AN ATHEOLOGY?   In a third response to atheism, let us consider the possibility of a comprehensive atheistic explanation of everything. I argued above that atheism is the belief that the ultimate explanation for the existence and nature of the universe is something other than God. It would seem that robust atheism, which demands evidence for belief in God, would feel obligated to identify this "something" and show how it explains everything else without reference to God or anything like God. As is true of all apologetics, atheist apologetics risks undermining its own cause should its explanation prove less than persuasive. Let us examine one of the few comprehensive atheist systems to see whether it accomplishes what it claims.

In the eighteenth century, Baron d'Holbach wrote what came to be called the "atheist's bible." In *The System of Nature* (1770), d'Holbach developed a comprehensive system that purportedly explained everything in terms of matter-in-motion. "The universe, that vast assemblage of every thing that exists," he explains, "presents only matter and motion: the whole offers to our contemplation nothing but an immense and uninterrupted succession of causes and effects."[24]

Thinkers from Plato and Aristotle to Descartes and Newton had distinguished matter from motion. Matter does not have the power of movement within itself; that must be added by an active spiritual mover. For Plato and Aristotle, both origin and continuation of movement require a nonmaterial mover, which they called "soul." According to Newton's theory of inertia, only change in motion requires a mover. Constant movement is relative to the observer. Nevertheless, even for Newton, the origin of motion requires an active mover. Newton's theory of gravity implied that the universe would eventually collapse inward; hence, it could not be eternal and in perpetual motion. Newton and Samuel Clarke, his theologian follower, concluded from this theory the necessity of a creator.[25]

D'Holbach challenged the long-accepted assumption that matter and motion are two different things. Why believe that this assumption is more likely

---

24. D'Holbach, *System of Nature*, 1, p. 14.

25. In 1704, Clarke delivered his Boyle Lectures, *A Demonstration of the Being and Attributes of God, More Particularly in Answer to Mr. Hobbes, Spinoza and Their Followers.* In 1711, these lectures were published together with *A Discourse Concerning the Unchangeable Obligations of Natural Religion, and the Truth and Certainty of the Christian Revelation.* For an extensive discussion of Clarke, see Michael J. Buckley, S.J., *At the Origins of Modern Atheism* (New Haven, CT: Yale University Press, 1987), pp. 166-93.

than its opposite? No compelling reason can be given for preferring one over the other. D'Holbach concludes: "Motion is produced, is augmented, is accelerated in matter, without the concurrence of any exterior agent: it is, therefore, reasonable to conclude, that motion is the necessary consequence of immutable laws, resulting from the essence, from the properties inherent in the different elements, and the various combinations of these elements" (p. 20). He says, even more compactly: "Motion is a manner of being, which matter derives from its peculiar existence" (p. 22).

D'Holbach builds his system on the hypothesis that motion is an aspect of matter and requires no spiritual explanation.[26] Neither the motions of the planets, nor the growth of plants and animals, nor any other change requires a spiritual source. D'Holbach's theory of evolution lacked the sophistication of later theories, such as Darwin's; nevertheless, he argued that, given matter-in-motion and infinite time, the evolution of our world is conceivable and inevitable.[27] D'Holbach does not hesitate to explain in material terms everything we usually view as spiritual. Love between parent and child, love of country, and desire for food are merely different manifestations of the same attractive forces that cause mud to harden into rock. Revulsion toward certain sights and smells, hate, and war are caused by the same forces that repel the poles of two magnets. Thoughts are merely states of the material brain. Freedom is illusory, for every effect is determined wholly by its cause: the human being "never acts as a free agent" (p. 101).

Dynamic matter is the ultimate reality and explanation of all phenomena. To sustain this thesis, d'Holbach transfers many of the traditional attributes of God to matter. In Volume 2 of *The System of Nature,* he examines the work of Samuel Clarke, Newton's theological disciple: *The Demonstration of the Being and Attributes of God.*[28] D'Holbach works out his materialist metaphysics in response to Clarke's twelve theses on the existence and nature of God. In Part I, "The Being of God," Clarke argues his first seven theses: God is (1) eternal, (2) unchangeable and independent, (3) necessary, (4) incomprehensible, (5) demonstrable in existence and some attributes, (6) infinite and omnipresent, and (7) one. In each case, d'Holbach responds that we can think of these perfections as belonging to matter as reasonably as we can think of them as belonging to God. Indeed, if matter really is the ultimate substance of all things, it must possess these perfections. Matter must be one if it is the fundamental reality; it must

---

26. See Buckley, *Origins of Modern Atheism,* pp. 277-88.

27. Richard Dawkins, in *The Blind Watchmaker* (New York: Norton, 1986), pp. 6-7, says that Darwin was the first person to make it possible to be an intellectually fulfilled atheist.

28. See Buckley, *Origins of Modern Atheism,* p. 174, for an outline of the *Demonstration.*

be omnipresent if it is the substance of all things. It must be eternal, since, as the explanation of all things, it cannot itself have come into being. And it must be infinite, because to be finite is to be limited by another, and there is no other.

D'Holbach next deals with Part II of the *Demonstration,* "The Principal Attributes of the Divine Nature," where Clarke argues his last five theses. The ultimate ground of all things, argues Clarke, must be (8) intelligent, (9) free, (10) omnipotent, (11) wise, and (12) infinite in moral perfections.[29] In response, D'Holbach argues that the ultimate reality (matter) does not possess these attributes. These qualities are merely human attributes projected onto nature. In a passage that anticipates Feuerbach and Freud, d'Holbach speculates: "Man having placed himself in the first rank in the universe, has been desirous to judge of every thing after what he saw within himself, because he has pretended that in order to be perfect it was necessary to be like himself. Here is the source of all his erroneous reasoning upon nature and his Gods" (p. 30).

It is very interesting that systematic atheism finds it impossible to rid the world of some ultimate reality that possesses many of the traditional attributes of God. To begin by saying that there is no God and that matter is the ultimate reality certainly sounds like atheism. But when we hear that matter is also one, eternal, infinite, independent, necessary, incomprehensible, and omnipresent, we begin to sense that matter is being transformed into something spiritual, something "like God." And when d'Holbach denies that the ultimate reality possesses spiritual attributes, he gives the impression of making a capricious decision to keep "matter" from becoming even more God-like.

The Agnostic Option

Many of our contemporaries find atheism too harsh and self-certain. But they do not believe wholeheartedly in God. They think they can find in agnosticism a comfortable place between belief and unbelief.[30] They justify themselves intellectually by claiming that there is simply not enough evidence to prove or disprove the existence of God. Thomas Huxley says: "It is wrong for a man to say he is certain of the objective truth of a proposition unless he can provide evidence which logically justifies that certainty. That is what agnosticism asserts and in my opinion, is all that is essential to agnosticism."[31] It makes little sense,

---

29. D'Holbach, *System of Nature,* 2, pp. 30-34.

30. The term "agnosticism" was coined by Thomas H. Huxley in 1869. For references, see *Evangelical Dictionary of Theology,* s.v. "Agnosticism."

31. "Agnosticism," available at http://www.infidels.org/library/historical/thomas_huxley/huxley_wace/part_02.html (accessed July 30, 2004).

Huxley and other agnostics reason, to conform one's life completely to either hypothesis. Most agnostics, it would seem, determine to live as if it does not matter whether God or anything like God exists. Of course, the problem with this way of thinking is that it *does* matter whether God exists. Clearly, agnosticism can be satisfying only if one does not know what the word "God" means. It treats the issue of God's existence as it would treat the possible existence of an earth-sized planet in a solar system in a galaxy that is five billion light years distant. What difference does it make? As we have already seen, theoretical atheism implies a radically different understanding of the cosmos and human existence than most people assume. We shall see below what a qualitative difference affirming the existence of God (Father, Son, and Holy Spirit) makes to our understanding of the cosmos and human existence. Agnosticism that comes to truly understand the word "God" can no longer remain content with itself; it will not rest until it discovers the truth of the matter.

God's Self-Demonstration

In the Bible, God demonstrates his existence, identity, and attributes. God's historical revelation to Abraham, Moses, and the people of Israel was not needed to convince them of the existence of a divine reality. All ancient peoples believed in a divine world. God's actions recorded in Scripture presuppose his revelation in nature as the origin of this universal belief. God makes his "eternal power and divine nature" clear in the things he has made (Rom. 1:20). However, as I have observed in the discussion of revelation, natural theology and religion pervert God's natural revelation. Hence, God's self-demonstration in history centers on differentiating himself from the idols of the nations.[32]

Central to the story of God's self-demonstration in Scripture is proving that he alone is God. Delivering the Israelites from slavery involved demonstrating God's control over the natural forces that Egypt worshiped: river, storm, death, and all the rest. At the giving of the law, God's first demand was: "You shall have no other gods before me." And the second was: "You shall not make for yourself an idol in the form of anything in heaven above or on the earth beneath or in the waters below" (Exod. 20:3, 4). The conquest of Canaan demonstrated further God's superiority over the gods of those peoples. But one of the central motifs of the Old Testament historical literature (Joshua, Judges, and 1 and 2 Kings) is Is-

32. I am sympathetic with Wolfhart Pannenberg, *Systematic Theology,* vol. 1, trans. Geoffrey W. Bromiley (Grand Rapids: Eerdmans, 1991), p. 192, where he argues that, in God's self-demonstration, "an existing knowledge of the divine was modified by special experiences."

rael's constant temptation to worship the gods of its pagan neighbors. Apparently, only after the exile and return from captivity in Babylon do the people as a whole grow firm in their determination to worship only the Lord.

One often hears complaints from modern readers about how the Israelites (and their neighbors) could have been so silly as to worship the forces of nature or ritual images representing them. Such a perspective is possible only because we have benefited from the lessons Israel learned in its history with God. Apart from that experience, polytheism, the belief in many divine beings, is plausible — perhaps even obvious. Nature confronts us as a display of many powerful forces. The sun, moon and stars, storms, the fertility of animals and the fecundity of plants, the oceans, rivers, the mountains — all of these confront us as powerful and mysterious. And they are necessary to life, health, and happiness. Nothing was more natural to the ancient person than the belief that each of these forces was a separate divinity.

If it is natural to believe in many gods, it is just as natural to view the divine as a means to human ends. Therefore, the nations thought of the divine in human terms, as being subject to flattery, manipulation, and bribery. Their relationship to their gods was economic: they did not understand the divine as the end of all things but as a source of worldly blessings. Furthermore, since pagans viewed the natural powers as divinities, the gods mirrored the amoral character of nature. Thus ancient myths portray the gods as having the same moral faults as their human devotees do. The pagan worshiper mirrors the character of his gods.

In the history of Israel, however, God demonstrates himself as the Lord of all nature and history and the sovereign Creator of the natural powers. Thus the divine reality can no longer be identified directly with natural forces. Nor can God's intentions and character be directly experienced in these forces. As an example of this revolution, consider these three biblical statements about wine:

> He makes grass grow for the cattle, and plants for man to cultivate, bringing forth food from the earth: wine that gladdens the heart of man, oil to make his face shine, and bread that sustains his heart (Ps. 104:14-15).

> Do not gaze at wine when it is red, when it sparkles in the cup, when it goes down smoothly! In the end it bites like a snake and poisons like a viper (Prov. 23:31-32).

> Do not get drunk on wine, which leads to debauchery. Instead, be filled with the Spirit. Speak to one another with psalms, hymns and spiritual songs. Sing and make music in your heart to the Lord (Eph. 5:18-19).

Notice the contrast between these biblical texts and Euripides' statements in his play *The Cyclops* (408 B.C.). In the first quotation Odesseus plots in his own mind how he will get Cyclops drunk; in the second he dialogs with Cyclops about Bacchus, the god of wine:

Odesseus: Then when he falls asleep, o'ermastered by the Bacchic god, I will put a point with this sword of mine to an olive-branch I saw lying in the cave, and will set it on fire; and when I see it well alight, I will lift the heated brand, and, thrusting it full in the Cyclops' eye, melt out his sight with its blaze.

[later]

Odesseus: Hearken, Cyclops; for I am well versed in the ways of Bacchus, whom I have given thee to drink.

Cyclops: And who is Bacchus? some reputed god?

Odesseus: The greatest god men know to cheer their life.

Cyclops: I like his after-taste at any rate.

Odesseus: This is the kind of god he is; he harmeth no man.

Cyclops: But how does a god like being housed in a wine-skin?

Odesseus: Put him where one may, he is content there.

Cyclops: It is not right that gods should be clad in leather.

Odesseus: What of that, provided he please thee? does the leather hurt thee?[33]

In Euripides, the pagan understanding of the divine stands out clearly. Wine is not merely a creature that can be used properly or misused. Wine is Bacchus himself: the action of the wine *is* the action of the god. All other natural powers are understood in the same way. The pagan lives in a world "full of gods" (Thales, 624-546 B.C.),[34] which he experiences directly in his daily encounter with nature. The Bible, in contrast, views wine, bread, oil, and grass as God's creatures, given for the use of humankind. They are signs of God's good will, but they are not themselves divine. Hence, their actions and effects cannot be identified directly with God's actions and effects. Since God created them for certain purposes and not others, they can be misused.

God's self-demonstration as the sole Creator and Lord of heaven and

33. "Cyclops," in *The Plays of Euripides,* trans. Edward P. Coleridge (London: George Bell and Sons, 1904), pp. 460-62.

34. Philip Wheelwright, ed., *The Presocratics* (New York: The Odyssey Press, 1966), p. 47. Thales's observation is preserved by Aristotle in *On the Soul.*

earth implied a complete revolution in the pagan concept of the divine. The divine nature was shown to be one and something that transcended the created world. Since the divine was removed from the chaos, irrationality, and contradiction of nature, God could be considered morally perfect. Since the divine action and will can no longer be read directly from events in nature, God can be known only indirectly in nature and directly only through his Word. I shall take up these issues in much greater detail when I deal with God's attributes.

Arguments for God's Existence

The church and her theologians have always been convinced that God reveals himself in nature and that all things bear witness to their Creator. The psalmist sings: "The heavens declare the glory of God and the firmament shows his handy work" (Ps. 19:1). Paul asserts that God's "eternal power and divine nature" are made known clearly by the things he has made (Rom. 1:20). The church fathers agree that God's glory shines forth from his creation. Listen to Athanasius (c. 296-373):

> Since then, there is everywhere not disorder but order, proportion and not disproportion, not disarray but arrangement, and that in an order perfectly harmonious, we needs must infer and be led to perceive the Master that put together and compacted all things, and produced harmony in them.[35]

Gregory of Nyssa (c. 330–c. 395) is no less eloquent:

> The one who has heard those heavenly announcements, by which, in the words of the Prophet, "the glory of God is declared," and, traveling through creation, has been led to the apprehension of a Master of the creation; he has taken the true Wisdom for his teacher, that Wisdom which the spectacle of the Universe suggests; and when he observed the beauty of this material sunlight he had grasped by analogy the beauty of the real sunlight; he saw in the solid firmness of this earth the unchangeableness of its Creator; when he perceived the immensity of the heavens he was led on the road towards the vast Infinity of that Power which encompasses the Universe; when he saw the rays of the sun reaching from such sublimities even to ourselves he began to believe, by the means of such phenomena, that the activities of the Divine Intelligence did not fail to descend from the heights of Deity even to each one

---

35. Athanasius, *Against the Heathen*, 38.1 (*NPNF*, 2nd ser., 4, p. 24).

of us; for if a single luminary can occupy everything alike that lies beneath it with the force of light, and, more than that, can, while lending itself to all who can use it, still remain self-centred and undissipated, how much more shall the Creator of that luminary become "all in all," as the Apostle speaks, and come into each with such a measure of Himself as each subject of His influence can receive![36]

Having discussed natural revelation already, I wish to focus here on another question. Even if we are sure that God is revealed in his creation — in the cosmos and in human beings — the question arises whether the experience we have of this revelation can be articulated in an argument for God's existence, without irretrievable loss.

Arguments for the existence of God move from common human experience to the existence of God as the explanation for that experience. Some arguments begin with our experience of the physical world and some from intellectual or moral intuition. The cosmological arguments were summed up in their classic form by Thomas Aquinas (*Summa Theologica*, 1.2.3, and *Summa Contra Gentiles*, 1.13) in his famous five ways: from motion to a first mover; from causes in the world to a first cause of the world; from the existence of contingent beings (beings that might not have existed and depend on something else for their existence) to a necessary being; from the imperfect things of the world to the absolute standard of perfection; and from the order and design in the world to the transcendent Designer.

Cosmological Arguments

Thomas begins with the argument from motion, by which he means not just an object's movement in space but any movement from potentiality to actuality. This comprehensive understanding of motion includes things as diverse as the movement of the planets, the growth of plants, and the action of the human will. As our experience confirms, something in a state of potentiality will remain in that state forever — until something else activates it. A baseball, for example, requires a pitcher to activate it into a 90-mile-per-hour fastball. A wheat seed needs moisture, warmth, and sunlight to move it from a potential wheat plant to a full-grown stalk. The human will needs an object of desire — food or rest or beauty — to set it in motion. This is our universal experience. We also observe that every mover or activator itself requires activation by yet another

---

36. Gregory of Nyssa, *On the Early Death of Infants* (NPNF, 2nd ser., 5, pp. 377-78).

mover. The pitcher, the sun, and the food also require something to move them from a state of potentiality to actuality. Does this chain continue backward forever, or is there a first mover that is eternally active of itself and needs no activation by another? Thomas rules out the first alternative, an infinite series of finite movers, as impossible:

> But this cannot go on to infinity, because then there would be no first mover, and, consequently, no other mover, seeing that subsequent movers move only inasmuch as they are moved by the first mover; as the staff moves only because it is moved by the hand. Therefore it is necessary to arrive at a first mover, moved by no other; and this everyone understands to be God (*SumTh*, 1.2.3).[37]

A second cosmological argument moves from our experience of a series of efficient causes to a first efficient cause. Efficient causality is the most familiar of Aristotle's four kinds of causes.[38] The builder is the efficient cause of a house, as lightning is of a forest fire and rain is of a flood. We notice that everything in our worldly experience is an effect and sometimes a cause. One thing (a forest fire) is caused by another (the lightning), which was caused by yet another activator. The line of causality goes in both directions, back in time and forward in time; and nothing in our experience is both cause and the effect in the same respect. A forest fire does not cause itself, "for so it would be prior to itself, which is impossible." Hence, there must be a first efficient cause, "to which everyone gives the name of God."

The third cosmological argument moves from the contingency of the world to a being that exists of absolute necessity. We know of nothing in our world whose existence is absolutely necessary. To put it another way, we know of no being that cannot not be. Flies come into being and pass out of being every two weeks or so. Even stars and galaxies form and die. In everything we experience only contingent beings, the kinds of beings that come into being and go out of existence. But everything that comes into being does so with the help of something else. If everything were contingent, however, why is there something rather than absolutely nothing? Might there be only contingent beings? Aquinas responds to this suggestion: "But it is impossible for these always to ex-

---

37. Anton C. Pegis, ed., *Basic Writings of Saint Thomas Aquinas*, vol. 1 (New York: Random House, 1945), p. 22. All of the following references to the *Summa* are from *SumTh*, 1.2.3 and can be found in Pegis, *Basic Writings*, pp. 22-23.

38. See Aristotle, *Physics*, 2.3, in *Basic Writings of Aristotle*, ed. Richard McKeon (New York: Random House, 1941), pp. 240-42. The causes are material, formal, efficient, and final causality, all of which are necessary to any actual material thing.

ist, for that which can not-be at some time is not. Therefore, if everything can not-be, then at one time there was nothing in existence. Now if this were true, even now there would be nothing in existence . . . which is absurd." Since we know that the world exists, we know that there must be "some being having of itself its own necessity, and not receiving it from another, but rather causing in others their necessity. This all men speak of as God."

The fourth cosmological argument builds on our conviction that the properties of things can be quantified. Things are good, better, and best, or they are big, bigger, and biggest, or they are hot, hotter, and hottest. This way of grading things makes no sense, according to Aquinas, unless we admit the existence of an absolute maximum that is the standard and cause of all the rest. "Therefore, there must also be something which is to all beings the cause of their being, goodness, and every other perfection; and this we call God."

Thomas calls his fifth way the argument from "the government of things." In nature we observe that natural bodies and living but unintelligent beings act to achieve ends. A seed grows to produce a plant and eventually many seeds. Countless species of plants and animals live in all kinds of environments and use innumerable strategies of survival and reproduction. The world is full of goal-seeking activity.[39] According to Aquinas, "whatever lacks knowledge cannot move toward an end, unless it be directed by some being endowed with knowledge and intelligence . . . therefore some intelligent being exists by whom all natural things are directed to their end; and this being we call God."

These five proofs are not so much five different arguments as five distinct aspects of one argument. According to Joseph Owens, "[t]hey all proceed from sensible beings to their efficient cause, subsistent being."[40] In our experience of the world, we do not find an adequate explanation of the world itself; we do not find something that makes all further questions needless. Every being and every event in the world calls for something outside itself to explain its movement, its place in a chain of causes, its being, its perfections, and its goals. However, we cannot believe that there is no final explanation, no end to the ceaseless reference to something else. We believe the principles of causality and of sufficient reason even if we cannot prove them; we believe that, for every being or event, there must be some adequate cause or sufficient explanation of its being and

---

39. The argument from the government of things is sometimes confused with the design argument developed during the Enlightenment. The design argument was vastly extended, amplified, and endlessly illustrated in the 17th and 18th centuries. One of the first thinkers to take this approach was John Ray; see his treatise *The Wisdom of God Manifested in the Works of Creation* (London, 1692).

40. Owens, *An Elementary Christian Metaphysics* (Houston: Center for Thomistic Studies, 1985), p. 350.

activity.[41] There must be a cause of all causes and an explanation of everything, which itself needs no explanation. Pointing out the vastness and extremely old age of the universe cannot replace demonstration of a first cause. As Sertillanges puts it, such reasoning is like saying that "a brush will paint by itself provided it has a very long handle."[42]

The cosmological arguments came under theological and philosophical attack in the eighteenth century. Bishop Joseph Butler initiated the theological critique of the argument, and the philosophical rejection was led by David Hume and Immanuel Kant. In *The Analogy of Religion* (1736), Butler attacked the Deists, who thought their natural theology and religion, derived from theistic proofs, was superior to Christianity. He highlighted the moral ambiguity and stark evil found in nature and showed how these things undermine Deists' claims. The very same objections that can be posed to a Bible-based religion, according to Butler, can be raised to a nature-based one.[43] Butler had no intention of creating a climate of skepticism by undermining the Deists' arguments, but it followed nonetheless.

David Hume, in his *Dialogues Concerning Natural Religion,* exploited Bishop Butler's arguments for the cause of skepticism. His objection was that a deity sufficient to explain the design in the world, though great, need not be the infinite and perfect God of traditional theism. For, even though the world is very large, it is still finite and requires only a finite explanation. Hume says that we should "renounce all claim to infinity in any of the attributes of the Deity. For as the cause ought to be proportioned to the effect, and the effect . . . is not infinite . . . what pretensions have we . . . to ascribe that attribute to the divine Being?"[44] Additionally, the world contains examples of successes and failures, good *and* evil. Hence, argues Hume, we are justified in concluding that the Creator is morally indifferent to the world.

Immanuel Kant criticized the cosmological argument for assuming that the same kind of causal reasoning we apply to events within the world applies to the world's relationship to its transcendent "cause." Kant argues: "The principle of causality has no signification whatever and no mark for its use except

41. Leibniz makes a cosmological argument that is in many ways similar to Aquinas's. Leibniz appeals to the principle of sufficient reason, which is broader than the principle of causality. Even things that have no cause must have a sufficient reason for their existence. See Leibniz, *On the Ultimate Origination of the Universe* (1697).

42. Quoted in Reginald Garrigou-Lagrange, O.P., *Providence,* trans. Dom Bede Rose, O.S.B. (1937; reprint, Rockford, IL: Tan Books and Publishers, 1998), p. 11.

43. Joseph Butler, *The Analogy of Religion* (New York: Frederick Ungar, 1961).

44. *David Hume On Religion,* ed. Richard Wollheim (New York: Meridian Books, 1964), p. 139.

only in the world of sense. Yet here [in the cosmological proof] the principle was to serve precisely for getting beyond the world of sense."[45]

Entering deeply into the debate about the validity and probative value of the cosmological arguments is not necessary for my purposes; but perhaps some comments are in order. First, we might wish to ask Kant how he knows that causality "has no meaning and no criterion for its application save only in the sensible world." Given the Christian view of God, we can see that we should not think of God as the "cause" of the world in the same sense that a match causes a fire or a stone breaks a window. God is the Creator of the world, not a finite cause within the world. But Kant rejects the Christian revelation, so he cannot speak with authority about God's relationship to the world. How, then, does he know the limits of the principle of causality? Second, Kant's criticism of the principle of causality exacts a heavy toll on our cognitive ambition. If we can no longer assume that the phenomena of our experience bear even an analogous relationship to their hidden causes, it appears that we are shut up within our own subjectivity. We can have no knowledge of anything beyond ourselves. Of course, there is no way to prove the principle of causality. But think of the costs of denying it. Ironically, the drastic nature of Kant's criticism bears witness to the appeal and power of the cosmological arguments. If, in order to defeat them, we must deny the mind's capacity for any objective knowledge, then they must be deeply rooted in our cognitive processes. I will reserve my final assessment of the cosmological arguments until I have canvassed other kinds of argument.

The Moral Argument

If cosmological arguments move from our experience of the world to its cause, moral arguments move from our experience of moral law to the supreme Lawgiver. Immanuel Kant and John Henry Newman appeal to moral sense as pointing to the existence of God, the moral lawgiver.[46] Apparently, all human beings have a sense of right and wrong, make moral judgments, and have a sense of justice. When we use such words as *right, wrong, justice, injustice, good,* and *evil,* we believe we are making sense. Unless we deem this intuition irrational and declare these words vacuous, there must be an objective moral order. One need

45. Kant, *Critique of Pure Reason,* unified edition, trans. Werner S. Pluhar (Indianapolis: Hackett Publishers, 1996), p. 592.

46. Newman, *A Grammar of Assent* (Garden City, NY: Doubleday, 1955), pp. 97-107. Kant's argument is found in *Critique of Practical Reason,* 2.2.5, trans. Lewis White Beck (New York: Macmillan, 1956).

not think of conscience as an intuition of God. One can think of the moral sense as data that needs a sufficient explanation. The explanation must also have a moral character, for any nonmoral explanation (physical, biological, or psychological) for the moral simply destroys morality. And only persons have a moral character. Therefore, God is a postulate necessary to validate our moral experience.

Though this argument has not lacked critics, many have found it compelling. Most people would reject the conclusion that love, mercy, and justice, on the one hand, and hatred, cruelty, and injustice, on the other, are ultimately reducible to the same (nonmoral) factors. However, without God or something like God, we seem to be forced to that implausible and unhappy conclusion. Evolutionary naturalism, for example, explains the moral sense in terms of natural drives instilled in our genes by natural selection for their survival value: that is, such qualities as sociability and altruism tend to help the species survive. Whatever one thinks of the explanatory power of this hypothesis and others like it, it does not account for the moral sense in moral terms. It reduces morality to the irrational process of random mutation and natural selection. Consciously preserving and cultivating a sense of moral obligation — of determining to do the right thing while believing that these feelings were put into us by irrational processes — strikes me as a piece of self-deception unmatched by anything believers are said to achieve.

The Ontological Argument

The ontological argument is the most intriguing and most difficult of the theistic proofs. It begins not with our experience of the world but with the idea of God and argues to God's existence. Augustine lays the foundation for the argument in the following statement:

> For on this principle it is that He is called Deus [God]. For the sound of those two syllables in itself conveys no true knowledge of His nature; but yet all who know the Latin tongue are led, when that sound reaches their ears, to think of a nature supreme in excellence and eternal in existence. For when the one supreme God of gods is thought of, even by those who believe that there are other gods, and who call them by that name, and worship them as gods, their thought takes the form of an endeavor to reach the conception of a nature, than which nothing more excellent or more exalted exists. . . . All, however, strive emulously to exalt the excellence of God: nor could any one be found to believe that any being to whom there exists a superior is God.

And so all concur in believing that God is that which excels in dignity all other objects.[47]

Anselm of Canterbury gave the argument its classic form:

> God cannot be conceived not to exist — God is that, than which nothing greater can be conceived — That which can be conceived not to exist is not God. And it assuredly exists so truly, that it cannot be conceived not to exist. For, it is possible to conceive of a being which cannot be conceived not to exist; and this is greater than one which can be conceived not to exist. Hence, if that, than which nothing greater can be conceived, can be conceived not to exist, it is not that, than which nothing greater can be conceived. But this is an irreconcilable contradiction. There is, then, so truly a being than which nothing greater can be conceived to exist, that it cannot even be conceived not to exist; and this being you are, O Lord, our God (*Proslogium*, 3).[48]

Like Augustine, Anselm began with the conviction that the word *God* may be used properly only of a being "than which nothing greater can be conceived." According to Anselm, we can conceive of the greatest possible being. Such a being possesses all the properties of being (sometimes called "perfections") to the maximal degree; that is, God is conceived as the most perfect being. Anselm suggests a thought experiment: first, think of the greatest possible being as not existing; now think of the greatest possible being as existing. Which is greater? A so-called "greatest possible being" that does not exist cannot really be the greatest possible being; for it lacks something perfection demands, that is, necessary existence. Hence, the idea of the nonexistence of God is a contradiction in terms. Once you become clear about what *God* means, you will see that God exists necessarily and cannot not exist.

The ontological argument has been rejected and defended for almost a thousand years by some of the greatest philosophical and theological minds.[49] Thomas Aquinas rejected it: he insisted that we know from other means (from faith and reasoning from God's works) that it is God's very nature to exist. God cannot not exist. Anselm is certainly correct here, for he is voicing the Christian understanding of God as the uncreated Creator of the world. Therefore, Thomas observes, we know that the proposition "God exists" is self-evident *in*

---

47. Augustine, *On Christian Doctrine*, 1.6-7 (*NPNF*, 1st ser., 2, p. 524). In *Confessions*, 7.5, Augustine explains how the principle that it is impossible to conceive "that which is better than you" shaped his thinking about God and freed him from many Manichean errors.

48. In *Basic Writings*, pp. 8-9.

49. Descartes, Leibniz, Wolfe, Hegel, and Hartshorne thought it valid, and many contemporary philosophers (but by no means all) follow Kant in rejecting it.

itself; that is, we know that God *is* his own existence. God does not depend on anything outside himself for his being. But the fact that God exists is not self-evident *to us*. We do not know this from the words alone, but only from God's works. Aquinas explains:

> Now because we do not know the essence of God, the proposition is not self-evident to us; but needs to be demonstrated by things that are more known to us, though less known in their nature — namely, by effects. . . . [Even if we grant] that everyone understands that by this word "God" is signified something than which nothing greater can be thought, nevertheless, it does not therefore follow that he understands that what the word signifies exists actually, but only that it exists mentally. Nor can it be argued that it actually exists, unless it be admitted that there actually exists something than which nothing greater can be thought; and this precisely is not admitted by those who hold that God does not exist.[50]

If we could see God's essence, we would see that God exists and exists necessarily; but by common consent of the Christian tradition, we cannot see God's essence. God is incomprehensible by finite minds. Simply having the thought of the most perfect being in our minds is not the same as seeing the essence of God. But without seeing God's essence (or having this truth demonstrated from God's works or receiving it in faith) we cannot get past the distinction we make in all other cases between what something is and whether it exists. Aquinas thus admits the validity of the ontological argument for those who are in a position to see God's essence — God himself and perhaps the redeemed — but not the validity for the rest of us.

Kant also rejected the ontological argument. He objected that the argument assumed the false idea that existence is a perfection or attribute of a thing. Imagine a $100 bill; now pull a $100 bill out of your wallet. Kant observes: "A hundred actual thalers do not contain the least more than a hundred possible thalers. For, the possible thalers signify the concept and the actual thalers signify the object and the positing thereof in itself; hence if the object contained more than the concept, then my concept would not express the entire object and thus would also not be the concept commensurate with this object."[51] The concept of God, Kant concludes, is not changed by the real existence (or nonexistence) of God. Therefore, according to Kant, conceiving the nonexistence of God does not involve a contradiction.

In this objection Kant has moved further away from the Christian under-

---

50. Aquinas, *SumTh*, 1.2.1 (*Basic Writings*, pp. 19-20).
51. Kant, *Critique of Pure Reason*, p. 584.

standing of God. Unlike Anselm and Thomas Aquinas, Kant does not know from other sources (revelation and God's works) that God is self-existent, that is, that existence is an attribute of God. He applies the distinction between what a thing is and whether it exists to God as well as to other things. Whatever might otherwise be thought of the ontological argument, Christian theology must reject Kant's assumption that God can be rightly thought of as a contingent being, as the kind of being that might not be. If we cannot agree with Anselm and think of God's existence as self-evident for us, we must at least acknowledge, with Thomas, that God's existence is self-evident *in itself.*

I cannot hope to bring closure to this debate. We need not, however, simply let the opposing viewpoints stand side by side as if nothing further can be said. As Hans Küng has pointed out, "there is food for thought" in this discussion.[52] Even if we do not see the ontological argument as proof of God's necessary existence, it brings the distinctive Christian understanding of God into bold relief. God exists in a way that no other being exists and can exist. Other beings might not have been, whereas God is not subject to nonbeing. Existence is one of God's attributes: God is "that than which nothing greater can be conceived." Because God created the world from nothing, we cannot conceive of a greater reality than God by thinking of God and the world together: God plus the world is not greater than God alone. The good in the world was in God before it was in the world.[53] Thus, when God made the world, God did not add any greatness to himself. And thus we can assure ourselves that God did not create the world out of necessity or for selfish reasons. Creation is pure grace and overflowing love. I shall develop these thoughts in greater detail in the appropriate section of the discussion of God's attributes.

Many other theistic arguments have been formulated. A brief list would include: (1) The argument from "common consent," which points to the probative value of the near universal human belief in a divine being or beings. (2) A set of epistemological arguments. For example, most of us believe that mathematical truths exist even before mathematicians discover them. Since mathematical truths are not material in nature, how can they exist before human beings think them, unless thought within a divine mind? We believe that such things as trees, squirrels, and frogs exist even when we are not experiencing them. We assume that these beings are composed of parts according to a "design plan" that can be reconstructed by the natural sciences.[54] Apart from a di-

52. Küng, *Does God Exist?* p. 535.

53. Sokolowski, *God of Faith and Reason*, pp. 8-11.

54. I am borrowing the term "design plan" from Plantinga, *Warrant and Proper Function*, p. 13.

vine mind that knows the design plan, how can we account for this assumption? Indeed, the premise of the intelligibility of the world seems to presuppose a divine mind. (3) Many pragmatic arguments have been proposed. The most famous is "Pascal's wager": since reason cannot attain absolute certainty of God's existence, we must bet on the existence or the nonexistence of God. Pascal argues that it makes more sense to wager on God's existence: for if God exists, you gain your soul, but if God does not exist, you lose only some cheap thrills. However, if you wager on God's nonexistence and it turns out that God exists, you will lose your soul.[55]

The Usefulness of the "Proofs"

How shall we evaluate the arguments for the existence of God from the perspective I have taken in this chapter? It is clear that many of the church's wisest and best servants valued these arguments to one degree or another. No segment of the church, Orthodox, Roman Catholic, or Protestant, has rejected them in principle. Nevertheless, it is also true that the church and her best theologians have seldom exaggerated their value. Rarely has a theologian considered these arguments coercive or producing absolute knowledge. Never were they said to produce knowledge adequate to salvation or to qualify as surrogates for faith. They were seen, at most, to be useful in confirming or reinforcing faith in God. If we accept this assessment, which I do, two final questions arise. First, what are the theological presuppositions of their usefulness? Second, how are they useful?

I have already concluded here that Scripture teaches that God witnesses to himself through the structures and events of nature. And I have rejected the idea that creation is a godforsaken place devoid of divine light. To the contrary, I exclaim with Psalm 19 that "the heavens declare the glory of God!" But I have also warned, with Paul in Romans 1, that the sinful mind's "thinking became futile and their foolish hearts were darkened." Natural religion and natural theology always pervert God's revelation in nature. Therefore, the theological presuppositions of the theistic arguments are the twin scriptural teachings that God witnesses to himself in nature and that this witness cannot be understood rightly apart from God's special revelation.

The theistic arguments attempt to put into words the self-witness of God in creation, and thus they have a legitimate theological foundation. However, it is important to observe that an argument is not the only way to articulate what

---

55. Pascal, *Pensées,* trans. A. J. Krailscheimer (London: Penguin Books, 1966), pp. 149-53.

we see and hear when we pay attention to God's creation. Doxology or praise is Scripture's preferred form of speech about creation: doxology spontaneously connects the beauty, majesty, and sublimity of creation with the Creator. Creation praises God and evokes praises: "Let them praise the name of the Lord, for he commanded and they were created" (Ps. 148:5). The theistic arguments are a step removed from doxology and hence a step removed from the wonder that evokes doxology. A cosmological argument for God's existence, for example, takes the focus off the wonderful creation itself and places it on propositions about the creation. Those propositions supposedly contain the conceptual content of some aspect of the wonderful creation: causality, movement, or order. From that point on, the creation itself recedes from view; for in arguments we move not from wonder to doxology, but from propositions about creation to propositions about God.

There are, of course, those who attend to creation and still are not moved to praise God. Attempting to convince them with arguments may help, but it may make matters worse. For constructing arguments for God's existence introduces even more possibilities for doubt. Even those who praise God as they look at creation may not grasp the truth of an abstract proposition about nature. We may be distracted by such side issues as the nature of causality and the definition of design. Introducing a chain of reasoning between God's self-witness in nature and the conclusion that he exists legitimates questioning every link in the chain. Claiming too much probative power for an argument may actually undermine confidence in the conclusion. Finally, debates may erupt about whether proving a first cause, prime mover, or moral lawgiver is the same as proving that *God* exists.

Having duly noted these cautions, I believe that the arguments for God's existence can play a useful part in the life of faith. It seems obvious that, if it is permissible to gaze on the heavens and praise God, it is legitimate to explore the qualities of the heavens that cause us to praise him. It also seems appropriate to consider the praise-evoking qualities of other creatures. However, it is very important to turn away soon from these abstractions back to God's self-witness in creation and in Scripture. We may return with a greater sensitivity, with sharpened eyes and more attentive ears, to see and hear creation praise its Creator. The various arguments (cosmological, moral, and ontological) explore many facets of the creation that point to God from diverse angles. In considering the manifoldness of creation we gain a fuller realization of the rich meaning of the statement "God exists." We can play the part of secondary witnesses by telling others what we see and hear; but the primary witness to God's natural revelation is nature itself. George MacDonald says the following:

In what belongs to the deeper meanings of nature and her mediation between us and God, the appearances of nature are the truths of nature, far deeper than any scientific discoveries in and concerning them. The show of things is that for which God cares *most*. . . . It is through their show, not through their analysis, that we enter into their deepest truths. . . . Nature as well exists primarily for her face, her look, her appeals to the heart and the imagination, her simple service to human need, and not for the secrets to be discovered in her and turned to man's further use.[56]

What God's Existence Means

God is not solely a word on our lips or an idea existing only in our minds or a conclusion to an argument. God is not merely a final comfort or a last resort when other things prove inadequate to sustain and satisfy us. God really exists! Everything the word "God" says is true and active. God exists most certainly because God cannot not be; nothingness has no power over God. Being, light, truth, good, and beauty — these are unassailable because they are God's eternal attributes. There is not the slightest possibility that chaos, nothingness, darkness, falsehood, evil, and ugliness will establish a foothold in God. God is the bedrock of being without whom nothing else would exist or happen. Every other being exists because God gives it being. Therefore, everything in creation bears witness to God's reality by its very existence. Moreover, the moment-by-moment existence of creation is a continuous act of God. If action is a mark of existence, God demonstrates his existence in infinite redundancy. If we do not see God's action because of its constancy, it is because we have not yet grasped what the word "God" means.

The Cosmic Meaning

God really exists, and the cosmic implications are astounding. Grasping the full depth and breadth of those implications would require the work of a lifetime. Even this book-length study can only begin to probe them. Thus I will conclude this chapter with a few indicators of how to begin this joyful task. Belief in God's existence gives what atheism takes away. God gives light and warmth and meaning to the universe, which, according to atheism, is dark and cold and meaningless. First, because God (Father, Son, and Holy Spirit) exists, we can be

---

56. C. S. Lewis, ed., *George MacDonald: 365 Readings*, p. 65.

confident that the universe exists for a reason. It is not a brute fact. The loving God created it freely from nothing for his own good reasons. And since the eternal God, full in his own being, does not need the world, we can be sure that those reasons involve nothing selfish. God made the world in an act of pure selfless love and overflowing goodness.

The second cosmic implication follows from the first: the world is full of meaning. The universe is not directionless and chaotic. God guides it toward a goal that he has set. God's loving act of creation will take its final shape over time as a concrete actuality. That purpose will be achieved by means of events that take place within the universe in partnership with the God who frees, empowers, and works in every worker. The relationships these events sustain to their divinely given purposes constitute their final meanings. Even if we cannot know the final meaning of any particular event, we can be confident that it is not absurd and its significance will not be annihilated as the ages pass and human beings forget.

Third, unlike the atheist, the believer can affirm confidently that there is a rationality that structures and orders all things. Mind and will and personhood are not merely secondary products of mindless matter. Since God made the world for a reason, we can know that the world was an idea before it was a material fact. It is grounded in God's mind and his eternal council. Since he created it and sustains it, the universe is intelligible to God in every detail. Nothing is hidden, dark, or obscure to him. Hence, even if we cannot comprehend it in every detail, we can assert confidently that the universe is intelligible in itself. We can join our minds to the cosmic rationality in the quest to understand the works of God. As we experience the manifold beauty and order of heaven and earth, we can allow joy to arise in our hearts unclouded by the sad thoughts that plagued the poet Matthew Arnold on that evening on Dover Beach:

> . . . the world, which seems
> To lie before us like a land of dreams,
> So various, so beautiful, so new,
> Hath really neither joy, nor love, nor light,
> Nor certitude, nor peace, nor help for pain,
> And we are here as on a darkling plain,
> Swept with confused alarms of struggle and flight,
> Where ignorant armies clash by night.[57]

Fourth, there is a cosmic plan. If God created the universe with a goal in mind, and that goal will be achieved by means of events within the universe, we

---

57. "Dover Beach" (1867), in *The Poems of Matthew Arnold 1840-1867* (1913; reprint, London: Oxford, 1940), p. 402.

can be confident that God knows those events and how they are related to each other and to the goal. The universe will not spin out of control and leave us to the tender mercies of chance and fortune.

Fifth, things such as trees and human beings are real and substantial in their wholeness. They are not mere chance compositions of material parts, ephemeral constellations that have being only in the human psyche. The eternal God knows them as wholes, as intelligible plans or essences, even apart from their material embodiment. He planned them and uses them according to his will. We know that nature is not a liar because we know that God is not a liar. We do not find the truth of nature only by analysis and reduction. To borrow George MacDonald's words again, "In what belongs to the deeper meanings of nature and her mediation between us and God, the appearances of nature are the truths of nature, far deeper than any scientific discoveries in and concerning them."[58]

The Existential Meaning

The existential implications of God's existence are staggering. An inexpressible joy begins to well up in our hearts as we contemplate them. Let me speak to you directly. First, you are in this world for a reason. You are not an accident or a chance product of blind forces. Nothing would happen without God, and God never does anything without a reason. Just as God created the world for a reason, he made you for a reason. But why *this* world, you may wonder, and why *me?* You may not discover all the intricacies of the reason, but you can rest confident in this: God made you because he loved you and wanted you to know his love and experience the joy of loving him in return.

Second, you were planned before the creation of the world. You were created for a purpose. You have an important mission, something great to do with your life. Your mission's greatness cannot be measured by anything visible to you or others; it can be measured only by the greatness of the One who sent you. Thus you are responsible and must be faithful to your commission by carrying out your mission. Your success or failure as a human being can be measured only by whether you are faithful to God's plan for you. It does not matter whether you are rich or poor, attractive or plain, healthy or ill, popular or unknown. God knows his plan for you, and you are irreplaceable.

Third, since God's eternal purpose is the objective meaning of the universe as a whole and of each event within it, the meaning of your life is rooted in real

58. Lewis, *George MacDonald: 365 Readings,* p. 65.

and eternal meaning. You don't need to pretend that your life means some-thing; you need not attempt heroically and futilely to create your own meaning. You simply don't have to worry about it: your life *is* meaningful. Your sense of meaning, your perception of meaning, can also be rooted in reality. You may not be able to see it with your own eyes, but every day, every event, every en-counter, every word, and every deed, no matter how insignificant it may seem to you and others, is weighty with God's meaning. God has work for you to do. Each event in your life, though seemingly trivial in itself, is decisive for the des-tiny of the world and the shape of eternity. There are no insignificant lives, no little people, and no born losers. There are no grounds for boredom, for the movement of time is no mere repetition. There are no empty moments, no or-dinary times, and God never stops working. God fills all our times with unceas-ingly new opportunities to work with him in accomplishing something that will last forever.

Fourth, because God is real, you can root your values in the real order of value. God is the greatest good, and loving God above all things frees you to love other things in the right way and to the right extent: that is, you can love them in their proper order related to that final end. That objective order of love is determined by God's will, and it terminates in his goals. Augustine never tires of emphasizing the necessity of loving God above all things and all things in God. Quoting Tobit and alluding to the Gospel of Matthew, he says: "'Happy is the person who loves you' (Tobit 13:18) and his friend in you, and his enemy be-cause of you (Matt. 5:44). Though left alone, he loses none dear to him; for all are dear in the one who cannot be lost."[59]

Fifth, you as a person — as John, Carol, or Matt — are real. You are real because God knows you *as you*, not merely as a composite of mindless stuff. You stand before God as a unique reality called into a person-to-person rela-tionship with the Father, Son, and Holy Spirit. You are more real than the stuff of which your body is made. It exists for your sake, to serve and sustain you, so that you might stand before God as a person. God knew *you* before he created the stuff out of which you are made. And you will live before him ages upon ages after the elements that compose your body have been dispersed through-out the universe. God loved you and called you by name long before your par-ents gave you the name you now wear. God's love is the power that makes you a person, one who is able to respond in love. In Augustine's *Confessions*, being a person means having a relationship with ourselves that is grounded in God's eternal love for us and knowledge of us. He confesses to God, "To hear you speaking about oneself is to know oneself" (p. 180). Self-knowledge, according

59. Augustine, *Confessions,* trans. Henry Chadwick (New York: Oxford, 1991), p. 61.

to Augustine, is God's gift: "For what I know of myself I know because you grant me light" (p. 182).

Sixth, you can accomplish something real and lasting. Apart from God, nothing you can do will last. Your most enduring monument will eventually crumble to dust. You will die, your wealth will be turned over to others, and your fame will fade. But what you do for God will last forever. You may not be able at present to see the significance of your work, but you can "always give yourselves fully to the work of the Lord, because you know that your labor in the Lord is not in vain" (1 Cor. 15:58). He will remember it, preserve it, resurrect it, and incorporate it into the glorious, redeemed world he is making. Peter encourages us to rejoice now in the hope of that future:

> Praise be to the God and Father of our Lord Jesus Christ! In his great mercy he has given us new birth into a living hope through the resurrection of Jesus Christ from the dead, and into an inheritance that can never perish, spoil or fade — kept in heaven for you . . . and even though you do not see him now, you believe in him and are filled with an inexpressible and glorious joy, for you are receiving the goal of your faith, the salvation of your souls (1 Pet. 1:3-9).

4

Where Being Means Loving: The Tri-unity of God

The Christian church came to know God through Jesus Christ, in the power of the Holy Spirit, in a way that compelled it to confess that God *is* Father, Son, and Holy Spirit. This doctrine of God is confessed by Roman Catholic, Orthodox, and Protestant churches. Gregory Nazianzus (A.D. 329-389) represents the voice of tradition when he says:

> But when I say God, I mean Father, Son and Holy Spirit. For Godhead is neither diffused beyond these, so as to bring in a mob of gods; nor yet is it bounded by a smaller compass than these, so as to condemn us for a poverty-stricken conception of deity, either Judaizing to save the *monarchia*, or falling into paganism by the multitude of our gods. For the evil on either side is the same, though found in contrary directions. This then is the Holy of Holies, which is hidden even from the Seraphim, and is glorified with a thrice repeated Holy, meeting in one ascription to the title Lord and God.[1]

Having a place in a church's creed, however, does not guarantee that the doctrine of the Trinity plays a vital role in the lives and thought of its members, clergy, and theologians. In liberal Protestant churches, confessing the Trinity has long since lost cognitive meaning, and liberal theologians, if they attend to the doctrine of the Trinity at all, treat it as a symbol pointing to something in religious experience. Even in confessional churches, those without robust teaching and preaching, traditional formulas become opaque and cease to illuminate the mind and stir the heart. Moreover, many evangelical and conservative believers tend toward biblicism in their approach to doctrine, and thus they feel uncomfortable with the metaphysical language of the traditional creeds.

1. Gregory Nazianzus, *Oration 38*, 8 (*NPNF*, 2nd ser., 8, p. 347).

104

In dealing with the subject of the Holy Trinity, as with no other, we must acknowledge our limitations. I do not pretend to offer anything more in this chapter than an introduction for beginners. As I write, I have in mind conservative believers, confessionalists, and biblicists. I think of my beginning theology students and members of my congregation who confess God as Father, Son, and Holy Spirit, but who would not feel competent to explain or defend the doctrine. And they certainly do not understand their Christian experience in Trinitarian terms. Therefore, my goal is to specify the claims made by the traditional doctrine of the Trinity, indicate its biblical basis, explore some of its implications, and show its relevance to Christian experience. Applying the approach outlined in earlier chapters, I will examine tradition in the light of Scripture, with the help of reason, and with a view to experience.

The Traditional Doctrine of the Trinity

It is important to distinguish between the reality of the Holy Trinity, the Trinitarian form of Christian knowledge, and the explicit doctrine of the Trinity. All Christian doctrine bears witness to the one God who *is* Father, Son, and Spirit: that is, everything God *does* is from the Father, through the Son, and in the Spirit. And every Christian response to God occurs in the Spirit, through the Son, and to the Father. Therefore, every Christian doctrine bears a Trinitarian aspect. Thomas Torrance rightly claims that the doctrine of the Trinity constitutes the "fundamental grammar of Christian dogmatic theology."[2] The doctrine of the Trinity teaches explicitly about the Trinitarian form of God's being and action. Naturally, the doctrine of the Trinity does not say everything there is to say about God. For the Holy Trinity has attributes other than being triune and engages in actions other than the inner Trinitarian begetting of the Son and proceeding of the Spirit. In all our discussions of these other attributes and actions, however, we must never speak of any God other than the Holy Trinity.

In Western theology, theologians tended to discuss the existence and attributes of God before they discussed the doctrine of the Trinity.[3] This procedure can lead to misunderstanding. Thomas Aquinas writes in *Summa Theologica* first of the existence and attributes of the divine unity (1.1-26); he deals with the divine persons later (1.27-43). Thomas argues that the existence

2. Thomas Torrance, *The Christian Doctrine of God: One Being, Three Persons* (Edinburgh: T&T Clark, 1996), p. 82.

3. Karl Rahner, *The Trinity*, trans. Joseph Donceel (London: Burns and Oates, 1970). Rahner dates this practice to the time when "the *Sentences* of Peter Lombard were superseded by the *Summa* of St. Thomas" (p. 17).

and some attributes of God can be known by reason, whereas other things about God — for example, that God is triune — can be known only by revelation. Does his separation between the divine unity and the divine tri-unity represent a possible overlap of the Christian doctrine of God with rational theism and various non-Christian monotheisms? Does it imply that the Christian doctrine of God is composed of a rational part and a mysterious part? If so, the doctrine of the Trinity, rather than permeating all Christian theology, stands at risk of becoming an isolated treatise that can be omitted without obvious loss to the main body of theology.

Aquinas and the Western theologians that followed him, both Roman Catholic and Protestant, held firmly to the doctrine of the Trinity and defended it against critics. None of them intended to marginalize or cast doubt on it. Nevertheless, Western theology from the Middle Ages onward gives the impression that the doctrine of the Trinity, though true and important, could be left out without major revisions in the rest of the doctrine of God. This division left the Western doctrine of God vulnerable to the contention of the Socinians, Deists, and Unitarians: that a non-Trinitarian (yet Christian) doctrine of God is possible.

It matters little where in the doctrine of God a theologian treats the explicit doctrine of the Trinity, the first chapter or the last. What is of greater importance is that all Christian knowledge of God is expounded as knowledge of the Father, through the Son, in the power of the Holy Spirit. I have placed this doctrine in Part One, "Knowing God," because I want to emphasize that all Christian knowledge is Trinitarian in form and substance.

The traditional dogma of the Trinity came to its definitive formulation in the Niceno-Constantinopolitan Creed (A.D. 381). The Nicene Creed was adopted by the Council of Constantinople, and it brought to a close the fourth-century controversy about the Trinity. It was accepted by the ancient ecumenical church and has remained a treasured statement of the Trinitarian faith for the worldwide church. That formulation reads as follows:

I believe in one God the Father Almighty; Maker of heaven and earth, and of all things visible and invisible. And in one Lord Jesus Christ, the only-begotten Son of God, begotten of the Father before all worlds [God of God], Light of Light, very God of very God, begotten, not made, being of one substance [essence] with the Father; by whom all things were made; who for us men and for our salvation, came down from heaven, and was incarnate by the Holy Ghost of the Virgin Mary, and was made man; and was crucified also for us under Pontius Pilate; he suffered and was buried; and the third day he rose again, according to the Scriptures; and ascended into heaven, and sitteth on the right hand of the Father; and he shall come again, with glory, to judge both the quick and the dead; whose kingdom shall have no end. And [I believe] in the Holy Ghost, the Lord and Giver of life; who proceedeth from the Father [and the Son]; who with the Father and the Son together is worshiped and glorified; who spake by the Prophets. And [I believe] in one Holy Catholic and Apostolic Church. I acknowledge one baptism for the forgiveness of sins; and I look for the resurrection of the dead, and the life of the world to come. Amen.[4]

The Creed affirms the oneness of God, who is Father, Son, and Holy Spirit; it distinguishes among the persons but maintains the unity of the divine nature. Being begotten not made, the Son is of "one substance with the Father." The Son is "God" just as the Father is. The Spirit is to be "worshiped and glorified" along "with the Father and the Son." The familiar distinction between "person" and "substance," though implicit, is not highlighted in the Nicene Creed. However, it is clear that the names Father, Son, and Spirit imply distinction and unity among the three. Explaining and clarifying the nature of these relationships in detail was not the aim of the Creed. The bracketed phrase "and the Son" was not present in the original (Greek) version of the Nicene Creed. The Western church added it later, and that occasioned a great split between the Western and Eastern churches.

As I have observed in the earlier discussion of tradition, specifying just what tradition teaches is not as easy as compiling authoritative statements on a subject. Therefore, one cannot fully articulate and specify the church's traditional understanding of the Trinity by quoting the Nicene Creed; nor could one do that by quoting all the other creeds and respected church fathers and theologians on the subject. A distinction always remains between the inexhaustible truth of the Trinity and the words that bear witness to this truth. Therefore, the church must continue to seek to understand, preserve, and teach the truth of its faith in the triune God. Even with these limitations in mind, however, I believe that we can assume we have in this creed a serviceable summary of the traditional doctrine of the Trinity. We must now ask about its biblical grounding, its internal consistency, and its coherence with other Christian teaching. My goal is not to foment doubt but to confirm faith.

4. Philip Schaff, ed., *The Creeds of Christendom*, vol. 2, rev. David S. Schaff (1931; reprint, Grand Rapids: Baker Book House, 1990), pp. 58-59. Schaff puts the Western additions in brackets.

The Triune Teaching in Scripture

Does Scripture, as tradition affirms, teach the doctrine of the Trinity? I must admit at the outset that Scripture does not teach this doctrine in exactly the same words or in the same compact and dense form as it appears in the creeds. Furthermore, though rich in triune teaching, Scripture never deals with the precise issues that necessitated the doctrine's formulation in the Nicene Creed. For Scripture never directly addresses the nature of the immanent relationships among the persons of the Trinity. Scripture does not explain how we can affirm three divine persons without thinking of them as three Gods or subordinating the Son and the Spirit to the Father. Nor does it explain how the three persons can be conceived to be one without losing their distinctness. Nevertheless, at the time that it promulgated the Nicene Creed, the church affirmed that the doctrine of the Trinity does nothing other than preserve and make explicit the teaching of Scripture.

I will examine a variety of texts that offer different insights into the Trinity. I do not claim to *prove* that Scripture teaches the doctrine. I shall aim for a more modest goal: to show that the traditional doctrine has a solid claim to a scriptural warrant. I can only indicate here what I believe would be upheld by a more detailed study. Following a traditional pattern, I will sample:

1. Texts that are explicitly Trinitarian or display a Trinitarian pattern
2. Texts that state or imply the deity of a person of the Trinity
3. Texts that distinguish the persons
4. Texts that affirm the unity of the divine nature
5. The Trinity in the Old Testament

Trinitarian Texts

Matthew 28:18-19

At the end of the Gospel of Matthew, Jesus commands his disciples to go into the world, make disciples of all people, and baptize "them in the name of the Father and of the Son and of the Holy Spirit." The Father is listed first, but the continued parallelism is striking. The baptismal rite of initiation is to be performed in the name of the Father *and* of the Son *and* of the Holy Spirit. Unless the Son and the Spirit were of equal dignity with the Father, how could they be set alongside the Father in this way? On the other hand, it is equally implausible that Jesus would use three names if the three were not distinct. It is even more implausible that he intended the distinctions to imply that there are three Gods.

Second Corinthians 13:14

Paul bestows the following Trinitarian benediction on the Corinthians: "May the grace of the Lord Jesus Christ, and the love of God, and the fellowship of the Holy Spirit be with you all." Again, the Trinitarian parallelism is arresting. Each divine person is a source of blessing: grace from the Son, love from God (the Father), and fellowship from the Holy Spirit. In the New Testament, these blessings can be bestowed by any one of the divine persons. For example, Paul asks, "Who shall separate us from the *love of Christ?*" (Rom. 8:35), and then answers that nothing "will be able to separate us from the *love of God* that is in Christ Jesus our Lord" (8:39). Later in Romans, Paul speaks of the *"love of the Spirit"* (15:30). The Trinitarian impact of the New Testament benedictions arises not so much from the nature of the blessings imparted. It comes from the almost thoughtless way the divine persons are listed together. Love, grace, and fellowship are divinely bestowed blessings of the one God, whether attributed to Father, Son, or Spirit.

Matthew 3:13-17

The church fathers noticed the triune pattern in the narrative of Jesus' baptism (cf. Mark 1:9-11; Luke 3:21, 22; John 1:32-34).[5] As Jesus is baptized, the Spirit descends in the form of a dove, and the Father declares, "This is my Son, whom I love; with him I am well pleased" (Matt. 3:17). This scene supports the traditional doctrine that Father, Son, and Spirit must be distinguished. The Son obeys the Father and receives the Spirit (who descends from the Father); the Father speaks about the Son; the Son hears the Father and sees the dove-formed Spirit.

Ephesians 3:14-19

Here Paul prays to the *Father* to strengthen the Ephesians through the *Spirit*, "so that *Christ* may dwell in your hearts by faith." He asks that they be given power to know "the love of Christ" that "surpasses knowledge" so that they "may be filled to the measure of all the fullness of God." How can one read this

---

5. For references, see Thomas Oden, *Systematic Theology*, 1 (San Francisco: Harper and Row, 1987), p. 203.

text in a non-Trinitarian way? What love but divine love "surpasses knowledge"? What power but divine power can enable a finite creature to "grasp" a love that "surpasses knowledge"? Who but God can fill us with the "fullness of God"?

We would, in an exhaustive study, discuss many other texts under this heading: 1 Cor. 12:1-6; Jude 20, 21; John 14:17; Acts 2:33; Rev. 1:4-6; 2 Thess. 2:13-17; Eph. 2:18; 4:4-6; and 1 John 5:4-6.

Deity-Affirming Texts

A second group of texts states or implies the deity of the Father or the Son or the Holy Spirit. The church fathers, the theologians of the Middle Ages, and the theologians of Protestant orthodoxy divided the scriptural proofs for the divinity of the Persons into four categories: the Person is either explicitly called God, or worshiped as God, or given divine attributes, or described as acting as only God can.[6]

The Father

It hardly needs to be argued that the one Jesus addressed as Father (Abba) is God. The one addressed as "Our Father who art in heaven" can be only the God of Israel who created the world and called, punished, and saved Israel. Paul salutes the Romans with "Grace and peace to you from God our Father" (Rom. 1:7; cf. James 1:27). There is "one God and Father of all" (Eph. 4:6). The Father is holy (John 17:11), the origin of "all things" (1 Cor. 8:6), "glorious" (Eph. 1:17), and the one "who is over all and through all and in all" (Eph. 4:6). True worshipers must worship the Father "in spirit and in truth" (John 4:23). God the Father deserves "praise" from us (2 Cor. 11:31; Eph. 1:3; 1 Pet. 1:3), "thanksgiving" (Eph. 5:20; Col. 1:3; 3:17), and "glory" (Rom. 15:6; Phil. 2:11; 4:20). The Father raises the dead (Gal. 1:1; 4:6), sends the Son (John 5:23; 10:36; 1 John 4:14; cf. 1 John 4:19), sends the Holy Spirit (Acts 2:33), and foreknows the future (1 Pet. 1:2).

---

6. Johannes Wollebius, *Compendium of Christian Theology* (1626), quoted in Heinrich Heppe, *Reformed Dogmatics,* rev. and ed. Ernst Bizer, trans. G. T. Thomson (1950; reprint, London: Wakeman Great Reprints, n.d.), pp. 123-24. See also Richard A. Muller, *Post-Reformation Reformed Dogmatics: The Rise and Development of Reformed Orthodoxy,* vol. 4, *The Triune God* (Grand Rapids: Baker Academic, 2003), pp. 149-50, 245 (hereafter *PRRD*).

The Son

There can be no doubt that the central issue at the origin of Christianity, and thus in the New Testament, is Christological: Who is Jesus and what did he do? The New Testament answers that he is the Messiah, the Son of God, the Son of man, the servant of the Lord, God, and the Word. It affirms that through him God created and now sustains the world, reconciles sinners to himself, and will judge the world in righteousness. The New Testament answer to the Christological question implies an answer to the Trinitarian question, though the New Testament did not specifically address this question. The two sets of issues are bound together. Any anti-Trinitarian answer to the question of the Trinity will undermine the New Testament answer to the Christological question. If it were clearly understood that the Son is a mere creature, it would also be obvious that the Christological titles Messiah, the Son of God, the Son of man, the servant of the Lord, God, and the Word were merely honorific (like an honorary doctorate). Why, then, was there the first-century controversy over who Jesus was and what he did?

Traditional interpretation argues that the New Testament gives Jesus Christ names and titles that can only be applied to deity. The Gospel of John begins by identifying Jesus as the Word: "In the beginning was the Word, and the Word was with God, and the Word was God" (John 1:1). Later in John's prologue, he identifies the Word with the one who "became flesh and made his dwelling among us" (1:14). This Word was "with" God and "was" God. This way of putting it implies both distinction and identity with God: hence, the one who became incarnate "was God." Thomas (the doubter) exclaimed at the sight of the resurrected Christ, "My Lord and my God" (John 20:28). Jesus did not reply to Thomas with a rebuke for being called Lord and God, but with a blessing (20:29). In another New Testament text, Titus is told to wait patiently for "the glorious appearing of our great God and Savior, Jesus Christ" (Titus 2:13).[7]

John assures his readers that Jesus Christ is "the true God and eternal life" (1 John 5:20).[8] In Philippians, Paul describes Jesus Christ's move from his native existence in the "form of God" to take up the "form of a slave." Because of his humility and obedience, the Father has given him "the name that is above every

---

7. The Socinians disputed the traditional interpretation of this text. The "great God" and "our Savior Jesus Christ," they teach, refer to two different persons (*Rocovian Catechism*, 4.1, quoted in Muller, *PRRD*, 4, p. 310); see Muller, *PRRD*, 4, pp. 309-14, for the orthodox refutation of the Socinian interpretation.

8. For the anti-Trinitarian interpretation of this text and the orthodox Reformed responses, see Muller, *PRRD*, 4, pp. 308-9.

name, that at the name of Jesus every knee should bow, in heaven and on earth and under the earth, and every tongue confess that Jesus Christ is Lord" (Phil. 2:6-11). What must we conclude about Jesus Christ, whose native existence is "in the form of God," whose name is above every name, and before whom every created being in the universe must bow the knee!

Jesus is called "Lord." He is not designated "lord" in a relative sense, in recognition of human authority; rather, he is acknowledged as "Lord" in an absolute sense. Jesus is Lord of the Sabbath (Matt. 12:8; Mark 2:28; Luke 6:46). Jesus Christ, according to Peter in his sermon to Cornelius and his household, is "Lord of all." Later in the New Testament, he is "Lord of both the dead and the living" (Rom. 14:9); he is the "Lord of glory" (1 Cor. 2:8); "Lord of lords and King of kings" (Rev. 17:14; 19:16); and "our only Sovereign and Lord" (Jude 4).

In the New Testament, Jesus is called Lord countless times. Reading these texts carefully discloses many subtle patterns and nuances, of which I wish to note three. In two places (1 Cor. 8:6 and Eph. 4:4-5) Paul speaks of "one God" and "one Lord." A superficial glance at these texts might lead us to think that they might cause difficulties for the Trinitarian teaching. After all, they speak of "one God" and then place Jesus Christ in another category. But further consideration dispels this first impression.

The first text comes from 1 Corinthians: "For us there is but one God, the Father, from whom all things came and for whom we live; and there is but one Lord, Jesus Christ, through whom all things came and through whom we live" (8:6). Here Paul contrasts pagan polytheism, in which there are many gods and lords, with faith in the one God, the Father, and in the one Lord, Jesus Christ. If we argue that the "Lord" cannot be "God" because he is not the Father, it follows that "God" (the Father) cannot be "Lord" because he is not "Jesus Christ." For the text says there is only one Lord, and it seems most implausible to deny lordship to God, since lordship in Scripture is a divine attribute.

The second text comes from Ephesians: "There is one body and one *Spirit* . . . one *Lord,* one faith, one baptism; one *God and Father* of all, who is over all and through all and in all" (Eph. 4:4-5). This text brings out the different unifying elements of the Christian faith to inspire believers to "keep the unity of the Spirit through the bond of peace" (Eph. 4:3). Again, the one Spirit and the one Lord are set alongside the "one God and Father." Does this mean that the Spirit and the Lord are being excluded from the divine nature? The approach in this text creates the same problems that it did in the preceding text. There is only one Spirit and one Lord. Is God, therefore, not Spirit? Is God not Lord? The Trinitarian interpretation makes these texts intelligible. By distinguishing between the three divine persons and the one divine nature, we can understand that God the Father exercises his lordship only through the Son and his power only in the Spirit. The Father, the Son, and the Spirit differ in person but all have the divine attributes of lordship, oneness, and spirituality.

A second pattern of parallelism occurs in New Testament texts that quote the Old Testament where the name "Lord" is used. In these Old Testament texts, there is no doubt that "Lord" refers to the one God of Israel. In several New Testament texts, the Lord Jesus Christ is assimilated to the Lord God. Consider Romans 10:9-13: "if you confess with your mouth 'Jesus is Lord' . . . you will be saved. . . . As the Scripture says, 'Anyone who trusts in him will never be put to shame' . . . for 'everyone who calls on the name of the Lord will be saved.'" Here Paul explains the saving significance of the required confession of Jesus as Lord by quoting two Old Testament texts, Isaiah 28:16 and Joel 2:32. The first refers to the stone the Lord plans to lay in Zion, a "tested" and "precious cornerstone": trust in him (the stone) will not disappoint. In the second text, Joel looks forward to the "great and dreadful day of the Lord" when the Lord will pour out his "Spirit on all people," and "everyone who calls on the name of the Lord will be saved" (Joel 2:28-32). Clearly, Paul understands Jesus to be the same "Lord" (or "Lord" in the same sense) as the Lord mentioned by Joel. How can one avoid the conclusion that confessing that Jesus is Lord is equivalent to confessing him as God?

We meet another example of the parallel between the Old Testament Lord and Jesus Christ in 1 Corinthians 2:16: "For 'who has known the mind of the Lord that he may instruct him?' But we have the mind of Christ" (1 Cor. 2:16). Here Paul quotes Isaiah 40:13, which asks a series of rhetorical questions meant to show the Lord's greatness by which he judges and redeems Israel. No one knows the "mind of the Lord," he reminds his readers in this text, but "we have the mind of Christ." A few verses earlier Paul had extolled the wisdom of God revealed in Christ by the Spirit. Only God's Spirit knows God, "even the deep things of God" (2:10). Only the one who has the Spirit can know such things. Then Paul drives the point home by claiming that "we have the mind of Christ." Apparently, Paul claims to have the "mind of Lord" precisely because in the power of the Spirit he has "the mind of Christ." How could we read this text in an anti-Trinitarian way? In Ephesians 6, the Lord's strength and "mighty power" is set side by side with God's armor as resources to withstand the devil (vv. 10-11). And in Colossians 2, Jesus is declared to be "Lord" because in him "all the fullness of the Deity lives in a bodily form" (vv. 6-10).

The New Testament also refers to Jesus as "Son of God," "only Son," and "the Son." The title "Son of God" by itself is ambiguous. In the Old Testament there are many "sons of God." Israel is God's son (Exod. 4:22, 19:5; Isa. 63:8; Jer. 31:9; Hos. 11:1; Mal. 1:6; and many others); it is often used as an honorific title for the judges and kings of Israel (Ps. 2:7; 82:26, 27; 2 Sam. 7:11-14). Christians become "sons of God" by adoption (Rom. 8:15, 23). But Jesus is the Son of God in a sense that differs from those other "sons of God." The angel announced to Mary that she would conceive by the power of the Holy Spirit and that the "holy one" she would bear would be called the "Son of God" (Luke 1:35). In the Synoptic Gospels, the devil and the demons recognize Jesus as the "Son of God" and connect this status with the power to perform miracles and to bring judgment on the demonic world (Matt. 4:3, 6; 8:29; Mark 3:11; Luke 4:3, 9). The ruling Jewish leaders understood Jesus' claim to be the "Son of God" as blasphemous (Matt. 26:63; John 19:17). Some found Jesus' claim that God was his "own Father" to be equivalent to "making himself equal with God" (John 5:18). Clearly, the New Testament understands Jesus' sonship as a metaphysical status. He is not a mere prophet with delegated authority.

Jesus is not simply a son of God; he is *the* Son of God. At Jesus' baptism the voice from heaven said, "This is my Son in whom I am well pleased." At the transfiguration, the voice from the cloud distinguished Jesus from Moses and Elijah, saying, "This is my Son, whom I love. Listen to him!" (Mark 9:2-8). The Son and the Father have a unique relationship, says Jesus: "No one knows the Son except the Father, and no one knows the Father except the Son and those to whom the Son chooses to reveal him" (Matt. 11:27). The Gospel of John and the Johannine letters emphasize Jesus' unique sonship: "No one has ever seen God, but God the One and Only, who is at the Father's side, has made him known" (John 1:18; cf. 3:16; 1 John 4:9). Paul refers to Jesus as God's "own Son," implying Jesus' unique sonship (Rom. 8:35). The Father is so identified with the Son that whoever "does not honor the Son does not honor the Father, who sent him" (John 5:23).

Jesus' sonship is eternal and natural, and Paul confirms this in his discussion of the resurrection and cosmic redemption in Romans 8. The whole creation is groaning and waiting "in eager expectation for the sons of God to be revealed" (v. 19). The creation will be liberated from its decaying state into "the glorious freedom of the children of God" (v. 21). In anticipation, we who enjoy the firstfruits of the Spirit "wait eagerly for our adoption as sons, the redemption of our bodies" (v. 23). Clearly, being a son of God is not a legal fiction, an honorific title with no metaphysical dimension. Becoming a son of God (even an adopted one) requires the creative power of the Spirit and involves the resurrection into glory and eternal life; that is, it is a metaphysical transformation. Why would Paul understand the transition into adoptive sonship as glorious metaphysical birth unless he already understood Jesus' unique sonship as a metaphysical station?

In conclusion, the New Testament understands Jesus to be the "Son of God" in more than an honorific sense. The New Testament takes the analogy of the human relationship of father and son very seriously. Whereas kings, angelic beings, and the saints in heaven are sons of God by adoption, Jesus is the natural Son, having the same divine nature as the Father.[9]

In the second of the traditional proofs of the Son's divine status, Jesus Christ is understood to have divine attributes. The Son is uncreated and eternal. "Before Abraham was, I am"(John 8:58), Jesus claimed, identifying himself with the "I am who I am" of Exodus 3:14. Asserting that the Word is coeternal with the Father, the Gospel of John begins in imitation of Genesis 1:1: "In the beginning was the Word . . ." (John 1:1). The Word of "eternal life," which "was from the beginning," has now appeared (1 John 1:1-4). Christ "created all things" and is "before all things" (Col. 1:16, 17). "Through him all things were made; without him nothing was made that has been made" (John 1:3). Only the uncreated God can create. The author of Hebrews, arguing the Son's superiority to the angels, applies the words of Psalm 102 to the Son: "But you remain the same, and your years will never end" (Heb. 1:12). That same author assures us: "Jesus Christ is the same yesterday and today and forever" (Heb. 13:8).

The Son has divine knowledge: "But Jesus would not entrust himself to them, for he knew all men. He did not need man's testimony about man, for he knew what was in a man" (John 2:24-25; cf. 1:48; Matt. 28:20). The Son has divine power: Christ is the "power of God" (1 Cor. 1:24). The Lord Jesus Christ exercises power over all things, and on this basis Paul assures us that Christ, "by the power that enables him to bring everything under his control, will transform our lowly bodies so that they will be like his glorious body" (Phil. 3:21). The Son sustains the created universe "by his powerful word" (Heb. 1:3). I admit that the argument from divine attributes, though by no means negligible, is the weakest link in the longer chain. This should not be surprising, because the New Testament focuses on the Son in his state of humiliation, in his "form" as a slave (Phil. 2:7). The argument from divine works is much stronger.

The Son is described as working as only God can work: the Son created all things and preserves them in being (John 1:3; Col. 1:16, 17; Heb. 1:3, 10; John 5:7; 1 Cor. 8:6); the Son will raise the dead "at the last day" (John 6:39, 40, 44, 54); Christ will judge the world. Jesus promises "that very word which I spoke will condemn him at the last day" (John 12:48; cf. John 5:22). Paul speaks of the "judgment seat of God" in Romans 14:10; but in 2 Corinthians he speaks of the judgment seat of Christ: "For we must all appear before the judgment seat of Christ" (2 Cor. 5:10; cf. Rom. 2:6; 1 Cor. 4:4, 5; 11:32; 2 Tim. 4:1, 8). Jesus also forgives sins. When he said to the paralytic of Capernaum, "Son, your sins are for-

---

9. See Muller, *PRRD*, 4, pp. 278-87, for the Arian and Socinian arguments against the metaphysical and eternal sonship of the Son and the orthodox responses.

given," his critics complained: "Why does this fellow talk like that? He's blaspheming! Who can forgive sins but God alone?" (Mark 2:5-7). Jesus' response was not to question their logic; rather, he implied that they should extend it to the miracles. Are miracles any less a sign of divine authority than forgiving sins? he asks rhetorically (Mark 2:9). It is through Christ that we have been reconciled to God (Rom. 5:11; 2 Cor. 5:18, 19). Who but God can do these things?

The Son is worthy of worship. In the great throne scene in Revelation 5, the four living creatures and the twenty-four elders fall down before the Lamb and worship. They are soon surrounded by millions of angels, who join the worship proclaiming, "Worthy is the Lamb, who was slain, to receive power and wealth and wisdom and strength and honor and glory and praise!" In a third movement, the crowd is joined by every creature "in heaven and on earth and under the earth and on the sea, and all that is in them, singing 'To him who sits on the throne and to the Lamb be praise and honor and glory and power'" (Rev. 5:8-13). To his detractors Jesus declares: "He who does not honor the Son does not honor the Father who sent him" (John 5:23). "You trust in God," says Jesus to his disciples, "trust also in me" (John 14:1). Christian baptism is administered in the name of the Son as well as of the Father and the Spirit (Matt. 28:19). The Eucharist, the central act of Christian worship, celebrates the death of Christ and facilitates our participation in the body and blood of the Lord (1 Cor. 11:17-31). The last words of the book of Revelation are the ancient Christian prayer to Jesus, "Come, Lord Jesus" (Rev. 22:20; cf. 1 Cor. 16:22). At his martyrdom Stephen prayed, "Lord Jesus, receive my spirit" (Acts 7:59), which reminds us of Jesus' words from the cross: "Father, into your hands I commit my spirit" (Luke 23:46).

The Holy Spirit

The Holy Spirit is not an impersonal force emanating from God in mechanical fashion.[10] The Spirit speaks. While Peter was thinking about the vision he had just received, "the Spirit said to him, 'Simon, three men are looking for you. So get up and go downstairs. Do not hesitate to go with them, for I have sent them'" (Acts 10:19-20; cf. Acts 13:2). The Spirit teaches (John 14:26), witnesses (Rom. 8:16), gives gifts (1 Cor. 12:4-11), intercedes (Rom. 8:27), judges (Acts 15:28), hears (John 16:13), speaks (Rev. 2:7), determines (1 Cor. 12:11), and grieves (Eph. 4:30).

---

10. Most Socinians of the seventeenth century understood the Spirit to be a divine power but not a divine person. The English Socinian John Biddle, dissenting from the majority view, argued that the Holy Spirit is a created being. See Muller, *PRRD*, 4, pp. 335-45, for the Socinian view of the Holy Spirit and the orthodox refutations.

The Holy Spirit is God. The titles "Holy Spirit" and "Spirit of God," though not unequivocal in themselves, indicate the divine nature of the Spirit when they are taken with the other lines of evidence. For example, in Paul's discussion of the Spirit's work of revealing the "deep things of God," he draws an analogy between human self-knowledge and the Spirit's knowledge of the "thoughts of God" (1 Cor. 2:10-14). Just as a human being's "spirit" knows the thoughts of the human being, God's Spirit knows his thoughts. The analogy will not hold unless the Spirit of God is God, just as the human spirit is human; hence, the Spirit's knowledge of God is divine self-knowledge.

The Spirit is eternal (Heb. 9:14) and knows all things (1 Cor. 2:10-14). The Virgin Mary conceived by the power of the Holy Spirit (Luke 1:35). The Spirit works miracles: he whisks away Philip (Acts 8:39), empowers the apostles at Pentecost (Acts 2), inspires prophets to speak the word of God (2 Pet. 1:21), and does signs and wonders (Rom. 15:19; Gal. 1:1-5; 3:5). When Ananias and Sapphira lie to Peter about their gift, Peter replies first to Ananias: "You have not lied to men but to God" (Acts 5:4; cf. 1 Thess. 4:8). A while later he replies to Sapphira: "How could you agree to test the Spirit of the Lord?" (Acts 5:9). Clearly, he closely identifies God and the Spirit. The Spirit sanctifies (Rom. 8:9; 15:16; 1 Cor. 6:11), gives us access to the Father (Eph. 2:18), enables the new birth (John 3:5; Titus 3:5-7), raises Jesus from the dead (Rom. 1:4), makes us sons (Gal. 4:4), brings freedom (2 Cor. 3:8-9), strengthens (Eph. 3:14-19), and gives life (John 6:63).

Though the data in the New Testament supporting the divine nature of the Spirit is not as extensive as that supporting the divine nature of the Son, it is sufficient. We noted earlier a pattern in many texts that groups the Father, Son, and the Spirit together. We need only recall two: Baptism is to be administered "in the name of the Father, and of the Son *and of the Spirit*" (Matt. 28:18-20). Paul's benediction reads, "May the grace of the Lord Jesus Christ, and the love of God, and the fellowship of the *Holy Spirit* be with you all" (2 Cor. 13:14).

Person-Distinguishing Texts

Many New Testament texts distinguish the divine persons. Traditional theologians argued that some biblical texts speak of the Father essentially, as the entire Godhead, and some speak personally, distinguishing the persons of the Trinity. Zacharias Ursinus (1534-83) laid down this rule in his *Commentary on the Heidelberg Catechism:* "When the name of the Father is opposed to the Son, it is taken personally, and signifies the first person of the Godhead . . . but when it is opposed to creatures it must be understood essentially, and signifies the whole divine essence."[11] Malachi 2:10 ("Have we not one Father?"), Hebrews 12:9 ("the Father of our spirits"), and Acts 17:26-28 ("God who made the world") speak of the Father essentially. John 17:8 ("Father, glorify your Son"), Matthew 3:17 ("this is my Son"), and Matthew 28:19 ("in the name of the Father") refer to the Father as a person distinct from the Son and the Spirit. Jesus addresses the Father (Matt. 11:25; Luke 10:31; 23:34, 46; 22:42; John 11:41; 17:1-26); and he speaks about the Father to others (Matt. 5:16, 45; 6:1; 7:11; 10:32, 33; Mark 11:25; Luke 11:13; John 4:53; 4:19; 8:20, 49, 54; 11:25, etc.).

The personhood of the Spirit has been disputed.[12] Yet the biblical evidence for the personal distinction between the Father and the Spirit, when taken as a whole, is quite strong. After the Spirit descended on Jesus at his baptism, the Spirit "drove" him into the desert to be tempted (Mark 1:12). Jesus promises that the Spirit will "take of what is mine and make it known to you" (John 16:14). The Spirit speaks to believers (Acts 10:19, 20) and to the Father for us (Rom. 8:26, 27). The Father speaks to the Son (Mark 1:11; Luke 3:22; John 12:28) and sends the Spirit (John 14:26; Gal. 4:6) and the Son (John 5:23, 36, 37; Rom. 8:3; 1 John 4:14).

The Son is a distinct person. The Modalists of the patristic era, whom I shall discuss below, denied the personhood of the Son. In the modern era, the distinct personhood of the Son is rarely denied. The Gospel writer distinguishes between the Word and God by indicating that the Word was "with God" as well as being God (John 1:1). The same author distinguishes Jesus from his Father: "Jesus knew that the time had come for him to leave this world and go to the Father. . . . Jesus knew that the Father had put all things under his power, and that he had come from God and was returning to God" (John 13:1-3). The texts cited above show the distinct person of the Father; and since they record the Son's self-distinction from the Father, they also show the personhood of the Son. In numerous texts from the New Testament letters, the Son, the Father, and the Spirit are distinguished by being set alongside each other (2 Cor. 13:14; Eph. 2:18; 3:14-19; 1 Cor 12:1-6, et al.). The persons are distinguished by name and by role in the economy of revelation and salvation, which the church has taken as indicative of real distinctions in God.

11. Ursinus, *Commentary on the Heidelberg Catechism,* trans. G. W. Willard (1852; reprint, Phillipsburg, NJ: Presbyterian and Reformed, n.d.), p. 140.

12. Muller calls it an intense debate (*PRRD,* 4, p. 345) and cites Francis Turretin, *Institutes of Elenctic Theology,* trans. George Musgrave Giger, ed. James T. Dennison, Jr. (Phillipsburg, NJ: Presbyterian and Reformed Publishing, 1992), 3.30.1-2, as an example.

Texts That Unify the Persons

The New Testament rarely treats the unity of the divine nature as a disputed matter, and it does so directly only in response to a pagan challenge (Acts 14:15, 16; 17:22-31; 1 Cor. 8:4; 1 Thess. 1:9). Ordinarily, it takes the biblical faith in the one God for granted. Whereas the New Testament bends over backward to show the divine nature of the Son, it does not respond explicitly to the charge that this belief somehow compromises the unity of the divine nature. It never seems to contemplate a charge that it teaches that there are three Gods.

The Trinity in the Old Testament

Does the Old Testament contradict the doctrine of the Trinity, as many Jewish scholars claim? Does the Old Testament explicitly teach the doctrine of the Trinity, as many of the church fathers claimed? Does it teach it implicitly? Does it merely not contradict it? Is the Old Testament doctrine of God illuminated by the doctrine of the Trinity?

The Christian doctrine of the Trinity must assume at minimum that the Old Testament does not contradict the doctrine. The church fathers, theologians in the Middle Ages, and orthodox Protestants made the much stronger claim that the Old Testament explicitly teaches the Trinity.[13] They found it taught in Genesis. At the creation of humankind, God says, "Let us make man in our image" (Gen. 1:26).[14] After the fall, God observes, "Behold, man is become as one of us" (Gen. 3:22; cf. Gen. 11:7). From the first mention of the Spirit of God in Genesis 1:2 ("The Spirit of God moved over the waters"), and continuing throughout the Old Testament, the Spirit of God is distinguished from God and yet acts as God.[15] The Spirit creates (Ps. 33:6-7; 104:29-30; Isa. 32:14-15), gives wisdom (Isa. 11:1-3), is God's presence (Ps. 139:1-8), bestows God's power (Judg. 3:9, 10; 14:6; 1 Sam. 10:6), speaks God's word (2 Sam. 23:2-3; 2:1-2; Mic. 3:8), does miracles (1 Kings. 18:12; Ezek. 8:3), and leads (Ps. 143:10).

The church fathers saw a reference to the entire Trinity in Psalm 33:6: "By the word [Word] of the Lord were the heavens made, their starry host by the breath [Spirit] of his mouth."[16] The fathers saw a reference to the pre-incarnate

13. For a defense of this claim, see Turretin, *Institutes of Elenctic Theology*, vol. 1, 3.26.1, p. 274.

14. Typical are the references in Augustine, *On the Trinity*, 12.6 (*NPNF*, 1st ser., 3, p. 157); see also Hilary, *On the Trinity*, 4.17 (*NPNF*, 2nd ser., 9, p. 76).

15. See Ambrose, *On the Holy Spirit*, 2.1 (*NPNF*, 2nd ser., 10, p. 115).

16. For example, Irenaeus, in *Against Heresies*, 1.22.1 (*ANF*, 1, p. 347).

Son in the figure of the "angel of the Lord" that appeared in the burning bush in Exodus 3. The angel says: "I am the God of your father, the God of Abraham, the God of Isaac and the God of Jacob" (Exod. 3:6; cf. Gen. 18:1-19; 19:1ff.).[17] The angel continues to speak as the Lord throughout this encounter. Furthermore, the threefold repetitions in the Old Testament impressed the older theologians as references to the Trinity (see Num. 6:24-26; Isa. 6:3).[18]

To the modern reader, the church fathers' Old Testament interpretation may seem implausible. With our greater sense of the historical relativity of ideas, we tend to think that a Trinitarian view of God was completely beyond the historical horizons of the Old Testament. Hence, its presence there would be about as anachronistic as the Mona Lisa wearing a digital watch. I will not rest my case for the doctrine of the Trinity on the persuasiveness of traditional interpretations of the Old Testament; however, before we dismiss it completely, we should consider two things. If we are persuaded that the New Testament truly teaches and teaches truly that God is Father, Son, and Spirit, we must then also presume that God always has been triune. Given this assumption, it would seem plausible to expect that earlier revelations would have had a triune form. Indeed, as we have seen, the New Testament itself makes this assumption explicit. The church fathers, then, were reading the Old Testament with a legitimate assumption they shared with the New Testament authors themselves. Those who reject the traditional exegesis will need to explain how they can do so without also rejecting the theological assumption on which it was built.

The second caution about rejecting traditional exegesis is this: the modern historicist assumption may itself be anachronistic, for it presupposes the existence already in the Old Testament of an abstract, philosophical monotheism that was developed only later in Neo-Platonism, and by medieval Jewish and Islamic scholars. In the Old Testament itself, we find a sense of richness in God and encounter many forms in which God makes himself present and acts on behalf of his people: the name, the wisdom, and the face of the Lord, the glory of the Lord, the angel of the Lord, and the spirit of the Lord. The Lord commanded that a temple be built "for my Name" (Deut. 12:5, 11, 12; 1 Kings 5:5; 8:16-19; Jer. 7:12). God will "put my Name there" (1 Kings 9:3). Apparently, the name is a mode of God's presence. Moses was not allowed to see God's face, but he was given permission to see God's "glory" pass by (Exod. 33:22). The "glory" of God can fill the temple (1 Kings 8:11). In Ezekiel's vision, the glory of the Lord is a visible and mobile mode of God's presence: "Then the glory of the Lord rose

---

17. Augustine, *On the Trinity,* 2.12-13 (*NPNF,* 1st ser., 9, pp. 47-49).

18. For references to the Trinitarian interpretation of these texts from the perspective of orthodox Reformed theology, see Muller, *PRRD,* 4, p. 227.

from above the cherubim and moved to the threshold of the temple. The cloud filled the temple, and the court was full of the radiance of the glory of the Lord" (Ezek. 10:4; cf. Ezek. 1:28; 11:23).

The Spirit is identified with God's presence (Ps. 51:11; Isa. 63:10-11). The Word of God appears sometimes as a person. The word that "goes out from my mouth," says the Lord, "will not return to me empty, but will accomplish what I desire and achieve the purpose for which I sent it" (Isa. 55:11). Wisdom acts as God's power in creation (Prov. 8:22-23). The face of God seems to be another mode of God's presence (Gen. 32:30; Ps. 24:6). The angel of the Lord is mentioned by Isaiah as "the angel of his presence" (Isa. 63:9).

The common concern in these texts seems to be for the presence of the transcendent God among his people. God dwells with his people in these forms. These "dwellings" (from *Shekinah,* the Hebrew word for dwelling) became the objects of speculation in Rabbinic Judaism. In these writings, *Shekinah* is associated with the name, the glory of the Lord, and the angel of the Lord. All of them are "dwellings" representing immanent forms of the transcendent God. In the Kabbalah, a later mystical school of Judaism, the *Shekinah* takes the form of the suffering God who shares the fate of his people.[19] The New Testament applies these Old Testament dwellings to Christ and the Spirit. "The Word became flesh and made his dwelling among us" (John 1:14). "Don't you know that you yourselves are God's temple and that God's Spirit lives in you?" (1 Cor. 3:16). In the New Testament, Christ is the presence of the glory of God. Unbelievers cannot see the "light of the gospel of the glory of Christ, who is the image of God. . . . For God . . . made his light shine in our hearts to give us the light of the knowledge of the glory of God in the face of Christ" (2 Cor. 4:4-6).[20]

Even if we cannot build an independent case for the traditional doctrine of the Trinity on the Old Testament data alone, it is clear that the Old Testament theme of God's dwellings raises questions about the mode of God's self-mediation that present difficulties for abstract, philosophical monotheism. The dwellings theme harmonizes well, however, with the Trinitarian pattern of the New Testament. The doctrine of the Trinity explains the transcendent God's capacity to reveal himself and dwell among his people without interposing a series of semidivine or created mediators. As I indicated at the beginning of this

---

19. Gershom G. Scholem, *Major Trends in Jewish Mysticism,* 3rd ed. (1954; reprint, New York: Schocken, 1961), pp. 244-86. For a study of the self-limitation and suffering God motif in Rabbinic Judaism, see Maureena Fritz, "A Midrash: The Self-Limitation of God," *Journal of Ecumenical Studies* 22 (1985): 703-14.

20. For a Jewish-Christian dialogue in which the Old Testament dwellings play an important part, see Pinchas Lapide and Jürgen Moltmann, *Jewish Monotheism and Christian Trinitarian Doctrine,* trans. Leonard Swidler (Philadelphia: Fortress Press, 1981).

chapter, I cannot claim in this short space to have proved that the New Testament (much less the Old Testament) teaches the doctrine of the Trinity. I think, however, that I have made a strong case, a case that we can now put to the theological test.

Theological Examination of the Doctrine of the Trinity

Now that we have established that the doctrine of the Trinity is firmly grounded in the Bible, we must answer a series of theological questions. We can strengthen our confidence in the church's teaching on the Trinity by (1) showing that the Trinitarian doctrine's presuppositions are sound; (2) ruling out alternative explanations for New Testament teaching; and (3) demonstrating that the Trinitarian doctrine is internally consistent and consistent with other aspects of the Christian faith.

The Gospel, the Economic, and the Immanent Trinity

Many religious and Bible-centered Christians find the move from the proclamation of the gospel and the worship of God, Christ, and the Holy Spirit in the church to the formal doctrine of the Trinity to be puzzling, impious, and alienating. They find it puzzling because of the complicated new terminology and logical moves it introduces, impious because analysis appears to be substituted for praise, and alienating because they do not recognize their experience in the formulas. Their feelings are sometimes justified, for the doctrine of the Trinity is frequently handed to them as a formula that is to be believed and recited without understanding, by people who themselves understand it no better than they do. This chapter is largely an effort to address the concerns of these good Christians.

I believe that we can gain greater understanding if we reflect on the way the doctrine of the Trinity arose (and arises again and again) in the Christian mind. In *The Christian Doctrine of God*, Thomas Torrance, a Scottish theologian of the Trinity, discerns three levels of the Christian mind's grasp of the doctrine.[21] Gaining greater understanding of the doctrine of the Trinity is largely synonymous with ascending through these levels. In this chapter I have already dealt with the first level, the "evangelical and doxological." First, we meet the Trinity in the pages of the Gospels and in our experience of salvation through Christ,

---

21. Torrance, *The Christian Doctrine of God*, pp. 83-111.

reconciliation with the Father, and sanctification and worship in the Spirit. We meet the Trinity in our baptism in the name of the Father, the Son, and the Holy Spirit and in our thanksgiving in the Supper of the Lord. According to Torrance, this level contains an "incipient theology" of the Trinity, in which our minds grasp "intuitively, and as a whole, without engaging in analytical or logical process of thought" (p. 89). This level is foundational for our knowledge of God. We do not leave it behind when we move to the second level. Just as the data of experience are foundational and indispensable for even the most abstract scientific theories, the scriptural data and the life of worship must be preserved in all subsequent Christian thought (pp. 84-90).

Nevertheless, we must enter a second, now explicitly theological, level. Analysis and thought are necessary, for we cannot suppress the question of whether the one we meet in Jesus and the Holy Spirit is the true and eternal God. The answer we give to this question is vital, for if we are "unable to relate Jesus Christ and our redemption in and through him intelligibly to the inner Life of God . . . faith withers away" (p. 90). In this second level we make explicit the doctrine implicit in triune patterns and structures in the "saving and revealing acts in Jesus Christ" (p. 91). We attempt to connect the entire set of scriptural patterns, statements, and narratives, seeking the underlying coherence of God's revelation in Christ. In God's acts of revelation and salvation, we always find the three (Father, Son, and Spirit) perfectly united in act and being.

At this level we articulate what is often called the economic Trinity. The idea of the economy of salvation finds its roots in the New Testament. In Ephesians, Paul draws a distinction between the mystery "in God" and the economy. He praises God for commissioning him to preach to the "Gentiles the unsearchable riches of Christ, and to make clear to everyone the administration [Greek: *oikonomía*] of this mystery, which for ages past was kept hidden in God, who created all things" (Eph. 3:9; cf. 3:2). The "economy" is the visible and temporal administering of God's eternal plan "to bring all things in heaven and on earth together under one head, even Christ" (Eph. 1:10). Already, then, in the New Testament we see distinction and unity between God's external and temporal work of salvation and God's internal and eternal life. The internal life of God is a mystery — "hidden in God"; the external activity (the economy) is "made known" and "put into effect" in time (1:10).

Although we focus our thought on God as *revealed* in the doctrine of the economic Trinity, the Christian mind cannot rest until it addresses the question of the extent to which the economic Trinity gives us knowledge of the inner life and being of God. Already in the economy we are convinced that Jesus Christ is of one substance *(homooúsios)* with the Father. If, in our skepticism or misguided humility, we fail to ascend to the third level, we place in doubt the previous two levels. For, if in Christ we do not learn something of God's eternal and inner life, we place in question God's economic tri-unity (second level) and Christ's deity and our salvation (first level). Hence, with "fear and trembling," we must move to the third level, the immanent Trinity.

The Christian mind has always held the conviction that "what God is toward us in Christ Jesus, he is inherently and eternally in himself in his own being" (Torrance, p. 99). This conviction holds true on all three levels and is the motive force that propels us to ascend from the first to the second and from the second to the third level. Hence, in articulating the doctrine of the Trinity, the church fathers assumed that the way God works in his actions of creation, revelation, and salvation reflects the way God really is. The distinction and unity between the economic and immanent Trinity is deeply imbedded in the church's doctrine. Rejecting it would have far-ranging implications. If, in order to protect God's transcendence, we deny that we meet the reality of God in the time, space, and flesh of the economy, God would become an unknown reality hidden behind the economic appearances. This agnostic principle could not be limited to the issue of God's tri-unity but would extend to every aspect of the knowledge of God. Is God really loving? Is God really just? Is God really good? Denying the unity between the economy and the immanent life of God would foreclose the possibility of answering these questions.

In contrast to the church fathers, some contemporary theologians deny any distinction between the economic and immanent life of God. They collapse the immanent Trinity into the economy, a move that limits God's freedom and makes creation and salvation necessary moments in the divine life. God's life and the world process become intertwined in a way that resembles pantheism. Catherine LaCugna builds (dubiously) on Karl Rahner's famous epigram: "The 'economic' Trinity is the 'immanent' Trinity, and the 'immanent' Trinity is the 'economic' Trinity."[22] "The doctrine of the Trinity," says LaCugna, "is not ultimately a teaching about 'God' but a teaching about *God's life with us and our life with each other*."[23] Colin Gunton's view of LaCugna hits the mark: "Far from ensuring the relevance of Trinitarian categories, the outcome of such a process is to destroy it. God's personal otherness from the world is needed if there is to be a true establishing of the world in its own right."[24]

---

22. Rahner, *The Trinity*, trans. Joseph Donceel (New York: Crossroad, 1997), p. 22.

23. Catherine Mowry LaCugna, *God for Us: The Trinity and the Christian Life* (San Francisco: Harper, 1991), p. 228.

24. Gunton, *The Promise of Trinitarian Theology* (Edinburgh: T&T Clark, 2003), p. xix; Gunton, "Review of Catherine LaCugna, *God for Us*," *Scottish Journal of Theology* 47 (1994): 135-37. See also Paul D. Molnar, *Divine Freedom and the Doctrine of the Immanent Trinity: In Dia-*

Jürgen Moltmann makes the identity of the immanent and the economic Trinity the centerpiece of his thought.[25] In *The Crucified God*, Moltmann rejects "the distinction made by the early church between theology as the doctrine of God and economy as the doctrine of salvation."[26] He declares bluntly: "Anyone who really talks of the Trinity talks of the cross of Jesus and does not speculate in heavenly riddles" (p. 207). In *The Trinity and the Kingdom*, Moltmann begins to speak cautiously of an immanent Trinity within a "doxological" theology.[27] The doxological Trinity, however, is not complete from eternity apart from world history. "The economic Trinity completes itself and perfects itself to the immanent Trinity when history and experience of salvation are completed and perfected. When everything is 'in God' and 'God is all in all,' then the economic Trinity is raised into and transcended in the immanent Trinity" (p. 161). Instead of his earlier rejection of the distinction, Moltmann proposes a rule to guide our language about the economic and immanent Trinity: "Statements about the immanent Trinity must not contradict statements about the economic Trinity. Statements about the economic Trinity must correspond to doxological statements about the immanent Trinity" (p. 154).[28]

This rule makes the economic Trinity prior to the immanent Trinity in every respect and leaves no room for God's freedom in relationship to the economy. It robs us of a principle of negation by which to distinguish those aspects of the economy that reflect the attributes of God from those that belong to creatures. Hence it requires us to read the conditions under which God works in the economy — time, space, suffering, and change — into the being and life of God. Molnar has not overstated his indictment of Moltmann when he concludes: "We have here a prototypical compromise of God's freedom as ex-

---

logue with Karl Barth and Contemporary Theology (London: T&T Clark, 2002). Molnar comes to a conclusion that is similar to Gunton's (pp. 3-6).

25. For a criticism of Moltmann, see Paul D. Molnar, "The Function of the Trinity in Moltmann's Ecological Doctrine of Creation," *Theological Studies* 51 (1990): 673-97; and *Divine Freedom*, pp. 29-32. See also Roger Olson, "Trinity and Eschatology: The Historical Being of God in Jürgen Moltmann and Wolfhart Pannenberg," *Scottish Journal of Theology* 36 (1983). Olson says that in Moltmann "historical events become determinative of God's eternal being" (p. 217).

26. Moltmann, *The Crucified God*, trans. R. A. Wilson and John Bowden (New York: Harper & Row, 1974), p. 67.

27. Moltmann, *The Trinity and the Kingdom*, trans. Margaret Kohl (Minneapolis: Fortress, 1993), pp. 151-61. For more on the doxological Trinity, see Jürgen Moltmann, *The Spirit of Life: A Universal Affirmation*, trans. Margaret Kohl (Minneapolis: Fortress, 1992), pp. 301-6.

28. For studies of Moltmann's shift to some appreciation of the immanent Trinity, see Richard Bauckham, *The Theology of Jürgen Moltmann* (Edinburgh: T&T Clark, 1995), pp. 155-57, and Warren McWilliams, "Trinitarian Doxology: Jürgen Moltmann on the Relation of the Economic and Immanent Trinity," *Perspectives in Religious Studies* 23 (Spring 1996): 25-38.

pressed in the Bible and in the tradition. It is no longer the case that the one God is the single transcendent subject of his actions in his Son and Spirit. Rather, his transcendent being and action is defined by his need to be man, his need to suffer and his need for another outside himself."[29]

In contrast to Moltmann and LaCugna, I will work from the traditional assumption that is shared by such modern theologians as Barth, Torrance, Molnar, and Gunton: that the immanent Trinity can be known from the economic Trinity without being identical to it.

Alternatives to the Doctrine of the Trinity

Some may think that the doctrine of the Trinity is but one among many ways to account for the New Testament data. In the second through fourth centuries, different thinkers within the church explored alternatives in great detail and with great erudition. By the end of this era the church had excluded every alternative but the (now) traditional one. The main alternatives hold in common that there is one divine nature and three actors (Father, Son, and Spirit) in the divine economy. These assumptions correspond in a straightforward way to the New Testament data. The alternatives diverge in their understandings of how the three actors are related to the one divine nature and to each other. Their answers to these problems can be placed into two categories: subordinationism and modalism. *Subordinationism* affirms genuine distinctions among the persons but denies that they share the same nature. It theorizes that the Son and the Spirit occupy a lower level of being to that of the Father, who alone is fully God; it preserves the distinct persons of the Son and Spirit at the price of their deity. *Modalism,* by contrast, affirms that the three actors share one divine nature, but it denies the genuine distinctions among the persons. It sees Father, Son, and Spirit as names under which the same God appears in the divine economy; it preserves the deity of the Son and Spirit at the price of their distinct personhood.

Subordinationism

Subordinationism is a general category that covers a variety of theories. I will examine three. In the late second century, Theodotus the Cobbler came to Rome advocating a theory now called adoptionism, or dynamic monarchism. Like all subordinationists, Theodotus aimed to preserve the unity and monar-

---

29. Molnar, *Divine Freedom*, p. 226.

chy of God. He sought to do this by contending that Jesus was a pious man, born of a virgin by the power of the Holy Spirit, but not God by nature. Jesus was filled with the Holy Spirit (who is the Christ) at his baptism.[30] In this way, Theodotus sought to do justice to the data of Scripture without compromising the unity and monarchy of God. A second — and more important — adoptionist was Paul of Samosata, Bishop of Antioch (c. A.D. 260). He constructed a much more sophisticated theory: that the *Logos* and the Spirit are not persons eternally existing alongside the Father, but are attributes of God. The man Jesus, endowed with the Spirit from birth, became one in mind and will with God and received the Logos through the Spirit at his baptism. Though joined to God by grace, Jesus was not God by nature. There is only one person in God. Paul's views were rejected and he was deposed at a synod in Antioch (A.D. 268).[31]

The third subordinationist theory, that of Arius (c. A.D. 250–c. 336), is by far the most important. Arius's theory, like others before it, focuses on protecting the unity and monarchy of God. God, says Arius, is unbegotten, undivided, uncompounded, and unchangeable. On the other hand, Jesus the Son is begotten and changeable: he had a beginning in time and, in Arius's infamous formula, "there was when he was not."[32] Therefore, the *Logos* is not of the same divine nature as the Father. This created *Logos* took the place of Jesus' human soul at his conception by the Holy Spirit. Here Arius's theory resembles that of Paul of Samosata, with the exception that the *Logos* that replaced the human soul of Jesus was not an uncreated attribute of God but a created *Logos*. Arius reinterprets the New Testament data consistently with this theory. The *Logos* incarnate in Jesus Christ, "although he is called God, he is yet not the true God, but by sharing in grace, just as all others also, he is called by name simply God."[33] The names, attributes, works, and worship that the New Testament gives to Jesus should not be taken in the strict sense, argues Arius. They are merely honorific, just as a saint may be called "holy" because of his or her love and submission to the Holy God.

30. John Behr, *Formation of Christian Theology,* vol. 1, *The Way to Nicaea* (Crestwood, NY: St. Vladimir's, 2001), pp. 142-44; Reinhold Seeberg, *Text-Book of the History of Doctrines, 2-vol. edition,* vol. 1, trans. Charles Hay (Grand Rapids: Baker, 1977), p. 163.

31. Seeberg, *Doctrines,* 1, pp. 164-66; Jaroslav Pelikan, *Christian Tradition: A History of the Development of Doctrine,* vol. 1, *The Emergence of the Catholic Tradition 100-600* (Chicago: University of Chicago Press, 1975), p. 176. See the detailed study of John Behr, *Formation of Christian Theology,* 1, pp. 207-35.

32. J. N. D. Kelly, *Early Christian Doctrines,* 2nd ed. (New York: Harper and Row, 1960), pp. 226-31.

33. Quoted in Athanasius, *Against the Arians,* 1.6. For discussions of Arius's teaching, see Seeberg, *Doctrines,* 1, p. 203; Pelikan, *Christian Tradition,* 1, pp. 193-200; Behr, *Formation of Christian Theology,* 2/1, pp. 130-50; and R. P. C. Hanson, *The Search for the Christian Doctrine of God: The Arian Controversy, 318-381* (1988; reprint, Grand Rapids: Baker Academic, 2005), pp. 3-18.

We see in Arius, according to Reinhold Seeberg, "the worst Christology imaginable."[34] Its startling implications were spelled out by Athanasius (A.D. 296-373), the great defender of Nicene orthodoxy, in his *Discourses Against the Arians:* the Trinity is not eternal but began in time with the creation of the *Logos* and the Spirit. The church administers baptism in the name of God and two creatures. God has not always been Father but became Father by creating the Son. According to Athanasius, the Arians "must of necessity say that there are two Gods, one Creator, the other creature, and must serve two Lords, one Unoriginate, and the other originate and a creature" (3.15).[35] Our knowledge of God is imperiled, for "how can he who beholds the mutable think that he is beholding the immutable?" (1.35).[36] How could a creature win salvation for us? Athanasius presses this question home: "[F]or if, being a creature, He had become man, man had remained just what he was, not joined to God; for how had a work been joined to the Creator by a work? Or what succour had come from like to like, when one as well as the other needed it? And how, were the Word a creature, had He power to undo God's sentence, and to remit sin?" (2.67).[37] The Council of Nicea (A.D. 325) condemned Arius's views and declared that the Son of God is "God of God, Light of Light . . . of one nature (Greek: *homooúsios*) with the Father."

As this brief consideration of subordinationism shows, it is impossible to harmonize the New Testament data with a theory that places the Son and the Spirit on a lower ontological level than the Father. Such theories require us to read every text that states or implies the deity of the Son and Spirit as metaphorical, hyperbolic, or honorific. Moreover, subordinationism fails to protect even the unity and monarchy of God, the purpose for which it was crafted. It gives the Son and the Spirit the status of semidivine beings (similar to the pagan gods), worthy of worship alongside the Father.

Modalism

Modalism uses another strategy to preserve the unity and monarchy of God while accounting for the biblical data. It understands Father, Son, and Spirit to be ways in which the one God appears and acts in the economy of salvation. But it denies genuine personal distinctions among them. Arriving at Rome in the late second century, Praxeas taught that the Father was born and suffered for

34. Seeberg, *Doctrines,* 1, p. 204.

35. *NPNF,* 2nd ser., 2, p. 402; cf. Basil the Great, who accuses the Arians of advocating a "great God and a small god" (*Letter 243, NPNF,* 2nd ser., 8, pp. 284-85).

36. Quoted in Seeberg, *Doctrines,* 1, p. 207.

37. *NPNF,* 2nd ser., 2, p. 385.

our sins.[38] Another modalist, Noëtus of Smyrna (c. 200), argued: "When indeed, then, the Father had not been born, He *yet* was justly styled Father; and when it pleased Him to undergo generation, having been begotten, He Himself became His own Son, not another's."[39] After he suffered and died, he raised himself from the dead.

Sabellius gave modalism its final form and bequeathed his name to it as an alternative designation for this heresy (Sabellianism). According to Sabellius, sonship is a possibility for the Father; therefore, God can be called "Son-Father." Father, Son, and Spirit are but three names for one person, as a single human person is body, soul, and spirit. Or "as, if it be in the sun, being in one object (I say) that there are three, having the energies of light-giving and heat and the form of roundness."[40] Modalism, unlike subordinationism, accounts well for the New Testament texts that teach the deity of the three persons. It must, however, explain away texts that show personal distinctions among them. Additionally, modalism undercuts the concept of revelation and undermines our confidence that we have genuine knowledge of God. If God appears as Father, Son, and Spirit in the economy but is not really triune, what is the true identity of the deity behind the three masks? Perhaps the true God differs greatly from the appearances through which he works.

Coherence and Consistency

Internal Coherence

The doctrine of the Trinity affirms that God is one nature and three persons. The unity of the nature in the persons and the distinction of persons in the nature are affirmed with equal force. Muslims, Jews, Socinians, and rationalists of all ages have dismissed the doctrine as self-contradictory.[41] However, the ratio-

---

38. Pelikan, *Christian Tradition*, 1, pp. 104-5 and 179-80, and Seeberg, *Doctrines*, 1, p. 167. Praxeas's views are known only because of the book *Against Praxeas* (1.5), which Tertullian wrote to refute him.

39. Quoted by Hippolytus, *Refutation of All Heresies*, 9.5 (*ANF*, 5, pp. 127-28). See Pelikan, *Christian Tradition*, pp. 178-80; see also Seeberg, *Doctrines*, 1, p. 167.

40. Seeberg, *Doctrines*, 1, p. 168, where he quotes Sabellius as preserved in Epiphanius, *Against Eight Heresies*, 62.1.

41. See Muller's discussion of the seventeenth-century anti-Trinitarians (*PRRD*, 4, pp. 74-99). The Socinians and the English anti-Trinitarians argued from biblicist and antitraditional premises that the doctrine of the Trinity is an unscriptural, "new" doctrine imposed on Christendom at the Council of Nicea. They also apparently adopted a nominalist metaphysics, which

nalist objection misses the point. The doctrine would contradict itself if it affirmed that God is one and three in exactly the same sense. But it does not do this. It affirms that God is one in a different sense than God is three: one *nature* and three *persons*. The question of the intelligibility of the doctrine of the Trinity must focus elsewhere. For the most part, it has focused on the distinction between nature and person.

It is important for us to remind ourselves that the church's doctrine of the Trinity did not arise from speculation but is grounded in the pattern of Scripture: it proclaims and preserves scriptural teaching. Its truth should be judged by its conformity to the teaching of Scripture and not by reason's ability to render it transparent or understand it completely. Without violating this principle, traditional theologians, insofar as it was possible, sought to grasp the intelligibility within the triune pattern of the scriptural revelation. To express this intelligibility, theologians used several analogies and philosophical concepts to help us grasp the distinctions among the persons within the one nature and the unity of the nature shared by distinct persons.

In his treatise *On the Trinity,* Augustine proposed a series of psychological analogies that have stimulated the theological imagination ever since.[42] After having composed an eight-book exposition of the Trinitarian faith that he has received from Scripture and tradition, Augustine attempts to understand the faith he has received. He says: "Let us believe that the Father, and the Son, and the Holy Spirit is one God . . . that the Father is not the Son, nor the Holy Spirit either the Father or the Son, but a trinity of persons mutually interrelated, and a unity of an equal essence. And let us seek to understand this, praying for help from Himself, whom we wish to understand" (9.1.1).[43] In Books 9 and 10, Augustine pursues two important anthropological analogies to the Trinity. The human mind, according to Augustine, is one substance but is composed of mind, knowledge, and love (Book 9) or of memory, intelligence, and will (Book 10).

In the first analogy, Augustine argues that the mind can know itself only if it duplicates its whole self in reflection and reunites itself through love. According to the second analogy, the whole mind is at once memory, understanding, and will, one substance but three distinct activities. Augustine's first analogy is relatively easy to grasp: we experience within our own consciousness both unity and diversity, yet the unity does not efface the diversity, and the diversity does not destroy the unity. In self-consciousness there is subject, object, and union

they used against the doctrine. For example, Muller (*PRRD*, 4, p. 98) quotes Crell, *Two Books . . . Touching on God the Father* (1665): "A person is in vain distinguished from his essence."

42. *NPNF,* 1st ser., 3, pp. 17-228.

43. *NPNF,* 1st ser., 3, p. 125.

of subject and object. I think of myself, and I think of myself *as me*. This analogy exerts strong attraction. The Father sees himself in his Word, and in the Holy Spirit is united to the Word as himself. Augustine concludes: "And so there is a kind of image of the Trinity in the mind itself, and the knowledge of it, which is its offspring and its word concerning itself, and love as a third, and these three are one substance" (9.12.18).[44]

Augustine is well aware of the limits and the dangers of appealing to these natural trinities. In Book 15 he reviews the previous fourteen books, pointing out the inadequacy of the analogies. The major weakness in all of them is that, though the mind knows, wills, loves, remembers, and understands, these activities are not persons; that is, knowledge itself does not know, will itself does not will, love itself does not love, memory itself does not remember, and understanding itself does not understand. Hence, the psychological analogies tend toward modalism. They take God's unity for granted and attempt to explain the threefold nature of the Godhead as somehow emerging out of the unity.[45] For the psychological analogies begin with one person existing in three modes or phases. We would open ourselves to great dangers if we mistook these limited analogies for rational knowledge of God. If, however, the goal in constructing these analogies is merely to stimulate the imagination to be open to the three-in-oneness of the Trinity, we can make careful use of them.

Because of its influence on the language of confession, the traditional distinction between nature (Greek: *ousía*) and person (Greek: *hypóstasis*) deserves more detailed consideration. In order to understand the patristic concept of person, we must set aside the modern understanding of a person as "an individual centre of consciousness" and of being as an impersonal general category. As I hope to unpack it below, to be a person is "to be one whose being consists in relations of mutual constitution with other persons."[46] According to Prestige and Torrance, *hypóstasis* (person) for Athanasius and the Nicene Fathers indicates "a reality *ad alios*" (for another), or something concretely independent. The term *ousía*, on the other hand, was used for a "reality *in se*," that is, "in its intrinsic constitution."[47] Athanasius and his followers understood *ousía* "not as static but as *living being* and not as dumb but as *speaking being*, and hence *personal being*."[48] This sense of "being" originated not from current philosophical

44. *NPNF,* 1st ser., 3, p. 133.

45. Gunton criticizes Augustine heavily for submerging the "distinguishable identity" of the divine persons "into the all-embracing oneness of God" (*Promise of Trinitarian Theology,* p. 42).

46. Gunton, *Promise of Trinitarian Theology,* p. 195.

47. G. L. Prestige, *God in Patristic Thought,* 2nd ed. (London: SPCK, 1952), p. xxix.

48. Torrance, *The Christian Doctrine of God,* p. 116 (italics in original).

usage, which tended to think of *ousía* as impersonal and generic, but from God's self-naming as "I Am" (Exod. 3:14; LXX: *egò eimí*) and Jesus' echo of that text in his "I am" *(egò eimí)* sayings in the Gospel of John.[49] According to the Nicene fathers, the Son is *homooúsios* with the Father and therefore, in Torrance's apt expression, "What God is in his *parousia* [presence] with us he is in his *ousía* in the highest, and what he is in his *parousia* with himself he is in his *ousía* among us."[50]

The Cappadocian theologians Gregory of Nazianzus, Gregory of Nyssa, and Basil the Great, in their defense of the Nicene faith, advocated the expression "one *ousía*, three *hypostasai*."[51] Basil and his brother, Gregory of Nyssa, concluded that defending the Nicene faith required them to make a clear distinction between *ousía* and *hypóstasis*.[52] In a move that created misunderstanding and controversy, Basil distinguished the terms by placing *ousía* on the general level and *hypóstasis* on the particular level. The term *ousía* was used for the nature common to James, Harry, and Joan, who are instances of humanity; the term *hypóstasis* designates the particularities marked by personal names, the properties that distinguish each instance of human nature from all others. In *Letter 38* (until recently ascribed to Basil the Great), Gregory of Nyssa explains his view of the person/nature distinction:

> My statement, then, is this. That which is spoken of in a special and peculiar manner is indicated by the name of the hypostasis. Suppose we say "a man." The indefinite meaning of the word strikes a certain vague sense upon the ears. The nature is indicated, but what subsists and is specially and peculiarly indicated by the name is not made plain. Suppose we say "Paul." We set forth, by what is indicated by the name, the nature subsisting.[53]

However, applying this distinction to the Trinity poses a difficulty. If James, Harry, and Joan are three humans who share one nature, are the Father, Son, and Holy Spirit three Gods who are divine because they participate in an impersonal divine nature?[54] To rebut this charge, Gregory of Nyssa and Basil ar-

49. Torrance, *The Christian Doctrine of God*, p. 103. See esp. John 8:59: "'I tell you the truth,' Jesus answered, 'before Abraham was born, I am!'"

50. Torrance, *The Christian Doctrine of God*, p. 132.

51. Prestige, *God in Patristic Thought*, pp. 233-35.

52. Pelikan, *Christian Tradition*, 1, pp. 218-23; Behr, *Formation of Christian Theology*, 2.2, pp. 298-99.

53. *NPNF*, 2nd ser., 8, p. 138. See Lucian Turcescu, *Gregory of Nyssa and the Concept of Divine Persons* (New York: Oxford, 2005), pp. 47-48, for a scholarly discussion about authorship.

54. Gregory of Nyssa responds to this charge in his treatise *That There Are Not Three Gods* (*NPNF*, 2nd ser., 5, pp. 331-36).

gued that the *hypóstasis* of the Father is the principle of unity in the Trinity. The Father (as person) is the "cause" *(aitía)*, "fountain" *(pegé),* and "origin" *(arché)* of the Trinity.[55] The Son and Spirit are God *because* of the Father. In Robert Jenson's judgment, Gregory of Nyssa teaches that "God is the Father as he is the source of the Son's and the Spirit's deity; God is the Son as he is the recipient of deity from the Father; God is the Spirit as he is the spirit of the Son's reception of deity from the Father."[56] According to Torrance, this way of speaking of the unity of the Trinity retains an echo of subordinationism and has led to many of the disagreements between the Western and Eastern churches.[57]

According to Torrance, Gregory Nazianzus, Epiphanius of Salamis, and Pseudo-Cyril pursued a more fruitful path in sync with the thought of Athanasius. Gregory Nazianzus, in response to the insinuation of subordination into the Trinity, developed an understanding of the persons of the Trinity as eternal and substantial relationships *(schesis)* within the divine *ousía.* "Father is not a name either of an essence or of an action . . . it is the name of the Relation in which the Father stands to the Son, and the Son to the Father. For as with us these names make known a genuine and intimate relation, so, in the case before us too, they denote an identity of nature between Him That is begotten and Him That begets."[58] For impersonal beings, relationships are external and accidental. A particular apple's being is not dependent on its relationship to other concrete things. I could not be a father without having children, but fatherhood is not my being. I would still be a human being even if I were not a father. The relationships among the Father, Son, and Spirit, however, are essential to the divine being. God *is* Father, Son, and Spirit; there is no other God. The Father is the Father by virtue of his relationship to the Son and Spirit, and the Son and the Spirit are what they are by virtue of their relationship to the Father.[59] Unlike the relationships between human fathers and their children, the Father *is* his fatherhood, the Son *is* his sonship, and the Spirit *is* his ineffable relationship to the Father and the Son. And God *is* Father, Son, and Spirit.

Understanding the persons of the Trinity as substantial relationships renders it impossible to limit the monarchy, the origin, and thus the foundation of the unity of the divine being to the person of the Father. The monarchy "is a Unity constituted in and by the Trinity."[60] Epiphanius of Salamis insisted that the mon-

55. Thomas Torrance, *The Trinitarian Faith: The Evangelical Theology of the Ancient Catholic Church* (Edinburgh: T&T Clark, 1988), p. 241.

56. See Robert Jenson, *Systematic Theology,* vol. 1 (New York: Oxford, 1997), pp. 104-6.

57. Torrance, *The Christian Doctrine of God,* pp. 178-79.

58. Gregory Nazianzus, *Oration 29,* 16 *(NPNF,* 2nd ser., 7, p. 307).

59. Torrance, *Trinitarian Faith,* pp. 320-21.

60. Torrance, *Trinitarian Faith,* p. 321.

archy of God belongs to the entire Trinity and not just to the Father. "In proclaiming the divine Monarchia we do not err, but confess the Trinity, and the
Trinity in unity, one Godhead of Father, Son, and Holy Spirit."[61] The Trinity is a
unity, a whole by virtue of the mutual indwelling of the three persons, which John
of Damascus, following Pseudo-Cyril, called *perichoresis*. Jesus, speaking to his
disciples, says that he dwells "in the Father and the Father in me" (John 14:10).
Athanasius, Hilary, and other church fathers saw in this text a claim that the Father and the Son mutually indwell each other and thus share the same being.[62]

The notion of indwelling had long been applied to God's permeating presence in the created world and to the Spirit's indwelling of Christians. It was applied by Gregory Nazianzus and Maximus the Confessor to Christology to illuminate the union of the two natures of Christ.[63] The term *perichoresis* was first
used to refer to the Trinitarian relationships by Pseudo-Cyril.[64] Though the concept of mutual indwelling of the Trinity had long been held, the term *perichoresis*
provided a simple but powerful tool for expressing this idea.[65] John of Damascus
adopted the Pseudo-Cyrillian terminology, and through John it became an established feature of the traditional doctrine of the Trinity.[66] He argues:

> The subsistences dwell and are established firmly in one another. For they are
> inseparable and cannot part from one another, but keep to their separate
> courses within one another, without coalescing or mingling, but cleaving to
> each other. For the Son is in the Father and the Spirit: and the Spirit in the
> Father and the Son: and the Father in the Son and the Spirit, but there is no
> coalescence or commingling or confusion.[67]

The idea of mutual indwelling makes analogical use of our experience of
spatial objects. Physical objects can stand beside each other, but they cannot oc-

61. Torrance, *Trinitarian Faith*, p. 329. For a fuller discussion of Epiphanius's contribution
to the doctrine of the Trinity, see pp. 326-40.

62. For references, see Torrance, *The Christian Doctrine of God*, pp. 169-71.

63. Prestige, *God in Patristic Thought*, pp. 291-96. Maximus was apparently the first to use
the noun *perichoresis*, which he applied to the human nature of Christ being permeated by the
divine nature. The term *perichoresis* is somewhat misleading in Christology, since the human
nature of Christ does not permeate the divine nature in the same way the divine does the human.

64. Pseudo-Cyril, *De Sacrosancta Trinitate*, pp. 22-27; see Prestige, pp. 282-301.

65. Prestige, p. 297. Basil of Caesarea (or Gregory of Nyssa), for example, understood God
as "a sort of continuous and indivisible community" (*Letter 38*, 4, quoted in Gunton, *Promise of
Trinitarian Thought*, p. 10).

66. Prestige, p. 299.

67. John of Damascus, *Orthodox Faith*, 1.14 (*NPNF*, 2nd ser., 9, p. 160).

cupy the same space. The mutual indwelling of physical objects is inconceivable. Even if we think of space in a metaphorical sense, we cannot conceive of mutual indwelling. Two numbers or concepts may stand "beside" each other within mathematical or conceptual space, but they do not mutually indwell. The space of a general concept is larger than the space of any finite number of particulars contained in it. The set of real numbers includes the set of integers but also includes numbers that are not integers. And the mutual indwelling of two concepts could be conceived only as identity, which excludes distinctions. Gregory of Nyssa sees an analogy to mutual indwelling in a human mind filled with two different sciences.[68] Maximus appeals to the traditional analogy of the heat that permeates the red-hot knife, which burns as it cuts.[69]

The plausibility of the concept of mutual indwelling *(perichoresis)* for illuminating the doctrine of the Trinity is not finally rooted in these natural analogies. It is rooted rather in the analogy with the traditional teaching that God, as Spirit, indwells all things. The being and action of creatures do not pose barriers to the divine presence. Nor does its complete permeation by God violate the distinct being and action of the creature. Application of indwelling to the persons of the Trinity is an obvious extension of the idea of God's indwelling of creatures. The Father, in the Spirit, can indwell the Son without ceasing to be the Father or displacing the Son. Likewise, the Son, in the Spirit, can indwell the Father without ceasing to be the Son and without crowding out the Father. In the Spirit, the Father is perfectly open to the Son and the Son to the Father. The Father, Son, and Spirit occupy the same divine "space," which is the one divine being. Indeed, their mutual indwelling *is* the divine being.

We must not allow the original spatial reference to lure us into conceiving of the mutual indwelling of the divine persons in an impersonal way. The "space" of the Trinity is "personal space," for the being of God is personal through and through.[70] Therefore, the mutual indwelling is best conceived of as the total openness and giving of Trinitarian love; the divine being is a "being for one another."[71] The Father loves the Son in the Spirit and the Son loves the Father in the Spirit. This love is concretely actual in the eternal circle of self-giving, receiving, and returning.[72] God is love!

Clearly, we have reached the limits of thought. The distinction between person and nature, the concept of relationship, the analogy of a community-of-persons, the analogy of the human mind, and all other concepts and analogies

---

68. Prestige, pp. 266, 289, 295.
69. Prestige, pp. 293-94.
70. Gunton, *The Promise of Trinitarian Theology*, p. 110.
71. Torrance, *Christian Doctrine of God*, p. 163.
72. Torrance, *Christian Doctrine of God*, pp. 129, 163, 202.

can take us only so far. Applied literally, they lead to misunderstandings. God remains free and greater, even in his revelation, than anything we can imagine or think. Thus we are forced to partially negate all analogies in our approach to God. This negative aspect of theology, which the Greek church fathers called "apophatic" theology, is of great importance for Trinitarian theology and all our language about God.[73] I shall discuss this method in detail in the section on the divine attributes.

Consistency with Other Christian Teachings

I have argued that the doctrine of the Trinity is securely rooted in Scripture and have concluded that it does not contradict itself. We are left with one last question: How does the doctrine of the Trinity cohere with other Christian teachings? Finding that the doctrine of the Trinity illuminates and is illuminated by other major Christian doctrines would greatly enhance our confidence that it truly articulates and preserves Scripture's teaching. To this end, I will reflect briefly on a series of central Christian teachings.

Let us consider first the doctrine of the incarnation. Scripture teaches, and the church has always confessed, that Jesus Christ is the incarnate Son of God. "The Word became flesh and made his dwelling among us" (John 1:14). The one who had the form of God "made himself nothing, taking the very nature of a servant, being made in human likeness" (Phil. 2:7). These texts and others teach clearly that the Son existed as a person before he became incarnate. The Nicene Creed affirms that "[f]or us and for our salvation he came down from heaven." The Definition of Chalcedon declares: "[B]egotten before all ages of the Father according to the Godhead, and in these latter days, for us and for our salvation, born of the Virgin Mary, Mother of God, according to the Manhood."[74] The doctrine of the Trinity complements belief in the incarnation of God. The Son, not the Father or the Spirit, became incarnate; nonetheless, God truly became incarnate because the Son is of the same nature as the Father. The Father did not obey, endure humiliation, suffer, and die; the Son did.

Rejecting the doctrine of the Trinity would raise several troubling questions about the incarnation. What kind of being became incarnate and died for our sins? If Jesus Christ was merely a spirit-inspired man, the incarnation is an

---

73. See Dumitru Staniloae, *The Experience of God: Orthodox Dogmatic Theology,* vol. 1. *Revelation and Knowledge of the Triune God,* pp. 95-117. Gunton rightly warns that the Christian understanding of the incomprehensibility of God focuses not so much on impersonal ideas such as the transcendence of God's infinitude as on the otherness of his personal being (*The Promise of Trinitarian Theology,* p. 202).

74. Schaff, *The Creeds of Christendom,* 2, p. 62.

illusion. What if, like Arius, we think of Jesus Christ as the incarnation of a created being? Then we would have to admit, of course, that our human nature has not been joined to the true God, the source of eternal life. Furthermore, we could not think of God as Father from all eternity. It soon becomes apparent that denying the doctrine of the Trinity would leave the doctrine of the incarnation in tatters.

The Trinity is also very important to the Christian doctrine of creation. We can make three points here. First, the New Testament affirms that the Word was the one through whom all things were created (John 1:3; Col. 1:16, 17; Heb. 1:3, 10; John 5:7; 1 Cor. 8:6). The doctrine of the Trinity is consistent with this scriptural teaching. The Son, though distinct from the Father, is God. Viewing him as the Creator does not attribute the power to create to a creature, and thus it avoids a significant problem. For how could a creature without the power to give itself being, give being to others? If it can give being to others, it must have the power of life and being within itself; hence it must be God. Second, the doctrine of the Trinity explains how God's act of creation can be understood as free and gracious. The relationship of the Father to the Son is one of eternally giving being (not creating but begetting). Therefore, the Father-Son relationship provides the model for the Creator-creation relationship, so that, in creating the world, God did not begin to be fountain of being or active or gracious. If this were so, God would have been enhanced by the creation of the world and thus motivated by this increase of good.

The Christian faith proclaims that God is eternally loving, wise, knowing, and willing. The doctrine of the Trinity grounds these personal attributes in God's eternal nature. God did not need to create a world to become loving, wise, knowing, and willing. The Father loved and knew the Son from all eternity. When the Father loves the world through his Son in the power of his Spirit, he does nothing out of character. An abstract monotheism cannot explain the personal characteristics and actions of the biblical God. For knowing and willing require distinction and otherness, and loving requires other persons. But if God does not love, know, and will eternally, creation, if conceivable at all, would have to be understood as an automatic emanation from the being of God.

Christian belief in divine self-revelation is illuminated greatly by reflection on the doctrine of the Trinity. Do we know God as a person or do we know a mere cosmic law? According to Scripture, God can be known only through God's initiative. We know God through the Word in the power of the Holy Spirit. According to Jesus, "Anyone who has seen me has seen the Father" (John 14:9). In the words of Paul, we know the "light of the knowledge of the glory of God in the face of Christ" (2 Cor. 4:6). The revealer is God; for no other has access to God. The thing revealed is God; otherwise, the true God is not revealed. The power that connects the thing revealed to the revealer must also be God; otherwise, we can have no confidence that what is revealed really is the revealer. The Father reveals himself in Jesus Christ, who is God revealed. The Holy Spirit is the communion or "bond of the Trinity" that allows the Father to know and love himself in his Son, and hence enables us to know and love the Father through the Son.[75]

After formulating the scriptural teaching in a concise way and exercising our imaginations and intellects with analogies and speculative distinctions in an attempt to understand, we are still left with a mystery. Some may ask, why bother attempting to understand, since we shall fail anyway? The exercise is vital to the life of faith and praise. It is one thing to accept as a matter of tradition that the Holy Trinity is a profound mystery; it is quite another to contemplate that mystery and thereby be drawn further into it and overwhelmed with the greatness of God. It is one thing to mouth the word "mystery," and it is another to stand in the presence of the holy mystery. Gregory of Nazianzus expresses this beautifully in his *Oration On Holy Baptism*:

> No sooner do I conceive of the One than I am illumined by the Splendour of the Three; no sooner do I distinguish Them than I am carried back to the One. When I think of any One of the Three I think of Him as the Whole, and my eyes are filled, and the greater part of what I am thinking of escapes me. I cannot grasp the greatness of That One so as to attribute a greater greatness to the Rest. When I contemplate the Three together, I see but one torch, and cannot divide or measure out the Undivided Light.[76]

75. Epiphanius, *Anchoratus*, 6.8. See Torrance, *The Christian Doctrine of God*, p. 126, for a discussion of this idea.

76. Gregory Nazianzus, *Oration 40*, 41 (*NPNF*, 2nd ser., 7, p. 375).

THE DIVINE ATTRIBUTES

5

Where Words Praise and Silence Adores:
The Divine Attributes

Etiquette forbids speaking about people in their presence; speaking for others when they can speak for themselves breathes insult; and explaining the feelings of a friend as she listens exudes presumption. Yet we dare to speak about the all-present, ever-listening God! Theologians pen tomes about the divine nature, and preachers fill the air with God's commands and comforts. Talk show hosts, celebrities, and our hair stylists ventilate their opinions about God directly from the gut. Can we hope to avoid the judgment that the God-in-storm pronounced on Job and his companions? "Who is this that darkens my counsel with words without knowledge?" (Job 37:2). What a terrifying prospect for those who work in words and sculpt in sound. How much better silence than "words without knowledge"!

Though safer than presumptuous speech, silence is no certain shelter from divine judgment. Silence without love, a silence of indifference or forgetfulness or despair or sloth, is no better than speech without knowledge. Where God is concerned, there is no safe path: to speak we risk presumption, but to remain silent we risk sloth. God is too transcendent for words but too important for silence. Let our speech, then, consist of confession and praise and our silence of penance and adoration. But where do we learn how to confess and praise, to repent and adore?

Thinking the Incomprehensible
and Speaking the Ineffable

An Unusual Question

What is God? I know this is an unusual way to speak about God, and it may seem to violate what I just said about speech and silence. After all, we are dealing with the supremely personal God. God is not a "what" but a "who." True. But we cannot avoid inquiring about what it means to be God any more than we could, in previous chapters, avoid asking whether God really is triune or what it means that God exists. I want to address this odd question because it brings to the table an important issue. For in our understanding of finite things, we distinguish between what a thing is (its essence or nature) and whether it is (its existence). But in the special case of God, as our discussion of Anselm's ontological argument has made clear, existence is identical to essence. It is God's nature to exist.

If we are to grasp the traditional doctrine of the attributes, I must explain some distinctions that traditional theologians have used to express their theology. Let us consider briefly two important distinctions: the distinction between essence and existence and the distinction between substance and accident. In creatures, in contrast to God, we must distinguish between the essence and the existence of a thing.[1] Suppose that a day comes when apple trees become extinct and all apples in the world have been eaten. As sad as that would be for those of us who love apples, this unfortunate circumstance will not change what it means to be an apple. An apple's essence does not depend on the existence of apples. The second distinction — between substance and accident — allows us to distinguish between one apple and another. Joseph Owens explains the difference: substance "is an essence or nature that calls for being through itself and not through another," while an accident "has its being in dependence on a substance."[2] Two apples must have the same nature or they would not both be apples; but they must differ in some respect, or they would be completely identical — one apple rather than two. The qualities that distinguish them fall into the category of "accidents." An apple can be rotten, red, six ounces in weight, sour, or bumpy. Apples are not by nature rotten, red, or sour; but they can be. Where do these accidental features come from? In traditional theology, informed as it was by Aristotelian metaphysics, accidents arise most obviously from the conditions of the material world. Matter, time, and space allow an essence to be instantiated in more than one example because they make possible accidental variations. In the material world, things can be identical only in essence and never as existing things. Hence, when we answer the question about what a thing is, we do not include accidental features in our answer.

Now we return to our strange question: What is God? Immediately, we are faced with a difficulty in our quest to understand God that we do not encounter

---

1. See Joseph Owens, *An Elementary Christian Metaphysics* (Houston: Center for Thomistic Studies, 1963), pp. 131-42.

2. Owens, *Christian Metaphysics*, pp. 144-45.

in our attempts to understand created things. We *define* a thing by placing it into a general class and differentiating it from other members of the class. The classic example is Aristotle's definition of humanity: "Man is a rational animal." That is, human beings are animals that possess reason. However, according to traditional Christian doctrine, God cannot be defined.[3] For, according to our faith, God is absolutely and necessarily unique: there is no set of beings of the species "divine." There is and can be only one God. God is not a member of a general class that includes, for example, all nonmaterial beings, within which various types of nonmaterial beings can be defined by differentiation. God is the unlimited, infinite origin of all things; God is God, apart from other things. Therefore, God cannot be defined.

The question "What is God?" also poses another difficulty. The ability to define something is practically synonymous with the power to comprehend it. Traditional Christian theologians, however, have argued that God is incomprehensible. Gregory Nazianzus speaks of the difficulty of comprehending created things and then says, "Far more than these things their transcendent cause, the incomprehensible and boundless nature pass understanding."[4] He tells of his own efforts to know God, comparing his search to Moses' ascent of the mountain and the high priest's entrance into the holy of holies:

> I penetrated the cloud, became enclosed in it, detached from matter and material things and concentrated, so far as might be, in myself. But when I directed my gaze I scarcely saw the averted figure of God, and this whilst sheltering in the rock, God the Word incarnate for us. Peering in I saw not the nature prime, inviolate, self-apprehended (by "self" I mean the Trinity), the nature as it all abides within the first veil and is hidden by the Cherubim, but as it reaches us at its furthest remove from God, being so far as I can understand, the grandeur, or as divine David calls it the "majesty."[5]

In commenting on this text by Gregory, Vladimir Lossky argues that the Eastern Church fathers' teaching on divine incomprehensibility is based on revelation and cannot be known from philosophy. "This awareness of the incomprehensibility of the divine nature," Lossky contends, "thus corresponds to an

---

3. For a discussion of Thomas Aquinas's treatment of this issue, see Etienne Gilson, *The Philosophy of Thomas Aquinas,* trans. Edward Bullough, ed. G. A. Elrington (New York: Dorset Press, n.d.), pp. 102-3.

4. *Oration 28,* 5; St. Gregory of Nazianzus, *On God and Christ: The Five Theological Orations and Two Letters to Cledonius,* trans. Lionel Wickham and Frederick Williams (Crestwood, NY: St. Vladimir's, 2002), p. 40.

5. Gregory Nazianzus, *On God and Christ,* pp. 38-39.

experience: to a meeting with the personal God of revelation."[6] Accordingly, John of Damascus introduces the first chapter of *The Orthodox Faith* with this heading: "That the Deity is incomprehensible, and that we ought not to pry into and meddle with the things which have not been delivered to us by the holy Prophets, and Apostles, and Evangelists" (1.1).[7]

In the Middle Ages, Thomas Aquinas argued that "whoever knows a thing so as to comprehend it, knows it as perfectly as it is knowable." But only God knows himself as perfectly as he is knowable; hence, "the created intellect cannot possibly comprehend the divine substance." The human mind is finite and "a finite power cannot of its operation rise to the level of an infinite object."[8] The post-Reformation orthodox Reformed also maintained the doctrine of divine incomprehensibility. Hugh Binning says: "This is the chief point of saving knowledge, to know God; and this is the first point or degree of true knowledge of God, to discern how ignorant we are of him, and to find him beyond all knowledge."[9] Must we give up, then, on answering the question "What is God?"

The Analogy of Faith and the Divine Attributes

Were it not for God's self-revelation, we would have to give up any hope of insight into God's nature and remain silent. However, were it not for God's self-revelation, we would not know that God is indefinable and that we should remain silent. We would continue chattering baselessly about the nature of the divine. Already, in our discussion of the question of God's nature, we have presupposed the Christian faith and made use of Christian knowledge of God. Such circularity is unavoidable in a theology that sees itself as faith seeking understanding. In theology, the part gains its full meaning only in light of the whole, and the whole can be grasped only by coming to see the relationships among all the parts. It does not matter where you begin as long as you traverse the whole.

I shall move from considering the economy of God's actions to speaking of God's being, just as I did when discussing the Trinity. Only by examining God's

6. Lossky, *The Mystical Theology of the Eastern Church* (Crestwood, NY: St. Vladimir's, 1998), p. 34.

7. John of Damascus, *ANF*, 2, p. ix.

8. Aquinas, *Summa Contra Gentiles*, 3.55, in *Basic Writings of Saint Thomas Aquinas*, vol. 2, ed. Anton C. Pegis (New York: Random House, 1945), p. 99; see also *SumTh*, 1.12.7.

9. Hugh Binning, *The Common Principles of the Christian Religion*, 8, in *The Works of The Rev. Hugh Binning, M.A.*, 3rd ed., ed. Rev. M. Leishan, D.D. (London: A. Fullarton and Co., 1851), p. 40.

works and words of self-revelation that are recorded in Scripture can we grow in our understanding of the One who does these things. As we raise our minds from God's works to the Worker of them, we ask what characteristics or attributes or properties of the Worker are revealed in the works. In studying the divine attributes, I shall examine the church's teaching by the norm of Scripture, interpreted with the help of tradition and reason with a view to experience and praise.

In speaking about God on the basis of his works and words, I shall speak of divine attributes. Some theologians prefer other terms: perfections, properties, characteristics, appellations, virtues, or names.[10] Many modern theologians refuse these terms, arguing that they depersonalize God by turning our attention away from the economy of salvation toward abstract qualities in an impersonal divine nature. When we are dealing with persons we should focus on personal identity, which is determined by interpersonal relationships and shaped by a history of personal experience and actions. Hence, they prefer narrative or dramatic ways of speaking of God. In his ten-page treatment of the divine attributes, Robert Jenson rejects the traditional method of deriving the attributes. Refusing to speak of God apart from the economy of salvation, he proposes that "every true proposition of the form 'God is . . .' is slogan for the gospel's pivotal claim or for some version of the actual gospel proclamation."[11] The "pivotal" claim is that "Jesus is risen."

Jenson and others make an excellent point, but why must we choose between the two? It makes sense to take the nature and existence of a person for granted temporarily so that we can focus on personal identity. But the nature of the character we are describing still matters. Suppose I say, "He looked at me all day with mournful eyes and sat patiently as I worked on the book." Would it make a difference to you whether I spoke of my son or my cat? Would it matter whether I spoke of my dog or God when I say, "He loves everyone"? It does matter what loves us. It matters that the character in a narrative and the identity in the drama is God, God Almighty.

We must use the word "attribute" with caution. In ordinary usage, an attribute is any characteristic of a thing, whether accidental or essential. But, as I have already indicated, it is not appropriate to think of God as having accidental attributes. Furthermore, the word "attribute" resonates with subjective over-

10. For a discussion of the many terms used by the post-Reformation orthodox Reformed, see Richard A. Muller, *Post-Reformation Reformed Dogmatics: The Rise and Development of Reformed Orthodoxy*, vol. 3, *The Divine Essence and Attributes* (Grand Rapids: Baker Academic, 2003), pp. 198-99 (hereafter *PRRD*).

11. Robert Jenson, *Christian Dogmatics*, vol. 1, ed. Carl E. Braaten and Robert W. Jenson (Philadelphia: Fortress, 1984), p. 183.

tones. Consequently, Karl Barth prefers the term "perfection" because "it points at once to the thing itself instead of merely to its formal aspect, and because instead of something general it expresses at once that which is clearly distinctive."[12] According to Barth, God is perfect in his "one, simple, distinctive being." But God is rich in his simplicity and so lives "his perfect life in the abundance of many individual and distinct perfections."[13] As Barth indicates, the terms "perfection" and "property" turn our attention to the objective being rather than our subjective perception of God. Nevertheless, I shall use the term "attribute" and attempt to guard against its subjective connotations. It is so widely used that substituting another term would create unnecessary confusion. Furthermore, no word is without its problems.

Do the many attributes point to real, objective distinctions within God? Or do they result solely from our limitations as creatures? For example, when we say that God is loving or just or holy, do these attributes name three different things within God or do they designate our varying responses to God? The first alternative would make God a composite being and imply all the limits to which compound beings are subject. For Friedrich Schleiermacher, on the other hand, "all attributes which we ascribe to God are to be taken as denoting not something special in God, but only something special in the manner in which the feeling of absolute dependence is to be related to Him."[14] Here, our knowledge of God is threatened, for the divine attributes have become merely effects in us of our encounter with an unknowable mystery. Is there a way between these two extremes?

Thomas Aquinas charts a middle course. According to Aquinas, God is simple in his own being. The attributes cannot name *real* distinctions in God; for this would imply that God is composed of parts.[15] On the other hand, the attributes are not merely synonyms but have a "foundation in the thing."[16] Each points to a different aspect of the divine nature, which is simple in itself. In the attributes, our knowledge of God, though genuine, is "imperfectly un-

12. Barth, *Church Dogmatics*, vol. 2, pt. 1, ed. G. W. Bromiley and T. F. Torrance, trans. T. H. L. Parker et al. (Edinburgh: T&T Clark, 1957), p. 322 (hereafter *CD*).

13. *CD*, 2/1, p. 322.

14. Schleiermacher, *The Christian Faith*, trans. H. R. Mackintosh and J. S. Stewart (Philadelphia: Fortress, 1976), p. 194.

15. According to Muller, the modifier "real" *(realis)* in Aquinas's term "real distinctions" means "thingish," not "genuine." That is, the attributes are genuine distinctions but not distinct things that must be united in some way (Muller, *PRRD*, 3, p. 56).

16. Aquinas, *Commentary on the Sentences*, 1.2.1.3, quoted in Steven R. Holmes, "'Something Much Too Plain to Say': Towards a Defense of the Doctrine of Divine Simplicity," in *Listening to the Past: The Place of Tradition in Theology* (Grand Rapids: Baker Academic Books, 2002), p. 51.

derstood through these conceptions."[17] We are creatures and can know God only "from creatures," in language derived from creatures.[18] Hence, we can know God only insofar as he resembles creatures. In other words, the validity of our knowledge of God in the attributes presupposes an analogy between the Creator and creatures. How do we know there is such a likeness? And how do we judge the extent of the analogy?

A metaphor can be known to be a legitimate analogy only by someone who has direct and nonmetaphorical knowledge of the thing that the analogy is meant to explain. Suppose I travel in a time machine to North America in 3000 B.C. For some reason, I want to explain to the native inhabitants what an airliner is. I could draw analogies between eagles, arrows, spears, and the moon — and an airliner. Clearly, *I* would be the one in a position to make analogies and judge their validity and effectiveness, whereas my audience would not. The one who makes analogies does not need them, and the one who needs them cannot make them. With my help, the ancient Americans would be able to construct a mental image of an "airliner." However, even given my best efforts to explain, the image evoked in their minds would probably differ greatly from the real thing. Nevertheless, it would bear a resemblance. In the same way, God alone can make genuine analogies to himself and judge the adequacy of the images of him created in our minds. Therefore, apart from God's self-revelation, we can have no confidence in analogies that supposedly give us a likeness of God.

In my earlier discussion of revelation I excluded the option of natural theology. Hence, we cannot establish the validity of attribute language by reason alone, but only in reference to God's self-revelation. Only here can we know God as Father, Son, and Holy Spirit. Only Scripture can establish that the triune God created the world from nothing and that God has bestowed on creatures attributes that bear some resemblance to him. Only in Scripture do we learn that God has become a creature in Jesus Christ, thereby establishing the definitive analogy between himself and his creation. Scripture provides a pattern of attribute language by which to judge our own usage. This pattern, which the orthodox Reformed, long before Karl Barth, called the "analogy of faith," provides a matrix of meaning within which the attributes interpret each other.[19]

Since we have in Scripture and in the Word made flesh the self-revelation

---

17. *SumTh,* 1.13.4 (*Basic Writings,* 1, p. 118).

18. *SumTh,* 1.13.4 (*Basic Writings,* 1, pp. 117-18). See Otto Weber, *Foundations of Dogmatics,* vol. 1, trans. Darrell L. Guder (Grand Rapids: Eerdmans, 1981), p. 410, for his discussion of Thomas's view of the attributes.

19. See Muller, *PRRD,* 2, pp. 493-97, for a discussion of the Reformed method of interpreting Scripture according to the analogy of faith. For Barth's use of the analogy of faith, see *CD,* 1/1, pp. 243-47.

of God, we need not labor anxiously to establish the adequacy of our knowledge of God in the attributes. The attributes are God's condescension to us. Our creaturely limitations do not limit God's ability to communicate. God is not a prisoner of his own transcendence. He is the author not only of attribute language but also of our capacity to understand it. We can, therefore, have confidence that this way of speaking of God is adequate for God's purposes. In faith, we know that we know the true God: "We know also that the Son of God has come and has given us understanding, so that we may know him who is true. And we are in him who is true — even in his Son Jesus Christ. He is the true God and eternal life" (1 John 5:20).

The Grammar of Attribute Language

Our faith in God's self-revelation gives us confidence that we are permitted to encourage each other with sentences such as, "God is good and worthy of praise." That same faith founds our belief that this sentence speaks truth about God. God really is good and worthy of our praise in his own deepest nature. Nevertheless, our faith also instructs us not to equate human goodness with divine goodness. This two-sided conviction — one positive and the other negative — places us in a situation that calls for careful consideration. We are told that we can speak of God truly in the language of creatures, but we are cautioned that we must not equate the attributes of creatures with those of the Creator. Can we do justice to both concerns and find a way to make the language of creatures serviceable in speaking truly about God? That is to say, what are the rules for the use and misuse of language about God?

In a very influential scheme, Dionysius the Areopagite (c. A.D. 500) proposed two ways by which we can move from the attributes of creatures to the highest knowledge of God.[20] In his *Mystical Theology,* Dionysius speaks of the affirmative and negative ways of speaking about God. In the affirmative class fall the doctrine of the Trinity and other dogmas of the church, the divine names or attributes, and all the metaphors Scripture uses to speak of God. These affirmations, he cautions, do not give us knowledge of God's essence, which is "beyond all affirmation" (p. 198), but knowledge of the light streaming from it. The way of mystical negation is superior to the way of affirmation (pp. 196-99). It begins by negating the possibility of sense perception of God, for God resembles nothing in the sensible world. It then progresses through the hierarchy of intellectual ideas, denying that

---

20. See *Dionysius the Areopagite on the Divine Names and the Mystical Theology,* trans. C. E. Rolt (Berwick, ME: IBIS Press, 2004).

any act of understanding can grasp the being of God. God is beyond intellect. The end of the negative way is a wordless, thoughtless, and timeless union with that "divine Darkness which exceedeth all existence" (p. 192).

Augustine articulates the negative way differently, more argumentative or dialectical and less mystical than does Dionysius. In his struggle to think his way out of Manichaeism, Augustine devises a way to test our conceptions of God. The Manicheans taught that God suffers from and is limited by evil. But Augustine believes that God is the highest, best, and greatest reality conceivable. There can be no "soul capable of conceiving that which is better than you, who are the supreme and highest good."[21] Something that can be injured and limited is corruptible. Augustine knows that the incorruptible is better than the corruptible, and he argues that we must remove from our conceptions ideas that imply God's corruptibility. For, "had it been the case that you [God] are not incorruptible, I could in thought have attained something better than my God."[22] Augustine thus lays down a principle of excellence to test the worthiness of all our conceptions of God: we should never attribute to God something less perfect than we can conceive.[23]

Anselm of Canterbury (c. 1033–c. 1109), inspired by Augustine's principle of excellence, understands God to be "that than which a greater cannot be conceived."[24] Anselm's definition has negative and positive implications.[25] Negatively, God is unlimited: like Augustine, Anselm denies to God any attribute that would limit him: space, time, body, composition, and other characteristics of creatures. His definition implies also the positive rule that "God is whatever it is better to be than not be. . . . What good, therefore, does the supreme good lack, through which every good is?" Anselm concludes from this principle that "thou art just, truthful, blessed, and whatever it is better to be than not to be. For it is better to be just than not just; better to be blessed than not blessed."[26]

Thomas Aquinas, like Augustine and Anselm before him, understood God to be "that, than which a greater cannot be conceived." After giving his proofs of God's existence, Aquinas begins to address "the manner of [God's] existence."

21. Augustine, *Confessions,* 7.4, trans. Henry Chadwick (New York: Oxford University Press, 1991), p. 114.

22. *Confessions,* 7.4, p. 114.

23. Augustine articulated a more sophisticated form of this principle in his *Christian Doctrine,* 1.6-7 (*NPNF,* 1st ser., 2, p. 524).

24. Anselm, *Proslogium,* 3, in *Saint Anselm: Basic Writings,* 2nd ed., trans. S. N. Deane (La Salle, IL: Open Court, 1968), pp. 8-9.

25. Katherin A. Rogers, *Perfect Being Theology* (Edinburgh: Edinburgh University Press, 2002), pp. 11-12.

26. Anselm, *Proslogium,* 5, p. 11.

In doing this, he proposes to "consider (1) how He is not; (2) how He is known by us; and (3) how He is named."[27] Aquinas uses the Augustinian conviction of God's transcendent greatness to help him understand what God is not. God cannot be a body, for example, because "God is the most noble of beings," and body is not the most noble of beings. "Therefore it is impossible that God should be a body."[28] In his discussion of the names of God, Aquinas delineates an affirmative way to speak about God: God is the "cause" of all creatures. Every "perfection" that is embodied in creatures is from God and resembles the absolute perfection of God, just as every effect resembles its cause.[29] "Now since the intellect knows God from creatures, it knows Him as far as creatures represent him. But it was shown above that God prepossesses in Himself all the perfections of creatures, being Himself absolutely and universally perfect. Hence every creature represents Him, and is like Him . . . as the excelling source of whose form the effects fall short, although they derive some likeness thereto."[30] When we say "God is good," we mean more than "God is the cause of goodness." We mean: "God causes goodness in things because He is good."[31]

Reformed scholasticism adopted from the medieval tradition the pattern of knowing and speaking of God according to the ways of negation, affirmation, and causation. Edward Leigh summarizes:[32]

(1) All perfections which we apprehend, must be ascribed unto God, and that after a more excellent manner, than can be apprehended; as that he is in himself, by himself and of himself: that he is one, true, good, and holy.
(2) We must remove from him all imperfections whatsoever; he is Simple, Eternal, Infinite, Unchangeable.
(3) He is the supreme cause of all.

According to Richard Muller, the Reformed scholastics do not think of the three ways as primarily rational and speculative. They always "coordinated the rational exercise with biblical arguments and thereby approach the three ways more as patterns of classification than as a basis for deduction."[33]

How shall we evaluate the traditional language about God? If these three "ways" are proposed as ways of gaining knowledge of God by moving from crea-

27. SumTh, 1.3 (Basic Writings, 1, p. 25).
28. SumTh, 1.3.1 (Basic Writings, 1, pp. 25-26).
29. Aquinas develops this point in SumTh, 1.4.3 and SumTh, 1.44.1.
30. SumTh, 1.13.2 (Basic Writings, 1, pp. 114-15).
31. SumTh, 1.13.2 (Basic Writings, 1, pp. 114-15).
32. A Treatise of Divinity, 2.1 (London, 1647), p. 2.
33. PRRD, vol. 1, Prolegomena to Theology, p. 167.

tures to God through reason alone, we should reject them. I have already shown that we cannot establish the analogy of creation to the Creator apart from revelation. Likewise, we cannot be sure that, in speaking of the infinite maximum of a good quality in a creature, we are thereby speaking of the triune God. Nor can we know, apart from God's self-revelation, that negating aspects of creatures we consider to be imperfect will automatically yield knowledge of God.

While I reject natural theology, I cannot imagine speaking about the God revealed in Scripture apart from the forms of speech articulated by the tradition. Are Augustine, Anselm, Aquinas, and all the rest wrong when they say that we should ascribe to God the highest perfection we can imagine? Was it because they were seduced by Greek rationalism that they urged us to remove from our conception of God everything imperfect, defective, and evil? Scripture itself uses the language of analogy, affirmation, negation, and causality. We are urged to ascribe to the Lord every good, great, and glorious thing we know. "Ascribe to the Lord the glory due his name" (Ps. 96:8). "Praise the Lord, O my soul. O Lord my God, you are very great; you are clothed with splendor and majesty" (Ps. 104:1). How can we give God the "glory due his name" if we are forbidden to reach for the best and highest we can conceive and deny whatever we think to be imperfect and evil?

Objections to the Traditional Grammar

Before we conclude this section, let us consider briefly two objections to the traditional approach to language about God. Some writers want to simplify matters and avoid the careful thought necessary to balance the positive and negative concerns. For lack of a better term we can call them biblicists. Let us stick to the language of Scripture, they plead. We cannot go wrong if we speak of God the way the Bible does. There is no need to heighten the perfections and remove the imperfections of creatures. The language of the Bible *defines* appropriate speech about God. I can agree with biblicists that we are allowed to speak of God as the Bible does and even that biblical usage defines appropriate language about God. But this does not solve the problem of what we should *think* when we hear those words and what we should *teach* on the basis of them. When the Bible speaks of God as a rock, a fortress, or a king, what should we think? When the Bible speaks of God's eyes, ears, and arms, what do we teach on the basis of these passages? Any interpretation of the metaphors and similes of Scripture will require an appeal to a set of rules defining what is appropriate and inappropriate to think and say of God.

Open theism also attacks the defenders of the traditional doctrine of God for applying the rules of negation and heightening to the language of Scripture. The God of Scripture, they point out, suffers, changes, dwells in time and space, repents, forgets, does not know the future, and gets angry. But traditional theologians refuse to take these texts at face value; instead, they remove all these "imperfections" and claim that Scripture speaks of God as having human-like qualities only to help us understand God's attributes and actions, which bear only a human resemblance to them. Open theists insist that traditional theologians prefer their rationally derived "perfect being theology" to the God of Scripture.[34] John Sanders indicts Calvin and other "orthodox" and "classical theist" Christians for using the Augustinian principle of negation:

> It is commonplace for theologians to claim that biblical anthropomorphisms are "accommodations" on God's part to our limited abilities to understand. . . . Sometimes appeal is made to what any being with the title "God" must be like. God, it is claimed, is a term for which only certain properties are "fitting" (*dignum Deo*). Any God worth his salt must conform to our intuitive notions of deity or get out of the deity business. Since the biblical depiction does not, according to some people, measure up to what is fitting for God to be, the doctrine of divine accommodation is enacted to protect the Bible from charges of falsehood.[35]

In this statement Sanders makes open theism sound like a sophisticated version of biblicism whose primary concern is taking the Bible seriously. This impression is misleading. Open theism aims primarily to undermine the traditional doctrine of God and replace it with another view. The biblicism of the open theists is but a means to that end. Their criticism of the Augustinian principle — that we ought never to attribute to God something less perfect than we can conceive — appears disingenuous. For open theists do not think their view of God places God in an inferior position or that God is *less* perfect than we can conceive. On the contrary, they think their doctrine of God does a better job of removing imperfections and heightening perfections. William Hasker, for example, explains that

> the difficulties with perfect being theology do not, in my view, stem from the assumption that God is an absolutely perfect being — that he is "whatever it

---

34. William Hasker, "A Philosophical Perspective," in *The Openness of God: A Biblical Challenge to the Traditional Understanding of God,* ed. Clark Pinnock, Richard Rice, et al. (Downers Grove, IL: InterVarsity Press, 1994), pp. 131-34.

35. Sanders, *The God Who Risks: A Theology of Providence* (Downers Grove, IL: InterVarsity Press, 1998), p. 33.

is better to be than not to be." Rather, difficulties have arisen because people have been too ready to assume that they can determine, easily and with little effort, what perfection is in the case of God — that is, what attributes a perfect being must possess.[36]

The real methodological difference between them and the traditional theologians is their view of what qualities are imperfect and need to be removed and what qualities are good and may be heightened. Unfortunately, this dispute cannot be resolved by invoking (or rejecting) the simplistic canons of biblicism. A decision between the two alternatives must be based on a comparison of the best examples of the completely developed systems.

I understand the three ways, not as our reaching up to God, but as God's condescension to us. God manifests himself in our world, in history, in language, and in the human flesh of Jesus Christ. God establishes the analogy, the negation, and the affirmation. I will follow the pattern of Scripture and take care to be guided by the three ways laid out in the tradition. As to the issue of what imperfections we should deny and what perfections we should heighten, I believe that the intuitions of the tradition, of Dionysius, Augustine, Anselm, Aquinas, and the Protestant Scholastics are fundamentally correct. It is better to be spirit than body, to be knowing than ignorant, immortal than mortal, simple than compound, and impassible than subject to suffering. Whether or not my faith in the soundness of the tradition is misplaced will be for others to decide, but I hope that they will decide only after I have presented my whole case.

Classifying the Attributes

Rather than discussing them in random order, traditional theologians have grouped the attributes into classes. They have usually placed those attributes into two groups, the first corresponding to God's transcendence, his complete independence from the creation, and the second corresponding to God's immanence, his intimate presence in creation. The orthodox Reformed speak of incommunicable and communicable — or absolute and relative — attributes, or the attributes of sufficiency and efficiency. According to the *Leiden Synopsis* (1624), the incommunicable attributes are those that "in themselves, according to their own pure understanding, are not communicated to creatures, but in some way only partially and comparatively." Among these are unity, immutability, and infinity. The communicable attributes are those that "are of God in

---

36. Hasker, "A Philosophical Perspective," p. 132.

such a way that they may also be communicated to creatures, and they may truly be shared by them, and therefore they are said to be analogous on account of the order which they have from God with respect to God and creatures."[37] John Owen (1616-83) provides an example of absolute/relative classification. He observes:

> The properties of God are either absolute or relative. The absolute properties of God are such that they may be considered without supposition of any thing else whatever, toward which their energy and efficacy should be exerted. His relative [properties] are such as in their egress and exercise, respect some things in creatures, though they naturally and eternally reside in God.[38]

The Reformed theologian Petrus van Mastricht (1630-1706) classifies the attributes into a threefold pattern corresponding to three questions: What? how great? and what sort of? In the first category Mastricht places such attributes as "spirituality, simplicity, and immutability"; in the second he lists "one, infinite, great, immense, omnipresent, and eternal"; and in the third he lists "intellect, will, and affections . . . majesty, glory, and blessedness."[39] Orthodox Lutheranism often divided the attributes into the negative and the positive attributes. The negative attributes are "those by which the imperfections found in creatures are removed from God": they include "unity, simplicity, immutability, infinity, immensity and eternity." The positive attributes are those "by which perfections are simply affirmed concerning God." These include "life, knowledge, wisdom, holiness, justice, truth, power, goodness, [and] perfection."[40]

Romanian Orthodox theologian Dumitru Staniloae divides the attributes into super-essential and spiritual attributes. The "super-essence" of God is beyond all created essences and thus is "totally unknown with respect to what it is in itself." We can know it only as it "manifests itself by entering into relation with us and making itself known to us in a series of dynamic attributes." These attributes can be conceived negatively by freeing them from the "aspect of insufficiency" found in the corresponding attributes of creatures. The super-essential attributes include infinity, simplicity, and eternity. The spiritual attrib-

---

37. Quoted in Otto Weber, *Foundations of Dogmatics*, p. 421.

38. Owen, *Vindiciae evangelicae*, quoted in Muller, *PRRD*, 3, p. 218.

39. Van Mastricht, *Theoretico-practica theologia*, 1.12-23; quoted in Muller, *PRRD*, 3, pp. 222-23.

40. Heinrich Schmid, *Doctrinal Theology of the Evangelical Lutheran Church*, trans. Charles A. Hay and Henry Jacobs (1899; reprint, Minneapolis: Augsburg Publishing House, 1961), pp. 118-19. Polanus, on the Reformed side, also used the negative/positive classification; see Muller, *PRRD*, 3, p. 220.

utes refer to God's life as a Trinity of persons and are manifested in the world in God's personal actions toward creatures. They include omniscience, justice, mercy, and holiness.[41]

I shall adapt the division of attributes proposed by Karl Barth, who groups them into those of divine freedom and of divine love. This classification has several advantages. While the concept of freedom has a negative aspect, corresponding to the removal of all limits, it also has a positive ring: it speaks of unfettered and full life. Love emphasizes the overflowing, filling, and giving abundance of God's life. The activity of the free and unlimited divine life is love. Furthermore, classifying the attributes into these two classes does not set them up as opposites that need to be reconciled. For we can grasp immediately, if not completely, the unity of freedom and love, since they are both inherent in personal life. Therefore, Barth speaks of God as "the One who loves in freedom."[42] This is not so much a definition of God as a shorthand description of the triune God we meet in Scripture.

The Unity of the Attributes

Traditional theology insists that God's attributes are unified in God's simple nature and that the attributes are God himself, not merely accidental qualities or appearances. God *is* his attributes or perfections. Of course, the statement "God is his attributes" does not mean that God is the concepts and words we think when we speak of him. It means that the attributes refer to the perfections of God's essential nature, which he freely enacts. Otherwise, in knowing the attributes we would not know God. God is not merely just, as though acting justly were merely one of God's possibilities; God *is* justice. Human beings are just only to the extent that they are like the One who is justice. God *is* love, and God *is* infinity. Because God is his attributes, his attributes are united in the completely harmonious and infinitely rich being of God. Of course, humans cannot fully grasp this unity. However, seeking to understand this harmony is a major task of a theology of the attributes.

Speaking of God as his attributes may strike some as detracting from God's personhood. This concern is understandable. Saying that God *is* justice or infinity or even love gives the impression of reducing the living God to an imper-

---

41. Staniloae, *The Experience of God,* vol. 1, *Revelation and Knowledge of the Triune God,* trans. and ed. Ioan Ionita and Robert Barringer (Brookline, MA: Holy Cross Orthodox Press, 1994), p. 141.

42. *CD,* 2/1, p. 257.

sonal abstraction. To counter this tendency, I shall emphasize that God's being (or nature) is not a static thing but a dynamic and living reality. God is action as well as being. The living God's existence is his action of being, and his eternal activity is his being. Instead of using abstract nouns to name God's attributes, we can just as well use verbs. God loves perfectly, and God is his loving action. God acts justly and is his action of doing perfect justice.

Since the words we use for God's attributes refer to God's one, simple nature without being synonyms, we cannot grasp the full meaning of an attribute by isolating it from all the others. On the contrary, only by exploring the relationships among the attributes can we grow in our understanding of each attribute and enrich our understanding of God. God is love, and God is freedom. The words "love" and "freedom" refer to the same simple reality; yet neither one alone can say all that needs to be said. Hence we gain greater insight by thinking them together: God is loving freedom and free love; God is just mercy and merciful justice; God is infinite wisdom and wise infinity. Using verbs and adverbs rather than nouns and adjectives, we can say that God loves freely and exercises freedom lovingly. God bestows mercy justly and exercises justice mercifully. We could continue this procedure for all the attributes in an almost infinite array of combinations of nouns and adjectives or verbs and adverbs. And as we engage in this exercise, the individual attributes grow more and more transparent to the God who is these things in perfect unity. This approach to the attributes works like a reverse prism that unites all the distinct colors of the spectrum into the original light, except that this light is too bright to take in. It begins to dawn on us that we are in the luminous presence of the one who is greater than all we can imagine or think. At this point our theology finds its fulfillment in doxology: silence, praise, and adoration.

The traditional lists of the attributes vary in the terms they use, but they include the following terms (or ones that are synonymous): oneness, simplicity, independence, infinity, eternity, immutability, impassibility, omniscience, omnipresence, omnipotence, wisdom, will, love, mercy, holiness, freedom, goodness, benevolence, patience, righteousness, justice, truth, grace, blessedness, glory, and beauty. With few exceptions, the church and her teachers have agreed for centuries that the attributes listed here are supported in Scripture and point adequately to the triune God that she worships. As we discuss these attributes individually, we will see that there have been differences of opinion about the exact meaning of some of the attributes. But on the whole the church has maintained a remarkable consensus on the doctrine of the attributes, so much so that the doctrine summarized by this list is often called the classical (or traditional) doctrine of God. In keeping with the method in this book, I shall take this consensus with utmost seriousness.

The Biblical Teaching on the Attributes

Before I examine each attribute individually, let us consider five ways that Scripture teaches about the divine attributes: (1) Scripture addresses God by several names that imply certain attributes; (2) sometimes the Bible makes explicit statements of attribution of the form "God is thus and so"; (3) some biblical statements attribute to God certain actions, and such statements take the general form "God does (or does not do) thus and so"; (4) the Bible narrates or describes events in which God acts; (5) finally, Scripture praises or thanks God for who he is or what he has done.

In this section and other sections where I cite biblical "proof-texts," only rarely will I enter into an exegetical discussion or cite studies by modern biblical scholars. I will not attempt to demonstrate that the traditional doctrine of God rests on interpretations of the Bible that meet the standards of modern biblical scholarship. Whatever the merits of such a project in other contexts — they are at least debatable — I make no pretense of accomplishing it here. I do not offer Scripture citations as *proof* of the church's teaching. I am making a less ambitious claim: my goal is to highlight the texts that traditional theologians have cited and to show that, at least on the surface, the traditional doctrine of God has scriptural warrant.

Modern biblical scholars often accuse traditional theology of "proof-texting," that is, of lifting verses of Scripture out of context and using the words to support doctrine without any concern for their historical and literary sense. There is no doubt that some traditional theologians have been guilty of this practice, as are some modern theologians. But Richard Muller has demonstrated that, in the case of the post-Reformation Reformed theologians, for example, this criticism is based on misunderstanding and ignorance and is guilty of doing the very thing it accuses others of doing. Many of the Reformed theologians began their careers as exegetes of Scripture and wrote massive commentaries on Scripture.[43] When they cite a text of Scripture in their theological work without extensive commentary, they assume that the reader understands that the "proof-text" points back "to the work of an exegetical tradition in which he was an active participant."[44] Admittedly, premodern exegetes do not use the methods of contemporary biblical interpretation; but they cannot justly be accused of carelessness or mindless dogmatism in their use of biblical texts. Muller demonstrates the extensive learn-

43. Muller, *PRRD*, 2, pp. 309-10.
44. Muller, *PRRD*, 2, pp. 309-10; see pp. 442-44 for an extensive treatment of the post-Reformation Reformed approach to the interpretation of Scripture.

ing of the traditional exegetes/theologians in the languages, literatures, and histories of the Bible and the ancient world and their painstaking grammatical and historical work as they studied Scripture. Many of the differences between premodern and modern biblical interpreters boil down to theological or philosophical disagreements.[45]

The Biblical Names of God

In the Bible, God is called by many names. Names were of greater significance in the ancient world than they are today: the name of a thing was supposed to correspond to the inner nature of the thing. The church fathers, the Protestant Reformers, and the post-Reformation orthodox Reformed were fascinated with the many names of God in Scripture. For the Reformers, "the names of God provided the Reformed with a primary source and focus for the *locus de Deo*."[46] The later Protestant scholastics viewed their discussions of the divine names "as the ground for all discussion of the essence and attributes."[47] For reasons I will delve into below, I cannot follow the tradition in this practice.

After making a covenant with Abram, God changed Abram's name to Abraham to reflect his new identity (Gen. 17). Jacob received a new name, Israel, after his struggle with God at the brook Jabbok (Gen. 32). As we noticed when discussing the doctrine of the Trinity, the "name" is a mode of God's presence (Deut. 12:5, 11, 12; 1 Kings. 5:5; 8:16-19; 9:3; Jer. 7:12). The third commandment reads: "You shall not misuse the name of the Lord your God, for the Lord will not hold anyone guiltless who misuses his name" (Exod. 20:7). Hence, a study of the biblical teaching on the attributes must consider the biblical names for God: *Yahweh, El, El Shaddai, El Elyon, El Olam, El Bethel, El Roi, El Berith, El Elohe-Israel, Elohim, Baal,* and *Adon.*

The name *Yahweh* holds a special place in the Bible, and speculation about its etymology and meaning is endless and inconclusive. The only text in the Old Testament that offers a clue to its meaning is Exodus 3:13-15: Moses asks the voice speaking from the burning bush his name, and God replies, "I am who I am." The Septuagint, the pre-Christian Greek translation of the Old Testament, translates the Hebrew expression "I am who I am" as *ego eimi ho on,* or "he who is." This translation led to the view that the name *Yahweh* expresses what is

45. See Muller, *PRRD*, 2, pp. 309-10.
46. Muller, *PRRD*, 3, p. 246.
47. Muller, *PRRD*, 3, p. 248. For a full discussion of the post-Reformation Reformed treatment of the divine names, see Muller, *PRRD*, 3, pp. 246-70.

known as God's aseity, or self-existent being. Contemporary scholars generally reject the Septuagint's interpretation.[48]

Old Testament scholars debate whether it means "I am here, present" or "I cause to be what comes into existence."[49] It does not appear that we are able to shed much light on the attributes of God merely from a linguistic study of the name Yahweh. However, Otto Weber draws three theological lessons from it. First, God has a personal name, which indicates that God is and acts as a person. Second, if we connect Exodus 3:14 with the whole Old Testament message, we can see that the church fathers were correct to see in the text an assertion of sovereignty and independence. God is who he is and is defined as God only in reference to himself. Third, "we learn that statements about God cannot be separated from those about God's covenant."[50] Yahweh is known as who he is in his deeds: election, calling, saving, and judging of his people in the history of salvation. Whereas the etymology of his name is obscure, Yahweh's acts define his identity clearly.

El is both a generic Semitic name for deity and a particular Canaanite god; its root meaning seems to be "power."[51] It is used of God most often in the Pentateuch narratives and in the poetic literature (Gen. 28; Num. 23:8, 19, 22-23; 24:4, 8, 16, 23; Ps. 16:1; 17:6; 85:8). *El* is also used in combinations that give more concrete attributes to God. God is called *El Shaddai* (Gen. 49:25; Num. 24:4, 16): perhaps it originally meant "the god of the mountain,"[52] and it was translated into Greek as *pantokrator* (ruler of all) in the Septuagint. Under the influence of the Septuagint, it is most often translated "God Almighty." The name *El Elyon*, God Most High, appears in the Melchizedek story in Genesis 14. Abraham recognizes *El Elyon* as "the maker of heaven and earth" (Gen. 14:22). References to this name also occur in the New Testament (Mark 5:7; Acts 7:48; 16:17; Heb. 7:1).

El Roi is used of God in the story of Hagar and may mean "the God who sees me" (Gen. 16:3).[53] *El Berith* (God of the Covenant) is used in Judges 9:46. *El*

48. Gerhard von Rad, *Old Testament Theology,* vol. 1, trans. D. M. G. Stalker (New York: Harper & Row Publishers, 1962). Von Rad argues that this text assures Moses of God's presence and hence emphasizes relative being rather than absolute being, "being there" as opposed to being absolutely considered (p. 180). For a similar conclusion, see Walther Eichrodt, *Theology of the Old Testament,* vol. 1, trans. J. A. Barker (Philadelphia: Westminster, 1961), p. 190.

49. *The Interpreter's Dictionary of the Bible,* vol. 2, ed. George A. Buttrick (Nashville: Abingdon, 1962), p. 410 (hereafter *IDB*).

50. Weber, *Foundations of Dogmatics,* 1, p. 418.

51. *IDB,* 2, p. 411.

52. *IDB,* 2, p. 412.

53. *IDB,* 2, p. 412.

Elohe-Israel (God of Israel) identifies the God whom Israel has known in her history. *Elohim* is a general name for deity; it often designates Yahweh as the sole deity, as in Elijah's challenge to the people of Israel: "If Yahweh is God *(Elohim)*, follow him; if Baal [is God] follow him" (1 Kings 18:21). The contest with the prophets of Baal proves that only Yahweh has the attributes of deity. It is debatable whether *Adon,* which means "lord," should be considered a name or a title. It can be used of human lords, but it can also be used appropriately of the "Lord of all the earth" (Josh. 3:11, 13; Ps. 97:5; Mic. 4:13; Zech 4:14; 6:5).

A study of the divine names alone cannot found the doctrine of the divine attributes: we cannot gain a precise understanding of the names isolated from their narrative and doxological contexts. We must bring to light the total biblical teaching on the attributes before we can attempt this task. Nevertheless, we can already see the outlines of the Christian doctrine of God taking shape. God is the sovereign maker and ruler of heaven and earth, who relates to his people as a You in his covenant with them. The God of Israel, the Lord of all, is the only one worthy of the designation "deity."

Statements of Direct Attribution

Whereas we have found it rather difficult to assess exactly what attributes the names of God imply, we find hundreds of texts in Scripture that directly attribute to God certain perfections or properties or characteristics. Scripture attributes to the Lord exclusive deity: "The Lord is God; besides him there is no other" (Deut. 4:35, 39; 1 Kings 8:60; 2 Chron. 33:13; Ps. 100:3); God is one (Deut. 6:4); God is just and righteous (Ps. 11:7; cf. 2 Chron. 12:6); God is loving (Num. 14:18; cf. 1 Kings 10:9; Ps. 100:5; 1 John 4:8, 16); God is great (Ps. 95:3); the Lord is king (Ps. 10:16; cf. Ps. 95:3; Isa. 33:22; Jer. 10:10; 1 Tim. 1:17); the Lord is good (Ps. 100:5; cf. 34:4). We could continue this list indefinitely with texts that assert that God is compassionate, merciful, gracious, faithful, holy, powerful, all-knowing, jealous, and spiritual.

Statements about God's Actions

Scripture refers to God's actions on almost every page and explicitly or implicitly points from those actions to the attributes of the divine Agent. The relationship between God's actions and his attributes is well illustrated by a text from Deuteronomy that emphasizes the unique nature of God's deity and greatness shown in his deeds:

Has any other people heard the voice of God speaking out of fire, as you have, and lived? Has any god ever tried to take for himself one nation out of another nation, by testings, by miraculous signs and wonders, by war, by a mighty hand and an outstretched arm, or by great and awesome deeds, like all the things the Lord your God did for you in Egypt before your very eyes? You were shown these things so that you might know that the Lord is God; besides him there is no other (Deut. 4:32-35; cf. Deut. 32:39-42; 1 Chron. 17:20-22).

God created all things (Gen. 1:1; cf. Is. 42:5; Mark 13:19; Acts 4:24; Eph. 3:9; Rev. 4:11; 10:6). He will "judge the world in righteousness" (Ps. 9:8; cf. Joel 3:12; Deut. 1:17). God makes covenant and gives promises (Gen. 9:15; Heb. 8:8; 9:15; Ps. 119:140; 2 Cor. 1:20). God speaks (Exod. 20:1; Heb. 1:1). God is present everywhere (Jer. 23:23, 24; Ps. 139:7-12). God knows the future (Isa. 42:9; cf. 44:6-8; 48:3-8). God is unlimited: "The Lord does whatever pleases him, in the heavens and on the earth, in the seas and all their depths" (Ps. 135:5, 6).

Scripture also uses the language of negation to contrast God with creatures. God is not fickle and changeable: "God is not a man, that he should lie, or a son of man, that he should change his mind" (Num. 23:19; James 1:17; Heb. 1:12). Unlike humanity, God is immortal and invisible: "God, the blessed and only Ruler, the King of kings and Lord of lords, who alone is immortal and who lives in unapproachable light, whom no one has seen or can see" (1 Tim. 6:15-16; 1:17; Rom. 1:23). God is not subject to the decay of time as is creation, for he is eternal (Ps. 102:3-27; cf. Ps. 90:2; Rev. 1:8). God is inscrutable (Isa. 55:8-9; Rom. 11:3-36; 1 Cor. 2:11). God is in no way subject to evil (James 1:13).

Narratives of God's Actions

In some cases, the Bible narrates the actions of God without reflecting on them. The creation narrative of Genesis (Gen. 1–2), the story of Abraham's "sacrifice" of Isaac (Gen. 22:1-18), the Joseph story (Gen. 37–50), the Exodus (Exod. 1–15), the giving of the law at Sinai (Exod. 19–24), the desert wanderings (Num. 13–27), and the conquest of Canaan (Josh. 1–12) presuppose and imply many attributes of God. In the creation narrative, for example, things are created at God's command, "Let there be" (Gen. 1:3, 6). There is no battle or struggle to overcome chaos. For God, creation is easy. God creates the heavenly bodies, just as he creates the fish and birds. They are not gods, but lights with very practical functions. In the story of Abraham, God demonstrates that he has the right to demand the life of Isaac, Abraham's "beloved son"; yet God provides a ram to take Isaac's place. The story of Joseph brims with lessons about God's providential control of the world. God gives Joseph dreams that reveal the future, but these very dreams also cause his brothers to rage with jealousy, thereby setting in motion events that would lead to the future that the dreams anticipated. Human actions and intentions — arrogance, jealousy, compassion, and lust — all work together to accomplish not what human beings desire in those feelings but what God wills.

In the Exodus story God shows faithfulness and compassion toward his enslaved people and demonstrates his sovereign power even in a foreign land. One by one, in a series of plagues, the gods of Egypt are shown to be impotent against the power of the Lord. At the giving of the law at Sinai, God demonstrates his holiness in the awesome scene. He demands exclusive worship from the people and complete respect for his name. As the Creator and Israel's redeemer, he claims exclusive right to life and property. In the desert wanderings, we see God's judgment visited on the people as well his provision for them in the desolate places of their travels. In the conquest of Canaan, God once again demonstrates his universal sovereignty and power as he fights for the people against the gods and people of the land and keeps his promise to Abraham.

The Praise of Israel and the Church

The attributes of God are raised to special prominence in the Bible's prayers, psalms, poetry, and doxologies. After being delivered from Egypt, Moses and the people sing a song praising the Lord: "I will sing a song to the Lord, for he is highly exalted. . . . Your right hand, O Lord, was majestic in power. . . . Who is like you among the gods, O Lord? Majestic in holiness, awesome in glory, working wonders" (Exod. 15:1-18; cf. Deut. 32:1-43). The Psalms of Israel are filled with praise: "O Lord, our Lord, how majestic is your name in all the earth!" (Ps. 8:1). Isaiah saw a vision of the Lord surrounded by heavenly creatures crying, "Holy, holy, holy, is the Lord Almighty; the whole earth is full of his glory" (Isa. 6:1-3). Paul's doxology at the end of Romans 11 is justly famous:

> Oh, the depth of the riches of the wisdom and knowledge of God! How unsearchable his judgments, and his paths beyond tracing out! "Who has known the mind of the Lord? Or who has been his counselor?" "Who has ever given to God, that God should repay him?" For from him and through him and to him are all things. To him be the glory forever! Amen (Rom. 11:33-36; cf. Jude 24-25).

The book of Revelation overflows with praise and adoration. The living creatures incessantly praise God: "Holy, holy, holy is the Lord God Almighty, who was, and is, and is to come" (Rev. 4:8). Angels cry, "Worthy" (5:12), and the heavenly company falls down and cries, "Amen! Praise and glory and wisdom and thanks and honor and power and strength be to our God for ever and ever. Amen!" The seven angels with the seven last plagues sing the song of the Lamb: "Great and marvelous are your deeds, Lord God Almighty. Just and true are your ways, King of the ages. Who will not fear you, O Lord, and bring glory to your name? For you alone are holy. All nations will come and worship before you, for your righteous acts have been revealed" (Rev. 15:3-4). After Babylon, the fierce enemy of God's people, is destroyed, the great multitude in heaven shouted: "Hallelujah! Salvation and glory and power belong to our God, for true and just are his judgments. . . . Hallelujah! For our Lord God Almighty reigns. Let us rejoice and be glad and give him glory" (Rev. 19:1-2, 6).

Summary of Biblical Data on the Attributes

Biblical teaching on the divine attributes is extensive and detailed, so much so that even this survey has grown quite long. But we have seen enough to conclude that the church's traditional teaching on the attributes is well grounded in the teaching of Scripture. For Scripture proclaims that God is loving, holy, just, good, and merciful. He is faithful and present; he cares, and he guides the world by the counsel of his good will and leads it unfailingly to its appointed destination. His power, knowledge, and presence know no limits. His life knows no boundaries in time or space. He has no rivals and is worthy of our adoration and praise. "Great is the Lord, and most worthy of praise!" (Ps. 48:1).

6

Love Transcendent:
Divine Love, Righteousness, and Holiness

God Is Love

Toward the middle of the twelfth century, the Italian Cardinal Haimeric wrote to Bernard of Clairvaux (1090-1153) to ask him this question: "Why should we love God, and what is the measure of that love?" Bernard wrote his book *On Loving God* as a response to that question. It begins this way: "You want me to tell you why God is to be loved and how much. I answer, the reason for loving God is God Himself; and the measure of love due to Him is immeasurable love." Bernard approaches his task with the assumption that, if we realized who God is and how much he loves us, we would know why we should love him and how much:

> And first, of His title to our love. Could any title be greater than this, that He gave Himself for us unworthy wretches? And being God, what better gift could He offer than Himself? Hence, if one seeks for God's claim upon our love here is the chiefest: Because He first loved us (1 John 4:19). Ought He not to be loved in return, when we think who loved, whom He loved, and how much He loved? For who is He that loved?[1]

God's loving acts on our behalf reveal God's heart to such an extent that John can say, "God is love" (1 John 4:8). John's equation provides an astounding answer to Bernard's last question ("Who is He that loved?"): Love itself loved us. God, who is love, loved us with the love he is. Another great spiritual writer, this one from the seventeenth century, says in a commentary on 1 John 4:8:

---

1. Bernard of Clairvaux, *On Loving God*, ch. 5. Available at http://www.ccel.org/ccel/bernard/loving_god.vii.html (accessed April 2, 2005).

"*God is love* . . . he who loves Him not, does not know Him, for how could we know love without loving it?"[2] May we learn to know love and love it.

Scriptural Teaching

Creation is a gift. What words can carry the weight of thanksgiving that is due our Creator? God created the heavens and the earth and "gives breath to its people and life to those who walk on it" (Isa. 42:5). God "gives autumn and spring rains in season" and "assures us of the regular weeks of harvest" (Jer. 5:24). God "gives all men life and breath and everything else" (Acts 17:25). Jesus bore witness to the generosity of God in creation when he gave thanks for the five loaves and two fish (Mark 6:41). And Paul approves of eating meat for the one who "gives thanks to God" (Rom. 14:6).

God's creatures had no right to exist before God created them. And God had no obligation to create the world one way rather than another: "Shall what is formed say to him who formed it, 'Why did you make me like this?'" (Rom. 9:20). God had no needs that motivated him to create a world (Acts 17:25). But God's generous act of creation is the first manifestation of his eternal love toward us.

God made covenants with Noah, Abraham, the people of Israel, and with the church. Nothing before creation required God to create and nothing in creation requires God to establish a relationship with humanity in the covenant. The Lord tells his people that he did not choose them because of their fine qualities. The reason was less flattering but more comforting: "It was because the Lord loved you and kept the oath he swore to your forefathers" (Deut. 7:7-8). In making those covenants, God promises not to abandon his creatures to fate or fortune. In other words, God binds himself to be with us and for us without being required to do so.

But human beings broke the covenant and spurned God's love: our first ancestors became the first sinners and set the trajectory for their children. The sea had hardly closed on the Egyptians when the Israelites began grumbling faithlessly in the desert and then fashioned a golden calf to lead them back to Egypt. At the threshold of the Promised Land, the people believed the report of the ten faithless spies and rebelled against the Lord. Israel's prophets indicted her for breaking the covenant. Jeremiah records the Lord's complaint: "They have returned to the sins of their forefathers, who refused to listen to my words"

2. Francois Fenelon, *Spiritual Counsel on Divers Matters Pertaining to the Inner Life*, 2. Available at http://www.ccel.org/ccel/fenelon/progress.iii.i.html (accessed June 28, 2005).

(Jer. 11:10). Sadly, the Lord's plaintive words in Isaiah apply to every age: "All day long I have held out my hands to an obstinate people . . . a people who continually provoke me to my very face" (Isa. 65:2-3).

Paul indicts the nations for their "godlessness and wickedness" (Rom. 1). The gentiles do not have the Jewish covenant or law; nonetheless, they are without excuse. They do not "give thanks" to their Creator (Rom. 1:21). Rather than looking up to God, they worship lower things, images of "mortal man and birds and animals and reptiles" (1:23). They explore every lust and desire and every illicit pleasure. Paul ends that first chapter of Romans with a litany of evils that would inspire any jury to exact the maximum penalty: "They have become filled with every kind of wickedness, evil, greed, and depravity . . . . They not only continue to do these very things but also approve of those who practice them" (1:28-32).

God had no obligation to create, no obligation to make a covenant with human beings, and certainly no obligation to forgive and save ungrateful sinners. But he did. God's love is demonstrated definitively by the incarnation and death of Christ. The Father waits for the prodigal to return home (Luke 15:11-32). The Son of God washes feet (John 13:1-17). Christ, though rich, "became poor" so that we might become rich (2 Cor. 8:9). The love of Christ "compels us, because we are convinced that one died for all" (2 Cor. 5:14). Though existing in the "form of God," he humbled himself to die on a cross for sinners who arrogate to themselves the prerogatives of God (Phil. 2:5-11). Even though we deserved wrath and judgment, God forgave us because of his "great love for us" (Eph. 2:4).

God's love is unlike any other: he gives being to those who are nothing; he establishes fellowship with the ungrateful; and, most amazingly, he loves godless rebels, forgives their sins, and takes their punishment on himself! God's love is revealed as sovereign and free of all restraints and all ends outside itself. His love is not determined in any way by its object. In creation God created the object of his love from nothing. In making covenant, God established a loving relationship that did not exist beforehand. And in reconciliation God loved us, not because we were just, but in order to create a justified people. God is love!

Theology of the Love of God

We cannot presume to fully grasp the character of God's love; yet we remember that Paul prays that his Ephesian readers "grasp how wide and long and high and deep is the love of Christ, and to know this love that surpasses knowledge" (Eph. 3:18-19). Though we cannot define God's love in a way that makes it transparent, let us consider a preliminary definition to set the stage for the following discussion.

Divine Love Defined

One contemporary theologian defines God's love in terms of God's relationship to his creatures: God's love is his "self-giving affection for his image-bearing creatures and his unselfish concern for their well-being that leads him to act on their behalf and for their happiness."[3] Though it is certainly true that God loves the world, this definition does not bring out the essential nature of God's love, and it risks making it a mere contingent response to creation. Another contemporary theologian treats divine love under the heading "God's self-love."[4] The dangers of such a concept should be obvious. Because love and self-centeredness cannot be easily reconciled, I believe it is best to avoid the notion that God loves himself. God has no self-relationship apart from the Trinitarian relationship. Wolfhart Pannenberg rightly insists that the persons of the Trinity do not love themselves in each other but are themselves in their love for the others.[5] Following the medieval teaching (e.g., Aquinas, *SumTh,* 1.20.1), the orthodox Reformed tended to define God's love with reference to the good. God loves himself as the highest good. In his love for creatures, explains Francis Turretin (1623-1687), God wills to communicate "himself to the creature and (as it were) wills to unite himself to it and do it good" (1.3.20).[6] While the Reformed view can be interpreted benignly, it could create confusion. For God's love is not secondary to a prior impersonal good that moves God to love. The goodness of God *is* the love of God; the good that God bestows on us *is* the love that God is.

I shall define God's love as the *free, total, and unconditional self-giving, -receiving, and -returning that constitute the eternal life of the Trinity.* In love, the Father eternally gives himself to the Son (John 17:24); the Son receives the Father and returns himself to the Father in complete obedience (John 15:9, 10); the Fa-

---

3. Jack Cottrell, *What the Bible Says About God the Redeemer* (Joplin, MO: College Press, 1987), p. 336.

4. John Frame, *The Doctrine of God: A Theology of Lordship* (Phillipsburg, NJ: Presbyterian and Reformed, 2002), p. 416. In fairness to Frame, I should note that his treatment of God's self-love is thoroughly Trinitarian.

5. Pannenberg, *Systematic Theology,* vol. 1, trans. Geoffrey Bromiley (Grand Rapids: Eerdmans, 1991), p. 426.

6. Turretin, *Institutes of Elenctic Theology,* vol. 1, trans. George Musgrave Giger, ed. James T. Dennison, Jr. (Phillipsburg, NJ: Presbyterian and Reformed, 1992), p. 241. For details of the orthodox Reformed view, see Richard Muller, *Post-Reformation Reformed Dogmatics: The Rise and Development of Reformed Orthodoxy,* vol. 3, *The Divine Essence and Attributes* (Grand Rapids: Baker Academic, 2003), pp. 561-69 (hereafter *PRRD*).

ther gives his love through the Spirit (Rom. 5:5); and the Son renders obedience "through the eternal Spirit" (Heb. 9:4). It is the very nature of the Father to love the Son in the Spirit, and it is the very nature of the Son to return the love of the Father in the Spirit. God would not be God without this love any more than God would be God without omnipotence or independence or unity. But divine love is also free: the Father freely and joyously gives himself to the Son, and the Son freely and joyously returns the Father's love.[7] Nothing forces the Father to love the Son, and nothing compels the Son to return the Father's love. God is not a prisoner of his nature. In Trinitarian love we see unity of being and action and of necessity and freedom. God's love is necessary because it is his nature to love. His natural and necessary love is free because God is completely himself in his action of love. The inner Trinitarian love is the archetype of all other loves, and even God's love for the world must be understood in its light.

God's Love for the World

God reveals his love for the world in the incarnation of the Son of the Father in the power of the Spirit. His love for us is the gracious outreach of that inner Trinitarian love by which God is God: a *free, total, and unconditional self-giving, -receiving, and -returning.*[8] The Father sends the Son into the world to unite creation to himself: that is, the Father loves the world through the Son. The Son obeys the Father and returns the love of the Father. In the Son — because the Son has united himself to the world in the incarnation — the world accepts the love of the Father and obediently returns his love. God thus brings the world, through the Son, into the giving, receiving, and returning of the eternal divine life and love. Dumitru Staniloae describes this event beautifully: "Simultaneously the Son filled human nature with his divine love for the Father."[9]

One important difference, however, between inner Trinitarian love and di-

7. See Lewis Ayres, "Augustine, Christology, and God as Love: An Introduction to the Homilies on 1 John," in *Nothing Greater, Nothing Better: Theological Essays on the Love of God,* ed. Kevin J. Vanhoozer (Grand Rapids: Eerdmans, 2001), p. 88. Ayres shows how Augustine roots God's love in the Trinitarian relationship: for Augustine, "[t]he Father's act of generation and spiration involves an act of sharing himself absolutely as loving, continually self-offering communion."

8. Alan Torrance, "Is Love the Essence of God?" in Vanhoozer, ed., *Nothing Greater, Nothing Better.* Torrance addresses the issue of how we *know* about inner-Trinitarian love: "To the extent that the life of Christ denotes the irreducibly historical self-giving of God in the deliverance of a lost humanity, it constitutes the essential ground of our affirming the *agape* of God" (p. 131).

9. Staniloae, *The Experience of God,* vol. 1, *Revelation and Knowledge of the Triune God,* trans. and ed. Ioan Ionita and Robert Barringer (Brookline, MA: Holy Cross Orthodox Press, 1994), p. 243.

vine love for the world stands out: though God's love for the world is free because he is completely himself in his love, it is not essential and necessary. For God would be God even if there were no world outside the Trinity. That God loved the world from all eternity, gave it being in time, and wills to redeem it into eternity is sheer grace. It is an overflow, an excess, a mystery of divine love, and the proper response to it is amazement, gratitude, and self-abandoning love. Karl Barth speaks similarly of God's love for the world: "It implies so to speak an overflow of His essence that He turns to us. We must certainly regard this overflow as itself matching His essence . . . [but not demanded] by any law by which God Himself is bound and obligated."[10]

Divine Love Is Free

Let us explore the contrast between divine love and human love. We cannot love freely because we do not exist freely. We did not choose to exist or decide what to be, because we receive our being from another. We cannot give ourselves freely because we do not possess ourselves freely: that is, our giving to others is always conditioned by our need for them. We fear being absorbed or rejected by them, and this fear is not irrational. As sinners, we are more likely to enlarge ourselves at the expense of others than to return love for love. The self-giving of love risks the complete loss of self. Love is a kind of death.

But God *is* love. Nothing outside God determines God's nature as love. When God acts according to his nature, he is not obeying a law imposed from without. He is completely free and totally himself in his action. His infinite love does not need to be rationed. Since God does not depend on a reality outside himself, the purity of God's love cannot be poisoned by fear of lack and loss. God does not love because his beloved is lovely. Everything worthy about the object of God's love — even its very existence — is the result of God's love, not its cause. God does not fear rejection. The Son's love for the Father is unshakable, for it is just as necessary as it is free. And because of the incarnation of the Son, who loves the Father from all eternity, the world also participates in the free and necessary love the Son has for the Father. God's love for the world will not remain unrequited. The world's reception and return of the Father's love is assured; indeed, it is an accomplished fact.

Many people find themselves unable to believe that God really loves them. They suspect that God may have created us for a reason that is at odds with our ultimate joy. Are God's gifts — his commands and the limits he imposes — re-

---

10. Barth, *Church Dogmatics*, vol. 2, pt. 1, ed. G. W. Bromiley and T. F. Torrance, trans. T. H. L. Parker et al. (Edinburgh: T&T Clark, 1957), p. 273 (hereafter *CD*).

ally for our good? Does God have another agenda, perhaps *his* goodness or glory or sovereignty, that explains why he pays attention to us? Or is God just being God when he loves us, like an apple tree is just being itself when it produces its lovely fruit? Others think that God could not possibly love people with such shameful résumés as theirs. Let us put an end to these doubts: God's love has no ground other than his love. God does not love us because it brings him glory, for his love is his glory. He does not love "to possess and to enjoy."[11] Nor can his love be hindered by anything in us.

Barth rightly declares, "He loves because He loves."[12] There is no more basic explanation, "no *why* beyond itself."[13] God does not love us because of anything in us or anything he gains by loving us. C. S. Lewis is correct when he says, "God, who needs nothing, loves into existence wholly superfluous creatures in order that He may love and perfect them." Strangely, in my view, Gary D. Badcock accuses Lewis of portraying God in that statement as "a simple fool, or worse again, a masochist." For "who or what, after all, in all the universe gives itself up for nothing?"[14] I suppose Badcock expects us to answer, "Nothing and no one." But I argue that God did in fact "give himself up" for a "nothing." And that is the glory of his love.

Contrary Views: Is God's Love Really Free?

Is divine love really free? Is it so different from human love? In this subsection I will test my thesis by contrasting it with two contemporary alternative views of God's love.

Divine Love's Risk?

In his study *Satan and the Problem of Evil*, Gregory Boyd develops an approach to the problem of evil in which the concept of love plays a central role.[15] According to Boyd, God created the world out of love and for the purpose of es-

---

11. Donald G. Bloesch, *God the Almighty: Power, Wisdom, Holiness, Love* (Downers Grove, IL: InterVarsity Press, 1995), p. 145.

12. *CD*, 2/1, p. 279.

13. Thomas Torrance, *The Christian Doctrine of God: One Being, Three Persons* (London: T&T Clark, 1996), p. 244.

14. C. S. Lewis, *The Four Loves* (New York: Harcourt, Inc., 1960), p. 127; Gary D. Badcock, "The Concept of Love Divine and Human," in Kevin J. Vanhoozer, ed., *Nothing Greater, Nothing Better*, p. 43.

15. Boyd, *Satan and the Problem of Evil: Constructing a Trinitarian Warfare Theodicy* (Downers Grove, IL: InterVarsity Press, 2001).

tablishing loving relationships with personal beings. But God's project is risky because achieving it requires him to give his potential partners freedom to respond to his love with acceptance and love — or to refuse it. For the capacity to love always "entails the possibility of its antithesis." Therefore, God had to make evil possible if he wanted to make a world where love is possible. It is "not logically possible," says Boyd, for God to achieve this end without risking the possibility that great evil will be unleashed (p. 17). Boyd articulates six theses in the course of his argument, the first two of which concern the nature of love.

Boyd's first thesis postulates that "love must be chosen." By its very nature, love must arise freely in the heart of the lover. For Boyd, "the possibility of saying no to God must be metaphysically entailed by the possibility of saying yes to him" (p. 53). The power to love and the power to refuse love are the same power. Thus, if God chooses to create creatures with the power to love, God has no further choice about whether they shall have the power to withhold love. The second thesis postulates that "freedom implies risk" (p. 86). According to Boyd, for a choice to be genuinely free, it cannot be preceded by something that determines it in advance; hence, there is no way for God to know the future free actions of creatures as certainties. But, since God knows all possibilities, he knew at the time of creation that human beings might "choose to oppose him" (p. 91). However, Boyd concludes, God did not know this for a fact, and thus we cannot hold God accountable for creating the world knowing that evil would break out and plague creation.[16] However, this easy method of securing God's innocence and preserving a sort of human freedom may become less attractive when we realize what we are asked to surrender in return: the sovereign and triumphant freedom of divine love.

Divine Love's Need?

Vincent Brümmer, in his studies *The Model of Love* and *Speaking of a Personal God*, develops a theory of God's personhood and explores the implications of God's relationship with his creatures.[17] According to Brümmer, three kinds of relationships among persons are possible: manipulative, agreements of rights and duties, and fellowship. Only the last rises to the level of love, for only in fellowship does "each partner choose to serve the interests of the other and not

---

16. See also Clark H. Pinnock, *Most Moved Mover: A Theology of God's Openness* (Grand Rapids: Baker Academic, 2001). Note, esp., ch. 3, "The Metaphysics of Love," where Pinnock uses a philosophically derived concept of love to determine what is possible for God.

17. Brümmer, *The Model of Love: A Study in Philosophical Theology* (Cambridge, UK: Cambridge University Press, 1993); see also Brümmer, *Speaking of a Personal God: An Essay in Philosophical Theology* (Cambridge, UK: Cambridge University Press, 1992).

primarily his own." In such a relationship each partner depends on the other. "It is logically impossible for either partner to establish or maintain the relationship by him- or herself" (*Speaking*, p. 141). For Brümmer, love must "be a relationship of give and take, otherwise it cannot be love at all" (*Model*, p. 161). Brümmer declares that these principles apply to divine love as well as to human love. Therefore, he rejects the idea that God's love is pure giving *(agape)* and introduces into God the concept of longing *(eros)*. By creating humans and giving them the freedom by which they can choose to love or not love, God becomes "dependent on the freedom and responsibility of human persons in order to enter into loving relations with them" (*Model*, p. 143). God thereby "assumes vulnerability in relation to them" (*Model*, p. 143). Brümmer speaks for many other contemporary theologians who reject the idea that God's love is pure benevolence and advocate God's need for responding love from the world.

A similar view is developed by process thinkers and others. Charles Hartshorne says: "To love is to rejoice with the joys and sorrow with the sorrow of others. Thus it is to be influenced by those who are loved." Paul Fiddes contends: "To love is to be in a relationship where what the loved one does alters one's own experience." Sallie McFague rejects self-giving love and replaces it with a relational model. She explains: "The model of God as lover, then, implies that God needs us to help save the world." Gary Badcock recognizes the danger of speaking "strictly" about God having needs. Nonetheless, he does speak tentatively and (I think) imprecisely about God needing our love: "The evidence suggests that God wants a response of love, and that in this sense — because he is love, perhaps — the response of love is something that is appropriate for God to need. We cannot ultimately penetrate the heavens to speak of what God is from eternity to eternity, but in the world of God's outreach and of human response it seems to this extent entirely appropriate to speak of God's 'need' of the world."[18]

Response to the Critics: Yes, God's Love Really Is Free

The line of thought pursued by Brümmer and Boyd is only too plausible. If a risky and needy love rings true to our experience, this is because it is based on our experience. Boyd's and Brümmer's theories do not begin with inner Trini-

18. Charles Hartshorne, *A Natural Theology for Our Time* (LaSalle, IL: Open Court, 1967), p. 75; Paul Fiddes, *The Creative Suffering of God* (Oxford: Clarendon Press, 1988), p. 50; Sally McFague, *Models of God: Theology for an Ecological, Nuclear Age* (Philadelphia: Fortress, 1987), p. 130; Gary D. Badcock, "The Concept of Love: Divine and Human," in *Nothing Greater, Nothing Better*, p. 45.

tarian love and move toward God's love for the world. They begin with the fragmentary human experience of love and attempt to clarify it conceptually and lay out the conditions necessary for its exercise. They do not judge human love by divine love; they bind divine love to human love as we know it. Brümmer is very clear about this: "If God is a God of love, as believers claim, then all this [his philosophical analysis of love] applies also to the sort of relation which God wants to establish and maintain with human persons" (*Model*, p. 142).

Boyd acknowledges that inner Trinitarian love is essential and necessary, and hence does not involve risk. Unfortunately, he considers it an exception to the rule instead of the norm for other loves. Because he defines freedom in libertarian fashion, that is, as something open to alternatives, Boyd cannot think of inner Trinitarian love as free. Boyd is half right, for it is repugnant to think of the Father as free to *refuse* to love the Son and the Son the Father.[19] But Boyd neglects the other half of the truth: it is equally repugnant to deny that the Father and the Son love each other *freely* just because their love is essential to their being. In contrast to Boyd, I believe that doing justice to God's love requires us to affirm that inner Trinitarian love is both free and essential — and normative for other loves. I will develop this important thesis further in my discussion of divine freedom.

It is regrettable that Brümmer and Boyd do not found their understanding of God's love for the world on a Trinitarian basis. They imagine that God attempts to establish previously nonexisting relationships with autonomous individuals the way we try to make new friends — by sharing our stories, gifts, smiles, and enjoying activities together. Without wishing to deny that such things have something to do with our relationship to God, I insist that we recognize that the Father's loving relationship with the world is centered and made concrete in the human being who is also his beloved Son. Without humans' cooperation or choice, God united himself to human nature and liberated it for love. In Jesus Christ, God brings the world into the circle of inner Trinitarian love. For God loves his Son freely and without any possibility of not loving him. In the man Jesus our humanity freely returns God's love without any possibility of refusal; that is, in the Son and through the power of the Spirit, humanity receives God's love and pours out its life on the cross in free obedience. In the person of the Son, the world receives *and returns* the Father's love and finds its true realization and freedom in self-abandonment to God.

I shall reflect at length on divine freedom later, but it is not too early to contrast the view I am defending with those who, like Boyd and Brümmer, define freedom so that it excludes essentiality or inner necessity. If we were to ap-

---

19. Boyd, *Satan and the Problem of Evil*, p. 53.

ply their concept of freedom to the inner life of God, the Christian understanding of God would fall apart. We could not assert God's necessary existence without denying that he exists freely. Or, if we affirmed God's essential freedom, we would be forced to deny that he is essentially loving, holy, just, living, infinite, or good. To be free in a libertarian way, God would have to be able to act in opposition to these things. God's deity would become a chaotic infinite power. God might be or do anything — or nothing!

However, if we begin from God's self-revelation as the Holy Trinity and the incarnate Son, rather than with our own insights, we will affirm that God is *all* his attributes essentially. We will not pit one against the other. God is love *and* God is freedom. God loves essentially *and* freely. God is free not because he could have been (and can be) other than himself or because he can just as well not love as love. God is free because he is himself completely in his action, which is his eternal life. God is free precisely in his "inability" to contradict himself. Divine freedom is the norm for all other freedoms, and I shall apply it rigorously in future chapters.

The Amazing Nature of Divine Love

We experience amazement even in human love. The experience of being loved is often accompanied by a sense of surprise, because love always has within it an element of gratuity. The difference between love and a commercial transaction is dramatic: love acts unconditionally, whereas a commercial transaction depends on an agreeable response. Central to the experience of being loved is the sense of wonder that our beloved loves us. Our experience would be soured were we to discover the reason. It is precisely its unfounded nature that makes love so wonderful and enjoyable.

Divine love is utterly amazing because it crosses spans, overcomes oppositions, and harmonizes contradictions. When we see oppositions, we look for a third thing to bridge the gap and mediate between the contradictory elements; or we give up the effort to reconcile them. We do not expect one of the elements to act as the mediator. But God, in his incomprehensible love, reaches across the infinite divide and unites himself with his enemy.

The First Barrier: Nothingness

God is God, the fullness of being and joy. Of ourselves, we are nothing, and we have nothing that God has not given us. Why, then, did God create us? Why should God love a nothing? What can we add to his being or joy? But God bridges the gap in love, and he gives being to something that is not. Why? Because he loved us. Beyond that, reasoning must give way to wonder and praise.

God's activity is weighty, worthy, and effective. God gives the command, and it is done. What God does matters, and what he says counts. The Psalms of Israel witness to this: "How many are your works, O Lord! In wisdom you made them all; the earth is full of your creatures" (Ps. 104:24). In contrast to God, what can we do? That which *is* nothing can *do* nothing. Our existence and capacity for action are gifts; indeed, they are constantly being given to us. But let us lay aside this fact for a moment and assume that our capacity for action is our possession. What can we do that matters? Time sweeps away all our deeds, so that even the "greatest" of them is like writing in the sand. With mighty efforts we rearrange atoms into an order that pleases us — in architecture, statuary, paintings, writing, and empires — but entropy soon randomizes them into the chaos from which they came. Compared to the universe, our actions amount to nothing; they do not register on the scales of the universe. Atomic war or universal peace on earth is all the same to the universe beyond our solar system. Surely the writer of Ecclesiastes was correct: "'Meaningless! Meaningless!'" says the Teacher, "'Utterly meaningless! Everything is meaningless.' What does a man gain from all his labor at which he toils under the sun? Generations come and generations go, but the earth remains forever" (Eccles. 1:2-4).

Why, then, should God care about us? Are we a factor God must take into account? Does God need us in some way? Certainly not. Nevertheless, God cares about us and freely makes us a factor in his eternal plan to redeem creation and bless it with his unveiled presence. And we stand amazed.

The Second Barrier: Sin

God is holy and just. In all his deeds God is true to himself and faithful to his promises. In contrast, we act in opposition to our true selves and break our covenant promises. Rather than acknowledging God's gifts with grateful hearts, we take our lives for granted; or, even worse, we use them as if we had created ourselves. When we ought to honor God by conforming to his holiness and justice, we follow our own foolish inclinations and reject the divine wisdom embodied in God's law.

Even if we admit that God has bridged the gaps between being and nothingness, between meaning and meaninglessness, why should the righteous and holy God reach out to an ungrateful and arrogant sinner? That which is nothing might at least arouse pity, since its pitiful state is not its own doing. But the ungrateful lawbreaker who considers himself wiser than God clearly deserves the consequences of his actions. Divine righteousness on one side and human unrighteousness on the other, God's holiness above and our unholiness beneath — how can God bridge such chasms? And why would he do so if he could?

To our amazement, God wills to have fellowship with the unrighteous: he chooses to save sinners from the consequences of their actions. When Jesus ate with sinners, those who did not expect God's love to be so amazing took offense (Mark 2:17). Paul experienced firsthand the surprising nature of God's love: "Christ Jesus came into the world to save sinners — of whom I am the worst" (1 Tim. 1:15). In Christ, God reconciled sinners to himself, "not counting men's sins against them" (2 Cor. 5:19-21). Why does God forgive sinners and reconcile them to himself by taking on their sin? Because he loves us with a love that "surpasses knowledge" (Eph. 3:19), and that provokes our wonder and amazement.

The Third Barrier: Rejection

God bridges the gaps between being and nothingness, between meaning and meaninglessness, and between righteousness and unrighteousness. Even these crossings amaze us beyond all comprehension. Yet there is one more contradiction that God's love conquers, and this one is even more amazing, if that is possible. It is utterly unbridgeable and without analogy. In creation, covenant, and forgiveness, God reaches out to us; yet time after time we reject his grace, spurn his love, and refuse his forgiveness. Perhaps a "no" to God's law could be forgiven. But what hope is there for the one who rejects a pardon because he feels no need of forgiveness? Can God's grace overcome human rejection of his grace? Paul gives a startling answer to this question: "The law was added so that the trespass might increase. But where sin increased, grace increased all the more, so that, just as sin reigned in death, so also grace might reign through righteousness to bring eternal life through Jesus Christ our Lord" (Rom. 5:20-21).

In the incarnation and atonement we confront the bottomless depth of God's love. God overcomes our arrogance with his humility; he conquers our disobedience with his obedience; he negates our "no" with his "yes." And his love displaces our hate. What we could not do, did not want to do, he did for us. "When we were God's enemies, we were reconciled to him through the death of his Son" (Rom. 5:6-10; cf. Eph. 2:1-5).

Jesus Christ is God's amazing love for us: realized, embodied, and perfected in the world. He is God's perfect love for us *and* our perfect love for God in the same person. In him God gives being to our nothingness, displaces our meaninglessness with his meaning, overcomes our sin with his righteousness, and negates our rejection by his acceptance. God is love!

The Holiness of His Love

As we begin to speak of God's holiness, we are not speaking about something foreign to his love. If we could see God's love as it really is, we would see his holiness as well. For God's love is a holy love. God's love differs from all others, and it opposes anything that would oppose it. It is holy precisely because it is *God's* love.

The Holy God in Scripture

The Hebrew root *qds* may mean "separation," or it may indicate "brightness."[20] Whatever the root meaning, a holy thing differs from ordinary things and must be separated from them. The Septuagint translated the Hebrew *qds* as *hagios*, and the New Testament follows the Septuagint in using *hagios* and its derivatives almost exclusively.[21] In Scripture we find many holy things. Particular times are holy: "And God blessed the seventh day and made it holy" (Gen. 2:3). There are holy places: "Do not come any closer," God said. "Take off your sandals, for the place where you are standing is holy ground" (Exod. 3:5). The plan for the Tabernacle includes a holy place and a most holy place (Exod. 26:33; cf. Lev. 16:2). The people of Israel are a holy people, "a kingdom of priests" (Exod. 19:6). The tabernacle and (later) the temple furniture, utensils, and altar are all holy (Num. 4:15, 19-20; 7:9; 10:21). However, other things become holy only in their relationship to the holy God. They are made holy by God's commands (Gen. 2:3), God's appearances (Exod. 19:10-24), or divinely approved ceremonies (Lev. 8:10; cf. Exod. 29:1-44).

God is holy by nature, whereas other things are holy only derivatively: "I am the Lord your God; consecrate yourselves and be holy, because I am holy" (Lev. 11:44). After God's deliverance of the Israelites from Egypt, Moses sang: "Who among the gods is like you, O Lord? Who is like you — majestic in holiness, awesome in glory, working wonders?" (Exod. 15:11). As Joshua challenged the Israelites to choose for or against God, he chided them: "You are not able to serve the Lord. He is a holy God; he is a jealous God. He will not forgive your rebellion and your sins" (Josh. 24:19). The Psalms of Israel voice the holiness of God: "Worship the Lord in the splendor of his holiness; tremble before him, all the earth" (Ps. 96:9). The prophet Isaiah speaks often of God as the "Holy One of Israel" (Isa. 1:4; 40:25; cf. Isa. 12:6; 17:7; 45:11; 47:4).

---

20. *The Anchor Bible Dictionary,* s.v. "Holiness: The Old Testament."
21. *The Interpreter's Dictionary of the Bible,* 5 vols., ed. George A. Buttrick (Nashville: Abingdon, 1962), s.v. "Holiness" (hereafter *IDB*).

The New Testament assumes the Old Testament teaching on the holiness of God and thus rarely teaches it explicitly. However, Jesus prays: "Our Father in heaven. Hallowed be your name" (Matt. 6:9). The word translated into English as "hallowed" *(hagiastheto)* is related to the word *hagios* ("holy"). Jesus' prayer echoes the words of Psalm 111:9: "Holy and awesome is his name." Jesus prays in the Gospel of John: "Holy Father, protect them by the power of your name" (John 17:11). And Peter takes up the Old Testament theme of holiness: "But just as he who called you is holy, so be holy in all you do; for it is written: 'Be holy, because I am holy'" (1 Pet. 1:15-16). The book of Revelation proclaims the exclusive holiness of God: "Who will not fear you, O Lord, and bring glory to your name? For you alone are holy" (15:4). It hails back to themes in Isaiah and Ezekiel when it pictures the heavenly scene in which the living creatures cry, "Holy, holy, holy is the Lord God Almighty, who was, and is, and is to come" (Rev. 4:8).

As I have indicated above, the concept of holiness marks some sort of separation. What is the nature of this separation? We can delineate the specific character of the partition by canvassing the various associations, demands, and responses to God's holiness. God, being holy, is unapproachable. On pain of death, Aaron may not come into the Most Holy Place "whenever he chooses" (Lev. 16:2). Moses cannot approach the burning bush simply because he is curious; for even the ground surrounding it is holy (Exod. 3:5; cf. Exod. 19). God will not be used for human ends. All of our dealings with God must be at his invitation.

The holiness of God is associated with fire, opposition, and judgment. Moses sees a "burning" bush (Exod. 3:2; cf. 19:18; 24:17; Deut. 4:12; Ezek. 1:4-28). God's fire symbolizes divine judgment (Ezek. 10:2; Rev. 8:5-7; 13:13; 14:18; 20:9). The author of the Epistle to the Hebrews, quoting Deuteronomy, warns the disobedient: "Our God is a consuming fire" (Heb. 12:29). God's holy fire can also make one holy. Isaiah saw "the Lord seated on a throne, high and exalted." Those around the throne praised God, saying, "Holy, holy, holy is the Lord Almighty; the whole earth is full of his glory." At this, Isaiah confesses his sin and unworthiness: "Woe to me . . . my eyes have seen the King, the Lord Almighty." Then one of the heavenly beings approaches Isaiah "with a live coal," which will purify Isaiah for God's service (Isa. 6:1-7).

God is holy, and hence he is jealous. He will tolerate no other gods or images (Exod. 20:4-6; 34:14; Deut. 4:24; cf. 1 Cor. 10:22). He hates hypocrisy and injustice, which desecrate his holiness (Isa. 1:14; Ps. 11:5; Hos. 9:15). Ezekiel prophesies God's holy judgment and wrath on Gog. When this happens, says the Lord, "I will show my greatness and my holiness, and I will make myself known in the sight of many nations. Then they will know that I am the Lord" (Ezek.

38:23). God's holiness implies his purity from all defects, especially from moral defects: "Your eyes are too pure to look on evil; you cannot tolerate wrong" (Hab. 1:13; Deut. 23:14). God's holiness is associated with his greatness (Ps. 77:13; Ezek. 38:23), righteousness (Isa. 5:6; Rev. 15:4; cf. Eph. 4:2), and glory (Isa. 6:3; 41:16).

The human response to God's holiness speaks volumes about its nature. All the Israelites "trembled violently" at the sights and sounds of the Sinai revelation (Exod. 19:18). Fear, dread, and terror seized those confronted by the holy God. "The Lord Almighty is the one you are to regard as holy, he is the one you are to fear, he is the one you are to dread" (Isa. 8:13; cf. Deut. 7:21). To acknowledge the holiness of God is to "stand in awe of the God of Israel" (Isa. 29:23). His name is "holy and awesome" (Ps. 111:9), and we should "tremble before him" (Ps. 96:9). "The fear of the Lord is the beginning of wisdom" (Prov. 9:10). The author of Hebrews reminds us that, in "holy fear," Noah built an ark to save his family (Heb. 11:7). The victorious saints in heaven sing: "Who will not fear you, O Lord, and bring glory to your name? For you alone are holy" (Rev. 15:4).

Theology of God's Holiness

To speak of God's holiness is to point to his transcendence, his utter difference from creatures and their actions. We can agree with Staniloae when he observes: "Holiness can be said to reveal to us all the divine qualities in a concentrated way. It is the luminous and active mystery of the divine presence. In it there is concentrated all that distinguishes God from the world."[22] God is pure and perfect, infinitely beyond us in quality of being, life, and action. If God were merely holy, perhaps we could simply keep our distance and survive. But God is holy *love*. And because God is holy love, he will not leave us alone: he opposes sin, death, and everything defective in us. His judgment falls on everything that opposes his love and grace. "For the Lord your God is a consuming fire, a jealous God" (Deut. 4:2; cf. Heb. 12:26).

Holy Opposition

God's opposition to us is the dominant theme of the attribute of holiness. Thomas Ridgley (c. 1667-1734) observes that holiness is the attribute "whereby God is infinitely opposite to every thing that tends to reflect dishonour or reproach on his divine perfections . . . a harmony of all his perfections, as they are

22. Staniloae, *The Experience of God*, 1, pp. 222-23.

opposed to sin."[23] God's life, character, and actions are immeasurably superior to ours. That God is holy means that he is mysterious and unpredictable. We cannot assume that God will value what we value and want for us what we want for ourselves. Yet God's opposition to us is not an annihilating force bent on our destruction. It is positive opposition, the opposition of infinite fullness, life, and being. The Creator stands sovereign over the creature. The very existence of the God whose faithfulness, justice, and love are perfect condemns all falsehood, injustice, and selfishness.

God's holy opposition to us is not our destruction but our salvation, because it is the opposition of love. This Opponent is "for us" and not against us (Rom. 8:31). In his love, God opposes whatever contests his good will for us. He wills that we be holy as he is holy; therefore, he opposes all unrighteousness within us. He wills that we be free; therefore, he opposes whatever enslaves us. He wants us to know the joy of receiving and returning his love; therefore, he condemns our ungratefulness and selfishness. He is the only source of our good and hence he will not have us worshiping other gods. He wills to give us eternal life; he would have us let go of this moral life that death may be "swallowed up in victory" (1 Cor. 15:54; cf. Isa. 25:8).

God's holiness is sanctifying holiness. It not only destroys but purifies. The "holy, holy, holy" God purified Isaiah's lips with his holy fire (Isa. 6:1-7). The temple furnishings, the priesthood, and the people of Israel as a whole were made holy by means of the divinely ordained ceremonies of purification and atonement. Sinners are made holy by the washing of baptism and the sanctifying work of the Holy Spirit; and God makes his church holy through the Holy Spirit, who descended as a flame of fire at Pentecost. Paul says to the Corinthian Christians: "But you were washed, you were sanctified, you were justified in the name of the Lord Jesus Christ and by the Spirit of our God" (1 Cor. 6:11).

Holy Love

God is holy in that he maintains his distinctive being in all that he does. He does not let go of his holiness in his acts of love, mercy, and grace. He shows himself to be holy precisely in his love. His love toward us is the very distinctive love — total, free, giving, receiving, and returning — that he is in his own triune life. As the Father gives himself to his Son, and his Son pours out his life in service and obedience, God is acting as very God. Jesus Christ, who is God's love for us, is also God's holiness for us — God's holy love. God does not cease

---

23. Ridgley, *Body of Divinity*, vol. 1, ed. Rev. John M. Wilson (New York: Robert Carter & Brothers, 1855), p. 103.

to be the holy God when he unites himself to our flesh. On the contrary, he sanctifies our flesh. When Jesus touched the lepers, he did not become unclean; they became clean (Matt. 8:1-3). He ate with sinners without becoming a sinner (Mark 2:15-17). In washing his disciples' feet, Jesus showed himself to be the Lord even of his lordship (John 13:1-17). Precisely by refusing to exercise power selfishly, he showed himself omnipotent; precisely by suffering all things, he showed himself impassible. He took on the guilt of the world without becoming guilty. He experienced death without becoming death's victim; rather, through death he gained the victory over death.

I cannot agree with those who believe that God's love and his holiness are opposed to one another. Jack Cottrell, for example, thinks that these two attributes were in "perfect harmony" until the fall of humanity. The fall, however, placed them "in a state of tension and opposition" and created a dilemma for God: "How can God fulfill the requirements of both love and holiness toward sinners at the same time?"[24] God resolved this inner divine tension by way of the atonement accomplished in Jesus Christ. This line of thought does not do justice to the doctrine of the attributes or to the doctrine of the atonement. If God is God apart from the world and all his attributes refer to his one simple essence, nothing that happens in the world can change God or create a "tension" within his being. With respect to the atonement, Cottrell's position makes the atonement as much about solving a divine problem as a human one. But sin is *our* problem — and God solves it. There is no dilemma for God.

Holy Mystery

God's holy presence inspires "infinite humility" — shame because of our corruption, guilt because of our sin, and terror because of our impotence.[25] For these reasons, our first reaction is to flee from God's holy presence (Ps. 139:7). Like the Israelites at Sinai, we want to keep our distance. The terrified people said to Moses, "Speak to us yourself and we will listen. But do not have God speak to us or we will die" (Exod. 20:19). Like Peter, we want the holy Jesus to "go away" from us sinners (Luke 5:8). Our desire to get away from the holy God can also be expressed as revulsion at God's holy condescension in Jesus Christ. Peter rebuked Jesus for prophesying the Messiah's crucifixion (Mark 8:32), and he refused to allow Jesus to wash his feet (John 13:8). The cross of Christ is "foolish" to the Greeks and offensive to the Jews (1 Cor. 1:18-25). But God chose

---

24. Cottrell, *The Faith Once For All: Bible Doctrine For Today* (Joplin, MO: College Press, 2002), pp. 92-93.

25. Staniloae, *The Experience of God*, p. 223.

to manifest his holy love in things that appear weak and foolish, things that are ordinarily despised (1 Cor. 1:26-31).

On the other hand, God's holiness exerts attractive force. Moses was fascinated by the appearance of God in the bush (Exod. 3:3). How disappointing it would have been had Jesus "gone away" at Peter's request. Nothing like us can save us. For all other creatures are vulnerable to the same corrupting and enslaving forces as we are. Only purity can cleanse us. Only immortality can rescue us from death. Only the incorruptible can protect us from corruption. Only the absolutely independent is absolutely dependable. Only the "weakness" of suffering love and the despised self-emptying of the cross can achieve the justifying, holy obedience that is the glory, holiness, and salvation of humanity.

Domesticating the Holy

It is a truism that the holy is the central motif of religion. As I observed in the section on natural religion, human beings are forced to deal with the divine in some way. We know we depend on something or someone beyond us. We have no choice: we need that reality. We must stay within its good graces, yet we fear it. For that which gives can take away, and that which bestows being can annihilate being. We take the attitude of Confucius, who said, "Respect spiritual beings but keep them at a distance."[26] Of course, it is not possible to ignore the divine altogether, hence the utility of religion.

Human beings use religion to deal with this problem: religion's function is to manage the holy. What do the divine beings want from us? How do we ensure enough of their goodwill to fulfill the needs of life? On the other hand, how do we get them to leave us alone so that we can live our lives as we desire? Religion mediates between us and the divine. It isolates us from the high energy of the holy. In religion, we receive the laws, ceremonies, sacrifices, and prayers by which we can manage the holy. Whatever we have left after we have completed our religious duties is ours to do with as we please. Religious activity is like paying taxes: you give up what you must, and then you try to forget about your loss so that you can enjoy what is left.

The holy God of Scripture will not be managed by religion: he demands everything from us. Perhaps the holy could be managed if it were merely a matter of difference and distance. But the holy God is love. He will not be satisfied with an occasional sacrifice or prayer. He will not give in to our request for holy

---

26. Confucius, *Analects*, 6.20, quoted in Niels C. Nielsen et al., eds., *Religions of the World* (New York: St. Martin's Press, 1983), p. 269.

indifference, for some space to be ourselves, for a little spot of ground to call "mine."[27] He will not leave us alone. He will give us no space and no time to experiment with corruption, slavery, injustice, sin, falsehood, and death. He loves us, and therefore he will not be satisfied with anything but our total, free, receiving, and returning love. God is holy; God is love; God is holy love — these are terrible and wonderful words.

Rather than flee God's holiness or attempt to manage it with religion, we should seek it with our whole being. In *The Experience of God*, Staniloae reflects on the Greek fathers' understanding of the saintly life. The more the human soul confronts the holiness of God, the more "it sees only itself in its nothingness and humility and is convinced that nobody else in the world is so unworthy" (p. 223). Contrary to what one might expect, this humbling experience leads to a new level of boldness before God, "an opening of conscience, a sincerity of communicability" that "resembles the boldness of a child innocent of sin, while in addition it possesses maturity of conscience and the joy of it" (p. 224). With no pretense of having to "be something," there is "nothing that hinders us from manifesting ourselves in all sincerity before him; we are no longer acting out a role that leads us to a point where we end up no longer knowing ourselves and living always in the fear of being unmasked" (pp. 223-24). This quest for holiness is not limited to the Greek fathers. The English Puritan Edward Leigh expresses this sentiment so beautifully that I am compelled to quote it at length:

> We should labor after holiness, to go quite out of ourselves, and all creatures, and go wholly as it were unto God, making him the ground, measure and end of all our actions, striving above all things to know him, esteem him, and set all our powers upon him. This is the felicity of the creature, to be holy as God is holy; this is the felicity of the Saints in Heaven, they care for nothing but God, are wholly and altogether carried to him and filled with him. He is all in all unto them, as he is all in all unto himself. In being thus carried to him, they are united to him and enjoy him and are blessed.[28]

The Righteousness of God

According to Scripture, God always does right and always acts justly. Even in those actions where his love and holiness claim our attention, God is altogether

27. C. S. Lewis, *Surprised By Joy: The Shape of My Early Life* (New York: Harcourt Brace Jovanovich, 1955), p. 172.
28. Leigh, *Treatise of Divinity*, 2.13 (London, 1647), p. 105.

righteous. If we could see God's love in its fullness, we would see his righteousness as well as his holiness. For God's righteousness does not consist in his conformity to a standard of justice outside and above him. It is not a matter of God giving everyone his due (good or evil) as determined by an external standard. Rather, God's righteousness is his complete self-consistency and faithfulness to himself in all his actions.[29] What God is in his own being, he is in his actions toward his creatures. God always does what is worthy of himself. God is righteous in that his holy love, grace, and mercy toward us perfectly reflect his own praiseworthy and eternal Trinitarian life.

Righteousness in Scripture

Scripture affirms God's perfect righteousness. The psalmist proclaims, "Your righteousness reaches to the skies, O God" (Ps. 71:19; Ps. 119:137). Daniel, even when contemplating God's judgments on Israel, concludes, "The Lord our God is righteous in everything he does" (Dan. 9:14). His righteousness consists in his unwavering condemnation of evil and approval of goodness. The Psalms extol God's righteous judgments: "They will sing before the Lord, for he comes, he comes to judge the earth. He will judge the world in righteousness and the peoples in his truth" (Ps. 96:13). The prophet Ezekiel announces God's judgment: "As for you, my flock, this is what the Sovereign Lord says: 'I will judge between one sheep and another, and between rams and goats'" (Ezek. 34:17). Paul sees God's "righteous decree" embodied in his wrath toward the wickedness and idolatry of the nations (Rom. 1:32). God alone is the perfect and righteous Judge (1 Cor. 4:4-5; Heb. 12:23; James 5:9; John 8:50).

Because God is righteous, he delivers the oppressed and vindicates the innocent: "The Lord works righteousness and justice for all the oppressed" (Ps. 103:6). Because God is righteous, he demands righteousness from human beings: "For the Lord is righteous, he loves justice; upright men will see his face" (Ps. 11:7). But human beings often disappoint: "And he looked for justice, but saw bloodshed; for righteousness, but heard cries of distress" (Isa. 5:7).

However, the righteousness of God is not always obvious in the events of life; therefore, maintaining confidence in God's righteousness requires faith. Sometimes, God's righteousness takes the strange form of affliction: "I know, O Lord, that your laws are righteous, and in faithfulness you have afflicted me"

---

29. Cottrell, *The Faith Once For All*, p. 77. Cottrell correctly declares: "[T]hat God is righteous means he is always consistent with himself; he is always true to himself or in perfect harmony with himself."

(Ps. 119:75). Jeremiah speaks for many when he says: "Why does the way of the wicked prosper? Why do all the faithless live at ease?" (Jer. 12:1). Other than the book of Job, Psalm 73 is perhaps the most poignant statement of a position we can call troubled faith: "Surely God is good to Israel, to those who are pure in heart . . . [but] I envied the arrogant when I saw the prosperity of the wicked. . . . Surely in vain have I kept my heart pure; in vain have I washed my hands in innocence. . . . When I tried to understand all this, it was oppressive to me till I entered the sanctuary of God; then I understood their final destiny" (Ps. 73:1-17).

The psalmist's complaint is framed with statements of faith. He begins with an affirmation of God's goodness that is based on the experience he narrates in the second half of the psalm. Then he confesses that, by relying on his own observations, he almost lost faith. His experience had called into question the righteousness of God's judgment. It seems that God blesses the wicked and punishes the righteous. However, entering the sanctuary of God opens his eyes to the reality of God's righteousness and allows him to anticipate future divine judgment on the wicked: "Surely you place them on slippery ground; you cast them down to ruin. How suddenly are they destroyed, completely swept away by terrors!" (Ps. 73:18-19). In the Bible, the fact that God is righteous in all his ways is a statement of faith, not an observation of experience.

Theology of God's Righteousness

Traditional theologians, to achieve greater understanding of God's righteousness and take into account the full spectrum of biblical teaching, distinguished various types of divine righteousness. Such distinctions do not imply real differences in God's justice; rather, as John Owen maintains, they speak of "the universal and essential rectitude of the divine nature variously considered."[30] God's righteousness can be considered absolutely or in relation to creation. God's absolute righteousness, in Turretin's view, is the "rectitude and perfection of the divine nature . . . belonging to him as God."[31] God's absolute righteousness will be our primary focus in this study, but apart from God's righteous action in creation, we could know nothing of his essential righteousness.

Let us consider now the interconnected issues of the knowledge, the definition, and the basis of God's righteousness. Believers affirm that God always does right, that he is righteous in all his ways. On what basis, however, do we

---

30. John Owen, *Dissertation on Divine Justice,* quoted in Muller, *PRRD,* 3, p. 484.
31. Turretin, *Institutes of Elenctic Theology,* 3.19.3, p. 235.

pronounce this judgment? Do we observe invariably that God meets an independent abstract legal or ideal standard? No. We cannot learn of God's perfect righteousness by observation, and we cannot determine that God is righteous by comparing his actions to a standard independent of him. Thinking that God's righteousness can be judged by an external standard, according to Calvin, is "foolish" and "very wicked." Speaking for the Reformers and the orthodox Reformed, he affirms: "The will of God is so much the highest rule of righteousness that whatever he wills by the very fact that he wills it, must be considered righteous."[32]

As I explained in the section on revelation, our knowledge of God is based on God's self-knowledge. Only God knows God, and thus only God can reveal God. Only God can reveal that he is triune, that he is holy, and that he is love. Likewise, only God can make known his perfect righteousness. God demonstrates his righteousness not by showing that he measures up to a higher standard. Just as God is not God because he conforms to the idea of the divine, God is not loving or good or righteous because he conforms to the idea of love or good or righteousness. Just as God *is* love, God *is* righteousness. Other righteous deeds are just only insofar as they resemble God's deeds. God demonstrates his righteousness in that he is always himself in his actions. Hence, I will define God's righteousness as *God's complete self-consistency and faithfulness to himself in all his actions.*

Arbitrary Righteousness?

Defining God's righteousness as I have raises concerns for some. Am I saying that whatever God does is right simply because he does it? If so, have I not evacuated all meaning from the affirmation that God is righteous? Does it boil down to saying that God does what God does? What, then, is the purpose of saying God is righteous "in all his actions"?

However legitimate the concern that gives rise to these questions may be, in their present form they presuppose something I have already rejected: that we can legitimately speculate about God apart from who he has revealed himself to be. I maintain that God's actions are righteous because *God* does them and remains true to himself in doing them; but the word "God," as I use it, refers not to an infinite and arbitrary potential for any imaginable action. God is Father, Son, and Holy Spirit. God is righteous because he acts only and always as Father, Son, and Holy Spirit. God is righteous because, just as he is holy love

---

32. Calvin, *Institutes*, 3.23.2, in *Institutes of the Christian Religion*, vol. 2, ed. John T. McNeill, trans. Ford Lewis Battles (Philadelphia: Westminster, 1960), p. 949.

by nature, he is holy love in all his actions toward us. There is no God above, beside, or behind the loving God revealed in Jesus Christ. God will not and cannot act contrary to the love that he is in his triune life. This is the meaning of the affirmation that God is righteous in all his ways.

Divine righteousness can be defined neither by reference to an eternal law of justice alongside God nor by an arbitrary act of God's will. The first alternative would make God dependent on a reality beyond him. God would not *be* his righteousness; rather, righteousness would be an accidental property that God might or might not possess relative to an external standard. God would not be "that than which no greater can be conceived" (Anselm). The second alternative would also deprive God of his righteousness (and all other moral attributes) by identifying God's essence with sheer will. If God *is* will alone, then all the other attributes are just names that give us no knowledge of God's eternal nature. With such a presupposition as a foundation, we could not define God's righteousness as "God's complete self-consistency and faithfulness to himself in all his actions." For we could not think of God as having a stable identity or nature to which he could be faithful in his actions. I agree, in substance if not in wording, with Calvin's evaluation of this teaching as "a devilish blasphemy forged in Hell."[33] In contrast to these views, I would insist that God *is* his attributes: he is love *and* holiness *and* righteousness. He will not and cannot act in contradiction to himself.

The Unity of Righteousness and Love

The second theological issue is related to the previous discussion. How is God's righteousness related to his other attributes, especially love, mercy, and grace? The unity and harmony of all the attributes is a foundational assumption of this study. Therefore, the challenge here is not finding a way to reconcile the independently defined attribute of righteousness with the equally independently defined attributes of love, grace, and mercy. From the very beginning I have maintained that we cannot understand one attribute in isolation from the rest. Every discussion of an attribute in isolation — we cannot avoid such discussions — must be considered preliminary.

Let us return to my definition of God's righteousness as *God's complete self-consistency and faithfulness to himself in all his actions.* In constructing this definition, I have already taken the other attributes into account; for it differs radically from definitions I might have developed by way of considering righteousness in an isolated way. I did not define righteousness as "giving everyone

---

33. From Calvin's *Sermons on Job* (quoted in Muller, *PRRD*, p. 478).

his due" or "the habit of conforming to an ideal moral standard." Both of these definitions would conflict with God's attribute of absolute independence, because they would make God's righteousness dependent on something outside God. In addition, the former would contradict the attribute of God's gracious love, which is self-giving without reference to the worth of the receiver. The definition I have given is consistent with those attributes, as well as with all the rest.

God's righteousness does not compete with his love. God is righteous because in all his deeds he loves us with his eternal triune love. His love does not indulge our lust, overlook our pride, make light of our sloth, or turn a blind eye to our falsehood. God's love is righteous, for he loves us precisely in that he gives himself and only himself. And he is holy and righteous. God is righteous when he loves us because his love demands — and accomplishes — our love in return. In his righteous love, God shows himself to be holy, completely set apart from all others.

Jesus Christ as God's Righteousness — and Ours

In a third theological affirmation, I contend that Jesus Christ is the righteousness of God incarnate. We have already seen that Jesus Christ is the love of God incarnate. Now we shall see that Jesus is God's righteousness precisely because he is God's love. "God demonstrates his own love for us," explains Paul, "in that while we were still sinners, Christ died for us" (Rom. 5:8). In dying for sinners, the Son of God faithfully enacts the eternal love of God toward us and hence embodies the righteousness of God. God does not deny or contradict himself in the cross of Christ. He is completely true to himself and so is altogether righteous in his action. In Christ, the determining center and defining essence of God's righteousness are revealed.

How can Jesus Christ embody this righteousness when he forgives sin, declares the transgressor righteous, and lets the guilty go free? Recall that the Lord warned: "Do not deny justice to your poor people in their lawsuits. Have nothing to do with a false charge and do not put an innocent or honest person to death, for I will not acquit the guilty" (Exod. 23:6-7). Isaiah contrasts the righteousness of God with unjust judges: "But the Lord Almighty will be exalted by his justice, and the holy God will show himself holy by his righteousness . . . [but cursed are those] who acquit the guilty for a bribe, but deny justice to the innocent" (Isa. 5:16, 23). And what about the proverb: "Acquitting the guilty and condemning the innocent — the Lord detests them both" (Prov. 17:15)? Does God, in Jesus Christ, overlook, indulge, or make light of unrighteousness?

By no means does God "acquit the guilty" in the sense of the texts quoted above. On the contrary, he punishes the guilty and destroys the sinner on the cross. God does not tolerate sin in the least; rather, he exercises his full fury on it. The sinner got the full measure of justice in Jesus Christ. In Barth's words, the cross "first reveals the full implication of the wrath of God, of His condemning and punishing justice . . . [and] discloses too the full implication of sin, what it means to resist God, to be God's enemy, which is the guilty determination of our human existence."[34] However, Paul declares that "God made him who had no sin to be sin for us, so that in him we might become the righteousness of God" (2 Cor. 5:21). God's destruction of the sinner is not all there is to God's righteousness. God is just in that he never "acquits the guilty"; but he is also "the one who justifies those who have faith in Jesus" (Rom. 3:26). God executes the sinner, but he also raises the dead.

Jesus Christ is human as well as God. He is God's righteousness, but he is ours as well. The Father said about him: "This is my Son. With him I am well pleased." In him, God has made a truly holy and righteous human being. He is the "righteous One" (Acts 22:14) who suffered for us and has become "our righteousness, holiness and redemption" (1 Cor. 1:30). In achieving the redemption of humanity in Jesus Christ, God maintained his righteousness. In Jesus Christ, God has given himself fully to humanity, and humanity has given itself fully to God in return. Sinful humanity has been put to death in Jesus: "One died for all, and therefore all died" (2 Cor. 5:14-15). God counts Jesus' divine and human righteousness as ours as well. This is the gospel: "For in the gospel a righteousness from God is revealed, a righteousness that is by faith from first to last" (Rom. 1:17). The righteous God does not merely pronounce just judgments on the unjust; God also conquers unrighteousness by converting the sinner and raising him from the dead. His righteousness is holy and loving, creative and life-giving: a righteous-making righteousness and a justifying justice. And this sets God's righteousness apart from all others.

Questioning God's Righteousness

We have to deal with the so-called problem of evil at many points in theology: in the doctrine of creation and providence, in the doctrine of reconciliation, and in eschatology. We deal with it for the first time here in a preliminary way in the doctrine of God. In their attempts to answer the problem of evil, many modern theologians and philosophers of religion propose extensive revisions in the doctrine of God. To maintain God's righteousness, some give up God's

---

34. *CD*, 2/1, p. 398.

omnipotence, omniscience, and providential control. If God cannot prevent evil, or does not know when specific evils will happen, or cannot fully control the course of events, God cannot be held responsible for the evil that occurs in the world. Ostensibly, these sacrifices are designed to protect God's righteousness; however, as we shall see, these revisions actually place God's righteousness in jeopardy.

I have affirmed that God is righteous in all his ways and that whatever God does is right and worthy of himself. How can we maintain this confession confidently in the face of evil? How could the one who is righteous in all his ways have created a world in which death, sin, pain, disease, and cruelty exist in such abundance? How may the existence of evil be harmonized with the belief that God is omnipotent or that God controls the world in his providence? Why does God allow evil to trouble us? And can evil be redeemed?

I cannot give adequate answers to all these questions at this point; but I want to emphasize a truth that will prove foundational to my future answers. In dealing with the problem of evil, we must never compromise the premise that God is righteous in all his ways. I have shown that this premise is not and cannot be grounded in observation; hence it cannot be threatened or overturned by our experience. Any argument against God's righteousness based on our subjective response to the suffering and trouble in the world can have no real force. Consider David Basinger's definition of evil: commonly recognized evils "are inherently undesirable in the sense that these states of affairs, in and of themselves, not only lack inherent value but actually detract from or diminish the value of our world"[35] Theologians who, like Basinger, go about revising the doctrine of God because God's righteousness is threatened by the trouble and suffering in the world are already defeated before they begin. For this project is based on at least two false premises: the first is that God's righteousness can be known and measured by independent standards; the second states that God would not be righteous if he really intended the world to be as we experience it. Nothing good can follow from such fundamental mistakes.

The first premise, as I have made clear already, deprives God of his righteousness. On the assumption that God is righteous only because he measures up to an independent moral standard, we can no longer say that God *is* his righteousness. We are admitting the possibility that God might not prove righteous. In contrast to this frightening thought, I have defended the thesis that God cannot be unrighteous because God is righteous by nature. The second premise — that God would not be righteous if he really intended the world to be as we ex-

---

35. Basinger, *The Case for Freewill Theism: A Philosophical Assessment* (Downers Grove, IL: InterVarsity Press, 1996), p. 85.

perience it — involves a judgment that identifies our fear and loathing of suffering and trouble with the voice of truth. A righteous God, the defenders of God reason, could not intend the suffering and trouble we experience. The intuition at the heart of this judgment is not really about the quantity of suffering but with its very presence. It views any object of fear and loathing as something for which God has to answer.

How can such reasoning avoid the conclusion that a righteous God would not intend *any* suffering and trouble for his creatures? Such a view is not compatible with the belief that God is the Creator and providential guide of the world. To guarantee that God is righteous, on these premises, we would have to deny that God has anything to do with the world, and that would strip away even the Christian façade from this faithless theism. Limiting God's power, knowledge, and control may allow God to keep a sort of "righteousness"; unfortunately, however, it also makes it irrelevant. Robert Neville comes to a similar conclusion in his critique of A. N. Whitehead's process metaphysics. He argues:

> But suppose evil is chosen only by people, and only in independence from God. Why should we want in the first place to exempt God from responsibility for evil? Because of an antecedent commitment to God's goodness. But to deny God responsibility by denying divine causal agency is not to lend *support* to the doctrine of divine goodness; it only strikes down a counter argument. And the price of this move is to make the actual course of events *irrelevant* to God's moral character; this goes counter to the religious feeling that God's moral character is *revealed* in events, for better or worse.[36]

In the doctrine of God I have set out, God's righteousness consists in his faithfulness to himself. That God is righteous is grounded in God's own being and life: God *is* righteousness. God is righteous because God is himself in all his actions. God is righteous because, just as he is holy love in his nature, he is holy love in his actions. In times of trouble and suffering, our holding on to this truth will provide comfort and hope.

---

36. Neville, *Creativity and God: A Challenge to Process Theology,* new ed. (Albany: SUNY Press, 1995), p. 11.

7

Love's Humility, Charity's Skill:
Divine Grace, Mercy, Patience, and Wisdom

The Grace of God

On June 18, 1882, the great British Baptist preacher Charles Haddon Spurgeon rose to deliver his Sunday morning message in the Metropolitan Tabernacle. The text of the day was Ephesians 2:7: "That in the ages to come he might show the exceeding riches of his grace in his kindness toward us through Jesus Christ." Spurgeon's sermon expresses what every sober theologian attempting to articulate the treasures of God's grace ought to feel:

> This morning I have a text before me which is a great deal too full for me — I can never draw out all its supplies. I have gone round the walls of this city text; I have counted its towers and marked well its bulwarks, but I am utterly unable to express myself by reason of joyous astonishment! I feel as if I must sit down and lose myself in adoration. I am a poor dumb dog over such a theme![1]

Never has a "dumb dog" barked so eloquently! Even in print, the sermon forces you to sit and "lose yourself in adoration" at the grace of God. I can hope only to yap a prosaic imitation of his "joyous astonishment."

In my treatment of God's love, I emphasized God's gift of himself and all good things to us. I argued that God's love for us is not motivated by our worth. God loves the unworthy, and, even more astoundingly, God loves the ungrateful, unreceptive, and unloving. In this earlier discussion, I described only gener-

---

1. Spurgeon, "The Exceeding Riches of Grace," *The Metropolitan Tabernacle Pulpit,* vol. 28, #1665. Available at http://www.spurgeongems.org/vols28-30/chs1665.pdf (accessed June 1, 2006).

ally the unmotivated nature of God's love. Now I shall focus in detail on that gratuitous quality.

God loves us freely. No law above him or quality within us compels God to love us. God's gift of our existence in creation, his turning to us in election and covenant, and his reconciliation of us in Jesus Christ are matters of grace, sheer grace. In grace, the infinite God takes notice of us and condescends to us. In grace, the holy God forgives our sin and overcomes our opposition to him. Grace is not something in addition to God, something God might or might not be. We can trust that God is gracious because God *is* grace, and he is himself in all his works. In acting graciously toward us, however, God does not take sin lightly. His grace is holy and righteous. For, in being gracious to us, God graces us with himself, the holy and righteous one. Consequently, the name Jesus Christ speaks of God's grace most fully: he is both God's free gift and the freely giving God. He is the reconciling God and the reconciled human being in one person.

The Gracious God of Scripture

Scripture teaches the graciousness of God. When Moses encountered God on Mount Sinai, God proclaimed: "The Lord, the Lord God, the compassionate and gracious God, slow to anger, abounding in love and faithfulness" (Exod. 34:6). This refrain is often repeated in Scripture (2 Chron. 30:9; cf. Neh. 9:17, 31; Ps. 86:15; 103:8; 111:4; 116:5; 145:8). In his grace God forgives sin. Hosea urges Israel to pray this prayer: "Forgive all our sins and receive us graciously that we may offer up the fruit of our lips" (Hos. 14:2). The Psalms remind us that "[t]he Lord is compassionate and gracious . . . . He does not treat us as our sins deserve or repay us according to our iniquities . . . . As far as the east is from the west, so far has he removed our transgressions from us" (Ps. 103:8-12).

The New Testament extols God's grace in almost every line. We have the forgiveness of sins "in accordance with the riches of God's grace" (Eph. 1:7; 2:7-9). We are justified "freely by his grace through the redemption that came by Jesus Christ" (Rom. 3:24). The gentiles are saved "through the grace of our Lord Jesus," just as Jews are (Acts 15:11). The Christian teaching about God's grace is such good news that it can be called "the gospel of God's grace" (Acts 20:24). Paul opposes God's grace to sin: As sin "reigned in death," grace must "reign through righteousness" to bring "eternal life through Jesus Christ our Lord" (Rom. 5:21; cf. 2 Thess. 2:16). The "grace of God" brings salvation to all (Titus 2:11). By the "grace of God," Jesus "might taste death for everyone" (Heb. 2:9).

The gracious God not only forgives sin, he transforms and empowers for a holy and righteous life. Paul boasts that God's grace toward him "was not without effect" (1 Cor. 15:10). The grace of God "teaches us," Paul instructs Titus, "to say 'No' to ungodliness and worldly passions, and to live self-controlled, upright and godly lives in this present age" (Titus 2:12). When Barnabas and his colleagues came to Syrian Antioch from Jerusalem, they "saw evidence of the grace of God" in the believers (Acts 11:23). And as Barnabas and Paul left the synagogue in Pisidian Antioch, they urged their hearers "to continue in the grace of God" (Acts 13:43).

Grace is always a gift, for we "are justified freely by his grace" (Rom. 3:23-24; cf. 5:15-17). God's grace is "freely given us in the One he loves" (Eph. 1:6; 2:7). Consequently, God's grace excludes the idea of merit. Toward the end of his long discussion of Israel's relationship to the gospel, Paul concludes that God's grace, not human choice or merit, is the decisive factor in the history of salvation (Rom. 11:5-6). Paul protests to the wavering Galatians that the law cannot bring righteousness. Our righteousness comes to us through Christ (Gal. 2:21; 3:18). The "gospel" of works is a "different gospel" and is not good news at all (Gal. 1:6). Attempting to achieve justification by works of the law causes one to "fall from grace" (Gal. 5:4). That salvation comes by grace means that it is not based on "anything we have done but because of his own purpose and grace" (2 Tim. 1:9).

In Scripture, God's grace is often a component in blessings. The beautiful blessing Moses pronounces on the Israelites is classic: "The Lord bless you and keep you; the Lord make his face shine upon you and be gracious to you; the Lord turn his face toward you and give you peace" (Num. 6:24-26; cf. Ps. 67:1). Paul's familiar blessing on the Corinthians includes a reference to grace: "May the grace of the Lord Jesus Christ, and the love of God, and the fellowship of the Holy Spirit be with you all" (2 Cor. 13:14). The grace of God is often shorthand for God's providential care. The writer of the Acts of the Apostles refers to the commissioning of Paul and Barnabas in Antioch as the time when "they had been committed to the grace of God" (Acts 14:26).

Finally, the grace of God does not always meet with repentance, thanksgiving, and joy. Isaiah observes: "Though grace is shown to the wicked, they do not learn righteousness" (Isa. 26:10). Paul addresses his fellow Jews, accusing them of mistaking God's grace for blanket approval: "Or do you show contempt for the riches of his kindness, tolerance and patience, not realizing that God's kindness leads you toward repentance?" (Rom. 2:4). Though the law in its own way manifests God's grace, it meets with resistance. Paul deals with the profound implications of this resistance in Romans: "The law was added so that the trespass might increase. But where sin increased, grace increased all the more" (Rom. 5:5; cf. Gal. 3:19). This "increase" of grace reached its maximum in Jesus Christ, who brought "eternal life" to those who dwelt in death (Rom. 5:21).

Amazing Grace

In view of the message of Scripture, I shall now develop several theses on God's grace and answer some objections to them. I shall focus directly on grace as an attribute of God and discuss grace as it is operative in creation, salvation, and sanctification only insofar as it points to God's gracious nature. Unfortunately, many theologians postpone treating God's grace until they deal with the doctrine of reconciliation. Robert Preus points out that the general theme of God's goodness in the post-Reformation Lutheran doctrine of God, which includes the attributes of holiness, mercy, grace, and righteousness, "is quite incomplete, lacking in balance, and disappointing."[2] These themes were covered in greater depth in discussions of the salvation worked by Christ. Much modern theology continues this practice. Wolfhart Pannenberg's doctrine of God, for example, devotes only ten pages to the attributes of divine love.[3] Karl Barth is the great exception to this pattern: he devotes eighty-eight pages to the same subject.[4] I think it is very important to develop these themes within the doctrine of God because this enables us to emphasize that God is these attributes eternally and apart from reference to the world.

The Reformers and their immediate successors were correct to emphasize that in speaking of grace we speak of God and not of a human quality put in us by God. "Grace, properly speaking," explains John Calvin, "is in God and it is the effect of grace that is in us."[5] Edward Leigh explains: "God's graciousness is an essential property, whereby he is in and of himself most gracious and amiable . . . and freely bountiful unto his creatures cherishing them tenderly without any desert of theirs."[6] In twentieth-century theology, Barth placed special emphasis on the identity of God and his grace: "Grace is an inner mode of the be-

---

2. Robert Preus, *The Theology of Post-Reformation Lutheranism,* vol. 2, *God and His Creation* (St. Louis: Concordia, 1972), p. 94 (hereafter *TPRL).*

3. Pannenberg, *Systematic Theology,* vol. 1, trans. Geoffrey Bromiley (Grand Rapids: Eerdmans, 1988), pp. 432-42.

4. Barth, *Church Dogmatics,* vol. 2, pt. 1, eds. G. W. Bromiley and T. F. Torrance, trans. T. H. L. Parker et al. (Edinburgh: T&T Clark, 1957), pp. 351-439 (hereafter *CD).*

5. Calvin, *Commentary on Romans,* in *Calvin's Commentaries,* vol. 8, *The Epistles of Romans and to the Thessalonians,* trans. Ross Mackenzie, ed. David W. Torrance and Thomas F. Torrance (Grand Rapids: Eerdmans, 1960), p. 115.

6. Leigh, *Treatise of Divinity,* 2.11 (London, 1647), p. 84.

ing of God Himself."[7] And Roman Catholic theologian Karl Rahner also insists that God has not merely created gifts, but he communicates in his gracious action: "God communicates *himself . . .* he makes man share in the very nature of God"[8] In what follows I shall adhere to this rule.

Grace Is God's Unlimited Love

Grace is God's love viewed as free with respect to the worth of its object. In his grace God demonstrates his love "to those who only deserve evil."[9] God's love for us is always a matter of grace. God grants us fellowship with himself, not as a reward or bribe, but as a gift. God does not need our love or respect or worship. Nothing we are and no potential we have moves God to love us and seek fellowship with us. He loves with the love he is.

However, understanding grace as love unlimited raises questions. Does this mean that God gets no rewards for loving us? Do we not make a difference to God? Is God indifferent to the way we respond to his love? In reply to these questions, I must first point out that they presuppose something I have already rejected: that divine love contains an element of desire, of need, of potential happiness or unhappiness. Process philosopher Charles Hartshorne makes this presupposition explicit when he asserts that love is a "participation in the good of others, so that some sort of value accrues to the self through the very fact that value accrues to another self."[10] Many ordinary believers, too, cannot imagine a love that is without need and yet finds joy in loving us. They cannot think of how God can love us if he is already infinitely happy, or why God cares about us when we can add nothing to him.

At first hearing, this objection resonates with some of our dearly held beliefs. For it does not ring true to Scripture to deny that we make a difference to God. It would be a strange love indeed that is indifferent to the beloved. However, before I address the element of truth in this objection, I must speak to its underlying mistake. Its superficial plausibility hides a proud and despairing rejection of God's grace. God's love always comes to us as grace; but in order to accept it *as grace,* we must acknowledge our emptiness, dependence, vulnerability, and unworthiness. Since we find this humiliating, we refuse to believe that

---

7. *CD*, 2/1, p. 353.

8. Rahner, ed., *Encyclopedia of Theology: The Concise Sacramentum Mundi* (New York: Crossroad, 1975), s.v. "Grace: II. Theological."

9. Herman Bavinck, *Reformed Dogmatics*, vol. 2, *God and Creation*, trans. John Vriend, ed. John Bolt (Grand Rapids: Baker Academic, 2004), p. 214.

10. Hartshorne, *Man's Vision of God and the Logic of Theism* (Chicago: Willett, Clark and Company, 1941), p. 115.

God's love is purely gracious. We suspect that God wants something from us, something we might not want to give up. Like Adam and Eve, we grow to distrust God, preferring our own instincts of self-interest to his word of command and promise. We fancy that we can add something to what God has given us, that God would be less happy without us than with us, and that we hold veto power over God's plan for his creation. In our proud despair, we embark on the hopeless project of proving to ourselves that we do not need God's grace.

As we can see, inserting a component of desire into God's love does not protect it from indifference. It actually plunges us into uncertainty. If we think God's love is conditioned by something in us, we will always doubt it. For if his love depends on finding something lovely in us — even potentially — we can never rest in his love as the final certainty in our lives and absolute ground of all hope. And, insofar as he loves us for something we possess, he does not really love *us*.

Only the complete graciousness of God's love can guarantee its constancy and our value. Indifference? If indifference implies inaction, God's love is the opposite of indifference. He gives himself to us for our sake, acts always in our true interest, and ever seeks our welfare. Even if God is not moved to love us by something in us, he nevertheless moves toward us and for us. God does not love us because we are valuable; his love for us makes us valuable. In love, he chose us and created us. In love, he forgave us and reconciled us to himself in Jesus Christ. In his grace he is always ahead of us.

But do we matter to God? Getting at this question will require a little analysis. Whether or not your food has been poisoned certainly matters to your health. Whether or not the map you are using is current may determine the success of your trip. Studying for an exam usually makes a difference in the grade you get. In these cases something matters because it is a necessary means to an important end. The presence or absence of this factor affects the outcome dramatically. When we say people matter to us, we identify their welfare with ours: that is, if something bad happens to them it detracts from our joy. And if something good comes to them, we rejoice. God matters supremely because God is goodness itself and the source of all good things. Without God nothing matters, and because of God nothing else really matters. By faith we know that, even if we lose all things — possessions, friends, family, life — but retain God, we have lost nothing. This does not mean that we do not love family, friends, and life. Rather, it means that we love them truly only when we love them as gifts from God, with God's love, and for God's sake. In other words, these things really matter only if, in loving them, we love God in them.

Now let us return to the question posed earlier: Do we matter to God? Yes, we matter to God. But it is not because we are the means to some end, the achievement of which is necessary for God's happiness. God's end is the same as our end: God. If what I suggested above is true for us — that losing everything but God is no real loss — then it is certainly true for God as well. God loves all things in God and for God's sake. In other words, we matter to God because God has freely chosen to love himself in us and us for his sake. Or, to speak more precisely, the Father loves the Son in us and us for his sake. There is no higher love and no greater honor than to be cherished for God's sake. And to be loved for God's sake by *God* is the deepest ground and clearest sign of our immeasurable worth.[11]

God's Grace Is God's Condescension to Us

In his love, God condescends to us. Not only is God's love unlimited by us, it is unlimited by God. God is not a prisoner of his greatness, holiness, and omnipotence. God transcends his transcendence. He is "the only One who is really in a position to condescend, because He alone is truly transcendent, and stands on an equality with nothing outside Himself."[12] He can measure his love to our needs. The one who fills the universe dwells within us and pours his love into our hearts (Rom. 5:5; 8:11). He who created the world became a creature to speak face to face with creatures. The Holy One became "sin for us, so that in him we might become the righteousness of God" (2 Cor. 5:21). Omnipotent, he becomes "weak" to the weak and wise, a "fool" to the foolish (1 Cor. 1:25). The one whose native form is God took on the form of a slave and "made himself nothing" for our sakes (Phil. 2:7). The immortal God took on our mortality and died on a cross that we might share in his immortality. The impassible God suffered as a human being so that we might be raised to eternal life. God's love is not a holy and distant well-wishing. He comes near. Nothing in us or in God required him to do this. Why did he do it? Because he loved us. There is no deeper explanation.

I shall mention here something that I shall develop at length later in this study. In God's condescension, he does not cease to be great. He does not give up his lordship when he washes feet. He does not have to leave heaven to become present on earth. Dwelling within our hearts does not compromise his transcendence. Bearing our sin does not pollute his holiness. He remains immortal even as he dies on a cross. He does not cease to be impassible even in his suffering for us. On the contrary, his greatness is displayed most fully in his condescension, his wisdom in his foolishness, and his power in his weakness.

---

11. My argument is similar to Augustine's in *On Christian Doctrine*, 1.22; 1.32.
12. Barth, *CD*, 2/1, p. 354.

He is most present to us in his hiddenness. His immortality can encompass death, and his suffering on behalf of others is the greatest demonstration of his impassibility.

Jesus Christ Is God's Grace Triumphant

I have already emphasized that God's grace is his freedom to love without limits. He is not limited by our unworthiness or by his holiness. Now I must show that God's love is not limited by our resistance to it. We are inclined to think of God's love as his goodwill, his benevolence unlimited by our lack of worth. Understood in this way, God's gracious love would be a standing offer of fellowship at the ready, should we find ourselves inclined to accept it. The problem with this view is that we are never inclined of ourselves to accept the offer. We need grace because we are sinners, and we are sinners because we have resisted God's grace. God is gracious in all his actions toward us, in election, creation, covenant, and the giving of the law. At every point, however, we prove ourselves sinners against his grace. Barth insists that "we know and rightly understand our sin only when we have realized it to be enmity against the grace of God. And we turn from our sin only when we return to the grace of God."[13] If God's grace in Jesus Christ were merely an offer of forgiveness and redemption, the effectiveness of which depends on our autonomous inclination to accept, we would be lost. We have no such inclination, and we cannot simply decide to have it. If we were so well disposed to the grace of God, we would not be sinners in such desperate need of it! But we are sinners, and God's grace is directed toward "sinners," the "ungodly," and God's "enemies" (Rom. 5:6-8).

According to Scripture, God's grace in Jesus Christ differs from his grace in creation, covenant, and law. It differs not in its nature as God's gift of himself or in its freedom but in its effect. In Jesus Christ, God triumphs over the human resistance to his grace. In Romans 7, Paul shows why the law, which is "holy, righteous, and good" in itself, cannot produce a righteous human being. God's command "Do not covet" calls on us to renounce desire for anything that is not a gift from God. It demands that we accept and depend on God's grace. "But," Paul explains, "sin, seizing the opportunity afforded by the commandment, produced in me every kind of covetous desire" (Rom. 7:8). God's command to live by his grace alone is bound to meet with resistance in the sinner, who is a transgressor precisely because he does not wish to live dependent on grace.

Even when sinners recognize that God's law is right, they cannot of themselves obey it wholeheartedly (Rom. 7:18-19). Resistance to God's grace lies so

13. Barth, *CD*, 2/1, p. 357.

deep within us that even our good works are tainted. "So I find this law at work: When I want to do good, evil is right there with me" (7:21). According to Paul, our very awareness that we are doing good is a sign that we have already departed from the good. As we become conscious of our good works, we attribute the good to ourselves and become proud of our goodness. In realizing that we are being humble, we have ceased to be humble. Indeed, our fall from the good is the cause of our awareness of our "goodness."

The vicious logic of the law and sin, Paul concludes, leads to complete despair of salvation: "What a wretched man I am! Who will rescue me from this body of death?" (7:24). Our wretchedness consists not so much in our breaking God's commands as in our futile efforts to obey them. We do not need another "offer" of grace, which would in effect constitute another law and would lead only to more sin. We need to be rescued. And that is what God did for us in Jesus Christ. Despair yields to joy as Paul turns away from human wretchedness to God's triumphant grace: "Thanks be to God — through Jesus Christ our Lord!" (7:25).

Continuing his argument in Romans 8, Paul explains how Jesus Christ rescues us from our wretched state. In Jesus Christ, God "did" for us what we could not do for ourselves, even with the help of the holy, righteous, and good law. Jesus responded to God's grace perfectly: to the gift of creation with thanksgiving, to the blessing of the covenant with faithfulness, and to the gift of the law with obedience unto death. In Jesus Christ — and this is the secret of the atonement — the gracious God triumphed over the endemic human resistance to grace. He became one of us that he might be both the just God and the justified human, the gracious God and the graced human, the holy God and the sanctified human. In Jesus Christ, God's grace has achieved its goal. In him, God's grace appears, not as simple goodwill, potential reconciliation, a mere offer of fellowship with God, but our salvation realized. "Thanks be to God — through Jesus Christ our Lord!" (Rom. 7:25).

The Unity of Grace with Holiness and Righteousness

In view of what I have said about God's triumphant grace, I am bound to be questioned about the righteousness and holiness of such grace. Does God set aside his holiness and righteousness to be gracious to sinners? In his grace, does God ignore or excuse sin? In keeping with my fundamental view of the divine attributes, I must give unequivocally negative responses to each of these challenges.

In opposition to the presumptions behind those questions, God is righteous and holy *because* he is gracious to sinners. In his grace — precisely as grace — God shows his holy intolerance for sin. In grace, the holy God takes up residence within unholy humanity without becoming unholy or making peace with the defilement of humanity. Through the Holy Spirit he purifies, sanctifies, and makes humanity a dwelling fit for the divine presence. His fierce grace burns until all our impurities are removed. Likewise, in his grace God exercises his righteous judgment against sin: by grace God "condemned sin in sinful man" (Rom. 8:3). His wrath toward sin is at the same time his grace to the sinner. His righteous judgment on sin is gracious because sin is not our friend or our essence — but our jailor and mortal enemy. The holy and righteous God graciously gives himself in fellowship with unholy and unrighteous humanity and in this way creates a new humanity, holy and righteous. That fellowship, as I have already made clear, is named Jesus Christ.

A so-called grace that ignored or tolerated humanity's sin and misery could not be the grace of God. God's grace for the sinner takes the form of wrath toward sin and liberation for the sinner. Only diabolical cynicism could transform God's gift of freedom *from* the power of sin into a (false) freedom *for* sin. There is no freedom in sin: there is only slavery, falsehood, destruction, and death. God's gracious "yes" to us must include a stern "no" to the sin that enslaves us. The opposition of his holiness and the judgment of his righteousness are only the negative sides of his grace. Therefore, God's holiness, righteousness, and graciousness indwell each other in perfect unity.

Great Is His Mercy

Whereas in grace God gives himself to the undeserving, in mercy God gives himself to the suffering. Accordingly, Edward Leigh defines God's mercy as "a disposition toward the creature considered as sinful and miserable by his sin. . . . It is a readiness to take a fit course for the helping of the miserable, or it is an Attribute in God whereby the Lord of his free love is ready to succor those that be in misery."[14] In his great mercy, God comes to the aid of fallen creatures. God takes up the cause of the sick, dying, and sin-cursed; he reaches out in compassion to the guilty, wretched, and miserable to forgive, heal, and comfort. God's mercy is gracious because we do not deserve it, loving because he gives himself freely, holy because he maintains his distinct being in his mercy, and righteous because he remains true to himself in his pity.

---

14. Leigh, *Treatise of Divinity,* 2.11 (London, 1647), p. 87.

The Merciful God of Scripture

Scripture praises God's great mercy and compassion: "The Lord is good to all; he has compassion on all he has made" (Ps. 145:9). Jesus urges us to be merciful "just as your Father is merciful" (Luke 6:36). Paul designates God as "the Father of compassion and the God of all comfort" (2 Cor. 1:3-4). James reminds those suffering trials that God overflows with "compassion and mercy" (James 5:11). Peter praises God because of "his great mercy" (1 Pet. 1:3). Those in distress call on God's mercy: "Answer me, O Lord, out of the goodness of your love; in your great mercy turn to me" (Ps. 69:16; Ps. 86:3). The lepers, demon-possessed, lame, and blind called on Jesus to have mercy (Matt. 15:22; 17:15; 20:30).

God is merciful to the penitent. The Psalmist pleads: "O Lord, have mercy on me; heal me, for I have sinned against you" (Ps. 41:41). Jesus offers the penitent tax collector's prayer as a model: "God, have mercy on me, a sinner" (Luke 18:13). God demonstrates his mercy in his great patience with wayward Israel: "But in your great mercy you did not put an end to them or abandon them, for you are a gracious and merciful God" (Neh. 9:31). Jesus Christ embodies God's mercy. Confronted by a leper begging for healing, Jesus extends mercy: "Filled with compassion, Jesus reached out his hand and touched the man. 'I am willing,' he said. 'Be clean!'" (Mark 1:41). Speaking to the gentile Christians, Peter reminds them: "You had not received mercy, but now you have received mercy" through Christ (1 Pet. 2:10). And Jude urges us to "wait for the mercy of our Lord Jesus Christ" (Jude 1:21).

God remains free and sovereign in his mercy. The Lord declares to Moses: "I will have mercy on whom I will have mercy, and I will have compassion on whom I will have compassion" (Exod. 33:19). Paul draws on this text in his treatment of Israel and the church in Romans 9–11. God's compassion does not depend on human activity "but on God's mercy" (9:16). We have no grounds to complain about God's actions, for God is free to extend mercy or withhold it (9:18). For mercy's sake, God freely ignores relative degrees of righteousness among human beings and places them all in the category of sinners so that he can extend mercy to all alike: "For God has bound all men over to disobedience so that he may have mercy on them all" (11:32).

Perspectives on God's Mercy

God's Mercy Is God's Love Directed to the Suffering

When we think of suffering, most often we think of agonizing physical pain, a sense of loss and bewilderment at the death of a loved one, or fear and anxiety in the face of our own death. But defining suffering in those terms narrows the concept to include only self-conscious suffering, suffering that is experienced as painful. A theological understanding of suffering must encompass more than that. In the most general terms, we can define suffering as the *state of being deprived of the good we were created to enjoy.*[15] This state comes upon us consciously and painfully when we lose a good that we have enjoyed. Losing a parent, a spouse, or a child cuts away part of our being and leaves us empty and grieving.

On the other hand, our suffering may be a state so familiar to us that we are not even aware of its character. We were made to love God with our whole being and to find in him our only good in life and death. Our sin has become so much second nature to us, however, that we have never experienced the full measure of this good. Hence, we are not aware of the depth of our suffering in living without it. Augustine observed: "Today I have more pity for a person who rejoices in wickedness than for a person who has the feeling of having suffered hard knocks by being deprived of a pernicious pleasure or having lost a source of miserable felicity."[16] If we could know the fullness of God's love for us and the joy of giving ourselves completely in return, the loss of this relationship would constitute the worst fall and the most painful suffering possible.

God knows our suffering, and he is more aware of its extent and depth than we are: "He remembers that we are dust" (Ps. 103:14). He knows that we are nothing and walk on the edge of nothingness. He knows the suffering we endure because of our sin. In our unbelief, we live as if God were not good or trustworthy. In our pride, we act as if we knew our true needs better than our Maker does. In our laziness, we give in to our immediate lusts and refuse to rise up to the freedom God offers. Losing sight of the truth, we justify our actions with a web of lies in which we play God and give to God the devil's role. We project a world in which death is life and life is death, slavery is freedom and freedom is slavery, and evil is good and good is evil.[17] But it will not work: however tightly we weave the web of self-deception, we cannot change God's world — the only real world — in the least. God is still God, our only good. We are

---

15. In the section on impassibility below, I will work with the following fuller definition: Suffering involves (1) a painful and undesirable state of mind, (2) induced by an external source, (3) that inflicts or threatens to inflict damage and loss to us.

16. Augustine, *Confessions*, 2.3, trans. Henry Chadwick (New York: Oxford, 1991), p. 36.

17. Barth developed his profound doctrine of sin as a threefold negation of God's grace: pride, sloth, and falsehood. Human pride negates the humility of the Son of God (*CD*, 4/1, pp. 358-513). Human sloth refuses to take up the freedom offered in the rising of the Son of God (*CD*, 4/2, pp. 378-498). Human falsehood attempts to hide from and suppress the truth manifested in Jesus Christ (*CD*, 4/3, 1, pp. 368-478).

still God's creatures, made to love him. Our refusal to love him is what constitutes our suffering, futility, wretchedness, misery, and hopelessness.[18]

We can be grateful that God's knowledge of our suffering is more than theoretical. His knowledge is accompanied by his compassion, and his compassion becomes our salvation through his mercy. He does not want us to suffer and be deprived of the good for which he made us. He loves us. God does not enjoy our suffering; nor does he stand at a distance, unmoved by our misery, or even delay his mercy a second. He is compassionate and merciful. He reaches out to us immediately and takes up our cause. In creation, he mercifully gave being to those who had been nothing. In his kind providence, he walks beside us in constant care, though we take his care for granted. In Jesus Christ, he addresses the taproot of our suffering by taking on our nature, bearing our sin and suffering.

God Is Free in His Compassion and Mercy

Human compassion is limited: it is not fully free, nor is it purely active. In its most primitive form, our compassion arises in us passively, an automatic response to stimuli. We require sights, sounds, and memories of suffering to activate our compassion. Sometimes we refuse to extend mercy even when we do feel compassion. This is because we have other feelings and desires that conflict with natural compassion. Compassion without mercy is plentiful and cheap. Because our perception of suffering is limited, our compassion is correspondingly impaired. We do not really "suffer along with" others, as the Latin-derived word "com-passion" and the Greek-based word "sym-pathy" would lead us to think. We do not feel the feelings of others or suffer their losses. We feel our own feelings and suffer our own losses. We suffer at the sight of others' sufferings. And thus compassion can become a very self-centered emotion manifested either in secret thankfulness that we are not suffering or in resentment toward the sufferer for causing our compassion.

But God is truly compassionate and sympathetic. God does not *become* compassionate because we suffer; nor does his compassion fluctuate with changes in our circumstances and emotions. God is eternally compassionate and fully sympathetic always. For God's compassion is not something other than his eternal triune love. Thus there is no need to define God's compassion in terms of divine suffering. I shall deal with this issue thoroughly in the section on impassibility. For now I shall simply state that God's love is an eternal self-giving, receiving, and self-giving-in-return among the triune persons without even the

---

18. See Barth's section entitled "The Misery of Man," where he treats the suffering-caused sin (*CD*, 4/2, pp. 483-98).

possibility of emptiness and loss. When God directs his love to suffering creatures, his love remains the same eternal self-giving, receiving, and self-giving-in-
return that God is eternally. After God has "wiped away every tear," and we know
the eternal joy of his unveiled presence, God's love for us will be just as compassionate as it was in the hour of our deepest suffering. In its eternal richness,
God's changeless love meets every need of a changing world. God loves no less
for loving us eternally! God's mercy is no less compassionate for its constancy!

Unlike our knowledge, God's knowledge of suffering is direct and unlimited. God does not need to interpret signs and symbols to understand us. God
knows our suffering in its reality. Hence God's compassion, unlike ours, does not
consist in his own suffering occasioned by the sights and sounds of our suffering. He knows our suffering as *our* suffering. He knows its causes and its remedy.
To object that God cannot be compassionate without himself suffering is as
cruel as it is shallow. I have already shown that human compassion — obviously
being used as the norm in this protest — embodies far from genuine knowledge
of others' sufferings, and its superficial resemblance to love and mercy makes it
all the more subject to abuse. These pitiless sufferers declare that they will not be
comforted unless their suffering causes others to suffer with them. It is not
enough that God fully understands our suffering, loves us, and has mercy on us;
we want to see God suffer as proof of these things. Such desires are foolish as well
as callous; for, if God really suffered in his compassion, it would be an infallible
sign that he did not understand our suffering fully. He would be caught up in his
own suffering, which would remain a barrier to understanding our suffering. On
the contrary, God understands nothingness, sin, hell, evil, suffering, and death
better than their victims know them. And he knows our suffering better than we
do precisely because he does not undergo it or suffer with it.

The merciful God does not suffer with us, but this does not make him cold
and heartless, as some critics claim. It empowers him to have compassion on *us*
without being distracted by his own pain. He can be fully present to us without
fearing loss of himself. He can extend mercy to us without anxiety about mercy
for himself. God is free in his compassion and mercy. And that is very good
news for the suffering.

God's Mercy Is One with His Righteousness and Holiness

God would not be merciful if he abandoned his holiness and righteousness in
his merciful actions. A mercy devoid of holiness and righteousness could touch
us only superficially, treating merely the symptoms of our suffering. God would
not be merciful if his mercy consisted simply in foregoing punishment for our
sins or in removing the physical pain and psychological disturbance that ac-

company our suffering. Rather, in his mercy God insists on removing the cause of our suffering. If suffering is the state of being deprived of the good we were created to enjoy, mercy consists in supplying this good. God is the good we were created to enjoy; sin is our refusal of this good; unholiness is our lack of this good; and suffering is the loss we endure in this sad state. God's mercy must be righteous to remove sin and holy to displace unholiness. God's mercy wars against sin as "unmercifully" as his righteousness does. God is true to himself in his mercy. God maintains his holiness in his mercy, for his mercy is unique and transcendent in character. In Jesus Christ, the compassionate God meets us at the point where our loss is complete and our suffering is deepest. The righteous and holy God, in his mercy, annihilates the cause of our suffering in the cross of Jesus. Jesus Christ abandoned himself, on our behalf, in obedience to his Father, and in doing so he achieved for us the goal of our existence: to live in a relationship with our Maker in which we know him as Love and love him above all things.[19] This is something for which to praise God!

The Patience of God

In exercising his holy and righteous love, God also manifests his patience. His grace and mercy are always accompanied by his forbearance. It will deepen and enrich our understanding of God's holy love to grasp how its every expression manifests his infinite and eternal patience. Though God's love is patient, we can imagine a "love" that is impatient in its desire. Rather than giving its object time and space to love in return, it absorbs it immediately. God's love is patient in that it gives us time and space to exist, grow, and love in return. Since it is completely one with his holiness, righteousness, and freedom, God's patience cannot be mistaken for weakness, indifference, limitation, or indulgence. God is patient in sovereign freedom and condescending love, and thus he evokes our amazement and praise.

God's Patience in Scripture

The Lord "is a compassionate and gracious God, slow to anger, abounding in love and faithfulness" (Exod. 34:6). God manifests his patience by putting up with the sin and rebellion of his people in view of their future repentance and return. Peter

---

19. Barth argues vigorously and extensively for the unity of mercy and righteousness (*CD*, 2/1, pp. 376-83).

reminded his readers of God's patience in giving Noah's contemporaries time to repent (1 Pet. 3:20). And 2 Peter responds to the criticism of God's delay of salvation and judgment: "He is patient with you, not wanting anyone to perish, but everyone to come to repentance" (2 Pet. 3:9). Paul speaks of some who attempt to take advantage of God's "kindness, tolerance, and patience." They do not realize that "God's kindness leads you toward repentance" (Rom. 2:4).

God's patience with sinners also can be directed toward manifesting his own glory. For God is not patient *because* human beings are rebellious any more than he is gracious because his creatures are unworthy or merciful because they suffer. God is as free in his patience as he is in his grace and mercy. Isaiah reminds the people of God's sovereign patience: "For my own name's sake I delay my wrath; for the sake of my praise I hold it back from you, so as not to cut you off. . . . I will not yield my glory to another" (Isa. 48:8-11). In Romans 9, Paul adds his witness to the free and sovereign nature of God's patience. God's patience toward sinners is not a sign of approval but a way of allowing evil to manifest its true nature and making "the riches of his glory known to the objects of his mercy" (v. 23). In Paul's own conversion, he sees an example of God's freedom in his "unlimited patience" (1 Tim. 1:16).

The ultimate goal (and thus the ultimate ground) of God's patience is Jesus Christ, for "in his forbearance he had left the sins committed beforehand unpunished — he did it to demonstrate his justice at the present time, so as to be just and the one who justifies those who have faith in Jesus" (Rom. 3:25-26). Scripture is very clear, however, that God's patience does not imply an indulgence or forgetfulness. Although the Lord is "slow to anger," he "does not leave the guilty unpunished" (Num. 14:18; Nah. 1:3). For this reason, Isaiah warns the descendents of David not "to try the patience of my God" (Isa. 7:13). Paul, the apostle of grace, writing in the "book of grace," solemnly warns: "God cannot be mocked" (Gal. 6:7).

Theology of God's Patience

Divine Patience Defined

Grace is God's loving gift of himself to the unworthy, and mercy is God's loving gift of himself to the suffering. God's patience is his *loving gift of space and time for creatures to exist and develop and act alongside him as genuine others.*[20] God shows his patience not only by tolerating the ignorance, foolishness, and sin of

---

20. In this definition I am influenced by Barth, *CD*, 2/1, pp. 409-10.

already existing creatures; he also shows it in his willingness to create anything at all and to live with something not himself. However, it would seem that attributing patience to God calls into question his deity, because, from a certain point of view, the very existence of something other than God represents a rupture in being, a wound in reality, and a fall from grace. From this perspective, creation could be viewed as a parody of God, a suffering shadow existence that ought not to be. A perfect God — again, from a certain point of view — should be impatient with the imperfection of creation. Indeed, an impatient God would never allow that rupture to occur or would close it as soon as it made its appearance.

However, Scripture declares, and the history of salvation demonstrates, that God is patient. He makes time and space for his creatures, giving them being, room for movement, and freedom for action. God rules creation in a way that does not absorb or annihilate or crowd it out. As I have observed above, God demonstrates his unlimited patience, first, in creation itself: he creates and sustains another reality. In his providence, God walks with creatures in space and time as they grow and actualize their divinely given potential. Along the way, he tolerates creation's weaknesses, hesitancies, and reversals. For the sake of his redemptive plan, God puts up with the sins of humanity and condescends to exist side by side with his enemies. Patiently, as Leigh beautifully expresses it, God "doth long bear with sin which he hateth, sparing sinners . . . that he might bring them to repentance."[21]

God Exercises Patience Freely

Why does God exercise such patience? Human beings are forced to wait in any case, patiently or impatiently. We cannot move in space without expending time, and we cannot find relief from suffering or bring our desires to fulfillment instantly. But nothing forces God to wait. Time and space are gifts to his creatures and not laws of being to which he must submit. God does not need to move in time to act or change locations to be present. We have no moral claim on his patience, for no obligation requires God to coexist with finite, time-bound, and sinful creatures. His patience is pure grace, love unlimited, and mercy unprovoked. And as he bears with us, God expresses his righteousness because he is being true to his eternal identity. In his patience he is holy, because he maintains his unique and transcendent being in his patient condescending.

Let us then assume that God is free in his patience and that God does not

21. Leigh, *System or Body of Divinity*, 2.13 (London, 1654), p. 186.

have to create the world or put up with it. What does it mean that God none-theless created the world and exercises patience with it? I have defined God's patience as his gift of space and time for creatures to exist and develop and act alongside him as genuine others. Does God's free decision to show patience with the world imply that he freely limits himself so that the world can exist and act alongside him? Must God draw back to make room for creatures? Emil Brunner says: "God *limits Himself* by creating something which is not Himself, something 'over against' Himself, which he endows with a relative indepen-dence."[22] Rachel Muers detects an element of "passivity" and suffering in God's patience: "Patience implies not only the gift of time, but also the acceptance of time."[23] W. H. Vanstone says that God "hands Himself over" to the world, that "in loving the world he gives to the world the terrible power to have meaning to and for Himself."[24] Are these writers correct? Must God cease being insofar as the creature is? Must God stop acting so the creature can act? Are divine free-dom and human freedom mutually exclusive?

I have anticipated these questions in my discussions of divine love and righteousness, and I will return to them again and again in future chapters. In-deed, answering these questions is a major aim of this book, and my case for answering each of them with a resounding "No" will require me to work my way through the entire doctrine of God issue by issue as I seek to show the su-periority of the alternative.

In discussing divine patience I will focus on two problems with the divine self-limitation theory: (1) it pits the attribute of patience against the other at-tributes, and (2) it denies that God is essentially and eternally patient. Concern-ing (1), I have already laid down the principle that God's attributes do not limit each other but are harmonious and mutually enriching. Thinking of divine pa-tience as self-limitation implies that God's patience restricts his freedom, holi-ness, omnipotence, omnipresence, and other attributes. God's decision to be patient would limit God's freedom for certain actions. God could not, for ex-ample, prevent violent people from causing suffering to others without contra-dicting his decision to give sinners freedom and time to repent. God could not exercise all his power because he has given some power to creatures. God could not control the world fully because, in his patience, he has given some control to his creatures. God could not know the future exhaustively because he has given creatures the ability to determine some of the future unilaterally. Be-

22. Brunner, *The Christian Doctrine of God*, trans. Olive Wyon (Philadelphia: Westminster, 1949), p. 251 (italics in original).
23. Muers, "Silence and the Patience of God," *Modern Theology* 17 (2001): 86.
24. Vanstone, *The Stature of Waiting* (New York: Seabury, 1983), p. 111.

lievers should not seriously consider taking this path.[25] On the contrary, I believe we should cling to what is a basic presupposition of this book: God's attributes do not limit but enrich each other.

The proposal that God's patience limits his other attributes arises partly from a mistaken concept of patience. Divine self-limitation theories assume that God's patience is a kind of inaction, withdrawal, and disengagement from the world. We understand human patience as a kind of self-restrained inaction, a combination of action and inaction. Because we are limited by space and time, two of us cannot inhabit the same place at the same time. Because individual desires sometimes conflict — for example, you want to practice the drums and I want to meditate quietly, or I want the last piece of cheesecake and so do you, or you have a high tolerance for disorder around the house and I am a neat freak — two people cannot always do what they will. Patience is the action of will whereby we restrain our outward actions in view of our objective limits. In patience, we adjust to the limits imposed on us by time, space, power, society, and moral law. Patience is necessary in human life, for we are inherently limited: we must vacate some time and space to allow other people their own existence and action.

In contrast to human waiting, God's patience is completely active. I can call on Barth for support here: "There can be no question of a neutral juxtaposition of God and the creature and therefore of a restraint on the part of God which signifies inaction."[26] When God gives us space and time, he *gives* them — actively and constantly. They have no being apart from God's constant action of creating and sustaining them. If God abandoned space and time, they would cease to be, and there would be no room or time for anything. Whereas our patience must respond to the conditions of our existence, God's patience faces no such barriers. He can be present to us in our space and time without displacing us. Far from threatening us, God's power and knowledge set us free for our own existence, knowledge, and action. In his patience God displays his wisdom: he accomplishes his will in a way appropriate to creatures.

The second problem with the divine self-limitation theory of divine patience concerns its understanding of patience as something temporary and nonessential in God's nature. Because it sees patience as the self-limitation and nonactivity of God, it does not wish to acknowledge that God's patience is eternal, because that would imply that God is eternally and essentially limited.

25. For examples of the approach I am criticizing, see Paul S. Fiddes, *Participating in God: A Pastoral Doctrine of the Trinity* (Louisville: Westminster John Knox, 2000), pp. 152-90, and Donald Gray, "On Patience: Human and Divine," *Cross Currents* 24 (1975): 421.

26. Barth, *CD*, 2/1, p. 411.

God's choice for self-limitation, his patience, is entailed in his decision to create the world: that is, the attribute of patience presupposes the existence of the world. If we assume this connection, it places us in a dilemma: Is God's patience an arbitrary decision unrelated to his eternal nature? This option is unacceptable because it would apply equally to all of God's attributes, and thus it would cast our knowledge of God into doubt. Or does God's nature change and gain further attributes with the creation of the world? This alternative makes God dependent on the world, which undermines God's freedom and independence.

However, understanding God's patience as purely active enables us to see it as an essential attribute without forcing us to think of God as essentially limited. This move roots God's patience in God's essential nature and thus secures our knowledge of God. It also gives us great comfort. God can be patient with us because he is eternally patient. But how can God be patient without a world upon which to exercise patience? If we view patience not as suffering the existence of another but as treasuring a genuine other, we will have no difficulty of grasping how God can be eternally patient. Patience is clearly an aspect of God's eternal triune love. The Father gives himself to the Son through the Spirit; the Father is the space and time where the Son lives; the Son returns himself to the Father in the Spirit and is the space and time where the Father lives. God's space and time is his self-distinction and fellowship as Father, Son, and Spirit. The triune persons dwell within each other in the perfect union and distinction of eternal love. The union is constitutive of the distinction, and the distinction is constitutive of the union. To put it another way, the distinction of patience makes the union of love possible, and the union of love makes the distinction of patience necessary.

God does not need to make room for us by limiting his presence in the space and time allotted to us. God has infinite space and time for us already, for God is his own space and time. The persons of the Trinity are no less God and no less distinct because they mutually indwell each other. In the same way, God does not need to become less God to make room for us to live in him and with him. God is patient love in that he gives himself as the space in which we can exist and live and enjoy the freedom he offers.

Jesus Christ Incarnates God's Patience

God is patient with us so that we can exist and develop and act alongside him as genuine others. But what hope is there that such patience will succeed? Universally, human beings show contempt for God's patience. They want to exist and develop and act not as genuine persons in loving relationships with God but as autonomous, self-centered beings. If it depended on us, God's patience would be for nothing; or, worse, it would show that divine patience is merely holy indifference that waits for us to destroy ourselves. In Jesus Christ, however, God reveals the reason and ground for his patience. In him, the old humanity dies and a new humanity is created and lives a new life of righteousness and holiness. In Jesus Christ, God takes time and space for us. As Barth succinctly puts it, "For the sake of the One, God has patience with the many."[27] In the union of our nature with the divine nature of the Son of God, God's space becomes our space, God's time our time, and God's freedom our freedom. In Jesus Christ, God gives himself fully to humanity, and humanity gives itself fully to God. Thus does divine patience achieve its goal.

The reality of Jesus Christ definitively refutes the divine self-limitation theory. God does need to give up space, time, and freedom to make room for creation. In the person of Jesus Christ, God unites himself with human nature without ceasing to be God. Nor is human nature destroyed or diminished or swallowed up by its union with the divine nature. The person Jesus Christ is both God and human: in him, God freely loves in mercy, grace, and patience. In him, humanity is liberated to love God in return and to show mercy, grace, and patience to others. In the incarnation, the union of God and humanity is so complete and harmonious that God does not need to hold back his divinity to make room for us. It is precisely in exercising the fullness of his divinity that God has room for us. And it is specifically in being truly human that we find our home within the infinite space and undiminished glory of God. As God gives himself completely to us and we give ourselves completely to him in return, we find that we have become persons, "genuine others," alongside God for the first time.

The Wisdom of God

Scripture and tradition agree in extolling the wisdom of God. Who can contemplate his works or review his mighty acts without breaking out in praise and concluding, with Paul, "To the only wise God be glory forever through Jesus Christ! Amen" (Rom. 16:27)? Barth characterizes God's wisdom by relating divine knowing and willing: "God not only wills, but knows what He wills."[28] He knows how to love us. And he knows how to maintain his holiness and righteousness in his love for us. He knows how to exercise grace, mercy, and patience so that his love is made effective in us. His wisdom is his knowledge of

27. CD, 2/1, p. 418. Barth says later that, in Jesus Christ, God has "created and established the ground for His patience" (p. 419).
28. Barth, CD, 2/1, p. 423.

how to accomplish his loving will perfectly. Even if we cannot trace it out, God's wisdom is perfect and worthy of praise: "Oh, the depth of the riches of the wisdom and knowledge of God! How unsearchable his judgments, and his paths beyond tracing out!" (Rom. 11:33).

Wisdom in Scripture

Scripture marvels at God's wisdom. Isaiah praises the Creator for his works and proclaims that "his understanding no one can fathom" (Isa. 40:28). The angels, the elders, and the four living creatures surrounding God's throne exclaim: "Wisdom and thanks and honor and power and strength be to our God" (Rev. 7:12). Most instructive for the Old Testament view of divine wisdom is the prayer of Daniel in which he praises God for the many evidences of his wisdom: "Praise be to the name of God forever and ever; wisdom and power are his. He changes times and seasons; he sets up kings and deposes them. He gives wisdom to the wise and knowledge to the discerning" (Dan. 2:20-23; cf. Jer. 10:12). Daniel points to creation's display of God's wisdom, to God as the source of human wisdom, and to the wisdom of God's providential governance of the world. The psalmist, too, expresses amazement at the wonder of creation and credits God with wisdom in his creative acts: "In wisdom you made them all; the earth is full of your creatures" (Ps. 104:24; cf. Prov. 3:19; Isa. 40:28).

All true wisdom finds its source in God. As Moses laid his hands on Joshua, the latter was "filled with the spirit of wisdom" (Deut. 34:9). At the beginning of his reign, Solomon asked God for wisdom (1 Kings 3:7-9), and God gave the young king "wisdom and very great insight" (1 Kings 4:29; cf. 10:24; 3:28). Proverbs and Psalms credit all true human wisdom to God (Prov. 2:6). Psalm 119 praises God for the wisdom embodied in his words and laws: "I have more understanding than the elders, for I obey your precepts" (119:100).

The New Testament continues the theme of divine wisdom. Paul prays for the Ephesian church to receive from God "a spirit of wisdom and revelation, so that you may know him better" (Eph. 1:17). Again, for the Colossian Christians, Paul never stops praying, "asking God to fill you with the knowledge of his will through all spiritual wisdom and understanding" (Col. 1:9). James tells those who lack wisdom to ask for it and God will give it to them (James 1:5). At the end of Paul's discussion of God's mysterious action of bringing the gentiles to faith through the unbelief of Israel, he breaks out in praise of God's wisdom in conceiving and carrying out this plan (Rom. 11:33). The salvation in Christ, which becomes a visible reality in the church, manifests God's wisdom "to the rulers and authorities in the heavenly realms" (Eph. 3:10).

Throughout Scripture, divine wisdom is contrasted to human folly and false claims to wisdom. Implying the insignificance of human wisdom as compared to the divine, Isaiah asks: "Whom did the Lord consult to enlighten him, and who taught him the right way? Who was it that taught him knowledge or showed him the path of understanding?" (Isa. 40:14). Human wisdom is no match for the Lord's wisdom: "There is no wisdom, no insight, no plan that can succeed against the Lord" (Prov. 21:30). Paul takes up this theme in the first two chapters of 1 Corinthians and applies it to God's use of the cross to save the world. He quotes Isaiah 29:14 as his text: "I will destroy the wisdom of the wise; the intelligence of the intelligent I will frustrate" (1 Cor. 1:19). The world, with all protestations of wisdom, did not gain true knowledge of God. By revealing himself in the cross of Christ, God exposed the wisdom of the world as foolishness. Worldly wisdom does not even approximate the wisdom of God; rather, it contradicts it and opposes it. This opposition is manifested in the actions of the "rulers of this age," who "crucified the Lord of glory" (1 Cor. 2:8). God's wisdom is not something that can be grasped by observing the ways of the world or reflecting on the human mind. This way leads to idolatry and foolishness. God's wisdom can be known only in Christ and through the power of the Spirit (2:10-16). Jesus Christ is the "wisdom of God" (1:24). In him God has accomplished "our righteousness, holiness and redemption" (1:30). In Christ, God has achieved his eternal plan in a way that is fitting and effective.

Theology of Wisdom

In his wisdom God knows how to accomplish his good will; God knows why he does what he does. God never acts capriciously or by trial and error; he is never unsure of his goal or uncertain of the way to reach it. In all his ways he follows his eternal plan and never makes mistakes. Thomas Ridgley (c. 1667-1734) lauds God's wisdom as "doing whatever he does in the fittest season, and in circumstances all of which tend to set forth his own honor . . . so that he can see no reason to wish it had been otherwise ordered, or to repent thereof."[29] Hence, God's wisdom is more than his omniscience: God not only knows all things speculatively, he knows how to accomplish all things in ways that perfectly embody his love, righteousness, and holiness. We can define God's wisdom, then, as *God's perfect understanding of how to accomplish his loving, holy, and righteous will.*

29. Ridgley, *Body of Divinity,* vol. 1, ed. Rev. John M. Wilson (New York: Robert Carter & Brothers, 1855), p. 99.

Human and Divine Wisdom

What is wisdom? Clearly, wisdom is more than speculative or scientific knowledge. It is "know-how" rather than "knowledge that." Yet wisdom is not mere skill. For you can be a good bricklayer, tennis player, or accountant without being a wise person. Wisdom is "know-how" for life, for successful human living in all its dimensions and relationships. In seeking to accomplish its goals, wisdom takes into account all the regularities and the contingencies of our existence. It adjusts itself to the laws of physics, chemistry, and biology. In its relationships with other people, wisdom will make plans and act on reliable knowledge of human psychological, economic, political, and social behavior. In wisely recognizing its own limits, wisdom makes its plans flexible to accommodate the unexpected. Wisdom also includes a moral component, for irrational drives war within us. A wise person will exercise self-control in situations where anger, lust, and pride urge us to shortsighted and destructive actions. And human wisdom will take account of the divine as it understands it; for the wise person will make plans and act in view of all factors that can influence outcomes.

However, the wisdom available to human beings, even the wisest, is limited. If wisdom is the capacity that guides our actions toward success, experience proves that we have less of it than we need. Wisdom channels our power toward achieving a goal, and everything depends on aiming at the right goal. A crafty person's success at committing a bank robbery or a seduction would not prove his wisdom but his lack of it. Not even a well-intentioned person always chooses the right goals. Indeed, since we are sinners, apart from God's supernatural help through the Spirit, our loves, which determine our goals, are all misplaced. One's technical skill as a driver is of little consolation if one is headed toward the wrong destination.

Even if we could select the right goals and arrange them according to their true priority, we do not have the knowledge to achieve them. On the physical level, at least in things bigger than atoms and smaller than the universe, the world is fairly regular and predictable. By extrapolation, we can predict the consequences of throwing a rock at a window or driving a car off a bridge or breathing cyanide. On some levels, human behavior is predictable: if it is not always at an individual level, it is at least at a statistical level. It is likely that you will receive a negative response if you yell an obscenity at your neighbor. In the economic sphere, if the "guaranteed" return on your investment sounds too good to be true, you should trust your instincts. But the predictability of an action declines in inverse proportion to the number of factors and interacting systems involved. Two or more deterministic physical systems often interact in ways that are unpredictable from within either system: an x-ray strikes a gene and causes a mutation, or while you are hiking, you cross paths with a rattle-snake. Even if the outcomes of interacting events are theoretically predictable, over time the number of factors grows exponentially and approaches infinity. Reality is so complex that we cannot make accurate predictions very far into the future. In large, chaotic systems such as bodies of water or masses of air, very small variations in conditions at a particular point in time can produce vastly different conditions at a later point.

Our lack of knowledge goes hand in hand with our lack of power. If wisdom is "know-how," it would seem that it is linked inextricably to power. Do you really know how to do something if you cannot do it or get it done? Surely, knowing how to do something means knowing *how to get it done.* The proof of wisdom is in the success of the deed. You may be able to make a wish without power, but you will not be able to make a plan.[30] Therefore, we are at least as limited in our wisdom as we are in our power. On the other side of the equation, it seems that exercising power requires wisdom. For power apart from wisdom is but chaos and destruction. Power, strictly speaking, is the ability to accomplish an aim. Energy without knowledge leads to destruction, and knowledge without power promotes frustration.

But God's wisdom is unlimited. Unlike us, God always works toward the right goals in the right order, for he is righteous in all his ways. God does not contend with the necessities that constrain us and the contingencies that surprise us. God is the Creator and sustainer of the world and all its "laws." The physical laws operative in the universe do not restrict God's possibilities. They are exactly as God willed them. There are no superuniversal laws, laws that determine the kind of universe God can make. Therefore, physical laws cannot constrain God's ability to do what he wills; rather, they obey his will. For God, there are no contingencies. The contingencies of our world may seem undetermined by previous events, but even the most far-fetched and unpredictable events depend on something. And all things depend on God. Even if the positions and energy levels of subatomic, quantum events prove to be indeterminate with reference to all their previous states, they are not independent and indeterminate to the God who sustains them.

If God's wisdom is not limited and fallible like ours, it is also not like the all-knowingness of the Deists' God. Deists conceived of God as a "perfect observer" residing outside the universe. According to this view, God's wisdom

---

30. Brunner rightly connects wisdom and power when he says: "The Wisdom of God . . . might be described as the ideal aspect of Divine Omnipotence . . . for this Divine Wisdom is the Power of God in its absolutely unlimited spiritual creativity" (*The Doctrine of God,* p. 283).

consists in his infallible ability to predict events within the universe by extrapolating from deterministic physical laws and the positions and energies of all things within the universe. However, God does not act *on* the universe, as in the Deist theory, or *in* the universe as we do; rather, the universe as a whole and in every part is God's action. Nothing happens independently of his action. And God knows his own action, which is in part what we mean when we say that God is wise.

For us, the further away in the future an event is, the more unpredictable it is. This is true because, as I have observed above, the passage of time allows for more and more complicating interactions among events and systems of events. However, time does not present the same challenge to God that it does to us. God does not act *in* time any more than he acts *in* space; rather, he gives us time as he acts on our behalf. For time is not a neutral medium within which events occur: time comes into being as God accomplishes his good will in a way appropriate to the creation. Time is God's creature, not God's jailer, and it presents no problem for his wisdom. God can act in such ways that the result of his actions will continue to embody perfectly his intentions, no matter how much time passes. For each "passing" moment is also God's action and will never overturn his previous intentions. Hence, God has the know-how (wisdom) to do whatever he wants.

God's wisdom is unlimited because, unlike creatures, his power is unlimited. To limit God's wisdom would be to limit his power and, conversely, limiting his power would also limit his wisdom. If God's wisdom is his know-how to achieve any goal, his power is his ability to do anything he wills simply by willing it. For example, in creation God moved things from a state of nothingness (if nothingness can be conceived as a state) to a state of existence by his word. In this sense, creatures have no power of their own. We could not even make a wish if we were not alive, and we do not come to life or remain alive because we will it. In creatures, willing something to exist does not make it exist. Consequently, we must always use means to achieve our ends. Our bodies, as well as our tools and machines, are means we use to accomplish our goals. But God *is* his power and so does not need other powers — such as a body, tools, or machines — to accomplish his goals. His power is unlimited. God can do anything he wills, and he wills only good things. Therefore, God's wisdom is unlimited.

God's wisdom is not a set of skills added to his essential nature. It is rather "the inner truth and clarity with which the divine life in its self-fulfillment and its works justifies and confirms itself and in which it is the sum and criterion of all that is clear and true."[31] As Barth's words suggest, God's existence is not a

31. Barth, *CD*, 2/1, p. 426.

brute fact, an enigma, but is completely luminous to him. God knows perfectly what he is and who he is, that is, God knows how to be God. The Father knows how to love the Son in the Spirit, and the Son knows how to love the Father in return by the Spirit. God knows why and how to create the world through the Word and the Spirit. And God knows how to be gracious to us while maintaining his righteousness and holiness. Jesus Christ embodies the same "wisdom" by which God is God eternally (1 Cor. 1:18-25). In Jesus Christ, God demonstrates that he knows how to save sinners, how "to reconcile the world to himself" (2 Cor. 5:19), and how to bring creation into the "glorious freedom of the children of God" (Rom. 8:21). Jesus *is* that salvation, reconciliation, and glorious freedom. Therefore, Jesus *is* the wisdom of God.

Limited Wisdom?

Is God infinitely wise, wise enough to accomplish everything he wills? Or is God wise enough to accomplish only some of what he desires or to achieve only an approximation of what he wills? Some modern thinkers, in their attempts to answer the problem of evil and make conceptual room for human freedom, hedge their statements about God's wisdom. They do not define God's wisdom as God's knowledge of how to accomplish his good will perfectly. Rather, they define it as God's knowledge of how to accomplish the best goals achievable, using the best means available in the most efficient way possible. This definition does not necessarily contradict my definition. As long as one understands that what is achievable, available, and possible are determined by God alone, the two definitions amount to the same thing. Unfortunately, this is not how its advocates understand it: they use this weaker definition of wisdom to maintain that God is "wise," while they deny that God is always able to accomplish his will. God's inability to achieve his will, according to this theory, absolves God of blame for the evil in the world. God is doing the best he can.

John Sanders, in *The God Who Risks*, understands God's wisdom as his ability "to work with the sort of world he decided to create, despite the fact that things do not always go as God desires."[32] Not everything happens in our world "precisely as God intends. God experiences setbacks and even defeats" (p. 183). But we can be thankful that God is "adept," "omnicompetent," and "resourceful." He is "wise enough" to deal with the challenges he faces, and God has a good "track record" in accomplishing his general will (p. 234; see also p. 183). Indeed, God has already "achieved a fair degree of victory" (p. 234). God's wisdom is displayed in his "competency and resourcefulness in working to achieve

---

32. Sanders, *The God Who Risks* (Downers Grove, IL: InterVarsity Press, 1999), pp. 181-82.

the goal of this project" (p. 234). As the title of Sanders's book indicates, God is a "risk taker" who has "placed his bet that he can establish a trusting, loving relationship with us through Jesus" (p. 234). However, Sanders does admit that God may fail to achieve all "the specific goals he would like to see fulfilled" (p. 236). It would appear that Sanders does not think of God's wisdom, as I have defined it, as God's *perfect understanding of how to accomplish his loving, holy, and righteous will.*

Jack Cottrell's view of divine wisdom comes closer to the traditional view than does Sanders's view; nevertheless, it also falls short. Cottrell offers the wisdom of God as great comfort to believers. He correctly warns that "[o]nly someone who is wiser than God has a right to sit in judgment upon his providence." However, Cottrell's definition of wisdom raises some concerns: "Wisdom is the ability to choose the best possible end, and then to choose the best possible means of achieving that end." The questionable nature of this definition manifests itself when he urges us to trust "that a world with free-will creatures is the best possible world, even though such creatures have the ability to sin." Does Cottrell presuppose that there is some ground other than God for what is "possible," which would thereby limit the wisdom of God?[33]

Why is God unable to accomplish his will perfectly? Because, according to this theory, what things are achievable, available, and possible are not determined solely by God. There are laws other than God's will that define what is achievable, limit what is available, and determine what is possible. For example, God cannot both determine the universe to turn out exactly as he wills *and* allow created beings to exercise freedom. The conclusion to this line of thought is disquieting: God does *not* know how to accomplish his will completely in any universe that contains you and me. It gives little consolation to reply, "No one else knows how either," or "God did not have to create a world containing free beings," or "That's because it is inherently impossible." We are still left with a God who does not know how to achieve his goodwill perfectly. We must contend with the possibility that God may fail to achieve the purpose for which he created this universe. How can we praise God with such thoughts troubling our minds?[34]

I will address this issue in much greater detail in my treatment of the at-

33. Cottrell, *The Faith Once for All: Bible Doctrine for Today* (Joplin, MO: College Press, 2002), p. 83.

34. Bruce A. Ware, *God's Lesser Glory: The Diminished God of Open Theism* (Wheaton, IL: Crossway Books, 2000). Not without some justification, Ware calls Sanders's doctrine of providence an "assault on God's wisdom" (p. 143). Ware questions Sanders's optimism about God's ability to bring things to a good conclusion, observing that "high risk and high confidence seem impossible together" (p. 157).

tributes of divine freedom. Here I must content myself to say that there are no laws, and can be no laws, above and beyond God that limit God's freedom and thus his wisdom. God is lord of the achievable, sole provider of the available, and definer of the possible. Hence, sound Christian theology must declare that God knows how to accomplish his goodwill perfectly. His wisdom knows no limits, and that is why it is worthy of our highest praise.

The Unity of Wisdom with the Other Attributes

Viewing the other attributes from the perspective of God's wisdom enriches them, and wisdom in turn is enriched by them. For a "love" without wisdom would be no more than sentiment without effect. And wisdom without love would be reduced to craftiness without morality. Grace without understanding would be but whimsical indulgence, and understanding without grace rises only to the level of cold calculation. An unwise mercy does more harm than good by its clumsy kindness, whereas wisdom without mercy surveys suffering heartlessly. Patience without wisdom inspires no confidence of success. But wisdom without patience inspires terror. While in his righteousness God always does right, in his wisdom he always does the best. And for the loving God, the right thing and the best thing are always the same. In his holiness, God maintains his unique being in all his acts, and in his wisdom he acts in ways that will accomplish his will in all things. God is always wise in his holy acts, and always holy in his wise deeds.

God is infinitely wise in all he does because he is wisdom itself. For in his triune life, God is God in the most perfect way. God is not God automatically and unconsciously, but freely. God is not on a journey of self-discovery in which he comes gradually to understand his nature and learns how to act as God more effectively. God knows how to be God. God knows the why, the how, and the wherefore of his deity. He knows, therefore, how to be God in relationship to his creation. He is "the only wise God" (Rom. 16:27), and he deserves glory and wisdom and power forever and ever.

More on the Relationship of Wisdom and Patience

In light of current issues in theology, the wisdom of God's patience and the patience of his wisdom deserves special consideration. In the previous section on divine patience, I defined God's patience as *his gift of space and time for the creature to exist and develop and act alongside him as a genuine other.* There I took issue with the contemporary theory that God's patience is equivalent to his self-limitation. According to this theory, God must limit his presence, freedom, and action to make room for human presence, freedom, and action. After this study of divine wisdom, I believe we see clearly that the divine self-limitation theory fails to take into account the wisdom of God's patience and the patience of his wisdom.

According to the divine self-limitation model, God's patience does not demonstrate his wisdom, that is, *his perfect understanding of how to accomplish his loving, holy, and righteous will.* God does not know how to do this in a world containing free beings. So, if God is to have any hope of seeing his will even approximated, he must withdraw and allow the achievement of his loving, holy, and righteous will to become contingent on the freedom, necessity, and chance that are operative in the created world. Perhaps this action demonstrates a sort of wisdom that makes the best of a bad situation, but it falls short of divine wisdom as Scripture presents it.

This theory begins with the presupposition that genuine human freedom and unlimited divine freedom are incompatible and concludes that God's patience manifests his limitation as much as his wisdom. If we begin, instead, with the presupposition that God is wise in his patience (because he is wise in all his actions) and patient in his wisdom, we will come to a very different conclusion. In his wisdom, God knows how to accomplish his will in a way that fits the creature. God's patience is not his forced absence but his free condescending, his hidden and mysterious, yet nonetheless full, presence. God knows how to be the Creator and the Redeemer of his creatures. Jesus Christ is God's patience *and* his wisdom. He manifests what is always true: in his patient actions, God knows what he is doing and why he is doing it. In the incarnation and the cross, God hides but does not withdraw; for under the veil of the flesh and in the darkness of the cross, the power of God accomplishes the impossible. Foolish and godforsaken in outward appearance, God's infinite patience bursts forth, in Christ, as his unlimited wisdom and power. Squinting in the light of wisdom's true glory, with our shredded theories at our feet, we can neither continue our foolish chatter nor remain completely silent. We have to praise him:

> Oh, the depth of the riches of the wisdom and knowledge of God! How unsearchable his judgments, and his paths beyond tracing out! "Who has known the mind of the Lord? Or who has been his counselor?" "Who has ever given to God, that God should repay him?" For from him and through him and to him are all things. To him be the glory forever! Amen" (Rom. 11:33-36).

8

Where Life Lives Triumphant:
Divine Freedom, Life, Spirituality, and Personhood

Life! Could a word stir us more and resonate with greater harmony in our souls? It resounds with hope, energy, meaning, and joy. Life — full, deep, and expansive! Everyone wants it and everyone seeks it. But we are not satisfied with mere biological life. We want to grow and explore; we want to think and know; we want to dream and create. We want life freed from the mere mechanical processes of the physical and biological spheres. We want a freedom that enables us to possess ourselves, to create, and to actualize our potential. And we want to know and be known and love and be loved. We want the distinct personal identity-in-relationship that can be achieved only in community with other persons.

Scripture declares and tradition echoes that God lives. God lives of himself, and in him life itself lives. God lives free from death in all its forms. He lives free from automatic processes and unconscious depths; he lives free from ignorance of his "origin" and fear of his end. He freely wills and enacts his entire being. He possesses himself entirely, yet he is not enclosed within himself. In his triune life he lives as love, as complete openness and fellowship. Life! We want it and seek it. But we will find it only in him who is life itself, life eternal.

Divine Freedom

In treating the attributes of the divine love I differentiated God's love, holiness, grace, mercy, righteousness, patience, and wisdom from those of all other beings. God is these things in an unlimited way, that is, God loves in complete freedom. Without ceasing to speak of the loving God, I will now focus directly on this differentiating factor: divine freedom.

Scripture

According to Scripture, God lives in complete freedom. He is what he is independent of anything else. "I am who I am," the Lord says to Moses from the burning bush (Exod. 3:14). "I am the Lord your God," declares the Lord over and over, without any effort to establish his lordship on anything but his claim (Exod. 20:2). No other power can share rule with the Lord: "I will not give my glory to another or my praise to idols" (Isa. 42:8). God is completely independent of all other powers because he does not "need anything" (Acts 17:25) and "has life in himself" (John 5:26). All other things depend on him while he depends on nothing outside himself. "For from him and through him and to him are all things" (Rom. 11:36).

The Tradition

The tradition has been unanimous in its praise for God's absolute freedom from all other powers. Whatever terms traditional theologians use — transcendence, independence, necessity, infinity, aseity, absoluteness — they assert clearly that God is what he is and does what he does in complete freedom. He does not depend on anything outside himself. He is complete and all-sufficient in his Trinitarian life.

According to G. L. Prestige, many of the early fathers expressed the idea of divine independence with words that began with the Greek prefix *hyper*.[1] Irenaeus, speaking of God, says that "out of his transcendence *(hyperoche)*, not out of our own nature, do we possess eternal life."[2] The Greek fathers also emphasized divine freedom by using the "alpha privative" to negate concepts unworthy of divine transcendence. One of the most significant negative words is *agenetos*, which means uncreated, or without beginning. According to Prestige, "the *ageneton* exists *per se*; its cause lies within its own being. As being independent of all other existences it enjoys perfection."[3] Jaroslav Pelikan argues that the patristic use of the "alpha privative" in apophatic theology (a theology that speaks only about what God is not) is above all a "theory of language" that reg-

---

1. G. L. Prestige, *God in Patristic Thought*, 2nd ed. (London: S.P.C.K., 1952), pp. 25-54.

2. Irenaeus, *Against Heresies*, 5.2.3, quoted in Prestige, *God in Patristic Thought*, p. 25. Prestige gives numerous examples. This practice is illustrated in abundance in Dionysius the Areopagite, *The Divine Names* and *Mystical Theology*, trans. C. E. Rolt (Berwick, ME: IBIS Press, 2004).

3. Prestige, *God in Patristic Thought*, p. 46. Prestige continues: "What it obviously means can best be described, not in a specifically Hegelian sense, but in general idea, as 'The Absolute'" (p. 47).

ulates what we say about God and protests the arrogance of our thinking that we can comprehend the infinite God.[4] However, apophatic theology also served to underscore God's freedom from all finite conditions. It "probed the mysteries of all the ways in which the divine being was set apart from all created beings."[5] In addition, the Greek fathers prefixed the reflexive word *autos* (self) to positive qualities such as being, life, principle, deity, good, and truth to emphasize that God does not have those qualities by participation in the ideas of these things. God *is* these things "of himself."[6]

Anselm of Canterbury (c. 1033–c. 1109) articulated the doctrine of divine freedom, or aseity, concisely in his influential *Monologium*. Reasoning by examining and excluding unworthy alternatives, Anselm concludes that the being through whom all things exist, must exist "through itself."[7] But how may we conceive of this? This self-existent being could not have created itself, for this is absurd: "Seeing that this Being, then, does not exist before itself, by no means does it derive existence from itself."[8] And we've already ruled out its creation by another. Anselm sums up the negative side of divine freedom (aseity) this way:

> The supreme Substance, then, does not exist through any efficient agent, and does not derive existence from any matter, and was not aided in being brought into existence by any external causes. Nevertheless, it by no means exists through nothing, or derives existence from nothing; since, through itself and from itself, it is whatever it is.[9]

At last, Anselm ventures to speak of the positive side of God's freedom, which is an impossible task in the end. He begins by repeating the negative side, as if to guard, one final time, against mistaking the following metaphor — because that's what it is — for a literal description of God's essence:

> Finally, as to how it should be understood to exist through itself, and to derive existence from itself: it did not create itself, nor did it spring up as its

4. Pelikan, *Christianity and Classical Culture: The Metamorphosis of Natural Theology in the Christian Encounter with Hellenism* (New Haven: Yale University Press, 1993), p. 40. Quoting Gregory of Nyssa, Pelikan says, "It tells us under what conditions [it was permissible to] conceive of God as existing."

5. Pelikan, *Christianity and Classical Culture*, p. 208.

6. See Barth, *Church Dogmatics*, vol. 2, pt. 1, ed. G. W. Bromiley and T. F. Torrance, trans. T. H. L. Parker et al. (Edinburgh: T&T Clark, 1957), p. 302.

7. St. Anselm, *Monologium*, 3, in *Saint Anselm: Basic Writings*, trans. S. N. Deane, 2nd ed. (LaSalle, IL: Open Court, 1968), p. 42 (hereafer *CD*).

8. *Monologium*, 6, p. 48.

9. *Monologium*, 3, p. 48.

own matter, nor did it in any way assist itself to become what it was not before, unless, haply, it seems best to conceive of this subject in the way in which one says that *the light lights* or is *lucent,* through and from itself. For, as are the mutual relations of *the light* and *to light* and *lucent (lux, lucere, lucens),* such are the relations of *essence,* and *to be* and *being,* that is, *existing* or *subsisting.* So the supreme *Being,* and *to be* in the highest degree, and *being* in the highest degree, bear much the same relations, one to another, as *the light* and *to light* and *lucent.*[10]

We can detect here a reference to the Trinity of an Augustinian type, that is, of deriving the three from the one. Anselm uses the ancient metaphor of the light, its action of giving its light, and the illumination so often used by the church fathers in their Trinitarian meditations. For Anselm, then, the mystery of the Trinity is the final explanation of God's aseity and freedom.

The Protestant Reformers and the post-Reformation Orthodox continue the tradition of exalting the freedom of God above all encumbrances, internal and external, spiritual and material. In commenting on John 5:26, Calvin says: "For God is said to have life in Himself, not only because He alone lives by his own inherent power, but because He contains the fullness of life in himself and quickens all things."[11] Wolfgang Musculus (1497-1563) speaks of God as

sufficient of himself, that not only has he all of himself, but he also suffices himself, that he has no need either of any of the things which he has, and which he has made and created. He is sufficient to himself through all things and unto all things. . . . He should not have been a point the richer, albeit he had created a thousand worlds.[12]

The orthodox Reformed understood God's aseity in a twofold way. First, God is all-sufficient in himself. In the words of Edward Leigh, God's "life is his own, he liveth of and by and in himself. . . . He is life, and the fountain of life to all things."[13] For Thomas Ridgley, God is sufficient unto himself because his "being and perfections are underived . . . . He is self-existent or independent."[14]

---

10. *Monologium,* 6, p. 49 (all italics in original).

11. *Calvin's New Testament Commentaries,* vol. 4, *The Gospel According to John 1–10,* trans. T. H. L. Parker (Grand Rapids: Eerdmans, 1959), p. 131.

12. Musculus, *Loci Communes,* 43; quoted in Richard Muller, *Post-Reformation Reformed Dogmatics: The Rise and Development of Reformed Orthodoxy,* vol. 3, *The Divine Essence and Attributes* (Grand Rapids: Baker Academic, 2003), p. 369 (hereafter *PRRD*).

13. Leigh, *System or Body of Divinity,* 2.3 (London, 1654), p. 140.

14. Ridgley, *Body of Divinity,* vol. 1, ed. John M. Wilson (New York: Robert Carter & Brothers, 1855), p. 83.

Second, God is independent of creation. God does not need creation in any sense. And having created it, he is not conditioned in the least by it; he remains forever free. Binning takes God's aseity, not as a cold and speculative doctrine, but as one of great comfort:

> God is independent altogether, and self-sufficient. This is his royal prerogative wherein he infinitely transcends all created perfection. He is of himself, and for himself; from no other, and for no other . . . you ought to follow the streams up to it, and there to rest, for you can go no farther. . . . How can we think of such a Fountain-Being, but we must withal acknowledge ourselves to be shadows of his goodness, and that we owe to him what we are, and so consecrate and dedicate ourselves to his glory! How can we consider such a Self-Being, Independent, and Creating Goodness, but we must have some desire to cleave to him and some confidence to trust in him![15]

Theology of Divine Freedom

As I have noted in the survey of Scripture and tradition, God's freedom has negative and positive aspects.[16] Negatively, God depends on nothing outside himself and is limited in no way by another reality. God is not limited by his nature or attributes, by beings spiritual or things conceptual, by his creatures, by time and space, by matter, chance, or natural law, by the limits of creatures, or by the free actions of human beings — even their sins. No law above, beside, or within God determines, restricts, or conditions him in any way. God's nature and existence are not his fate, that is, they are not mere presuppositions or foundations of God's free action. God is the free Lord of his divinity, so that what God is and does, he does in perfect freedom. Barth articulates the freedom of God's being succinctly: "For as God is not an it but a He, so He is not a He who has first to partake in an it in order to be this He."[17]

However, God's freedom is positive in a more profound sense than it is negative. We must move beyond showing the ways God is not limited by other things. For even the indeterminacy of infinite chaos or the void of absolute

---

15. Binning, *The Common Principles of the Christian Religion,* in *The Works of The Rev. Hugh Binning, M.A.,* 3rd ed., ed. Rev. M. Leishan, D.D. (London: A. Fullarton and Co., 1851), pp. 4, 45.

16. I am following Karl Barth in making this distinction; see *CD,* 2/1, p. 301. We make this division due to our limitations. The positive and negative are one in the simplicity of God: God's unlimitedness is the same as his fullness.

17. Barth, *CD,* 2/1, p. 299.

nothingness have a sort of freedom in that they are not determined by anything outside of them. But God is not indeterminate or empty. God is God in supreme concreteness, full, rich, and perfect. In his freedom, God is complete and possesses himself completely. God is alive, aware, and powerful — all in the absolute freedom of his self-determination. In himself and from himself and to himself, God is beautiful and bountiful, joyful and glorious. God is his own infinite goodness, and God perfectly possesses this goodness as his own act and being.

As we enter our discussion of the attributes of divine freedom, let me remind the reader that none of our concepts is powerful enough to comprehend God, and no words are adequate to express his greatness. Conceptual analysis can take us only so far. We seem able to understand certain concepts fairly well, as long as they are set in opposition to others. Three of the most important concepts for this book are the one and the many, freedom and necessity, and nature and person. Along with all traditional theology, this study assumes that God transcends these polarities. Yet we cannot find a conceptual way to get beyond these dichotomies and comprehend clearly God's transcendence. As the reader can see from the two preceding paragraphs, I am struggling to find words adequate to God's greatness. Sometimes my expressions sound paradoxical, doxological, mystical; for less sympathetic readers, they may seem contradictory. Theology is, in Anselm's classic definition, "faith seeking understanding." While this is true, it is vital to underscore the word *seeking*. We seek to understand the one we meet in faith in the church; and we must not claim to have understood.

If we cannot claim to understand so that we no longer need to seek understanding, still less can we claim to have found the right words to express fully God's greatness. In this section and the following sections, my goal will be to seek understanding and to find the best ways possible to express God's greatness. While no words can express God's unique freedom and transcendence adequately, some words and expressions do this better than others. I am seeking ways to speak of God that honor him, and doing so sometimes requires speaking in paradoxical or mystical or dialectical ways. Sometimes it requires that we shut up and sit in silence, which is difficult to do in a book. Our speech and silence about God must keep us on the move, transcending every concept and every expression as we seek to know him who is beyond understanding and to express the greatness of the ineffable God.

Explaining and defending my view of divine freedom requires me to give attention to several additional attributes. I see these traditional attributes not as capturing the holy divine essence in human concepts, but yet as the best ways to honor the God we worship in the church and as the best ways to point us to the transcendent God. In this chapter I shall consider life, spirit, and person; in succeeding chapters I shall investigate God's unlimited power (omnipotence) and knowledge (omniscience), his freedom with reference to space (omnipresence) and time (eternity), his singularity (uniqueness), his freedom from composition and from the possibility of decomposition (simplicity and immortality), his freedom from desire, need, and loss (impassibility and immutability), and his beauty, joy, and glory.

Moving from one attribute of the divine freedom to another, we must keep in mind their harmony with each other and with the attributes of the divine love. Each attribute of freedom will enrich our understanding of all the others and add depth to the attributes of the divine love. We must not forget for a moment that the omnipotent, omniscient, and impassible God is the one who loves us and is gracious and merciful toward us. We must hold his righteousness, holiness, and patience in mind as we consider the one who is immortal, omnipresent, and immutable. The one who is glorious is also wise. God is the one who loves in freedom, and if we now probe the meaning of his freedom, we must not forget that God's freedom is the freedom of his *love*.

Challenges to Divine Freedom

THE PRIORITY OF DIVINE SUBSTANCE OVER THE DIVINE PERSON (OR "SUBJECT")[18] Traditional Christian teaching about God's freedom faces many challenges, some very subtle; but thinking through them will help us deepen our understanding of the concept. The oldest and most persistent challenge posits an impersonal divine reality that exists eternally alongside (or within) the individual gods. This view preceded the Old Testament and served as the milieu within which ancient Israel struggled to remain faithful to the Lord. Whether in Ancient Near Eastern or Mediterranean myths or in the abstractions of Greek metaphysics, all nonbiblical religions give priority to the divine substance over the divine personhood. After surveying religions from five continents, Yehezkel Kaufmann concludes:

> Yet all these embodiments involve one idea which is the distinguishing mark of pagan thought: the idea that there exists a realm of being prior to the gods and above them, upon which the gods depend and whose decrees they must obey. Deity belongs to, and is derived from, a primordial realm . . . . The gods are not the source of all that is, nor do they transcend the universe.[19]

---

18. Barth argues this point using the term "subject" instead of "person" (*CD*, 2/1, p. 300).

19. Kaufmann, *The Religion of Israel from Its Beginnings to the Babylonian Exile*, trans. Moshe Greenberg (New York: Schocken Books, 1972), pp. 21-22.

From the pagan perspective, the divine substance itself is not a person or a subject and thus is not concrete and free. The divine nature fills the gods with awesome powers, but being gods and having divine powers comes upon them as a fate. The divine nature constitutes the necessity that founds and limits the freedom of the individual gods. As individuals, they are empty; they exist and act only because they participate in the divine substance, which is their fate and not their choice. Even if they are immortal, they are not so freely.[20]

In his study "Is God Essentially God," philosopher James Sennett proposes a sophisticated theory that defends aspects of this ancient perspective.[21] He argues that Yahweh is not essentially but contingently morally perfect: "There are at least two reasons to believe that Yahweh's failure to bear moral perfection in some worlds is essential to his being God in the actual world" (p. 299). The first is that moral perfection is possible only if borne contingently; the second is that "contingent moral perfection may make Yahweh greater than essential moral perfection" (p. 300). A being who "cannot do wrong," says Sennett, is less perfect than one who can do wrong but does not. Needless to say, such a view strays far from the tradition I am defending. A being who can "sin," even if he does not, is not God, because that being's character stands under the judgment of an independent moral standard (to offer just one reason).

I considered this opposing viewpoint earlier, and I shall address it in greater detail when I consider the attributes of personhood, unity, and simplicity. Here I simply point out that the biblical view of God aggressively rejects this view and takes pains to root out its every vestige. By rejecting the divisibility of the divine substance and the priority of the divine substance over the divine person, the Bible destroys the theoretical foundation of polytheism, magic, and witchcraft. Instead, it asserts the uniqueness and freedom of the Lord. The personal name of God (YHWH) indicates the whole, undivided person/substance of the divine reality. The Lord is not *a god*; God is the Lord. There is no divine substance that is not the divine person of the Lord. The one God is the Creator of every other thing. No idol can harness his power and make it available for human use. Prayer to the Lord replaces magic and witchcraft, which attempts to tap into the divine substance directly.[22] In the biblical view, there is only one God — the Lord. Because he created all things from nothing by his command, there is no reality that is not under his personal control.

---

20. Kaufmann, *The Religion of Israel,* pp. 40-58.
21. Sennett, "Is God Essentially God?" *Religious Studies* 30 (1994): 295-303.
22. Kaufmann, *The Religion of Israel,* p. 109.

SELF-LIMITED FREEDOM?   A second challenge to God's freedom comes from the hypothesis we have confronted several times in this study already, the divine self-limitation theory. In chapter 7, I argued that this theory does not do justice to God's patience or wisdom. Here I shall show that it cannot do justice to God's freedom. The theory's defenders claim that God is limited by his relationship to the world and that this limitation explains why God does not prevent all evil and suffering. God does not will suffering and death or any other evil; he does the best he can, but he cannot prevent or stop all of it. Nonetheless, according to this theory, God's freedom is ultimately unlimited.[23] For, even though the de facto existence of the world limits God's options for action, God did not have to create this world or any other world. God is free to undo his creation at any time. We don't have to choose between a God who is by nature limited or a God who is absolutely illimitable and unrelated to the world. According to Richard Rice, "we have the option that an omnipotent God voluntarily decides to share his power with his creatures and henceforth cooperates with them in reaching his objectives for the universe."[24] God freely created the kind of world (a world with free beings) that would constrict his further actions as long as he stands by his original free decision to create. God is unlimited in his freedom because no reality *outside* him limits him. God freely limits himself for the sake of the world he loves.

Does this clever theory do justice to divine freedom? It argues that the limits on God's freedom of action in the world are purely his self-chosen limits, matters of his will in no way imposed from outside. Unfortunately, this strategy is as incoherent as it is creative. For, according to this theory, although God does not have to create any of many possible worlds, *if* he creates and maintains a world with free beings, his freedom of action *will be* limited. Notice that, though God is free to create or not create, God is not free to create without limiting his freedom. This means that, prior to creating any kind of world, God is restricted as to the kind of world he can create. But this situation itself is a "world," an uncreated and eternal and necessary predicament or state of affairs. In other words, God is limited eternally by something outside his will, by a sort of fate, a necessity beyond the reach of his freedom.

In my view, the implications of this theory raise serious concerns about "possible worlds" metaphysics of divine freedom. If one imagines God before a set of "*possible* worlds," which he can actualize or not, one has already placed

---

23. See Richard Rice, "Process Theism and the Open View of God," in *Searching for An Adequate God: A Dialogue between Process and Free Will Theists*, ed. John B. Cobb, Jr., and Clark H. Pinnock (Grand Rapids: Eerdmans, 2000).

24. Rice, "Process Theism and the Open View of God," p. 191.

God in a *necessary* world. The set of all possible worlds is what it is by necessity. Therefore, the actual "world" (the "maximally consistent state of affairs") in which God finds himself is not grounded in his freedom but in prior necessity. To put it another way, God exists eternally in a metaphysical space accompanied by other eternal objects that define that space and determine God's place in it.[25]

The self-limitation theory thus secretly presupposes the ancient nonbiblical worldview in which the gods are fated with their own natures and the natures of other things.[26] Against this view, I shall defend the thesis that neither God's existence nor his nature come upon him as a fate with which he must simply live. Instead, they are his free action, completely in his possession. I shall also reject the notion that one divine action could become a sort of fate for succeeding divine actions, which the self-limitation theory explicitly affirms. On the contrary, God's actions are completely harmonious: they do not limit each other.

INFINITE OR PERFECT? A third problem that animates the discussion of divine freedom is the difficulty of reconciling the notions of the infinite and the perfect.[27] These two ideas correspond to what I have called negative and positive freedom, respectively. Belief in God's negative freedom assures us that God labors under no limits, an idea that is also entailed in the concept of the infinite. Positive freedom asserts that God is full, complete, and lacking nothing good (this is also asserted by the concept of divine perfection). The problem is this: perfection implies closure, or boundedness; the infinite implies openness, or unboundedness. Thus "perfection" appears to be a relative

---

25. The quoted definition of "possible worlds," which comes from Alvin Plantinga, can be found in Jay Wesley Richards, *The Untamed God: A Philosophical Exploration of Divine Perfection, Simplicity and Immutability* (Downers Grove, IL: InterVarsity Press, 2003), p. 54.

26. For my criticism of divine self-limitation theories, see Ron Highfield, "Divine Self-Limitation in the Theology of Jürgen Moltmann: A Critical Appraisal," *Christian Scholars Review* 32 (2002): 47-71; Highfield, "The Function of Divine Self-Limitation in Open Theism: Great Wall or Picket Fence?" *Journal of the Evangelical Theological Society* 45 (2002): 279-99; Highfield, "Does the World Limit God: Assessing the Case for Open Theism," *Stone-Campbell Journal* 5 (2002): 69-92; and Highfield, "The Problem with the 'Problem of Evil': A Response to Gregory Boyd's Open Theist Solution," *Restoration Quarterly* 45 (2003): 165-80.

27. For an extended discussion of this issue, see Philip Clayton, *The Problem of God in Modern Thought* (Grand Rapids: Eerdmans, 2000), pp. 117-82. Other thinkers discuss essentially the same problem when discussing the compatibility of freedom and perfection: see W. L. Rowe, "The Problem of Divine Perfection and Freedom," in *Reasoned Faith*, ed. Eleonore Stump (Ithaca, NY: Cornell University Press, 1993), pp. 223-33; see also Thomas V. Morris, "Perfection and Creation," in *Reasoned Faith*, pp. 234-47.

concept. An individual nature, say a flower seed, reaches perfection by realizing the full potential of its nature. To attain perfection, a flower does not need to achieve a mysterious superfloral state. Its perfection is the full realization of its natural possibilities. A flower does not need to be infinite to be perfect. Indeed, it is impossible to conceive of an infinite flower. An overflowing coffee cup is no fuller than one that is level full. A thing's definiteness, finiteness, and closedness seems to be necessary to its perfection. The more potential a nature has, the richer and more glorious its perfection. Nevertheless, whatever potential a being possesses, the attainment of its perfection implies closure.

Infinity seems to imply, on the other hand, complete openness, indeterminacy, and never-ending movement. If God is infinite, does this mean that he is nothing determinate? If God is never "this" or "that" because every this or that is determinate and closed, is God anything in particular? If God is neither "here" nor "there" because here and there are determinate and particular, is God anywhere? If perfection implies a determinate identity, and determination implies finitude, how can God be infinite? How can God be open *and* closed, infinite *and* perfect?

Perhaps there is a philosophical solution to this problem. If Charles Hartshorne's answer is any indication, I doubt that any plausible philosophical solution would resemble the God revealed in Jesus Christ, the Father, Son, and Holy Spirit. Hartshorne attempts to harmonize the two concepts by redefining divine perfection as unsurpassability. God's actual goodness (perfection) cannot be surpassed by another being because the word "God" names all good so far realized in the world. God is infinite in that he is "self-surpassing surpasser of all." God has infinite potential and will keep surpassing himself infinitely.[28] God is the most perfect being with infinite potential to become even better.

Should we identify the infinite, adopting Anaximander's definition, with the indefinite or continuous?[29] Should we think of divine perfection as the perfect realization of the all potential within the world, which we can conceive only as the complete realization of human potential?[30] In any case, this path is closed to theology. For the church's understanding of the perfection of God is deter-

<hr/>

28. Hartshorne, *Man's Vision of God* (LaSalle, IL: Open Court, 1941), p. 20.

29. See H. P. Owen, "Infinity in Theology and Metaphysics," in *The Encyclopedia of Philosophy*, 4, pp. 190-93. Owen says: "Thus, in classical Greek philosophy infinity represents a substratum which is formless, characterless, indeterminate. It is a pejorative term. An entity is good to the extent that it is limited by form" (p. 190).

30. Clayton, in *The Problem of God*, treats the problem of projection that plagues the traditional practice of deriving God's attributes by heightening human virtues to perfection (pp. 171-77).

mined by God's self-revelation and not by raising humanity to perfection. The unity of God's freedom is a premise of the Christian doctrine of God: though not limited in any way, God is concrete, specific, or self-determinate. The Christian concept that unites these two aspects of God's freedom is the idea of personhood. This important concept will occupy our attention in the last section of this chapter.

IS GOD A LIBERTARIAN? A fourth challenge to the traditional doctrine of God's freedom comes from those who espouse the view of freedom known as the freedom of indifference, or libertarian freedom. According to this view, one is free for a certain action if one has the power to act or refrain from acting before the action. I act freely only if, before I act, my action is undetermined and my eventual action is determined by me alone. Duns Scotus articulated a classic form of the libertarian theory. For Scotus, free will is a power but "not one according to which the will has acts successively, but it has them at the same moment. For it can have an opposite act of willing . . . willing at a, it can not-will at a."[31] The process of determining an action is called a choice. For libertarians, though many factors can influence a choice — after all, in deliberation we weigh the factors — no factor or accumulation of factors actually determines the choice. The free subject does that.

I will put aside for the moment the issue of whether this concept of freedom can serve to inform a Christian understanding of human freedom and deal with its appropriateness to divine freedom. Is God's freedom a freedom of indifference? In the libertarian theory, a being's freedom is its state of indeterminacy accompanied by its power to determine its future state. In other words, the libertarian theory understands freedom as (indeterminate) potentiality. Freedom ends when potential is actualized and the indeterminacy is resolved into something definite. It follows from this that there must be a temporal distinction between the potential and the actual. Freedom characterizes only the potential, so the two states cannot exist simultaneously. The second consideration concerns how the indeterminate is resolved to a determinate state. In a choice, an individual ends deliberation in a decision that determines the action. Deliberation involves weighing many (but for beings with limited knowledge, not all) factors that condition the desirability of possible courses of action. The impetus to action, and hence to deliberation, is desire. According to the libertarian view of freedom, indeterminacy, desire, deliberation, decision, action — at least all of these are involved in a free action.

31. Duns Scotus, *Lectura,* 1.9, quoted in Eleonore Stump, "Persons: Identification and Freedom," *Philosophical Topics* 24 (1996): 183-214.

Applying a libertarian model to divine freedom would have far-reaching implications for the Christian doctrine of God. We would need to make major adjustments to the other divine attributes to render them consistent with divine libertarian freedom. I will revisit these issues in detail during the course of my study of the attributes of divine freedom, where we can set them against the traditional understanding of the appropriate attribute. Here I will briefly note five of the most radical revisions implied by the libertarian model. First, God's freedom would have to be understood as a state of indeterminate potentiality. This view returns to the sub-Christian view of the priority of substance over person that I have discussed above. God's *possession* of this potential could not be a free action, for then it would be actual and determinate, and thus not free. In other words, *that* God is free would be God's fate and not an aspect of his freedom!

Second, to remain free, the divine life must consist of an unending movement from potentiality to actuality. Hence, God lives his life moment by moment in time. This inserts composition into the life of God. What force holds God's fragmentary experiences together? Is it a reality beyond God or a more primitive pole within God's being, for example, an impersonal divine substance? Third, because actuality is already a determined state, insofar as God is actual, God is not free. Traditional theology has always held (rightly, I believe) the relationship to be reversed: divine freedom has the nature of full actuality rather than maximum potentiality. According to traditional theology, God is pure act and hence absolutely free. Only if God is eternally and purely actual can God possess himself perfectly — his existence, essence, and action — and hence be perfectly free. A being with unrealized potential cannot possess itself perfectly, for it has no definitive identity.

Fourth, the idea of divine desire raises a problem, because the concept implies that God is partly empty and thus needs something other than himself to complete himself. If God's freedom is his potentiality and God realizes himself moment by moment, the character of God's developing identity must be directed and determined in some measure by an external reality, toward which God moves in desire. Fifth, deliberation is required only of beings that do not yet have the truth, and decisions are needed only because of the press of time and by beings that have no prospects of arriving at complete and certain knowledge in a timely manner. Practical deliberation is always a matter of probabilities, and decisions always involve risks. A choice is always a chance.[32]

---

32. The discussion between Samuel Clarke and Gottfried Leibniz is one of the great debates about divine freedom. Clarke defended a libertarian view and Leibniz a compatibilist view. See *The Leibniz-Clarke Correspondence*, ed. H. G. Alexander (Manchester, UK: Manchester Univer-

DOES DIVINE FREEDOM CONFLICT WITH HUMAN FREEDOM? The final view that calls the traditional concept of divine freedom into question arises from a desire to protect human freedom from divine encroachment. Those who prefer this view fear that attributing unlimited freedom to God will annihilate human freedom. If all reality is determined by God's will, human freedom is an illusion. In order to make room for human freedom, we must deny that God's freedom extends that far. According to this view, God can do many things that he does not do. And one reason he does not do some things he otherwise might want to do is his desire to allow room for human freedom to determine a portion of reality. "Autonomous freedom," as the power of self-determination is called, is especially important in morality. Ultimately, human beings must decide whether they will say "yes" or "no" to God's offer of himself in fellowship. Without the (indifferent) freedom to refuse God's fellowship, genuine fellowship would be impossible: one can genuinely accept God's fellowship only if one could have refused it.

I do not need to treat this objection as extensively as the others because it is based on assumptions I have discussed above. It assumes that freedom, divine and human, must be understood as the freedom of indifference, and it stands or falls with this assumption. However, viewing freedom through this lens guarantees the incompatibility of divine and human freedom; indeed, it guarantees the conflict of all "free" beings with each other. For one being to have unrestricted freedom, all others must give up freedom completely. For everyone to retain some freedom, each would have to restrict action to a finite space reserved for free action. In other words, we would need to establish, through something like political compromise, a set of rights and duties that places all free beings within mutually exclusive spheres of autonomous action and agreed-upon spheres of cooperative action. This defines other free beings either as "limits" on my freedom or objects on which I can exercise my freedom. As Sartre said, "There's no need for red-hot pokers. Hell is — other people."[33] That is to say, other beings deny me absolute possession of myself.

The fear that unlimited divine freedom would erase human freedom is based on a false premise that rests on a defective view of freedom. The answer

---

sity Press, 1978). For a study of the Leibniz-Clarke debate on divine freedom, see W. L. Rowe, "Clarke and Leibniz on Divine Perfection and Freedom," *Enlightenment and Dissent* 16 (1997): 60-82. Even the literature about this subject is enormous. For a convenient summary of the issues and an extensive bibliography, see W. L. Rowe, "Divine Freedom," *Stanford Encyclopedia of Philosophy.* Available at http://plato.stanford.edu/entries/divine-freedom/#1 (accessed Feb. 10, 2006).

33. Jean-Paul Sartre, "No Exit," in *Four Contemporary French Plays,* intro. Ruby Cohn (New York: Random House, 1967), p. 111.

to this fear will unfold as I develop an alternative view of divine (and human) freedom. As I have already hinted, the solution to this problem is to be found in the concept of divine personhood underlying the biblical view of God and made explicit in the church of the fourth century. In preparation for that discussion, I will now consider the attributes of life and spirit.

The Living God

God is alive. God is free from every form of decay and death. God lives free from dead matter, unconscious depths, repetitious processes, and nothingness. He overflows with life. God is fully aware of himself and all things; he is centered and integrated. God is powerful, self-moved, and active. God is full of meaning, purpose, intelligence, and joy. All other living things must be connected to a life-giving source that sustains their lives. But God is his life, which is eternal, immortal, and life-giving life.

Life in Scripture

Scripture repeats so often and emphasizes so strongly that God is truly alive that "living" becomes one of God's titles or names. At the giving of the law, the elders of the people of Israel came to Moses in great fear and asked him to mediate between them and God. "For," they explained, "what mortal man has ever heard the voice of the living God speaking out of fire, as we have, and survived?" (Deut. 5:26; cf. Dan. 6:20). The prophet Hosea prophesies that a time will come when the people of Israel will be called "sons of the living God" (Hosea 1:10). Peter confesses Jesus as the Christ, "the Son of the living God" (Matt. 26:63). Unlike the "lifeless" idols of the nations, God is alive (Ps. 106:28). Elijah taunts the prophets of Baal on Mount Carmel; yet, despite their pleas, their god does not act (1 Kings 18:27-29). Isaiah pokes fun at those who make idols from firewood and then bow down to them as if they were alive and could save them (Isa. 44:9-23). At Lystra, Paul urged the pagan crowd to turn from "these worthless things to the living God, who made the heaven, the earth, the sea, and everything in them" (Acts 14:15). The Thessalonians turned away from their idols "to serve the living and true God" (1 Thess. 1:9). For Paul, the church is the "temple of the living God" (2 Cor. 6:16).

That God is alive means that he speaks (Deut. 5:26), acts powerfully (Josh. 3:10), sees and hears (2 Kings 19:16), saves (1 Tim. 4:10), and judges and punishes (Heb. 10:31; Rev. 7:2). God's aliveness is associated with his truth: "But the Lord is the true God; he is the living God, the eternal King" (Jer. 10:10; 1 Thess. 1:9). Not only alive, God is the Lord and giver of life: human life is a gift from the Creator (Gen. 2:7). God "gives life to everything" (1 Tim. 6:13; Acts 17:25). Jesus taught that those who believe on him will gain eternal life, "for as the Father has life in himself, so he has granted the Son to have life in himself" (John 5:26).

God's life had no beginning and will have no end. He lives eternally. God alone is "immortal" and "lives in unapproachable light" (1 Tim. 6:16; cf. 1:17; Rom. 1:23). Therefore, he alone can bestow eternal life on us. The Spirit, the water, and the blood of Jesus Christ testify that "God has given us eternal life, and this life is in his Son" (1 John 5:11). Jesus Christ is "the true God and eternal life" (1 John 5:20). Believers, therefore, "live in hope of eternal life, which God, who does not lie, promised before the foundation of the world" (Titus 1:2).

Theology of Divine Life

Perfect Life

When the Bible affirms that God is alive, it is not speaking about biology but about existence and power. Therefore, a technical biological definition of life would be of little aid in understanding God's life. The Bible draws on our common experience with living things, especially with ourselves. Three characteristics of life surface over and over in the preceding biblical teaching about the divine life: to be alive is to be an integrated whole, to be aware, and to be active.[34] To be capable of awareness or action, a living being must be a unified whole and have an individual identity. All living beings within our experience are composed of parts — atoms, molecules, cells, and organs. In a living organism these parts are integrated and coordinated by something we can call a "design plan" and a unified unifying force we can call "soul."[35] The design plan and the soul make a centered, living being out of the nonliving parts. A pile of sand is not an integrated whole, for its identity as a "pile of sand" is imposed on it by us. It does not arise from within.

Already in the concept of an integrated whole is implied the concept of

---

34. In dialogue with Aristotle, Thomas Aquinas says: "All things are said to be alive that determine themselves to movement or to operation of any kind, whereas those that cannot by their nature do so cannot be called living, unless by some likeness." *SumTh*, 1.18.2, in Anton C. Pegis, ed., *Basic Writings of Saint Thomas Aquinas*, vol. 1 (New York: Random House, 1945), p. 188. Aquinas centers on the principle of self-movement; but my definition is essentially identical because self-movement presupposes self-possession, or unity and awareness.

35. Alvin Plantinga, *Warranted Christian Belief* (New York: Oxford, 2000), p. 13.

awareness. For a center, which in a sense is the whole, must be aware of itself in its parts; otherwise it would not be a whole. The capacity for awareness is the ability to receive and communicate information. The grains of sand in a pile touch each other, but they are not aware of each other. For a grain is no more an integrated whole than a pile; it has no capacity for receiving and communicating information. A living being, no matter how primitive, because it is an integrated whole, has the capacity to receive information from its environment and respond to that information. The plants in my garden window respond to the sunlight by turning toward it to position themselves to receive more light. The idea of awareness, as this last example shows, includes the concept of action. For responding to information communicated from the environment is a sort of action. A purely passive awareness is impossible to imagine since the capacity that enables a being to receive information also bestows the capacity to communicate information.

No creature achieves perfect life. Not even human beings are fully alive. We exemplify a high degree of integration, awareness, and ability to act compared to other creatures; however, these attributes fall far short of perfection. Taking these in reverse order, there is much about me over which I have no control. Many things happen within me that are not my deliberate action. I can lift my arm, walk, and speak when I will, but there are thousands of psychic, organic, cellular, and molecular processes that occur within me without my being aware of them. And, though all these processes are highly integrated by my body's design plan and soul, they are poorly integrated into my self, the "me" of which I am conscious. I do not possess the whole of my being. The integrating power of my design plan and my soul are not enough to unify me into a perfect whole, where each part is fully present to the whole and the whole is fully present to each part.

God is perfectly alive. Gregory of Nyssa (c. 330–c. 395) says, "The Godhead is very life."[36] God's infinitely rich being is perfectly integrated in a way that surpasses the distinction we must make between part and whole. He is not a composite being made up of preexisting parts held together by a design plan and a soul. God needs no external composing force or source of life. He is immortal. For what is death but the disintegration of the whole into its parts? He is his life because he is the cause of his wholeness; and for that same reason he can be the giver of life to others.

God is perfectly aware of his entire being. God is not sustained in existence by a hidden force he does not control. He does not live by means of a body designed by another and operating without his awareness. He has no subconscious mind. He has no receding past or mysterious future, so that God loses some of what he was or can only anticipate what he will be. God is fully present

36. Gregory of Nyssa, *Against Eunomius*, 8.5 (*NPNF*, 2nd ser., 5, p. 210).

to himself — eternally. He sees clearly every corner of his being. God does not receive his existence or essence passively but enacts his entire being. If the ability to act is the ability to determine oneself, God is perfectly self-determining. Edward Leigh distinguishes between God's life and the life of creatures in this way: "His life is his nature or essence, he is life itself; theirs the operation of their nature, he is life, they are but living. His life is his own: he liveth of and by and in himself; their life is borrowed from him, in him we live and move. . . . He is life, and the fountain of life to all things."[37]

Combining these three qualities of life enables us to see that life is an attribute of freedom. To have unlimited freedom means to live unlimited life, to be perfectly whole, completely self-aware, and absolutely self-determining. Divine life corresponds to what I have called above the "positive" aspect of divine freedom: fullness, activity, knowing, identity, richness, and joy.

God Lives as Love

Now we are in position to see that the divine life is love — the giving, receiving, returning activity discussed earlier. Of course this is not the impression of life we get from observing the living creatures we know. Life looks more like selfishness — taking, being taken from, and taking back. One creature feeds on another, absorbing it for selfish use; life for one creature means death for others. One creature devours another and ends its life only to become food for still another. From this vantage point, the existence of creatures looks as much like death as it does life. This is true in a manner of speaking, because, like death, individual living things exist only by absorbing life from outside. They do not generate it within, for they are not one with life itself. Creatures are leaky containers through which life passes. Most of their energy is spent working to draw in enough life to replace today's seepage.

But God is love, and God is life. God lives by, in, through, and for love.[38] God's wholeness, awareness, and self-determination are the activities of his love. The unity of God's wholeness is not an impersonal coordination of disparate factors but the action of uniting persons in love. For love is the only way to unite persons as persons. The Father, Son, and Spirit are bound together by love, which they give, receive, return, and share. The act of triune love is an infinite circle of joy in giving, receiving, and returning. In love, the persons of the

---

37. Leigh, *System or Body of Divinity,* 2.3 (London, 1654), p. 140.

38. Thomas Aquinas expresses God's perfect life in intellectual terms: "In God to live is to understand. God thinks himself" (*SumTh,* 1.18.4, *Basic Writings,* p. 193). While this is true, it needs to be stated in Trinitarian terms. God thinks, loves, experiences, and moves himself as Father, Son, and Holy Spirit.

Trinity mutually indwell each other and are, in this way, completely one even in their distinctness. Dumitru Staniloae has put it this way: "In God the love between 'I's is perfect and therefore the unity between them is surpassing. Even so the distinct 'I's are not abolished within this unity, otherwise the living relationship between them would be impossible."[39]

Only love opens one person to another so that the one may become aware of the other as a person. Consequently, the mutual giving of triune love is also a mutual knowing. Because their love is complete, the mutual knowledge of the triune persons is perfect. Love is also the character of God's self-determination. By eternally begetting the Son, the Father determines himself to be the Father, the one who loves the Son. By eternally causing the Spirit to proceed, the Father defines himself as the giver of the Spirit of life. The Son is the Son because of the love of the Father. The Spirit is the Spirit of the Father's love. Hence, God's self-definition is a work of love.

God is not a lifeless monad, so "unified" and without distinctions that he disappears into a dimensionless point, a lifeless, unfeeling unity that might as well be nothing. God's unity is the passionate love among Father, Son, and Holy Spirit. God's awareness is not that of a dispassionate, omniscient observer. God knows because he loves. God's self-determination is not that of a selfish being who lives in fear of being absorbed by other selfish and fearful beings. No, God defines himself as love by loving without holding anything back. His love knows no fear, feels no need (not even the need to love!), and has no limit. God is full of life — activity, wholeness, love, and joy — and because his life is his love, he invites others into his life to share the fellowship with him we call eternal life. God gives life by loving others with the love by which he lives eternally. Quoting Staniloae again, "In the divine, love is all."[40]

God's Life Has a Name

Jesus Christ is the name of that eternal life that God has promised us (1 John 1:1-4). For Jesus Christ is the embodiment of God's love for us. He is "our life" because he is the center that makes us whole, that gives us meaning, and that sets the direction for our lives (Col. 3:3-4). In his resurrection he integrates body and soul perfectly into the life of the Spirit. In his church we are liberated for a fellowship in which we begin to experience now the eternal life to come. Christ is our life because in him we have fellowship with the Father and the Son. We

---

39. Staniloae, "The Holy Trinity: Structure of Supreme Love," in *Theology and the Church*, trans. Robert Barringer (Crestwood, NY: St. Vladimir's, 1980), p. 79.

40. Staniloae, "The Holy Trinity," p. 79.

experience the love of the Father and begin to love him in return. Christ and the Spirit set us free for love and life. In love God created us for love, so that love defines our being: for us, to exist is to be loved and to live is to love. Just as God's life act is love, so too must we love if we are to live. Only by loving can we grasp our existence and make it our act. Paradoxically, then, we can possess ourselves fully only by returning ourselves to God in gratitude.

God Is Spirit

God does not live as creatures do, in a fleshly body, vulnerable, mortal, and limited to a small segment of time and space. The living God is spirit. As spirit, God is invisible and immortal. He is unity, power, life-giving life, presence, self-awareness, knowledge, and action — without the limits of matter, time, and space. Spirit is a mode of life not possible for creatures of the biological world; therefore, it differentiates divine life from all other life. Spirit is the cause of life, the power of life, and life itself. Biological life lives only as long as it participates in the life of spirit. Spirit lives of itself — eternally.

Spirit in Scripture

The classic text for the doctrine that God's mode of life is spiritual is found in the Gospel of John. In his discussion with the Samaritan woman, Jesus points her beyond Jerusalem and Mount Gerizim, the places of worship for Jews and Samaritans, respectively: "Yet a time is coming and has now come when the true worshipers will worship the Father in spirit and truth, for they are the kind of worshipers the Father seeks. God is spirit, and his worshipers must worship in spirit and in truth" (John 4:23-24). Here Jesus reminds the Samaritan that God does not live in a way that limits his presence to specific places. God is spirit: he is present to every time and space. Worshipers are not guaranteed an audience with God only when they enter a particular holy place. True worship must relate to God in keeping with God's mode of life, that is, "in spirit" — in response to the prompting of the ever-present Spirit of God.

In his discussion with Nicodemus, Jesus brings out another contrast that is common to Scripture, the contrast between spirit and flesh. Nicodemus misunderstands Jesus' teaching requiring him to be "born again," thinking that Jesus is referring to a second physical birth. But Jesus corrects him, saying that he must be "born of water and the Spirit. Flesh gives birth to flesh, but the Spirit gives birth to spirit" (John 3:5-6). Mortal life can produce only mortal life; but the life

Jesus brings derives directly from the immortal Spirit, and it is thus immortal life. In another context in the Gospel, Jesus said, "The Spirit gives life; the flesh counts for nothing. The words I have spoken to you are spirit and they are life" (John 6:63). In the Old Testament, Isaiah contrasts flesh and spirit as well: "But the Egyptians are men and not God; their horses are flesh and not spirit" (Isa. 31:3). Notice the parallelism: the flesh-spirit contrast is parallel to the human-divine contrast. God as spirit exercises invincible power; men and horses, which are but flesh, "stumble," "fall," and "perish." Even the demonic powers are "spiritual" and are more powerful than "flesh and blood" (Eph. 6:12).

Paul's discussion of the resurrection in 1 Corinthians 15 brings out these contrasts clearly. Some in the church doubt the resurrection of the body because they imagine it as returning to the life of the flesh. Paul agrees with the doubters that "flesh and blood cannot inherit the kingdom of God" (15:50), but disagrees that the only alternative is a denial of resurrection. Rather, he argues that the resurrection body will be a "spiritual body" (15:44). The physical body is "perishable," clothed in "dishonor," beset by "weakness," at home only in the "natural" sphere. But the resurrection body will be imperishable, glorious, powerful, and spiritual. The one is "earthly," the other "of heaven" (15:48). Paul continues in the next verse: "And just as we have borne the likeness of the earthly man, so shall we bear the likeness of the man from heaven" (15:50).

In other Scripture texts, God's Spirit is associated with God's pervasive presence: "Where can I go from your Spirit? Where can I flee from your presence?" (Ps. 139:7). The Spirit imparts power (Judg. 3:9-10; 1 Sam. 10:6; Acts 1:8; 1 Cor. 2:4; 1 Thess. 1:5; Eph. 3:14-19). The Spirit gives wisdom (Isa. 11:1-3). Creation and life are works of the Spirit (Gen. 1:2; Isa. 32:14-15; Ezek. 26:26-27; Ps. 104:29-30). The Spirit knows God directly, and only those empowered by the Spirit can also know God (1 Cor. 2:10-16). The Spirit has power over death (Rom. 8:11), and the Spirit imparts love and sonship (Rom. 5:5; 8:15).

Theology of Spirit

God is spirit.[41] In Scripture, spirit is a mode of life independent of "flesh," that is, a physical body.[42] Spirit is the superior form, free of many of the limitations

41. For the modern history of the idea of spirit in Spinoza, Kant, Fichte, Hegel, Kierkegaard, Marx, and Dilthey, see Karl Rahner, ed., *Encyclopedia of Theology: The Concise Sacramentum Mundi* (New York: Crossroad, 1975), s.v. "Spirit"; see also Wolfhart Pannenberg, *Systematic Theology*, 1, pp. 370-84.

42. Evangelical theologian Clark Pinnock, in *Most Moved Mover: A Theology of God's Openness* (Grand Rapids: Baker Academic, 2001), pp. 33-35, toys with the idea of God's embodiment.

of physical existence. Life is not defined exclusively by the physical existence with which we are familiar. Nonphysical modes are possible; however, spirit is not synonymous with the nonmaterial realm. Spirit, Wolfhart Pannenberg declares correctly, "is not to be equated with *nous* [mind] but as creative and life-giving dynamic."[43] Plato's forms, for example, exist in an ideal realm, but this does not make them spirits. Numbers, geometric definitions, and ethical norms are not alive, for they are not centered, aware, and active. Unlike concepts, life and spirit are not static. Furthermore, even if we add the idea of process to the nonmaterial world, we still do not arrive at the spiritual. A dynamic process without wholeness, awareness, and the ability to act does not attain the level of life, much less spirit. Since spirit is a mode of life, with a center, awareness, and action, I need not repeat my earlier discussion of these qualities and their application to God.[44] I shall assume them here and focus instead on some issues that arise at the level of spirit.

God is spirit, but spirit is not synonymous with God. Just as beings other than God live, beings other than God live as spirit. In Christian theology, the great divide in being is not between material and nonmaterial or between flesh and spirit; it is between Creator and creature. God creates and sustains all beings, even nonmaterial concepts. Therefore, the existence of spiritual beings, which God sustains without the mediation of a physical body, is no more a mystery than the existence of physical beings. Both live only by the grace of God. Our sense that we understand God's sustaining action in the physical world better than we do in the spiritual realm is purely illusory. Such created spiritual beings as angels draw their life (centeredness, awareness, and activity) from God just as much as physical beings do. They live without some of the limitations of flesh, but they depend on God for that life as much as the lowliest creatures do.

How does the doctrine of God's spirituality relate to the doctrine of the person and nature of the Holy Spirit? An adequate Christian theology of God's spirituality must speak not only of the divine nature common to the triune persons but also of the triune relations. Focusing solely on the spirituality of divine nature can be taken as support for two opposing but equally destructive errors. On the one hand, we should take care not to abstract an impersonal nature from the concrete existence of the Father, Son, and Spirit. This would transform the triune persons into mere instantiations of an impersonal nature. On

43. Pannenberg, *Systematic Theology,* 1, p. 382.

44. For Pannenberg's reflections on spirit's relationship to human life, see Pannenberg, *Anthropology in Theological Perspective,* trans. Matthew J. O'Connell (Philadelphia: Westminster, 1985), pp. 522-32.

the opposite extreme, we should not think of the spiritual nature of God as a fourth person in the Godhead. It is important to maintain that the Father and the Son are spirit just as much as is the Holy Spirit. For the Holy Spirit is the Spirit of the Father and of the Son: the Spirit proceeds eternally from the Father, and the Father does everything he does through the Son and in the Spirit. Hence, the Father's and the Son's spirituality is the being and act of the Holy Spirit. God has no impersonal spirit. All of God's acts are spiritual, and all of God's spiritual acts are personal.

The Tri-Personal God

The supremely living and spiritual God is not an impersonal force or an abstract and general divine nature. God is — to speak loosely for the moment — a specific individual, a particular being, a concrete identity: that is, God is a person.[45] I am aware that using the word "person" in reference to God inevitably causes confusion; that's because, in everyday language, the word "person" means an individual human being. We think especially of the particular character that sets one person apart from other persons, as illustrated in this statement of Henry Fielding (1707-54): "There is a certain person in the world, who in a certain person's eye, is a more agreeable person than any person, amongst all the persons, whom persons think agreeable persons."[46] Even in this quote the word "person" retains some of its older meaning: "a character sustained or assumed in a drama or the like, or in actual life."[47] I was recently reminded of the possibilities for confusion in this term by the puzzled looks I received from a general audience when I referred to God as a person. They thought I was implying that God is a human being. Once they made me aware of their concern, I explained to them the broader and more technical meaning the word has in Christian theology.

Because of the confusion caused by the word "person," Barth suggested using the term "mode of being" in its place. Robert Jenson proposed the term "identity" as a workable alternative.[48] While both of these suggestions have merit, they also have drawbacks. Even if I were to use another term in the place of "person," it would still be necessary to explain the traditional term. I see no

---

45. It is more accurate to say, as I shall argue in this section, that God is a perfect community of persons. For a helpful critique of the Western concept of person as applied to God, see F. LeRon Shults, *Reforming the Doctrine of God* (Grand Rapids: Eerdmans, 2005), pp. 41-65.

46. Fielding, *Love in Several Masques*, III.x.39 (London: John Watts, 1728).

47. *Oxford English Dictionary*, s.v. "Person."

48. Jenson, *The Triune Identity* (Philadelphia: Fortress, 1982), pp. 105-11; see also Jenson, *Systematic Theology*, vol. 1 (New York: Oxford University Press, 1997), p. 119.

alternative, then, but to attempt to explain the special meaning of the term "person" when it is used of God.

Person in Scripture

Scripture does not explicitly articulate the concept of person; but the necessary building blocks are there. First, God is a concrete, centered identity, an "I." "I am who I am," the Lord replied to Moses' request for the divine name (Exod. 3:14). "I am the Lord your God" is how the preface to the Ten Commandments begins (Exod. 20:2). Second, though the Lord is a concrete "I," he is not an individual in the sense of being one among many actual or possible gods. As I emphasized in the section on divine freedom, the Lord alone is God (Deut. 6:4). Not only is the Lord divine, divinity is the Lord. The biblical assertion that God is one does not indicate the unity of an impersonal divine nature. Israel's polytheistic neighbors could have agreed with this, as could later Greek and Roman pagans. Rather, it proclaims the concentration of divinity in one "I," the person of the Lord, a view that is completely incomprehensible on pagan premises. Third, God is completely free to do whatever he wills: "Our God is in heaven; he does whatever pleases him" (Ps. 115:3; cf. Ps. 135:6). Nothing limits God. Fourth, the biblical doctrine of creation asserts that God created all things by his word. "And God said, 'Let there be light,' and there was light" (Gen 1:3; cf. Ps. 33:9; 148:5). "All things" were created through the Word and "without him nothing was made that has been made" (John 1:3; cf. Col 1:6; 1 Cor. 8:6). God requires nothing for creation but his command. He created the world out of nothing (Heb. 11:3; cf. Rom. 4:17). At the foundation of the cosmos lies not necessity but freedom. In Scripture, personal freedom takes precedence over impersonal necessity.

Theology of Personhood

The concepts of life and spirit find their fulfillment in the concept of personhood. Life adds centeredness, awareness, and action to the concept of bare existence. But the perfection of these qualities is not attainable in physical life. Spirit is life independent of the physical, which allows a fuller realization of the elements of life. Nevertheless, freedom from "flesh and blood" does not necessarily include complete independence; for a created spirit's existence, essence, and capacity for action come upon it as a fate. However free it is from the limits of space, matter, and perhaps time, a created spirit cannot fully possess its own being. However centered it is, it remains eccentric because of its external origin.

However aware of itself it is, it cannot encompass its dependence and related-ness to God. However free for action it is, it cannot free itself for freedom; it can act only in the freedom given to it.

The Christian concept of person, brought to its definitive form in the late fourth century, perfects the concept of life and spirit. As I shall develop the con-cept, a person is a concrete living and spiritual identity in relationship to other concrete living and spiritual identities whose existence and essence are its own free act. There is no backward or outward reference to an impersonal nature with which the person is fated.[49]

Combining the four biblical building blocks, we have the essential content of the concept of person. For clearly God is a concrete "I" in Scripture: he is the sole bearer of divinity (divinity himself), completely free, and bound by no ne-cessity in heaven or earth, because these powers are products of God's freedom. In other words, God is supremely personal. There is only one thing missing: for-mal pursuit of the issue of being (ontology). This does not indicate any substan-tive lack in the biblical view of God's personhood. It simply means that in the Bi-ble there is no need or interest in explaining the meaning of God's personhood in metaphysical terms. To say that the Lord created, sustains, and rules the world, and thus deserves our undivided devotion, is to declare the perfect freedom and personhood of God just as much as later metaphysical formulae do. However, when Christianity took the message of the free Lord and Creator to the Greek and Roman worlds, it met an uncongenial set of presuppositions about what could and could not be. To the Greek mind, the Christian faith appeared to con-tradict the necessary order of being. Christian theologians needed to find a way to explain the biblical view of God in the familiar language of being in a way that overturned the Greek order of being and set up a persuasive alternative.

Background in Greek Religion and Theology

We should not think of Greek philosophy in isolation from Greek religion.[50] In a real sense, Greek metaphysics is an abstract formalization and defense of two foundational presuppositions of Greek polytheistic religion.[51] The first presup-

49. See Lucian Turcescu, *Gregory of Nyssa and the Concept of Divine Persons* (New York: Oxford University Press, 2005); see also Turcescu, "The Concept of Divine Persons in Gregory of Nyssa's *To His Brother Peter, on the Difference Between Ousia and Hypostasis,*" *The Greek Or-thodox Theological Journal* 42 (1997): 63-82, for a detailed study of the most philosophical of the Cappadocian fathers.

50. Philip Wheelwright, ed., *The Presocratics* (New York: Odyssey Press, 1966), pp. 1-5.

51. Indeed, it may be, as Robert Sokolowski argues, that these two presuppositions charac-terize all pagan religions. It is a kind of natural religious position. See Sokolowski, "Creation

position is the priority of substance over person. Greek religion distributed religious devotion among many gods. Like all ancient nonbiblical religions, however, it assumed that the individual gods derive from and depend on a vast ocean of divinity. The gods are gods by virtue of their participation in this more fundamental divine nature, and this divine nature itself is not a person. Thus, deep within Greek religion lies the intuition that nature or substance has priority over person or freedom. For Greek thinkers, personhood and freedom are always "something added to his being" and have "no bearing on his true 'hypostasis,' something without ontological content."[52]

The second presupposition is the continuity of all being. In all ancient religions the substance of the world we experience, if not its appearance, is everlasting or eternal. John Zizioulas contends that "from the Presocratics to the Neo-Platonists this principle ['ontological monism'] is invariably maintained in Greek thought."[53] Even if the divine is the best and highest aspect of the world, it is nevertheless part of the world.

It should not amaze us that the first Greek philosophers asked the two following questions: What is the *one* reality foundational to the many things in the world? And how do the many things of the world derive from this one foundational reality?[54] Clearly, these two questions arise out of the two presuppositions foundational to Greek religion. The earliest Greek philosophers looked for the one foundation of all things among the things themselves. Accordingly, Thales (c. 585 B.C.) declared that "all is water," and Anaximenes (c. 546 B.C.) said that "all is air."[55] Parmenides (c. 480 B.C.) understood that what is common to all the different things of the world cannot be one of those things. A thing must exist to have other attributes and qualities. Everything that is, *is,* regardless of *what* or *how* it is. Hence, for Parmenides, "being" is the one foundational reality. Furthermore, being cannot change, or it would not be. About being he said, "It is and cannot not-be."[56] Therefore, being is static, permanent, and changeless; change, motion, coming to be, and going out of being are illusory.[57]

---

and Christian Understanding," in *God and Creation: An Ecumenical Symposium,* ed. David B. Burrell and Bernard McGinn (Notre Dame, IN: University of Notre Dame Press, 1990), pp. 179-92; see also Sokolowski, *The God of Faith and Reason: Foundations of Christian Theology* (Washington, DC: The Catholic University of America Press, 1995).

52. John Zizioulas, *Being as Communion* (Crestwood, NY: St. Vladimir's, 1997), pp. 32-33.
53. Zizioulas, *Being as Communion,* p. 29.
54. Fredrick Copleston, S.J., *A History of Philosophy: Greece and Rome,* vol. 1, pt. 1 (Garden City, NJ: Image Books, 1962), pp. 83-93.
55. Wheelwright, *The Presocratics,* pp. 44, 60.
56. *The Presocratics,* p. 96.
57. *The Presocratics,* p. 97.

Heraclitus (c. 500 B.C.) held the opposite view: for him, the foundational reality is change, flux, chaos. Nothing within our experience remains constant, except change: "Everything flows and nothing abides; everything gives way and nothing stays fixed."[58] There is no permanence. Plato (c. 429-347 B.C.) attempted to reconcile the Parmenidean and Heraclitean viewpoints, but did not challenge the two underlying presuppositions. He argued that we must admit a third category: becoming. Being itself is unchanging, but there is a realm of flux or nonbeing. When being and nonbeing interact, as they do in this world, the result is becoming.[59] Becoming is an imperfect realization of being. Plato thus affirms a basically Parmenidean preference for static being over chaos and flux but is able, after a fashion, to account for the multiplicity and change we observe in the world. Again, notice how the two presuppositions underlie Plato's formulation of both the problems of metaphysics and his answers.

The Greeks certainly developed a concept of the individual. The individual is the smallest unit into which a species can be divided and remain an example of the species.[60] An individual god is an example of divine beings. An individual human being still embodies the necessary attributes of the species; a half a human being does not. However, the species has priority over the individual. There is nothing of substance in the individual that is not in the species. Those things unique to the individual are of no substance, no true being. For they come into being and go out of being with the coming and going of that individual. Reality is unchanging and universal. What is unique and what comes and goes out of being are, at best, becoming.[61]

The Greeks also made a place for the person. The Greek word *prosopon* (person) and the Latin *prosopa* function similarly. The word *prosopon* comes to its definitive meaning in the Greek theater. The Greek tragedians attempted to dramatize the human situation as they understood it. All-determining fate, law, and custom bound humanity with steel bands. The characters might assert their individual freedom and unique identity with as much heroism as they could muster. But in the end, all individual rivers converge in the sea: the individual is washed away, and only the universal, the necessary, and the species re-

---

58. *The Presocratics*, p. 70.

59. For Plato, the changing world perceived by the senses owes its "quasi-existence . . . to an imperfect participation in the full and perfect existence of the other [ideal world]" (W. K. C. Guthrie, *Greek Philosophers from Thales to Aristotle* [New York: Harper and Row, 1960], p. 90). See also Frederick Copleston, S.J., *A History of Philosophy*, 1/1, p. 201.

60. The English word "individual" retains an echo of its archaic meaning of "not divisible." See *OED*, s.v. "Individual."

61. Zizioulas, *Being as Communion*, p. 28.

main. A *prosopon* was a mask worn by an actor so he could take up a role: thus a "person" is a role, an act, a superficial and temporary disguise. The *prosopa* of the Romans is also a role, but a role in society: father, citizen, soldier. The individual becomes a legal person by taking up a role; the substance of the person is not the individual as such but society as species. One has no being, rights, or status as an individual but only as a bearer of the universal.[62]

Neither Greece nor Rome had any conceptual way to establish the genuine reality or *substance* of the individual person (divine or human) in his or her freedom and uniqueness. The ancient polytheistic presupposition that substance has priority over person made this impossible. Only after Christian theologians succeeded in articulating an adequate ontological explanation of the divine persons of the Holy Trinity could the freedom and uniqueness of the human person enter the list of fundamental ideals in the Christian world.[63]

God as Tri-Personal Love

For the most part, the church of the third and fourth centuries remained conscious of the biblical doctrine of God's freedom: that the Lord alone is God, that the world is the product of God's freedom,[64] that God is completely free, and that God is an "I." Yet, the two master presuppositions of Greek religion and theology made up a massive attraction to the educated mind. Even among those who acknowledged the biblical Trinity, there was a tendency to look behind the three concrete identities or persons for the one (impersonal) substance. Or, in the other direction, there was a tremendous impulse to derive the threeness of God from the impersonal divine substance of God, in a way that was similar to Plotinus's attempt to derive the multiplicity of the world from the One. Both of these tendencies operate within the presuppositions of Greek religion: the need to find the impersonal one behind the manifoldness of the world and the need to explain how the multiplicity of the world derives from the unity of its single substance. They lead ultimately to dissolution of persons — divine and human — into the all-embracing substance.

How shall we escape the pagan presuppositions? The Cappadocian fathers,

---

62. Zizioulas, *Being as Communion*, pp. 31-35. For the use of *prosopon* and *prosopa* in the church fathers, see G. L. Prestige, *God in Patristic Thought*, pp. 157-68; see also Vladimir Lossky, *The Mystical Theology of the Eastern Church* (Crestwood, NY: St. Vladimir's, 1998), pp. 51-53.

63. Lossky, *Mystical Theology*, p. 53; see also Thomas F. Torrance, *The Christian Doctrine of God: One Being, Three Persons* (Edinburgh: T&T Clark, 1996), pp. 102-3.

64. G. Florovsky, "The Concept of Creation in Saint Athanasius," *Studia Patristica* 6 (1962): 36-67.

Basil the Great, Gregory of Nyssa, and Gregory of Nazianzus, propose a way.[65] In what John Zizioulas calls an "ontological revolution," the Cappadocians identified *prosopon* (person) with *hypostasis* (concrete existence).[66] Thus they gave personhood an ontological status. Zizioulas notes: *"Hypostasis was needed precisely in order to add to the relational character of prosopon an ontological content."*[67] In a second modification of Greek thought, according to Zizioulas, the Cappadocians identified the "cause" *(aitia)* of the divine nature with the Father. We cannot escape the pagan Greek conception of divinity as long as we assume that God's divinity — the unity of the divine nature, the begetting of the Son, and the Spirit's procession — is derived from an impersonal divine nature. This approach will always land us on pagan soil, with God's existence and essence being his fate rather than his free act. Orthodoxy insisted that, though the begetting of the Son by the Father and the procession of the Spirit from the Father are not acts of creation in time, nonetheless they are relations of origin. A decisive break with the pagan presuppositions, Zizioulas insists, came with the insight that the inner Trinitarian relations originate (again, not in time) from the person of the Father rather than from an impersonal divine substance.[68] If God is to be God freely and not as a fate, his divinity must be his free act. Zizioulas says:

> Thus when we say that God "is" we do not bind the personal freedom of God — the being of God is not an ontological "necessity" or a simple "reality" — but we ascribe the being of God to His personal freedom. In a more analyti-

65. In general I follow what Zizioulas says in *Being as Communion*. However, I must register certain reservations. Zizioulas's insistence, with the Cappadocians, that the inner Trinitarian relations originate from the *person* of the Father could very easily lead to the subordination of the Son and the Spirit to the Father. I can accept Zizioulas's formula only if, by the expression "Person of the Father," he means the "Personal Being of the Father." Colin Gunton, *Act and Being: Towards a Theology of the Divine Attributes* (Grand Rapids: Eerdmans, 2002), pp. 104-8, while largely sympathetic to Zizioulas's position, cautions against the "voluntarist terms in which this freedom is expressed" (p. 106). He proposes a position close to what I shall argue in this section: "May we say that the triune life is free by virtue of the free but ordered perichoresis . . . of communion in which each of the hypostases is what he is from and through the others?" (p. 107). For T. F. Torrance's comments on this issue, see *The Christian Doctrine of God*, pp. 140-41.

66. Zizioulas, *Communion as Being*, p. 36.

67. Zizioulas, "The teaching of the Second Ecumenical Council on the Holy Spirit in Historical and Ecumenical Perspective," in *Credo in Spiritum Sanctum*, ed. J. S. Martins (Rome: Libreria Editrice Vaticana, 1983), p. 38, n. 18, quoted by Aristotle Papanikolaou, "Divine Energies or Divine Personhood: Vladimir Lossky and John Zizioulas on Conceiving the Transcendent and Immanent God," *Modern Theology* 19 (2003): 381, n. 52 (italics in original).

68. *Communion as Being*, pp. 40-42.

cal way this means that God, as Father and not as substance, perpetually confirms through "being" His free will to exist.[69]

With this move, which seems to be in line with the four biblical affirmations I have noted above, we escape from the ancient pagan premise that subordinates person to (impersonal) substance. Person now takes precedence over substance in the "order of being."[70] Speaking of the primacy of person over substance is a way of articulating a foundational datum of revelation: God is God freely. God exists, is triune, and is what he is in complete freedom. God's being *(ousia)* is not a fourth thing in addition to, behind, or underneath the Trinity. The divine being is the eternal communion among Father, Son, and Holy Spirit.[71]

What, then, is a person? A person, according to Boethius, is a "rational, individual substance."[72] Richard of St. Victor (d. 1173) added the notion of incommunicability, that is, uniqueness, to Boethius's definition.[73] In defending Boethius's definition against criticism, Thomas Aquinas says: "I answer that, 'Person' signifies what is most perfect in all nature — that is, a subsistent individual of a rational nature."[74] According to Piet Schoonenberg, the definition of Richard of St. Victor (and implicitly those of Boethius and Aquinas) "emphasizes the negative aspect of being a person." That is, to be one identity excludes being another. We must add a positive aspect to overcome the opposition, the concept of relationship.[75] To be a person is to be a person-in-relation to other persons. And if we add relationality to Thomas's definition of person, we can agree with him that person "signifies what is most perfect in all of nature."

---

69. *Communion as Being*, p. 41.

70. Orthodox theologian Vladimir Lossky, a harsh critic of Western theology, accuses it of elevating the unity of an impersonal essence over the Trinity of persons. Unlike Zizioulas, however, Lossky does not argue a *priority* of person over essence. He advocates a radical apophatic approach to theology whereby the antimony of the one and the three drive us to encounter the divine mystery (*Mystical Theology*, p. 80).

71. Aristotle Papanikolaou, "Divine Energies or Divine Personhood," pp. 357-85. According to Papanikolaou, Lossky rejects the idea of an ontology of the divine nature and limits our knowledge of God to the divine "energies," which are the works of God streaming out from the divine nature. Zizioulas, on the other hand, develops a relational ontology of divine personhood. While I am sympathetic to the apophatic approach because I want to respect the incomprehensibility of God, I am attracted to Zizioulas's relational ontology.

72. Boethius, *De duabus naturis,* 3, quoted in *Encyclopedia of Theology,* s.v. "Person."

73. Richard of St. Victor, quoted in *Encyclopedia of Theology,* s.v. "Person."

74. Aquinas, *SumTh,* 1.29.3 (*Basic Writings,* vol. 1, p. 295).

75. Schoonenberg, "God as Person(al)," in *A Personal God?* ed. Edward Schillebeeckx and Bas van Iersel (New York: Crossroad, 1977), pp. 81-82.

The term "person" takes on a special meaning when applied to God. In the section on divine freedom above, I have noted the conceptual difficulty of asserting both God's unlimited freedom and his determinate identity. There I anticipated this section by promising that the concept of person would unify these two. We can now define a person as *a living, spiritual, concrete identity, in relationship to other living, spiritual, concrete identities, whose entire being is its own free act*. Its existence and essence do not come upon it as a fate but are its own freely willed possessions. Its freedom, its relationships, and its uniqueness are not masks or roles but are its very substance.

Are the Son and the Spirit persons in the same sense that the Father is? If the Son is begotten of the Father, and the Spirit proceeds from the Father, how are the Son and Spirit persons in the sense defined above? Can the Son and the Spirit will their existence and essence as freely as the Father does? Is not the Father a person in a sense that the Son and Spirit are not? The answer to this question is decisive both for the theology of the Trinity and for human personhood and freedom.

According to traditional Trinitarian teaching, the members of the Trinity enact their identity, not in isolation, but only in their mutual loving relationships. The Father cannot be the Father apart from the Son and Spirit. *Being* is relational: each person of the Trinity lives in the other persons. *Freedom* is relational: the Son through the Spirit dwells in the giving freedom of the Father, and the Father dwells through the Spirit in the receiving freedom of the Son.[76] The Son's act of reception is just as free and foundational for the Father's identity as the Father's act of giving is for the Son's identity. The implications of this mutuality are profound: the divine persons are free to be themselves fully only in fellowship with each other. To put it another way, each person of the Trinity is freed to enact his identity by the receiving, returning, and giving love of the others. God is an eternal communion of persons-in-relation. Personhood always requires fellowship, and the freedom of the divine persons is in no way inhibited by their mutual relatedness. On the contrary, mutual love liberates each divine person to enact his being perfectly in these relationships. Being in relationship to other persons does not contradict the ideal of freedom. Love and freedom bring each other to perfection![77]

Can human beings become persons and experience true freedom? Or is a created person a contradiction in terms, since creatures cannot choose their ex-

---

76. For a similar view, see Colin Gunton, *Act and Being*, p. 107.

77. For a view of divine freedom very similar to the one I am proposing, see Robert W. Jenson, "An Ontology of Freedom in the *De Servo Arbitrio* of Luther," *Modern Theology* 10 (1994): 247-52.

istence and essence before they receive them? According to the Trinitarian faith, the eternal relationship between the Father and the Son is the archetype of the relationship we can have with the Father through the Son and in the Spirit. Of course, the archetypal relationship differs from ours. The Father's love for the Son is enacted as the eternal "begetting." The Father's love for us issues forth in the act of creating and adopting us through the Son and in the Spirit. The differences are profound, for God does not become Father by creating us, and we do not make God Father by receiving our being. The Son is "begotten not made," as the Nicene Creed makes clear; we are made not begotten. Nevertheless, we become persons temporally in a way similar to the way the Son receives his sonship eternally. The Son is a person because of the Father's giving love for him and his responding love to the Father. Similarly, the Father loved us in the Son and through the Spirit before the foundation of the world (Eph. 1:4-6). Empowered by the Spirit, who pours the Father's love into our hearts (Rom. 5:5) and transforms us into God's "children" (Rom. 8:14-17), we begin to love the Father in return and cry "Abba Father." In receiving and returning God's love, we discover our genuine personhood.

We recognize through the Spirit that we cannot attain our true being and freedom by remaining within ourselves, competing with others, and attempting to absorb them into ourselves. To the contrary, our true being is a being-in-relationship to the divine persons.[78] Our genuine personhood *is* the loving relationship God willed in election and established for us in Jesus Christ. In a sense, we *are* the love the Father has for us in the Son; that is, our existence and essence are an act of the Father's love for us. In that recognition, we are freed by the Spirit to accept the Father's love for us as our true life, authentic identity, and definitive future. As the Spirit enables us to receive God's love, and that divine love engenders our love for God in return, we begin freely to enact our own existence and essence, and thus we possess ourselves fully. As the Spirit causes God's love for us to become our love for God, we become free. Our true being has become our authentic act.

Robert Jenson expresses it beautifully: "Human freedom . . . is nothing less than participation in God's own triune rapture of freedom. . . . God frees us 'by the Spirit,' by that personhood in which he is his own freedom."[79] Divine freedom is thus the ground, model, and ever-present support of human freedom. The love of the divine persons for us makes us persons. For, if we do not originate from freedom, we can never possess ourselves in freedom. If there is no

78. In making the same point, T. F. Torrance speaks of God as the "personalizing Person" and of humans as "personalized persons" (*The Christian Doctrine of God*, pp. 159-60).

79. Jenson, "An Ontology of Freedom," p. 252.

eternal person, our personhood is not grounded in reality; it is just a mask. Therefore, far from limiting our freedom, God's unlimited freedom expressed in his love for us frees us for "the glorious liberty of the sons of God" (Rom. 8).

The priority of person over substance or nature applies to human nature as well to the divine nature.[80] Just as God is the loving fellowship among the persons of the Trinity, we *are* the loving fellowship we have with the triune persons — and with one another. Our human nature is not an impersonal abstraction. It originates in God's loving freedom and comes to concrete realization in our freed freedom and love-engendered love. Just as the Son lives and loves and acts freely in the Father through the Spirit, we can also share in his life, begin to love in the power of his love, and act freely within his freedom. In responding to God's loving gift of fellowship, we freely enact our nature by loving God and one another. Authentic human personhood *is* the fellowship of love we have with the triune God and one another in the body of Christ.

Conclusion

God's freedom is the freedom of a loving communion among the Father, Son, and Holy Spirit. The actions of loving and being loved, of giving, receiving, and returning, constitute the divine life — blessed, full, and overflowing. In the freedom of the Spirit, the divine persons indwell each other completely, are perfectly transparent to each other, and are known by each other utterly. As a communion of persons, and in fullness of life and the transparency of the Spirit, the triune God lives, loves, and knows in perfect freedom. For the love freely bestowed among the triune persons *is* the divine being: God's existence and essence. Great is the Lord and worthy of praise! For the Lord is the Life who gives life to the dead; the Lord is the Spirit who spiritualizes our physical bodies; and the Lord is the Person who makes us persons by loving us with the love he is.

80. Zizioulas, *Being as Communion*, pp. 54-59.

9

The Only "One and Only":
Divine Uniqueness and Simplicity

Divine Uniqueness

What could be more foundational to the biblical faith than belief in one God? The Shema of Deuteronomy declares: "Hear, O Israel: The Lord our God, the Lord is one" (Deut. 6:4). Christians agree with their Israelite forebears: there is only one God. Paul confesses: "There is one God, the Father, from whom all things came and for whom we live" (1 Cor. 8:6). The Nicene Creed begins: "We believe in one God the Father Almighty, Maker of heaven and earth, and of all things visible and invisible." But what does it mean? In the Western church we take this confession so much for granted that we fail to perceive its profound implications. For it declares that one person,[1] the Lord, the God with whom Abraham, Isaac, and Jacob dealt, the one who spoke to Moses, saying, "I am the Lord," is the exclusive bearer of the divine nature. The Lord is unique. There are no other gods, and there can be no other gods. This God is and can be only the Lord.

The Teaching of Scripture

Scripture proclaims that the Lord alone is God. The Lord demonstrates that he alone is God by his great deeds: "You were shown these things," says Moses, "so that you might know that the Lord is God; besides him there is no other. . . . Acknowledge and take to heart this day that the Lord is God in heaven above and

---

1. Here — and in other instances in this section — I am not using "person" in its precise Trinitarian sense. I mean one concrete and existing being.

on the earth below. There is no other" (Deut. 4:35, 39; 1 Kings 8:60). The Psalms urge worshipers to live according to this confession: "Know that the Lord is God. It is he who made us, and we are his; we are his people, the sheep of his pasture" (Ps. 100:3).

Israel addressed the Lord as the sole God in its prayers and worship. In his distress over the Assyrian Sennacherib's blasphemy, Hezekiah prayed: "You alone are God over all the kingdoms of the earth" (2 Kings 19:15-19). In his prayer of national repentance, Nehemiah prayed: "Blessed be your glorious name, and may it be exalted above all blessing and praise. You alone are the Lord" (Neh. 9:5-7; cf. Isa. 44:24). And David praised God, saying: "How great you are, O Sovereign Lord! There is no one like you, and there is no God but you, as we have heard with our own ears" (2 Sam. 7:22).

Scripture denies the genuine divinity of other gods just as strongly as it affirms the true deity of the Lord: "For all the gods of the nations are idols, but the Lord made the heavens" (Ps. 96:5; cf. 1 Chron. 16:26). The idols of the peoples are "worthless" (Deut. 32:21; 1 Kings 16:13, 26; Jer. 10:8; 14:22; 16:19; Ps. 36:1); they are "man-made" (Deut. 4:28; Ps. 115:4; Acts 19:26), as well as false and fraudulent (Jer. 10:14; 16:19, 20; Acts 19:26); they cannot see, hear, or speak (Ps. 115:5; Jer. 10:5; Hab. 2:18; 1 Cor. 12:2); they cannot move, save, or do anything good or bad (Isa. 41:22-23; 45:20; Jer. 10:5; 14:22). Idols are lifeless things, made of wood, stone, gold, and silver (Deut. 4:8; Isa. 45:20; Ps. 115:4; Jer. 10:8-9). Jeremiah sums up the biblical attitude toward idols: "Do men make their own gods? Yes, but they are not gods!" (Jer 16:20). Paul, echoing Jeremiah, reminds the Galatians that "when you did not know God, you were slaves to those who by nature are not gods" (Gal. 4:8).

Scripture condemns worshiping other gods in the strongest possible terms. The first and second commandments of the Decalogue state this unequivocally: "You shall have no other gods before me" (Exod. 20:3). The Lord demands all our love, heart, soul, and strength (Deut. 6:4-5), and the Lord declares, "You shall acknowledge no God but me, no Savior except me" (Hosea 13:4). Worshiping other gods is compared to adultery (Ezek. 6:9; 16:17; 20:24; 23:37; Lev. 17:7), and it evokes the Lord's anger (2 Kings 2:17; Jer. 8:19). Idols are detestable (Deut. 29:17; 2 Chron. 15:8; 34:3; Jer. 4:1; Ps. 78:58).

Scripture declares idols to be nonexistent and without power; but it does not speak with the same certainty about the gods represented by the idols. Surely, the "gods" are not truly divine — as is the Lord God. But there are other alternatives. Are they fallen angels, demons, or personified natural powers? Some scholars attempt to develop from Scripture an elaborate theology of the gods. I do not wish to get sidetracked by this issue, but I admit that there is some evidence in Scripture that the gods exist in more than the human imagination. If angels and demons exist and can act, can they, perhaps, masquerade as gods? Paul seems to equate the pagan gods with demons (1 Cor. 10:20): he speaks of the "god of this age," who has blinded people to the gospel's truth (2 Cor. 4:4), and "the ruler of the kingdom of the air," who is at work in the dis-obedient (Eph. 2:2). The important point to notice is that the existence of a realm of created spiritual beings who are in rebellion against God and are mas-querading as gods does not in the least undermine the biblical doctrine that the Lord alone is God.

It would be difficult to overstate the radical changes in the pagan worldview that are demanded by the biblical doctrine of the Lord's uniqueness. Karl Barth does not exaggerate when he says: "No sentence is more dangerous or revolutionary than that God is One and there is no other like him . . . besides God there are only His creatures or false gods and beside faith in Him there are religions only as religions of superstition, error, and finally irreligion."[2] Shifting one's view of the world, of morality, and of religious devotion from the presup-position of a general divine nature to the unique divine person changes every-thing. The world of nature, with its powerful forces and mysterious processes, becomes secular. The natural processes of generation, birth, growth, and death lose their divine status. The earth, sea, sky, sun, moon, and stars no longer di-rectly reveal the face of the divine. Since divinity is a person, human beings can be considered directly related to the divine as persons, as images of God; thus they must be respected. In religion, all impersonal and manipulative ap-proaches to the divine become irrational and blasphemous; using magic, idols, and manipulative rituals is forbidden. The world is no longer fragmented, with many competing power centers, but unified by its personal origin outside itself. And the human personality is correspondingly unified.[3]

Theology of God's Uniqueness

In a sense, the biblical teaching about God's uniqueness speaks for itself. How-ever, as I noted in the introduction, we tend to confess the one God and pass on to other things without grasping the far-reaching implications of this confes-sion. In this section I shall explore several of these implications.

2. Barth, *Church Dogmatics,* vol. 2, pt. 1, eds. G. W. Bromiley and T. F. Torrance, trans. T. H. L. Parker et al. (Edinburgh: T&T Clark, 1957), p. 444 (hereafter *CD*).

3. For these ideas, see Yehezkel Kaufmann, *The Religion of Israel: From Its Beginnings to the Babylonian Exile,* trans. Moshe Greenberg (New York: Schocken Books, 1960), to whom I re-ferred in my treatment of divine freedom.

God's Unique Uniqueness

There is only one God. Most of us know that much. But we may not have considered how unique God's uniqueness is. He is the only genuine "one and only." Ordinarily, when we say something is "unique," a double-headed dime for instance, we designate it to be, by definition, the only one of its kind. Uniqueness of this kind, however, does not capture the full meaning of the divine uniqueness. For, even if there were only one double-headed dime, there *could* be more, which would make the dime in question a member of the class of double-headed dimes. God, however, is unique in a unique way: God cannot be classified with other beings *like* him because there can be none like him. Thomas Aquinas says it truly: "Genus is prior to what it contains. Nothing is prior to God either really or mentally. Therefore God is not in any genus."[4] To express it another way, God is not *a* god; God is not even the only god; for God is not a member of the class "gods."

Not only are there no other gods; the very idea of another God is a contradiction in terms. David Burrell, commenting on Aquinas, concludes: "So when Aquinas denies even this much discrepancy in God [the distinction between essence and existence], he is asserting that the very notion of many possible gods is incoherent. For once the pretenders have been eliminated there is only one God possible."[5] I argued in the section on the divine person that the divine "I" freely enacts his nature. I say here, by extension, that God freely and eternally classifies or names himself as divine. And just as God *is* his nature, God *is* his class.

If God were not unique in this strong sense, he would not be free, because the idea of God or a general divine nature would have priority over the divine person. The Lord would be God because he participated in an impersonal divine nature. There could be no explanation for why the Lord is in fact unique. For the Lord's uniqueness would not result from his freedom. Were God not unique in his uniqueness, God could not define himself and possess his existence and essence in freedom; that is, God would not be a person in the sense we have described above.

Uniqueness Is Personal and Incommunicable

It should be clear from the previous discussion that the biblical declaration of God's uniqueness does not speak merely of the divine nature. The confession

4. *SumTh*, 1.3.5, in Anton C. Pegis, ed., *Basic Writings of Saint Thomas Aquinas*, vol. 1 (New York: Random House, 1945), p. 31.

5. Burrell, *Aquinas: God and Action* (Notre Dame, IN: University of Notre Dame Press, 1979), p. 23, commenting on *SumTh*, 1.3.4.

"God is one" or "there is only one God" asserts not only that the divine nature is one. As I have said many times in this study, the Babylonians, Egyptians, Canaanites, Greeks, and Romans could agree without hesitation. Rather, the Bible asserts, in the face of paganism, that there is only one divine person, the Lord, the God of Abraham, Isaac, and Jacob. Everything that is properly called divinity is summed up by the name of the Lord: the Lord is God, and God is the Lord. There are and can be no other gods.

Because God is unique, his divinity is incommunicable. In the Greek understanding, divinity is an abstract quality or an impersonal power that can be shared by many things in different concentrations. It is like the color red: something can be intensely red, moderately red, or only faintly red. At the top of the scale is the most divine thing, but there is a descending chain of lesser and lesser divine beings.[6] This pagan conceptual scheme explains why some heretics in the early church could call Jesus divine but not divinity itself. However, if God is unique in the sense I have described, there is a radical break between the divine and all other things. There is no natural scale of greater or lesser participation in the divine nature. We relate to God as persons, in fellowship, love, and mutual indwelling. We do not relate to the divine as an impersonal substance in which we participate by nature or grace.

Karl Barth expresses concern that traditional theology from Augustine to Aquinas to the orthodox Reformed tended to treat God's uniqueness as if it were a rational truth rather than a fact of revelation. The tradition gives the "impression," complains Barth, that God is "*ens vere unum* and not the God of the doctrine of the Trinity and of Christology, although this is in flat contradiction to the way in which this recognition originally forced itself on the Church."[7] We need not agree wholly with Barth's judgment on the tradition to appreciate his caution.[8] It is not enough to derive the uniqueness of the divine *nature* from the laws of logic and being, because this move is not the same as proving that the Lord — Father, Son, and Spirit — is the only God and the only possible God. We know this is true, as our survey of the scriptural teaching shows, only because the Lord proved himself to be the one God, the only possible bearer of the divine nature.

6. Robert Jenson, *Systematic Theology,* vol. 1 (New York: Oxford, 1997), p. 94.

7. *CD*, 2/1, p. 447.

8. See Richard A. Muller, *Post-Reformation Reformed Dogmatics: The Rise and Development of Reformed Orthodoxy,* vol. 3, *The Divine Essence and Attributes* (Grand Rapids: Baker Academic, 2003), pp. 241-54, for a summary of the orthodox Reformed on the subject of the divine unity (hereafter *PRRD*).

The One God as Father, Son, and Spirit

Adhering to "monotheism" does not necessarily guarantee that we will rightly confess God's uniqueness. Barth warned about this danger: "Necessarily, then, we must say that God is the absolutely One, but we cannot say that the absolutely one is God."[9] To hold tenaciously to the abstract concept of oneness as if the number one itself were God begs the question of what and who this One is. In Scripture the oneness of God is important because of who and what the One is. Unless God himself answers these questions, we will be tempted to substitute one of the powers and forces of nature or one of our own attributes. It would be just as idolatrous to worship Zeus or one of the gods of India or Arabia as the one God as it would be to worship the whole pantheon. In its teaching about divine uniqueness, Scripture urges us to seek, worship, and imitate exclusively that One who is Father, Son, and Spirit.

The doctrine of the Trinity makes clear that Christian theology does not derive its teaching about God's uniqueness from abstract meditations on the number one. As a first impression, one might think that the doctrine of the one God being Father, Son, and Spirit is self-contradictory, or at least paradoxical. And if someone is not determined to derive the Christian doctrine of God from God's revelation, it will prove an insurmountable problem. As I have explained in the chapter on the Trinity, the church sought to articulate its Trinitarian faith in a way that affirmed the unity of God. The Father, Son, and Spirit are three *hypostases* or persons within the one divine nature. Each is the fullness of the divine nature, but they are not three separate gods. The Father, Son, and Spirit mutually indwell each other, so that there is only one (tri-)personal God.

The doctrine of the Trinity claims to do more than preserve a "self-evident" divine uniqueness: it claims to be the true and most profound doctrine of God's oneness. The inner relatedness of God as Father, Son, and Spirit guarantees that God is concretely — not just abstractly — one. If we attempt to conceive of God as one in abstraction from all difference and relation, God disappears into a dimensionless point without attributes or identity or character or relationships. Monotheisms that are in reaction to Christian doctrine of the Trinity — Judaism, Islam, and modern Deism — tend toward such abstraction. This abstraction bears little resemblance to the personal God of Scripture. The doctrine of the Trinity, however, urges us to understand God's unity as the perfect harmony of the mutually indwelling Father, Son, and Spirit. This internal relatedness of the divine being opens a space within the one God so that God becomes a distinct and concrete character and identity. God can be a real per-

---

9. *CD*, 2/1, p. 448.

son to us because God *is,* in his own eternal life, the communion among three persons. For Christian theology, God is not the abstract "One" generated by the dynamics of the human mind but the concrete *Someone* who speaks to us from the Father, through the Son, and in the Holy Spirit!

Divine Simplicity

The doctrine of uniqueness denies the repeatability of the divine person, while the doctrine of simplicity denies that the divine nature is compound. Uniqueness deals, as it were, with the external environment; simplicity deals with the internal nature of the divine being. So far in this study I have presupposed divine simplicity, insisting that God *is* his attributes and that each attribute refers not to a part but to the whole divine nature. Furthermore, I have presupposed that our knowledge of God will be deepened when we contemplate the different attributes as mutually enriching each other.

Consequently, this book stands or falls with the doctrine of divine simplicity. I am comforted that the simplicity of God's nature is the traditional teaching of the church; nevertheless, many contemporary Christian theologians voice sharp criticism of that doctrine. They insist that the issues of God's uniqueness and God's simplicity are separable, that one can affirm uniqueness and deny simplicity. In the present circumstances, I cannot presuppose the doctrine of simplicity, or merely assert it; I must explain and defend it against current challenges. In the following pages I shall argue that the two issues of uniqueness and simplicity are inseparable, that it is impossible to deny one and affirm the other, and that the simplicity follows from the uniqueness of God.

The Tradition

For several compelling reasons, the church's teachers have always asserted the simplicity of the divine nature. According to Gregory of Nyssa, "[w]e believe that the most boorish and simple-minded would not deny that the Divine Nature, blessed and transcendent as it is, is 'single.' That which is viewless, formless, and sizeless, cannot be conceived of as multiform and composite."[10] According to Augustine, "we do not say that the nature of the good is simple, because the Father alone possesses it, or the Son alone, or the Holy Ghost alone . . . but we say it is simple, *because it is what it has,* with the exception of the rela-

---

10. Gregory of Nyssa, *Against Eunomius,* 1.19 (*NPNF,* 2nd ser., 5, p. lviii).

tion of the persons to one another."[11] Dionysius the Areopagite (c. 500) declares that "all the Names proper to God are always applied in Scripture not partially but to the whole entire Godhead, and that they all refer indivisibly, absolutely, and unreservedly, and wholly to the wholeness of the whole and entire Godhead."[12] John of Damascus (c. 675–c. 749), summarizing the teaching of the most respected teachers of the ancient church, says:

> The Deity is simple and uncompound. But that which is composed of many and different elements is compound. If, then, we should speak of the qualities of being uncreated and without beginning and incorporeal and immortal and everlasting and good and creative and so forth as essential differences in the case of God, that which is composed of so many qualities will not be simple but must be compound. But this is impious in the extreme.[13]

Anselm of Canterbury articulates the traditional teaching on divine simplicity concisely: "For this Being it is the same to be just that it is to be justice; and so with regard to attributes that can be expressed in the same way: and none of these shows of what character, or how great, but what this Being is."[14] The Synod of Rheims (1148) affirmed the traditional doctrine of divine simplicity in response to certain teachings of Gilbert de la Porrée (1080-1154), bishop of Poitiers. That synod affirmed that (1) God is his Deity; (2) the distinctions among the persons of the Trinity do not compromise the unity of the nature; (3) God is his attributes; and (4) the incarnation does not partition the divine nature.[15] Thomas Aquinas summarizes the tradition, the consensus in his own day, and his previous arguments for divine simplicity in this way:

> For there is neither composition of quantitative parts in God, since He is not a body; nor composition of matter and form . . . nor His essence from His existence; neither is there in Him composition of genus and difference, nor of subject and accident. Therefore, it is clear that God is nowise composite, but is altogether simple.[16]

---

11. Augustine, *City of God*, 11.10 (*NPNF*, 1st ser., 2, pp. 210-11 [italics added]).

12. Dionysius the Areopagite, *Divine Names*, 2, in *Dionysius the Areopagite on the Divine Names and The Mystical Theology*, trans. C. E. Rolt (Berwick, ME: Ibid Press, 2004), p. 65.

13. John of Damascus, *Orthodox Faith*, 1.9 (*NPNF*, 2nd ser., 9, p. 12).

14. Anselm of Canterbury, *Monologium*, 16, in *Saint Anselm: Basic Writings*, 2nd ed., trans. S. N. Deane (LaSalle, IL: Open Court, 1968), p. 64.

15. Muller, *PRRD*, 3, p. 37. These propositions were taken from Bernard of Clairvaux, *Libellus contra capitulum Gilberti* (see Muller, *PRRD*, 3, p. 37. n. 50 for reference).

16. *SumTh*, 1.3.7, in *Basic Writings*, 1, p. 34.

The Protestant Reformers and generations of orthodox Protestant theologians who follow them affirm the traditional teaching on divine simplicity. Ulrich Zwingli (1484-1531) connected the doctrine of divine simplicity to God's immutability and freedom from composition.[17] Guillaume Farel (1489-1565) understands God to be "a simple Essence, spiritual, indivisible, and incomprehensible."[18] Philip Melanchthon, in the later editions of his *Loci communes,* affirms that "in God, power, wisdom, righteousness, and other virtues are not contingent things, but are one with the Being; divine Being is divine power, wisdom, and righteousness, and these virtues are not to be separated from the Being."[19] Calvin understands God to be "a single, simple essence, in which we comprehend the three persons."[20] We must, Calvin insists, keep the biblical teaching on simplicity in mind constantly, "lest anyone imagine that God is threefold, or think God's simple essence to be torn into three persons."[21]

The post-Reformation scholastic Benedict Pictet explains that divine simplicity is "nothing more than the intimate connection and entire unity of all the attributes of God and their oneness or identity with the divine essence itself."[22] Bernhardus De Moor (1682-1771) defines divine simplicity succinctly as "the most perfect unity of divine essence and attributes, excluding all real composition."[23] According to Leonhard Rijssen (c. 1636-1700), the doctrine of divine simplicity demands that we view "the divine nature not only as devoid of all composition and division, but indeed, incapable of componibility and divisibility."[24] Finally, we can allow the Puritan William Perkins (1558-1602) to speak for many orthodox Protestant theologians when he says:

> The Simpleness of his Nature, is that by which he is void of all Logical relation in arguments. He hath not in him subject and adjunct. Hence it is manifest that to have life and to be life, to be in light and to be light, in God all are one. Neither is God subject to generality or specialty: whole, or parts; matter, or that which is made of matter: for so there should be in God divers things,

---

17. Zwingli, *On Providence,* 1 (Muller, *PRRD,* 3, p. 273).

18. Muller, *PRRD,* 3, p. 273.

19. Melanchthon, *Melanchthon on Christian Doctrine: Loci communes 1555,* trans. and ed. Clyde L. Manschreck (Grand Rapids: Baker Book House, 1965), p. 8.

20. *Institutes* 1.13.20, in *Institutes of the Christian Religion,* vol. 1, ed. John T. McNeill, trans. Ford Lewis Battles (Philadelphia: Westminster, 1960), p. 144.

21. *Institutes* 1.13.2, p. 122.

22. Pictet, *Christian Theology,* 2.8, trans. Frederick Reyroux (London: Seeley and Burnside, 1834), p. 99.

23. De Moor quoted in Muller, *PRRD,* 3, p. 277.

24. Rijssen, quoted in Muller, *PRRD,* 3, p. 278.

and one more perfect than another. Therefore whatsoever is in God is his essence, and all that he is, he is by essence.[25]

Theology of Divine Simplicity

The doctrine of divine simplicity negates the limits found in composite things, but it does so in service of the perfection and freedom of God; and we can avoid many pitfalls by keeping both facets in mind always. Negatively, the doctrine of simplicity denies that God's wholeness, fullness, and perfection is a composite of separable entities or properties. Positively, it affirms that God's wholeness is his free action of self-determination, which is transparent and fully present to him. The doctrine of simplicity affirms that God is — or, more accurately, God enacts — his attributes. The Christian doctrine of divine simplicity argues that God is indivisible but rich and full in his indivisibility.

Divine Simplicity Affirmed

On the one hand, Scripture compels us to confess God's perfection, uniqueness, immortality, transcendence, independence, and eternality. On the other hand, Scripture requires us to speak of God as Father, Son, and Spirit and allows us to speak of God as possessing many different attributes. The doctrine of simplicity demonstrates why we must affirm the perfect unity of the divine nature or give up, among other attributes, God's immortality, independence, and uniqueness. The challenge is to do so without negating the distinctions among the three divine persons and the many divine attributes. Let us apply the logic of simplicity to these three attributes before we address the challenge of maintaining the distinctions mentioned.[26]

God is immortal; this is an article of faith. But analysis leads us to the insight that no compound being can be immortal by nature. Were we to attribute composition to God, we would thus undermine our confidence in his immortality. For every composite being is in principle subject to decomposition, even if it happens to remain whole forever. For a composite being, to break apart is to cease to exist. But the Scriptures clearly affirm that God is immortal and that he alone has the capacity to bestow immortality (1 Tim. 1:7; Rom. 2:7; 2 Tim. 1:10). God's immortality is more than the mere fact that he does

---

25. Perkins, *A Golden Chaine or the Description of Theology*, 2, in *The Works of William Perkins*, ed. Ian Breward (Berkshire, UK: Sutton Courtenay Press, 1970), pp. 179-80.
26. My reasoning corresponds for the most part with that of Aquinas (*SumTh*, 1.3.7).

not die: he is free from the very possibility of dying. This is true of no compound being.

God is completely independent and self-existent. Speaking of God as composite would contradict these truths of faith, for every composite whole exists only because of its parts and their relations. The idea of a composite whole, therefore, presupposes preexisting parts, a composing force, and a plan for the relationships among the parts.[27] And all of these are at least logically prior to the whole. Let us consider each of these in turn. In a compound the parts can exist independently of the whole. The bricks in a building, the cells in my liver, and the carbon atoms in a benzene molecule can exist before and independently of the particular whole they constitute. If God were composed of parts (in this sense), his existence could not be his own free act, for he would depend on the continued existence of the parts for his own existence. And these parts do not depend on God for their existence; they are either completely independent or dependent on something else. Either way, God would depend on something outside himself for existence.

Thinking of God as composite would require us to ask about the force that holds God together. No part of a whole is the whole or the plan for the whole. Therefore, there must be some composing force that can bring the parts together into the proper relationships. In the material world such composition requires expending energy. Even composing a piece of music, which is not a physical reality, requires the brain to use some electrochemical energy. The energy of composition cannot come from the thing being composed. Thus, again, a compound God would depend on something outside and prior to himself for his existence.

The last of these three is the design plan for the whole. Every composite whole is the particular kind of whole it is because of a design plan that makes it a building, a liver cell, or a benzene molecule. The design plan is logically prior to the existing whole for which it is the plan. Applying this notion to God would require that we view the idea of god (that is, the divine nature) as prior to the existence of God. Here we meet again the pagan presupposition that substance is prior to the person: a composite God would be a god and not the Lord.

Maintaining God's uniqueness requires that we affirm his simplicity. Though the Bible does not explicitly discuss divine simplicity, it is undisputed among Christian theologians in all traditions that it affirms divine uniqueness. Careful consideration will show that the doctrine of divine uniqueness cannot be sustained without affirming divine simplicity. Suppose the name "God" ap-

---

27. I am sure that someone will notice that these are three of Aristotle's four causes: material, formal, and efficient. The fourth is final causality.

plies to a composite whole. What is the ontological status of the parts, the composing force, and the design plan, all of which are implied by the idea of a composite whole? If these things are prior to God, why not consider *them* divine in some sense? For, if they make God divine, they have power to confer divinity. And what can confer divinity but the divine? If God is not essentially love or wisdom or power or goodness, what is to keep us from thinking of *them* as a pantheon of gods? At the very least, it compromises God's unchallenged uniqueness. Furthermore, there is no apparent reason why the parts, composing force, and design plan of a particular whole cannot find realization in other wholes. Hence, if one denies divine simplicity, one can give no reason why the "Lord" could not be merely one of many gods.

Now we have come full circle: we can thus see clearly why we cannot deny divine simplicity without denying divine uniqueness. The doctrine of simplicity asserts that God *is* his attributes. We applied this presupposition in our section on divine uniqueness to show that the Lord is not merely *a* god. Uniqueness is not an accidental property of God but his essential nature: there can be no other God. So even the doctrine of divine uniqueness (assuredly a biblical doctrine) cannot be sustained without assuming divine simplicity.

Simplicity Denied

The traditional doctrine of divine simplicity faces severe criticism from contemporary theologians, who criticize it on biblical grounds, and from philosophers, who criticize it on logical grounds.[28] In the latter half of the nineteenth century, the liberal theologian Albrecht Ritschl and his disciples William Herrmann and Adolf von Harnack began a sustained critique of the use of metaphysical and scientific language in theology.[29] They considered the patristic church's use of Greek metaphysical categories to explain and defend the Christian gospel a falling away from its original purity. For Ritschl,

28. Among the philosophical critiques are Alvin Plantinga, *Does God Have a Nature?* (Milwaukee: Marquette University Press, 1980); Christopher Hughes, *On a Complex Theory of a Simple God: An Investigation in Aquinas' Philosophical Theology* (Ithaca, NY: Cornell University Press, 1989); and Nicholas Wolterstorff, "Divine Simplicity," in *Philosophical Perspectives, 5, Philosophy of Religion,* ed. James Tomberlin (Atascadero, CA: Ridgeview Publishing, 1991). I will not address Hughes's or Wolterstorff's views. In principle (if not in detail), Plantinga's criticisms voice the concerns of the other two, and my answer to Plantinga applies equally to Hughes and Wolterstorff.

29. Albrecht Ritschl, "Metaphysics and Theology," in *Albrecht Ritschl: Three Essays,* trans. Philip Hefner (Philadelphia: Fortress, 1972); William Herrmann, *Die Metaphysik in der Theologie* (Halle, 1876); Adolf von Harnack, *History of Dogma,* vol. 1, 3rd ed., trans. Neil Buchanan (Eugene, OR: Wipf & Stock, 2000).

the patristic concept of God was a "metaphysical idol,"[30] and its inclusion in the Christian doctrine of God was "an unheard-of interference of metaphysics in the religion of revelation."[31] The task of theology, as they saw it, was to rid theology of ontological speculation and restore the original moral and religious message of the historical Jesus. The influence of Ritschl's critique endures to this day, even among those who reject his moralistic interpretation of Christianity.

Acknowledging his agreement with Ritschl, Emil Brunner, in *The Christian Doctrine of God,* contends that the patristic theologians "failed to notice the contradiction between the speculative method of the Greek thinkers and the way of reflection prescribed for the Christian theologian by that which has been 'given' in revelation."[32] The doctrine of divine simplicity is "a speculative *theologumenon* . . . which has nothing to do with the God of the Christian faith." It is "simply the undifferentiated *Monas* of Neo-Platonism modified by Theism" (pp. 293-94). Clark Pinnock adapts the Ritschl-Brunner critique for his defense of open theism. He offers Augustine's and Aquinas's doctrines of God as examples of how "there has been a Christianization of Greek, and a Hellenization of Christian thought." He makes his view of the doctrine of divine simplicity clear: "God is to be thought of as movement, not simple, immutable substance. He is internally and externally dynamic and relational. 'Simplicity' is, along with impassibility, one of the most alien of the Greek-influenced attributes of God."[33]

As an example of the philosophical critique of divine simplicity, let us consider Alvin Plantinga's 1980 Aquinas Lecture, entitled *Does God Have a Nature?* According to Plantinga, the doctrine of simplicity asserts that "no distinctions can be made in God . . . he is the very same thing as his nature."[34] Plantinga acknowledges the appeal of the intuition that motivates the doctrine, that is, it is necessary to protect the "sovereignty and aseity" of God (p. 28). Nevertheless, he rejects the doctrine for this reason: if "God is identical

---

30. Ritschl, *Theologie und Metaphysik* (Bond, 1887); quoted in Wolfhart Pannenberg, "The Appropriation of the Philosophical Concept of God as a Dogmatic Problem of Early Christian Theology," in *Basic Questions in Theology,* vol. 2, trans. George H. Kehm (Philadelphia: Westminster, 1971), p. 120.

31. Quoted in Pannenberg, "Appropriation of the Philosophical Concept of God," p. 120.

32. Brunner, *Dogmatics,* vol. 1, trans. Olive Wyon (Philadelphia: Westminster, n.d.), p. 243. Brunner acknowledges the influence of Ritschl and of Hermann Cremer's *Die Christliche Lehre von den Eigenschaften Gottes* (The Christian Doctrine of God's Attributes).

33. Pinnock, *Most Moved Mover: A Theology of God's Openness* (Grand Rapids: Baker Academic Books, 2001), pp. 71, 84.

34. Plantinga, *Does God Have a Nature?* p. 27. Hereafter page references are given parenthetically in the text.

with each of his properties, then each of his properties is identical with each of his properties, so that God has but one property" (p. 47). This cannot be true because, according to the Christian conception, God has many properties, and these properties are not identical. Even more damning, "if God is identical with each of his properties, then since each of his properties is a property, he is a property — a self-exemplifying property" (p. 47). But if God is a property, then God is not a person and could not have created the world or know anything or love anybody.

Is the Christian doctrine of divine simplicity, as Brunner and Pinnock contend, a product of Greek natural theology? Did traditional theologians rule out all distinctions within God and replace the living God with an absolutely undifferentiated monad? Does it reduce God, as Plantinga argues, to an abstract property? I will address the "Theory of Theology's Fall into Hellenistic Philosophy" in more detail in the section on impassibility.[35] It is enough to say here that the advocates of the fall theory attempt to place the church fathers in a "false dilemma": between absolute simplicity, which allows for no distinctions, and composition, which violates God's independence.[36] Since they deny that God is composite, critics reason, traditional theologians must think of God as an abstract monad. Evaluated from a Christian point of view, such a doctrine is an easy target for the withering criticism heaped upon it by its critics. The problem with such criticism is that we have every ground to deny that any traditional theologian "ever took it to mean this, given that the tradition has consistently affirmed not only divine simplicity but also the Trinity, the meaningful identification of divine attributes, and the creation of the world by God."[37] I agree with Steven Holmes that "it seems utterly implausible to think that generation upon generation of church fathers and theologians — even church councils — failed to notice so stark a contradiction."[38]

Plantinga and other philosophical critics treat the traditional doctrine of simplicity as if it were a statement about what God is, thus misunderstanding

---

35. For critiques of the fall thesis, see Paul L. Gavrilyuk, *The Suffering of the Impassible God: The Dialectics of Patristic Thought* (Oxford: Oxford University Press, 2004), p. 46; W. V. Rowe, "Adolf von Harnack and the Concept of Hellenization," in *Hellenization Revisited: Shaping a Christian Response within the Greco-Roman World* (Lanham, MD: University Press of America, 1994), pp. 69-99; Roy Kearsley, "The Impact of Greek Concepts of God in the Christology of Cyril of Alexandria," *Tyndale Bulletin* 43 (1992): 307-29; and Wolfhart Pannenberg, "The Appropriation of the Philosophical Concept of God as a Dogmatic Problem of Early Christian Theology."

36. Gavrilyuk, *The Suffering of the Impassible God*, pp. 5-6.

37. Muller, *PRRD*, 3, p. 41.

38. Steven R. Holmes, "Something Much Too Plain to Say: Towards a Defense of the Doctrine of Divine Simplicity," in *Listening to the Past: The Place of Tradition in Theology* (Grand Rapids: Baker Academic, 2002), p. 51.

the apophatic function of this doctrine. Plantinga's misreading surfaces when he says, "It is exceedingly hard to grasp or construe this doctrine, to see just what divine simplicity is."[39] Holmes comments wryly on Plantinga's admission: "That it is 'not easy to see what' the simple essence of God 'might be' is precisely what the tradition (including Aquinas) insisted in asserting God's incomprehensibility."[40] Frederik Immink reminds us that the traditional doctrine of divine simplicity is "a logical characterization of the exalted divine being" rather than a positive speculation about the divine essence.[41]

Along the same lines, David Burrell shows that Aquinas, in his thinking about divine simplicity, is "engaged in the metalinguistic project of mapping out the grammar appropriate *in divinis*. He is proposing the logic proper to discourse about God."[42] Burrell argues that Aquinas's doctrine of simplicity performs only the negative function of telling how we may not speak of God and does not give us a positive foundation for a doctrine of God. Brian Davies contends that "from first to last the doctrine of divine simplicity is a piece of negative or apophatic theology and not a purported description of God."[43] It functions to remind us that "God is ontologically basic."[44] It is designed to show us how not to speak of God. It warns us not to take literally our affirmations about God — God is this or that — since our language cannot escape speaking after the manner of composition.

A Christian Answer to the Simplicity Problem?

Can the Christian doctrine of divine simplicity escape the dilemma of having to choose between composition and undifferentiated unity? On the negative side, Christian doctrine rejects the idea that the divine nature is compound for the reasons we have discussed; but, unlike Neo-Platonism, it affirms that the divine nature is infinitely rich and full, triune, personal, and loving, and it does

39. Plantinga, *Does God Have a Nature?* p. 28.
40. Holmes, "Something Much Too Plain to Say," p. 53.
41. Immink, *Divine Simplicity* (Kampen, The Netherlands: J. H. Kok, 1987).
42. Burrell, *Aquinas: God and Action,* pp. 16-17.
43. Davies, "Classical Theism and the Doctrine of Divine Simplicity," in *Language, Meaning, and God: Essays in Honor of Herbert McCabe,* ed. Brian Davies (London: Cassell, 1987), p. 59.
44. Steven R. Holmes, "Something Much Too Plain to Say," p. 52. Katherin Rogers also argues that Plantinga and Wolterstorff misunderstand the teaching of Aquinas. God "neither has properties nor is he a property. . . . God is simply act" (*Perfect Being Theology* [Edinburgh: Edinburgh University Press, 2000], p. 27). See also Rogers, "The Traditional Doctrine of Divine Simplicity," *Religious Studies* 32 (1996): 165-86.

not hesitate to speak of God's action, thought, and life. God is the Creator and sustainer of the universe. Christian theology rejoices that God has revealed himself in space and time, in word and deed. Most of all, Christian theology glories in the incarnation, cross, and resurrection of the Son of God. God has taken on flesh in Jesus Christ so that John can assure his readers that human eyes have seen and human hands "have touched" the Word of Life (1 John 1:1).

Simplicity as Harmony?

A Christian doctrine of divine simplicity must understand simplicity not as the simplicity of nothingness or of monotony, but as perfect harmony within God's infinitely rich and full being. But we find ourselves stricken with a poverty of concepts to express God's rich simplicity. Take harmony, for example: harmony is a wholeness that unites many things in a way that transforms the individual elements into anticipations of the whole and the whole into the fulfillment of the individual elements. But the harmony with which we are familiar is compound, a whole composed of parts: notes in a melody, petals on a flower, or scenes in a play.

To think rightly of God's simplicity as harmony requires us to remove from it the idea of composition. But doing this seems to reduce harmony to monotony. Avoiding this reduction will require that we retain the concept of distinction while we remove the concept of composition. Distinction implies negation or difference, however, for one thing is distinguished from another by difference, by not being in some way what the other is and by being in some way what the other is not. How can distinction not bring composition in its wake? We cannot grasp it.[45] But according to traditional teaching, not being able to grasp something about God is not sufficient reason to reject it. Even if we cannot clearly grasp what we are saying, we must affirm, for example, both that love and justice refer to the simple being of God, and that the distinction between the two is more than verbal. It has a basis in God's simple being.

Simplicity in Many Aspects?

Perhaps we can speak of distinctions among the attributes as *aspects* of the ultimate divine simplicity. An aspect is the appearance of a thing viewed from a particular location; viewed from another vantage point, the thing appears in a differ-

---

45. See Leonard Hodgson, *The Doctrine of the Trinity: Croall Lectures 1942-1943* (New York: Charles Scribner's Sons, 1944), for an interesting attempt to think unity and multiplicity together as harmony.

ent way. Are the differences we observe real and objective (within the thing itself), or do they exist only in the appearances? The concept of an aspect is neutral on this point. Without repeating material from the chapter on the divine attributes, I find it helpful to remind readers that Aquinas understood the divine attributes to be different aspects of the simple being of God. We can refer to Venus truly as the "morning star" or the "evening star" because of the different times in which it is visible to us on the earth. In the same way, to say "God is wise" and "God is love" are two different ways of saying God is God. We can account for the difference between the two expressions mostly (but not wholly) by calling attention to the inadequacy of human language and thought to grasp the simple being of God in one concept.[46] Indeed, even with multiplication of attributes, we cannot comprehend God. Nonetheless, Thomas argues that we are not totally ignorant of God's simple being. To say "God is wise" is to say something true about God. In other words, Thomas does not go from the identity of God with his attributes (divine simplicity) to the agnostic conclusion that God has no attributes.

Trinity and Simplicity

It is ironic that the critics of the doctrine of simplicity see it as a threat to the doctrine of the Trinity.[47] The church fathers appealed to the simplicity of the divine nature in *defense* of the Trinity. John of Damascus, according to Holmes, "interweaves simplicity, Trinity, and Incarnation so thoroughly that one must assume that he regarded them as necessarily linked doctrines."[48] Indeed, for John of Damascus, "divine simplicity may be derived from standard Trinitarian positions."[49] Gregory of Nyssa appealed to the doctrine of divine simplicity when arguing against Eunomius, who declared that the Son, though divine, was less than the Father. Gregory says:

> Nothing which possesses wisdom or power or any other good, not as an external gift, but rooted in its nature, can suffer diminution in it; so that if any

46. Aquinas believed that the attributes are not synonymous: they have a "foundation in the thing" (*Commentary on the Sentences*, 1.2.1.3, quoted in Steven R. Holmes, "Something Much Too Plain to Say," p. 51).

47. It was the Socinians who *denied* the doctrine of the Trinity and who attacked the doctrine of simplicity. Turretin says: "The Socinians [in the *Rocovinian Catechism*, 3.1] agitate this controversy with us since they deny that simplicity can be attributed to God according to the Scriptures and think it should be expunged from the number of the divine attributes for no other purpose than to weaken more easily the mystery of the Trinity by establishing composition of divine essence" (*Institutes of Elenctic Theology*, 3.7.1; vol. 1, p. 191).

48. Holmes, "Something Much Too Plain to Say," p. 62.

49. Holmes, "Something Much Too Plain to Say," p. 63.

one says that he detects Beings greater and smaller in the Divine Nature, he is unconsciously establishing a composite and heterogeneous Deity. . . . If he had been thinking of a Being really single and absolutely one, identical with goodness rather than possessing it, he would not be able to count a greater and a less in it at all. . . . It is, indeed, difficult to see how a reflecting mind can conceive one infinite to be greater or less than another infinite. So that if he acknowledges the supreme Being to be "single" and homogenous, let him grant that it is bound up with this universal attribute of simplicity and infinitude. If, on the other hand, he divides and estranges the "Beings" from each other, conceiving that of the Only-begotten as another than the Father's, and that of the Spirit as another than the Only-begotten, with a "more" and "less" in each case, let him be exposed now as granting simplicity in appearance only to the Deity, but in reality proving the composite in Him.[50]

According to the Nicene doctrine, God is Father, Son, and Holy Spirit, three persons, one substance. Clearly, the Christian doctrine of God does not envision the divine nature as an absolutely unrelated monad. The being of God is internally related. Nevertheless, the divine nature is uncompounded. The three persons of the Trinity are not three gods but three ways in which God is God, three relationships in which God is related to God. The three divine persons are not "parts" that make up the divine being that just happen to find themselves related in the triune way. The persons *are* their relationships, so that, unlike "parts," they have no substance apart from their relations. A brick, in contrast, maintains its substance apart from its relationship to the building of which it is a part. It could acquire another identity by entering into other relationships: it could become a doorstop, a boat anchor, or a weapon.

The triune persons have no substance and no identity apart from their relationships. They are, as Aquinas (and Gregory of Nazianzus before him) puts it, "substantial relations."[51] According to Aquinas, "[p]ersonal properties are the same as the persons because the abstract and the concrete are the same in God. For they are the subsisting persons themselves, as paternity is the Father Himself, and filiation is the Son, and procession is the Holy Ghost."[52] Each tri-

---

50. Gregory of Nyssa, *Against Eunomius*, 1.19 (*NPNF,* 2nd ser., 5, p. lviii). For an extended discussion of Gregory's teaching on divine simplicity, see Basil Krivocheine, "Simplicity of the Divine Nature and the Distinctions in God, According to St. Gregory of Nyssa," *St. Vladimir's Theological Quarterly* 21/2 (1977): 76-104. Krivocheine documents Gregory's extensive efforts to show how there can be distinctions in God without violating divine simplicity.

51. Aquinas, *SumTh,* 2.40.41-44, in *Basic Writings,* 1, pp. 382-89; Gregory Nazianzus, *Oration 29,* 16.

52. *SumTh,* 2.40.41, in *Basic Writings,* 1, p. 382.

une person/relation is a concrete instance of the whole divine nature related to itself in a certain way.

Let us press the brick analogy to the extreme. Let us say that the builder integrates a brick so perfectly into the building that it becomes wholly absorbed into its relationship to other bricks. The brick would then no longer be a mere part with a substance different from the building and with other possible relationships and identities. It would be purely a relationship of the whole building to itself. Lest you think my brick analogy is far-fetched, consider John of Damascus's similar metaphor to make his point about the Trinity: "We speak of those things as imperfect which do not preserve the form of that which is completed out of them. For stone and wood and iron are each perfect in its own nature, but with reference to the building that is completed out of them, each is imperfect: for none of them is itself a house."[53] Father, Son, and Spirit are each the whole deity, not components of the deity; they are relationships within the deity.

How does this line of thought help us with the problem of articulating God's rich simplicity and simple richness? I must emphasize that the attributes are not divine persons. God is Trinity. There are no more or fewer and can be no more or fewer divine persons. So we cannot understand the attributes as "substantial relations," since that would increase the number of persons beyond three. Nevertheless, Trinitarian thought, based as it is on God's self-revelation, breaks through the iron logic of the philosophical doctrine of simplicity by pushing us beyond the dialectical relationship between undifferentiated simplicity and complexity.[54] John of Damascus witnesses to this when he speaks of the persons of the Trinity as "united without confusion and divided without separation (which indeed transcends thought)" and as differing "from each other, being *indivisibly divided* not by essence but by the distinguishing mark of their proper and peculiar subsistence."[55] For John of Damascus and other representatives of the traditional doctrine of God, the ultimate beginning point and final terminus for thought is the triune God, who is simple in his complexity and complex in his simplicity. Hence, even though the attributes are not divine persons, we have grounds for believing that God's nature is rich in its simplicity. We do not contradict God's simplicity by contending that attributes allow us truly and in some measure to grasp the richness and fullness of God's uncompounded nature.

53. John of Damascus, *Orthodox Faith,* quoted in Holmes, "Something Much Too Plain to Say," p. 62.

54. Colin Gunton addresses this problem in *The One, the Three and the Many: God, Creation and the Culture of Modernity* (Cambridge, UK: Cambridge University Press, 1992).

55. John of Damascus, *Orthodox Faith,* 1.8 (*NPNF,* 2nd ser., 9, p. 10b).

Person and Simplicity

In a final attempt to grasp something of the rich and full simplicity of God, I refer to the concept of person developed in the section on divine freedom. As I have said above, the doctrine of simplicity aims to protect God's uniqueness and independence. The doctrine that person is prior to substance functions in the same way. If person is prior to substance, and God freely enacts his existence and essence, God possesses himself completely. His being is completely transparent to himself, and he is totally present to himself. The rich fullness of his being is his own free action. In other words, God freely enacts his attributes. Gregory of Nyssa says that God "is never changed by the impulse of choice, but always wishes what He is, and is, assuredly, what He wishes."[56] God is his act of being. Steven Holmes articulates this beautifully: "God does one thing, and that is to be God — perfectly, eternally, and incomprehensibly."[57]

Recall the definition of divine simplicity: God is his nature (or attributes). Saying that "God freely enacts his attributes" brings out another dimension of the statement "God is his nature." The latter statement, on the surface, leaves the nature of God's nature in obscurity. Is God an abstraction or a property? But the statement that God freely enacts his nature leaves no doubt that God is what he is freely. God can be rich without being composite, because God's simplicity is his free action. When we look at it in this light, we can see that God's simplicity is not nothingness or monotony. It is not a boring fate God must bear. God's freedom is rich and full as well as completely one with itself.

56. Gregory of Nyssa, *Against Eunomius*, 3.6 (*NPNF,* 2nd ser., 5, italics added).
57. Holmes, "Something Much Too Plain to Say," p. 52.

10

Where All Times Meet:
Divine Omnipresence and Eternity

When I was a child I was afraid of the dark. Sometimes I would wake up in the middle of the night to be surrounded by still, quiet darkness. I would cry out, "Mama! Daddy! Are you there?" My mother's kind voice, muffled by the walls between us, would say, "I'm here. Don't be afraid." Comforted, I would embrace my pillow and fall back into sweet sleep. Was it darkness I feared, or was it something else? As I held my father's hand or clung to my mother's skirt, darkness held no terror. I could tweak its nose and feel no fear. So I believe that it was not darkness itself but abandonment and aloneness that I dreaded. Our need for a loving presence is deeply rooted in our souls, and in the doctrines of omnipresence and eternity God says to us: "I am here. I have been and always will be here for you. Do not be afraid." These teachings provide much more than an occasion for controversy or an opportunity to practice our dialectical skills. They speak to our hearts: "You will never be alone. Take courage for the journey."

God's Omnipresence

God is everywhere. Where God is not is nowhere and nothing, for God is the maker of heaven and earth. Space, time, matter, and energy exist because he is there for them. Were he to withdraw his presence, they would cease to be. This biblical teaching, because of its significance for our understanding of God and the life of faith, deserves greater attention than it receives in contemporary theology.

The Scriptural Teaching

Scripture speaks of God's omnipresence primarily for the sake of his presence to his people. The affirmation that God is always everywhere assures us that God is here now. He is able to help and to judge. This concern is evident in the classic text for omnipresence, Psalm 139: "Where can I go from your Spirit? Where can I flee from your presence? If I go up to the heavens, you are there; if I make my bed in the depths, you are there." Solomon dedicates the Jerusalem temple with an acknowledgment that a human-made temple cannot hope to contain the one who made heaven and earth (1 Kings 8:27). Jeremiah warns his listeners that God can judge them wherever they go because he fills heaven and earth (Jer. 23:23-24). Paul speaks of the "one God and Father of all, who is over all and through all and in all" (Eph. 4:6).

According to Scripture, God is everywhere, and everything is thoroughly open to him. But God is not everywhere and always open *to us*. Though he is everywhere, God makes his presence felt in holy places at sacramental times. The Lord met the people of Israel on Mount Sinai (Exod. 19), and Moses entered the "presence" of the Lord as he entered the "tent of meeting" (Exod. 33). After standing in the "presence" of God, Moses' face became so radiant that he had to put on a veil in order to speak to the people (Exod. 34:29-35). When the tabernacle was completed, God's glory filled it and traveled with the people on their wilderness journey (Exod. 40:35-38). Just before they entered Canaan, Moses reminded the people: "You are standing today in the presence of the Lord your God" (Deut. 29:10). When the Lord struck dead seventy men from Beth Shemesh for looking into the Ark of the Covenant, which they had stolen, the survivors complained, "Who can stand in the presence of the Lord, this holy God?" (1 Sam. 6:20).

Sometimes Scripture generalizes God's presence to mean his favor, his attention, or protection. As the book of 2 Kings reflects on the conquest and exile of unfaithful Israel and Judah, it explains that God "thrust them from his presence" (2 Kings 17:18-20). In the final judgment, the wicked will be "shut out from the presence of the Lord and from the majesty of his power" (2 Thess. 1:9). Angelic beings apparently experience the presence of God constantly. In the book of Job, Satan stands in the "presence of the Lord" among other heavenly beings (Job 1:12; Zech. 6:5; 2 Pet. 2:11). Gabriel reprimanded the doubting Zechariah by announcing: "I am Gabriel. I stand in the presence of God" (Luke 1:19). According to the book of Hebrews, Christ did not enter an earthly temple. "He entered heaven itself, now to appear for us in God's presence" (Heb. 9:24).

The Christian hope is to live in the unveiled presence of God forever. Paul anticipates the day when we will appear "in the presence of our God" (1 Thess. 3:13). The resurrection will usher us into God's presence (2 Cor. 4:14), where we shall "see face to face" (1 Cor. 13:12). In a sense, we are already "with" Christ, Paul says, because "your life is now hidden with Christ in God" (Col. 3:3). But as long as we are alive, we are still "away from" and not yet "at home with the Lord" (2 Cor. 5:8).

The Tradition

The Fathers

The church fathers spoke of God's omnipresence as his "immensity" and "infinity": God "contains" but is not contained by the universe; God is immense in that he "fills and embraces the whole universe with His being, but He Himself cannot be encompassed by it."[1] Not even the whole universe can circumscribe and limit his infinite presence. Stanislaus Grabowski summarizes the patristic view of God's omnipresence in this way: "Through immensity and infinity all spatial limitations are removed from God, and God cannot be present by a circumscriptive presence. As a result of these attributes God is present to all beings in the universe at the same time."[2]

The Apostolic Fathers continue the biblical practice of appealing to divine omnipresence to warn offenders of God's judgment. In his *Epistle to the Corinthians* (A.D. 96), Clement of Rome asks, "Whither, then, shall any one go, or where shall he escape from Him who comprehends all things?"[3] Justin Martyr (c. A.D. 100–c. 165) denies that the universe can contain God: "For the works do not contain the maker, who was before them, and lends existence to them, and preserves them by his power."[4] Clement of Alexandria (c. A.D. 150–c. 215) argues that, although God is far above human comprehension,

> [h]e is very near in virtue of that power which holds all things in its embrace. . . . For the power of God is always present, in contact with us, in the

1. Stanislaus J. Grabowski, *The All-Present God: A Study of St. Augustine* (St. Louis: B. Herder Book Co., 1954), p. 33. (Note that I have changed the tense of this sentence from past to present.) I depend on the section of Grabowski's book entitled "Tradition and the Divine Omnipresence" (pp. 33-49) for most of what follows.

2. Grabowski, *The All-Present God*, p. 33.

3. Clement of Rome, *The Epistle to the Corinthians*, 28 (*ANF*, 1, p. 12). For other references, see Grabowski, *The All-Present God*, pp. 33-34.

4. Justin Martyr, *Against the Sabellians*, 9, quoted in Grabowski, *The All-Present God*, p. 41.

exercise of inspection, of beneficence, of instruction. . . . For God is not in darkness or in place, but above both space and time, and qualities of objects. Wherefore neither is He at any time in a part, either as containing or as contained, either by limitation or by section. . . . And though heaven be called His throne, not even thus is He contained, but He rests delighted in the creation.[5]

Arnobius, in his apology *Against the Pagans* (c. A.D. 300), criticizes the Roman belief that the divine nature is bound to particular locations and able to act only when present. For him it is axiomatic that it "belongs specially to the gods to fill all things with their power, to be not partly at any place, but all everywhere, not to go to dine with the Ethiopians, and return after twelve days to their own dwellings."[6] For Hilary of Poitiers (c. A.D. 315-367), God is "infinite, for nothing contains Him and He contains all things; He is eternally unconditioned by space, for He is illimitable."[7] Athanasius (c. A.D. 296-373), arguing for the divinity of the Word of God, appeals to God's omnipresence as a sign of his divine status:

The marvelous truth is, that being the Word, so far from being Himself contained by anything, He actually contains all things Himself. In creation He is present everywhere, yet is distinct in being from it; ordering, directing, giving life to all, containing all, yet is He Himself the Uncontained, existing solely in His father.[8]

Cyril of Alexandria (d. A.D. 444), famous for his struggle with Nestorius (d. c. A.D. 451) over the relationship between the humanity and divinity of Christ, declares: "The divine hand embraces every place and every creature, containing and preserving in their being created things, infusing life to those beings which are devoid of life and inserting intellectual life [into beings] capable of intelligence."[9] Later in the same work Cyril says: "God is not in place, nor is He circumscribed by space: for this He cannot suffer who is without quantity, extension and body."[10]

Augustine discussed God's omnipresence in many of his writings and even

5. Clement of Alexandria, *Stromata*, 2.2; cf. 7.2 (*ANF*, 2, p. 348).

6. Arnobius, *Against the Pagans*, 6.4 (*ANF*, 6, p. 508).

7. Hilary of Poitiers, *On the Trinity*, 2.6 (*NPNF*, 2nd ser., 9, p. 53).

8. Athanasius, *On the Incarnation*, 17, in *St. Athanasius On the Incarnation* (Crestwood: St. Vladimir's, 2003), p. 45.

9. Cyril of Alexandria, *On St. John's Gospel*, 1.9, quoted in Grabowski, *The All-Present God*, p. 133.

10. *On St. John's Gospel*, 9.9, quoted in Grabowski, *The All-Present God*, p. 35.

wrote an entire treatise on the subject.[11] He addresses those who imagine that whatever is real must occupy space: "He who made heaven and earth is neither heaven nor earth . . . these are not God. Do not imagine for thyself some grandiose and beautiful human: God is not circumscribed by a human form: He is not contained by place, He is not held by space."[12] John of Damascus, summarizing previous patristic thinking on omnipresence, concludes: "God, then, being immaterial and uncircumscribed, has not place. For He is His own place, filling all things and being above all things, and Himself maintaining all things. . . . But it must be understood that the Deity is indivisible, being everywhere wholly in His entirety and not divided up part by part like that which has body, but wholly in everything and wholly above everything."[13]

The Medieval Scholastics

In the scholastics of the Middle Ages we begin to find nuanced analyses of the concept of divine omnipresence: thinkers reflected on the ground, modes, and extent of omnipresence; they dealt with such issues as God's presence in Hell and in evil people and whether God is present in creation by essence or by power only. Anselm of Canterbury (c. 1033-1109) argues for omnipresence from creation's need of divine action to sustain its existence: "But if this is true . . . it follows that, where this Being is not, nothing is. It is, then, everywhere, and throughout all things, and in all."[14] Anselm further argues that it is more accurate to say that God is "everywhere" *(ubique)* than to say that he is in "every place" *(in omni loco)*. This way of speaking brings out the fact that God is not only in all places but "in all existing things."[15] In his treatise on the Trinity, Anselm argues that God is present to all things in essence as well as in power. For God's power is essential to God's being; therefore, God is essentially present wherever he works.[16]

Peter Lombard (1100-1160), author of the most used textbook of theology

11. Augustine, *Letter 187*, in *Fathers of the Church, Letters*, vol. 4, trans. Sr. Wilfred Parsons, S.N.D. (New York: Fathers of the Church, Inc., 1955), pp. 221-55. See also Adrian Fuerst, *An Historical Study of the Doctrine of the Omnipresence of God In Selected Writings Between 1220-1270* (Washington, DC: Catholic University of America Press, 1951), p. 7, n. 28. There Fuerst catalogs a long list of references to omnipresence in Augustine.

12. Augustine, *Sermo*, 4.4.5, quoted in Grabowski, *The All-Present God*, p. 76.

13. John of Damascus, *Orthodox Faith*, 1.13 (*NPNF*, 2nd ser., 9, p. 16b).

14. Anselm of Canterbury, *Monologium*, 13, in *Saint Anselm: Basic Writings*, 2nd ed., trans. S. N. Deane (LaSalle, IL: Open Court, 1962), pp. 60-61.

15. Anselm, *Monologium*, 23, p. 82.

16. Anselm, *De Fide Trinitatis*, 4. See the comments by Fuerst, *Omnipresence of God*, p. 14.

of the Middle Ages, proposed three modes by which God is present to everything: by presence, power, and essence.[17] Alexander of Hales (c. 1186-1245) proposes two reasons why we must affirm God's omnipresence. First, God is the cause of creation's continued existence. Were God not present, creation would cease to exist. Second, God, as infinitely perfect, possesses the power to be present but transcends the imperfection of spatial limitation. Thus God can be perfectly present to one thing without having to withdraw from other things.[18] Albert the Great (c. 1200-1280), teacher of Thomas Aquinas, sharpens the traditional point that God's continual sustenance of creation requires his omnipresence. We know that God does not use a medium to sustain creation, reasons Albert, because He created the world from nothing, which rules out created mediators. And since creation and sustenance require the same divine power, God must be directly present to all things.[19]

In his *Summa Theologica,* Aquinas himself addresses God's omnipresence in four articles. First, "God is in all things . . . as an agent is present to that upon which it acts." God causes things to exist "as long as they are preserved in being. . . . Therefore, as long as a thing has being, so long must God be present to it." Second, God is in every place and gives "it being and locative power. . . . Indeed He fills every place by the very fact that He gives being to the things that fill places." Third, Aquinas gives his interpretation of the traditional threefold mode of divine presence — presence, power, and essence: "God is in all things by His power, inasmuch as all things are subject to His power; He is by His presence in all things, inasmuch as all things are bare and open to His eyes; He is in all things by His essence, inasmuch as He is present to all as the cause of their being." Fourth, Aquinas argues that to be omnipresent is proper to God alone. No material and spatial thing can be genuinely omnipresent. Only God can be present to every part and to the whole of creation, "not by a part of Him, but by His very self."[20]

---

17. Lombard, *Libri IV Sententarium,* 1.37.1; see Fuerst, *Omnipresence of God,* p. 17. This threefold distinction appears to contain a tautology, presence and essence being synonymous. Fuerst points out that Lombard quotes this text from a commentary on the *Canticle of Canticles,* 5:17. This text had been mistakenly attributed to Gregory the Great and hence was viewed as authoritative. Subsequent commentators on Lombard's *Sentences* felt obligated to harmonize the three modes by showing a plausible distinction between presence and essence.

18. Alexander of Hales, quoted in Fuerst, *Omnipresence of God,* pp. 43-48.

19. Albert the Great, quoted in Fuerst, *Omnipresence of God,* pp. 86-87.

20. Aquinas, *SumTh,* 1.8.1-4, in *Basic Writings of Saint Thomas Aquinas,* vol. 1, ed. Anton C. Pegis (New York: Random House, 1945), pp. 67-69. For a developmental view of Aquinas's thinking on divine omnipresence, see Fuerst, *Omnipresence of God,* pp. 171-200.

Protestant Scholastics

Protestant scholastic theologians faithfully preserved the traditional doctrine of omnipresence taught by the church fathers and medieval scholastics. According to Ezekiel Hopkins (1633-1690), the "omnipresence of God is simply necessary, not only for preserving and upholding his creatures in their beings and operations, but necessary to our very being."[21] Benedict Pictet (1655-1724) roots God's omnipresence in his action of creating and preserving the world: "God is omnipresent by virtue of his power, energy, and operation. He is omnipresent in regard to his *operation,* for he works all in all, giving to all the creatures their being, and preserving them, bestowing on all of them their strength and power and action."[22]

Protestant scholastics made two noteworthy modifications (or shifts in emphasis) in traditional doctrine. First, although their predecessors had made a connection between God's infinity and his omnipresence,[23] post-Reformation Reformed and Lutheran theologians placed this connection at the center of their thinking, discussing omnipresence and eternity under the heading of infinity. William Perkins (1558-1602) explains the order: "The infiniteness of God is two-fold: his eternity, and exceeding greatness. God's eternity is that by which he is without beginning or ending. God's exceeding greatness is that by which his incomprehensible nature is everywhere present, both within and without the world."[24] Second, many Reformed scholastics distinguished more sharply than their predecessors had between immensity and omnipresence. Immensity is taken to refer to God's unlimited nature "in distinction from the created order," while omnipresence "refers to him in positive relation to the world," as being present in all things.[25] Leonhard Rijssen (c. 1636-1700) explains this distinction as follows: "It is God's immensity by which, devoid of measure and limit, God is everything that is. This immensity is distinguished from omnipresence; the for-

---

21. Hopkins, *On the Omnipresence of God,* quoted in Richard A. Muller, *Post-Reformation Reformed Dogmatics: The Rise and Development of Reformed Orthodoxy,* vol. 3, *The Divine Essence and Attributes* (Grand Rapids: Baker Academic, 2003), p. 343 (hereafter *PRRD*).

22. Pictet, *Christian Theology,* 2.7, trans. Frederick Reyroux (London: Seeley and Burnside, 1834), pp. 95-96.

23. See Aquinas, *SumTh,* 1.8.1.

24. Perkins, *A Golden Chaine or the Description of Theology,* 2, in *The Works of William Perkins,* ed. Ian Breward (Berkshire, UK: Sutton Courtenay Press, 1970), p. 178. For the Lutheran views, see Robert D. Preus, *The Theology of Post-Reformation Lutheranism,* vol. 2, *God and His Creation* (St. Louis: Concordia, 1972), p. 75 (hereafter *TPRL*).

25. Muller, *PRRD,* 3, p. 338. According to Preus, *TPRL,* 2, p. 85, Lutheran theologians, with the exception of Calov, "speak much more of an operational divine omnipresence than of God's immensity."

mer states an eternal and absolute attribute of God, while the latter denotes a dwelling locally which exists in time."[26]

Summary of the Tradition

Let us summarize the essential points of the doctrine of omnipresence handed to us from the tradition. (1) God is wholly, absolutely, and essentially present to all things and all places in a way appropriate only to God. (2) God's presence to things and places does not limit him in any way, as, for example, a container is limited by what it contains or as the content is circumscribed by the container that holds it. (3) God's omnipresence in creation does not follow upon the existence of creation; rather, it is God's active presence that gives existence to creation and sustains its being. (4) God is immense and unlimited in his own eternal nature apart from creation. Indeed, God's essential immensity grounds God's power to be omnipresent in creation.

Theology of Omnipresence

As is true with other divine attributes, we readily confess God's omnipresence but rarely think seriously about it. Consequently, we don't find ourselves praising God for his omnipresence and, indeed, are at a loss to explain its praiseworthiness. And the thought of God's constant presence is even disturbing to some. In this section I will examine God's omnipresence in a way designed to bring its praiseworthiness to light.

The Meaning of Presence and Omnipresence

We can hardly begin to speak of God's omnipresence before we gain some idea of what it means for one thing to be "present" to another. In our ordinary experience, presence is associated with physical proximity. When are you present to a thing? When you can see it? Touch it? Hear it? How close do you have to be? Three feet? Ten feet? A mile? A light-year? Clearly, however, there is more to presence than spatial proximity. Suppose, for example, two magnets touch each other. In a sense, they are present to each other; but they are not fully present, because only two external faces touch each other. The other faces and inner aspects of the magnets are still at a distance and thus are not present to each

---

26. Rijssen, quoted in Heinrich Heppe, *Reformed Dogmatics,* rev. and ed. Ernst Bizer, trans. G. T. Thomson (1950; reprint, London: Wakeman Great Reprints, n.d.), p. 66.

other. Nor would they be present to each other if we ground them to powder and mixed them together. This would destroy the two wholes only to multiply the number of particles — smaller wholes — that would again exist in mere proximity. We would not have increased the presence.

Following this pattern of analysis will lead us to the concept of perfect presence as the presence of one whole thing to another whole thing; that is, it requires mutual indwelling without displacement. Hence, two spatially extended objects can never be absolutely present to each other. They cannot indwell each other because physical things repel and displace each other. Furthermore, spatially extended objects never fully achieve wholeness because they are divisible into parts. No one part can commune with the whole of another physical body.

For these reasons, when we speak of presence, we usually do not have nonliving things in mind; only living things can possess their wholeness. Presence, moreover, is not a matter of spatial proximity for living beings any more than it is for rocks. Even if two people can touch each other, they are not thereby fully present to each other. Human beings are more than material beings. Because they have a spiritual dimension, they can be centered and have their wholeness to some degree as their possession. Thus holding hands, looking at a friend's face, or speaking a word can become more than mere external proximity. Through these means we can present our inner selves to other people. For personal beings, "presence" means "personal presence" and entails awareness, knowledge, communication, and interaction among persons. Persons commune and enjoy each other's presence through symbolic actions or words.

It seems, then, that only persons have any hope of becoming fully present to each other. For, even though people communicate by means of their bodies, persons are not bodies. Presence is more than being there beside another. Building on the understanding of personhood that I developed in the discussion of freedom — that only a person can possess himself or herself fully and freely — I conclude that only a person can *present* himself or herself fully to another person. Such a presentation of the self must be understood as a free gift, an act of love. Therefore, full presence is a perfect union, a mutual indwelling that can be accomplished only in the mutual giving of perfect love.

If we understand presence as I have developed it so far, God's *omnipresence* must entail more than God's mere proximity to all things, more than God's nearness to the external surfaces of things. Rather, it means that God lives inside and outside all things, that he indwells and contains all things. He does not merely passively observe his creation. God's presence to all things is the active relationship of love in which he gives being and acknowledges the identity of all things. God's omnipresence is thus an aspect of his love. Omnipresent love, wide and deep and long and high! And his omnipresent love is the power by which he gives being to the objects of his love. Now that is praiseworthy!

Omnipresence in Relationship to Uniqueness and Simplicity

God can be omnipresent because he is unique and simple. Were there more than one god, none could be omnipresent. For, as John of Damascus says, "Where the one would be, the other could not be."[27] Nothing composed of parts can be fully present to itself or to another thing. Full presence, as we have seen, requires the mutual indwelling of wholes within each other, which is impossible for composite beings. But God is unique and simple: his fullness and richness is concentrated, as it were, into a dimensionless whole (neither large nor small). He can be absolutely near because he has no external surfaces that repel other beings. God can be fully present to any and every point in the universe, for he is neither present by being large in a way that is infinitely divisible nor by being small in a way that is infinitely repeatable.

How, then, can a simple God be present to a composite universe? The short answer to this question is that the universe *is* simple to God because it is the result of his own simple action. The action by which God creates and sustains the universe is not multiple or spread out in time, as if God needed to create the world in stages, first creating space, then matter, and finally assembling the pieces into a whole. Just as God exhaustively knows his creation by knowing his action, he is fully present to the world because he is fully present in his action. God can be fully present to every part of creation at the same time because his simple act integrates each "part" perfectly into the whole, so that the part and the whole are not in different places. The part is but an aspect of the whole of creation and reflects a different feature of the simple richness of God's being and action. An adequate defense of this idea must be delayed until we treat the doctrine of creation. One point will be enough to give us an idea of the direction such a treatment must take: in Christ the "fullness of the Deity lives in bodily form" (Col. 2:9), and "in him all things hold together" (Col. 1:17-19). In other words, Christ is the mutual indwelling of God and creation in one person. In Christ, God is omnipresent.

Eternal Omnipresence and Divine "Space"

Does God's attribute of omnipresence make sense only with reference to a space-time world? Indeed, our first thoughts of omnipresence envision a spa-

---

27. John of Damascus, *Orthodox Faith*, 1.5 (*NPNF*, 2nd ser., 9, p. 4).

cious world that God somehow permeates. Yet, if we take the doctrine of the Trinity seriously, we can see that God must be eternally omnipresent, apart from creation and incarnation. The tradition, I have noted, distinguished between God's immensity and his omnipresence. The Reformed scholastics correctly made this distinction in opposition to those who wished to limit God's omnipresence to creation. However, if the scholastics had been thinking in a consistently Trinitarian way, they might have used the term "omnipresence" for God's eternal self-presence as well as for his presence to the world. While I have no objection to using the term "immensity" for God's eternal nature, my goal of thinking in a radically Trinitarian way forces me to use "omnipresence" instead.

God is eternally omnipresent in his own Trinitarian life. In love, the Father presents himself to the Son in the Spirit, and the Son receives that love and in return presents himself to the Father in the Spirit. To put it in traditional terms, Father, Son, and Spirit mutually indwell each other: the Father lives *in* the Son and the Spirit, the Son lives *in* the Father and the Spirit, and the Spirit lives *in* the Father and the Son. They are absolutely present to each other. Therefore, God is eternally omnipresent, for God is present to himself in the mutual indwelling of the Trinity.

Does this make God spatial? Many modern authors think so, and they criticize traditional theology harshly for denying divine spatiality. While it is true that tradition rejected the idea of God's spatiality, it is not correct to charge it with replacing the triune God of love with an abstract, spaceless cause of space. Both Karl Barth and Luco J. van den Brom, each in his own way, accuse Augustine, Aquinas, and other traditional theologians of making this substitution. Barth scolds Augustine for playing games in his assertion that God is "everywhere" *(ubique)* and "nowhere" *(nusquam)* at the same time and for thinking of God as "the non-spatial principle" of space. Barth concludes that the bishop of Hippo turned God into "the lifeless and loveless God of pure human invention."[28] Barth seems unaware or (more likely) unsympathetic toward the patristic method of coupling negation and affirmation to purify our language about God. When Augustine says God is everywhere and nowhere at the same time, he is not equating God with the absolute negation of space, which would make him vulnerable to Barth's critique. Rather, Augustine is affirming God's unique way of being present without the limitations of *created* space.

Van den Brom treats Augustine's statement (God is everywhere and nowhere) as a "dilemma" that begs for a rational solution, and he views the history

---

28. Barth, *Church Dogmatics,* 4 vols., trans. G. W. Bromiley and T. F. Torrance (Edinburgh: T&T Clark, 1936-1969), 2/1, pp. 471-72 (hereafter *CD*).

THE DIVINE ATTRIBUTES

of the doctrine as animated by successive attempts to escape from its horns.[29] Augustine's statement is not a rational dilemma but a paradoxical way of speaking, common among the church fathers, designed to remind us that God is beyond the power of human language to comprehend. Augustine and other traditional theologians did not deny that God "is His own place," to use the words of John of Damascus.[30] They deny only that God suffers the limitations space places on creatures.

In keeping with the tradition, we should continue to affirm that the Father, Son, and Spirit are not extended and separated in created space and time.[31] Nor do the persons of the Trinity need a spatial medium in order to meet and relate to each other. However, in agreement with Barth and van den Brom,[32] I find it important to affirm that God is spatial in a very special sense. The free and eternal relations among Father, Son, and Spirit constitute a divine "space."[33] The divine nature is the "place" where the divine relations occur, and the divine nature is the free action of Father, Son, and Spirit. This is the place where God lives in love, where he decrees his good will, where he knows and loves the world, and where we shall be with him forever. Barth is right when he says, "If no space exists that belongs only to God and to nothing else, God Himself is again spaceless, and therefore lifeless and loveless."[34] God is his own space.

Divine Space and Created Space

The spaciousness of God's nature makes *possible* God's coexistence with creation, with created space. We must take care, however, to avoid blurring the ontological distinction between divine and created space. Divine space is related to created space just as the divine nature is related to created nature — as Creator to creation. The divisible space of physical extension is not an aspect of divine space or an unoccupied corner of God's being. Nor is its possibility

29. Van den Brom, *Divine Presence in the World: A Critical Analysis of the Notion of Divine Omnipresence* (Kampen, The Netherlands: Kok Pharos Publishing, 1993), p. 171.

30. John of Damascus, *Orthodox Faith,* 1.13 (*NPNF,* 2nd ser., 9, p. 16b).

31. For a contemporary defense of divine spacelessness, see Paul Helm, "God and Spacelessness," in *Contemporary Philosophy of Religion,* ed. S. Cahn and D. Shatz (Oxford: Oxford University Press, 1982), p. 107.

32. Van den Brom, *Divine Presence in the World,* pp. 231-65.

33. Clearly, I am working with a relative view of space, as do Barth and van den Brom and many modern theologians. Space is not an empty container that makes possible the co-presence of things within it. Rather, space is constituted by the presence of things in relation to other things. Van den Brom provides a definition of relative space as "the generalized next-to-each-other relation extended to subsume all possible objects" (*Divine Presence in the World,* p. 114).

34. Barth, *CD,* 2/1, p. 474.

286

grounded in a Platonic superspatial heaven where multitudes of ideas, numbers, and concepts relate in distinction. Apart from created space, there is only the space constituted by the mutual love of Father, Son, and Spirit. The possibility of created space is grounded in the inner Trinitarian relationships. The actual existence of our space is constituted by God's free action of relating in love to creation. God did not create space so that he could relate to his creatures; rather, space is constituted by that relationship. Hence, God's omnipresence does not depend on the existence of our space; rather, God creates space by presenting himself to the world in self-giving love.

Now that I have safeguarded the distinction between divine space and created space, we can venture to relate the two. I must emphasize at the outset that Christian theology has no vested interest in supporting any particular theory of physics. Physics and the other natural sciences study the relationships among things *within* the created universe, not God's Trinitarian relationships or God's free relationship to the universe. To put it another way, physics studies the universe's self-presence, while theology studies God's presence to himself and to the world. If God's self-relatedness constitutes divine space, and the universe's internal relatedness constitutes the space of creation, what space is constituted by God's relationship to the universe? The answer to this question can only come from a Christologically informed doctrine of creation in which the proper order of priority is observed: the Trinitarian relationships, Christ as the place where God meets the world, and, finally, the created space constituted by inner worldly relationships.

The Christian doctrine of creation is thoroughly Trinitarian.[35] The Father creates the world through the Son and in the Spirit. The Son is not a creature and the world is not divine; but in Scripture the Father's eternal relationship to the Son is the archetype of God's relationship to the world. In election, creation, reconciliation, and redemption, the Father acts toward the world only *through* the Son and in the Spirit. God creates us and our space by inviting us, through the Son, to join the circle of fellowship with the Father, Son, and Spirit. In a sense, then, God creates our space (and time) by freely inviting us into the divine "space," where he is eternally omnipresent. The meeting place of divine space and created space, as we noted earlier, is Christ: they are united, as the Creed of Chalcedon puts it, "without confusion, transmutation, division, or contrast."[36]

---

35. No one in contemporary theology has done more to revive a Trinitarian theology of creation than has Colin Gunton; see his book *The Triune Creator: A Historical and Systematic Study* (Grand Rapids: Eerdmans, 1998).

36. Philip Schaff, *Creeds of Christendom*, vol. 2, *The Greek and Latin Creeds*, rev. David S. Schaff (1931; reprint, Grand Rapids: Baker, 1990), p. 62.

Does Omnipresence Imply Pantheism or Panentheism?

Does God's omnipresence imply that the world *is* God? If God permeates the world in the manner of omnipresence, perhaps the world is a manifestation of God. If God is present in the world not only by power but also by essence, perhaps God is the essence of the world. Pantheism identifies divine and created space by transferring the divine self-relatedness of the Trinity to the world. The self-relatedness of the world, in pantheism, is interior to the divine being. God's omnipresence in the world is guaranteed because the underlying substance of the world is divine. There is no created being.[37] Most Christian theologians reject pantheism because it contradicts too many other Christian doctrines, most obviously the doctrine of creation. Referring to the world as "creation" without distinguishing its being from God's being would be an abuse of the word. If there is no being but God's being, there is no creation. It is true that in the act of creation God gives — constantly gives — the world its being, and the being of the world presents itself to itself in human consciousness. But this is not the same as saying that God is the being of the world and appears to himself in human consciousness as the world. For Christian theology, God would still be God in undiminished greatness even if there were no world.

Contemporary Christian theologians often suggest the theory of panentheism as a way of understanding God's omnipresence in the world that avoids the pitfall of pantheism (total immanence) on the one hand and of deism (total transcendence) on the other. The word *panentheism* literally means "all-in-god-ism." Its basic thesis is that the world is *in* God and God is in the world without being limited to the world. It aims to preserve an intimate relationship between God and the world without making the two identical. As we have seen, the traditional doctrine of omnipresence teaches that the world is in God and God is in the world. If this were all the advocates of panentheism meant, I would have no objections. However, the decisive question is whether God's relationship with the world limits God in any way. Traditional theology denies that the world's presence in God and God's presence in the world limits God; but most self-designated advocates of panentheism argue that the existence of the world limits God to some degree.

Some theologians advocate panentheism in a rather vague sense, without drawing on any well-developed system, and in that case it is hard to tell what they mean by it. But the most developed contemporary panentheist theories

---

37. See van den Brom, "As Thy New Horizons Beckon: God's Presence in the World," in *Understanding the Attributes of God*, ed. Gijsbert van den Brink and Marcel Sarot (New York: Peter Lang, 1999), pp. 88-89, for a short exposition of this option. See van den Brom, *Divine Presence in the World*, pp. 126-45, for a longer version.

draw either on the dialectical system of Hegel or the process thought of A. N. Whitehead. I will address Whitehead's thought later, especially in the section on immutability. But let us deal briefly with Hegel here. Hegel constructs a philosophical system that avoids a simple identity of God and the world. Nevertheless, in Hegel's system the whole of reality encompasses God and the world. The interaction between God and the world produces a higher stage of reality ("Absolute Spirit") than either one alone. The world is a stage in the life of God, and thus the history of the world is identical to the history of God.

Jürgen Moltmann is perhaps the most influential contemporary theologian advocating a Hegel-type panentheism. He identifies the economic with the immanent Trinity, God's time and space with the world's time and space, and hence reads the history of salvation as the life of God.[38] Suffering, change, and evil play their parts in God's self-realization as the "all in all" of the (eschatological) immanent Trinity. God is not yet omnipresent. For creatures to exist, God must withdraw his presence. The reconciliation of creation by way of the suffering of God in history, especially by way of the cross, will accomplish the omnipresence of God as an eschatological goal. God draws the negatives of history into himself, overcoming them by suffering their wounds.

Panentheism, as developed by Hegel and adapted by Moltmann, blurs the biblical distinction between God and the world and for that reason throws the doctrine of omnipresence into confusion. Does the world live by the absence or by presence of God? Is the world a genuine other to God, or is it God's temporary shadow that will eventually be swallowed by the all-encompassing light? The biblical teaching is clear: God's loving presence gives the world its own presence, and it is God's utter distinction and independence from the world that makes his absolute presence to what is other than him possible.

Omnipresence as Love

Pantheism contends that God is already omnipresent in the world by virtue of identity, and panentheism understands God to be growing toward such omnipresence. The traditional doctrine, in contrast, understands God's omnipresence as the presence of his powerful love to his beloved creatures. We must develop this thought a bit further here. In his love, God wills that creatures exist beside him and live in his presence. He does not love us because we exist in his

---

38. Moltmann develops these ideas in *The Trinity and the Kingdom,* trans. Margaret Kohl (Minneapolis: Fortress, 1993); see also Moltmann, *God in Creation: A New Theology of Creation and the Spirit of God,* trans. Margaret Kohl (Minneapolis: Fortress, 1993); and *The Spirit of Life: A Universal Affirmation,* trans. Margaret Kohl (Minneapolis: Fortress, 1992).

presence; we exist before him because he loves us. His omnipresence is based on his universal love, in which he gives being to all creation. God's loving and self-giving presence founds the world's capacity for self-presence, its space. He gives creatures to themselves and to each other by giving himself to them.

The world has no possibility of existence apart from the life-giving presence of God. Therefore, space in Christian theology is an ethical as well as an ontological concept. Divine space is the mutually indwelling love of the Trinity. Christ-space is the place where we meet God's love for us and in the power of the Spirit love him in return. Christ indwells us through the Spirit, and through the Spirit we live in Christ. Created space is (or will be eschatologically) the mutual indwelling of God's creatures. God's command and the presence of the Spirit urge us to spiritualize created space by making all our relationships ones of self-giving love in response to and imitation of God's love. The eschatological redemption of created space will remove the distance — physical and ethical — that separates God's creatures from each other and will enable them to indwell each other in love. God created space by love and for love and maintains it in love.

Ways of Being Present

God is present to all things, for it is God's presence that gives them being and the power of presence. In Scripture, however, it seems that God is sometimes present and sometimes not, or that he is present in different modes and intensities. Is God really more or less present at different times and places? Was God more present at Mount Sinai, the Jerusalem temple, or in the incarnate Son than he is to the remotest star or to the smallest microbe? The answer to these questions must be negative. God is absolutely present to all things at all times in the most intimate way possible, for he constantly gives them being. But God can be present in ways that are additional to his general omnipresence. Traditional theologians perceived the necessity of distinguishing God's special presence from his general omnipresence. Benedict Pictet, for example, says that, in addition to God's general omnipresence, God can be present "in a peculiar manner in certain places and persons, where he gives the signs and effects either of his majesty, or his glory, or his grace."[39] On these occasions, God adds to his hidden act of sustaining and guiding creation his special activity related to his will to save creation from its "bondage to decay" (Rom. 8). God is present to us and active in us always, but he can make us aware of his presence to whatever degree he wishes. Therefore, when we say "God is present," we usually mean:

39. Pictet, *Christian Theology,* 2.7, p. 96.

"God is present to my consciousness" or "I have a sense of God's presence" or "God is an object of my experience." Our perception, however, is not the final test of God's presence.

God can be omnipresent without ever becoming an object of our experience. For his presence is the origin of our existence, not a datum of our experience. His presence conditions all our experience so that he can, if he wills, remain hidden at the root of our being. The theophanies of Scripture and even the incarnation itself do not increase God's presence in the world. Nor do the times of God's silence and hiddenness decrease his presence. Unlike creatures, God can be fully present without disturbing any of the ordinary patterns in creation. God can be present without giving off or blocking light waves. God does not disturb the balance of gravitational forces or displace any creature from its space by his presence.

God is free, however, to become an experience for us. He can speak in audible sounds, for example, or appear as light, or he can make himself touchable in the flesh of Jesus Christ. His Spirit can open us to his presence, and in the sacraments he can establish and maintain fellowship with us in redemptive ways. The Christian hope is for a final revelation of God, for the eschatological revelation of his glory. But in all these it is we who change, not God. He is always here, "not far from any one of us." It is we who must "seek him and perhaps reach out for him and find him" (Acts 17:27). He is already with us.

Understandably, believers long for special experiences of God, for "signs and effects" of God's gracious presence. But here, at the conclusion of this section, I want to emphasize the power and comfort the believer can experience in contemplating in faith the *doctrine* of omnipresence. Among the things human beings fear more than death, being left alone surely is near the top of the list. We fear it because we cannot survive physically in this world alone. But more that that, we fear it because we need relationships with others to provide identity, meaning, and joy in living. More than almost anything we want to love and be loved. But to love and be loved requires knowing other people and being known truly by them. And this is not easy to have. Indeed it seems impossible, for we do not know ourselves well enough to "show" our true selves to others. Even more frightening, others might reject us even if we had the power to reveal ourselves. And how can we trust others who claim to tell us the truth about themselves?

At one of the many jobs I had to work my way through graduate school, I had a conversation that I will never forget. A fellow worker and I were preparing to punch the time clock and leave work for the day. I knew that this woman was twenty-seven years old and already divorced, but she seemed especially anxious and fidgety that evening. Just making small talk, and knowing that she was a partier, I asked what she planned to with the rest of the evening. She said, "I plan to go home, open a bottle of wine, and turn on the stereo as loud I can stand it until I fall asleep." Perhaps I should have kept my mouth shut, but I said, "Why do you want the stereo on so loud?" (I knew why she wanted the wine.) She said something like, "Because I can't stand silence." I sensed that I was standing in the presence of a desperately lonely and empty person. Not knowing what else to say, but wishing to say something helpful, I replied: "I have felt what you feel but not for a long time. I always have someone with whom to converse no matter where I am." She knew of whom I spoke. We punched our time sheets and left, and we never spoke of it again.

Many times since that day I have reflected on the difference believing in God's constant presence makes in my life. Believing in God's presence allows me to sustain a constant conversation with my Creator, so that I need never be alone. God's presence transforms my mind from a cold echoing void into a cozy place designed for intimate conversation. I do not know who I am, but I am in constant conversation with the One who knows me absolutely. I do not know whether you would love me if you knew me; but I know that the One who knows me completely loves me utterly. And with this I have all the knowledge of myself I need: I am the one whom God invites into his conversation space. I am the one whom God knows and loves. The cozy place God makes of our minds enables us to invite still others, without fear, into the conversation based on truth.

The comfort and joy afforded by the doctrine of omnipresence depends on the identity of the one we understand to be present. Listen to Jesus' words of comfort and connect them to omnipresence: "I will not leave you as orphans; I will come to you. . . . On that day you will realize that I am in my Father, and you are in me, and I am in you. . . . He who loves me will be loved by my Father, and I too will love him and show myself to him" (John 14:18-21).

The Eternal God

According to tradition and Scripture, our God has no beginning and will have no end. He does not forget, recede into the past, or fall victim to fortune. He does not change or grow old, for God's "time" is his perfect and full life, and this eternal life is not stretched out in successive moments or phases. God is free from every limit and imperfection creatures suffer by virtue of their temporal mode of being. God is fully present in all time as well as in all space. The creature's time does not shut God in or keep him out. Therefore, God has time for us and is always ready for us.

What Scripture Says

In Scripture the everlasting God proves a reliable help in time of need. Divine dependability differs from even the most dependable worldly powers. God is invulnerable to the forces of decay we associate with time. Psalm 90 states this contrast eloquently: "Before the mountains were born or you brought forth the earth and the world, from everlasting to everlasting you are God. You turn men back to dust, saying, 'Return to dust, O sons of men.' For a thousand years in your sight are like a day that has just gone by, or like a watch in the night" (Ps. 90:1-4; cf. Ps. 102:25-27; 2 Pet. 3:8).

Unlike our lives, which speak of vulnerability, fleetingness, and mortality, the mountains and earth give the impression of being impervious to change and decay. Nevertheless, the Lord lived before them, and, when they are gone, crumbled to dust, he will still be young. The Lord gave these creatures their time and, whenever he wills, he commands them to "return to dust." A thousand years — or any finite stretch of time — pass for God as quickly as does a day gone by or as three or four hours of the night while we are asleep. Hence, God is totally reliable and always available to help: "God is our refuge and strength, an ever-present help in trouble. Therefore we will not fear, though the earth give way and the mountains fall into the heart of the sea" (Ps. 46:1-2; cf. Deut. 33:27).

God is the foundation of all hope, for he is able to bring about the future he has promised. He does not grow old and tired (Isa. 40:28). He is the Lord of time and thus the God of hope. God is "before" all things and active at "the beginning," because God created all things (Gen. 1:1; cf. John 1:1-3). The Lord identifies himself as the one who "made all things, who alone stretched out the heavens, who spread out the earth by myself" (Isa. 44:24; Jer. 10:16). "From him and through him and to him are all things" (Rom. 11:36; cf. 1 Cor. 8:6). Christ is "before all things" (Col. 1:17). In election, God was active "before" creation: "For he chose us in him before the creation of the world" (Eph. 1:4; cf. 1 Pet. 1:20).

Sometimes, the words "everlasting" and "eternal" are used as titles or attributes for God. Paul speaks of the pagan blindness to God's "eternal power and divine nature" (Rom. 1:20; cf. 16:26). He speaks of God as the "King eternal, immortal, invisible, the only God" (1 Tim. 1:17). God lets himself be known to John as "the Alpha and the Omega . . . the one who is, and who was, and who is to come, the Almighty" (Rev. 1:8). Often in Scripture the everlasting God is praised as "from everlasting to everlasting" (Ps. 41:13; cf. 1 Chron. 16:36; 29:10; Ps. 106:48). The eternally living God is the only one who can give eternal life (1 John 5:11). According to the Scriptures, then, a creature can in a certain sense *possess* eternal life. But only God can *give* eternal life. God alone possesses eternal life without having receiving it from another. He is life eternal — life-giving life.

Four Summary Points

Some contemporary theologians and biblical scholars deny that the traditional doctrine of God's eternity or everlastingness can be discovered in the Scriptures or founded on them. Let us summarize the biblical teaching in preparation for assessing this claim. Scripture shows no interest in contemplating God's everlastingness as such; that is, it does not approach God's manner of life ontologically. Rather, Scripture refers to God's eternity only as a matter of praise, comfort, or confidence in the lives of God's people. Nevertheless, some things are affirmed and others are denied about God with reference to time as the basis for this praise, comfort, and confidence. Scripture clearly affirms that: (1) *God had no beginning and will have no end.* Unlike creatures, there was no time before God existed, and God will never cease to exist. There was, however, some sort of "before" the creature existed. (2) *God is present to every moment of our time.* He was present and available in the past, is now present, will be present to all future times. (3) *God is the Lord over time.* Time does not wear God out, dissipate his energy, or cause him to grow old and die. (4) *God's eternity is closely associated with his being the source of his own life and hence the source of all other existence and life.* Scripture is interested in everlasting life, not everlasting time. Time is not approached as a container in which life becomes possible but as a mode of life.[40]

Scripture does not explicitly address some issues that have generated much discussion in the history of theology: What relationship does God's eternity or everlastingness bear to our time? Are the two times the same? Does God's time include our time as a "segment" of an infinite series of moments? Or is eternity the negation of time, timelessness? Does God live his life in successive moments? Or are all the "moments" contemporaneous? Is God's eternity a motionless present? Whereas Scripture does not answer these questions explicitly, we need not remain completely silent. Combining the above four scriptural propositions with other biblical teachings yields insight

---

40. John Frame, *The Doctrine of God* (Phillipsburg, NJ: Presbyterian and Reformed, 2002), pp. 554-56, also summarizes scriptural teaching in four headings under which he names the ways God is free from the limiting characteristic of temporal creatures: "the limitation of beginning and end," "the limitation of change," "the limitation of ignorance," and "the limitation of temporal frustration."

into them and helps us decide among the many alternative answers that have been proposed.

The Tradition

The church fathers, following Scripture, proclaim that God alone possesses eternal life, life without beginning or end. Clement of Alexandria, after explaining how God's providence had enlightened the minds of some Greek authors, concludes that God is "an unbeginning principle. . . . For God did not make a beginning of being Lord and Good, being always what He is. Nor will He ever cease to do good, although He bring all things to an end."[41] Athanasius affirmed the eternity of God in the context of the debate with Arianism. Arius used the formula "there was a time when he was not" to point out the Son's ontological inferiority to the Father. Athanasius attacked Arius for dragging the divine nature into the vicissitudes of time.[42]

Gregory of Nyssa made clear his conviction that God's eternal form of life excludes temporal succession. God is "neither in place nor in time, excluding all limitation and every form of definition."[43] Complaining about those who take literally terms such as "before" and "after" in reference to the life of God, Gregory quips: "It is clear, even with a moderate insight into the nature of things, that there is nothing by which we can measure the divine and blessed life. It is not in time, but time flows from it."[44] Even when Scripture uses temporal terms to speak about God, as it does in Isaiah 44:6 ("I am the first and I am the last; apart from me there is no God"), it teaches "the doctrine of a single divine nature, continuous with itself, and without interruption."[45]

For Western Christianity, Book Eleven of Augustine's *Confessions* is the most well-known and influential treatment of divine eternity. To those who ask what was God doing "before" he created the world, Augustine declares that the question presupposes a false understanding of God's eternity:

41. Clement of Alexandria, *The Stromata or Miscellanies,* 5.14 (*ANF,* 2, p. 476).

42. For this story, see E. P. Meijering, "A Discussion in Time and Eternity," in *God, Being, History: Studies in Patristic Philosophy* (Amsterdam: North-Holland Publishing Company, 1975), pp. 81-88.

43. Gregory of Nyssa, *Orationes de beatitudinibus,* 3, quoted in Jaroslav Pelikan, *Christianity and Classical Culture: The Metamorphosis of Natural Theology in the Christian Encounter with Hellenism* (New Haven, CT: Yale University Press, 1993), p. 113.

44. *Contra Eunomium,* 3.7.23, quoted in Pelikan, *Christianity and Classical Culture,* p. 114.

45. *Contra Eunomium,* 3.3.10, quoted in Pelikan, *Christianity and Classical Culture,* p. 116.

Since, therefore, you are the cause of all times, if any time existed before you made heaven and earth, how can anyone say that you abstained from working? You have made time itself. Time could not elapse before you made time. But if time did not exist before heaven and earth, why do people ask what you were then doing? There was no "then" when there was no time.[46]

How, then, does eternity differ from time? God's eternity must not be compared to a "long time." A long time "is long only because constituted of many successive movements which cannot be simultaneously extended. In the eternal, nothing is transient, but the whole is present."[47] God's years "subsist in simultaneity, because they do not change; those going away are not thrust out by those coming in. But the years which are ours will not all be until all years have ceased to be."[48] For us, the present is fleeting. God's "today" is eternity; God is wholly present to his whole being.[49]

It was Boethius, however, who gave to the world the most compact and memorable definition of divine eternity, which, because of its vast influence, I quote here in its larger context:

The common opinion, according to all men living, is that God is eternal. Let us therefore consider what is eternity. . . . *Eternity is the simultaneous and complete possession of infinite life.* This will appear more clearly if we compare it with temporal things. All that lives under the conditions of time moves through the present from the past to the future; there is nothing set in time which can at one moment grasp the whole space of its lifetime. It cannot yet comprehend tomorrow; yesterday it has already lost. And in this life of today your life is no more than a changing, passing moment. And as Aristotle said of the universe, so it is of all that is subject to time; though it never began to be, nor will ever cease, and its life is co-extensive with the infinity of time, yet it is not such as can be held to be eternal. For though it apprehends and grasps a space of infinite lifetime, it does not embrace the whole simultaneously; it has not yet experienced the future. What we should rightly call eternal is that which grasps and possesses wholly and simultaneously the fullness of unending life, which asks naught of the future, and has lost naught of the fleeting past; and such an existence must be ever present in itself to control and aid itself, and also must keep present with itself the infin-

46. *Confessions,* 9.12, in *Saint Augustine Confessions,* trans. Henry Chadwick (New York: Oxford University Press, 1991), pp. 229-30.

47. *Confessions,* 9.11, p. 228.

48. *Confessions,* 9.14, p. 230.

49. *Confessions,* 9.14, p. 230.

ity of changing time. Therefore, people who hear that Plato thought that this universe had no beginning of time and will have no end, are not right in thinking that in this way the created world is coeternal with its Creator.[50]

Anselm of Canterbury continues the tradition of Augustine and Boethius. Anselm spends seven chapters of his *Monologium* in tightly reasoned arguments to establish his conclusions about God's eternity. "It is evident that this supreme Substance is without beginning and without end; that it has neither past, nor future, nor the temporal, that is, transient present in which we live."[51] Echoing Boethius, Anselm concludes: "Hence, if this Being is said to exist always . . . no better sense can be attached to his statement, than that it exists or lives eternally, that is, it possesses interminable life, as a perfect whole at once. For its eternity apparently is an interminable life, existing at once as a perfect whole."[52]

Aquinas begins his discussion of eternity with the question of whether Boethius' definition is a good one. He defends the famous definition, arguing that God's eternity consists of two facts: it is interminable, without beginning or end; and it excludes all succession, "being simultaneously whole."[53] For Aquinas, eternity follows from simplicity and immutability. Since God is not composed of parts and cannot change, the succession and change that time measures — hence time itself — has no place in the divine life.[54]

Protestant theologians of the Reformation and post-Reformation eras continued along the lines set out by Augustine, Boethius, and Anselm. Calvin, in commenting on Isaiah's critique of idolatry (40:28), explains: "[F]or if God is eternal, he never changes or decays, eternity being uniformly attended by this quality, that it is never liable to change, but always remains the same."[55] Edward Leigh emphasizes that "God is eternal. Eternity is a being without limitation of time, or a being without beginning, ending, or succession. Time is the continu-

50. Boethius, *Consolation of Philosophy*, 5, in *The Consolation of Philosophy*, trans. W. V. Cooper (London: J. M. Dent and Company, 1902), pp. 160-61.

51. Anselm, *Monologium*, 24, pp. 82-83.

52. *Monologium*, 24, p. 83.

53. Aquinas, *SumTh*, 1.10.1, in *Basic Writings*, 1, p. 75. For a discussion of how Aquinas's thought develops in these first questions of the *Summa Theologica*, see David B. Burrell, CSC, *Aquinas: God and Action* (Notre Dame, IN: University of Notre Dame Press, 1979), pp. 1-41.

54. In one of his early writings, Duns Scotus criticizes Aquinas for destroying temporal distinctions among different events in creation. If all events are contemporary with eternity, are they not contemporary with each other? In his later works Scotus corrects himself, defends divine timelessness, and shows how God's eternal presence does not efface temporal distinctions within the creation. See Richard Cross, "Duns Scotus on Eternity and Timelessness," *Faith and Philosophy* 14 (1997): 3-25.

55. Calvin, *Commentary on Isaiah*, quoted in Muller, PRRD, 3, p. 349.

ance of things past, present, and to come, all time hath a beginning, a vicissi-
tude, and an end, or may have . . . but God's essence is bounded by none of the
hedges."[56] Leonhard Rijssen, echoing Anselm and Aquinas, declares: "God is
utterly simple and immutable, and for this reason he cannot be said to change
temporally."[57]

Theology of God's Eternity

I have presented the texts of Scripture from which traditional Christian theologians constructed their doctrine of divine eternity and have quoted extensively
from the architects of the traditional teaching. Now we must ask whether or not
the traditional teaching remains a viable option for contemporary Christians. I
shall conclude that the traditional doctrine not only withstands recent criticisms leveled against it but provides a firm foundation for joy and hope. As one
well-known contemporary defender of the tradition expresses it: "We are filled
with joy at the thought of this Being-Eternity which includes all that is created
and contingent, including also our little being, our every act, every moment of
our lives."[58]

Time

The first step toward a greater understanding of God's eternity must be to clarify the concept of time as best we can. Our concept of eternity is shaped by our
understanding of its relationship to time. So we must specify which aspects of
time are like and which are unlike eternity. To do this, we must identify some
basic characteristics of time.

Time can be understood from different angles of our experience, and our
thinking becomes confused when we mix the different contexts. Apart from
theology, we can view time in at least four ways: chronologically, psychologi-
cally, physically, and ontologically. The first two are available to common experience, and the latter two involve more abstraction.[59] Chronological time iden-

56. Leigh, *System or Body of Divinity,* 2.4 (London, 1654), p. 147.

57. Rijssen, *Summa Theologiae,* 3.12, quoted in Muller, *PRRD,* 3, p. 351. For the Lutheran
view, which does not differ in substance from the Reformed view, see Preus, *TPRL,* 2, pp. 76-79.

58. Pope John Paul II, "The Loving God Has Revealed Himself as Eternity Itself," General
Audience, Sept. 4, 1985.

59. See Wolfgang Achtner, Stefan Kunz, and Thomas Walter, *Dimensions of Time: The
Structures of the Time of Humans, of the World and of God* (Grand Rapids: Eerdmans, 2002), for
another way of analyzing our experience of time.

tifies time with the observed movements of the heavenly bodies. Our watches are machines that are designed to move certain distances or vibrate at certain frequencies within a natural day or year. We grasp chronological time quantitatively, in terms of numbers of identical units. We usually answer the question "What time is it?" with a chronological answer.

Psychological time is very different. It cannot be merely quantitative, because different times have different qualities, characters, and textures. Psychological time does not necessarily move with the rotations of the heavenly bodies. Nor does it move at a steady rate: it can move fast or slow. Some times are boring, while others are exciting. Time can be empty or full. Psychological time includes a sense of duration, memory, and imagination (or anticipation). To the question "What time is it?" Charles Dickens might answer, "It was the best of times. It was the worst of times." If we were to be asked the question "What is time?" instead of "What time is it?" our first inclination might be to answer in psychological terms by speaking of past, present, and future. For we have a dim sense of the past, a vivid sense of the present, and we imagine a future that is projected by drawing a straight line from the past through the present to the future.

Philosophers of time disagree about whether time is really tensed, that is, composed of past, present, and future. Some argue that even though our experience is tensed we need not think that reality is tensed. Just as we do not regard the "here" of space as superior to the "there," we are not bound to regard the "now" of time as uniquely real as opposed to the past and future. The past-present-future relationships can be reduced to a tenseless before-after relationship. Others argue that reality is tensed to the core: that is, time is an inherent feature of being. Even God must experience himself and the world in a tensed fashion. Hence they would disagree with my placement of our sense of past, present, and future in the psychological category. This debate far outstrips my knowledge of contemporary philosophy. But it seems clear that, whatever else the tenses are, they are also psychological. Our experience of them depends on our powers of memory and imaginative anticipation.[60]

Physicists tell us not to be fooled by our chronological and psychological senses of time. In our daily lives we assume that time is an absolute feature of the universe: that is, there must be a "now" that is simultaneous for the entire universe. Suppose for me at this moment a volcano on one of Jupiter's moons were erupting; suppose, further, that there is a way to synchronize the clocks of all other observers (whatever their location or velocity relative to me) with my own. Common sense would dictate that each clock would mark the exact same

60. See J. J. C. Smart, "Time," in Paul Edwards, ed., *Encyclopedia of Philosophy,* vol. 7 (New York: Macmillan, 1967), pp. 126-34.

time for this event. According to Einstein's Special Theory of Relativity, however, this cannot be true. If we assume the constancy of the speed of light and the relativity of motion, we discover that the time an event happens differs for observers in different inertial frames of reference (that is, that are moving toward or away from each other). Einstein says: "Thus we see that we can attribute no *absolute* meaning to the concept of simultaneity, but that two events which, examined from a co-ordinate system, are simultaneous, can no longer be interpreted as simultaneous events when examined from a system which is in motion relative to that system."[61] This means that, for one observer, the "now" of your birth could be marked as after the "now" of your death for another observer. Therefore, to the question "What time is it?" the physicist will answer: "That depends on where you are and how fast you are moving."[62]

Finally, we can consider time in ontological terms and ask about its relationship to being. Aristotle viewed time as a mode of being of imperfect beings.[63] Imperfect beings exist partly in a state of potentiality, that is, a state of not-yet-being. Their natures have not yet been fully actualized; they do not possess their full being. Only by moving successively from various stages of potentiality to full actuality can they enact their being and bring it into actual existence. The measure of this movement is time. Aristotle thus defines time as "the number of motion in respect of before and after."[64] Temporal beings' lack of full actuality is the reason they need time. Time is thus a mode of being of beings that do not possess themselves fully but strive toward self-possession.

Nothing can actualize itself. A being that is merely potential requires help from a being that is already fully actual. (E.g., it takes a spark to kindle a flame.) A fully actual and perfect being is timeless: it has no unrealized potential and thus has no need to move, the measurement of which is time. The world is drawn forward toward perfection by its desire for full actuality, which is a reality only in the divine nature. For Aristotle, the divine is the "unmoved mover" of all.[65] The divine is timeless, for time is the proper and necessary mode of be-

61. "On the Electrodynamics of Moving Bodies," quoted in William Lane Craig, *Time and Eternity: Exploring God's Relationship to Time* (Wheaton, IL: Crossway Books, 2001), p. 42.

62. In my view, William Craig raises some serious questions about whether we ought to take Einstein's theory realistically (*Time and Eternity,* pp. 38-66).

63. Aristotle discusses space and time in *Physics,* 4, in *The Basic Writings of Aristotle,* ed. Richard McKeon (New York: Random House, 1941), pp. 289-300.

64. *Physics,* 4.11, quoted in Richard Sorabji, *Time, Creation and the Continuum: Theories in Antiquity and the Early Middle Ages* (Ithaca, NY: Cornell University Press, 1983), p. 84. Sorabji treats Aristotle's views extensively in this work.

65. Aristotle treats the ultimate origin of all motion in *Physics,* 8, in *The Basic Writings of Aristotle,* pp. 354-94.

ing only for imperfect beings and thus is an imperfect mode of being. A perfect being would not be perfect if it had an imperfect mode of being. Hence, the divine being is timeless.

Plotinus criticized Aristotle's treatment of time, assessing it as more a description than a definition. According to him, Aristotle never answers the question "What is time?" Plotinus begins with the concept of eternity and then defines time relative to eternity. Eternity is the fullness of life "instantaneously entire, complete, at no point broken into period or part."[66] Eternity contains, whole and unbroken, every good that is contained, scattered, and sequenced in time. Eternity, then, contains time latent within itself. Never-ending time is an image of eternity, refracted and spread out. Time comes to be as the striving of the world soul, "seeking perpetuity by way of futurity."[67] Time seeks to unfold the reality of eternity by perpetual reaching forward toward an infinite future. Even though time considered as a whole contains everything contained by eternity, it can never grasp its wholeness from within time. It can do this only from the perspective of eternity.[68]

It would not serve our interests to pursue in detail the complicated and controversial history of these four nontheological ways of viewing time. However true it is that we can gain an understanding of God's eternity only by viewing it in some relationship to time, we cannot arrive at an understanding of God's eternity merely by affirming or negating a human understanding of time. The most we can hope to gain from nontheological concepts of time is an expanded body of concepts or stimulation to our imagination, both of which can be of service to theology. Theology, however, must retain its freedom from nontheological systems.

Does God Live in Time?

Some modern authors think so. In this section I will focus on the view that God is unqualifiedly temporal, advocated by Nicholas Wolterstorff, and leave aside positions such as those of William Lane Craig, who conceives of God as timeless before creation and temporal afterward, and those of Alan G. Padgett, who

66. Plotinus, *Enneads*, 3.7.3; trans. Stephen Mackenna, abr. John Dillon (London: Penguin Books, 1991), p. 216.

67. *Enneads*, 3.7.4, p. 217.

68. See Sorabji, *Time, Creation and the Continuum*, pp. 138-56, for an explanation of Plotinus's understanding of time and eternity in its ancient context. For an appreciative appropriation of Plotinus's view of time and eternity for Christian theology, see Wolfhart Pannenberg, *Metaphysics and the Idea of God*, trans. Philip Clayton (Edinburgh: T&T Clark, 1990), pp. 69-90.

sees God as existing in "relative timelessness" or "pure duration" within which our "measured time" exists. My major objections to these positions concern the ways in which God is subjected to temporal change and relativity, which is why I will focus on the more radical position, "unqualified temporality."[69]

Wolterstorff argues that the data of Scripture do not support the traditional doctrine of divine eternity. He contends that Scripture speaks of God as a temporal being, and we ought to take this language "as literally true" unless we can generate compelling reasons not to do so.[70] A theology faithful to Scripture will understand God's eternity as everlastingness rather than timelessness. According to Wolterstorff, only a temporal being could do what Scripture attributes to God. In Scripture, God has a life history and experiences that life in moment-by-moment succession. God changes in response to what happens in creation as it happens. A timeless God would be incapable of such responsiveness, for a God without past, present, or future could not even know what time it is now. "One can know that something is presently happening only when it is."[71] An eternal God could know creation only in a tenseless way, which leaves out much important information.[72] Others have responded in detail to Wolterstorff and other contemporary advocates of a wholly temporal God.[73] Instead, I shall give some "compelling reasons" to accept the traditional teaching.

God Is His "Everlastingness"

In the four propositions we gleaned from Scripture, God's mode of life is contrasted and compared with ordinary human experience. Human beings come

69. For Wolterstorff's views, see the older and more technical article, "God Everlasting," in *Contemporary Philosophy of Religion*, ed. S. Cahn and D. Shatz (Oxford: Oxford University Press, 1982), pp. 77-98; see also Wolterstorff's more popular treatment, "Unqualified Divine Temporality," in *Four Views: God and Time*, ed. Gregory E. Ganssle (Downers Grove, IL: InterVarsity, 2001), pp. 186-213. For Craig's views, see *Time and Eternity* and "Timelessness and Omnitemporality," in *Four Views: God and Time*, pp. 129-60. For Padgett's theory, see his technical work *God, Eternity and the Nature of Time* (New York: St. Martins Press, 1992), as well as his more popular piece, "Eternity as Relative Timelessness," in *Four Views: God and Time*, pp. 92-110.

70. Wolterstorff, "Unqualified Divine Temporality," p. 187.

71. "Unqualified Divine Temporality," p. 206. Wolterstorff accepts the theory that reality is inherently tensed; the present is the only reality.

72. See also Richard Swinburne, *The Coherence of Theism* (Oxford: Clarendon Press, 1977), pp. 220-21. Swinburne rejects the idea of timeless divine knowledge of creation.

73. See Paul Helm, *The Eternal God: A Study of God Without Time* (Oxford: Clarendon Press, 1988) and "God and Spacelessness," in Cahn and Shatz, *Contemporary Philosophy of Religion*, pp. 99-110. Helm argues that Wolterstorff's arguments apply equally to space, which counts against them.

into being and go out of being. The creature's time is ambiguous; time gives and then takes away what it gives. It brings life, freedom, and joy, but it also bears dependency and mortality in its embrace. However, God is not subject to time's transitions. Therefore, viewing God's life from within the human frame of reference, Scripture pictures it as everlastingness.

But it is clear that Scripture makes much more than a quantitative distinction between God's life and our lives. God is holy, mysterious, and incomprehensible. We must take into account those qualitative differences in considering God's eternity. We cannot plumb its depths by equating God's eternity merely with his long life. We think of our lives as a finite series of moments or events with a beginning and an end. Naturally, then, our first thought of God's everlastingness will be formed by extending a timeline backward to the infinite past and forward to the infinite future. However, we must not forget that, unlike us, God is the basis of his life. His "everlastingness" is not an accidental quality so that God just happens to be everlasting. I noted in the section on God's uniqueness that we tend to view God's oneness as a mere accident, as if there just happens to be only one God. But we learned that God's uniqueness is unique, that there can be no other God. God *is* his oneness, and such oneness is not repeatable.

God's "Everlastingness" Is Unique

In the same way, God does not just happen to be everlasting, as if it were merely his fate to have no beginning and no end. His everlastingness, like his oneness and all his other attributes, is his free possession. He is his eternity, and there can be no other eternity like his. Perhaps we can imagine a god that in fact always was and always will be. But this being would not be God, for it would be eternal only by participation in an eternity not its own. But Scripture asserts that God is dependent on nothing outside himself. God is exempt not only from the *fact* of having come into being but from the very *possibility* of coming into being. Not only will God never die; God cannot die. He is his eternal life.

Two Objections to Exclusive Divine Temporality

Since God is his unique "everlastingness," we should not conceive of God's life as spread out in an infinite series of instants. We are never present to our whole lives. When we are born, we are not yet who we will be. At the end of our lives we will not yet be what we could have been, nor shall we encompass the whole of what we have been. We remember some events and bear in our bodies and souls some results of what we have been and done, but by no means all. Moreover, just as we reach the definitive whole of our lives, we lose our grasp on them in death.

The first reason to reject exclusive divine temporality then is that such a being cannot possess his life fully. If God lived in time, some of his life would no longer be and some of it would not yet be. God would thus not *be* his nature, for there would still remain a distinction between the possibilities of the divine nature and the particular god that God is. God's being and life and his existence and essence would be distinct in reality; God would be a god. But if God freely enacts his nature and possesses his life fully, there can be no "not yet" in God. His nature is fully actual eternally in his triune life.

A second reason we must reject the idea of a temporal God is that it compromises God's independence. If God's life were stretched out in time, he would depend on something outside himself to make him whole, to determine his definitive identity. As I suggested earlier, the whole life of a temporal being can be possessed only by a reality that encompasses and hence transcends the whole. A temporal God would be in the same situation that we are, dependent on a higher whole-making reality. Let us recall here the discussion of divine simplicity. If we conceive of God's life as composed of an infinite series of different states corresponding to different points on a time line, we run into the same difficulties we face in dealing with the notion of a composite God. What is the ontological status of the different states? Are they different gods? What is the composing force that holds them together in one identity? Is this "force" the real unchanging God behind the temporal God? What is the status of the design plan that determines the relationship among the states? Is this "design plan" the eternal foundation of God's deity?

Is God's Vivid Memory the Basis of His Unity?

Some advocates of a wholly temporal God answer these questions with the thesis that God holds his past and future together in his present consciousness by his vivid memory, which retains the past perfectly, and his perfect foreknowledge, which fully anticipates the future. Does this theory do justice to the God of Scripture? Can vividness of memory make up for the lack of presence and reality of God's past and future? Consider first the nature of memory. Memory is passive with respect to the original experience it remembers. The original experience impresses itself on the memory when it is present, and then passes out of existence. The present act of remembering and the (now) past act of experiencing are not the same. We do not "experience" the past by remembering it; we experience only our memory of it. We cannot make our past experience truly present no matter how vividly we have remembered it.

304

What are the implications of this theory for the life of God? According to this viewpoint, God must remember his past and anticipate his future as things that do not now exist, because, according to the view I am criticizing, "to exist" means "to exist now." This means that the "unified" self that God experiences in his temporal consciousness is a mixture of being and nonbeing, of consciousness of his present being, memories of his past being, and anticipations of his future being. Thus, in this view, God is not fully present to his *real* self. God's being is not his act; for, since God no longer controls what he was and does not control what he will be, God does not control his present identity. Surely this understanding cannot be worthy of the one of whom Paul said, "From him and through him and to him are all things" (Rom. 11:36).

Furthermore, according to this theory, the power of remembering the past, knowing the present, and foreknowing the future is the power (the "composing force") that holds the moments of God's life together. But this raises a question: Is this power temporal? If it is temporal, it too will be divided into past, present, and future and require another power to hold it together, which leads to an infinite regression. On the other hand, if God's power of memory is not temporal, we are faced with two alternatives: along with process theology, we could postulate a dipolar God, with an eternal, unchanging pole and a temporal, changing pole; or we could give up the theory of a wholly temporal God and affirm with tradition that God is eternal. I believe that listening to Scripture demands that we choose the latter.

A Timeless God?

If God does not live his life piecemeal, is he timeless? Critics assume, often without argument, that the traditional doctrine teaches the *absolute* timelessness of God. But even a cursory reading of Boethius's definition ("the simultaneous and complete possession of interminable life") shows that this charge is false. Which of these five words — simultaneous, complete, possession, interminable, or life — indicates the absolute negation of time? Even our lives contain an image of such eternal life. For our temporal existence in the fleeting present is a sort of simultaneous presence of some of our lives, which we possess incompletely. Boethius does not wish to negate time absolutely, for then he would have to negate *us* and our little imperfect image of God's "simultaneous and complete possession of interminable life." The Boethian definition negates only time's imperfections. Likewise, the tradition as a whole meant to exclude only the *imperfections* of temporal existence. Richard Muller, historian of post-Reformation Reformed dogmatics, concludes: "The historical sources do not offer a doctrine of 'timeless eternity' if that is taken to mean a doctrine of eternal being unrelated to time and incapable of dealing with temporal events as temporal."[74] Just as the critics of the doctrine of divine simplicity are mistaken to think that it taught that "in God there are no distinctions whatever,"[75] critics of divine eternity are beating a dead horse to fight against the traditional doctrine of an absolutely timeless God. There is no such tradition.

The insurmountable problems for the doctrine of God generated by the notion of absolute timeless eternity would have been clear to every traditional theologian. The first problem is methodological: How could we generate the idea of absolute timelessness except by negating the concept of time absolutely? Scripture certainly sets an example by negating all defect and evil when speaking of God: "God is light. In him is no darkness at all" (1 John 1:5). We are permitted to deny that God is imperfect or evil and remove from our concept of God any such component. But, since it is God's creation, time is not evil. Therefore, we must not derive the attribute of eternity by negating time absolutely. Time is certainly an imperfect mode of life, for creatures are finite and are not yet perfect. But time enables creatures to exist, live, and act. Hence, negating time fully will also negate life, existence, space, relationship, action, and all other positive aspects of creatures. An absolutely timeless God could hardly be distinguished from a nonexistent God.

Another problem arises when we consider the incarnation. The Son of God became human without ceasing to be divine. He took on the "form of a servant," including the form of temporality. Barth is correct to conclude that "we cannot understand eternity only as the negation of time."[76] The absolute negation of time would imply a heretical Christology of a Gnostic or Monophysite type, in which the human nature of Christ is overwhelmed by the divine.

Eternity as Duration?

To avoid the problems of an absolutely timeless God, some have argued that we can conceive of God's eternity as changeless duration without introducing time into the life of God.[77] In ordinary language, "duration" is a temporal term im-

---

74. PRRD, 3, p. 354.

75. Wolterstorff, "Divine Simplicity," Philosophical Perspectives 5 (1991): 531. This statement is mystifying. Traditional theologians spent rivers of ink defining the nature of the distinctions within the divine being, the most prominent being the distinctions among the persons of the Trinity.

76. CD, 2/1, p. 617.

77. Eleonore Stump and Norman Kretzmann, "Eternity," Journal of Philosophy 79 (1981): 429-58. Stump and Kretzmann defend a kind of extension or duration in eternity. Brian Leftow, Time and Eternity (Ithaca, NY: Cornell University Press, 1991), pp. 120-46, 267, considers dura-

plying continued existence over a segment of time. The average human being endures for about eighty years; the average mountain endures for, let's say, 100 million years. God endures forever. The traditional doctrine of eternity was intended to remove beginning and end and succession from God's life. Though it is possible to think of duration without beginning or end, I am not sure that duration can be purged of its connotations of successiveness. Even if we think of God's duration as changeless, it appears to retain the possibility of succession and measure. Thus the concept of eternity as changeless duration does not appear to differ fundamentally from the concept of everlastingness.

Perhaps duration can be useful as an analogy for eternity. However, when we take it literally, as a concept fully adequate to eternity, we connect God's duration too closely with the image of a highly durable creature, a mountain or the sun. Therefore, even thinking of eternity as pure duration distorts eternity. As a last resort to save the concept, we could attempt to conceive of duration without the possibility of succession and measure. But then it appears that we have lost touch with creaturely duration, which gives the concept its texture, and we are returning to the Boethian concept of eternity.[78]

The Trinitarian Relationships as God's "Time"

God's eternity is not merely the negation of time, for God is not impersonal, unrelated, and lifeless. God is active and full of life. God is the eternal act of love among the Trinity. The Father loves the Son in the Spirit and the Son loves the Father in the same Spirit. The Father's love takes the form of begetting. The Son is begotten and returns the Father's love in filial obedience. In creature-time, the one who begets and the one who is begotten are separate, and the father/son relationship comes into being in time. In God's life, the Father/Son relationship is eternal: there is no separation (spatial or temporal or ontological) between the one who begets and the one begotten. For the Father is always Father, and the Son always Son. The Father breathes the Spirit, and the Spirit is breathed by the Father.

As I have argued above, the persons of the Father, Son, and Spirit are substantial relationships, co-essential and co-eternal. Yet these eternal and substantial relationships retain their order: the "before" and "after" character of their relation-

tion as "Quasi Temporal Eternity" a "defensible position"; but he chooses not to work it into his own final position.

78. For criticism of the strategy of identifying eternity with pure duration from a defender of the tradition, see Katherin A. Rogers, "Eternity Has No Duration," *Religious Studies* 30 (1994): 1-16; and *Perfect Being Theology* (Edinburgh: University of Edinburgh Press, 2000), pp. 54-70. In *Time, Creation and the Continuum,* pp. 100-111, Sorabji also criticizes duration as an inadequate interpretation, especially of the thought of Parmenides.

ships are not reversible. The Son cannot beget the Father, and the Spirit cannot beget the Son or breathe the Father. The Father is "prior," and the Son and Spirit are anterior. Barth speaks of there being "order and succession" among the Trinity. "The unity," he continues, "is in movement. There is a before and an after. God is once and again and a third time, without dissolving the once-for-allness, without destroying the persons or their special relations to one another, without anything arbitrary in this relationship or the possibility of reversal."[79]

Let us connect our thinking about God's time with the preceding thoughts about God's space. I have argued that every relationship between two things presupposes a space that contains them. The triune persons, however, indwell each other; so God is his own space. There is no fourth thing (space) that contains them and enables them to relate. Let us apply this same reasoning to the issue of God's time. Every relationship between two things presupposes a time (as well as a space) that contains them, for there must be an order of priority between them. However, with the Trinity, the "before" of the Father and the "after" of the Son and Spirit indwell each other without ceasing to be distinct relationships. Barth spoke of this mutual indwelling of the Father, Son, and Spirit as "simultaneity."[80] They need no fourth thing (time) to hold them together and order them. God is his own time, his own simultaneity and duration.

In God's life, space and time merge. The "being with" relationship of space coincides with the before/after relationship of time. For the divine life consists of the distinct triune persons dwelling in the same "space" at the same "time." Their full presence to each other is at once the "presence" of space and the "presence" of time. The relationship of "with" (John 1:1) and the relationship of before-after (John 1:14) are identical with the eternal triune relations — Father, Son, and Spirit. God is, so to speak, his own space-time. Divine space-time (eternity) is the freely enacted divine nature constituted by the triune relations. Invoking again the principle that "person has priority over nature," I insist that the divine space-time does not enable the divine relationships. The relations among the divine persons constitute the eternal life of God.

Boethius's famous definition fits perfectly into the line of thought I am developing: "Eternity is the simultaneous and perfect possession of interminable life."[81] Eternity is living and active, not dead and static. That is, eternal life is not possessed, or made whole, by another, which functions as space and time for it. Eternal life possesses itself. It is its own simultaneity and perfection. The idea of

---

79. *CD*, 2/1, p. 615.
80. *CD*, 2/1, p. 608.
81. *The Consolation of Philosophy*, pp. 160-61. Barth praises Boethius's definition for its positive character: it does not define eternity as the negation of time but the full possession of life (*CD*, 2/1, pp. 610-11).

perfect wholeness implies spatial distinction and relationship without separation in space. The notions of simultaneity and perfection imply temporal distinctions and relationships without separation in time. God possesses his perfect life all at once, without having to become perfect by actualizing a given potential in time. These thoughts call to my mind the never-ceasing words of the four living creatures that surround the throne of the eternal God: "Holy, holy, holy, is the Lord God Almighty, who was, and is, and is to come" (Rev. 4:8). He is the only eternal God, who simultaneously and perfectly possesses his interminable life.

The Relationship of Eternity and Time

Studying the relationship of eternity and time is, strictly speaking, the work of the doctrine of creation. Since Trinitarian time makes created time possible, however, I must briefly consider the eternity/time relationship in the doctrine of God. The simultaneity (or mutual indwelling) of the "before" and "after" relationships of the Trinity ground the "before" and "after" of created time. If there were no divine before and after, there could be no created before and after. In other words, if God were absolutely timeless (the pure negation of time), there would be no begetting of the Son or breathing forth of the Spirit within God. The before/after relationship would be impossible. Nothing could exist "after" God, and thus the world could not exist in an "after" relationship to God, who is before all things. But understanding God's internal simultaneity allows us to conceive of the possibility of a relationship between eternity and time. "True eternity includes this possibility, the potentiality of time."[82]

In seeking to understand their relationship, let us not depersonalize this discussion by abstracting the relationship of eternity to time from the relationship of the Creator to the creature and of the divine persons to the human person. Eternity and time are not simply two concepts we can deal with on a purely logical plane. Eternity is God, and time is God's creature. Therefore, the relationship of eternity to time must be approached as an aspect of the Creator's loving relationship to creatures. Thus the relationship of eternity to time is a matter of grace. In the same loving act by which he makes room for us, God makes time for us. Just as God's presence makes "no where" into a spacious home for the creature, it makes "no when" into a "now" for creatures, overflowing with possibilities for the future.

By speaking to us, God brings us into the eternal conversation among the persons of the Holy Trinity. This dialogue founds our existence as persons.

82. Barth, *CD*, 2/1, p. 617.

Hearing the word of God establishes our existence, enables us to hear the words of others, and empowers us to become persons in relationship to each other. Only in dialogue can we distinguish ourselves from the world of impersonal processes and from other persons. Only then can we strive for fuller knowledge, growth, good, and perfection. Time is distinction and separation: between God and us, between us and the world, between us and other people, and finally, between our person and our nature. But just as God's omnipresence unifies our space, God's sustaining presence unifies our time. God's presence brings the here and there of our space and the before and after of our time into perfect wholeness. God's personal address to us thus establishes our time and opens the possibility of overcoming the separations without losing the distinctions. That is, knowing God is eternal life (John 17:3).

However, our wholeness is not yet *our* possession. But since it *is* God's possession, we can hope that it will be ours as well. This hope is grounded in the incarnation and resurrection of the eternal Son of God. By uniting himself to human nature in his own person, the Son brings human nature (and its time) into union with the eternal God, which is eternal life. Barth boldly declares the meaning of the incarnation for our question: "The fact that the Word became flesh undoubtedly means that, without ceasing to be eternity, in its very power as eternity, eternity became time. Yes, it became time."[83] In his resurrection Christ overcame for us the coming into being and passing out of being that is characteristic of time. He brought together the before and after, the here and there, of our lives and gave us the power of "simultaneous and perfect possession of [our] life" in union with God. God's eternity is thus joined to created time in what we can call Christ-time, an analogy to the concept of Christ-space that I developed above. In the incarnation of the Son of God, creation is drawn into God's eternity. Just as in the incarnation the divine nature of the Son does not cease to be divine and the human nature does not cease to be human, God's eternity does not annihilate time. It redeems and frees it from the futility and despair of fallen time. Eternity liberates time from the perpetual dying of the now, the fading of the past, and the uncertainty of the future. "For in Christ all the fullness of the Deity lives in bodily form, and you have been given fullness in Christ" (Col. 2:9).

Modes of Contemporaneity?

Let us draw one more analogy between God's presence to our space and his presence to our time. Do miracles, sacred moments, and the incarnation in-

---

83. *CD*, 2/1, p. 616.

crease God's contemporaneity with us? Again, the answer must be negative. Whatever is not contemporaneous with God does not exist and cannot act. Just as God is fully present always in our space, he is fully contemporaneous to our time. God is fully present to every event. Just as God's presence to us enables us to be here, it enables us to act, to become, and to move from here to there. We can be assured that God will be with us wherever we go because he is already there. Likewise, we can know that God will be present with us tomorrow, because he is already contemporaneous with our tomorrow.

God's contemporaneity with us may be viewed from three perspectives: in view of his act of *creation,* in view of his actions of *reconciliation,* and in view of his future *redemption.* In creation God gives time to creatures by giving them their existence. He gives them time so that they may come to possess their whole being through their own action in obedience to the divine command. Fallen time, the time of sinful humanity, is wasted, empty, futile, and misdirected. It aims not at self-possession through obedience but at self-destruction and nothingness through disobedience. In the time of reconciliation, fallen time is reclaimed, filled with significance and redirected by the incarnation, cross, and resurrection, and empowered by the Spirit. The time of redemption is the fulfillment of created time and the completion of the time of reconciliation. In the time of redemption the whole creation will be united to God's eternity. The times of creation, fall, reconciliation, and redemption are the subjects of later volumes, and I must remain content to enumerate them here.

In the times of miracles, in the time of the incarnation, and at other holy moments, we become aware of God's gracious contemporaneity in extraordinary ways. In these moments it seems as though God becomes active after a time of quiescence. But that impression is misleading, because God is always active. Jesus said to those who criticized him for performing a miracle on the Sabbath: "My Father is always at his work to this very day, and I, too, am working" (John 5:17). Just as God is always present in our space, even if hidden, he is always contemporaneous with our time, even if his action is imperceptible. The eschatological goal of our time, as I indicated, is perfect wholeness and contemporaneity with God. The incarnation, miracles, the sacraments, and other holy moments are real anticipations of the final revelation of God, when we shall "know as we are known" (1 Cor. 13:12). God's constancy and faithful care of the world give us the impression that God is not doing anything. How deceptive are the senses! The world and our lives are God's constant activity, a miracle for those with eyes to see it!

11

Where Knowing and Doing Converge: Divine Omniscience and Omnipotence

Small children love to play peekaboo and older children hide-and-seek. The ability to hide from others gives us a sense of control. If "knowledge is power," the ability to withhold knowledge is no less power. It was disquieting for me to realize for the first time that I could not hide from God. It was like waking up to realize that someone had been sitting at my bedside all night. To be known is to be vulnerable. A little later in life I realized something equally disturbing and even stranger: I don't know myself. I am who I am, and that should be simple. But I feel, think, and do things I don't understand. I cannot grasp my origin and cannot see my end. My past fades and my future hides. I am more question than answer, more deception than truth. I am many, not one.

Above the entrance to the Temple of Apollo at Delphi was the inscription "Know Thyself." The challenge would have been no greater had it said "Create Thyself." During the course of his life, Augustine of Hippo learned the importance of self-knowledge and the impossibility of achieving it from within ourselves. In Book Nine of the *Confessions,* Augustine asks God, "Who am I and what am I?" And he begins Book Ten with this prayer: "May I know you who know me. . . . Indeed, Lord, to your eyes, the abyss of human consciousness is naked. . . . What could be hidden within me, even if I were unwilling to confess it to you? I would be hiding you from myself, not myself from you." How, then, may we know ourselves? Augustine answers with a confession: "To hear you speaking about oneself is to know oneself. . . . For what I know about myself I know because you grant me light."[1] The way to self-knowledge is living aware

---

1. Augustine, *Confessions,* 9.1 and 10.1, in *Saint Augustine Confessions,* trans. Henry Chadwick (New York: Oxford, 1991), pp. 155, 179-82.

of the one who knows us thoroughly: listening to God, confessing sin, and praying for understanding.

Augustine places the two disquieting events I suggested above in a very different light. It will disturb us less to discover that God knows us absolutely if and when we realize that God's knowledge of us founds our existence and grounds our hope of knowing ourselves. Far from the sinister thought I first feared as a child, the doctrine of God's omniscience teaches that we are always known and loved by the omnipotent God who gave us being and calls us into fellowship with him. His knowledge is an aspect of his power, and his power is an aspect of his love. And his love is most worthy of praise.

The All-Knowing God

God knows all things. Nothing can hide from his sight, even if it dwells in the distant reaches of physical space, is under the obscurity of matter, or is inside the recesses of our hearts. Nothing escapes him by receding into the half-light of the past or by laying in wait in the distant future. God's way of knowing, like his way of being present, is perfectly effective. Since he indwells all things, is contemporary with all things, and empowers all things, God knows all things directly and thoroughly. Yet his knowledge of things, like his indwelling of them, does not distort them or violate their natures. Just as God's knowledge of himself does not constitute fate for him, God's knowledge of other things does not represent fate for them. In knowing things, God loves and creates and liberates them. Correctly understood, God's knowledge of all things is of great comfort, and it gives us another reason to praise him.

Omniscience in Scripture

Scripture testifies to the unlimited nature of God's knowledge. In some places the Bible states plainly that God "knows everything" (1 John 3:20). The writer of Hebrews declares: "Nothing in all creation is hidden from God's sight. Everything is uncovered and laid bare before the eyes of him to whom we must give account" (Heb. 4:12). God knows the human heart: "If we had forgotten the name of our God or spread out our hands to a foreign god, would not God have discovered it, since he knows the secrets of the heart?" (Ps. 44:20, 21). But God says, "I the Lord search the heart and examine the mind" (Jer. 17:9-10). It should not be surprising that the classic text for omnipresence is also the classic text for omniscience: "O Lord, you have searched me and you know me. You know when I sit and when I rise; you perceive my thoughts from afar. . . . Before a word is on my tongue you know it completely" (Ps. 139:1-12). God's presence to all things guarantees his knowledge of all things.

Jesus reminds those that "justify yourselves in the eyes of men" that "God knows your hearts" (Luke 16:15). In his teaching on prayer, Jesus counsels us to keep our words to a minimum because "God knows what you need before you ask him" (Matt. 6:8). Confidence in God's perfect knowledge of the human heart demands human honesty. In 2 Corinthians, Paul is forced to "boast" about his sufferings and spiritual experiences. Aware that some may think he is exaggerating, Paul reminds the Corinthians that God "knows I am not lying" (2 Cor. 11:31). In recounting his spiritual experience, Paul admits to uncertainty about its exact nature but is comforted in the thought that "God knows" (2 Cor. 12:2-3).

Unlike human beings, God knows the future. According to Isaiah 41–48, knowledge of the future is a distinctive mark of divinity. Through the prophet the Lord demands proof that unfaithful Israel's idols are really gods. The prophet says, let your idols "tell us what the future holds, so that we may know that you are gods" (Isa. 41:21-23). The Lord, on the other hand, declares "new things . . . before they spring into being" (42:8-9; cf. 44:7-8). God foretold what was to happen so that the people could not say, "My idols did them; my . . . god ordained them" (48:2-5).

The story of Joseph (Gen. 39–45) illustrates divine knowledge of the future in narrative form. Joseph dreams that his brothers and father will someday bow down before him. Joseph's brothers interpret his dream as a manifestation of his arrogance, and that would be the most likely interpretation if the dream had not come true. Through his brothers' treachery, Joseph finds himself first a slave and then a prisoner in Egypt. But God blesses Joseph even in prison and later raises him to a position second only to Pharaoh. In this position he is able to save his family from the seven-year famine. When Joseph finally reveals his identity to his brothers, he observes: "And now, do not be distressed and do not be angry with yourselves for selling me here, because it was to save lives that God sent me ahead of you" (Gen. 45:5-8).

Though prophecy is not limited to predicting future events, it sometimes does foretell the future. The book of Deuteronomy's instructions for testing prophetic claims clearly presuppose that God knows the future. If what the prophet says comes true, we may presume that the Lord gave him his message; if not, "that prophet has spoken presumptuously. Do not be afraid of him" (Deut. 18:21, 22). The divine predictions given to Abraham in Genesis 15 point to events far into the future: "Know for certain that your descendants will be strangers in a country not their own, and they will be enslaved and mistreated four hundred years" (Gen. 15:13-16).

Jesus knows the identity of the one who will betray him (John 6:64). At the Last Supper, Jesus mentions the betrayer: "I am telling you now before it happens, so that when it does happen you will believe that I am He" (John 13:19, 20). Jesus also foretells Peter's threefold denial (Matt 26:34). Peter, in his Pentecost sermon, says that what happened to Jesus was no mere unforeseen accident. No, "this man was handed over to you by God's set purpose and foreknowledge" (Acts 2:23). Jerusalem's persecuted believers express the same thought: "Indeed Herod and Pontius Pilate . . . did what your power and will had decided beforehand should happen" (Acts 4:27, 28). Jesus knows in advance of Peter's martyrdom (John 21:18, 19). John of Patmos tells his readers that God gave him this message about "what must soon take place" (Rev. 1:1).

The biblical themes of foreknowledge and predestination presuppose that the future is not a closed book to God. Paul finds great comfort in knowing that "those God foreknew he also predestined to be conformed to the likeness of his Son" (Rom. 8:29). "God chose us in him before the creation of the world . . . predestined us to be adopted as sons" (Eph. 1:4, 5; cf. 1 Pet. 1:2).

In preparation for our theological reflections on God's knowledge, I shall summarize the scriptural teaching in a modest way that I hope will provide a broad platform for discussing some of the more controversial questions: (1) God knows everything that can be known. Scripture is very clear that nothing can hide from God. If it is possible for any observer to know it, God knows it. Of course, this leaves open the question of what kinds of things are knowable. (2) God knows some (perhaps all) future events. Clearly, Scripture portrays God as knowing many future events. The future is not dark to God. It seems rash, however, to claim that the texts usually cited teach explicitly that God knows the future *exhaustively.* This claim must be established (if at all) by drawing inferences from texts and combining scriptural texts to construct theological arguments. (3) God's knowledge of "all things" is a matter for rejoicing and praising. In no way does God's omniscience constitute anything negative for creatures: there can be nothing depressing, fatalistic, or contradictory to genuine human dignity about the extent and depth of God's knowledge.

Theology of God's Knowledge

Scripture does not approach this issue theoretically. The Bible declares God's perfect knowledge of the human heart to warn us against the false hope that we can hide our sin from God or to comfort the persecuted with the thought that God knows their plight and their persecutors' deeds. The Lord knows; therefore, he can help. In Scripture, God's amazing knowledge is an object of praise, not a theological problem. However, when genuine questions arise, we must address them, even if Scripture does not deal specifically with them. Theology has to deal with several such questions. Does God know the future exhaustively? How can God foreknow genuinely free choices? Does God remember the past, or is God present to the past as if it were the present? How does God know the future?

What Is Knowing?

Discussing the nature and extent of God's knowledge presupposes that we have some idea of what it means to know something. Of course, this issue is notoriously complex and controversial, and I am under no illusion that my suggestions will convince everyone or plumb the depths of the subject. Nevertheless, I have no choice but to explain something of my understanding of knowing and knowledge.

Purely logical approaches to this subject seem to me to leave out the most important and interesting issues. Recent studies in the theory of knowledge by analytic philosophers, for example, define knowledge as "true, justified belief," or "true, warranted belief."[2] These approaches are getting at the problem of what it means to be a rational person that was bequeathed to the modern world by enlightenment thinkers such as René Descartes and John Locke. A rational person holds warranted or justified beliefs: knowledge is a combination of rationality and truth. I have knowledge only if I hold true beliefs on a proper basis. A lucky guess is not knowledge. Moreover, I may be justified, given my circumstances, for holding false beliefs. However, settling the issue of what kinds of beliefs should count for "knowledge" would not answer a couple more interesting questions: "What does it mean to know a thing?" and "What is truth?" Arguing that to know a thing means holding true, justified beliefs about it strikes me as wholly inadequate and even trivial. For what is the relationship between the belief resident in my mind (a proposition) and the thing itself? Is the belief a copy of the thing itself? Or is the belief the thing itself? Or, in yet another alternative, am I the thing itself, so that all knowledge is self-knowledge?

Do we think only a "copy" of the thing we know? The idea of a copy presupposes a copier, something that comes into direct contact with the thing to be copied and can act as a mediator between it and our minds. Do things send out

---

2. For a concise and readily available summary of current theories of knowledge, see Metthias Steup, "The Analysis of Knowledge," in *The Stanford Encyclopedia of Philosophy*. Available at http://plato.stanford.edu/entries/knowledge-analysis/ (accessed May 31, 2006); see also *The Encyclopedia of Philosophy*, ed. Paul Edwards (New York: Macmillan, 1967), s.v. "Knowledge and Belief."

copies of themselves "to whom it may concern"? Or do our minds reach out and copy them? Or, as a third possibility, does God put copies of things into our minds? The first two options reduce to the same one. If our minds can copy things, they must have access to the thing itself, and thus they do not really need a copy. And if things send out copies of themselves, since I am one of those things, my mind can copy one thing at least — me. However we decide the issue of how the copy gets into our minds, there is still a problem with the copy theory:[3] if the copy is not a perfect likeness, our knowledge is defective, but if it is a perfect copy, what is the difference between it and the thing itself? The philosopher and mathematician Gottlieb Frege raised this objection in 1918: "A correspondence, moreover, can only be perfect if the corresponding things coincide and so are just not different things."[4]

If we think the copy theory inadequate, perhaps we should imagine that things exist in a universal mind to which our minds are united by nature. The illusion that an external, nonmental world exists will break apart when we grasp this truth. Are the distinctions among things, therefore, also illusory — between us and the world, between the world and God, and between God and us? Is there only one reality? If that is so, thought and knowledge are also illusory, for thought presupposes a knower and a thing known.

I conclude that knowing involves the knowing mind's uniting with something that maintains its distinction from the knower even in the union. It must itself be present "inside" the knower, but not as a dark and opaque presence like a grain of sand to an oyster. It must be luminous and clear, but without losing its distinction from the knower. I shall put aside a discussion of whether human beings can attain such knowledge and move directly to God's self-knowledge, which is the model of perfect knowledge and the archetype of all other knowing, whether of God's knowledge of the world or of our knowledge of the world and God.

God's Self-knowledge

If we are to understand the doctrine of God's omniscience, we must begin with God's self-knowledge. God's self-knowledge is logically prior to his knowledge

---

3. Here I am referring to what philosophers call the "correspondence theory" of truth. For a survey of the history and literature of this subject, see Marian David, "The Correspondence Theory of Truth," in *The Stanford Encyclopedia of Philosophy*. Available at http://plato.stanford .edu/entries/truth-correspondence/ (accessed Sept. 27, 2005).

4. Frege, "Thoughts," in *Logical Investigations* (Oxford: Blackwell, 1977), p. 3, quoted in Stewart Candlish, "The Identity Theory of Truth," in *The Stanford Encyclopedia of Philosophy*. Available at http://plato.stanford.edu/entries/truth-identity/ (accessed July 17, 2006).

of the world, for the existence of the world, unlike God, is not necessary. Hence, God's self-knowledge is the model for all other knowledge. In the Trinitarian understanding that I am advocating in this study, the Father, Son, and Spirit are distinct in person and one in essence. In irreversible relationships, the Father begets the Son and breathes the Spirit. The triune persons are united in perfect love, and they are totally present to each other in their mutual indwelling. The mutual indwelling of the distinct triune persons provides a model of perfect knowing and knowledge. The knower and the known indwell each other — that is, they are absolutely present to each other — without ceasing to be distinct. In God, the knower and the known are substantial relationships within one essence. The Father, Son, and Spirit are not alien, dark, and mysterious to one another. They freely enact the same being. Their love is perfect giving, receiving, and returning; hence, their knowing is perfect.

God's Knowledge of Creation

If we did not believe that God knows himself perfectly, we would have no way to speak of God's knowledge of the world without projecting our way of knowing and its limits onto God. God would know himself by encountering something not himself and differentiating himself from it. In other words, to know himself, God would need the world. But the doctrine of the Trinity provides a way to speak of God's self-knowledge without such projection. Does God's knowledge of the world conform to the Trinitarian model? I answer with a cautious yes. Caution is required lest we wipe out the ontological distinction between God and his creation. We must not violate the principle that God does not need the world. God would be God in undiminished glory if he had not created. God created the world "from nothing," so the creation can add nothing to God's being. With this caution noted, I believe that we can safely affirm that God's perfect knowledge of creation conforms to the Trinitarian archetype.

Creation is not an alien eternal substance opaque to God. Creation is God's own action of giving existence to his eternal plan. A discussion of the ontological status of God's actions *ad extra,* that is, his acts toward creation rather than those by which he enacts his being, belongs in the doctrine of creation. I cannot do justice to God's eternal plan here; nonetheless, we can assert that God knows perfectly his plan and his actions. When God creates and sustains his creation, he knows perfectly what he is doing and why. Creation is God's act, and creatures are the results of this act. When I say "results," I do not mean to imply that God's act of creation ceases. No, God's act continues, for apart from God's continual sustenance, creation would cease to exist. Nor by using the term "results" do I imply that the intention of God's act is now alienated from itself so that the result is something essentially different from the act itself. In human acts of creation, the result never perfectly embodies the intention of the act, because we cannot create something from nothing. We must project our intentions into a preexisting medium that is less than perfectly malleable. In contrast, God requires no medium, and so there can be no resistance to his creative will. Therefore, we can see that God knows his creation as well as he knows his own action because it *is* his own action.

Does this mean, then, that everything is God and God's knowledge of the world is identical with his self-knowledge? No. God is not locked within himself so that he cannot create a being not himself. In creation, God gives existence, life, and freedom to other beings. Creatures derive from God's creative act and realize perfectly God's intention. Without ceasing to be God's act, and perfectly transparent to God, creatures exist distinct from God. They possess themselves without ceasing to be God's possession, and they act with their own intentions without ceasing to be acts of a God who has his own intentions. Apart from the doctrine of the Trinity, I could substantiate the preceding assertions only with a claim that sounds like another assertion: "That is just what the doctrine of creation means." But knowing that there are eternal distinctions and relationships within the one nature of the triune God allows us to contemplate a genuine creation. God's own nature is his free action. Therefore, what is to hinder God from freely creating natures other than his own? The eternal triune life consists in the mutual indwelling of distinct persons. Hence, there is nothing illogical or evil in the idea of nondivine persons existing distinct from each other and from God.

Now we can return to the question of whether God's knowledge of the world conforms to the model of God's perfect self-knowledge. First, I argued that, in knowing creation, God knows his own action. Second, I contended that, in knowing the world, God knows something different from himself. Combined, these two propositions articulate the ideal of perfect knowledge, the union of a knower and a distinct thing known.

Let us reinforce this point by shifting our attention from the inner Trinitarian relationships to Christology. I argued in the section on omnipresence that Christ is the space in which God is omnipresent to the world. I argued in the section on eternity that Christ is God's "time" for the world. Now I shall argue that Christ is the space-time in which God knows the world. According to Scripture, creation is accomplished from the Father, through the Son, and in the Spirit. "For by him [Christ] all things were created" and in him, "all things hold together" (Col. 1:16-17; cf. Heb. 1:3; John 1:3, 10). Through Son/Word, creation receives its existence and is maintained in being. The Word, not the Father or the Spirit, "became flesh and made his dwelling among us" (John 1:14). In the incarnation, creation was given a new relationship to God by being united with the divine nature in the person of the Son. It is not, as some popular writers have mistakenly mused, that God gained new insight into humanity and the rest of creation by becoming incarnate. God does not perform his acts of creation, incarnation, and atonement for God's sake, "as if he needed anything" (Acts 17:25). God does these things for our sake.

The incarnation changes creation's relationship to God but not God's relationship to creation. It was accomplished so that we could know God, not so that God could know us, to unite us to God and not to unite God to us, and to reconcile us to God and not to reconcile God to us. Indeed, both creation and incarnation presuppose God's intimate, perfect knowledge of creation. God knows the being and action of creatures apart from and prior to their own self-knowledge. God knows not only his design plan for stars, frogs, and human beings, but also their internal experience. God knows eternally not only what a frog or a human *is*, but also what it is *like* to be one. God did not dwell in ignorance of human experience, of pain, suffering, and death, before the incarnation. The incarnation meets perfectly our needs and hence presupposes that God already knows perfectly those needs. The incarnation reveals God's eternal and complete knowledge of creation in the Son.

Omniscience and Other Attributes

In keeping with my thesis that the divine attributes enrich each other, let us probe the relationship of omniscience to some other attributes. Certainly, the first attribute that comes to mind is omnipresence. If God is fully present to creatures, as I have argued, God also knows them fully. For God's presence is not a blind proximity. It is a spiritual and intellectual presence that sees, feels, and comprehends the total reality of that to which it is present. Omnipresence and omniscience stand or fall together. The same is true of omnipotence, for God's presence and knowledge of things is not passive but active. God is not merely a nearby onlooker. God is a knowing presence to a thing insofar as he gives and sustains its existence. He knows a thing's actions insofar as he empowers it for its action and acts in its action. Affirming God's omnipotence means declaring that nothing can exist or happen without God's empowerment, and thus nothing can exist or happen apart from God's knowledge. God knows what he does. But God's power has the character of love: his power is manifested in *giving* — giving being, life, and power for action. God knows us in his love for us.

Does God Really Know All Things?

Until recently, Christian theologians of all traditions and schools of thought agreed that God knows everything that was, is, and will be. Such is the teaching of Dionysius the Areopagite:

> For if God, in the act of causation, imparts Existence to all things, in the same single act of causation He will support all these His creatures the which are derived from Him and have in Him their forebeing, and He will not gain His knowledge of things from the things themselves . . . for the universal Cause, in knowing Itself, can scarcely help knowing the things that proceed from it and whereof it is the cause. With this knowledge, then, God knoweth all things, not through a mere understanding of the things but through an understanding of Himself.[5]

John of Damascus confirms this tradition, adding the qualifier that God's knowledge of all future good and evil acts does not determine them:

> Moreover, there is the property of knowing all things with a simple knowledge and of seeing all things, simply with His divine, all-surveying, immaterial eye, both the things of the present, and the things of the past, and the things of the future, before they come into being. . . . We ought to understand that while God knows all things beforehand, yet He does not predetermine all things. For He knows beforehand those things that are in our power, but He does not predetermine them. For it is not His will that there should be wickedness nor does He choose to compel virtue. So that predetermination is the work of the divine command based on fore-knowledge.[6]

In the West, Augustine speaks authoritatively of God's complete knowledge of all things:

> Nor did He become acquainted with them [creatures], so as to know them, at any definite time; but He knew beforehand, without any beginning, all things to come in time, and among them also both what we should ask of Him, and when; and to whom He would either listen or not listen, and on what sub-

---

5. *On the Divine Names*, 7.2, in *Dionysius the Areopagite on the Divine Names and The Mystical Theology*, trans. C. E. Rolt (Berwick, ME: Ibis Press, 2004), p. 151. For a discussion of divine knowledge based on Dionysius, see Dumitru Staniloae, *The Experience of God*, vol. 1, *Revelation and Knowledge of the Triune God*, trans. and ed. Ioan Ionita and Robert Barringer (Brookline, MA: Holy Cross Orthodox Press, 1994), pp. 200-201.

6. John of Damascus, *Orthodox Faith*, 1.14; 2.30 (*NPNF*, 2nd ser., 9, pp. 17, 42).

jects. . . . He does not know them because they are, but they are because he knows them.[7]

The fourteenth-century thinker William of Ockham (1280-1349) upheld the tradition without wavering, even if he refused to venture an opinion about how God knows:

> Therefore I reply to the question that it has to be held without any doubt that God knows all future contingent facts evidently and with certainty. But to explain this evidently, and to express the manner in which He knows all future contingent facts, is impossible for any intellect in this life.[8]

We could continue to quote traditional writers, such as Boethius,[9] Aquinas,[10] Calvin,[11] and countless Lutheran and Reformed Orthodox theologians,[12] all of whom defend the traditional view that God knows all things, past, present, and future.

Although thinkers took different positions on how God knows the future, the fact of God's knowledge of the future was not in dispute. Gottschalk (c. A.D. 804–c. 869) and others who, under the influence of Augustine, emphasized the sovereignty of divine grace, election, and predestination, understood God's knowledge of all things to be grounded in his all-determining will.[13] God determines everything to happen as it does; hence, he knows all things infallibly. Others, such as Boethius and John of Damascus, argue that God knows free choices because in his eternal presence he sees them.[14] Ockham, as stated

---

7. Augustine, *On the Holy Trinity,* 15.13 (*NPNF,* 1st ser., 3, p. 212).

8. William of Ockham, *Philosophical Writings: A Selection,* trans. Philotheus Boehner, OFM (New York: Bobbs-Merrill Co., 1964), p. 148.

9. Boethius, *Consolation of Philosophy,* trans. W. V. Cooper, ed. Israel Golancz (London: J. M. Dent and Co., 1902), pp. 140-68.

10. Aquinas, *SumTh,* 1.14.1-16, in *Basic Writings of Saint Thomas Aquinas,* vol. 1, ed. Anton C. Pegis (New York: Random House, 1945), pp. 135-61.

11. Calvin, *Commentary on Daniel* 2:20; 2:22, in *Calvin's Commentaries,* ed. David W. Torrance and Thomas F. Torrance (Grand Rapids: Eerdmans, 1960).

12. For an extensive study of this topic among the orthodox Reformed, see Richard A. Muller, *Post-Reformation Reformed Dogmatics: The Rise and Development of Reformed Orthodoxy,* vol. 3, *The Divine Essence and Attributes* (Grand Rapids: Baker Academic, 2003), pp. 392-432 (hereafter *PRRD*).

13. For the history of the post-Augustinian debates concerning grace and predestination, see Jaroslav Pelikan, *The Christian Tradition: A History of the Development of Doctrine,* vol. 3, *The Growth of Medieval Theology 600-1300* (Chicago: University of Chicago Press, 1978), pp. 80-95.

14. In general, the Eastern theologians have a greater tendency to understand God's pre-

above, refused to speculate on the "manner" in which God knows all things. Now we turn to the disputed issue of whether or not God knows the future exhaustively.

The sixteenth-century Spanish Jesuit Luis de Molina (1535-1600) broke with this tradition in some respects.[15] In response to the "Calvinist" view that we must deny free will to exalt divine grace, Molina wrote *A Reconciliation of Free Choice with the Gifts of Grace, Divine Foreknowledge, Providence, Predestination and Reprobation.*[16] In this work Molina argues that God not only knows himself and all his possibilities (called "natural knowledge") and all his actual works (called "free knowledge").[17] God also knows what every creature would do in every conceivable situation (called "middle knowledge"). The latter is called "middle" knowledge because it falls between God's knowledge of what he could do and what he chooses to do. Like natural knowledge, middle knowledge is necessary; but, like free knowledge (and unlike natural knowledge), it is about what will in fact happen, given certain circumstances.[18] Middle knowledge allows God to choose from all possible worlds to create the one he wants to create, without determining the choices of free creatures. God chooses to actualize the precise and infinitely complex set of circumstances in which each human being makes the choices God wants made. Molina explains his view:

> Before any free determination of his will. . . . He discerns what the free choice of any creature would do by his own innate freedom, given the hypothesis that He could create it in this or that order of things with these or those circumstances or aids — even though the creature could, if it so willed, refrain

---

destination as based on his foreknowledge of free choices. See John of Damascus, *Orthodox Faith,* 2.30. For a study of Eastern Christendom's struggle with dualism, Islam, and the Augustinian West, in which it defended free will and combated fatalism, see Jaroslav Pelikan, *The Christian Tradition,* vol. 2, *The Spirit of Eastern Christendom* (Chicago: University of Chicago Press, 1974), pp. 216-27, 234-35, 294-95.

15. See Alfred Freddoso, "Molina, Luis De" in *The Concise Routledge Encyclopedia of Philosophy* (London: Routledge, 2000).

16. *Liberi arbitrii cum gratiae donis, divina praescientia, providentia, praedestinatione et reprobatione Concordia.* For a translation of the section on divine foreknowledge, see *Luis de Molina On Divine Foreknowledge* (Part IV of the *Concordia*), trans. Alfred J. Freddoso (Ithaca, NY: Cornell University Press, 1988). This translation contains an 81-page introduction by Freddoso. William Lane Craig also summarizes Molina's teaching in ch. 5 of *The Problem of Divine Foreknowledge and Human Freedom from Aristotle to Suárez* (Leiden: Brill, 1980).

17. This twofold division of divine knowledge was standard in the Middle Ages. See Eef Dekker, "Was Arminius a Molinist?" *Sixteenth Century Journal* 27/2 (1996): 337-38.

18. Freddoso, "Introduction," in *Luis de Molina On Divine Foreknowledge,* p. 23.

from acting or do the opposite, and even though if it was going to do so, as it is able to freely, God would foresee *that* very act and not the one that He *in fact* foresees would be performed by that creature.[19]

Molina claims to have reconciled divine foreknowledge and human free will without compromising God's complete sovereignty. Every event in the history of creation is encompassed within the divine will, God "intending it as a particular or permitting it as a particular."[20] Without overpowering the freedom of any agent, God realizes perfectly the universe that he wills by choosing from among the possible universes the one that corresponds to his will. He chooses the universe in which Abraham obeys the command to leave Ur, Judas betrays Jesus, Peter denies the Lord three times, Paul persecutes the church before his conversion, you and I are born, I sit in a hotel at 1:31 p.m. (PST) on July 9, 2003, writing these lines, and you read these lines at some date in the future beyond this moment. A really ingenious theory with many modern adherents![21]

On the Protestant side, the Dutchman Jacob Arminius (1559-1609) of the University of Leiden came to disagree with the dominant teaching of the Reformed Church on divine knowledge, grace, predestination, providence, and free will. Like Molina, Arminius argued that God's omniscience and sovereign grace could be harmonized with free will by making certain distinctions within the divine will and knowledge. Instead of thinking of God's decision to create, judge, and save the world as one decree, which would entail that God determines everything that happens, Arminius conceives of four logically sequential decrees:

(1) Christ is to be the mediator of salvation and an expression of God's general will to save.
(2) God decrees to save all whom he foresees will repent and believe.
(3) God decrees the conditions or means under which human individuals are able to repent and believe.

19. *Concordia*, 4.49.11, trans. Freddoso, p. 119 (italics in original).

20. *Concordia*, 4.53.3.17, quoted in William Lane Craig, "Middle Knowledge: A Calvinist-Arminian Rapprochement," in *The Grace of God and the Will of Man*, ed. Clark Pinnock (Minneapolis: Bethany House Publishers, 1989), p. 153.

21. One prolific writer defending middle knowledge is William Lane Craig. Among his many works dealing with the subject, see *The Only Wise God: The Compatibility of Divine Foreknowledge and Human Freedom* (Grand Rapids: Baker Books, 1987); "Middle Knowledge: A Calvinist-Arminian Rapprochement," pp. 141-164; and *Divine Foreknowledge and Human Freedom: The Coherence of Theism: Omniscience* (Leiden: E. J. Brill, 1990).

(4) God determines to save those whom he foreknows will decide to believe and persevere, and damn those who do not.[22]

Observe that, while (1) expresses God's general will to save all, (2) places the final say-so within the power of human free choice. In (3), God makes use of his middle knowledge to discover what means to provide to make a free decision possible. And in (4), we see most clearly that, for Arminius, what people will actually decide determines God's knowledge of their decisions and his decree to save or damn them. Richard Muller explains further the significance of Arminius's distinctions:

> All of Arminius' distinctions . . . tend to display a mutual or reciprocal relation between God and the world rather than a purely sovereign or absolute relation. . . . The Arminian doctrine tends to emphasize the distinctions for the sake of arguing interaction between God and genuinely free or contingent events in the created order. . . . There is . . . a movement away from the strictest notion of divine simplicity and transcendence toward a view of God as conditioned and, somehow, limited by his relation to the temporal order.[23]

In the case of Arminius and such Arminians as John Wesley, even though God makes his fourfold decree in complete freedom, the decree is co-eternal with him.[24] Though God is conditioned by events that will happen in time, God's decisions in response to those events are not made in time. Hence, in the Arminian understanding, God has always possessed complete knowledge of all possibilities and of everything that will ever come to pass; that is, God is omniscient in the traditional sense.[25]

Criticism of the Molinist/Arminian system to exploit its central weakness began soon after its creation. Neither Molina nor Arminius could explain *how* God could foreknow what a free creature would do in a situation that God will never in fact make actual. Yet knowing that God has the power to do this is es-

22. For documentation and extensive discussion of these four theses, see Richard Muller, *God, Creation, and Providence in the Thought of Jacob Arminius* (Grand Rapids: Baker, 1991), pp. 162-63. For a shorter summary, see Muller's "Arminius and Arminianism," in *The Dictionary of Historical Theology*, ed. Trevor Hart (Grand Rapids: Eerdmans, 2000), pp. 33-36.

23. Muller, *God, Creation, and Providence*, pp. 189-90.

24. Wesley says: "God foreknew those in every nation who would believe, from the beginning of the world to the consummation of all things" (Sermon 58), quoted by David Hunt, "The Simple Foreknowledge View," in *Divine Foreknowledge: Four Views*, ed. James K. Beilby and Paul R. Eddy (Downers Grove, IL: InterVarsity Press, 2001), p. 70.

25. For the orthodox Reformed critique of the theory of middle knowledge in Molina and Arminius, see Muller, *PRRD*, 3, pp. 411-32.

sential to the theory of middle knowledge and all that flows from it. God cannot just look from eternity and see what is happening in the future, for the event in question will never happen; nor, for the same reason, can God look through a "time telescope" to see it from a distance within time.[26] Shifting the ground from seeing reality to believing propositions, as modern analytic philosophers do, does not rescue the situation. For to say that God believes all true statements and disbelieves all false ones does not settle the question of what makes a particular proposition true or false.[27] To say that God knows a conditional (an "if-then" statement) proposition's truth or falsity surely indicates that God knows directly the state of affairs that makes it true or false; otherwise, we are back to the "God-just-knows" answer. But in this case the conditional statement is counterfactual, that is, it refers to a state of affairs that will never exist.

The Socinians of the seventeenth century pressed Molina's and Arminius's ideas to their logical extremes, and in doing so they denied divine omniscience and simplicity and argued for the finitude of the divine essence.[28] Within contemporary theology, process thinkers and open theists explicitly deny the traditional doctrine of omniscience. Process philosopher Charles Hartshorne links the process understanding of omniscience to the Socinian view: "Have we any other reason [than thinking of God as immutable] for rejecting the old Socinian proposition that even the highest conceivable form of knowledge is of the past-and-definite as past-and-definite and of the future and partly indefinite as future and partly indefinite? . . . Is God all-knowing? Yes, in the Socinian sense. Never has a great intellectual discovery passed with less notice by the world than the Socinian discovery of the proper meaning of omniscience. To this day works of reference fail to tell us about this."[29] I shall address process thought in greater detail when I discuss omnipotence and immutability; but in this section I shall leave aside process thought and focus on open theism.

Clark Pinnock expresses his distaste for the "popular belief" that God knows the future exhaustively. He complains that such a belief "is not so much a biblical idea as an *old tradition*."[30] God knows the past and the present com-

---

26. David Hunt uses this term in "The Simple Foreknowledge View," p. 67.

27. Suarez, according to Freddoso, argued that all conditional statements about future contingents are either true or false; and since God is omniscient, God knows them as such (*Luis de Molina On Divine Foreknowledge*, pp. 78-79).

28. Muller, *PRRD*, 3, pp. 395, 418, 420, 424-32.

29. Hartshorne, *Omnipotence and Other Theological Mistakes* (Albany, NY: SUNY Press, 1984), pp. 26-27.

30. Pinnock, "Systematic Theology," in *The Openness of God: A Biblical Challenge to the Traditional Understanding of God*, ed. Clark Pinnock, Richard Rice, John Sanders, et al. (Downers Grove, IL: InterVarsity Press, 1994), p. 122.

pletely but knows the future only insofar as it is determined by the past. According to Pinnock, "God experiences temporal passage, learns new facts when they occur and changes plans in response to what humans do."[31] Elsewhere, Pinnock says, "God is dependent on the world for information about the world."[32] John Sanders refers to this view as "present knowledge."[33]

Open theists make a variety of arguments to support their view, including a biblical one. I shall examine three. First, open theists argue that a genuinely free act cannot be caused or determined or brought about by anything other than the free agent in the moment of decision. Not even God can know a future free act as a factual certainty. Therefore, defending the traditional doctrine of omniscience would require us to give up human freedom and accept causal determinism. According to open theists, there is no middle ground. William Hasker's essay *God, Time and Knowledge* is a sustained attack on all attempts to find this middle ground.[34] Illustrating the dilemma of foreknowledge, Hasker argues that, if God believes I will eat salad for lunch tomorrow, no one can bring it about that I will not eat a salad for lunch tomorrow. Thus it is now necessary for me to eat a salad for lunch tomorrow, and so I cannot eat my salad in freedom.[35] Of course, Hasker affirms libertarian free will, which he defines this way: *"An agent is free with respect to a given action at a given time if at that time it is within the agent's power to perform the action and also in the agent's power to refrain from the action."*[36] And because he accepts the disjunction between free will and foreknowledge, Hasker rejects foreknowledge.[37]

A second argument is articulated by Gregory Boyd and depends on the assumption that the future does not exist in any meaningful sense. Boyd asks whether God is less omniscient because he does not know that there is a mon-

---

31. *The Openness of God,* p. 118.

32. Pinnock, "God Limits His Knowledge," in *Predestination & Free Will: Four Views of Divine Sovereignty & Human Freedom,* ed. D. Basinger and R. Basinger (Downers Grove, IL: InterVarsity Press, 1986), p. 146.

33. Sanders, *The God Who Risks: A Theology of Providence* (Downers Grove, IL: InterVarsity Press, 1998), p. 198.

34. Hasker, *God, Time and Knowledge* (Ithaca, NY: Cornell University Press, 1998).

35. I am condensing a 7-proposition version of this argument made in *The Openness of God,* p. 148.

36. Hasker, "A Philosophical Perspective," in *The Openness of God,* pp. 136-37 (italics in original).

37. See John Martin Fischer, ed., *God, Foreknowledge and Freedom* (Stanford: Stanford University Press, 1989), for a collection of the most influential philosophical articles on the subject. Most of these studies were inspired by Nelson Pike's famous 1965 article denying the compatibility of foreknowledge and freedom ("Divine Omniscience and Voluntary Action," *The Philosophical Review* 74 [1965]: 27-46).

key sitting next to me when there is in fact no monkey sitting next to me. Of course not. We do not slight the divine dignity of God's knowledge when we observe that he does not know a nonexistent thing to exist or a falsehood to be true. In fact, God knows that there is no monkey sitting next to me. Indeed, he knows all the possibilities for this time and place, including the possibility of a monkey. If possible and imaginable future events do not exist, as in the case of the possible but nonexistent monkey, God's knowledge is not diminished by knowing them as possible rather than as existent. Similarly, God cannot know future free actions because "there is nothing there for God to know."[38] And propositions affirming or denying them can be neither true nor false, for nothing exists to make them true or false.

Elsewhere, Boyd attempts to reframe the debate with the traditional doctrine of foreknowledge as a disagreement about the nature of creation. In the traditional view, God decides eternally the course of creation from beginning to end. For Boyd, however, God settles some things from the beginning but leaves others open. He writes that God's knowledge includes not only "possibilities that might have been" [Molina] but also "other possibilities as what might be. Reality, in other words, is composed of settled and open aspects."[39]

In a third line of argument, open theists argue that the problem of evil is insurmountable if we accept the premise of God's exhaustive foreknowledge. God cannot know the future except as he determines it. If he knows it exhaustively, he determines it exhaustively. And if he determines it exhaustively and there is real evil and sin, he wills, determines, and carries out sin and evil. Since we cannot accept this last implication, we must reject exhaustive knowledge of the future. A detailed response to this argument would require much more space than I have here.[40]

Yes, God Really Does Know All Things

Though it will soon become obvious that I disagree with Molina, Arminius, and their contemporary advocates at decisive points, I applaud their adherence to traditional doctrines of divine providence and omniscience. Able defenders of Molinism have demonstrated its considerable power to achieve its goal of defending a robust doctrine of providence, omniscience, and predestination with-

38. Boyd, *The God of the Possible: A Biblical Introduction to the Open View of God* (Grand Rapids: Baker, 2000), p. 16.

39. In Beilby and Eddy, eds., *Divine Foreknowledge: Four Views*, p. 14.

40. See Ron Highfield, "The Problem with the 'Problem of Evil': A Response to Gregory Boyd's Open Theist Solution," *Restoration Quarterly* 45 (2003): 165-80.

out giving up indeterminist freedom.[41] Open theism, in contrast, calls for radical revisions in the traditional doctrine of God. The God of open theism learns, grows, changes, suffers, and reacts in dependence on the actions of free creatures. Because God does not know what we are going to do, he does not know what he is going to do in response. The "perfectly provident" God is reduced to someone who intends to accomplish as much good as possible in view of the limited cooperation lent to him by his creatures.[42] Heaven only knows how it will all turn out! On second thought, I guess Heaven does not know after all.

What are the consequences of denying God's exhaustive foreknowledge? I believe that they are much more far-reaching and damaging than open theists are willing to admit. Giving up God's knowledge of the future entails giving up everything that I have concluded in the previous section about God's eternity and viewing God's life as a series of moments. This move forces us to accept the consequences of denying God's simplicity, thereby throwing his uniqueness into doubt. Implied here is an acceptance of the pagan premise of the priority of the divine nature over the divine person. If God does not know the future, does he know the past? Suppose he remembers it perfectly. What is the difference between God's perfect memory and the actual events? Does God live in a present as we do and merely remember the past and project the future? If this is so, God's past acts are no longer in his actual possession. What gives wholeness to our lives or, more importantly, to God's life? Can God really maintain his lordship when the future is open-ended for him? Is God really the infinitely wise God "who knows how to get his will done" when he must improvise along the way in response to the unforeseeable decisions of human beings? Does God have perfect knowledge of himself when he does not know what he will do in the future because what he needs to do will be determined by what his creatures do? If God does not dwell in eternity, he must learn and grow as the future unfolds out of the possibilities of the present. If God is not eternal, he is not fully actual, and hence not fully free. The cascade continues and leaves no aspect of the doctrine of God untouched.

Taking Sides

Excessive hunger for rational coherence can be dangerous. Sometimes we must remain content to hold propositions that we are confident are true and

---

41. See Alfred Freddoso's introduction to his *Luis de Molina On Divine Foreknowledge* (Part IV of the *Concordia*). I could also mention Thomas Flint and William Lane Craig.
42. *Luis de Molina On Divine Foreknowledge*, p. 35.

compatible even when we cannot reconcile them to the satisfaction of everyone. The intuitions of traditional theologians serve us well in this discussion. Even when they disagreed about how to reconcile God's sovereignty and exhaustive foreknowledge with human freedom or election with the necessity of the church and her sacraments, they held to both sides of these polarities. It would be much wiser to confess these truths without grasping fully their unity than to allow our desire for rational symmetry to lead us to reject a vital truth of faith.

Nevertheless, as the reader may have gathered from the previous sections, I believe that the Augustine-Aquinas-Calvin-Bañez-Barth trajectory better preserves the emphasis of Scripture than do the other alternatives. I reject the open-theist solution because it simply pares away one whole set of biblical truths for the sake of facile answers. Molinism is probably as good as any available model for reconciling a robust libertarian view of freedom with the traditional doctrines of omniscience and providence. I consider the Arminian tradition a well-intentioned but ultimately unsuccessful effort to reconcile the biblical truths it confesses in common with older tradition.

According to Alfred Freddoso, there are two distinct but related questions that any discussion of foreknowledge must address: (1) the "source-question," which asks about the ground of God's knowledge of future contingents and (2) the "reconciliation-question," which asks about the harmony of foreknowledge with human freedom. Concerning the source question, I believe we should reject any answer that makes God dependent on anything outside himself for his knowledge. We are mistaken to base God's knowledge of our free acts on his observation of them. It matters little whether we conceive of God's knowledge as gained from his temporal presence, through a time telescope, or in his eternal presence to things. For this way of knowing implies that God depends on us and is changed by what we do. On the contrary, God knows all things through himself and is himself the source and ground of his omniscience. Garrigou-Lagrange's analysis of the situation should awaken in us a sense of what is at stake in this debate:

> God's knowledge cannot be determined by anything which is extrinsic to Him, and which would not be caused by Him. But such is the *scientia media,* which depends on the determination of free conditioned future; for this determination does not come from God but from the human liberty, granted it is placed in such particular circumstances. . . . Thus God would be dependent on another, would be passible in His knowledge, and would no longer be Pure Act. The dilemma is unsolvable: Either God is the first determining being, or else He is determined by another; there is no other alternative. In

other words, the *scientia media* involves an imperfection, which cannot exist in God. Hence there is a certain tinge of anthropomorphism in this theory.[43]

In view of my commitment to God's independence, I argue that God's knowledge of all things finds its source in himself, either in the self-knowledge of his eternal being, with its infinite possibilities for imitation, or in God's infallible knowledge of his immovable intentions for creation. The triune God needs no advisors or junior partners to help devise a plan for achieving his will. In his wisdom God knows how to accomplish his will. God knows the future exhaustively by knowing his own will, from which his actions flow. God does not need to guess or to learn what will happen. He knows well what he does. For absolutely nothing would happen apart from his working. God works in all workers, empowering them for their action.

The second question to be addressed is the matter of reconciling God's omniscience with human freedom. Since my answer to the source question is that God knows the free acts of his creatures by knowing his own action, my treatment of the reconciliation question fits better in the discussion of omnipotence. A brief statement will suffice here.

It seems to me that the Molinist-Arminian-Wesleyan models of reconciliation begin with a strong definition of libertarian freedom and trim divine independence and freedom to make room for this kind of autonomy. The Augustine-Aquinas-Calvin-Bañez-Barth tradition begins with a strong definition of divine independence and works to find a place for human freedom within that framework. My sympathies lie with this latter tradition. The Augustinian tradition insists that we not inflate the power and dignity of ordinary human freedom, the kind we exercise in everyday affairs. Such freedom is limited to matters we can grasp and evaluate by our reason. Thus the limit of reason marks also the limit of freedom. We are not free to decide about matters of which we are ignorant or deceived. Ordinary freedom applies only to objects presented to our consciousness. We cannot even make bad decisions about something of which we have no knowledge; our decisions about matters on which we are misinformed are about imaginary alternatives. And freedom surely has to do with truth and reality.

Furthermore, no mere human act can be free in an absolute sense; for we do not have absolute knowledge of our intentions or the results of the action we are contemplating. Advocates of libertarian freedom view the essence of freedom as indifference and indeterminism, but both aspects present difficulties

---

43. Garrigou-Lagrange, *The One God,* pp. 465-66, quoted in Freddoso, *Luis de Molina On Divine Foreknowledge,* p. 66.

when pressed. Total indifference rules out the use of reason in a free act. One of reason's functions is to overcome the initial indifference among alternative courses of action. On the other hand, the absence of an alien cause determining my choice does not guarantee that I will achieve what I intend or that I will not regret my choice as soon as I make it. It is a great weakness of the libertarian theory that stupid, blind, prejudiced, and wicked choices are judged as having just as much freedom as enlightened, virtuous, and just decisions. This is counterintuitive. Freedom is not something you either have or don't; it comes in degrees, like virtue, knowledge, and wisdom.

Libertarians see themselves as guardians of human responsibility for sin. Of course, the Christian faith holds people responsible for their sins and calls on them to repent. The faith also assumes, however, that people are redeemable (by God) and can repent. This assumption shows that human sinful acts are not so free as to express the definitive identity of the person; in that case we would be unredeemable. In one of the most hopeful moments in Scripture, the dying Jesus prays to his Father: "Father, forgive them, for they know not what they do." Yes, human beings are answerable for their sins; they have incurred guilt and need forgiveness. But human sin is forgivable because it arises out of blindness, ignorance, and deception more than out of cold-blooded, clear-eyed hatred of God. Thus God's liberating forgiveness can be the beginning of a new life. Responsibility, like freedom, is not an either/or matter. It, too, comes in degrees.

I shall argue in the section on omnipotence that we are not obligated to reconcile divine omniscience and omnipotence with the standard libertarian view. Such freedom clearly cannot achieve the self-possession at which it aims. It falls far short of the perfect freedom we are promised through Jesus Christ in the power of the Holy Spirit. We can be liberated into this freedom only by the omnipotent power of God. There is no conflict at all.

The Omnipotence of God

The Apostles' Creed begins this way: "I believe in God the Father, Almighty [pantokrator], Maker of heaven and earth." It uses omnipotence as a master attribute to sum up God's divinity. God is almighty. What more needs to be said? He can do whatever pleases him, because nothing is "too hard for the Lord" (Gen. 18:13). He creates, saves, and judges the world, and his actions do not deplete or diminish his power in the least. God is the ruler of all, the Almighty, the Lord of heaven and earth. But the creed does say more: "Jesus Christ, His only Son . . . suffered under Pontius Pilate, was crucified, died, and was buried." In Christ, God's power takes on the appearance of weakness and suffering. In his humiliation God demonstrates a power more marvelous than the power of force. For in the "weakness" and "suffering" of Christ, God overcomes human rebellion and sin, gives humanity a new heart, and raises humans from the dead to eternal life.

Divine Omnipotence in Scripture

Scripture holds God's unlimited power in such esteem that it ascribes it to him as a title: "The Lord Almighty is with us; the God of Jacob is our fortress" (Ps. 46:7; cf. Ps. 84:8; 88:9; Rev. 16:7). God's power is "incomparably great" (Eph. 1:19). God can do "immeasurably more than we ask or imagine" (Eph. 3:20). He is the "ruler of all things" (1 Chron. 29:12). Faced with powerful attackers, King Jehoshaphat of Judah prayed in the temple: "O Lord . . . Power and might are in your hand, and no one can withstand you" (2 Chron. 20:6). The psalmist says to the Lord, "All things serve you" (Ps. 119:91).

Upon hearing Sarah laugh at his promise of a child, the Lord asks Abraham, "Is anything too hard for the Lord?" (Gen. 18:13). Jeremiah confesses that the Lord made heaven and earth, and he concludes, "Nothing is too hard for you" (Jer. 32:17; 32:26). With God "all things are possible" (Matt. 19:26). As Jesus prayed in Gethsemane on the night of his betrayal, he could still hope that his Father would "take this cup from me" because he knew that "everything is possible for you" (Mark 14:36). God cannot be defeated. Job finally concluded this after God's self-demonstration in the whirlwind: "I know you can do all things; no plan of yours can be defeated" (Job 42:2). After rehearsing a litany of our most powerful enemies, Paul concludes that nothing in all creation "can separate us from the love of God that is in Christ Jesus our Lord" (Rom. 8:39). The Lord speaks confidently about his plans: "My purpose will stand, and I will do as I please. . . . What I have said, that I will bring about; what I have planned, that I will do" (Isa. 46:10-11).

Scripture does not hide the fact that there are other powers, but it is very clear that other powers and authorities depend on God (Rom. 13:1; John 19:11). The devil exercises power (Heb. 2:4; 1 Pet. 5:8; Rev. 2:10), and the "secret power of lawlessness is already at work" (2 Thess. 2:7). Death and Hades "were given power over a fourth of the earth to kill by the sword, famine and plague and by the wild beasts of the earth" (Rev. 6:8). However, all power comes from God. Anticipating the inevitable, Moses warns the people not to conclude that their strength and skill produce the things they enjoy. God gives you the power to work and the skill to accomplish your goals (Deut. 8:17; cf. 1 Chron. 29:12). God created all things in heaven and on earth, "whether thrones or powers or rulers or authorities" through Christ (Col. 1:15). Jesus gave his disciples "power and authority" to do miracles (Luke 9:1). We should fear God above all other powers; those powers can kill the body, but God can cast us into hell (Luke 12:4).

God demonstrates his power in many ways, most obviously by creating and sustaining the universe. "God made the earth by his power and founded the world by his wisdom" (Jer. 10:12; 32:17-19). Isaiah bids us lift our eyes to the skies and contemplate the "great power and mighty strength" of the one who made them (Isa. 40:26). According to Paul, God's divine power can be "understood from what has been made" (Rom. 1:20). God's power becomes personal in his saving deeds. In freeing his people from slavery, God strikes the land of Egypt and its Pharaoh to demonstrate his deity to the whole world (Exod. 4:16). As Jesus exercises divine power to deliver the possessed from demons the people exclaim, "What is this teaching? With authority and power he gives orders to the evil spirits and they come out!" (Luke. 4:36).

The magnitude of God's saving power is seen in the resurrection of Christ (Eph. 1:19-23). God will give us the victory over death and the grave "through Jesus Christ our Lord" (1 Cor. 15:57). The glorified Jesus, "by the power that enables him to bring everything under his control," will return and "transform our lowly bodies so that they will be like his glorious body" (Phil. 3:20, 21).

A new aspect of God's power comes to light in the gospel. Christ is the "power of God" (1 Cor. 1:24). In Christ, however, God's power appears as weakness, for it is through suffering and death that God saved the world from its greatest threat. Not by force of arms but "by his death" he "destroyed him who holds the power of death — that is, the devil — and freed those who all their lives were held in slavery by their fear of death" (Heb. 2:14). The Gospel of John points out that Jesus "knew that the Father had put all things under his power," even as he got up from the table and washed his disciples' feet (John 13:3). In response to Paul's request for relief from his "thorn in the flesh," the Lord replied, "My power is made perfect in weakness" (2 Cor. 12:7). Notice the relationship between suffering and power in this text from the Pastoral Epistles: "So do not be ashamed to testify about our Lord, or ashamed of me his prisoner. But join with me in suffering for the gospel, by the power of God" (2 Tim. 1:8). God's power is not force, intimidation, destruction, and domination; it is self-abandoning, giving, and suffering love.

The Traditional Teaching

For almost nineteen centuries the Christian church agreed on the basics of the doctrine of divine omnipotence. It faced very little serious opposition from without and practically none from within. Therefore, the doctrine outlined below well deserves to be called "the traditional doctrine of omnipotence." The Apostles' Creed in its Greek and Latin forms begins: "I believe in God the Father, *Almighty*."[44] And the Nicene Creed (A.D. 381) begins in the same way. Speaking for the Greek fathers, Dionysius the Areopagite proclaims that God's power transcends every power on earth and in heaven; in that sense, it is beyond our comprehension. However, according to Dionysius, we do not need to remain silent. We can say:

> God is power because in His own Self He contains all power beforehand and exceeds it, and because He is the Cause of all power and produced all things by a power which may not be thwarted nor circumscribed, and because He is the Cause wherefrom Power exists whether in the whole system of the world or in any particular part. Yea, He is Infinitely powerful not only in that all Power comes from Him, but also because He is above all power and is Very Power, and possesses that excess of Power which produces in infinite ways an infinite number of existent powers. . . . And, in short, there is nothing in the world which is without the Almighty Power of God to support and to surround it. For that which hath no power at all hath no existence, no individuality, and no place whatever in the world.[45]

John of Damascus says simply that God is "omnipotent, of infinite power, containing and maintaining the universe and making provision for all."[46] In the West, Augustine says that God

> without doubt can as easily refuse to permit what He does not wish, as bring about what He does wish. And if we do not believe this, the very first sentence of our creed is endangered, wherein we profess to believe in God the Father Almighty. For He is not truly called Almighty if He cannot do whatsoever He pleases, or if the power of His almighty will is hindered by the will of any creature whatsoever . . . . The will of the Omnipotent is never defeated.[47]

---

44. Philip Schaff, ed., *The Creeds of Christendom*, vol. 2, rev. David S. Schaff (1931; reprint, Grand Rapids: Baker, 1990), pp. 46-55. According to Schaff, the creed as preserved by Tertullian was the first to use the Latin term *omnipotentem*, an obvious translation of the Greek *pantokratora*.

45. Dionysius, *The Divine Names*, 8, pp. 154-57. Dumitru Staniloae uses Dionysius as his main example of the Greek fathers' teaching on the subject of divine omnipotence; see Staniloae, *The Experience of God*, vol. 1, *Revelation and Knowledge of the Triune God*, pp. 184-85.

46. John of Damascus, *Orthodox Faith*, 1.14 (*NPNF*, 2nd ser., 9, p. 17).

47. Augustine, *Enchiridion*, 96, 102 (*NPNF*, 1st ser., 3, pp. 267, 270); see also Augustine, *The Creed: A Sermon to Catechumens*, 2, where he says, in commenting on the first affirmation of the

Anselm of Canterbury, addressing the issue of why God's "inability" to do such things as lie or die or contradict himself do not compromise his omnipotence, concludes: "Therefore O Lord, the more truly art thou omnipotent, since thou art capable of nothing through impotence, and nothing has power against thee."[48] Aquinas's definition is very much in line with those of Dionysius, Augustine, and Anselm:

> God is called omnipotent because He can do all things that are possible absolutely. . . . For a thing is said to be possible or impossible absolutely, according to the relation in which the very terms stand to one another, possible if the predicate is not incompatible with the subject, as that Socrates sits; and absolutely impossible when the predicate is altogether incompatible with the subject, as, for instance, that a man is a donkey.[49]

The Protestant Reformers and their heirs, while shunning speculation, continue to teach that "God is omnipotent and unlimited in his dominion."[50] Luther's teaching on omnipotence focuses on God's power to save from sin and the devil.[51] Zwingli's teaching moves in the direction of determinism.[52] Calvin taught that God "can accomplish whatever he wills to do," but took care not to separate God's power from his righteous and good will.[53] The post-Reformation Reformed theologians refined the Reformers' teaching on omnipotence but added nothing of substance to the tradition. Benedict Pictet, for example, defines divine power as that "virtue by which God can do whatever is possible to be done. . . . The object of this power is every thing that God wills, which does not involve a contradiction, as that *a thing is, and is not, at the same time,* that *a circle is a square.* . . ."[54] Marcus Wendelin (1584-1652) defines God's power as "that by which God is able to do whatever is not alien to his nature and truth."[55] Accord-

creed, "He does whatsoever He will: that is Omnipotence" (*NPNF,* 1st ser., pp. 1-3). See also Augustine, *Reply to Faustus the Manichean,* 26.3-6, where he argues against the Manichean view that evil limits God.

48. Anselm, *Proslogium,* 7, in *Saint Anselm: Basic Writings,* 2, ed. and trans. S. N. Deane (LaSalle, IL: Open Court, 1968), p. 13.

49. Aquinas, *SumTh,* 1.25.3, in *Basic Writings,* p. 263.

50. Muller, *PRRD,* 3, p. 518.

51. Muller, *PRRD,* 3, p. 518.

52. Reinhold Seeberg, *Text-Book of the History of Doctrines,* trans. Charles Hay, vol. 2 (Grand Rapids: Baker, 1977), pp. 313-15.

53. Calvin, *Sermons on Job,* 157, quoted in Muller, *PRRD,* 3, p. 523.

54. Pictet, *Christian Theology,* 2.7, trans. Frederick Reyroux (London: Seeley and Burnside, 1834), p. 92 (italics in original).

55. Wendelin, *Christianae theologicae libri duo,* 1.1.27, quoted in Muller, *PRRD,* 3, p. 526.

ing to Muller, William Perkins provides "a basic early orthodox form of the doctrine in which most of the standard scholastic distinctions were stated or adumbrated."[56] Perkins says:

> God's Omnipotence, is that by which he is most able to perform every work. Some things notwithstanding are here to be excepted. First, those things whose action argueth an impotencie, as to lie, to deny his word. Secondly, such things as are contrary to the nature of God, as to destroy himself and not to beget his Son from eternity. Thirdly, such things as imply contradiction. For God cannot make truth false, or that which when it is not, to be. God's power may be distinguished into an absolute and actual power. God's absolute power is that by which he can do more than he either doth or will do. God's actual power is that by which he causeth all things to be, which he freely willeth.[57]

While the tradition achieved remarkable consensus about the *fact* of God's omnipotence, it did not attain complete unanimity about its meaning. Traditional theologians disagreed about the exact extent of God's power. Can God transcend the law of contradiction or sin or command us to sin? Can God change the past? Can God determine a creature's free act? In recent theology, however, some have begun to argue that the word "omnipotence" ought to be dropped altogether from our theological vocabulary and replaced with "almightiness," or some other word unburdened with problems that attend the traditional term.[58] In the following pages I shall address the traditionally disputed questions I have referred to above, as well as some recent and more fundamental challenges to traditional doctrine as such.

---

56. Muller, *PRRD*, 3, p. 530.

57. Perkins, *A Golden Chaine or the Description of Theology*, 2, in *The Works of William Perkins*, ed. Ian Breward (Berkshire, UK: Sutton Courtenay Press, 1970), p. 180.

58. See Charles Hartshorne, *Omnipotence and Other Theological Mistakes*, p. 26; David Ray Griffin, *Evil Revisited: Responses and Reconsiderations* (Albany, NY: SUNY Press, 1991), p. 56; Peter Geach, "Omnipotence," in *Contemporary Philosophy of Religion*, ed. Steven M. Cahn and David Shatz (New York: Oxford University Press, 1982). For responses to Geach's criticisms of omnipotence, see Thomas P. Flint and Alfred J. Freddoso, "Maximal Power," in *The Existence and Nature of God*, ed. Alfred J. Freddoso (Notre Dame, IN: University of Notre Dame Press, 1983), pp. 81-113; Gijsbert van den Brink, "Capable of Anything? The Omnipotence of God," in *Understanding the Attributes of God* (New York: Peter Lang, 1999), pp. 139-59.

Theology of Omnipotence

What Is Power?

As with the ideas of knowledge and presence, we need some preliminary clarity about the concept of power before we move into issues concerning God's power. Our common sense understanding of power arises from experience of our bodies, machines, and nature. We lift weight against the resistance of gravity and cycle against the resistance of the air. Body builders are generally stronger than other people, and racing cars have more power than do production cars. Power is the presupposition for movement against resistance. We speak of storms, waterfalls, oceans, stars, and supernovas as being powerful. Further consideration will show that these things, though they involve massive concentrations of energy and move against resistance, do not possess power. Power requires more than energy, even in massive quantities. Power involves energy, will, and intelligence. Energy must be concentrated so that it can be used for work; will is needed to choose a goal; and intelligence is required to direct energy toward a goal. When we speak of an animal's power, we have in mind what it can accomplish: running swiftly, flying high, or jumping long distances. Human beings are more powerful than animals because of their superior intelligence.

According to Hannah Arendt, though individuals possess strength, only groups possess power. She says: "Power corresponds to the human ability not just to act but to act in concert. Power is never the property of an individual; it belongs to a group and remains in existence only so long as the group keeps together."[59] In this reading, power is exclusively a political concept. Kyle Paseward points out that most discussions of power begin with the notion of political power as the paradigm case. For this reason most theorists of power define it as an external relation of domination. Paseward argues that an adequate concept of power must involve an ontology of power in which the ubiquity of power is recognized. Paseward also rejects the domination model of power and defines power as "communication of efficacy."[60] That is, authentic power confers being and freedom on another. In this section I shall develop a concept of God's power that bears some kinship to Paseward's theology of power.

Whether we define power in political or other terms, we recognize that our power is limited. We can do some things but not others. We can bring about

---

59. Arendt, *On Violence* (New York: Harcourt, Brace & World, 1970), p. 44, quoted in Kyle A. Pasewark, *A Theology of Power: Being Beyond Domination* (Minneapolis: Fortress, 1993), p. 212.

60. Pasewark, *Theology of Power*, pp. 1-3, 5.

many states of affairs but not all. Whenever we do something, we expend time and energy that could have been used to do something else. Because of our intelligence, we can overcome some of our physical limits through technology and social and political cooperation. Human beings can do things now that they could not do in the past: routinely travel at 550 miles per hour, perform heart bypass surgery, and search distant libraries through electronic networks. Perhaps even more amazing things will come within our power in the future.

However, there is no reason to think that our power will ever overcome all limits. We will always be able to imagine doing things we cannot do, things that are logically possible but physically impossible. Even if our imaginations were unlimited — there are reasons to doubt this — the universe is made of stubborn stuff that is resistant to our wills. We can imagine a universe with completely different laws and possibilities. But our universe has its own laws and possibilities that place limits on what we can do. We are not our own power, and thus we depend on something other than ourselves. Accomplishing something requires channeling and depleting the finite energy available to us. We cannot make things real simply by imagining and willing them; every power we exercise — life, intellect, nature, and will — comes to us as a gift.

Whatever more precise definition we might give it, power is the presupposition of action. It is the measure of our ability to actualize our ideas, to make things happen, and to cause things to come into being. We can distinguish, as Aquinas did, between passive power and active power.[61] We can act on the world to bring about change, to build a new house, to write a book or sing a song. But we also can be acted on by the world and changed. A child has the passive power, under the right conditions, to grow into a mature, healthy adult. Under the right teacher, some of us have the power to become professional photographers, doctors, or auto mechanics. Every action presupposes both kinds of power, for there must be an actor and a patient, that is, something that acts and something that receives the action and is shaped by it.

Our passive powers enable us to grow, develop our skills, and increase our knowledge. Human beings have great potential. So great is our potential that we cannot actualize all of it in a lifetime — indeed, not in a hundred lifetimes! Our potential, it is often said, is a mark of our greatness and of our superiority over animals. What is not pointed out as often is how this characteristic marks us as imperfect beings. For example, when a piano teacher says to a beginning student, "You have great potential as a pianist," the young pupil naturally takes it as a compliment. However, if one great pianist says to another, "You have great potential as a pianist," the other one would take it as an insult. One com-

---

61. *SumTh*, 1.25.1.

pliments a great pianist by speaking of her as "accomplished," that is, as having arrived at greatness, not as merely being in the process of becoming a pianist. When we view our passive powers positively, we are anticipating their full actualization. It is not good to have "no potential," better to have "great potential," but even better to be "accomplished." The accomplished person has so actualized her potential that it no longer exists, having been transformed into a fully activated skill. It is ironic that a perfect piano player no longer has any "potential" as a piano player.

God's Power as Purely Active

When we speak of God's power, ordinarily we have in mind God doing such things as creating and sustaining the world, empowering creatures, redeeming sinners, raising Jesus from the dead, and judging the world. God is not dead, inactive, and powerless, but is alive and active. We can see here some analogy between our power and God's power. However, the differences are profound. First, according to traditional theology, God's power is purely and eternally active, never passive. God is not merely "potentially great" but eternally great, that is, "accomplished." Therefore, God has no potential.[62] By saying that God has no potential, I do not mean that he cannot *do* anything. Rather, I mean that God can do all things effortlessly, without himself changing. God is already fully God.

God Is His Power

Human beings *have* power: active and passive power. We are alive, active, and awake — in a sense, self-moved. Whereas rocks cannot actualize their potential, human beings can strive toward perfection. But we cannot achieve it without help. We live and act depending on a source outside us and before us. But God is his own life, energy, and power. Any being merely having or using power depends on the availability of power. Such a being can cease to be or can run out of power. But God can never deplete his power, any more than he can exhaust his wisdom, love, or holiness. His power is indivisibly simple and omnipresent. For his power is his presence, love, and knowledge.

---

62. This is argued by Thomas Aquinas in *SumTh*, 1.3.3; 1.9.1. See also Michael J. Dodds, "St. Thomas Aquinas and the Motion of the Motionless God," *New Blackfriars* 68 (1987): 237; see also David Burrell, "Divine Practical Knowing: How an Eternal God Acts in Time," in *Divine Action: Studies Inspired by the Philosophical Theology of Austin Farrer*, ed. Brian Hebblethwaite and Edward Henderson (Edinburgh: T&T Clark, 1990), pp. 84-94.

Omnipotence Defined

In declaring God's omnipotence, I am in firm agreement with the tradition that (1) God is power itself, (2) God can accomplish all things, and (3) God empowers all other powers.[63] We need all three parts of this definition. If we were not to understand God as power itself, we could not consistently hold that God "can accomplish all things" or that he "empowers all other powers." The second aspect of my definition emphasizes that God's power should not be measured only by what God does. Creation is finite, but God's power is infinite. God can do all things, even things he does not will to do. The third aspect emphasizes that God's creatures depend on his power just as much for their continued existence and their own acts as they do for their coming into being.

Controversies surround all three parts of the definition. With reference to the first, those who deny divine simplicity will object to identifying God with this attribute or any other. Objecting to the second aspect, some have asked, can God really do "*all* things"? Can God do the logically impossible? Does God do all he can do? If God could do more than he does, does this mean that God has passive power — or potential — after all? And, with reference to the third affirmation, are other powers free if God must empower their action? Is God responsible for the evil deeds of other powers? I shall address these questions below. However, I must first ground our thinking about omnipotence in the eternal life of God.

Trinitarian Omnipotence

Would God be omnipotent without the world? Or can God exercise power only outside of himself? My answer to these questions must be in the negative, because, as with all God's attributes, we gain adequate understanding of divine power only by considering God's eternal life as Father, Son, and Spirit. But how

---

63. Aspects (2) and (3) of my definition correspond to the medieval distinction between *de potentia absoluta* and *de potentia ordinate*, God's power considered only with respect to his own being and God's power considered with respect to his will for creation. For an authoritative study of the nature and history of this distinction, see Lawrence Moonan, *Divine Power: The Medieval Power Distinction Up to Its Adoption by Albert, Bonaventure, and Aquinas* (New York: Oxford University Press, 1994). For Moonan's able defense of the continued necessity and usefulness of this distinction, see his article "On Dispensing with Omnipotence," *Ephemerides Theologicae Lovanienses* 65 (1989): 60-80. For a study of this distinction in the sixteenth and seventeenth centuries, see Frances Oakley, "The Absolute and Ordained Power of God in Sixteenth and Seventeenth Century Theology," *Journal of the History of Ideas* 59 (1998): 437-61; see also Oakley, *Omnipotence, Covenant and Order: An Excursion in the History of Ideas from Abelard to Leibniz* (Ithaca, NY: Cornell University Press, 1984).

can we conceive of God's eternal power apart from the world when I have argued that nothing about God is potential? How can a being with no potential do anything other than be? These questions find their answers implied in a thesis I developed earlier: God is God not simply as a state of being; God enacts his deity.

Some traditional thinkers made a *rational* distinction (that is, a mental distinction to help us grasp something beyond our comprehension) between the nature and the life of God.[64] There is no *real* distinction between the two. For the moment, however, allow me to press this distinction. If we consider the divine nature in the abstract and apart from God's life as the eternal communion of the persons, it would appear as a sort of potential God. It would contain all possible divine attributes and potential Trinitarian persons. Actualizing the infinite potential of the divine nature would require omnipotent power. It takes unlimited power to be God. To help us grasp God's independence from all other powers, Barth appeals to the distinction I am making: "We say that (as manifest and eternally actual in the relationship of Father, Son and Holy Ghost) He is the One who already has and is in Himself everything which would have to be the object of His creation and causation if He were not He, God."[65]

Of course, this is just a thought experiment, and there is no movement in God from potential to actual. But this experiment allows us to see activity and power — infinite power — in the eternal life of God. God fully, freely, and eternally enacts the divine nature. Although there never was a time when God was not fully actual, the eternal relationship of the persons and the attributes to the divine nature is that of actualization, a power relationship. Every "possible" good is a concrete actuality in the eternal triune life of God. Therefore, God is eternally omnipotent, apart from any reference to the world. God freely enacts his nature: the Father begets the Son and breathes the Spirit, the Son receives the Father and returns himself to the Father. God enacts his infinite attributes freely. In eternal omnipotence, God is God freely.

Examples of Omnipotence: Creation, Incarnation, and Resurrection

As I observed in the Scripture section, God's power is magnificently displayed in creation. However, none of God's acts can display omnipotence as long as we are thinking of God's power in a quantitative sense. The skeptic David Hume made this mistake when he objected that a finite creation could never

---

64. See Muller, *PRRD*, 3, pp. 365-67; see also Muller, *God, Creation and Providence in the Thought of Jacob Arminius*, pp. 116-26.

65. Barth, *CD*, 2/1, p. 306.

prove an omnipotent God.[66] However, this issue appears differently when one understands that God's power is God's own simple being and thus not a matter of quantity. God does not have to exert more power to create a universe than to create a mouse or an atom. Each of these acts requires omnipotence in the sense I have defined it. In each case, God empowers and calls into being something from absolutely nothing. Such a Creator must be his own power and his own being. If God were not power and being itself, he would be threatened by the loss of both and of succumbing to nothingness. He would not be the Lord of nothingness, but he would be vulnerable to it. But God demonstrates that he is the Lord of nothingness when he creates by his word and presence alone.

God creates from nothing, yet does this without dividing his power or being. This implies, as Aquinas recognized, that God's act of creation establishes a relationship rather than imparts a substance.[67] In the myths of the Ancient Near East, creation involved some form of imparting a substance: a carving up of the body of a dead god to make heaven and earth, or sexual generation in some form.[68] God said in Genesis, "Let it be," and creation was. By his address, God established a relationship to that which had no existence. God's speaking to a thing that had no existence as if it existed established its real existence. When God wills a thing to exist before him for the sake of his love, it comes into being. God's presence to a thing, love for a thing, and knowledge of a thing gives it being. God does not need to change or give up some of his life energy to create something. God's undivided presence and power constitute our existence and power for action. We gain existence by entering into a certain kind of relation with God, not by being given a piece of God. God's presence, love, and knowledge are not passive but active and powerful.

In the incarnation of the Son of God, God demonstrates his omnipotence in another way. By uniting human and divine nature in the person of the Son, God demonstrates that he so transcends the world that he is not defined by the world — either positively or negatively. The existence of the world does not make God greater, and the absence of the world would not diminish his majesty. In joining himself to human nature, God does not change or gain perfections that were not already eternally his. Human nature does not contradict or augment divine nature, for there is nothing good in it that is not already contained in the divine nature, and there is nothing evil about it that is God's

---

66. Hume, *Dialogues Concerning Natural Religion,* 5.

67. Aquinas makes this point in *SumTh,* 1.45.2-3.

68. See James B. Pritchard, *Ancient Near Eastern Texts Relating to the Old Testament,* 3rd ed. (Princeton, NJ: Princeton University Press, 1969). For examples from Egypt, see pp. 3-10; for the Akkadian creation myth, see pp. 60-72.

creation.[69] Evil is not a creature but a distortion and a negation of the creation, and the incarnation purifies human nature of the evil that plagues it. Natural possibilities or impossibilities do not limit God's power. Human nature does not have within itself the possibilities of the divine nature; but God has within himself the possibilities for human nature. Different things in the world displace each other because their natures are limited. But God contains the possibilities for all creatures, and thus God neither displaces nor violates creatures by joining them to himself. Every possibility in the world is already fully actual in God. Therefore, the incarnation is an act of omnipotence.

The resurrection of Christ is a third example of God's omnipotence. From a theological point of view, death is a negation of the creature's existence and thus a negation of the word by which creation comes to exist. In Scripture death derives from sin as its result and punishment: sin is the human negation of God's "yes" to the creature, to God's "let it be." Hence, it is also the self-negation of the creature: that is, in sin the human creature wills to be something other than what God wills for it. In effect, it wills to be nothing, because whatever God does not will is nothing and will be nothing eternally. It is impossible.[70] The dreams that project it are vanities, the words that describe it are lies, and the acts that strive to realize it are futile. Its end is death. God demonstrates again in the resurrection of Christ that he is the Lord of the possible and the impossible. Human nature within itself has no possibility for eternal life. But God expands it beyond its own possibilities and shows that he is the Lord of his creation. In saving Jesus from death, God reasserts his creative will and brings it to eschatological fulfillment. God demonstrates again that he is Lord over nothingness — God Almighty.

Omnipotence and the Other Attributes

Recent attempts to define "omnipotence" in general, apart from God's other attributes, are faced with insurmountable obstacles.[71] Omnipotence, like all divine attributes, is defined by what God is, and God is all his attributes. God is omnipotent in all his attributes because, in every attribute, God is fully actual. God is omnipotent love and loving omnipotence. His omnipresence is the presence of his limitless power, and his limitless power indwells and contains all things. His omniscience is all-powerful and his power is all-knowing; his power is eternal

69. For these ideas, see Robert Sokolowski, *The God of Faith and Reason: Foundations of Christian Theology* (Washington, DC: Catholic University of America Press, 1995), pp. 31-40.

70. Barth, *CD*, 4/1, pp. 409-10.

71. Moonan, in "On Dispensing with Omnipotence," and van den Brink, in "Capable of Anything?" voice significant criticisms of the "omnipotence-in-general" approach.

and his eternity is powerful. Since all his attributes are fully actual, they give to others what they are in themselves. God's life is life-giving life (1 Cor. 15:45); his love is love-engendering (1 John 4:19). His righteousness makes us righteous; his wisdom enlightens us. His holiness sanctifies us; his freedom frees us. His glory glorifies and his beauty beautifies; his knowledge of us enables us to know ourselves. His omnipresence gives space to things and makes them present to God, to themselves, and to other things. God is the power of all powers, and his eternity gives time to things. His power, then, is not an anonymous, ambiguous, or sinister force; rather, it is the fullness of his personal being "for us" (Rom. 8:31). There is not the slightest basis for imagining that God's power will ever be turned against us in a way that is not truly for us. As we shall see, understanding Christ crucified as the "power of God and the wisdom of God" transforms our understanding of God's power and exposes our fascination with coercive "power" as a vain and futile dream of nothingness.

Christ Crucified: The Power of God

In power, God freely enacts and possesses his own triune life. His action and possession take form as total giving, receiving, returning, and sharing. The triune persons live, not in themselves, but in each other by mutual indwelling. They never take from one another or dwell selfishly in themselves. Divine power is love, divine action is giving, and divine freedom possesses the self as given freely by another for the sake of giving again. The mighty power whereby God creates and sustains the universe is self-giving love. In creation, God gives himself to what was nothing and thereby makes it something. He bestows his presence on what was nowhere so that it would have a place to be. He makes something that had no time contemporaneous with himself so that it would have time. In creation God gives power to the powerless; so the power, freedom, and action of creatures must, if they are to effect anything, follow the way of divine power: loving, giving, and possessing the self as a gift for the purpose of giving. To act otherwise is to embrace nothingness, powerlessness, and slavery. It is not to act at all.

Unfortunately, fallen human beings do not believe that power comes to itself in loving and giving. They do not believe that freedom possesses the self as a gift for the sake of giving. Hence, they do not believe that God really is loving or giving or that God possesses himself freely for the sake of others. Power appears to fallen creatures as the action of absorbing things, taking from others, and possessing the self by expanding it to infinity for the sake of itself. Human beings naturally exercise this false power in the hope of becoming a self, securing the self, and expanding the self. They cannot love or thank or praise God;

therefore, they cannot love or thank or rejoice in their fellow human beings. Thinking that they will find their being in possessions, sensual pleasure, and flattery, they steal, kill, boast, lie, cheat, and, in a thousand other ways seek to secure and enrich the self. For all the frantic motion that goes along with the human rejection of the divine model of power, it accomplishes nothing — nothing at all. True power, on the other hand, accomplishes things, brings them into being, and makes them perfect. Self-centered power, pseudo-power can destroy things and cause heartache and sorrow by making idols and monuments to vanity, anxiety, and despair. But it cannot bring our created nature to the goal for which God made it: it cannot shape the world into its Christ-form destiny. It is all for nothing — vanity, futility, and lies.

Humanity's greatest need cannot be fulfilled, and its greatest enemy cannot be defeated, by pseudo-power. Our greatest need is to be loved by God and to love him in return, and we cannot possess ourselves except as a gift given for the sake of giving. To live, we must die. The false self, constructed by feeding on others and expanded by absorbing others, must be killed. It cannot coexist with the "new self, created to be like God" (Eph. 4:24). Our greatest enemy is whatever keeps us from loving God and possessing ourselves as a gift given for giving. Our greatest enemy is not poverty, death, sickness, or even the devil: it is we ourselves, the very ones whose needs are so great. This is why we cannot fulfill our own needs and defeat our enemy. We are trapped in the vicious circle of our fallen existence. The exertion of Herculean or Napoleonic or Einsteinian power would only propel us faster and faster around the same wretched circuit. The despairing words of Paul come to mind here: "Who will rescue me from this body of death?" (Rom. 7:24). The only possible answer follows: "Thanks be to God — through Jesus Christ our Lord!" (Rom. 7:25).

To meet our deepest needs and defeat our greatest enemy, God did not send an army of angels or make the rivers flow with wine and the fields perpetually ripe for harvest. God sent his Son to do for us what we would not and could not do for ourselves (Rom. 8:1-3). He sent him, as one of us, to love God and to possess his self as a gift given for giving. God sent his Son to give himself totally to his Father on our behalf. This act did not change the Son, for he loved the Father from eternity. But what a radical change for humanity! As human, the Son's total giving of himself had to take the form of death to break the wretched circle in which we orbit around ourselves. Every attempt to induce a moral reformation or to impart sacred knowledge or facilitate esoteric religious experiences would have been immediately subverted into more energy for the perpetual voyage around our own emptiness. But the cross of Christ is the absolute renunciation of the pseudo-power that thinks it can live by taking, imposing, domineering, and absorbing other beings.

This is not to say that the cross is the renunciation of all power. Far from it: Christ is the power of God (1 Cor. 1:24), and in the cross the Son of God is not passive. He does not merely endure the action of others. In the cross he is completely in charge and purely active, for in the cross he abandoned himself and gave himself utterly to the Father on our behalf. He accomplished for us in one act something that had not been accomplished by all the futile displays of arrogance, lust, and force since the beginning of creation. He realized God's final goal for humanity, a humanity that lives only by the words of God, receives its being with unmixed gratitude for the purpose of returning it in obedience and love.

Is God's Power Really Unlimited?

The second aspect of our definition of omnipotence declares that "God can accomplish all things." As witnessed in the affirmations of Dionysius, Augustine, Anselm, Aquinas, and other traditional theologians, the tradition did not mean by this declaration that God can do anything we can put into words. Scripture itself mentions several things God "cannot do": God cannot lie (Heb. 6:18) or deny himself (2 Tim. 2:13), and, analogous to these things, we understand that God cannot cease to exist, give up an attribute, or sin. With a few exceptions, the tradition has also agreed that God cannot do or bring about a contradiction: thus God cannot make a square circle or a married bachelor or a change in the past.

Defenders of this traditional view find themselves challenged from two different angles. First, many people feel very uncomfortable hearing someone begin a sentence with the words "God cannot," because it sounds as though we are limiting God's power. This reaction is not a new phenomenon. According to Peter Damiani (d. 1072), one such statement by Jerome (342-420) served for six hundred years as "an occasion for imputing a lack of power to God."[72] It is not unusual to hear someone assert, from a misguided reverence for God's omnipotence, that God can do *anything*, even bring about contradictions. Such concerns are not limited to ordinary believers. René Descartes, the great "father of modern philosophy," subscribed to this view. Descartes's position arises from the laudable motive of wanting to avoid making God "subject to

---

72. Damiani, *De divina omnipotentia*, quoted in Frances Oakley, "The Absolute and Ordained Power of God in Sixteenth- and Seventeenth-Century Theology," *Journal of the History of Ideas* 59 (1998): 441. In writing in praise of virginity, Jerome stated that not even the omnipotent God can "raise up a virgin after she has fallen" (cited in Oakley, p. 441, n. 14). For a fuller treatment of this issue, see Frances Oakley, *Omnipotence, Covenant and Order*, pp. 42-47.

the inexorable laws of logic as Jove was to the decrees of the Fates."[73] Descartes explains his view as follows:

> The mathematical truths which you call eternal have been laid down by God and depend on him entirely no less than the rest of his creatures. . . . In general we can assert that God can do everything that is beyond our grasp but not that he cannot do what is beyond our grasp. It would be rash to think that our imagination reaches as far as his power.[74]

Barth, whose views we will consider further below, appears to subscribe to a view similar to that held by Descartes.[75]

A second reaction to the tradition embraces the alternative that Descartes rejected in horror: that God is genuinely limited. Peter Abelard made it appear that God, in creating the world, was "incapable of doing anything other than he had in fact done," thus implying that God is limited in a "non-trivial" sense.[76] In the wake of the Reformation, the Socinians accepted the traditional view that God cannot accomplish a contradiction but argued that this condition implies the "finitude and limitation of the divine essence."[77] Peter Geach argues that the traditional view limits God by listing some logically possible things among those things that God cannot accomplish. It is logically possible for some beings to lie or die or make something they cannot destroy; but the tradition argued that God cannot do those things because they contradict the divine nature. According to Geach, the tradition unknowingly limits God's power by attributing to him a determinate nature that excludes some logical possibilities.[78]

Like the Socinians and Geach, Gregory Boyd considers God's inability to accomplish a contradiction a "non-trivial" limitation of God's power. This idea plays a central role in Boyd's project of constructing a theodicy that explains the origin and prevalence of evil in a way that clears God of responsibility for

---

73. Geach, "Omnipotence," p. 51.

74. Descartes, "Letter to Mersenne, 15 April 1630," in *The Philosophical Writings of Descartes III*, trans. John Cottingham, Robert Stoothoff, Dugold Murdoch, and Anthony Kenny (Cambridge, UK: Cambridge University Press, 1991), pp. 22-23, quoted in R. J. Snell, "Overcoming Omnipotence: The Crisis of Divine Freedom in Ockham and Descartes," *Quodlibet Journal* 5.1 (2003). Available at http://www.quodlibet.net/snell-freedom.shtml (accessed May 30, 2006).

75. *CD*, 2/1, pp. 532-38.

76. Lawrence Moonan, "On Dispensing with Omnipotence," pp. 70-71; see also the discussion in Oakley, *Omnipotence, Covenant and Order*, p. 45.

77. Muller, PRRD, 3, p. 535.

78. "Omnipotence," pp. 51-54. Like Geach, Nelson Pike, in "Omnipotence and God's Ability to Sin," *American Philosophical Quarterly* 6 (1969): 208-16, argues that omnipotence entails the ability to sin; but, unlike Geach, Pike contends that God has this ability.

it.[79] According to Boyd, since God cannot bring about a logical contradiction, God cannot create a being that is free to love but not free to withhold love. If God wants a world that contains loving beings, God has to risk creating beings that can do evil as well as good. By creating free beings, God has voluntarily limited his future options, since he had to give creatures room to do evil as well as good. Yet, according to Boyd, God's self-imposed limits do not compromise God's omnipotence, for God was under no necessity to create at all. God limited himself freely. Boyd concludes that, because of God's self-limitation, which is based ultimately on the law of contradiction, God is not culpable for the evil in the world, directly or indirectly. God is not directly culpable because free creatures are totally responsible for their own actions. And God is not indirectly culpable because, strictly speaking, he did not even choose to create beings that are capable of evil. This action was merely entailed in the act of creating beings capable of love, and thus it lacked full intentionality.

It seems to me that the traditional view can withstand these criticisms and avoid the pitfalls they step into. Sometimes we are simply confused by the clumsiness of language. The declaration that God cannot die or sin or lose an attribute only *seems* to deny a power to God. In reality, it denies a *lack* of power or perfection to God, for the "ability" to sin or die is a weakness, not a power. Sentences such as this contain two negatives, and one negates the other. We could just as easily state the same truth positively by saying God is perfectly alive or purely good. To say that God cannot die *affirms* that death has no power over him. Other beings can sin and die, but this does not mean they can *do* something God cannot do. Death is not something one does; it is one's undoing. And sin accomplishes nothing because it is based on falsehood, which is nothing and can never become something. That God cannot contradict his nature does not limit God's ability to act; on the contrary, as we shall see in greater detail in the next section, it is this very quality that constitutes God's freedom. God is free precisely because he is in his action what he is in his nature.

The traditional view of God and logical contradiction seems much preferable to Descartes's position (or Geach's or Boyd's variations). To affirm with Descartes that God can accomplish contradictions is to destroy our ability to think and speak about God. We could not make any affirmation about God without at the same time affirming its contradictory. The proposition "God exists" would be no truer than the proposition "God does not exist." Believing that God is good would not give us the right to deny that God is evil. We could

---

79. Boyd, *God at War: The Bible and Spiritual Conflict* (Downers Grove, IL: InterVarsity Press, 1997); see also Boyd, *Satan and the Problem of Evil: Constructing a Trinitarian Warfare Theodicy* (Downers Grove, IL: InterVarsity Press, 2001).

not accept God's revelation as the truth about God, for God is beyond truth and falsehood. Even the proposition "God can accomplish logical contradictions" is no truer than its opposite. Theology ends in self-destruction.

Contrary to Geach, the tradition contends that, when we say that God cannot accomplish logical contradictions, we are not limiting God. In order to limit God's power, we would need to say that there is at least one logically possible thing that God cannot accomplish. Unicorns and green planets are possible, while square circles and two-sided triangles are not. Only a lack of power and wisdom could explain why God could not create unicorns and green planets; but it demonstrates no lack of power to be "unable" to accomplish a square circle. The words square and circle standing alone refer to clear and meaningful concepts; but, stuck together, they refer to nothing at all — indeed, they are sheer nonsense.[80] A square circle is not something that is difficult to make; it is simply not a thing. The general statement taught by the tradition, "God cannot do a logical contradiction," makes a meaningful assertion. It says God cannot do nonsense. To put it positively, God is free of self-contradictory impulses. But if one substitutes for the meaningful term "logical contradiction" a nonsensical expression such as "square circle," which calls to mind no meaningful concept, the sentence itself becomes nonsense. The statement "God can (or cannot) make a square circle" makes no meaningful assertion. Statements such as this do not limit God or remove limits from God. They say nothing. And if they say nothing, they do not limit God's power.

Finally, we must do justice to Descartes's legitimate concern that we not place God under a set of laws. God is ultimate and absolute, answerable only to himself. Barth thought he detected in Aquinas and theologians influenced by him a tendency to place God under the law of contradiction. Aquinas spoke, not only of things impossible for God because of their contradiction to God's being, but also of the impossibility of things "which have an inherent contradiction."[81] Barth agrees with Aquinas that God cannot do contradictions, but he rejects Thomas's reasoning. "We cannot," says Barth, "accept the idea of an absolutely possible or impossible by which even God's omnipotence is to be measured. On the contrary we have to recognize that God's omnipotence is the substance of what is possible."[82] Barth is probably reading Thomas too unsym-

80. My analysis is similar to that of Aquinas, who, in *Summa Theologica*, 1.25.3, points out the linguistic meaninglessness of such expressions. Geach, in "Omnipotence," p. 52, disagrees with Aquinas and thinks such expressions, though false, are not "gibberish." Geach accuses Aquinas of not knowing the difference between self-contradiction and nonsense, a dubious charge.

81. *CD*, 2/1, p. 534.

82. *CD*, 2/1, p. 534.

pathetically here.[83] However, as is often the case, even when Barth may be mistaken in his criticism of the tradition, he is correct in his own doctrinal construction. Barth is correct in saying that God's power and will

> are not subordinate and responsible to any higher power and independent idea of what is possible and impossible for Him either as concerns Himself or as concerns His works. . . . We are forced to say that God is omnipotent in the fact that He can do everything that is in his power. His power is not that of any kind of power defined by any kind of idea of what is possible. On the contrary, God is power, the one, unique, and only power. And as such He is also the substance of everything that is possible.[84]

With Barth, I insist that God himself is the ground of the distinction between what is possible and what is impossible. Whatever has a possibility in God is possible, and what does not have its possibility in God is impossible. Ultimately, then, all true statements of the form "God cannot do this or that" reduce to the one statement that God cannot contradict himself. The possibility or impossibility of an action is determined by its consistency or inconsistency with God's nature and not by something extrinsic to God. Zurich theologian Johann Heidegger (1633-1698) articulates this truth in a compact and clear paragraph:

> The object of divine power is . . . the possible; not in itself, as though there were anything outside God, which has the cause of its possibility in itself, outside the power and will of God; but in the power and will of God, which alone is the foundation and root of all possibility. All things outside of God derive their essence and reality from the fact that, as God understands how to make them for His own glory, so He wills that they be and produces them. . . . Thus then that is possible, which God can will, order, call, do for His glory; impossible, which God cannot will, order, call, do for His glory.[85]

Descartes was not mistaken to insist that God is absolute and not subject to any régime of law above him. Instead, his mistake was to consider God's power apart from his identity and attributes disclosed in revelation. Though I deny

---

83. See *SumTh*, 1.25.3. Aquinas is not placing the law of contradiction above God: for Aquinas, as for Barth, the divine nature is the measure of the possible.

84. *CD*, 2/1, p. 535.

85. Heidegger, *Corpus Theologiae*, 3, quoted in Heinrich Heppe, *Reformed Dogmatics*, trans. G. T. Thomson, rev. and ed. Ernst Bizer (1950; reprint, London: Wakeman Great Reprints, n.d.), pp. 100-101.

that there is a law above God, I nonetheless affirm that God's power is not that of an indeterminate chaos about which nothing can be confidently affirmed. Rather, it is the loving power of our dear Father, our righteous and holy God, who is Father, Son, and Spirit.

Divine Omnipotence and Human Freedom

The question of the compatibility of divine omnipotence and human freedom plays a large part in contemporary discussions of God's power. If God exercises power in all things, how can human beings exercise freedom? We have viewed the issue of God and human freedom from several angles already under these subject headings: divine patience, divine freedom, omnipresence, and omniscience. In each setting I have argued that we need not diminish God to make room for creation. Here I shall argue that acknowledging God's unlimited power does not evacuate the creature of power, freedom, and genuine action. In contrast, I shall argue that only in the freedom of divine freedom can creatures exercise freedom, and only as empowered by divine power can creatures act to accomplish something real and lasting.

Some schools of thought explicitly deny the doctrines of divine omnipotence and creation from nothing.[86] God cannot do all things because another reality imposes limits on him. In a move that looks like an attempt to gain victory through surrender, these thinkers rejoice that the eternal limits on God make room for human freedom and explain the existence of evil. Other theologians, more in the mainstream, affirm omnipotence and the doctrine of creation from nothing but argue that God must restrain the use of his power so that humans can act in freedom and God can avoid responsibility for evil. They adopt what I shall call the Competitive Power Rule (hereafter, CP rule): if God exercises all power, humans can exercise none, but if humans can exercise some power, God cannot exercise all.[87]

I shall begin by pointing out two obvious exceptions to the CP rule. All parties to this debate acknowledge that (1) we were created and are sustained by

---

86. This is true of process theism as represented by Charles Hartshorne in *Omnipotence and Other Theological Mistakes,* and David Ray Griffin in *God, Power and Evil* (Louisville: Westminster, 1976); see also Griffin, *Evil Revisited: Responses and Reconsiderations.*

87. Clark Pinnock argues this in "Between Classical and Process Theism," in *Process Theology,* ed. Ronald Nash (Grand Rapids: Baker, 1989), where he says: "Thinking of God as literally *all*-powerful divests the finite universe of a degree of power" (pp. 316-17). See also Pinnock, *Most Moved Mover: A Theology of God's Openness* (Grand Rapids: Baker Academic, 2001), pp. 53-55.

God's power;[88] and (2) that we did not choose to become free beings but received our freedom from God. In these two instances, at least, God's omnipotent power does not limit our freedom; it makes it possible. God graciously gives it to us. Adherents of the CP rule view these two instances as exceptions to the general rule that God's action limits our freedom. In these cases, CP rule defenders admit that God's omnipotence does not limit our freedom. But once we exist and begin to exercise freedom, God must withhold some of his power so that we can act freely. But surely this cannot be right. Why would the divine act that bestows existence and freedom on us not indicate the way God relates to us generally? A rule with such massive exceptions cannot hold; it cries out to be revised so that it can account for the exceptions.

I see only two ways that we can make the necessary revision: we can apply the CP rule ruthlessly even to God's omnipotent act of giving us being and freedom, or we can allow this gracious act to become the central feature of a new rule. Let us consider the first option. According to the CP rule, our freedom and dignity rest on our ability to choose and act apart from God's power and gifts. Forcing the "exceptions" to conform to the CP rule would transform God's gracious acts of creating us and giving us freedom into outrageous violations of our freedom and thus into the greatest indignities ever perpetrated on us. For God did not ask us whether we wanted to bear the burden of existence or endure the anxiety of making choices. Think of all the "decisions" God made for us! We did not decide to be created male or female, tall or short, intelligent or mentally challenged. We did not decide where or when to be born, or into what family. If our dignity resides in the power to make ourselves through our choices, we have very little of it. It is hard to imagine, however, Christian theologians railing against God for "violating" our freedom not to exist. Most of us express gratitude for our lives. We understand that our existence and freedom are God's good gifts, which we gratefully embrace only long after we have received them. Hence, we can rule out the first option.

Consider the second option. Let us assume that God's powerful action of creation and his gift of freedom are typical of the relationship between omnipotence and human freedom and dignity. Let's call this new rule the Non-Competitive Power Rule (the NCP rule). This rule has the advantage of being consistent without blaspheming, and it rids us of the intolerable assumption that the divine activity that made freedom possible at its beginning makes it impossible thereafter. Instead, it assumes unity and harmony in God's actions

---

88. William Hasker, "An Adequate God," in *Searching for an Adequate God: A Dialogue Between Process and Free Will Theists,* ed. John B. Cobb Jr. and Clark H. Pinnock (Grand Rapids: Eerdmans, 2000), pp. 219, 225.

toward us. The power that called us into the freedom of being continues to make that life possible. How might this be?

From a certain perspective, we can view the act of creation as a great liberation: in creation, God "frees" us from the darkness of nothingness into the light of being. Without being or life or knowledge or power, nothingness is the opposite of freedom. In God's loving act of creation, God gave us space, time, knowledge, life, and power to act. God replaced the impotence of nothingness with the liberty of being, and by that same power and love God continues to protect us from falling back into nothingness and losing the freedom of being. As creatures made from nothing, we are threatened every moment by the paralysis of nothingness. We cannot secure ourselves against this threat. Only the omnipotent Creator is his own being and power. Our liberty is based on God's grace.

Up to this point, defenders of the CP rule might hesitantly agree with my analysis. They would admit that God created us and gave us all our powers and that our existence continues to depend on him. However, they would balk at extending the logic of creation to our free actions. Possessing existence and freedom is one thing, but exercising them is another altogether. God can give us existence and power to act freely, but God *cannot* give us our free acts, for then they would not be free. But the NCP rule insists that God *can* give us our free actions in the same way that he gave us our being and freedom. An action can be "mine" and "free," though I do not choose it *before* I do it. Given our common understanding of freedom, this seems highly implausible. However, continuing to follow the logic of the NCP rule will enable us to see how God can give us our free actions.

Consider the gifts of creation and freedom from another angle. Are my existence and my freedom mine? Is my body mine? Is my dignity mine? Yes. They are mine, though I did not choose or create them. They are mine because God gave them to me. Someone may object in this way: "They are not yours freely, however, and they can never be yours freely because you did not choose them." What a sad thought! If I can never possess myself freely because I did not choose to be what I am, I can never be mine, because I can never choose to be me before I exist. But the gospel is not that pessimistic: it promises us the "glorious freedom of the children of God" (Rom. 8:21). The NCP rule insists that being unable choose my existence and freedom *before* I receive them does not conflict with the hope expressed in Romans 8. Empowered by the Spirit, I can possess these gifts freely by dwelling in the freedom in which the all-wise God gave them to me. I can acknowledge myself as a gift and rejoice in the freedom by which God made this decision for me. By the Spirit, I am united with that original freedom and participate in that eternal decision by voicing my "Amen."

I am freed by his freedom: in and through his freedom I can enact myself freely. God does all things well.

According to the NCP rule, I can receive and freely possess my actions in the same way I acknowledge and freely possess my existence and my capacity for freedom. Before we can grasp this counterintuitive truth, we must recognize the difference between an act and an intention, and between those and a decision (or choice). An act is not an "event" that is separable from its lasting results. An act *is* what it accomplishes, that is, what it really accomplishes, not just the accompanying changes that are immediately apparent.[89] An intention is what I desire and imagine will be accomplished in my act. And a choice is the cessation of deliberation, so that I can act to achieve what I intend. In our acts we never achieve everything we intend to and only that. Reality simply does not bend that readily to our wishes. Our intentions are never free from error and sin, and they are never fully clear to us. And our choices are never based on complete and infallible knowledge of all possible consequences of our acts. A choice is always a chance.

On this analysis, it is clear that our acts (that is, what we actually accomplish) are not determined fully by our choices and intentions. Hence, if we define freedom as a condition in which our intentions and choices determine fully our acts, we will find freedom a rare item indeed. For we cannot fully and freely possess our acts *before* they are accomplished. For the most part, we don't know what we are doing or why we are doing it until well after the deed is done.

The theory of libertarian freedom attempts to avoid this problem by defining freedom in terms of intentions and choices alone and leaving action out of the definition. We are free if our intentions and choices are determined by us alone. Nothing external to me causes my choices, so at any moment before I make a choice, I could choose from the available alternatives. In response, theological compatibilists (for example, Jonathan Edwards) argue that we are free if nothing prevents us from choosing what we will and attempting to do it; but we are not free to will anything other than what we will.[90] On the whole, I think Edwards has the stronger argument. But I am approaching the issue of freedom from a different angle and will not take sides in the debate about free choice. I deny that being able to intend and choose for ourselves — whether or to whatever degree we can do this — constitutes the fullness of freedom. Of what

---

89. According to Alfred J. Freddoso, the medieval consensus was that an action is a "determination" of the patient. Apart from an effect, there is no act. See Freddoso, "God's General Concurrence with Secondary Causes: Pitfalls and Prospects," *American Catholic Philosophical Quarterly* 67 (1994): 138-39.

90. See Jonathan Edwards, *Freedom of the Will* (New Haven, CT: Yale University Press, 1957).

worth is a choice without the power to achieve what we intend or to measure our intentions according to truth? Clearly, we do not have this power.

However, a noncompetitive understanding of God's power enables us to conceive of how God can give us all good things ahead of or in spite of our imperfect choices and confused intentions — without limiting our freedom. We can possess our actions *if* God gives them to us, and our actions can express our genuine freedom if God's loving freedom encompasses them. He winnows our misguided intentions and directs our uninformed choices so that what *God* intends in our actions will be their lasting achievement. Our intentions will be frustrated, our choices thwarted, and our acts redirected unless they harmonize with God's will. But in the Spirit's power we can dwell in God's freedom, adopt his intention, and submit our choices to his wise judgment. Saying "thy will be done" is stepping into freedom, not running away from it. In this way we can possess our actions by faith and anticipate "the glorious freedom of the children of God."

According to Scripture, true freedom comes from the Spirit, and its fullness is an eschatological hope realized in Jesus Christ. What Jesus freely did — his righteousness, his decisions, and his actions — has been given to me in the same way that my existence was given to me. And I freely accept the gift of salvation in a way similar to the way I accept the gift of my existence. Christ is now my being, and his action is now my action. His gift to us and his actions for us do not violate our freedom. They set us free, truly free for the first time. Our freedom is realized in our willing what God has willed for us, in possessing ourselves as God in Christ already possesses us. The fulfillment of this hope can only be God's doing. Therefore, omnipotence does not threaten human freedom; rather, it is the only possible ground of our genuine freedom.

Am I advocating a cold determinism in which God is everything and humans nothing? Not at all. What I am advocating is something totally opposed to determinism. The charge of "determinism" and "fatalism" and the dreaded "predestination of Calvinism" dredges up portrayals of a heartless machine grinding out the future according to an impersonal cosmic law. It pictures a loveless supreme being who lords it over the world and beats it into the shape of his iron will without concern for the dignity of his creatures, a being who bears no resemblance to the God revealed in Jesus Christ. Instead, I am advocating that we understand God's power as omnipotent love. In his powerful love, God gives himself to us continually and thereby gives us to ourselves continually. What some slander as God's "determination" of our selves is really God's loving gift of our true selves to us. Far from advocating "determinism," I am advocating the only ground on which true and perfect freedom is possible. I cannot give myself to myself! My self must be the gift of omnipotence. Only omnipotence can give us existence and freedom; only omnipotence can empower our actions to realize our true being; and only omnipotence can enable us to possess ourselves and enact ourselves completely, to become authentic persons. Our true freedom comes by grace and not by works. It must be a gift.

Libertarian freedom — whether we possess something like it or not — is wholly incapable of achieving the goal of freedom, full self-possession. As I have shown above, libertarian freedom can never transform our existence, life, freedom, or anything we have been given into our own free possession. We can never choose these things *before* we receive them. Furthermore, even in our most considered decisions, we cannot choose all the results of our actions. The outcomes of our actions never match completely our intentions when we are performing them. Suppose I choose to make a left turn on my way home this evening but am killed by a drunk driver in making my turn. Of what comfort is it for my family to know that I made the turn "freely," according to the theory of libertarian freedom? How does that enhance my dignity? Would I have freely embraced my "choice" if I could have known in advance its consequences? Will I embrace it in a postmortem review? Freedom of action must surely include success in what the action intended. And here the wretchedness of libertarian theory comes into full view. We cannot choose our way to heaven, for we do not know the way. We cannot fulfill our intentions, for we do not know our hearts. We cannot take possession of ourselves, for we do not know who we are or "what we shall be" (1 John). We cannot even choose our way to the grocery store, because we cannot guarantee that we will arrive. Only if the omnipotent God gives us heaven, ourselves, and yes, a safe trip to the grocery store, do we have any hope of attaining them. We must admit, with Augustine, "Without you, what am I to myself but a guide to my own self-destruction?"[91] Let us then confess with renewed confidence and joy, "I believe in God the Father, Almighty!"

---

91. Augustine, *Confessions*, 4.1, p. 52.

357

12

Love's Passionate Serenity:
Divine Immutability, Impassibility, and Glory

The Immutability of God

The first question of the Heidelberg Catechism (1563) asks: "What is your only comfort in life and in death?" How should we answer? May we rely on our strong physical constitutions or our wealth or our righteousness? Even a young candidate for baptism or confirmation knows better than that. The things of this world are corruptible and temporary; a foundation solid enough for life and death must be immune to them. The Catechism suggests the only adequate answer: "That I, with body and soul, both in life and in death, am not my own, but belong to my faithful Savior Jesus Christ."[1] According to our faith, our lives find their certain foundation in God, who alone is completely faithful and does not change. God is not corruptible or fickle or temperamental; he does not grow better or worse or mature or decline. God does not lie, and he remains true to all his promises. "God is our refuge and strength, an ever present help in trouble. Therefore we will not fear, though the earth give way and the mountains fall into the heart of the sea" (Ps. 46:1-3). Because God remains God forever, he can remain *our* God forever.

I intend to defend the traditional but widely rejected doctrine of immutability, and thus I will also use the traditional term "immutability" rather than popular alternatives such as "faithfulness" or "constancy." These terms focus narrowly on God's ethical immutability, that is, his constancy of character. I want to be clear that I am not limiting God's immutability to his ethical character. Immutability, as a more general term, includes the ethical dimension cov-

---

1. Philip Schaff, ed. *The Creeds of Christendom*, vol. 3, *The Evangelical and Protestant Creeds*, rev. David S. Schaff (1931; reprint, Grand Rapids: Baker, 1990), p. 306.

ered by faithfulness and constancy, but it also affirms the immutability of God's nature, knowledge, and will.

Divine Immutability in Scripture

Scripture presents God's reliability as a message of great comfort and joy. The ground under our feet seems solid enough; yet we know that everything around us changes and decays. But God will be reliable always. Heaven and earth will perish; but God "remains the same," and his "years will never end" (Ps. 102:23-28). In contrast, our interests, moods, and characters change with changing circumstances. When the occasion calls for it, we will lie or renounce our promises. But God does not change. Through the oracle of Balaam, the Lord says: "God is not a man, that he should lie, nor a son of man, that he should change his mind. Does he speak and then not act? Does he promise and not fulfill?" (Num. 23:19). James assures us that God, who always gives good things, "does not change like shifting shadows" (James 1:16-17). Contrasting himself to his faithless people, God affirms: "I the Lord do not change" (Mal. 3:6-12).

In Scripture, God's faithfulness to others is grounded in his faithfulness to himself, his word, and his promises. He knows himself and is true to himself: thus he always speaks the truth to us. He promises what he knows he can fulfill: "My purpose will stand, and I will do all that I please" (Isa. 46:10). God is faithful and keeps his promises to a "thousand generations" (Deut. 7:9). The works of God's hands are "steadfast for ever and ever, done in faithfulness and uprightness" (Ps. 111:7-8). God's love and faithfulness endure forever (Ps. 100:5; 146:6). The word of God stands "eternal" and "firm" (Ps. 119:89; 33:11). God's promises are all "Yes" in Christ, and the seal of his spirit "guarantees" their fulfillment (2 Cor. 1:20-22). God can swear by himself that he will keep his promises because his purposes are "unchanging" and he cannot lie. For all these reasons, "we have this hope as an anchor for the soul, firm and secure" (Heb. 6:17-19).

God's faithfulness and immutability afford great comfort to his penitent and persecuted people. We can trust in God's forgiveness because he is "faithful and just" (1 John 1:9). In times of persecution we can put ourselves into the hands of our "faithful Creator" (1 Pet. 4:19). We can place our hope in the God "who does not lie" (Titus 1:2). God's word will prove true against all contradictions, says Paul: "Let God be true and every man a liar" (Rom. 3:3, 4). We cannot change God by becoming faithless, "for he cannot disown himself" (2 Tim. 2:13). We are changeable; God is not.

But it is also true that Scripture speaks of God as changing in some sense. In Genesis 6, God looks down on humanity's corruption and regrets that he has made humankind. Older translations say, "it repenteth me that I have made them" (ASV).[2] As Moses was descending Mount Sinai with the law in his hands, the Lord informed him that he had made up his mind to destroy the people because of their stubborn addiction to idols. Moses interceded for the people. "Then the Lord relented and did not bring on his people the disaster he had threatened" (Exod. 32:14).[3]

Entering the debate over the interpretation of these texts would require more space than I have and would lead me away from the plan of this book. However, it is worth noting that even those who cite these texts against the doctrine of immutability understand that the divine changes mentioned always serve a greater divine faithfulness and immutability of character.[4] Most agree that the "change" texts should not be interpreted to undermine God's faithfulness or imply that God is capricious or fickle. Traditional theologians also noticed the priority of immutability over changeability and interpreted the "change" texts in light of what is clearly a more basic principle of God's unchanging nature and character. Origen explains: "All those passages in Scripture in which God is said to lament, rejoice, hate, or be happy are written figuratively and in a human way."[5] It was Augustine, however, who laid down the principle that would have lasting influence on Western interpretation of Scripture and would become the standard answer to the scriptural argument for divine changeability:

> Therefore that which begins to be spoken of God in time, and which was not spoken of Him before, is manifestly spoken of Him relatively; yet not according to any accident of God, so that anything should have happened to Him, but clearly according to some accident of that, in respect to which God begins to be called something relatively. When a righteous man begins to be a friend of God, he himself is changed; but far be it from us to say, that God loves any one in time with as it were a new love, which was not in Him be-

2. See also 1 Sam. 15:11, 35, where God is said to repent that he had made Saul the king. Other similar texts are: Jon. 3:10; Amos 7:3, 6; Jer. 18:8; 1 Chron. 21:15; Ps. 106:45.

3. For biblical arguments for a changeable God, see Gregory A. Boyd, *God of the Possible* (Grand Rapids: Baker, 2000), pp. 53-87, 157-69; see also John Sanders, *The God Who Risks: A Theology of Providence* (Downers Grove, IL: InterVarsity Press, 1998), pp. 39-139; see also Clark H. Pinnock, *Most Moved Mover: A Theology of Openness* (Grand Rapids: Baker Academic, 2001), pp. 25-65.

4. Sanders, in *The God Who Risks,* is concerned to establish that God's changeability does not undermine the immutability of his wisdom, love, faithfulness, and almightiness. See especially pp. 173-94.

5. Origen, *Homily on Numbers 23:4,* quoted in Joseph M. Hallman, *The Descent of God: Divine Suffering in History and Theology* (Minneapolis: Fortress, 1991), p. 42.

fore, with whom things gone by have not passed away and things future have been already done.[6]

Scripture makes clear God's reliability and assures us that our confidence in him is well founded. God does not get tossed about by changing circumstances, and the forces of change, growth, decay, death, loss, and alteration do not rule him. As in its teaching on other attributes, Scripture shows no interest in questions about God's nature in isolation from his relationship to us as Creator, Lord, and Savior. The church, however, found it necessary to address questions about the nature of God's immutability that were not raised within the biblical horizon, questions such as these: Do Scripture's teachings about God's immutability of character and durability of existence imply the immutability of his nature, knowledge, and will? How can an unchanging God remain personal, loving, related, and engaged with creation?

Immutability in the Tradition

Even its severest critics admit that the doctrine of divine immutability was taught and celebrated in the church, almost without dissent, "from the time of the fathers through the seventeenth century."[7] For Augustine, God is wisdom and truth itself, and truth itself cannot change. One would have to be blind, he says, to question this axiom: "Now, no one is so egregiously silly as to ask, 'How do you know that a life of unchangeable wisdom is preferable to one of change?'"[8] Elsewhere he says: "In the first place mark, what is called 'Is.' Ye know what it is that is so called. That which is called 'Is,' and not only is called but is so, is unchangeable: It ever remaineth, It cannot be changed, It is in no part corruptible: It hath neither proficiency, for It is perfect; nor hath deficiency, for It is eternal."[9] According to Augustine, everyday experience teaches us that "the unchangeable is to be preferred before the changeable."[10] In his treatise on the Trinity, Augustine explains the principle in terms of being:

6. Augustine, *The Holy Trinity*, 5.16.16 (*NPNF,* 1st ser., 3, p. 96).
7. Richard Muller, *Post-Reformation Reformed Dogmatics: The Rise and Development of Reformed Orthodoxy,* vol. 3, *The Divine Essence and Attributes* (Grand Rapids: Baker Academic, 2003), p. 308 (hereafter *PRRD*). In the seventeenth century, Conrad Vorstius and the Socinians attacked the doctrine of immutability. For these objections, see Muller, *PRRD,* 3, p. 318.
8. Augustine, *On Christian Doctrine*, 1.9 (*NPNF,* 1st ser., 2, p. 525).
9. Augustine, *Homilies on the First Epistle of John,* 4.5 (*NPNF,* 1st ser., 7, p. 484).
10. Augustine, *Confessions*, 7.17.23 (*NPNF,* 1st ser., 1, p. 112).

Other things that are called essences or substances admit of accidents, whereby a change, whether great or small, is produced in them. But there can be no accident of this kind in respect to God; and therefore He who is God is the only unchangeable substance or essence, to whom certainly Being itself, whence comes the name of essence, most especially and most truly belongs. For that which is changed does not retain its own being; and that which can be changed, although it be not actually changed, is able not to be that which it had been; and hence that which not only is not changed, but also cannot at all be changed, alone falls most truly, without difficulty or hesitation, under the category of Being.[11]

In his *Summa Theologica*, Aquinas defends the traditional doctrine that God is "altogether immutable." He gives three reasons. First, God, as the Creator and first cause of all things, "must be pure act, without admixture of any potentiality." Change involves movement from potentiality to actuality. "Hence it is evident that it is impossible for God to be in any way changeable." Second, "everything which is moved, remains in part as it was, and in part passes away." And this requires composition; yet God is "altogether simple." Therefore, "it is manifest that God cannot be moved." Third, "everything which is moved acquires something by its movement, and attains to what it had not attained previously. But since God is infinite, comprehending in Himself all the plenitude of perfection of all being, He cannot acquire anything new, nor extend Himself to anything whereto He was not extended previously." Hence such movement does not belong to God.[12]

The Protestant Reformers and the post-Reformation Reformed theologians take up the tradition of immutability and defend it vigorously. For Ulrich Zwingli, God is "pure, genuine, complete, simple, and unchangeable."[13] Calvin is scandalized by those who dare "imagine some change in the essence of God." In contrast, he affirms that "piety recognizes or allows no name which intimates that anything new has happened to God in himself."[14] Benedict Pictet argues that divine immutability "denotes nothing else than such a state of the divine essence and attributes, as is not subject to any change. Now this immutability is proved by scripture. . . . Besides, that which possesses all perfection, cannot be changed. If God changed, he would do so either *for the better,* or

---

11. Augustine, *On the Holy Trinity,* 5.2.3 (*NPNF,* 1st ser., 3, p. 88).

12. Aquinas, *SumTh,* 1.9.1, in *Basic Writings of Saint Thomas Aquinas,* vol. 1, ed. Anton C. Pegis (New York: Random House, 1945), pp. 70-71.

13. Zwingli, *On Providence,* 1, quoted in Muller, *PRRD,* 3, p. 311.

14. Calvin, *Institutes,* 1.13.8, in *Institutes of the Christian Religion,* vol. 1, ed. John T. McNeill, trans. Ford Lewis Battles (Philadelphia: Westminster, 1960), p. 130.

for the worse, or *for something equal.*"[15] He speaks for all of the orthodox Reformed when he says: "[T]here is no mutation in God, neither in his essence, nor in his eternity, nor in his understanding, nor in his will. . . . This immutability of God is the fulcrum of our faith and the foundation of our hope."[16]

Theology of Divine Immutability

Divine immutability is the traditional doctrine, and this should motivate us to think carefully before we discard it. But can we defend it today?

Types of Change and Immutability

What does it mean for a thing to change or to remain constant? Apparently, some things cannot change without ceasing to be. The concept of a triangle or a circle, for example, cannot change. A two-sided figure is not a triangle in the least, and a set of points on a curved line, all of which are not equidistant from a point not on the line (the center), is not a circle at all. Now triangular and circular objects can be blue, red, or green, and they can vary in size, texture, or composition. They can change from possessing one of these properties to possessing another. However, none of these properties is essential to the definition of a triangle or a circle. They are accidental and have to do with the triangle's or the circle's embodiments in the material world. These examples show that an unchanging concept loses or gains accidental properties in its worldly embodiment.

In everyday experience we see change as development, maintaining equilibrium, or decay in concrete things. We see a baby grow into adulthood; we see seedlings grow into trees; we see new housing developments spring up; we see

---

15. Pictet, *Christian Theology*, 2.8, trans. Frederick Reyroux (London: Seeley and Burnside, 1834), p. 99.

16. Pictet, *Christian Theology*, 2.8, p. 99. For more on the Reformed view of immutability, see Muller, *PRRD*, 3, pp. 308-20; see also Heinrich Heppe, *Reformed Dogmatics*, rev. and ed. Ernst Bizer, trans. G. T. Thomson (1950; reprint, London: Wakeman Great Reprints, n.d.), pp. 67-68. Post-Reformation Lutheran dogmatics affirmed divine immutability as firmly as did the Reformed. See Robert D. Preus, *The Theology of Post-Reformation Lutheranism*, vol. 2, *God and His Creation* (St. Louis: Concordia, 1972), pp. 100-103 (hereafter *TPRL*); see also Heinrich Schmid, *Doctrinal Theology of the Evangelical Lutheran Church*, trans. Charles A. Hay and Henry Jacobs (1899; reprint, Minneapolis: Augsburg, 1961), pp. 118-19. Affirmations of divine immutability are to be found in the Reformed Belgic Confession (1561) and the Westminster Confession of Faith (1647), as well as the Roman Catholic *Dogmatic Constitution of the First Vatican Council* (1870).

the surf erode the foundation of a beach home; we see illness come upon a loved one and eventually overtake her in death. Above all, we experience change in ourselves — in our bodies and minds. Our bodies develop according to a pattern of progressive change, which we identify mostly with our genetic codes. Our minds appear programmed for curiosity. We learn, and then we use what we have learned as a foundation for more learning — and more. Other changes seem to be induced by chance or by our choices. Here too, however, we notice the continuity in the changes. If I remodel my house, I can speak of the "changes" I have made to it. But if I tear it down and build a new one, it hardly makes sense to speak of the new house as a form of the old one. We change radically in the course of our lives. The statement "I have changed so much that I am not the same person" makes little sense if we take it strictly. In all changes, I must remain the same in some way; otherwise, the changes could not be attributed to me.

The tradition, as we have seen from the statements of Augustine, John of Damascus, and Aquinas, denies that change applies to God. None of the conditions required for change pertains to God. For God has no accidental properties to gain or lose, and God is not located in a particular place and time so that he needs to move to become present in others. God has no potential to become something he is not: God is essentially perfect, fully actual from all eternity. God does not need to become better or more mature or wiser or more knowledgeable or more loving.

Value Aspects of Change and Immutability

We also view change within a framework of value. Change and immutability bring about or conserve good or evil, but change and immutability are not good or bad in themselves. Thomas Weinandy observes that "change as change is neither good nor bad, but it is good or bad depending on whether it increases or decreases the perfection of the creature."[17] Change appears in a positive light when we contemplate a natural endowment moving from a potential to an actual state as in learning a skill or maturing physically and emotionally. The prospect of change strikes us as hopeful when we contemplate the repentance, reformation, and healing of someone caught in an addiction or in a life of crime. However, we consider some changes as being for the worse: a loss of faith, getting caught in an addiction, contracting a bad marriage, falling ill, and becoming corrupt in character. Likewise, we evaluate immutability by the na-

17. Weinandy, OFM, *Does God Change? The Word's Becoming in the Incarnation* (Still River, MA: St. Bede's Publications, 1985), p. 128.

ture of the constant thing: we value the immutability of a good character, the reliability of the laws of nature, the stability of a currency, and the faithfulness of a spouse. We cherish the immutability of good things. We complain about the immutability of evil things or about things that could become better but stubbornly remain the same. The immutability of a toothache, a dripping faucet, failure at chemistry — these are unwelcome continuities. Therefore, I conclude that we value change and immutability for the sake of the good they make available to us. In summary, I can think of four possible value states of change and immutability: (1) change for the better, (2) change for the worse, (3) immutability of evil, and (4) immutability of good. Clearly, we prefer "immutability of good" over the others.

God, Immutability, and Change

I concluded above that change and immutability are not good or bad in themselves. Does this mean that we can attribute the positive aspects of change — as well as those of immutability — to God? I can venture an affirmative answer to that if we keep in mind an important difference between change and immutability. Change is a positive value only in the face of evil or imperfection. We value it for the sake of the good for which we hope. Only because we do not as yet have that good do we value change. Immutability, in contrast, is a positive value when good is possessed, and it is a negative value when we are beset by evil and imperfection. When we finally get the anticipated good, we will not want to change it. What is good in change is already wrapped up in the immutability of God's perfection. In Simon Tugwell's words, "All richness that we can only experience successively is there all at once."[18] We hope that God will change the world, since the world suffers from evil and imperfection; but we equally hope that God himself will not change. God possesses (and is) the highest good.

Traditional theology did not consider it appropriate to attribute change to God, whereas it did attribute immutability to him. Michael Dodds argues that Aquinas (representative of the tradition) understands the divine nature to be incomprehensible, and thus the crux of his discussion of immutability is how may we speak of God most appropriately. According to Dodds, Aquinas does not argue that by grasping the concept of immutability we grasp God's nature. Immutability is simply the most appropriate way to speak of God. Aquinas carefully distinguishes God's immutability from that of creatures. In the end, "immutability seems to signify divine being *(esse)* more appropriately [than

---

18. Tugwell, "Spirituality and Negative Theology," *New Blackfriars* 68 (1987): 261.

motion] since it more clearly indicates the distinction of divine being from all other things and the transcendence of divine being above all our human concepts and knowledge."[19]

When the tradition says that God is immutable, it means that God is God eternally, forever "dynamic and boundless perfection."[20] He is and always will be himself. In Scripture and the tradition this theme resonates with joy, confidence, and hope. God is good, powerful, patient, righteous, and loving — immutably. There is nothing negative in God's immutability. In no sense are we merely "stuck" with God. God is no eternally boring, one-dimensional repetition. God is immutable, "not because he is static, inert, or inactive [like a rock] but precisely because he is so much in act that it is ontologically impossible to be more in act."[21] Nothing evil or even not-yet-perfect resides in God: God is unchangeably full, rich, active, present, attentive, compassionate, and loving. Hence, learning to know God is an exhilarating, engaging, joyous, and glorious journey.

Contemporary Objections to Immutability

Many contemporary theologians, from a variety of perspectives, reject what they understand to be the traditional doctrine of immutability. Barth critiques the traditional doctrine as expounded by the Reformed theologian Amandus Polanus (1561-1610) when he says that Polanus's views do "not correspond in the least with the biblical passages" he cites in support of his position. The traditional doctrine identifies God as the *"pure immobile."* But it is not possible for such a God to have a "relationship between Himself and a reality distinct from himself. . . . [T]he *pure immobile* is death."[22] Apparently, Barth identifies (mistakenly) the tradition's notion of God's unmoveability — that is, his perfect and purely active life — with the immutability of death. Richard Muller points out the irony that Barth's own view of immutability ends up "being quite close to that of orthodoxy."[23] Preferring the word "constancy" to the term "immutability," Barth affirms that God is constant in "His knowing, willing and acting and therefore in His person." "The real truth is . . . that God is 'immutable,' and

19. Dodds, *The Unchanging God of Love: A Study of the Teaching of St. Thomas Aquinas on Divine Immutability in View of Certain Contemporary Criticism of this Doctrine* (Fribourg: Editions Universitaires Fribourg Suisse, 1986), p. 224.

20. Dodds, *The Unchanging God of Love*, p. 227.

21. Weinandy, *Does God Change?* p. 78.

22. *CD*, 2/1, p. 494.

23. *PRRD*, 3, p. 309.

this is the living God in His freedom and love, God Himself. He is what He is in eternal actuality."[24]

The open theist John Sanders argues that the traditional doctrine "undermines the personal and living God who establishes a covenantal relationship and remains faithful to it."[25] Though "the essence of God does not change," Sanders urges, God changes "in experience, knowledge, emotions and actions."[26] In his essay entitled "The Immutability of God," philosopher Norris Clarke cautiously criticizes the traditional doctrine for failing to aid contemporary "existential consciousness seeking an intellectual understanding of itself."[27] The "traditional doctrine of the God of philosophy," Clarke observes, "seems to many to be in conflict with the exigencies of the God of personal religion" (p. 44). Clarke seeks to make room within a Thomist framework for a kind of change in God. To that end he proposes a distinction between God's real being and his "intentional" being (p. 45). Intentional being is the existence of objects of knowledge in the consciousness of the knower. God's real being would remain unchanged, but his intentional being would have been different had he decided to create a world different from the one he created (p. 56).[28] And God remains the same even though his intentional being changes with the changes of the world (p. 50).

The most sustained and thoroughgoing critique of immutability, however, comes from the process philosophers Alfred North Whitehead and Charles Hartshorne and their theological followers.[29] Process thought challenges the

24. *CD*, 2/1, pp. 494-95.

25. Sanders, *The God Who Risks*, p. 186.

26. *The God Who Risks*, p. 187. For more criticisms of immutability from an open theist perspective, see Clark Pinnock, *Most Moved Mover*, pp. 85-88; Pinnock, "God Limits His Knowledge," in *Predestination & Free Will: Four Views of Divine Sovereignty & Human Freedom*, ed. D. Basinger and R. Basinger (Downers Grove, IL: InterVarsity Press, 1986), pp. 146-47, 155; Richard Rice, "Biblical Support for a New Perspective," in *The Openness of God*, pp. 28, 36, 47-49; John Sanders, "Historical Considerations," in *The Openness of God*, p. 79; Clark Pinnock, "Systematic Theology," in *The Openness of God*, pp. 117-18; William Hasker, "A Philosophical Perspective," in *The Openness of God*, pp. 129, 133; Clark Pinnock, "From Augustine to Arminius: A Pilgrimage in Theology," in *The Grace of God, The Will of Man*, ed. Clark Pinnock (Minneapolis: Bethany House Publishers, 1989), p. 24; and Pinnock, "Between Classical and Process," in *Process Theology*, ed. Ronald Nash (Grand Rapids: Baker, 1987), p. 322.

27. "The Immutability of God," in *God Knowable and Unknowable*, ed. Robert J. Roth, SJ (New York: Fordham University Press, 1973), p. 43.

28. Another Thomistic thinker, William J. Hill, argues for a position similar to Clarke's; see Hill, "Does the World Make a Difference to God?" *The Thomist* 38 (1974): 146-64; see also Hill, "Does God Know the Future? Aquinas and Some Moderns," *Theological Studies* (1975): 3-18. For a critique of Clarke and Hill, see Theodore J. Kondoleon, "The Immutability of God: Some Recent Challenges," *The New Scholasticism* 58 (1984): 293-315.

29. I will focus on their critique of the traditional doctrine rather than on the process alter-

foundational assumption of the traditional doctrine, that is, that a perfect being cannot change without becoming imperfect.[30] Hartshorne argues that the classical notion of perfection is self-contradictory. No being can possess the perfect actualization of every possible "value," because values conflict with each other. For example, you cannot paint your room red all over and blue all over at the same time; you cannot move and not move to Texas simultaneously; and you can't secure the advantages of working at home and also those of the office at the same time. Therefore, no being can possess the perfection of all possibilities.[31]

With the traditional idea of perfection set aside as incoherent, Hartshorne proposes an alternative model. According to Hartshorne, the traditional doctrine of immutability depends excessively on the way of negation. By negating change, plurality, potentiality, relativity, dependence, and other aspects of the world, the classical doctrine excludes all the "excellencies" in those things. And a being without the excellencies found in these qualities cannot be perfect. A perfect being must contain *all* excellencies, which implies that a perfect being must embrace stability *and* change, unity *and* variety, actuality *and* potentiality, and independence *and* dependence. Within Hartshorne's framework, "to be supremely excellent God must at any particular time be the greatest conceivable being, the all-worshipful being."[32] This means that God must not only be the most stable being but also the most changeable being. A perfect being must be able to adapt immediately to a constantly changing universe.

To encompass all the excellencies we experience in one being without contradiction, Hartshorne proposes a dipolar model of the divine nature. God has both an abstract and a concrete nature. God's "abstract nature" is his infinite potential, which never changes, whereas God's "concrete nature" is mutable

---

native they propose. For responses to the process view of God, see Weinandy, *Does God Change?*; E. L. Mascall, *He Who Is* (London: Libra Books, 1966); and Robert Neville, *Creativity and God: A Challenge to Process Theology* (New York: Seabury, 1980).

30. For this exposition of Hartshorne, I am indebted to Daniel A. Dombrowski, "Must a Perfect Being Be Immutable?" in *Hartshorne, Process Philosophy and Theology*, ed. Robert Kane and Stephen H. Phillips (Albany, NY: SUNY Press, 1989), pp. 91-111.

31. Hartshorne articulates this objection in many works. Perhaps his most concise statement on this subject is in *The Divine Relativity* (New Haven: Yale University Press, 1948), pp. 18-22. See also Hartshorne, *Man's Vision of God* (New York: Harper and Brothers, 1941), pp. 1-56; and Hartshorne, *The Logic of Perfection and Other Essays in Metaphysics* (LaSalle, IL: Open Court, 1962), pp. 33-44. For a sympathetic review of Hartshorne's arguments on this subject, see David A. Pailin, "The Utterly Absolute and the Totally Related: Change in God," *New Blackfriars* 68 (1987): 243-55; see also Santiago Sia, "The Doctrine of God's Immutability: Introducing the Modern Debate," *New Blackfriars* 68 (1987): 220-31.

32. Dombrowski, "Must a Perfect Being Be Immutable?" p. 99.

and finite.[33] Properties that would contradict each other if possessed in the same way by one being become compatible if possessed in different ways. In summary, for process theology, far from being excluded by the perfection of the divine nature, change is necessary to its perfection.[34]

In Defense of Immutability

A Caricature Is Not an Argument

What shall we say to these criticisms? First, let us deal with the critics' descriptions of the traditional doctrine. All of the critics mentioned present the tradition as if it were saying that God is unrelated, static, cold, aloof, unresponsive, and dead. But, as we have already seen, this caricature bears little resemblance to the God of the church fathers, Augustine, Aquinas, and orthodox Protestantism. For them, God is not "static" — a term that applies to something that has potential for movement but is stuck in its present state — but pure act.[35] God's immutability is not the immutability of a rock but the immutability of a perfectly dynamic and unlimited life. Michael Dodds, Gerald Hanratty, and Thomas Weinandy have given persuasive answers to Aquinas's critics.[36] Richard Muller has done the same for the post-Reformation Reformed theologians.[37] God's immutability does not render him unrelated and aloof; rather, it guarantees his ability to be absolutely present as our totally reliable Creator. If God were not immutable, he could not come near to us — as in the incarnation — without being changed by the relationship.[38] God could not be himself *for us.* Far from making God unresponsive and dead, his immutability assures us that God is life itself without any admixture of death (that is, mere potentiality). God is eternally and proactively our good in every situation.

33. Dombrowski, "Must a Perfect Being Be Immutable?" pp. 99-100.

34. See Lewis S. Ford, "Process and Thomist Views Concerning Divine Perfection," in *The University as Journey: Conversations with W. Norris Clarke,* ed. Gerald A. McCool, SJ (New York: Fordham University Press, 1988), pp. 115-29.

35. See Kondoleon, "The Immutability of God," p. 298, for his reasons why the term "static" should not be applied to God's immutability.

36. See Dodds, *The Unchanging God of Love;* Hanratty, "Divine Immutability and Impassibility Revisited," in *At the Heart of the Real,* ed. Fran O'Rourke (Dublin: Irish Academic Press, 1992), pp. 135-62; and Weinandy, *Does God Change?*

37. *PRRD,* 3, pp. 308-20.

38. On this point, see Weinandy, *Does God Change?* pp. 182-86.

A critique of the traditional doctrine of immutability that deserves our serious attention will have to move beyond the refutation by caricature that prevails in much of the literature. We are past the time when the critics were beating a dead horse; rather, they are beating a "nonexistent horse."[39]

Must Perfection Be Perfect?

The challenge to the argument from perfection, in contrast, presents a substantive argument and requires a serious response. The tradition argues that immutability follows from the premise that God is absolutely perfect, and something absolutely perfect cannot change without falling from perfection. Process thinkers and open theists attack this argument. I will focus on process thinkers in this section, because open theists borrow their arguments from process philosophy; thus, in answering process objections, I will have also answered open-theist objections. Process thinkers attempt to refute the traditional understanding of perfection in a twofold way: (1) by arguing that the classic understanding of perfection is self-contradictory; (2) by redefining perfection so that change in a perfect being does not bring about imperfection but maintains the highest level of perfection possible under new circumstances.

I acknowledge the difficulty of comparing internal elements of two vastly different systems: traditional theology and process philosophy. We need a clear statement of the most fundamental disagreement between the two, and Robert Sokolowski provides just such a statement. He identifies the Christian conviction that God is absolutely independent of the world as the definitive difference between Christian theology and all other ways of viewing the divine. Since God created the world freely, God would be God "in undiminished greatness and goodness even if the world had not been."[40] God plus the world is *not* greater than God alone. Process philosophy begins by rejecting this foundational conviction. "In the first place," Whitehead contends in his famous Gifford Lectures, "God is not to be treated as an exception to all metaphysical principles, invoked to save their collapse. He is their chief exemplification."[41] For process thought, God and the world fall under one grand system of metaphysical principles. God plus the world *is* greater than God alone. God cannot be the full actualization of all possible ex-

---

39. Muller, *PRRD*, 3, p. 310.

40. Sokolowski, *The God of Faith and Reason: Foundations of Christian Theology* (Washington, DC: The Catholic University of America Press, 1995), pp. 1-11; see also Sokolowski, *Eucharistic Presence: A Study in the Theology of Disclosure* (Washington, DC: The Catholic University of America Press, 1994), p. 19.

41. Whitehead, *Process and Reality: An Essay in Cosmology* (New York: Macmillan, 1929), p. 521.

cellencies, because this would make him independent of the world and exempt him from the world's principles. Clearly, when process thinkers criticize the traditional understanding of divine perfection, they are simply paraphrasing their more fundamental rejection of God's independence from the world.

Traditional theology sees things very differently. Since God exists in absolute independence from the world, there is no good in the world that does not find its origin in God. Since every good in the world originates from the one God, the ultimate harmony of good is axiomatic. The problem of incompatibility among goods arises from a departure from this axiom and a laying down of the opposing axiom that all beings must be subject to the laws and limits of the physical universe.

So far I have dealt with Hartshorne's criticisms on the level of fundamental assumptions. But I think his arguments are vulnerable even on an empirical level. Must some actualized goods inherently conflict with others? We can readily admit that we (as finite and created beings) cannot realize all the possibilities of our existence. But is this *because* genuine possibilities for excellence contradict each other? I may never achieve perfect kindness, but surely this is not *because* I cannot be kind in all imaginable ways. Might not the 9,000th kind deed simply be a repetition of the same perfect kindness that was exemplified in the 8,999 preceding kind deeds? Is the good of a blue room its blueness, or the good of a red room its redness? It must be something else. If it were its blueness as such, painting it red would make it evil. And if it is something else — for example, its ability to actualize some potential for happiness in our natures or to bring glory to God — then the good of a blue room may well be identical to the good of a red room, even though a room cannot be both red and blue at the same time. The very fact that we must choose one good while letting another one go indicates not a conflict of good with good but the partial and imperfect good in all finite things. Therefore, finite things point beyond themselves to an infinite good that makes them all good. Instances of *imperfect* realizations of the good are often incompatible; but I see no reason to think that perfect realizations of good will contradict each other. And for the tradition, God is the only perfect realization of the good.

According to the second prong of the process critique, a being that includes all the "excellencies" found in the world — including change, passivity, and potential — is more perfect than one that excludes some of these excellencies. This argument is open to criticism on at least three fronts. First, it misrepresents the tradition and then critiques the caricature it has created. Weinandy comments wryly on this situation: "This is a devastating array of criticisms. The only problem is finding someone or some position to whom or to which they refer."[42] The

---

42. Weinandy, *Does God Change?* p. 126.

traditional doctrine of immutability was not derived by totally negating the changing world. It also affirms the good in the world.[43] As I have argued above, neither immutability nor change is good in itself. Indeed, according to Aristotle, they are nothing at all in themselves: "[T]here is no such thing as motion [i.e., change] over and above the things."[44] Their value depends on what changes or remains the same.

The tradition did not affirm immutability in itself as the highest state of perfection. Rather, it affirmed the immutability *of the highest good* as the highest state. The Creator's immutable perfection includes unchangingly the good that can be achieved in created things through change. Divine immutability thus transcends the imperfections of both worldly immutability and change, while it includes and heightens their excellencies. Process thought's argument presupposes the false notion that change in itself is good: only if change is good in itself can it be a loss of good to exclude it. However, it should be clear to anyone that things can change for the worse as well as for the better.[45]

Second, process philosophy's redefinition is a strange sort of "perfection." It is no longer understood as the complete realization of the highest good, that is, as *absolute* perfection. God's perfection is, rather, the greatest realization of excellence possible at any one time. It is "perfection" only with respect to the finite actuality achieved to date. That is, God's "perfection" is in principle no different from that of any other finite being. God needs the world process to help him achieve more of his potential, which he will never fully achieve. Process philosophy's critique of the traditional argument from perfection fails because its concept of changeable perfection turns out to be "perfection" in name only. The word "perfect" cannot be meaningfully used of a being that possesses infinitely more potential than it has yet realized and is totally dependent on the world process for its continued self-realization. Instead of improving our concept of perfection by including change, process thought simply speaks in exalted terms of old-fashioned imperfection.

A Dipolar God?

Now we come to the third vulnerable point in the process alternative to immutability. Contemporary critiques of the traditional doctrine of immutability of-

43. See Dodds's discussion of Aquinas's use of the ways of causation and eminence in his doctrine of immutability (*The Unchanging God of Love*, pp. 208-27). See also Tugwell's defense of negative theology, "Spirituality and Negative Theology," *New Blackfriars* 68 (1987): 257-63.

44. *Physics*, 3.1, in *The Basic Works of Aristotle*, ed. Richard McKeon (New York: Random House, 1941), pp. 253-55.

45. Weinandy, *Does God Change?* p. 128.

ten posit a polarity within God. Hartshorne, as noted above, distinguishes between God's abstract and concrete natures; Clarke differentiates God's real being from his intentional being; and John Sanders discriminates between God's nature and God's experience of the world. In each case, God changes in some respects and remains immutable in others. Hartshorne's view is clearly more radical than Clarke's or Sanders's. For Hartshorne, God changes in his real being, his concrete nature. God does not change, of course, in his abstract nature. But the abstract nature does not really exist; it is merely potential. Let us leave aside Hartshorne and focus on the less radical proposals of Clarke and Sanders, which are more appealing to a wide range of theologians not willing to accept the finite God of process philosophy. As we shall see, however, theologies that retain some aspects of the traditional doctrine while accepting some aspects of process philosophy contain inconsistencies that push them toward one or the other original systems.

Supposedly, the concept of a dipolar God solves the problem, insoluble within the traditional framework, of how an unchanging God can relate to a changing world. God does not change in nature and character, these theologians are careful to say, but God does change in experience, emotions, and actions in relation to the changes in creation. According to this viewpoint, God is indeed eternally the fullness of deity: he never acquires moral flaws or needs to improve in character. He is who he is, eternally. However, in order to be able to relate to his changing creation, God must be able to change in experience. That is, knowing a thing that is changing requires a corresponding change in the divine mind. Examples of this principle could be multiplied. As I watch a sunrise or a passing train, my mental experience of the images, with their qualities, proportions, and relationships, is constantly changing. My mind changes from a state of not knowing to knowing to remembering these things. Furthermore, my emotional state also changes in response to the beauty or ugliness, the danger or harm or good of what I sense in the images.

Finally, the changes in my experience may call forth the need to act in response to new circumstances. As I have observed above, the human capacity to change in these ways is a relatively good thing; not being able to change in response to changing circumstances would be death. Imagine the comic scene of always being too slow to respond to surrounding change: you would cross the street after the light has turned red, raise your glove to catch the baseball after it hit you in the forehead, and laugh a minute after a joke's punch line has been delivered.

However, the surface plausibility of this proposal evaporates upon further thought. The original reason for proposing a dipolar view of God was that an unchanging God cannot relate to a changing world. The dualistic proposal does not solve this problem but pushes it back into God's own life. With the same logic, we can ask how the unchanging nature and character of God can relate to the changing experience and action of God. Must we posit another duality, and another, and so on to infinity? Furthermore, positing a duality in God because of the premise that an unchanging God is dead and impersonal does not remove the supposed "deadness" in God. It merely submerges it into God's unchanging pole.

The dipolar model projects into God the real distinction between essence and existence that limits and structures the being of all creatures. God's nature becomes merely his potential, while his existence is understood as the finite actuality of *some* of his potential. Whereas the tradition taught that we are *really* related to the fully personal God — to the unchanging and eternal fullness of the God who is pure act — dipolar theism teaches that we are *really* related to the finite actualization of the divine nature as it stands at the moment; we are only *potentially* related to the infinite divine nature.

Clearly, the dipolar proposal, even in its moderate form, will work a revolution in the doctrine of God. Such an approach must reject God's simplicity and insert composition into God. Its distinction between essence and existence undermines God's unique uniqueness as the only God and the only possible God. God's independence is threatened, for God could not be who he is without the world. The dipolar proposal requires that God's way of knowing be passive and temporal. In short, no aspect of the doctrine of God will remain unchanged.

Can an Unchanging God Respond to Our Needs?

One of the more popular rhetorical arguments against divine immutability asks us whether we want a God who is responsive to our needs or one who is unresponsive to them. If God cannot change, he cannot respond. Only a changing God can respond to our changing needs, the argument runs. The choice is obvious. The word "responsive" strikes a positive chord in us: it connotes someone who listens to our concerns and comes to our aid at once and in a way appropriate to our circumstances. On the other hand, the word "unresponsive" connotes an uncaring person deaf to our cries, someone who will not move a finger to help us. But the word "responsive" is not always positive either. A punch in the nose is just as much a "response" to a hearty greeting as a handshake is. We would prefer unresponsiveness to that kind of response! What is more important, receiving the good things we need from God *as a response* or *receiving* them from him? According to the tradition of immutability, God's eternal goodwill is manifested in time in his daily provision for us. God's loving care for us is better than responsive: it is immutably responsive or super-responsive. Because he is our eternal and unchanging good, he can be our good at every moment in time.[46]

The Impassibility of God

The traditional doctrine of God's impassibility is closely related to that of immutability.[47] One theologian defined impassibility as "immutability with regard to one's feeling, or the inner quality of one's inner life."[48] The doctrine of immutability affirms that God is not subject to change in any respect; the doctrine of impassibility declares that nothing can disturb God's heart or rob him of his joy. Unlike human beings and the gods of mythology, God is not subject to irrational or malformed passions. The doctrine does not assert that God has no heart, no feelings of love, wrath, joy, or jealousy. It asserts rather that God's "emotional state" — we are stretching language here — is in no way caused or conditioned by anything outside of God.[49] God's "emotions" are his own freely self-enacted being.

Scripture does not explicitly say, "Nothing can disturb God's heart or rob him of his joy." However, the same texts that assert God's immutability also teach his impassibility by implication; for, if God is not subject to change in any respect, he certainly cannot be deprived of his joy or driven to irrational behavior. On the other hand, Scripture speaks explicitly of God's love, anger, joy, and jealousy. It even speaks of God's sorrow, pain, and regret. And the suffering and death of the Son of God stands at the center of the Christian faith. In the passion of Jesus, God reveals the depth of his love for the world. Clearly, no theology that takes Scripture seriously can understand God's "emotional state" as the pure negation of passion. We must not replace the God of Scripture with a passionless, unfeeling, and cold abstraction. In the sections that follow I shall endeavor to develop a doctrine of impassibility that is consistent with Scrip-

---

46. For an incisive explanation of the traditional view of God's immutable action, see David B. Burrell, "Divine Practical Knowing: How an Eternal God Acts in Time," in *Divine Action: Studies Inspired by the Philosophical Theology of Austin Farrar*, ed. Brian Hebblethwaite and Edward Henderson (Edinburgh: T&T Clark, 1990), pp. 93-102; see also Michael J. Dodds, OP, "St. Thomas and the Motion of the Motionless God," *New Blackfriars* 68 (1987): 233-42.

47. According to Muller, *PRRD*, 3, pp. 309-10, the post-Reformation Reformed theologians divide their treatment of the issues we are discussing between the headings of immutability and the divine "affections."

48. Marcel Sarot, "Patripassionism, Theopaschitism and the Suffering of God: Some Historical and Systematic Considerations," *Religious Studies* 26 (1990): 368.

49. Weinandy, *Does God Suffer?* pp. 38-39, 70.

ture's teaching on God's immutability *and* its teaching on God's passionate love for the world.

Why Impassibility?

Scripture proclaims both that God is constant and that he is intimately related to our changing world. It proclaims that God is not subject to change; yet it declares that God loves the world, that he is angry at sin, and that the Son of God suffered in his flesh for our sins. Scripture does not directly address the question of how to reconcile these two lines of thought. In theological reflection, however, we must deal directly with this apparent tension, and in my reflections I will address several important questions. What is passion, and why does the tradition view it as an imperfection? Does the traditional doctrine of impassibility merely negate passion in God and view him as emotionless? Does God suffer in his dealings with the world, especially in the suffering of Christ? Does the doctrine of impassibility manifest God's praiseworthiness and comfort the suffering?

Passion and Impassibility

Since we are seeking to understand the doctrine of impassibility, we must clarify the concept of passion *(pathe)*. What is it about passion that the tradition found objectionable? The early Stoics viewed all emotions as irrational and hence inherently defective. They listed four basic passions that were to be eradicated: distress, pleasure, fear, and desire. Later Stoics, admitting that some passions were positive, developed the category of *eupatheiai,* good feelings, to balance off the bad ones. The Peripatetic school, Aristotle's disciples, considered the emotions neutral as long as they are held in moderation, an ideal they called *metriopatheia.*[50] As these three different views attest, there is "no one unified account" of the passions, human or divine, in Greek and Hellenistic philosophy.[51]

When we hear the English word "passion,"[52] our first thought may be of sexual passion. Sexual passion can be excited by sights, sounds, smells, and other external stimuli; it can also be induced by the release of chemicals from

---

50. Paul L. Gavrilyuk, *The Suffering of the Impassible God: The Dialectics of Patristic Thought* (Oxford: Oxford University Press, 2004), pp. 26-30.

51. *Suffering of the Impassible God,* pp. 21-22.

52. The Greek word *pathe* includes a wide range of meaning that cannot be captured in translation. The word "emotion" sounds less irrational than does the word "passion." See *The Suffering of the Impassible God,* p. 115, for references to scholarly discussions of translation problems.

within the body or introduced from without. We understand sexual passion, not as something constant and essential to a person's being, but as an intermittent state induced by a stimulus. The same holds true of other passions, such as anger, disgust, fear, love, and regret. In each case, our subjective state of mind is changed by something other than us. Our anger may be kindled by the insult of a passing motorist, or our disgust may be evoked by the sight of base actions. We fear whatever threatens to deprive us of something we need. We feel tender love when we see our little child asleep. On reflection, we regret doing something we ought not to have done. In all these cases, a subjective state of consciousness evoked by something outside us urges us toward certain actions. Something external facilitates a belief about a new state of affairs. We evaluate this state of affairs as good or evil, desirable or undesirable. This judgment, then, becomes a motive for action.[53]

In our analysis of change and immutability, we have discovered that neither is inherently good. We consider change good when it brings about something better, and we prefer immutability when it conserves something good. Change in emotional states displays the same ambiguity: we consider it admirable when someone is moved to compassion at the sight of suffering or stirred to righteous anger at injustice. However, when someone is moved to greed by the sight of our watch or ring, or to hate by the color of our skin, we consider it a change for the worse. Alternatively, we admire immutability in certain states of consciousness. We consider persons who are consistently loving, humble, and compassionate better people than those who move in and out of these states; and persons who are constantly vicious and full of greed, lust, and envy horrify us. The possible four states of immutability and change listed above apply to passions as well: (1) change for the better, (2) change for the worse, (3) immutability of evil, and (4) immutability of good. Again, in considering the passions, we find "immutability of good" to be preferable to the other alternatives, including even the first one. For, though change can bring good our way, it cannot guarantee that the good it brings will remain.

Impassibility and Its Function in Traditional Theology

We cannot do justice to the traditional doctrine of impassibility unless we keep its function and context in mind. In his study of impassibility in the church fathers,

---

53. My analysis of passion and emotion tends toward the "cognitive" theory of emotion, which has a long history. It is advocated today by William Lyons, *Emotions* (Cambridge, UK: Cambridge University Press, 1980). See the helpful summary of Lyons's book in Nicholas Wolterstorff, "Suffering Love," in *Philosophy and the Christian Faith*, ed. Thomas V. Morris (Notre Dame, IN: University of Notre Dame Press, 1988), pp. 213-14.

Paul Gavrilyuk concludes that impassibility functions generally as an "apophatic qualifier."[54] That is, it qualifies our language about God's emotions by warning us not to attribute evil and imperfection to God. Belief in God's impassibility played a pivotal role in Christianity's confrontation with pagan religion. In the face of pagan mythology, according to which the gods suffer such human-like passions as lust, greed, hatred, and envy, the church fathers denied that God ever does evil or ever exists in evil states of mind. Justin Martyr is typical: he points out that Christians no longer worship the immoral Dionysus, Apollo, Persephone, and Aphrodite because Jesus Christ taught believers to give themselves "to the unbegotten and impassible God."[55] According to Athenagoras (second century A.D.), "there is neither anger, nor desire and appetite, nor procreative seed" in the divine.[56] Irenaeus (c. 130–c. 200) affirms that "the Father of all is far removed from those affections and passions which have their place in humans."[57] In Gavrilyuk's judgment, the church fathers were "clearing the decks of popular theological discourse in order to make space for the God-befitting emotionally coloured characteristics such as mercy, love, and compassion."[58]

The church fathers did not understand God's impassibility to mean that God never experiences anything *like* emotion. In the judgment of G. L. Prestige, "[t]here is no sign that divine impassibility was taught with any view of minimizing the interest of God in his creation or his care and concern for the world that he had made."[59] On the contrary, they insisted that God knows the world and takes it into account. God loves his creation, is compassionate toward the suffering, wrathful toward the rebellious, and gracious toward the repentant. Impassibility functioned to distinguish God's "emotions" from their human namesakes. The church fathers insisted that God loves and exercises compassion and anger in a manner that befits God, that is, impassibly. Lactantius (A.D.240-320), for example, wrote an entire treatise defending the idea of the anger of God against those who thought it unworthy of God. God's anger is the reverse side of his eternal justice. God is immutable and impassible even in his anger.[60]

---

54. Gavrilyuk, *Suffering of the Impassible God,* p. 62.

55. Justin Martyr, *First Apology,* 1.25 (*ANF,* 1, p. 171).

56. Athenagoras, *A Plea for the Christians,* 21.4 (*ANF,* 2, p. 138).

57. Irenaeus, *Against All Heresies,* 2.15.3, quoted in Gavrilyuk, *Suffering of the Impassible God,* p. 50.

58. *Suffering of the Impassible God,* p. 51.

59. Prestige, *God in Patristic Thought,* 2nd ed. (London: SPCK, 1952), p. 11.

60. Lactantius, *De Ira Dei.* See Weinandy, *Does God Suffer?* pp. 97-107, for treatments of divine anger in Origen, Tertullian, Novation, and Lactantius. These writers agree that God can be angry, but, in Novation's words, "we are not to understand these to be asserted of him in the sense in which they are human vices" (p. 106).

The traditional doctrine of impassibility denies that God's love, compassion, wrath, and grace are passions in the ordinary sense of the term. God does not enter loving, compassionate, wrathful, and gracious states of mind at the instigation of external stimuli. For this would mean that his love and holiness are not his essential attributes: God's love and holiness would be caused by something outside him, and this would constitute a denial of God's essential independence. God is not passionate in the sense that his states of mind are triggered by another or come and go, or that his passions carry him along toward an action. God *is* his love, holiness, and compassion. God's attitude toward us cannot be altered by our actions and attitudes toward him, and we cannot make God's state of mind the plaything of our wills. We cannot, in our sullenness, hold God's joy for ransom.

The traditional doctrine also protects God's perfection, his pure actuality (more accurately "pure act").[61] The idea that God might change subjective states implies that God is not already perfectly loving, gracious, holy, and compassionate. If God loves universally and perfectly, could change ever be for the better? If God universally and perfectly judges and negates sin and evil, why expect change from him? The tradition declares that God's love, grace, holiness, and compassion are eternally perfect and thus do not need to change. They are already appropriate for every circumstance. Just as God is present in all space and time whether we are there or not, God maintains the same "state of mind" regarding the character of all events within the world. The reader will recall from the section on omnipresence that God is not less present elsewhere because he speaks from a mountain or joins himself to humanity in the person of the Son of God. Likewise, he is not less loving or holy toward other circumstances and at other times just because we experience his wrath or love or forgiveness here and now. And he is not more loving or gracious or patient with us just because we are aware of it on some occasions more than on others.

Passionate Impassibility

It should now be clear that the traditional doctrine of impassibility does not deny that God has all the good we see in passion and none of the evil or imperfection. We consider love, compassion, righteousness, and grace "passions" because we experience these good things as initiated by something outside us and

---

61. For a defense of impassibility from a Thomistic perspective, see Gerald Hanratty, "Divine Immutability and Impassibility Revisited," in *At the Heart of the Real*, pp. 135-62. Hanratty effectively rebuts the charge that an impassible God must be a "remote and impassive deity" (p. 155). He defends Aquinas's view that God's love and compassion are perfect *because* they are without suffering.

as compelling us toward actions we might not otherwise do. But their essential beauty and goodness do not consist in their being externally caused or in their alien power to move us. They are good and beautiful because these "states of mind" correspond to God's "state of mind." They fit our God-given nature, which is made in the image of God and is destined for union with God. Entering these "states of mind" at the instigation of external stimuli is a good thing only because *dwelling* in them is the better thing. God exists eternally in these states of mind. For love, compassion, righteousness, and grace are the uncaused and essential attributes of the God who "feels" them. This is the doctrine of impassibility. Far from declaring that God has no feelings, it declares that God is these "feelings" from all eternity. Indeed, the traditional doctrine of impassibility could better be described as *passionate* impassibility: that is, God's infinite and perfect passion is unchangeable. We cannot move God to love us more, have greater mercy on us, be more gracious to us, or exercise greater patience with us. He loved us from eternity, and his eternal love includes mercy toward the suffering, grace on the undeserving, and patience with the imperfect. His wrath is the eternal jealousy of his love that judges, condemns, and destroys everything that contradicts and would hinder his love for us.

Contemporary Critics of Impassibility

The doctrine of impassibility was held in high esteem by almost all theologians from every branch of the Christian tradition until recently. Perhaps no ecumenical doctrine of the church, however, has been abandoned so rapidly and thoroughly as the doctrine of impassibility. Indeed, contemporary discussions of the doctrine have become more of an occasion for scorning the church fathers, the medieval doctors, the Reformers, and anyone who defends it today than for serious theological reflection. Gavrilyuk complains about this state of affairs: "[S]uperficial criticism of divine *apatheia* on purely etymological grounds, without any serious analysis of its actual function in the thought of the Fathers, has become a convenient polemical starting point for the subsequent elaboration of a passibilist position."[62] The historical reasons for this defection and scorn are too complicated to explain here.[63] But those contemporary theologians who reject the doctrine charge that the church fathers replaced

62. *Suffering of the Impassible God*, p. 2.
63. For the early history of this abandonment, see J. K. Mosley, *The Impassibility of God: A Survey of Christian Thought* (Cambridge, UK: University of Cambridge Press, 1926); see also Bertrand R. Bransnett, *The Suffering of the Impassible God* (London: SPCK, 1928). Bransnett discusses several important authors whom Mosley does not discuss.

the passionate God of the Bible with the "absolute" of Greek metaphysics.[64] To hold to the doctrine of impassibility, they lament, is to offer an uncaring abstraction instead of a loving God to a hurting world. Furthermore, the critics claim, the doctrine of impassibility cannot account for the genuine suffering of Jesus. The doctrine of atonement is incomprehensible, they insist, unless God himself suffered on the cross for our sins. A. M. Fairbaim concludes: "There is no falser idea than that of the impassibility of God. . . . The very truth that came by Jesus Christ may be said to be summed up in the possibility of God."[65] The idea of a suffering God, the critics of impassibility say, is the only way to deal with the problem of evil. They find offensive the idea that God watches our suffering without suffering along with us.[66]

The Hellenization Theory

What can we say to these charges? Were the church fathers seduced into substituting the uncaring and impassible God of Greek philosophy for the loving and attentive God of the Bible? In his book Gavrilyuk labels this thesis the "Theory of Theology's Fall into Hellenistic Philosophy" and subjects it to a devastating criticism. He urges that "[t]he Theory of Theology's Fall into Hellenistic Philosophy must be once and for all buried with honours, as one of the most enduring and illuminating mistakes among the interpretations of the development of Christian doctrine" (p. 46). Gavrilyuk summarizes this theory in five points:

1. divine impassibility is an attribute of God in Greek and Hellenistic philosophy;
2. divine impassibility was adopted by the early fathers uncritically from the philosophers;
3. divine impassibility does not leave room for any sound account of divine emotions and divine involvement in history, as attested in the Bible;
4. divine impassibility is incompatible with the revelation of the suffering God in Jesus Christ;

64. A list of the advocates of this view would fill several pages. See T. E. Pollard, "The Impassibility of God," *Scottish Journal of Theology* 8 (1955): 353-64.

65. A. M. Fairbairn, *The Place of Christ in Modern Theology* (New York: Charles Scribner's Sons, 1916), p. 483.

66. For more recent critics of the doctrine of impassibility, see W. McWilliams, *The Passion of God: Divine Suffering in Contemporary Protestant Theology* (Macon, GA: Mercer University Press, 1985). Weinandy, in *Does God Suffer?* surveys recent authors and provides an extensive bibliography of authors dealing with the possibility/impassibility debate.

5. that fact was recognized by a minority group of theologians who affirmed that God is passible, going against the majority opinion (p. 177).

Gavrilyuk shows that each of these points is either false or misleading. The advocates of the "fall into Hellenism" assume that classic and Hellenistic philosophers were of one mind on the subject of divine impassibility. The critics need this first assumption because, if the church fathers were faced with options and impassibility were a debated doctrine, the accusation that the fathers were overwhelmed by the unanimous opinion of the Greeks would lose plausibility. The evidence, however, does not support the idea of such a consensus. As Gavrilyuk shows, there was a wide variety of opinion about divine impassibility within the Hellenistic world.[67] This philosophical pluralism also renders the second point of the "fall" theory suspect. "The Fathers could not possibly agree with the philosophers simply because the philosophers did not agree among themselves" (p. 36). With such a wide range of opinions available, there must have been a reason the fathers held tenaciously to divine impassibility. Far from uncritically adopting the views of the philosophers on impassibility, the church fathers critically appropriated the idea of impassibility in their quest for "God-befitting language" (pp. 14, 114, and 120-21). The function of impassibility in the church fathers was quite distinct from its function in any form of Hellenistic philosophy. As I have noted above, the church fathers used impassibility as an "apophatic qualifier" of divine emotions and rejected the idea of an unfeeling God (pp. 51, 60-63, 91).

In response to the third point of the "fall" theory, Gavrilyuk documents the church fathers' universal concern to affirm divine "God-befitting" emotions (love, joy, wrath, and compassion) and divine creation and providence against those who would deny them. I have already noted how Irenaeus, Lactantius, Tertullian, and Novation defended the biblical view of God against the Gnostics and Marcion.[68] It is noteworthy that Gavrilyuk points out that the Docetists and Gnostics were using impassibility to deny "any divine association with the unseemly human experiences of birth, suffering, and death" (p. 85). The fathers, contrary to the thesis of the "fall into Hellenism," held to the biblical faith in God as the Creator and to the real incarnation of the Word of God in the face of a demand made in the name of "un-

---

67. See *Suffering of the Impassible God,* pp. 21-37, for a survey. For other criticisms of the "fall" thesis, see W. V. Rowe, "Adolf von Harnack and the Concept of Hellenization," in *Hellenization Revisited: Shaping a Christian Response within the Greco-Roman World* (Lanham, MD: University Press of America, 1994), pp. 69-99; see also Roy Kearsley, "The Impact of Greek Concepts of God in the Christology of Cyril of Alexandria," *Tyndale Bulletin* 43 (1992): 307-29.

68. Weinandy, *Does God Suffer?* pp. 97-107.

qualified impassibility."[69] It was the Gnostics, not the orthodox fathers, who argued for the absolute negation of anything like passion in God.

In their struggle against these early anti-creation and anti-incarnation heresies, the fathers uttered many "theopaschite" (suffering God) statements. Ignatius speaks of "the passion of my God,"[70] and Hippolytus declares that "the impassible Word of God underwent suffering in the flesh."[71] This pattern continues in later centuries. Gregory of Nazianzus, in his second Easter sermon, explained it this way: "We needed an Incarnate God, a God put to death, that we might live . . . God crucified."[72] The advocates of the "fall into Hellenism" thesis either dismiss these statements as nonsense or cite them as evidence of a minority tradition that advocates a suffering God.[73] According to Gavrilyuk, in this strategy the advocates of the fall theory attempt to place the church fathers in a "false dilemma" between "unrestricted impassibility and an unrestricted passibility" (pp. 5-6). Instead, Gavrilyuk argues, the paradox expressed in the statement "the Impassible suffered" is expressive of the faith held by the church from the beginning. This faith was challenged in three fundamental ways. Doceticism denied "the reality of Christ's human experiences"; the Arians "gave up Christ's divine status"; and the Nestorians claimed "that divine actions and human experiences have different subjects" (p. 173). In each of these cases the orthodox fathers insisted that "the Impassible suffered," while their opponents insisted that the impassible cannot suffer. Each controversy forced the church to deepen its understanding of its paradoxical faith in the incarnation of God. The controversy with the Docetists solidified the church's commitment to a genuine incarnation. The long and painful Arian controversy established the church's faith in the incarnate "Christ's undiminished divinity" (p. 174). And, as Gavrilyuk points out, the Nestorian controversy brought this

---

69. *Suffering of the Impassible God,* pp. 2, 13, 20, 160-61, 171, 173. Gavrilyuk uses the term "unqualified impassibility" to designate the thoroughgoing removal of anything like emotion from God. Whereas contemporary advocates of the fall theory accuse the orthodox fathers of such a view, it was really their heretical opponents — such as the Docetists, Gnostics, and Arians — who advocated this view.

70. Ignatius, *Epistle to the Romans,* 6.3 (*ANF,* 1, p. 76).

71. Hippolytus, *Contra Noetum,* 15.3, quoted in *Suffering of the Impassible God,* p. 94. Gavrilyuk refers the reader to Michael Slusser, "Theopaschite Expressions in Second-Century Christianity as Reflected in the Writings of Justin, Melito, Celsus and Irenaeus" (Ph.D. diss., Oxford University, 1975). In an appendix to this work, Slusser compiles a long list of theopaschite citations from the second century.

72. Gregory of Nazianzus, *Oration 45,* 28-29 (NPNF, 2nd ser., 7, p. 433).

73. Jürgen Moltmann, in *The Trinity and the Kingdom,* trans. Margaret Kohl (Minneapolis: Fortress, 1993), p. 22, dismisses these statements as incoherent. Hallman, *The Descent of God,* pp. 46-109, advocates the "minority tradition" thesis.

line of development to a definitive conclusion by establishing that all experiences and passions and actions of the incarnate Son were those of the same subject, the only begotten Son of God. The one person of the incarnate Son of God, *homooúsios* with the Father, genuinely suffered in his flesh (p. 176).

Must God Suffer?

The critics of the traditional doctrine of impassibility argue that the divine nature is passible. Moving beyond the traditional teaching that the Son of God suffered in his flesh, they attribute suffering to the divine nature and all the persons of the Trinity, even apart from the incarnation.[74] For process theologian Paul Fiddes, "the cross is an actualization in our history of what is eternally true of God's nature. If indeed God suffers in the cross of Jesus in reconciling the world to himself, then there must always be a cross in the experience of God as he deals with a world which exists over against him."[75] Challenging one of the most cherished aspects of the traditional doctrine of God, Fiddes argues that "a suffering God is one who has potentialities within him which he has not yet actualized; only in this way can we speak of a God who suffers change in suffering."[76]

Jürgen Moltmann argues passionately for a suffering God:

> A God who cannot suffer is poorer than any man. For a God who is incapable of suffering is a being who cannot be involved. Suffering and injustice do not affect him. And because he is so completely insensitive, he cannot be affected or shaken by anything. He cannot weep, for he has no tears. But the one who cannot suffer cannot love either. So he is also a loveless being.[77]

What do the advocates of divine suffering mean by suffering? Process thinkers do not face great difficulties in defining divine suffering. Suffering means the same thing for God as it does for humans. God and humans, for all their differences, find themselves in the same situation: they are faced with a world that puts up resistance to their efforts to achieve good. In contrast, nonprocess advocates of divine suffering rarely clarify what they mean by suffering. Nicholas Wolterstorff is the only thinker I have found who explains the concept of suffering that he is working with. In his essay "Suffering Love," he says: "Suf-

---

74. Richard Bauckham, "'Only the Suffering God Can Help': Divine Passibility in Modern Theology," *Themelios* 3 (1985): 6-12.

75. Fiddes, *The Creative Suffering of God* (Oxford: Clarendon Press, 1988), p. 29.

76. Fiddes, *Creative Suffering*, p. 52.

77. Moltmann, *The Crucified God*, trans. R. A. Wilson and John Bowden (New York: Harper & Row, 1974), p. 222.

fering, when veridical, is an existential No-saying to something in reality."[78] We can understand the suffering character of this "No-saying" in human experience: our "no" to reality is ineffective and based on incomplete knowledge. But are we to imagine God's "No-saying" in this way? Does God's "no" meet with resistance? Apparently so for Wolterstorff. He argues that, because God loves the world, he experiences some of it joyfully and some of it sufferingly: "The claim of the tradition was that God's knowledge of the world gives him no vexation at all, no disturbance, no unhappiness. We have seen reason to think that that claim is false" (p. 229). For Wolterstorff, God's knowledge of the suffering in the world causes him vexation, disturbance, and unhappiness. But we are still left wondering about the nature of these negative emotions and what in God's nature renders him vulnerable to these passions.

No doubt this general silence about the nature of suffering is motivated by the difficulty of establishing a mediating position between the process view and the traditional view. Consequently, the non-process theologians' disparagement of the "uncaring" impassible God and pleas for a suffering and loving God may strike the attentive reader as not much more than rhetorical appeals to emotion. However, we must know what they mean by suffering before we can evaluate these claims.

In human experience, suffering is a passion. We suffer under the scourge of illness, torture, and the threat of death. We suffer when our children suffer from these things. We suffer at the very possibility of our suffering and at the suffering of those we love. In suffering we experience agony, dread, and hopelessness in the face of an external force that robs or threatens to rob us of the goods that sustain our lives and give us joy in the present and hope for the future. I conclude that suffering involves (1) a painful and undesirable state of mind, (2) induced by an external source, (3) that inflicts or threatens to inflict damage and loss to us. Everything that I have said about divine change and passion in general applies in the case of suffering. The question "Does God suffer?" inquires about the three things just listed. Does God ever experience a "painful and undesirable" state of mind that is induced by an "external cause"? Does God ever lose or come under threat of losing something necessary for his life and joy? I believe we must answer these questions with a firm and confident "no." If God could be made unhappy by evil, God would have been unhappy from eternity contemplating the possibility of evil; furthermore, he will be unhappy for eternity contemplating the history of evil. God cannot lose anything good, for he *is* his goodness, and he is the source of "every good and perfect gift" (James 1:17).

---

78. Wolterstorff, "Suffering Love," in *Philosophy and the Christian Faith,* ed. Thomas V. Morris (Notre Dame, IN: University of Notre Dame Press, 1988), p. 216.

Divine Love and Human Suffering

In view of the suffering of Jesus Christ, however, this "no" cannot remain the last word. Though I rejected the ideas that God changes and that God is subject to passion, I did not merely negate change and passion. I found something positive in them. In the same way, we cannot derive the attribute of impassibility merely by negating the concept of suffering. For suffering can have a positive as well as a negative meaning. As far as suffering tends toward nothingness, we must negate it. In suffering, good is taken from us incrementally; unchecked, suffering will accompany us all the way to annihilation. We suffer every time we give up a good. But sometimes we must give up one good for the sake of a greater one. We might choose to give up eating beef every night for the sake of our health. We might be willing to endure pain and sore muscles to improve our physical conditioning. Some are willing to "forsake all others" to enjoy married love. Many people find great joy in giving their time and money to help others in need. Mothers risk health and life and endure great pain to give life to their children. In some cases we find ourselves willing to suffer the loss of all things for the sake of something greater than ourselves. Jesus said, "Greater love has no one than this, that he lay down his life for his friends" (John 15:13).

Nothing is more beautiful than a love that gives its all for another. In our world, love must suffer because love must give to fulfill its nature: giving takes the form of giving up, of losing, of letting go. For we have a limited store of time, energy, and other goods, and to give them to others means having less for ourselves. But it is not the losing and hurting that we admire in suffering; it is the loving and the willing acceptance of loss and pain for the sake of another. And if that other is undeserving or a stranger or an enemy, we admire the willing sufferer all the more. According to our faith, God's love is manifest in the suffering of Christ, who died for the "ungodly" and his "enemies" (Rom. 5:6-8).

This text and many others declare unequivocally that God loves us and that he enacted his love in its purest form in the suffering and death of Christ. The Father gave his Son for us and gave himself to us in his Son. Christ's suffering and death were acts of the loving, righteous, and holy God. Undeniably, the Son of God suffered and died in his flesh. If we accept the Nicene faith that the Son is "very God of very God" and "of the same nature with the Father," is this not proof that God suffers? And did not the Father suffer, too, when he suffered the suffering of the Son?

My treatment of change and passion in general anticipates a negative answer to these questions. The Father did not suffer on the cross; the divine nature of the Son did not suffer on the cross. However, I cannot simply state this denial and move on. For this denial again raises the specter of a heartless God who cannot understand the suffering of the world. We must not lend any plausibility to such a distortion. God *is* love. From all eternity the Father gives himself completely to the Son in the Spirit; and in the Spirit the Son receives the Father and gives himself utterly to the Father in return. In God's triune life each person gives himself utterly to the others and dwells completely in the others. But the Father does not *suffer* in giving himself to the Son, nor does the Son in giving himself to the Father. The love among the persons of the Trinity is not painful but joyful, not forced but freely given. Indeed, it is in this mutual loving, giving, and indwelling that God lives his full, infinitely rich, and blessed life. The Father does not lose himself by giving himself to the Son: he *is* the Father only in his love for the Son. Nor does the Son lose himself by returning himself to the Father: he *is* the Son as he returns himself to the Father. God lives by and in love. God lives his infinitely full life precisely as each person "empties" himself in love for the others.[79]

When, in his love for the world, the Father gives himself to us in his Son, and the Son, in obedience to the Father, gives himself for us, the triune God does not change. For the Son *eternally* gives himself to the Father. In loving us and giving himself for us, the Son of God does nothing qualitatively different from what he had done from eternity.[80] The only difference is this: in his incarnate state, the Son of God gave himself in obedience to the Father *as a human being for all human beings.* Jesus did for us, and as one of us, what we should have done in our own right but would not and could not do. As a human being, the Son of God received his being gratefully from the Father and gave himself utterly to the Father in obedience. What he did in eternity as the Son of God, *homooúsios* with the Father, he did in time as the Son of God, *homooúsios* with us. In obedience to the Father, the incarnate Son gave himself in service to human beings. As he was a human being among other human beings, his divine loving and giving necessarily took the form of giving up, loss, and death. In this world, to love is to suffer — even for the Son of God.

Suffering accompanies every stage and every moment of human life. In life we are always lacking or losing, or standing under the threat of lacking or losing.

<hr/>

79. John M. Quinn, in "Triune Self-Giving: One Key to the Problem of Suffering," *The Thomist* 44 (1980): 196-97, develops a similar way of relating Jesus' suffering to the divine life of self-giving love while preserving divine impassibility.

80. The view I am advocating here resembles that of Hans Urs von Balthasar; see Gerard F. O'Hanlon, SJ, *The Immutability of God in the Theology of Hans Urs von Balthasar* (New York: Cambridge University Press, 1990); O'Hanlon, "Does God Change? — H. U. von Balthasar on the Immutability of God," *Irish Theological Quarterly* 53 (1987): 161-83. See also Steffen Lösel, "Murder in the Cathedral: Hans Urs von Balthasar's New Dramatization of the Doctrine of the Trinity," *Pro Ecclesia* 5 (1996): 427-39.

Death's shadow shades all of life, and suffering is constant. In the Son of God, however, humanity suffered *willingly and actively*. In love and utter obedience, this human being gave up to God completely what God had given to him. As human, the Son of God did in time what he does in eternity as God. In time, the Son receives his human nature in the power of the Holy Spirit, gives himself to the Father in return through the Spirit, and receives himself again in the resurrection by the power of the Holy Spirit. In this way God set humanity on a new foundation and gave it a new being; humanity, for its part, has become righteous, holy, immortal, and impassible in Christ. As the church fathers would put it, "the Impassible suffered that we who suffer might become impassible."

In answering the questions I have been addressing, traditional theology drew on the two natures/one person Christology that was championed by Cyril of Alexandria and came to definitive expression in the Council of Chalcedon (A.D. 451). While an extended treatment of Christology is beyond the scope of this study, and though some have invoked the two natures/one person Christology in a casual manner, I believe that it contains the only viable solution to the question of whether God suffers in Christ. According to orthodox Christian belief, Jesus Christ is both human and God, "truly human and truly divine." That is, divine and human natures are united in the person of the Son of God: though the natures are united in the Son's person, they retain their essential attributes. The Son of God does everything he does in his incarnate state *as* human — even his miracles. But he eats, walks, drinks, and breathes because he is human, and these activities are proper to human nature. He does not eat, drink, and walk *because* he is divine; as divine, the Son does not need to move in space or stay hydrated or take in fuel for energy. Paul speaks similarly when he says of Christ that "as to his human nature [he] was a descendant of David" (Rom. 1:3). Clearly, Paul does not think that the eternal Son is a descendant of David according to his divine nature.

When the Son of God suffered, he did not suffer as God but as human. He suffered in the same way that he ate, drank, and lived as a Jewish male — walking and sweating under the Middle Eastern sun. Belief in the Son of God's personal union with humanity does not justify the conclusion that God is Jewish or male, that he needs to eat and drink, that he sweats — or that God suffers. In Christ, God gives, loves, heals, and re-creates, but he does not change, suffer loss, die, or have his joy taken from him. Our salvation does not come through God's suffering. It is we, not God, who need to give up our ungrateful and selfish possession of ourselves so that we may receive our new selves created in the image of the Son of God. God is already selfless love, and it is we, not God, who need to give up this temporary life so that we might receive eternal life. God already lives in eternal joy. The impassible Son of God suffered for us *as human* so that we might share in his divine impassibility. If God is passible, we are lost. Our lives will be forever under the threat of lack and loss, and joy will forever elude us. But God is not passible, so we can rejoice in the hope of immortality, impassibility, and eternal life. Because God's hands are not busy wiping his own tears, they are free to wipe away ours.

The Glory of God

God is glorious in himself. His excellence, perfection, greatness, holiness, beauty, and worth shine forth wherever he allows himself to be known. His deeds, words, and laws manifest his glory. Heaven and earth radiate his majesty. In his revelation God manifests qualities that are so far beyond those we are familiar with that they overwhelm our capacity to take them in. They blind us with their light, and their beauty fills us with longing. His glory demands not our analysis but our praise. The angels announced to the shepherds the birth of the Messiah with their joyful refrain, "Glory to God in the highest!" (Luke 2:14). The heavenly beings who stand before God's throne continually sing, "You are worthy, our Lord and God, to receive glory and honor and power, for you created all things, and by your will they were created and have their being" (Rev. 4:11).

Glory in Scripture

Manifestations in Scripture of God's glory often appear as fire and brilliant light. At the time of God's revelation on Mount Sinai, "the glory of the Lord looked like a consuming fire on top of the mountain" (Exod. 24:17). When the angel of the Lord appeared to the shepherds to announce the birth of Jesus, "the glory of the Lord shone around them and they were terrified" (Luke 2:9). The gospel is the "light" of the "glory of Christ" (2 Cor. 4:4). God makes his "light shine in our hearts to give us the light of the knowledge of the glory of God in the face of Jesus Christ" (2 Cor. 4:15).

God manifests his glory in his actions of creation and salvation. In dealing with the stubborn Pharaoh, the Lord promises that he will glorify himself so that the Egyptians will know that he is the Lord (Exod. 14:4). The works of God evoke the people's praise, and they say "Glory!" (Ps. 29:9). As Jesus raised Lazarus from death, he manifested "the glory of God" (John 11:40). In wonder the psalmist sings, "The heavens declare the glory of God" (Ps. 19:1). Attributing glory to God is a common component of the praise of Israel and the church.

After the defeat of the Egyptian army, Moses sang: "Who among the gods is like you, O Lord? Who is like you — majestic in holiness, awesome in glory, working wonders?" (Exod. 15:11). After seeing the generosity of the people in their gifts for the construction of the temple, David praises God's power and "glory and majesty and splendor" (1 Chron. 29:11). The psalmist urges us to give God the glory due his name (Ps. 29:1; 105:3; 115:1; 135:5; cf. 1 Chron. 16:28, 29). The winged creatures of Isaiah's vision sing to one another: "Holy, holy, holy is the Lord Almighty; the whole earth is full of his glory" (Isa. 6:3).

The glory of God sometimes appears visibly among the people. While Aaron was speaking to the people, "the glory of the Lord" appeared in a cloud (Exod. 16:10). Often the glory of the Lord, in the form of smoke or a cloud, fills the place of worship, the tabernacle or temple (Exod. 40:34). Sometimes the presence of the glory of God precludes anyone from entering the sanctuary. When the Ark of the Covenant was placed in the temple, "the glory of the Lord filled the temple of God" (2 Chron. 5:13, 14). On the occasion of Ezekiel's call to prophesy, he saw "the appearance of the likeness of the glory of the Lord" (Ezek. 1:28). On another occasion he saw "the glory of the Lord standing" on the plain before him (Ezek. 3:23). In his temple vision Ezekiel saw the "glory of the Lord" at first rest above the cherubim and then move toward the entrance of the temple (Ezek. 9–11). Eventually, the "glory" moved out of the temple and the city, and it came to rest above a mountain on the east of the city (Ezek. 11:23).

Israel's prophets look forward to a day when the glory of God would be revealed in its fullness. Isaiah anticipates the day when "the glory of the Lord will be revealed, and all mankind together will see it" (Isa. 40:5). Habakkuk prophesies a time when the earth will overflow "with the knowledge of the glory of God" (Hab. 2:14), and the psalmist prays to God, "Let your glory be over all the earth" (Ps. 57:5). The hope for the definitive appearance of God's glory includes the hope of participation in God's glory. Filled with the glory of God, Zion will attract the nations with the "brightness" of its "dawn" (Isa. 60:1-3). Just as Moses' face shone from having been in the presence of God's glory, Christians "reflect the Lord's glory" and are "being transformed into his likeness with ever-increasing glory" (2 Cor. 3:18). By faith "we rejoice in the hope of the glory of God" (Rom. 5:2), for we endure his sufferings "in order that we may also share in his glory" (Rom. 8:17; cf. 1 Cor. 2:7; 2 Thess. 2:14). Christ's work, according to the author of the book of Hebrews, includes the task of "bringing many sons to glory" (Heb. 2:10; cf. 1 Pet. 5:10).

Jesus Christ is the "Lord of glory" (1 Cor. 2:8), who glorifies those who look to him (2 Cor. 3:18). We are called to share in "the glory of our Lord Jesus Christ" (2 Thess. 2:14), and we confess the name of Jesus "to the glory of God the Father" (Phil. 2:11). After urging his readers to "grow in the grace and knowledge of our Lord and Savior Jesus Christ," Peter blesses Christ: "[T]o him be glory for ever and ever. Amen" (2 Pet. 3:18). Unbelievers cannot see the good news of "the glory of Christ" (2 Cor. 4:4). The mystery Paul proclaims to the gentiles is "Christ in you, the hope of glory" (Col. 1:27). The Son, says the Hebrews writer, is "the radiance of God's glory" (Heb. 1:3).

Theology of God's Glory

Divine Glory Defined

Edward Leigh defines the glory of God as "the manifestation and shining forth of Excellency."[81] Barth speaks of divine glory as "the self-revealing sum of all divine perfections. It is the fullness of God's deity, the emerging, self-expressing and self-manifesting reality of all that God is. It is God's being in so far as this is in itself a being which declares itself."[82] I understand God's glory as *the manifestation and perception of the greatness, splendor, and excellence of God's being and actions.* Clearly, God's glory has to do with the communication, shining forth, and being seen of God's attributes. Glorious things — sunsets, flowers, and clear starry evenings — overwhelm us with their beauty and greatness. They stream toward us, engulf us, indwell us, and transform us with their stirring presence. Glorious things are glorious in their self-evidence; they ravish us with their beauty and force our admiration with their greatness. Before we have time to think, we are on our feet with attentiveness, on our knees with reverence, or on our faces in awe. God is glorious in all his attributes and actions; therefore, wherever God makes himself known, he reveals his glory. Nothing about God is dull, drab, ordinary, or routine. God is great, magnificent, and excellent in every aspect of his own life, and whoever knows him truly knows him as glorious.

Traditional theologians rightly distinguished between the glory intrinsic to God and the glory that accrues to him from creation's praise. In Leigh's words, God's glory may be understood as "the inward excellence and worth whereby he deserves to be esteemed and praised," or as "the actual acknowledging of it, for glory is defined as clear and manifest knowledge of another's excellence; therefore the glory of God is two-fold."[83] God manifests his glory in all his actions. His love is great, magnificent, and excellent; hence his loving actions are glorious. His mercy, righteousness, grace, and patience are equally great, excel-

---

81. Leigh, *Treatise of Divinity,* 2.15 (London, 1647), p. 111.
82. Barth, *CD,* 2/1, p. 643.
83. *Treatise of Divinity,* 2.15, pp. 111-12.

lent, and glorious. His acts of power, knowledge, and presence manifest his greatness and thus are glorious. All God's ways are glorious because he is eternally glorious in himself. Even apart from creation, God is perfect and great, and God knows his own perfection and greatness.

God's worthiness and excellence are manifested and perceived in God's own triune life. God lives eternally in glory. The Son knows the Father's greatness and dwells in his glory; the Father knows the Son's perfect sonship and sees his glory; the Spirit knows the glory of the Father and the Son and reveals that glory within the triune life. Glory, I conclude, is an essential attribute of God. God is God in that he is glorious. Not only is God great, magnificent, and excellent in all his attributes, but the light of his greatness fills the divine being. Not only is God essentially great, but his glory is essentially *known* as great. God *is* glory, for God *is* the knowledge of his greatness.

If God is glorious in himself, he is glorious wherever he dwells. As we have learned in the section on omnipresence, God's absolute presence to us does not entail our perception of God's presence. He is sovereign over his presence, which he can hide from us without thereby hiding us from himself. His glory likewise fills the universe, for God knows always and everywhere the greatness of his being and action. We, on the other hand, can see his glory only when and where God reveals himself. For his own good reasons he withholds his full revelation and thus his full glory from us. But in his own good time and at his own good pleasure God will manifest his glory for all to see. In the end, "every knee will bow" before God (Rom. 14:11, quoting Isa. 45:23). The revelation of his glory will also effect our glorification. When we see him in all his glory, "we shall be like him" (1 John 3:2; cf. Rom. 8:19-21).

Dealing fully with God's glory requires us to examine two related concepts, beauty and worthiness. I will deal with our response to God's glory, beauty, and worthiness in the final chapter; here I will focus on God's intrinsic glory. The two sections will thus complement each other.

Divine Beauty

Only a few passages in the Bible refer to God as beautiful, among which is the following: "One thing I ask of the Lord, this is what I seek: that I may dwell in the house of the Lord all the days of my life, to gaze upon the beauty of the Lord and to seek him in his temple" (Ps. 27:4). But this text and others do not give us a highly nuanced concept of beauty such as that found in Plato and the Platonists. Rather, they assume that we can recognize beauty when we see it and know what someone means when he or she refers to something as beautiful. Nevertheless, I believe we can benefit from some reflection on the experience of beauty.

Though it is possible to speak of a texture, a smell, or a taste as beautiful, most things we consider beautiful we experience through sight or hearing. We experience natural scenes as beautiful: waterfalls, sunsets, flowers, forests, and mountains. We see beauty in the human face, in a work of art, and in a human person. We also hear beauty in the music sung by birds or humans or music played on instruments. In all these things we find many different elements arranged in a harmonious pattern. For example, consider the many notes played by the different instruments of a symphony orchestra. A single note held or repeated indefinitely is annoying. Properly arranged, however, a piece of music can be a very pleasing whole that is composed of many different sounds and themes that move from beginning to completion. A rose is composed of many identical, curved petals that are arranged in different points in space on concentric circles, which allows light to be reflected from different angles, which in turn creates many different shades of the same color.[84]

As a third example, consider the beauty of a person. We consider a person beautiful when his or her character traits are in perfect harmony with one another and move toward the good of other persons. Courage, compassion, generosity, humility, and love stand in harmony with each other and with those same characteristics in other people. But selfishness, greed, and callousness in one person stand in total contradiction, not only to their contrary virtues, but also to selfishness, greed, and callousness in other people. Two honest people can live at peace, but two thieves cannot.

I think we can see this rule operating in our experience of beauty: the greater the number of elements and the greater disparity among them, the greater the difficulty of harmonizing them and the greater the beauty when this is accomplished. A simple melody played on one instrument can please us, but a complex symphony played by a full orchestra can enthrall and transform us. Chaos and contradiction repel and threaten us. What, then, can be more beautiful than chaos harmonized and contradictions reconciled?

God is beautiful because in him all the diverse elements of being indwell each

---

84. The nature of beauty is disputed. The most common view today is that "beauty is in the eye of the beholder." Needless to say, I reject the common view and hold to the view that something is beautiful because it possesses certain properties that can more or less be spelled out. For an extensive review of the history of the concept of beauty, see Wladyslaw Tatarkicwicz, "The Great Theory of Beauty and Its Decline," *The Journal of Aesthetics and Art Criticism* 31 (1972): 165-80. For the history of aesthetics, see *The Encyclopedia of Philosophy* (New York: Macmillan, 1967), s.v. "Beauty." For quick overviews of the debate, see the articles on beauty in Robert Audi, ed., *The Cambridge Dictionary of Philosophy*, 2nd ed. (Cambridge, UK: Cambridge University Press, 1999), and Simon Blackburn, ed., *The Oxford Dictionary of Philosophy* (Oxford: Oxford University Press, 1996).

other in perfect harmony.[85] The Father, Son, and Spirit indwell each other in perfect unity of being. The Father is the Father because he loves the Son with paternal love, and the Son is the Son by virtue of his filial love for the Father. One in being, distinct in person, and harmonious in will, the Trinity is the archetype of all beauty. All God's attributes are one and yet rich in their oneness: love and justice, mercy and judgment, person and nature, freedom and law — all these dwell in perfect harmony in God. All of God's works are beautiful. Creation is the beginning of salvation, and salvation is the completion of creation. His love lies hidden but real and effective in his works of judgment. And his acts of mercy and grace make his judgment effective in this world. God is the one who loves in freedom and who exercises freedom in love. God is the one who is — simultaneously and in perfect harmony — free, loving, righteous, merciful, gracious, omniscient, omnipotent, omnipresent, unchanging, patient, good, and glorious.[86]

In his work of reconciliation we see God's beauty in its most stunning expression. Love is certainly the most praised and the most beautiful virtue. In 1 Corinthians 13, Paul speaks of love in terms that remind us of the language of beauty: "Though I speak with the tongues of men and of angels and have not love, I am a noisy gong or a banging cymbal." Without love, our otherwise admirable actions lack something. This defect renders them ugly, empty, and useless (13:1-3). Love unites different persons. The love of a mother for her child is beautiful: the mother cannot feel her child's pain or fear, and the child is helpless and cannot reciprocate its mother's love on an equal basis; yet the mother unites herself to her child as if it were she and she were it.

Friendship is beautiful. Each friend finds him- or herself in the other. In friendship, two equals are pulled out of themselves into a greater whole in which both individuals are but elements harmoniously arranged. They are both the greater for the sacrifice of pretended self-sufficiency. Married love is more beautiful than friendship among equals, for it is a sacramental image of Christ's relationship to the church (Eph. 5:22-33). This teaching is reinforced by the observation I made earlier: the greater the difference, the more difficult and beautiful the harmony. The differences between any man and any woman are dramatically greater than they are between any two men or any two women. Therefore, the love, understanding, and harmony between them, if those can be achieved, are much more beautiful than the other harmonies.

However, the differences between friends, between mother and child, or be-

85. Barth, in *CD*, 2/1, p. 653, expresses a certain caution but feels compelled to treat God's glory as beauty.

86. Barth, in *CD*, 2/1, pp. 657-66, gives three examples of God's beauty: the harmony of all the attributes, the Trinity, and the incarnation.

tween a wife and her husband disappear when compared to those between God and his human creation. God is the Creator and we are his creatures; he is holy and we are unholy; he is righteous and we are unrighteous; he is eternal and we are temporal. Yet, for no reason in us, God condescends to care for us. How amazing! How beautiful! God called us into being out of nothing. We had no right to be, no claim on existence. But God freely and graciously gave us our lives. As soon as we become aware of our existence, however, we begin to assert various rights as we encounter God, the first of which is the right to self-possession. We imagine falsely and blasphemously that God has some secret self-interest in his dealings with us. Instead of thanking him as our gracious benefactor and obeying him as our wise Lord, we treat him as an enemy. Nevertheless, God remains true to his command of creation, which now must be fulfilled as the reconciliation of a rebel.

In Romans 5, Paul expresses his amazement at God's love for his wayward creatures. Christ died for the "ungodly," for "sinners" and for his "enemies." Through Christ's death God made "peace" with them. He justified them, reconciled them, and poured his love into their hearts by his Holy Spirit. Human beings may rise to noble sacrifices for family, country, and friends, and perhaps the honored memory will be worth the cost. But God demonstrates his matchless love in the death of Christ for his enemies. It might have been a quixotic gesture had it not accomplished the sanctification of the ungodly, the conversion of the sinner, and the reconciliation of the enemy. Here is the beauty and the glory of God's action in Christ: God brings his opposite into harmony with himself by negating himself. God humbles himself to do for his enemies what they considered themselves too good to do. The Son of God washes feet, carries his own cross, and dies a criminal's death. So much human ugliness, and yet so much divine beauty! For in this one loving act, God reconciles the world to himself, ridding it of its chaos and contradictions.

But in his humiliation God revealed his eternal glory, for his foot-washing and his cross and death did not hide God's glory but revealed it. The apparent self-negation was no negation at all. From all eternity God has been humble; there never was a self-centered God. The Father loves and gives freely, untainted by any secret self-interest. The Son shows his glory in filial obedience. The Son has known the Father's generosity, and the Father has known the Son's obedience from all eternity. The glory of God has been revealed in Christ. God is love. Free, sovereign, humble, and beautiful love!

Divine Worth

Now let us consider a second concept related to glory. Throughout Scripture worshipers address God as "worthy." The Psalter exclaims: "Great is the Lord and most worthy of praise; his greatness no one can fathom" (Ps. 145:3). The refrain "For great is the Lord and most worthy of praise" — the theme of this book — is found repeatedly in the worship of Israel (1 Chron. 16:25; Ps. 48:1; 96:4). In the book of Revelation, the heavenly beings praise the one sitting on the throne, extolling him as worthy of all glory and honor and power (Rev. 4:11). They also praise the Lamb as worthy of "power and wealth and wisdom and strength and honor and glory and praise!" (Rev. 5:11). Throughout the New Testament, Christians are urged to live lives worthy of their "calling" (Eph. 4:1), of the "gospel of Christ" (Phil. 1:27), of the "Lord" (Col. 1:10), of "kingdom of God," and "worthy of God" (1 Thess. 2:12).

The concept of worth finds its setting in the world of the economy, not simply of money and finance, but of comparative values. One thing's value is measured in terms of another thing. Something of worth merits our time, energy, and other resources. Our expenditures on the worthy thing are not wasted, but they are *worth* it. The idea of worth, like beauty, is an aesthetic concept. As Augustine pointed out, some things are valued for their usefulness and other things are valued as ends to be enjoyed. He explains: "For to enjoy a thing is to rest with satisfaction in it for its own sake. To use, on the other hand, is to employ whatever means are at one's disposal to obtain what one desires."[87] Useful things are valued only insofar as they can serve as means for attaining things of worth to be enjoyed for their own intrinsic qualities. Something that can neither be enjoyed nor used to attain something that can be enjoyed is worthless.

The Bible does not hesitate to speak of God in aesthetic terms, in terms of taste, desire, and thirst: "Taste and see that the Lord is good" (Ps. 34:8); the Lord's words are "sweet" to the taste (Ps. 119:103). God is the supreme object of "desire" (Ps. 73:25), and the righteous person "thirsts" for God (Ps. 42:1, 2). The poet of Psalm 63 expresses a desperate thirst and longing for God. God's love is "better than life" and worthy of lifelong praise. God is the origin and end of all ends, the good in all other goods, the joy in all other joys, and the beauty in all other beauties. To know God is to long for him, to praise him, and to love him above all other things. We sometimes exaggerate our praise of other good, beautiful, and great things. But God is worthy of our souls' highest praise, and we cannot exaggerate his greatness. He is the "pearl of great price," worth everything we own (Matt. 13:45, 46), and the "one thing needful" (Luke 10:42). Compared to the "surpassing greatness of knowing" him, everything else is rubbish (Phil. 3:8). "Great is the Lord, and most worthy of praise!"

---

87. Augustine, *On Christian Doctrine*, 1.4 (*NPNF*, 1st ser., 1, p. 523).

Does God Do Everything for His Own Glory?

I must now address a possible misunderstanding of God's glory. God's glory has nothing to do with a display of sovereign, arbitrary power simply for the sake of proving that God can do whatever he wills. As a proof-text for such a view, some have used Romans 9:22-23: "What if God, choosing to show his wrath and make his power known, bore with great patience the objects of his wrath — prepared for destruction? What if he did this to make the riches of his glory known to the objects of his mercy, whom he prepared in advance for glory — even us, whom he also called, not only from the Jews but also from the Gentiles?" But to use this text as proof for that view of God's glory ignores the fact that Paul states this view as a question. He is not declaring that God does in fact seek his glory in such an arbitrary manner. He merely refutes an implicit objection to the justice of God's ways. These questions cut the legs out from under the objection by asserting that, *even if* God were purely arbitrary, we would have no grounds for complaint. The creature simply has no standing to criticize the Creator. Paul's long argument (Rom. 9-11) concludes that God's providential action in history is neither an arbitrary demonstration of power nor a conditional response to our merits and actions: "For God has bound all men over to disobedience that he might have mercy on them all" (Rom. 11:12). In the end, God unites the "objects of wrath" and the "objects of mercy" in one category. To this amazing turn of events Paul erupts in praise: "Oh, the depths of the riches of the wisdom and knowledge of God . . . from him and through him and to him are all things. To him be the glory forever! Amen" (Rom. 11:33-36).

Samuel Hopkins (1721-1803), argues that we should be willing to be "damned for the glory of God," expressing the conviction that we should seek God's glory above all things, even our own salvation.[88] There is some truth to this conviction. But something about it troubles most of us, for this principle also implies the possibility that God might arbitrarily damn a person who was willing to be damned for God's glory. Let's probe this view. In it, God might give a person faith in Christ, the spiritual insight to see that the glory of God is the end of all things, and the will to then give up all things for God's glory; but then God might damn that person just to show that he can do whatever he wills.

Something has gone wrong here. The attribute of glory has been cut loose from the other attributes and from the revelation of God in Christ and has been elevated to the status of a super attribute. God's love, righteousness, mercy,

---

88. Quoted in Walter A. Elwell, ed., *Evangelical Dictionary of Theology* (Grand Rapids: Baker, 1984), s.v. "The New England Theology."

grace, and all the other attributes are robbed of their revelatory significance. For behind them all is the sheer arbitrary will of God to be known as the one who does whatever he wills. The humility, love, justice, and mercy that are revealed in the cross of Christ are thereby relegated to secondary status. We do not see in them God's deepest heart but rather a certain arbitrary attitude adopted toward a group chosen only for the purpose of demonstrating God's right to do as he wills. Furthermore, in this view, God's acts of justice and mercy do not show God to be essentially just or merciful. They show merely that God can do and be whatever he wants to be. In other words, God's acts do not reveal his character; they merely demonstrate his power, and power alone is not beautiful and thus not glorious. And we are plunged into the dark night of skepticism and despair.

Now it is certainly true that whatever God does is glorious. However, it is also true that whatever God does is loving, patient, merciful, and just. God is all his attributes. We must not make glory a master attribute, so that, for example, we conclude that God loves and acts justly or graciously or mercifully only when it brings him glory. This implies that God always seeks his glory but does not always love or act justly and graciously and mercifully. I reject this view. Indeed, God seeks his glory in all his actions, but it is equally true that he loves in all his actions. As Barth reminds us, "God's glory is God's love."[89] Let the reader recall my definition of God's glory: "the manifestation and perception of the greatness, splendor, and excellence of God's being and actions." All his attributes and actions are glorious all the time. He glorifies himself in his love for his enemies, in his mercy on the rebellious, and in his forgiveness of the ungodly. Everything God does is glorious, not because he asserts his will, but because he is true to himself in his actions and is most worthy of praise.

89. *CD*, 2/1, p. 645.

· III ·

ETHICS

13

Or the Stones Will Cry Out:
The Ethics of the Doctrine of God

Hugh Binning (1627-1653) entered Glasgow University at fourteen years of age and became a professor of philosophy there at nineteen. He became minister of Govan in Glasgow in 1650 and died three years later at the age of twenty-six. He devotes the first lecture of *The Common Principles of the Christian Religion* to explaining how glorifying God should be our chief occupation in life. According to Binning, God is most worthy of our praise, and we were made to praise him: "If I were a lark, I would sing as a lark; but as I am a man, what should I do, but praise God without ceasing? It is proper to us to praise God, as for a bird to chaunt. . . . All our thoughts of him, all our affections toward him, should have the stamp of singularity, such as may declare there is none like him, none beside him; our love, our meditation, our acknowledgment should have this character on their front. . . . And then a soul should, by the cords of affection to him and admiration of him, be bound to serve him."[1]

Binning's words capture well the goal of this chapter. I want to show how God's very being and action drive us to seek him, demand that we imitate him, and compel us to praise him. Every line in this book anticipates this chapter. Everything I have written thus far was meant to set before our minds the goodness, righteousness, and greatness of our God that we might seek passionately to know him, become like him in all our ways, and praise him with all our being.[2] I

---

1. *The Works of The Rev. Hugh Binning, M.A.*, 3rd ed., ed. Rev. M. Leishan, D.D. (London: A. Fullarton and Co., 1851), p. 6.

2. I agree with Geoffrey Wainwright that it is more than legitimate for a theologian to be motivated by a desire to praise God and lead others to praise God. However, Wainwright warns us that "to mention the praise of God as the theologian's motivation runs the risk of provoking dissent from colleagues anxious for academic neutrality" ("The Praise of God in the Theological Reflection of the Church," *Interpretation* 39 [1985]: 42).

have maintained all along that the knowledge of God is practical. We cannot know God without passion, longing, seeking, following, and praising. To know him is to praise him, for he is most worthy of praise. In knowing God we perceive that he is righteous, the model and power for all authentic action. Now I shall explore the ethics of the doctrine of God, as we seek to know how we may respond in a way that corresponds to him.

The Divine Command

God is lord of all. Authority and power unlimited belong to him. He is lord over his own being and action, and all things exist because of his will and command. Therefore, his will and command are the being and law of all beings. God's very being and life constitute a threefold command for us: to acknowledge his greatness by seeking him, following him, and praising him. When we spurn God's goodness, close our eyes to his excellence, and find him unworthy of praise, we move toward death, evil, and nothingness.

God's Command in Scripture

One cannot read Scripture without noticing the prominent role played by the commands of God, God's approval of obedience, and his disapproval of disobedience. God created the world with his word of command, "Let there be . . ." (Gen. 1:3, 6, 9, 14). The heavens should praise God, the psalmist urges, because "he commanded and they were created" (Ps. 148:5, 6). After Jesus had calmed the storm with a rebuke, his stunned disciples asked, "What kind of man is this? Even the winds and the waves obey him!" (Matt. 8:27).

God's commands can be directed to individuals or groups on unique occasions or given as general rules. The Lord commanded the first human couple not to eat of the tree of the knowledge of good and evil (Gen. 2:17). God demanded that Abraham sacrifice his son Isaac as a burnt offering (Gen. 22:2). In their meeting at the burning bush, the Lord commanded Moses to tell Pharaoh to let his people go (Exod. 8:1). Paul recalls that, on the road to Damascus, Jesus said to him, "Go, for I will send you far away to the Gentiles" (Acts 22:21).

From Sinai, the Lord gave the Ten Commandments: "You shall have no other gods before me. . . . Honor your father and your mother. . . . You shall not murder. You shall not commit adultery. You shall not steal . . ." (Exod. 20:3-17). Following the Decalogue, there are in Exodus and Leviticus many specific rules, regulations, and decrees concerning worship, idolatry, and various kinds of human relationships. Scripture not only records God's commands; it urges continuous obedience to them. The book of Deuteronomy, especially, emphasizes this:

> Hear now, O Israel, the decrees and laws I am about to teach you. Follow them so that you may live. . . . Observe them carefully, for this will show your wisdom and understanding to the nations. . . . So be careful to do what the Lord your God has commanded you; do not turn aside to the right or to the left. Walk in all the way that the Lord your God has commanded you (Deut. 4:1-32).

In view of the prominence of God's commands, it should not be surprising that Scripture understands the highest measure of moral character as a spirit of obedience. The Lord commends Abraham for being willing to sacrifice Isaac in obedience to him (Gen. 22:16, 17). The Bible commends Noah repeatedly because he did everything "just as God commanded him" (Gen. 6:22; 7:5, 9). The text of Exodus tells us over and over that Moses "did just as the Lord commanded him" (Exod. 7:6, 10, 20; 39:32, 42). Ezekiel looks forward to the day when the Lord will remove from the Israelites their stubborn hearts and give them a will to obey his laws (Ezek. 11:19, 20). Psalm 119 holds up the model of the obedient person who obeys God's decrees (v. 5), delights in his laws (v. 15), and wills to obey with all his or her heart (v. 34). Scripture praises the life of obedience to God's commands: "What does the Lord your God ask of you but to fear the Lord your God, to walk in all his ways, to love him, to serve the Lord your God with all your heart and with all your soul, and to observe the Lord's commands and decrees that I am giving you today for your own good?" (Deut. 10:12, 13).

In the Sermon on the Mount, Jesus makes clear that he is no antinomian: he does not plan to abolish the law or the prophets, but has come to fulfill them. The demands of the law will stand firm until the kingdom comes in all its fullness (Matt. 5:17-20). Jesus' teachings, far from loosening God's commands, intensify and renew them. Not only must you not murder, you must not even be angry with your brother. Not only must you not commit adultery, you must not even imagine committing adultery. Not only must you not lie under oath, you must not take an oath at all; simply tell the truth. Jesus closed the loopholes in divorce law. And he commanded that we turn the other cheek, go the extra mile, and love our enemies. In short, his command was: "Be perfect, therefore, as your heavenly Father is perfect" (Matt. 5:48).

Jesus sets an example for his followers by obeying his Father. "The world must learn that I love the Father and that I do exactly what my Father has commanded me" (John 14:31; cf. John 15:10). Jesus says to his hungry disciples, "My food is to do the will of him who sent me and to finish his work" (John 4:34). In the face of death, Jesus gives himself over to the will of his Father (Luke 22:42). Having set an example of love and humility by washing his disciples' feet, Jesus says, "A new command I give you: Love one another" (John 13:34). The test of love is obedience. "Whoever has my commands and obeys them, he is the one who loves me" (John 14:21). John, in his letters, continues this theme: "We know that we have come to know him if we obey his commands" (1 John 2:3, 4; cf. 1 John 3:22, 24). And later he says, "This is love for God: to obey his commands" (1 John 5:3).

Disobeying God's commands, on the other hand, is viewed in Scripture as great evil, failure, and folly. Adam and Eve's disobeying of God's command not to eat of the tree of the knowledge of good and evil is paradigmatic of all the evil that follows. Death, alienation, pain, and toil result from that first disobedience. In Deuteronomy, Moses prophesies the Israelites' disobedience and the punishment that will follow (Deut. 31:28). Speaking as God's oracle, Jeremiah looks back on Israel's history of disobedience, and he complains about her rebellion and stubbornness, laying blame for her trouble at her own feet (Jer. 11:7-23). Despite God's manifold blessings, Jerusalem "has rebelled against my laws and has not followed my decrees," Ezekiel charges (Ezek. 5:6). According to Paul, God will punish those who "do not obey the gospel of our Lord Jesus" (2 Thess. 1:8). Peter warns of the judgment to come on those "who do not obey the gospel of God" (1 Pet. 4:17).

Christian Ethics as the Theology of God's Command

Divine Command Ethics

My thinking on the nature of Christian ethics has been shaped decisively by Karl Barth's 270-page chapter in *Church Dogmatics* entitled "The Command of God."[3] However, whereas Barth uses the ethics section in his doctrine of God to lay a formal "foundation" for his later ethical studies in the doctrines of creation, reconciliation, and redemption, I am using it to treat human actions that I think are best understood as responses to the very being of God. Unlike Barth, I include what some would call "religious" acts within this ethics section: that is, seeking God and praising God. For me, knowing God is ultimately a practical matter, and *all* human action falls under the subject of ethics.

3. Barth,*Church Dogmatics*, vol. 2, pt. 2, eds. G. W. Bromiley and T. F. Torrance, trans. T. H. L. Parker et al. (Edinburgh: T&T Clark, 1957), pp. 509-781 (hereafter *CD*).

According to Scripture, authentic human action must be grounded in the will and command of God. What some philosophers call the "divine command theory" seems to me to be the pervasive teaching of Scripture.[4] No other foundation is adequate. We must not attempt to ground ethics in any aspect of the human being — in our biology, our psychology, or our social nature. Nor can we found ethics on human subjectivity, for human beings have no right to do as they please without reference to the command of God. Barth explains this with his characteristic bluntness: "For the man who obediently hears the command of God is not in any position to consider why he must obey it."[5] Nor can we ground ethics in an impersonal, cosmic process or law, whether spiritual or material, for the triune God is the foundation of all things. Emil Brunner rightly affirms this: "Here there is no 'intrinsic' Good. What God does and wills is good, all that opposes the will of God is bad. The Good has its basis and its existence solely in the will of God."[6]

Christian ethics rejects the help of mere theism, the abstract notion of an anonymous god generated by natural theology. Only an ethics that understands itself as a theology of the command of the triune God can do justice to Scripture and thus merit the title "Christian ethics." Dietrich Bonhoeffer speaks of the command of God with the same urgency and exclusivity as do Barth and Brunner: "The command of God . . . embraces the whole of life. It is unconditional; it is also total. It does not only forbid and command; it also permits. It does not only bind; it sets free; and it does this by binding . . . . God's commandment is the only warrant for ethical discourse . . . [it] is the total and concrete claim laid to man by the merciful and holy God in Jesus Christ."[7]

4. The body of recent philosophical literature dealing with the so-called divine command theory is enormous. A few examples are: Philip Quinn, *Divine Commands and Moral Requirements* (Oxford: Clarendon Press, 1978); Robert Merrihew Adams, *Finite and Infinite Goods: A Framework for Ethics* (Oxford: Oxford University Press, 1999), pp. 249-76; Edward Wierenga, "A Defensible Divine Command Theory," *Nous* 17 (1983): 387-407; William Alston, "Some Suggestions for Divine Command Theorists," in *Christian Theism and the Problems of Philosophy*, ed. Michael Beaty (Notre Dame, IN: University of Notre Dame Press, 1990), pp. 303-26; Mark C. Murphy, "Divine Command, Divine Will, and Moral Obligation," *Faith and Philosophy* 15 (1998): 3-27; Paul Rooney, "Divine Commands and Arbitrariness," *Religious Studies* 31 (1995): 149-65.

5. *CD*, 2/2, pp. 521-22.

6. Brunner, *The Divine Imperative*, trans. Olive Wyon (Philadelphia: Westminster, n.d.), p. 53.

7. Bonhoeffer, *Ethics*, trans. Neville Horton Smith (New York: Macmillan, 1955), p. 277.

Arbitrary Commands?

In preparing to develop a theology of the command of the triune God, let us first address an ancient objection that may have crossed the reader's mind already. If God's command determines the boundary between justice and injustice, between good and evil, is God, then, beyond good and evil? Are the concepts "good" and "evil" devoid of meaning? Plato articulated this objection in its classic form in his dialogue *Euthyphro*. Is an action right or good because the gods command it, or do the gods command it because it is good? Or as Socrates, Plato's mouthpiece, puts it: "The point which I should first wish to understand is whether the pious or holy is beloved by the gods because it is holy, or holy because it is beloved of the gods."[8] The first alternative, according to Plato, makes the distinction between good and evil arbitrary, for what the gods command today they could forbid to-morrow. The second alternative — Plato's choice — renders the gods irrelevant ethically.[9] The good exists independently of the gods and has its being eternally and unchangeably in an immaterial realm. The gods are just as dependent on the idea of the good as humans are. Gods and humans must grasp the general idea of the good in order to discern what is good in a specific instance. Humans can, through the power of their reason, grasp the idea of the good apart from the command of a god. Therefore, Plato concludes, the good is completely independent of the gods. It does not require divine help to exist or to reveal itself.[10]

However, Plato's argument is convincing only if we grant the pagan presupposition of the priority of nature over person. The gods, according to Plato and other pagan thinkers, are divine by virtue of their participation in an impersonal divine nature. Whereas the divine nature is immutable, the gods (as persons) are changeable. Hence, rooting the good in the command of the gods makes the good itself mutable and arbitrary. But if we reject the pagan presupposition and understand the triune God as constant and faithful, the problem Plato raises disappears. The will and command of God, as aspects of the immutable divine nature itself, do not change.[11]

8. *The Dialogues of Plato,* vol. 2, trans. and ed. Benjamin Jowett (1892; reprint, Bristol, UK: Thoemmes Press, 1997), pp. 80-84.

9. See Baruch A. Brody, "Morality and Religion Reconsidered," in *Readings in the Philosophy of Religion: An Analytic Approach,* ed. Baruch A. Brody (Englewood Cliffs, NJ: Prentice-Hall, 1974), pp. 592-603. Brody contends that the argument of Socrates does not defeat the affirmation that some of our moral obligations are based on the notion of God's creation and ownership of the world. For a criticism of Brody's argument, see John L. Hammond, "Divine Command Theories and Human Analogies," *The Journal of Religious Ethics* 14 (1986): 216-23.

10. See John M. Frame's concise discussion of the "Euthyphro Problem" in *The Doctrine of God* (Phillipsburg, NJ: Presbyterian and Reformed, 2002), pp. 405-9.

11. Erik J. Wielenberg argues that, even if God can rightly impose some obligations because

Understandably, Plato prefers an impersonal, immutable standard to an arbitrary and mutable one. However, with help from the Trinitarian principle of the ontological priority of person over impersonal nature, we can see that an impersonal good (or justice) cannot serve as our highest ideal. For these abstract principles have no relationship to themselves except as mediated by the world: hence, good cannot be its own good nor justice be for itself just. As Christopher Stead points out, understanding the highest reality as impersonal confronts us with "the paradox of a Being who is the source of all goodness but cannot be good."[12] The Platonic good can maintain its character as the "good" only if there is a world by which it is desired. Platonic justice is justice only as it judges the world. Apart from their relationship to the world, these principles lose their normative character. They just are. I conclude that Plato rejects an arbitrary understanding of the good only to fall into a fatalistic understanding of the good. Just as the gods are fated to be gods, the good is fated to be the good. Good is not good freely and by its own power: that is, Plato's highest reality, because it is not free, cannot be righteous or virtuous or admirable. We can desire it, but we cannot admire it or imitate it, and thus it cannot be our highest good. Our highest good must be personal.[13]

The Eternal Command of God

The distinctions between good and evil and right and wrong are grounded solely in the will and command of God. Nevertheless, these distinctions are not capricious or matters of sheer power. God is not good because he participates in the good, or righteous because he measures up to an external law. God *is* his nature, and because goodness and righteousness are his attributes, God *is* goodness and righteousness. Therefore, God's will and command are not capricious, because they always express his essential goodness and righteousness.

---

of his status as the benevolent Creator, not all moral obligations arise this way. Some arise in our relationships to other human beings, and some are based on "intrinsic values." See ch. 2, "God and Morality," in *Value and Virtue in a Godless Universe* (New York: Cambridge University Press, 2005), pp. 38-67.

12. Stead, "Divine Simplicity as a Problem for Orthodoxy," in *The Making of Orthodoxy: Essays in Honor of Henry Chadwick,* ed. Rowan Williams (Cambridge, UK: Cambridge University Press, 1989), p. 265. For a similar assessment of Plato's view of the good, see also Frederick Copleston, SJ, *A History of Philosophy,* vol. 1, *Greece and Rome,* part 1 (Garden City, NY: Image Books, 1962), p. 206.

13. See Paul Rooney, "Divine Commands and Arbitrariness," *Religious Studies* 31 (1995): 149-65. Rooney argues that divine commands can be "arbitrary" without being irrational, whimsical, or capricious.

Moreover, since God is constant (or immutable), his will and command are constant and reliable.

God's goodness and righteousness, though essential to him, are not his fate. Nothing outside himself causes him to be divine. As I have argued repeatedly in this book, God is what he is freely: that is, he freely enacts his nature. God's goodness and righteousness do not "just" exist; rather, they are his own free action. God, as it were, asserts his goodness and righteousness in opposition to nothingness, evil, and unrighteousness. And though these opponents have no power to resist him — indeed, they have no being at all — we must take into account that God knows what he is *not* as well as what he *is*. God knows what he does not will as well as what he wills. And he is just as free in his rejection of what he is not as he is in his enactment of what he is. Though there is and can be no other God, this does not mean that God is God *because* this is his only option.

As God's free acts, his goodness and righteousness are thus admirable as well as desirable. We desire what we believe will bring us joy and help us actualize our potential. In viewing God as the good, we desire him as the completion of ourselves. On the other hand, we admire what we believe we should imitate. In viewing God as the admirable, we recognize his perfection as freely achieved. As beings that can achieve perfection only in our freedom, we recognize God's righteousness as the standard for us, acknowledge our distance from his perfection, and long to be like him. Only in being like God can we freely and faithfully enact our true nature, which is "created to be like God in true righteousness and holiness" (Eph. 4:24). God's righteousness consists in his perfect faithfulness to himself. Our righteousness can consist only in our participation in God's faithfulness to himself. We must be empowered and freed by God to enact our God-given nature.

I believe that we are now prepared to see why we must understand God's command as an eternal aspect of the divine life or even a divine attribute. As I have noted, God's goodness and righteousness are not abstract and static properties but dynamic and free actions. If free actions arise out of self-determinations rather than unfolding automatically by a fatalistic necessity, God's actions can be viewed as accompanied always by his self-determination. God's self-determination can be understood as a kind of resolution, decision, or self-command. Therefore, to view God's being as an action is to view it as an eternal command and the eternal execution of this command.

Traditional theologians treated the issue of God's self-determination under the rubric of "the will of God." Though the will of God is one, traditional theologians understood that we must apprehend it according to its distinct objects. The most important among the many ways we can view God's will is to distinguish between God's willing of himself and his willing of creation. According to Marcus Friedrich Wendelin (1584-1652), "Will is the active principle *(principium imperans),* by which God, through himself, wills himself, and beyond himself, wills all things according to himself or to his glory."[14] Similarly, Amandus Polanus defines God's will as "His most wise propension toward Himself as the supreme end and towards the creatures as means for His own sake."[15] Leonardus Rijssen says that the divine will "is concerned either with God himself, his life and approbation, or with creatures."[16]

The traditional distinction between God willing himself and his willing of creatures is of great importance to our present discussion. I have chosen to speak of God's "command" rather than his will, not because I disagree with the tradition, but because I want to emphasize, in agreement with the tradition, the free and personal nature of God's willing of himself. For neither God's will toward himself nor his will toward the world is an impersonal force or blind urge. God eternally wills and freely enacts his own being. As I have urged above, God asserts his being, goodness, and righteousness against everything he wills not to be. His life, then, is at once an eternal command and the eternal execution of that command.

We can see this most clearly from the perspective of the doctrine of the Trinity. God's life, love, righteousness, and all his other attributes are exemplified in the Trinitarian relationships. This is also true of God's command. Though it is true to say with the tradition that God wills himself, it is more accurate to say that the Father wills the Son in the Spirit, and the Son in the Spirit wills the Father's will. The Father eternally begets the Son, who is one with the Father in being. In gratitude and obedience, the Son returns himself to the Father. In his incarnate state, the Son listens to the Father (John 8:28), teaches only what the Father has taught him (John 14:24), does as the Father does (John 8:28), submits to the will of the Father (Matt. 26:39), and carries out the Father's commands (John 15:10). The Spirit proceeds eternally from the Father and is sent by the Son to give life to the world.

Though we are allowed and even forced by Scripture to speak of the "obedience" of the Son, we must take care. Just as we cannot transfer the human suffering of the Son into the divine being without appropriate *apophatic* qualification, we cannot transfer the human obedience of the Son into the divine being

---

14. Wendelin, *Christianae theologiae libri duo,* 1.1.18, quoted in Richard Muller, *Post-Reformation Reformed Dogmatics: The Rise and Development of Reformed Orthodoxy,* vol. 3, *The Divine Essence and Attributes* (Grand Rapids: Baker Academic, 2003), p. 440 (hereafter *PRRD).*

15. See Heinrich Heppe, *Reformed Dogmatics,* rev. and ed. Ernst Bizer, trans. G. T. Thomson (1950; reprint, London: Wakeman Great Reprints, n.d.), p. 81.

16. Muller, *PRRD,* 3, p. 451.

without such qualification. Nevertheless, just as I have argued that the Son's suffering in his humanity corresponds to his eternal self-giving love to the Father, I contend here that the Son's human obeying of the Father corresponds to his eternal willing of the Father's will. Barth asserts an inner Trinitarian obedience in even bolder terms:

> As we look at Jesus Christ we cannot avoid the astounding conclusion of a divine obedience. There we have to draw the no less astounding deduction that in equal Godhead the one God is, in fact, the One and also the Another, that He is indeed a First and a Second, One who rules and commands in majesty and One who obeys in humility. The one God is both the one and the other.[17]

Within the triune God, then, is command and obedience, speaking and listening, and giving and receiving.

God's Command to Creatures

We are now able to understand why God does nothing new or whimsical when he commands his creatures to act in certain ways and forbids them to act in others. God exists as the triumph of good and right over evil and wrong. His command to us is the revelation of his triumph and the invitation to share in the glory of his victory. His command in all its forms is good, gracious, righteous, generous, and loving. This command, however, can be viewed immanently or economically: that is, it can be viewed as an attribute of his eternal being or as an aspect of his actions toward us in creation, reconciliation, and redemption.[18] Each vantage point discloses different facets of God's one command. Hence, each locus of doctrine must contain its own particular ethics section that deals with the command of God from that perspective. The ethics of creation will focus on the requirements of thanksgiving, responsibility, and caretaking. The locus of reconciliation will highlight repentance, faith, and love. The doctrine of redemption will bring hope, rejoicing, and glorifying God to the fore.

The ethics of the doctrine of God explains how the very being of God constitutes a command to us, explores the specific content of this command, and

---

17. *CD*, 4/1, p. 202. For a full statement of Barth's view of the obedience of the Son, see his section entitled "The Way of the Son of God into the Far Country" (*CD*, 4/1, pp. 157-210).

18. My fourfold way of treating the command of God corresponds essentially to Barth's method (see *CD*, 2/2, pp. 549-51).

describes how the command moves us to obey. As we have seen, simply by being good and full of life, righteousness, and joy, God invites and commands us to participate in that good. God's being, considered simply and apart from creation, reconciliation, and redemption, constitutes a command for us to seek him, follow him, and praise him. The moving power of God's goodness is that goodness itself, which is the only object worthy of our desire. Every other good is good only by participation in the good that is God, and the desire to participate in the good that is God motivates us to do what we are commanded. All God's commands demand and invite us to participate in his goodness. Simply by being righteous, God invites and commands us to imitate his righteousness. The moving power of God's righteousness is that righteousness itself, which is inherently admirable. Admiration for God's righteous life motivates us to imitate that life, for God's perfection is the standard and goal of our nature. Simply by being great, beautiful, glorious, and worthy, God commands and calls forth our praise.

Though each vantage point brings out a different facet of God's command and calls for a different response, we are dealing with the same command, which is God himself. Likewise, our responses to the command of God are but different facets of the one act of our being to which we are called by this command. God's command thus integrates our lives and harmonizes our actions. It gives us an identity, a genuine self rooted in the unchanging God. In this chapter I shall explore how our seeking, imitating, and praising of God are called forth, justified, and integrated by the very being of God.

The Ethics of the Doctrine of God

Seek Him!

God is boundless being, life, and joy, and from him alone these goods flow to all creatures; apart from him, we have no being or life or joy. Why, then, would we seek joy in finite things apart from him? Such vain seeking can lead only to disappointment, emptiness, and death. Apart from God, the goods we seek are nothing at all. Thomas à Kempis, speaking in the voice of Christ, says:

> From Me the small and the great, the poor and the rich draw the water of life as from a living fountain, and they who serve Me willingly and freely shall receive grace upon grace. He who wishes to glory in things apart from Me, however, or to delight in some good as his own, shall not be grounded in true

joy or gladdened in his heart, but shall be burdened and distressed in many ways. Hence you ought not to attribute any good to yourself or ascribe virtue to any man, but give all to God without Whom man has nothing.[19]

Scripture's Command to Seek Him

Scripture resonates with the message that God is our only good. The Psalms express the yearning the faithful feel to be with God: "One thing I ask of the Lord, this is what I seek: that I may dwell in the house of the Lord all the days of my life, to gaze upon the beauty of the Lord and to seek him in his temple" (Ps. 27:4). If we know God, we will seek him like a wanderer in the desert seeks water (Ps. 63:1; 143:6). Isaiah looks forward to a time when the people of Judah will sing these words: "Your name and renown are the desire of our hearts. My soul yearns for you in the night; in the morning my spirit longs for you" (Isa. 26:8, 9). We are told to seek God with all our hearts (Ps. 119:2). We are to "delight" in him (Ps. 37:4).

To the man who called him "good," Jesus replied: "No one is good — except God alone" (Luke 18:19). According to Paul's Areopagus speech, God set up the world in such a way "that men would seek him and perhaps reach out for him and find him, though he is not far from each one of us" (Acts 17:27). The writer of Hebrews instructs us that God "rewards those who earnestly seek him" (Heb. 11:6). James points us to the "Father of heavenly lights," because every "good and perfect gift" comes from him (James 1:17). Finally, Peter urges his converts to "crave pure spiritual milk . . . now that you have tasted that the Lord is good" (1 Pet. 2:2, 3).

Seeking God

In *seeking* God we are treating God as "good," or *the* Good. In this context, "good" does not mean benevolence but good-for-ness. Robert Adams argues that we should think of God's goodness primarily as excellence and only secondarily as the ground of our well-being or good-for-ness. I think that he is probably correct, all things considered. Thinking of God only as the source of our well-being would make God's good relative to and dependent on our needs and tempt us to treat God as a mere means to our ends. However, thinking of God's goodness as excellence emphasizes God's inherent and absolute goodness. I believe that we should not separate these two understandings of God's

19. Thomas à Kempis, *The Imitation of Christ*, trans. Aloysius Croft and Harold Bolton (Peabody, MA: Hendrickson Publishers, 2004), p. 66.

goodness. Thinking of God's goodness as excellence unrelated to our well-being would deprive us of any way to make a connection with it.[20]

My own view is that God's eternal life exhibits both kinds of goodness in the most profound unity. In this section I shall consider God as the absolute fulfillment of our nature, and in the next two sections I shall focus on God's inherent excellence. But the two must be thought of together if we are to grasp the deepest meaning of each. God is both good for us and excellent apart from any reference to our needs. And God is good for us precisely as he is excellent apart from us. For it is good for us to rejoice in God's inherent excellence.[21] To put it another way, we were made to love God — and even ourselves — for God's sake alone.[22]

Thinking of God's goodness in Trinitarian terms will help us understand God's goodness as good-for-ness without making God dependent on the world, and it will assist us in viewing it as excellence without making it unrelated to our needs. The Father is the infinite good of the Son and the Spirit, and the Son and the Spirit are each other's and the Father's good. The Father, Son, and Spirit delight in each other. And the perfect and selfless love among the Father, Son, and Spirit shines forth as infinite beauty and excellence and demands our attention, admiration, and praise.

When we are satisfied and secure, we forget that we are nothing and can do nothing apart from the grace of God. We lose our sense of dependence on reality outside ourselves. But take away our air or water or nourishment, and we soon begin to feel our vulnerability. If our environment is too hot or cold or violent, we cannot survive; we are needy, thirsty, and craving beings. We grasp, thirst, hunger, long, and hope for the things we need. The finite goods of this world evoke our desire and lure us into action so that we may enjoy them and quiet our disturbing desire. Most of us attend to the immediate source of enjoyment and satisfaction and rarely connect our desire and striving to the ultimate source of the goods with which we are occupied.

However much we need them, the finite goods for which we strive are themselves derivative and temporary. We depend on them, but they are not absolutely dependable; they might not have been, and eventually they will not be. They are not constant and eternal, not the good itself. They cannot end all desire and bestow perfect joy. And striving for them as if they were able to

---

20. Adams, *Finite and Infinite Goods,* pp. 13-14.

21. Adams argues a similar point. He says: "I wish to explore the idea that what is good for a person is a life characterized by enjoyment of the excellent" (*Finite and Infinite Goods,* p. 93).

22. See Bernard of Clairvaux's famous essay *On Loving God,* where he develops four stages of love. Available at http://www.ccel.org/ccel/bernard/loving_god.titlepage.html (accessed May 2005).

satisfy will lead only to disappointment and boredom. Finite goods point outside themselves to the source of the good they contain. "Seek me!" God commands. "Do not think you will find good in bread, health, and life apart from me."

Seeking God begins with knowledge and desire.[23] We must make the connection between the good in finite things and God, so that God becomes the chief object of our desire. Only then can our natural striving for the goods of this world be redirected toward the good that is God. We are physical beings: our stomachs were made for food, our lungs for air, and our eyes for light. We are also spiritual beings: our minds were made for truth and beauty, our hearts for love. But we are more. We were made, as persons, for fellowship with our Creator.[24] As Augustine and the Augustinian tradition remind us, we cannot find rest and perfect joy in anything but God.[25] Facilitating this insight is an important goal of the doctrine of God, which teaches us to think of God as "the fountain-source of all things."[26] God is holy, righteous, loving, powerful, patient, and free — everything that is a worthy object of our desire. Our doctrine of God can witness to that fact, but God alone can make himself present to us and assure our hearts that he alone is "the everlasting wellspring of all good things."[27]

Desire is a kind of hopeful pain.[28] Its emptiness is accompanied by a misty image of fullness. Apart from faith that God is the source of all good, our desire settles on finite things. We seek vainly in creatures the fullness found only in the Creator. However, when God presents himself to us as the good, as the fullness that corresponds to our emptiness, we must seek him. In revealing himself as

23. Adams uses the term "recognition" instead of knowledge (*Finite and Infinite Goods*, p. 20).

24. John M. Rist rightly criticizes certain medieval ethicists for attempting to distinguish a natural from a supernatural end for humanity. Rist defends an Augustinian view: that humanity was made to enjoy God and cannot achieve its end without reference to God (*On Inoculating Moral Philosophy Against God* [Milwaukee: Marquette University Press, 1999], pp. 66-67).

25. See Augustine, *Confessions;* and Thomas F. Martin, *Our Restless Heart: The Augustine Tradition* (Maryknoll, NY: Orbis, 2004).

26. Ulrich Zwingli, *Commentary on True and False Religion*, eds. Samuel Macauley Jackson and Clarence Nevin Heller (1929; reprint, Durham, NC: Labyrinth Press, 1981), pp. 71-72, quoted in Muller, *PRRD*, 3, p. 503.

27. Heinrich Bullinger, *The Decades of Henry Bullinger*, 2.2, trans. H. I., ed. Thomas Harding (Cambridge, UK: Cambridge University Press, 1849-1852), p. 216, quoted in Muller, *PRRD*, 3, p. 504.

28. Adams criticizes Plato for limiting *eros* to desire. Desire arises from emptiness, and it seeks *future* enjoyment. Adams wants to expand *eros* to include present enjoyment. Adams does this so that he can apply the concept of *eros* to God without implying that God is needy (*Finite and Infinite Goods*, pp. 133-36).

the good (and *my* good), he frees us from slavery to lesser goods and directs us to the ultimate good. He liberates us to enjoy those finite goods as God's gifts. Thankfulness enables us to enjoy the giver along with the gift. He commands us to seek him.

We cannot find God as we discover other things, by traversing space and uncovering something previously hidden. We cannot locate him among created things; nor can we find him inside our minds or underneath our feelings. God is already nearer to us than these things. As we learned in the section on omnipresence, God indwells and contains us; he empowers us and sustains us. We are present to him completely, and he knows us thoroughly. We cannot hide from him, but he is free to hide from us — or reveal himself to us — according to his will. We have no power to uncover him against his will. Therefore, our seeking can only take the form of the beseeching, listening, and waiting called prayer.

Seeking as Praying

More than an occasional request, prayer is a mode of life that corresponds to God as the source of all good things. Merold Westphal says: "The praying soul seeks to be fully present to God, but that is the always unfulfilled task of a lifetime."[29] The Christian life is a constant prayer. "Pray continually," Paul urges the Thessalonians (1 Thess. 5:17). "And pray in the Spirit on all occasions with all kinds of prayers and requests. With this in mind, be alert and always keep on praying for all the saints" (Eph. 6:18). Paul encourages the Philippians to let prayer replace anxiety (Phil. 4:6). Everything good comes from God, and every good that comes from God enters our lives as a gift freely bestowed.

For a Christian, all the different spiritual disciplines are but different forms of prayer. You can find God in the study of Scripture only as the answer to prayer. If you find God through the practice of contemplation, it will not be because of your powers of introspection, but because he wills to reveal himself graciously in answer to the prayer embodied in your practice. The practices of fasting, simplicity, and silence cannot make God present simply as a result of our performing them. They are best understood as different ways in which we beseech God to manifest himself to us.

The desire to pray is evidence not only of our seeking God; it is also a sign of having found him — or rather of having been found by him. The urge to pray is grace already at work; thus prayer is not only seeking but communing as well. A prayer is not a monologue but a conversation. God is always present,

---

29. Westphal, "Not About Me," *Christian Century* (April 5, 2005): 20.

and he is never silent, for the triune God is an "eternal conversation."[30] When God invites us to pray to him, he bids us join a conversation already in progress. This living conversation is the source of life and all good things. We live because God speaks our name; we become persons when we learn to speak God's name. If it is amazing that God speaks to us, it is much more amazing that God invites us to speak to him! "Seek and you shall find," says our Lord. How true this is, for seeking is the beginning of finding!

Follow Him!

In the previous section I concluded that God's goodness compels us to *seek* him. In this section I shall argue that God's righteousness obligates us to *imitate* him. Indeed, the very being of God commands us to follow him, even apart from a specific command directed to us.

Scripture's Command to Follow Him

In Scripture we are, on the one hand, urged to be like God and, on the other hand, warned against the desire to be like God. God created human beings in the "image" and "likeness" of God (Gen. 1:26). Apparently, however, it was a desire to be "like God, knowing good and evil" that lay at the root of the fall (Gen. 2:5). From the Tower of Babel story in Genesis 11 to the fall of Babylon the Great in Revelation 14, Scripture always considers it intolerable to compare oneself to God. The temptation to arrogate to oneself the prerogatives of God seems particularly strong in royalty. Pharaoh (Exod. 3–14), Nebuchadnezzar (Dan. 4), and Herod (Acts 12), serve as negative examples of those who compare themselves favorably with God and do "not give praise to God" (Acts 12:23). We must bear this negative possibility in mind as we pursue the study of God's command to "imitate" him.

Scripture holds up God as the standard of moral perfection that we should imitate. The Lord said to the liberated Israelites, "Be holy because I, the Lord your God, am holy" (Lev. 19:2; cf. Lev. 11:44, 45; 20:7, 26). God chose David as king because he was a "man after his own heart" (1 Sam. 13:14; cf. Acts 13:22). Jesus summarizes the Sermon on the Mount with his command to be like the Father: "Be perfect, therefore, as your heavenly Father is perfect" (Matt. 5:48). Peter, reflecting the teaching of Leviticus, urges this of his readers: "Just as he who

30. Robert Jenson, "Joining the Eternal Conversation: John's Prologue and Language of Worship," *Touchstone* 14/9 (November 2001).

called you is holy, so be holy in all you do" (1 Pet. 1:15). Paul asks us to lift our sights above worldly things and "to put on the new self, created to be like God in true righteousness and holiness" (Eph. 4:23-24). John holds up God's love for us as a model for our love for our brothers and sisters, so that "we will have confidence on the day of judgment, because in this world we are like him" (1 John 4:16, 17). Finally, all the texts in which we are told to follow the example of Christ (1 Cor. 11:1; Phil. 2:5-11; 1 Tim. 1:16; 1 Pet. 2:21) assume that Christ is "the image of the invisible God" (Col. 1:15; cf. 2 Cor. 4:4).

The Imperative of God's Existence, Nature, and Action

In the sections on freedom and omnipotence I have argued that God enacts his nature and existence freely. There I have emphasized the freedom and power in which God is God. In this section I will focus on the righteousness of God's act of being. Earlier in this chapter I have also argued that, even apart from creation, God's life must be viewed as an eternal command and the perfect execution of that command. Now I will press further to claim that the existence, nature, and acts of God, apart from any direct commands, constitute an imperative to imitate him.

How can God's sheer existence constitute a command to follow him? How can we derive an obligation from a mere fact? Does this derivation not commit what G. E. Moore called the "naturalistic fallacy," deriving the "ought" from the "is"?[31] According to Moore's logical analysis, we must not jump from the fact that God exists to the conclusion that God *should* exist, nor from the conclusion that God is good to the conclusion that God's goodness is what *ought* to be. Moore's reasoning appears to be sound when applied to other natural or metaphysical objects, but God's existence is no mere fact or accident. Unlike creatures, God exists freely and thus *is* his existence. Likewise, God *is* his righteousness and does not just happen to be righteous, for his righteousness is his own act. Thus God is both his existence and his righteousness, and by thinking these two attributes together we can see that God's free act of existence is righteous. Everything God does is righteous, and his fundamental act is existing. Therefore, the fact that he exists is right — is what ought to be.

Second, God's nature is his command in the same way that his existence is

---

31. George Edward Moore, *Principia Ethica* (Cambridge, UK: Cambridge University Press, 1968). See, esp., ch. 4, "Metaphysical Ethics" (pp. 110-41). The attempt to found an "ought" on a fact, argues Moore, "rests upon a failure to perceive that any truth which asserts, 'This is good in itself' is quite unique in kind — that it cannot be reduced to any assertion about reality, and therefore must remain unaffected by any conclusions we may reach about the nature of reality" (p. 114).

his command, for *what* God is, is no mere accident or fate. He is not a god. As we saw in the sections on the divine freedom and personhood, God enacts his own nature freely. And he is righteous in all his actions. What God *is*, therefore, is right: it is what ought to be. Third, God always does what is right. As I explained in the section on righteousness, God always acts righteously in that he always acts consistently with his nature. His actions display his essential righteousness. The way God acts then obligates us to imitate him, for the way he acts is according to the way things ought to be. In sum, God's existence, nature, and actions express his will perfectly and thus voice his command to be like him.

Now I must deal with another objection to the position I am defending. Even if I have established that God's existence, nature, and action are what ought to be and thus determine what we ought to be, we can still inquire about the relationship between "what ought to be" and what is possible. That is, are there other ways of being and acting than imitating God? For if there are other genuine ways of being and acting, we can ask why God exists and acts in one way rather than another. More to the point, we may wonder why God commands us to be like him rather than take up other ways of living. Until we resolve this difficulty, we can imagine that some of those ways of being might be preferable to the one God commands us to take up.

In addressing this question, let us recall the section above on God's uniqueness. In that discussion I concluded that God is the only God and the only possible God. There are no other ways of being God. That God exists is not a mere accidental quality of God. God exists necessarily. He *is* his existence and nature. Therefore, we can say with Thomas Aquinas that "God is His own being."[32] The point is this: just as God's righteousness, love, and holiness define what it means to be righteous, loving, and holy, the being and activity of God define what it means to be and to act. We can be only as we share in his being, and we can act only as we participate in his action. There are (and can be) no other ways of being and acting, for there are (and can be) no other gods. Just as other "gods" are nothing, other "ways of being" are nothing, and other ways of acting are futile and empty. Therefore, God's command to imitate him is no arbitrary choice to impose on us one of many possible ways of being. God commands us to accept and enact our genuine being — our only possible being — rather than dreaming of a being that is nothing and wasting our energies chasing vanities. God's command to imitate him is a command to be, to live, to be free, and to enjoy good. To refuse it is to embrace nothingness, death, slavery, and evil.

32. *SumTh*, 1.3.4.

The Wrong and Right Ways to Imitate God

There is an infinite distance between envy and admiration and between the forms of imitation they inspire. I noted above that there is a negative side to the imitation of God.[33] Although Scripture urges us to be like God, it condemns the human ambition of taking God's place and exercising his prerogatives. This prohibition raises a question: Are we missing something good by not being God and by acting like God? Is there a legitimate basis for human envy of God? Friedrich Nietzsche thought so: "If there were Gods, how could I endure it to be no God," he complained.[34] Nietzsche is not alone. The archetypal sin in Scripture is the desire to be "like God." This aspiration presupposes that God is someone it makes sense to envy. That is, the one who envies God imagines that God is very much like us, except that he has access to goods that we have been denied. In our envy we project our own wishes onto God and think of him as a self-centered being, exercising his unlimited power capriciously and selfishly. We picture God at the center of the universe, drawing all things irresistibly into himself like a divine black hole. In the final analysis, we view God as nothingness, chaos, evil, and death. And we want to be like our "god."

There is no such God, nor can there be. Nothing about the true God invites jealousy and envy. Indeed, God is the opposite of enviable in almost every way. His power is love. He exists eternally as the total giving, receiving, returning, and sharing among the Father, Son, and Spirit. Out of infinite abundance and pure grace God creates, reconciles, and redeems his creation. We see the unenviable nature of God most clearly in the cross of Jesus. As I argued in the section on impassibility, the cross reveals the eternal character of God as self-giving, receiving, returning, and sharing. The passion of Christ proves the nonexistence of the self-centered god. No one can look at that figure on the cross with envy. Yet "he is the true God and eternal life" (1 John 5:20).

We have access to the Father through the Son in the Spirit. Hence, our understanding of God's command to imitate him must center on the Son's relationship to the Father, and the power to imitate him must come from the Spirit.[35] The Father loves the Son and gives him everything. The Son receives the love of the Father and returns that love in complete self-abandonment.

33. Where I speak of "wrong ways to imitate God" (under the influence of Augustine, *Confessions,* 2), Barth speaks of "resistance," "hostility," "indifference," and "willfulness" to the grace of God (*CD,* 2/2, pp. 575-83).

34. Friedrich Nietzsche, *Thus Spake Zarathustra,* trans. Thomas Common, vol. 4, *The Complete Works of Friedrich Nietzsche,* ed. Oscar Levy (Edinburgh: T. N. Foulis, 1909), p. 99.

35. Barth roots the justice of God's command in the grace of God given to us in Jesus Christ (*CD,* 2/2, p. 559).

The Son and the Spirit share in the love of the Father. According to Scripture, the Father creates, reconciles, and redeems the world through the Son and in the Spirit. The Son and Spirit love the world with the love of the Father. Within the Trinity, that circle of love flows from the Father to the Son through the Spirit and returns from them to the Father. With reference to creation, the movement of divine love flows from the Father through the Son and the Spirit to the world. However, God wills to draw the world into the divine circle of love, so love moves not only from the Father through the Son and Spirit to the world, but also is returned by the world through the Son and Spirit to the Father.

Just as the eternal Son in the Spirit receives, returns, and shares the love of the Father with us, so must we receive, return, and share the love of the Father with others. Orthodox theologian Dumitru Staniloae's bold words highlight this goal: "As a work of raising us believers to intimate communion with God, salvation and deification are nothing other than the extension to conscious creatures of the relations that obtain between the divine persons."[36] In a first step toward obeying God's command to imitate him, we must receive the eternal love the Father has for us in the Son. We cannot earn or force it, for it is from that love that we exist and enjoy good. All things flow from the Father.

Perhaps it appears easier to receive God's love than to return or share it. We may think we can simply take advantage of it by not rejecting our existence, relishing the good things of this world, and enjoying the comforting aspects of religion. But it is not that easy, for even in receiving God's love we must abandon ourselves. God's love is our only good; without it we are nothing. To receive God's love as genuine *love* (that is, as a gift) we must acknowledge that we are not our own, have no rights against God, and depend on him absolutely. Receiving God's love requires us to possess ourselves only as God's gift that is to be returned to him, immediately confident that our loving Father will not abandon us. He will give us ourselves again and again — and again. We know that this is true because the Father, who loves the Son eternally, did not abandon him to the grave but raised him from the dead.

Imitating God requires a second step. Having received ourselves, we must return ourselves to the Father without hesitation. For only by giving up all claims to self-possession can we possess ourselves *as a gift*. We cannot possess ourselves *as our own*, for on our own we are nothing. The mystery of the Holy Trinity, the glory of the cross, and the secret of the Christian life is that only by

36. Staniloae, *The Experience of God*, vol. 1, *Revelation and Knowledge of the Triune God*, trans. and ed. Ioan Ionita and Robert Barringer (Brookline, MA: Holy Cross Orthodox Press, 1994), p. 248.

abandoning our self for the sake of others do we become a self with any substance. Receiving and returning are but two aspects of one event.

The third movement in the imitation of God is sharing the love of the Father with others. Two can give, receive, and return, but it takes three to share. Indeed, only sharing can validate the genuineness of giving and receiving. The Holy Spirit is the Trinitarian principle of sharing or fellowship. The Son and the Spirit share the love of the Father with each other and with the world. The Holy Spirit opens the divine circle of fellowship to include us. We cannot genuinely receive the love of God and return ourselves to the Father without sharing that love with others. The Son and the Spirit joyfully act as a means through which the Father extends his love to others. In the same way, our receiving of the Father's love entails that we renounce any basis for selfishness. Returning ourselves to the Father makes us available as means through which the Father may love others. When our trust in God's love allows us to abandon ourselves to God without fear of lack or loss, it also frees us to abandon ourselves for the sake of those whom God loves. Thus imitating God requires us to emulate the giving love of the Father, the receiving and returning love of the Son, and the sharing love of the Holy Spirit — one God blessed for ever and ever.

Praise Him!

"Great is the Lord and most worthy of praise!" (Ps. 96:4). God is not only good and righteous; God is perfect, admirable, and glorious in his own eternal life. His very being commands us to praise him. Each of his attributes and actions is perfect, and all of them dwell harmoniously together in infinite beauty as the perfection of perfections. We cannot dwell in his presence unmoved by his excellence.[37] We must praise him.

The Praiseworthy

The praiseworthy evokes our admiration and elicits our praise. We admire and praise things of beauty and value in nature and art: a sunset, a flower, an ocean, a mountain scene, a painting, a sculpture, or a cathedral. Let us leave nature aside for the moment, however, and focus on our admiration for human accomplishments. Art (for me at least) is never as beautiful as nature, but we are conscious of something in art that is not so obvious in nature: the accomplishment of the artist. In addition to the sheer beauty of the art, we experience

---

37. Barth, in *CD*, 2/1, p. 674, links glorifying God with following him.

wonder at the exceptional skill, insight, and genius of the artist. But if the artist were a god that created art by magic, we would not entertain such wonder. In admiring the art we are aware that the human creator shares our humanity; and, though the artist is endowed with great gifts, he or she does not transcend human possibilities. The artist makes it look easy; but if we became convinced that the work really was easy, our admiration would cease. Our admiration is greatly enhanced by the assumption that the artist spent much time and exerted great labor to develop these native gifts. It matters that the beauty was achieved at a cost. That is, our appreciation of art has a moral dimension.[38]

Let us then shift our attention from the beauty of art to the moral excellence of persons. According to Aristotle, moral excellence, like beauty in nature and art, is self-evidently recognizable. We simply admire the character of some individuals as morally excellent. Upon reflection, we discover that these individuals have certain virtues that excite our admiration: courage, temperance, justice, generosity, wisdom, and magnanimity.[39] Each of these virtues is a mean between two extremes: for example, courage is a mean between rashness and cowardice. In a morally excellent character, all these virtues fit together in harmonious relationships that strike us as beautiful. Like the great artist, the virtuous person is one of us and realizes possibilities that are ours as well. Yet the excellent moral character excites our admiration, not only because of its sheer beauty, but also because it is accomplished at great cost and is freely enacted. If we learned that it came easy to that person or that it was determined by some necessity, our admiration for the person's moral character would diminish.[40]

Christian moral philosophers often build on Aristotle's ethics of virtue by adding the supernatural virtues of faith, hope, and love to the natural virtues.[41] In doing so, they elevate our notion of moral excellence. Love is the chief Christian virtue, and, though it does not replace them, it gives a new and higher ori-

---

38. For a similar analysis of the relationship between skill and praise, see James D. Wallace, "Excellences and Merit," *The Philosophical Review* 83 (1974): 187-88.

39. In his *Ethics,* Aristotle discusses the moral virtues in Books 2-5, and the intellectual virtues in Book 6.

40. Aristotle lists three conditions under which a good act counts as praiseworthy: "The agent also must be in a certain condition when he does them; in the first place he must have knowledge, secondly he must choose the acts, and choose them for their own sakes, and thirdly his action must proceed from a firm and unchangeable character" (quoted in Wallace, "Excellences and Merit," p. 193). Lewis White Beck says that the praiseworthiness of actions depends on the conditions under which they are performed. And two of those conditions are that "they are reached through struggle and in opposition to other values which might have been attained through possible alternative actions" ("Character and Deed," *Philosophy and Phenomenological Research* 4 [1944]: 552). These two conditions correspond to "cost" and "freedom" in my analysis.

41. Aquinas discusses the "theological virtues" in *SumTh,* 2.1.62.1-4.

entation to all other virtues. Love, more than any other virtue, exemplifies the admirable qualities mentioned above: costliness, beauty, and freedom. In love we give ourselves to another in freedom. Love epitomizes all the other virtues, for all of them involve unselfish and free relationships with others. Love even includes the other theological virtues, faith and hope: "Love believes all things, hopes all things" (1 Cor. 13:7). We bestow our highest admiration on a character composed of all the virtues, balanced in harmony, and held together by love.

Our admiration for the praiseworthy must be expressed. We are moved by its excellence to an inner state of admiration. However, this inner feeling exerts an outward pressure, seeking expression and reinforcement. We must praise the praiseworthy thing. We can express our praise in silent attention or by falling prostrate to the ground. We can lift up our hands to the heavens or kneel to earth; we can weep with longing or shout with joy. Moreover, if the admiration in us is caused by the praiseworthy thing itself, others can admire and praise it as well. The praiseworthy thing must be shared, for experiencing others' praise for it confirms that our admiration is grounded in the praiseworthy thing itself and thus adds to our admiration and praise. Hence, we must praise it before others and hope that they, too, have seen, admired, and will praise it. It is too wonderful to be taken in alone.[42]

God Is the Praiseworthy

Other things are praiseworthy in a limited sense, but God is unlimitedly praise-worthy. Indeed, since he is all his attributes, God is the praiseworthy itself. We cannot value him more than he merits, admire him beyond his worth, or praise him more than he deserves. God's virtues are perfect and his character complete, and he acts in perfect love and freedom. He exercises perfect mercy and righteousness without conflict. The Lord is boundless but fully present to the smallest particle. Though his power is inexhaustible, he stoops to empower the weakest of his creatures. He is completely constant in the incessant activity of his life. Though God dwells in eternity, he gives time to creatures so that they may live with him.

God is infinite, omniscient, omnipotent, omnipresent, independent, impassible, immortal, and so on. But these alone do not evoke our praise. We do not admire and praise God just because he is more powerful, long-lasting, and knowing than we are. We admire and praise him because, as the transcendent one, God is also free and loving; and as the free and loving one, he is also tran-

---

42. John Kleinig, in "What's the Use of Praising God?" *Lutheran Theological Journal* 38 (2004): 87, emphasizes the communal nature of praise.

scendent. As self-sufficient, God could remain wrapped up in himself, but he does not. He goes out of himself, freely making himself present to the most insignificant of creatures. We admire him because, as great, he stoops down to the small, in mercy to the suffering, in grace to the guilty, and in patience to the rebellious.

I noted earlier that our admiration for a work of art would diminish if we discovered that the artist were a god who could produce the art object by magic or necessity. Unfortunately, we often think of God this way and thus blunt our ability to admire and praise him. If being God and doing what he does is easy for him (like magic), how can we admire him? Robert F. Creegan voices this objection in these words: "All praise is for achievement in some quest . . . we do not praise one for having a certain status. We may greatly admire one for that, but still we do not praise one for that."[43] Or, if God is God by necessity and acts as God by necessity, why does he deserve praise? Philosopher William L. Rowe articulates the objection this way: "If God necessarily creates this world and, therefore, cannot avoid creating it, and, in addition, this world necessarily includes us, then it would make no sense for us to thank God or be grateful to God for creating us."[44] Though I have already answered these questions implicitly in this chapter, let us address them explicitly.

Do God's works cost him anything? We can find the answer to this question only by again probing our faith that God is love and does all he does in love. Of course, the idea of "cost" cannot be applied to God strictly. The actions by means of which he has created and cares for his creatures do not "cost" him something in the sense that God must give up "some" of his goodness, happiness, power, or life so that creatures may have some of these things. This would imply that God's attributes are finite and divisible. Nevertheless, love is costly to God in this sense: in love God gives himself wholly and unconditionally to the object of his love. If God were not already (eternally) perfect love, creating the world would be very costly to him in the strict sense. That is, to create the world, an isolated and self-absorbed God would need to give up his serene state — presumably the highest good for him — and open himself to suffering and loss.

But God exists eternally as self-abandoning love among the Father, Son, and Spirit. As we learned in the section on impassibility, God's eternal self-giving is not painful but joyous, not loss but gain. The divine life is infinitely full precisely because it is self-abandoning, and self-abandonment is a loss only

43. Creegan, "Remarks on the Phenomenology of Praise," *Philosophy and Phenomenological Research* 6 (1946): 422.
44. Rowe, *Can God Be Free?* (Oxford: Clarendon Press, 2004), pp. 113-14.

on the assumption that self-containment is the higher good. The revelation of the triune God in Jesus Christ demonstrates once and for all that it is not. God exists in complete openness. The persons of the Trinity live eternally in each other, so that God has never been a self-contained being. Indeed, we could not admire and praise a self-enclosed God even if he endured the cost of opening himself to our existence. For opening himself to us would cast into doubt his genuine self-containment and create suspicion that his overtures were based on underlying necessity or secret need. We can admire and praise God without holding back only if God is free of need — and gives himself to us anyway. Hence, I must revise the earlier principle where I said that our admiration for a work of art or an excellent character is proportioned to the cost required for its achievement. We can now see that it is not the harm done to the giver that evokes our admiration and praise; rather, it is the presence of the giver in the gift, made available freely and unselfishly. We do not admire and praise God because he harms himself to help us; we admire and praise him because he gives himself to us as our good, freely and unselfishly.

Having addressed the question of whether we can admire and praise God if his actions cost him nothing, we now turn to the question of whether we can admire and praise God if his actions flow *necessarily* from his divine nature. We treat God and his benefits, more often than not, as if they were part of the necessary structures of the universe. If we consider them in that way, perhaps we could view God as the highest good and thus desire him and seek him as necessary for our happiness. But we could not admire and praise God simply for being what he is and doing what he does. Contemplating God's existence might arouse longing and desire, but it could not spark admiration and praise. Observing the workings of a machine might engage our curiosity, and grasping a logical proof might give intellectual satisfaction; but neither one would evoke admiration and praise.

But to think of God in this way is to forget that God is God freely. Here, as elsewhere in this study, we must labor to escape the pagan premise of the priority of impersonal nature over personhood. God is not God because this is his fate. Traditional theologians rightly spoke of God's necessary existence and attributes, but this necessity was never conceived as fate or limit. Rather, it refers to the essential nature of God's existence and attributes: God exists and is what he is freely. For freedom is just as much an essential divine attribute as is necessity. Indeed, God's necessity is an essential aspect of his freedom. If God did not exist essentially (hence, necessarily), he would be subject to external coercion, and that would imply a lack of freedom. God's "necessity" lies in his free enactment of every aspect of his being, and his freedom is freed from all arbitrariness by his necessity. God exists in the perfect union of infinity and perfection, subject and object, and freedom and necessity that we earlier called personhood.[45]

If we are to think rightly about God, we will not say to ourselves, "God is God. So what?" No, when we come to understand that God is God freely, we will say, "God is God. Praise God!" His glorious being is his free act. That God exists is amazing, surprising, and glorious. Rowe says it aptly: "It appears that only if God is in some way causally responsible for his own perfect nature can we be justified in morally praising God for the perfect acts required by his essential nature."[46] Fortunately, Rowe goes on to argue that God is in fact responsible in that way. To put it in Trinitarian terms, the Father wills to exist for the Son and the Spirit, and the Son and the Spirit will to exist for the Father. The triune God wills to exist for us. God's omnipotence, omnipresence, mercy, love, righteousness, wisdom, patience, and his other attributes are his free acts. No fate forces him to be this way. We meet *God* in his acts, not fate acting through him. The freedom of which I speak is not the freedom of contingency or indifference, that is, of those things that might not have been. God does not freely exist because he might not have been, but because he possesses himself completely. His is the freedom of self-possession, that is, of pure actuality or of perfect personhood.

We can admire and praise God simply for existing as God, because he does not have to exist. His existence is his free action, and thus it is admirable and praiseworthy. We can admire and praise him for all his attributes and actions because he did not have to be or act in this way. Everything about God is an act of love and freedom. Therefore, everything about God — his existence and attributes as well as his actions toward us — is a matter of character and virtue. God's infinite excellence is his own achievement (not fate); hence, he deserves our infinite admiration and praise.

Perfecting Our Admiration and Praise

God is praiseworthy from all eternity and in every respect. Every good and beautiful thing we receive and desire points beyond itself to the gracious giver who gives himself totally in all his gifts. God exists and lives as a command to praise him. Therefore, we must praise him with our whole being, at all times, places, and in all our actions and words. The psalmist understands this: "Praise

---

45. According to Muller, traditional theologians opposed necessity to "impossibility" and freedom to "coercion": that is, freedom and necessity are not contraries. See Muller, *PRRD*, 3, p. 434, n. 360.
46. Rowe, *Can God Be Free?* p. 150.

the Lord, O my soul; all my inmost being, praise his holy name" (Ps. 103:1). "I will praise the Lord all my life; I will sing praise to my God as long as I live" (Ps. 146:2). Likewise, Paul urges the Romans to offer themselves as "living sacrifices, holy and pleasing to God" (Rom. 12:1). Although every act of life can praise God in its own way, in order for us to achieve its highest expression, our praise must come into speech as personal address. All our actions take place *before* God, but our praise speaks *about* "the greatness of God in virtues and deeds" to others or is directed *to* him in the presence of others.[47] This is why Scripture urges us to sing to the Lord in the company of God's people.

In Scripture, wherever there is thanksgiving and praise, there is singing. Moses begins his victory song: "I will sing to the Lord, for he is highly exalted" (Exod. 15:1). In view of God's new work of redemption, Isaiah urges Judah to sing a "new song" to the Lord (Isa. 42:10). He urges the heavens to "sing for joy," the earth to "shout aloud," and the mountains and trees to "burst into song" in praise of God (Isa. 44:33). The Psalter witnesses to the place of praise in the life of God's people: "Praise the Lord with the harp; make music to him on the ten-stringed lyre. Sing to him a new song; play skillfully, and shout for joy" (Ps. 33:2-3; cf. Ps. 96:1; 149:1).

The New Testament continues to urge the people of God to praise him with their lips. Paul writes to the Ephesians: "Speak to one another with psalms, hymns, and spiritual songs. Sing and make music in your heart to the Lord" (Eph. 5:19; cf. Col. 3:16). James counsels the troubled to pray and the happy to "sing songs of praise" (James 5:13). There is singing before the throne of God, according to the book of Revelation. The four living creatures "never stop saying: 'Holy, holy, holy is the Lord God almighty who was, and is, and is to come'" (Rev. 4:8). The twenty-four elders lay their crowns before the throne and say, "You are worthy, our Lord and God, to receive glory and honor and power" (Rev. 4:11). At the appearance of the Lamb, the twenty-four elders "[sing] a new song" to the Lamb (Rev. 5:9; cf. Rev. 14:3). Finally, all the angels join in the praise, and "in a loud voice they [sing]: 'Worthy is the Lamb, who was slain, to receive power and wealth and wisdom and strength and honor and glory and praise!'" (Rev. 5:12; cf. Rev. 15:3-4)

Barth pictures humanity joyfully, if belatedly, joining the chorus of heaven and earth as it glorifies God:

And when a man accepts again his destiny in Jesus Christ . . . he is only like a late-comer slipping shamefacedly into creation's choir in heaven and earth,

---

47. Geoffrey Wainwright, "The Praise of God in Theological Reflection of the Church," *Interpretation* 39 (1985): 35.

which has never ceased its praise. . . . In the eternal glory before us . . . man too will live in his determination to be the reflection and echo of God and therefore the witness to the divine glory that reaches over to him, rejoicing with the God who Himself has eternal joy and Himself is eternal joy.[48]

I do not intend to limit the praising of God to singing in harmony or in poetry or even in words alone. However, admiration for God must express itself in actions and words: nonresponsiveness is not an option. Even the presence of natural beauty or a great work of art requires and compels a response. How much more would a lack of responsiveness to God's greatness indicate an absence of understanding? Seeing God's greatness without praising him would constitute a contradiction and induce great pain. We must praise him, and we must urge others to praise him! As Jesus entered Jerusalem, the crowd sang his praises: "Blessed is the king who comes in the name of the Lord. Peace in heaven and glory in the highest." Some of the Pharisees asked Jesus to rebuke his disciples for their display, but Jesus replied: "I tell you that if they keep quiet, the stones will cry out" (Luke 19:37-40).

48. *CD*, 2/1, pp. 648-49.

Bibliography

Achtner, Wolfgang, Stefan Kunz, and Thomas Walter. *Dimensions of Time: The Structures of the Time of Humans, of the World and of God.* Grand Rapids: Eerdmans, 2002.

Adams, Robert Merrihew. *Finite and Infinite Goods: A Framework for Ethics.* Oxford: Oxford University Press, 1999.

Alston, William. "Some Suggestions for Divine Command Theorists." In *Christian Theism and the Problems of Philosophy,* edited by Michael Beaty, 303-26. Notre Dame, IN: University of Notre Dame Press, 1990.

Anselm. *Saint Anselm: Basic Writings.* 2nd ed. Edited and translated by S. N. Deane. LaSalle, IL: Open Court, 1969.

Aquinas, Thomas. *Basic Writings of Saint Thomas Aquinas.* 2 vols. Edited by Anton C. Pegis. New York: Random House, 1945.

Arendt, Hannah. *On Violence.* New York: Harcourt, Brace & World, 1970.

Aristotle. *The Basic Writings of Aristotle.* Edited by Richard McKeon. New York: Random House, 1941.

Arnold, Matthew. *The Poems of Matthew Arnold 1840-1867.* Reprint of 1913 title. London: Oxford, 1940.

Athanasius. *St. Athanasius On the Incarnation.* Translated and edited by A Religious of C.S.M.V. Crestwood, NY: St. Vladimir's Press, 2003.

Augustine. *Confessions.* Translated by Henry Chadwick. New York: Oxford University Press, 1991.

Ayres, Lewis. "Augustine, Christology, and God as Love: An Introduction to the Homilies on 1 John." In *Nothing Greater, Nothing Better: Theological Essays on the Love of God,* edited by Kevin J. Vanhoozer, 67-93. Grand Rapids: Eerdmans, 2001.

Badcock, Gary D. "The Concept of Love: Divine and Human." In *Nothing Greater, Nothing Better: Theological Essays on the Love of God,* edited by Kevin J. Vanhoozer, 30-46. Grand Rapids: Eerdmans, 2001.

Barth, Karl. *Church Dogmatics.* 4 vols. Translated by G. W. Bromiley and T. F. Torrance. Edinburgh: T&T Clark, 1936-1969.

Barton, John. *Holy Writings, Sacred Text: The Canon in Early Christianity.* Louisville: Westminster John Knox, 1997.

―――. "Marcion Revisited." In *The Canon Debate,* edited by Lee Martin McDonald and James A. Sanders, 340-54. Peabody, MA: Hendrickson, 2002.

Basinger, David. *The Case for Freewill Theism: A Philosophical Assessment.* Downers Grove, IL: InterVarsity Press, 1996.

Bauckham, Richard. "'Only the Suffering God Can Help': Divine Passibility in Modern Theology." *Themelios* 3 (1985): 6-12.

―――. *The Theology of Jürgen Moltmann.* Edinburgh: T&T Clark, 1995.

Bavinck, Herman. *Reformed Dogmatics.* 3 vols. Edited by John Bolt. Translated by John Vriend. Grand Rapids: Baker Academic, 2003-2006.

Beck, Lewis White. "Character and Deed." *Philosophy and Phenomenological Research* 4 (1944): 547-53.

Behr, John. *Formation of Christian Theology.* 2 vols. Crestwood, NY: St. Vladimir's Seminary Press, 2001.

Bernard of Clairvaux. *On Loving God.* Available at http://www.ccel.org/ccel/bernard/loving_god.vii.html (accessed April 2, 2005).

Binning, Hugh. *The Works of The Rev. Hugh Binning, M.A.* 3rd ed. Edited by Rev. M. Leishan, D.D. London: A. Fullarton and Co., 1851.

Blackwell, Richard J. *Galileo, Bellarmine, and the Bible.* Notre Dame, IN: University of Notre Dame Press, 1991.

Bloesch, Donald G. *God the Almighty: Power, Wisdom, Holiness, Love.* Downers Grove, IL: InterVarsity Press, 1995.

Bobrinskoy, Boris. *The Mystery of the Trinity: Trinitarian Experience and Vision in the Biblical and Patristic Tradition.* Crestwood, NY: St. Vladimir's Seminary Press, 1999.

Boethius. *The Consolation of Philosophy.* Translated by W. V. Cooper. London: J. M. Dent and Company, 1902.

Bonhoeffer, Dietrich. *Ethics.* Translated by Neville Horton Smith. New York: Macmillan, 1955.

Boyd, Gregory. *God at War: The Bible and Spiritual Conflict.* Downers Grove, IL: InterVarsity Press, 1997.

―――. *The God of the Possible: A Biblical Introduction to the Open View of God.* Grand Rapids: Baker Books, 2000.

―――. *Satan and the Problem of Evil: Constructing a Trinitarian Warfare Theodicy.* Downers Grove, IL: InterVarsity Press, 2001.

Braaten, Carl E., and Robert W. Jenson, eds. *Christian Dogmatics.* 2 vols. Philadelphia: Fortress Press, 1984.

Bransnett, Bertrand R. *The Suffering of the Impassible God.* London: SPCK, 1928.

Brody, Baruch A. "Morality and Religion Reconsidered." In *Readings in The Philosophy of Religion: An Analytic Approach,* edited by Baruch A. Brody, 592-603. Englewood Cliffs, NJ: Prentice-Hall, 1974.

Bruce, F. F. *The Canon of Scripture.* Downers Grove, IL: InterVarsity Press, 1988.

Brümmer, Vincent. *The Model of Love: A Study in Philosophical Theology.* Cambridge, UK: Cambridge University Press, 1993.

———. *Speaking of a Personal God: An Essay in Philosophical Theology.* Cambridge, UK: Cambridge University Press, 1992.

Brunner, Emil. *The Christian Doctrine of God.* Translated by Olive Wyon. Philadelphia: Westminster Press, 1949.

———. *The Divine Imperative.* Translated by Olive Wyon. Philadelphia: Westminster Press, n.d.

Buckley, Michael J. *At the Origins of Modern Atheism.* New Haven, CT: Yale University Press, 1987.

Burrell, David. *Aquinas: God and Action.* Notre Dame, IN: University of Notre Dame Press, 1979.

———. "Divine Practical Knowing: How an Eternal God Acts in Time." In *Divine Action: Studies Inspired by the Philosophical Theology of Austin Farrar,* edited by Brian Hebblethwaite and Edward Henderson, 93-102. Edinburgh: T&T Clark, 1990.

———. *Knowing the Unknowable God.* Notre Dame, IN: University of Notre Dame Press, 1986.

Butler, Joseph. *The Analogy of Religion.* New York: Frederick Ungar Publishing Company, 1961.

Calvin, John. *Calvin's Commentaries.* 22 vols. Edited by David W. Torrance and Thomas F. Torrance. Grand Rapids: Eerdmans, 1960.

———. *Institutes of the Christian Religion.* Edited by John T. McNeill. Translated by Ford Lewis Battles. Philadelphia: Westminster Press, 1960.

Campenhausen, Hans von. *The Formation of the Christian Bible.* Translated by J. A. Baker. Philadelphia: Fortress Press, 1972.

Candlish, Stewart. "The Identity Theory of Truth." In *The Stanford Encyclopedia of Philosophy.* Available at http://plato.stanford.edu/entries/truth-identity/ (accessed July 17, 2006).

Casey, Michael. *The Battle Over Hermeneutics in the Stone-Campbell Movement.* Lewiston, NJ: Edwin Mellen Press, 1998.

Chemnitz, Martin. *Examination of the Council of Trent.* Translated by Fred Kramer. St. Louis: Concordia Publishing House, 1971.

Clarke, Norris. "A New Look at the Immutability of God." In *God Knowable and Unknowable,* edited by Robert J. Roth, S.J. New York: Fordham University Press, 1973.

Clayton, Philip. *The Problem of God in Modern Thought.* Grand Rapids: Eerdmans, 2000.

Clifford, W. K. *The Ethics of Belief and Other Essays.* London: Watts and Co., 1947.

Clouser, Roy. *Knowing with the Heart: Religious Experience and Belief in God.* Downers Grove, IL: InterVarsity Press, 1999.

———. *The Myth of Religious Neutrality: An Essay on the Hidden Role of Religious Beliefs in Theories.* Notre Dame, IN: University of Notre Dame Press, 1991.

Congar, Yves M. *Tradition and Traditions: An Historical and a Theological Essay.* New York: Macmillan Company, 1967.

Copleston, Fredrick. *A History of Philosophy.* 9 vols. Garden City, NY: Image Books, 1962-1967.

Cottrell, Jack. *The Faith Once For All: Bible Doctrine For Today.* Joplin, MO: College Press, 2002.

———. *What the Bible Says About God the Redeemer.* Joplin, MO: College Press, 1987.

Craig, William Lane. *Divine Foreknowledge and Human Freedom: The Coherence of Theism: Omniscience.* Leiden: E. J. Brill, 1990.

―――. "Middle Knowledge: A Calvinist-Arminian Rapprochement." In *The Grace of God and the Will of Man,* edited by Clark Pinnock, 141-64. Minneapolis: Bethany House Publishers, 1989.

―――. *The Only Wise God: The Compatibility of Divine Foreknowledge and Human Freedom.* Grand Rapids: Baker Books, 1987.

―――. *The Problem of Divine Foreknowledge and Human Freedom from Aristotle to Suárez.* Leiden: Brill, 1980.

―――. *Time and Eternity: Exploring God's Relationship to Time.* Wheaton, IL: Crossway Books, 2001.

―――. "Timelessness and Omnitemporality." In *God and Time: Four Views,* edited by Gregory E. Gannsle, 129-60. Downers Grove, IL: InterVarsity Press, 2001.

Creegan, Robert F. "Remarks on the Phenomenology of Praise." *Philosophy and Phenomenological Research* 6 (1946): 421-23.

Cross, Richard. "Duns Scotus on Eternity and Timelessness." *Faith and Philosophy* 14 (1997): 3-25.

Davies, Brian. "Classical Theism and the Doctrine of Divine Simplicity." In *Language, Meaning, and God: Essays in Honor of Herbert McCabe,* edited by Brian Davies, 51-74. London: Cassell, 1987.

Davis, Caroline Franks. *The Evidential Force of Religious Experience.* Oxford: Clarendon Press, 1989.

Dawkins, Richard. *The Blind Watchmaker.* New York: Norton, 1986.

D'Holbach, Baron. *The System of Nature.* 2 vols. Translated by H. D. Robison. Kitchener, Ont.: Batoche Books, 2001.

Descartes, René. *The Philosophical Writings of Descartes.* Translated by John Cottingham, Robert Stoothoff, Dugold Murdoch, and Anthony Kenny. Cambridge, UK: Cambridge University Press, 1991.

Dekker, Eef. "Was Arminius a Molinist?" *Sixteenth Century Journal* 27/2 (1996): 337-52.

Dionysius the Areopagite. *Dionysius the Areopagite on the Divine Names and the Mystical Theology.* Translated by C. E. Rolt. Berwick, ME: IBIS Press, 2004.

Dodds, Michael J. "St. Thomas and the Motion of the Motionless God." *New Blackfriars* 68 (1987): 233-42.

―――. *The Unchanging God of Love: A Study of the Teaching of St. Thomas Aquinas on Divine Immutability in View of Certain Contemporary Criticism of this Doctrine.* Fribourg: Editions Universitaires Fribourg Suisse, 1986.

Dombrowski, Daniel A. "Must a Perfect Being Be Immutable?" In *Hartshorne, Process Philosophy and Theology,* edited by Robert Kane and Stephen H. Phillip, 91-111. Albany, NY: SUNY Press, 1989.

Dorner, I. A. *Divine Immutability: A Critical Reconstruction.* Translated by Robert R. Williams and Claude Welch. Minneapolis: Fortress Press, 1994.

Duns Scotus, John. *Philosophical Writings.* Translated by Allan Wolter. Indianapolis: Hackett, 1987.

Edwards, Jonathan. *Freedom of the Will.* New Haven, CT: Yale University Press, 1957.

Eichrodt, Walther. *Theology of the Old Testament.* 2 vols. Translated by J. A. Barker. Philadelphia: Westminster Press, 1961.

Eliade, Mircea. *The Sacred and the Profane.* New York: Harper Torchbooks, 1961.

Elwell, Walter A., ed. *Evangelical Dictionary of Theology.* Grand Rapids: Baker Book House, 1984.

Euripides. *The Plays of Euripides.* Translated by Edward P. Coleridge. London: George Bell and Sons, 1904.

Fairbairn, A. M. *The Place of Christ in Modern Theology.* New York: Charles Scribner's Sons, 1916.

Fénelon, François. *Spiritual Counsel on Divers Matters Pertaining to the Inner Life.* Available at http://www.ccel.org/ccel/fenelon/progress.iii.i.html (accessed June 28, 2005).

Ferguson, Everett. "Factors Leading to the Selection and Closure of the New Testament Canon: A Survey of Some Recent Studies." In *The Canon Debate,* edited by Lee Martin McDonald and James A. Sanders, 295-320. Peabody, MA: Hendrickson Publishers, 2002.

Fiddes, Paul. *The Creative Suffering of God.* Oxford: Clarendon Press, 1988.

———. *Participating in God: A Pastoral Doctrine of the Trinity.* Louisville: Westminster/ John Knox Press, 2000.

Fielding, Henry. *Love in Several Masques: A Comedy, As It Is Acted at the Theatre-Royal, by His Majesty's Servants.* London: John Watts, 1728.

Fischer, John Martin, ed. *God, Foreknowledge and Freedom.* Stanford, CA: Stanford University Press, 1989.

Flew, Anthony. *The Presumption of Atheism.* London: Pemberton, 1976.

———. "The Presumption of Atheism." In *Contemporary Perspectives on Religious Epistemology,* edited by R. Douglas Geivett and Brendan Sweetman, 19-32. New York: Oxford University Press, 1992.

Flint, Thomas P., and Alfred J. Freddoso. "Maximal Power." In *The Existence and Nature of God,* edited by Alfred J. Freddoso, 81-113. Notre Dame, IN: University of Notre Dame, 1983.

Florovsky, Georges. "The Concept of Creation in Saint Athanasius." *Studia Patristica* 6 (1962): 36-67.

Ford, Lewis S. "Process and Thomist Views Concerning Divine Perfection." In *The University as Journey: Conversations with W. Norris Clarke,* edited by Gerald A. McCool, S.J., 115-29. New York: Fordham University Press, 1988.

Frame, John. *The Doctrine of God.* Phillipsburg, NJ: Presbyterian and Reformed Publishing Company, 2002.

Frankford, Henri, et al. *Before Philosophy: The Intellectual Adventure of Ancient Man.* Baltimore: Penguin Books, n.d.

Freddoso, Alfred J. "God's General Concurrence with Secondary Causes: Pitfalls and Prospects." *American Catholic Philosophical Quarterly* 67 (1994): 553-85.

———. "Molina, Luis De." In *The Concise Routledge Encyclopedia of Philosophy.* London: Routledge, 2000.

Fritz, Maureena. "A Midrash: The Self-Limitation of God." *Journal of Ecumenical Studies* 22 (1985): 703-14.

Fuerst, Adrian. *An Historical Study of the Doctrine of the Omnipresence of God in Selected*

Writings Between 1220-1270. Washington, DC: Catholic University of America Press, 1951.

Gamble, Harry Y. *The New Testament Canon: Its Making and Meaning.* Minneapolis: Augsburg/Fortress, 1985.

————. "The New Testament Canon: Recent Research and the *Status Quaestionis.*" In *The Canon Debate,* edited by Lee Martin McDonald and James A. Sanders, 267-94. Peabody, MA: Hendrickson Publishers, 2002.

Gannsle, Gregory E., ed. *God and Time: Four Views.* Downers Grove, IL: InterVarsity Press, 2001.

Garrigou-Lagrange, Reginald. *Providence.* Translated by Dom Bede Rose, O.S.B. Reprint of 1937 title. Rockford, IL: Tan Books and Publishers, 1998.

Gavrilyuk, Paul L. *The Suffering of the Impassible God: The Dialectics of Patristic Thought.* Oxford: Oxford University Press, 2004.

Geach, Peter. "Omnipotence." In *Contemporary Philosophy of Religion,* edited by Steven M. Cahn and David Shatz, 46-60. New York: Oxford University Press, 1982.

Gerson, Lloyd P., ed. *Cambridge Companion to Plotinus.* New York: Cambridge University Press, 1996.

Gilson, Etienne. *The Philosophy of Thomas Aquinas.* Translated by Edward Bullough. Edited by G. A. Elrington. New York: Dorset Press, n.d.

Grabowski, Stanislaus J. *The All-Present God: A Study of St. Augustine.* St. Louis: B. Herder Book Co., 1954.

Gray, Donald. "On Patience: Human and Divine." *Cross Currents* 24 (1975): 409-22, 443.

Gregory of Nazianzus. *On God and Christ: The Five Theological Orations and Two Letters to Cledonius.* Translated by Frederick Williams and Lionel Wickham. Crestwood, NY: St. Vladimir's Seminary Press, 2002.

Grenz, Stanley J. *Rediscovering the Triune God: The Trinity in Contemporary Theology.* Minneapolis: Augsburg Fortress, 2004.

Griffin, David Ray. *Evil Revisited: Responses and Reconsiderations.* Albany: SUNY Press, 1991.

Gunton, Colin. *Act and Being: Towards a Theology of the Divine Attributes.* Grand Rapids, Eerdmans, 2002.

————. *The One, the Three and the Many: God, Creation and the Culture of Modernity.* Cambridge, UK: Cambridge University Press, 1992.

————. *The Promise of Trinitarian Theology.* Edinburgh: T&T Clark, 1991.

————. "Review of Catherine LaCugna, *God for Us.*" *Scottish Journal of Theology* 47 (1994): 135-37.

Guthrie, W. K. C. *Greek Philosophers from Thales to Aristotle.* New York: Harper and Row, 1960.

Hallman, Joseph M. *The Descent of God: Divine Suffering in History and Theology.* Minneapolis: Fortress Press, 1991.

Hammond, John L. "Divine Command Theories and Human Analogies." *The Journal of Religious Ethics* 14 (1986): 216-23.

Hanratty, Gerald. "Divine Immutability and Impassibility Revisited." In *At the Heart of the Real,* edited by Fran O'Rourke, 135-62. Dublin: Irish Academic Press, 1992.

434

Hanson, R. P. C. *The Search for the Christian Doctrine of God: The Arian Controversy, 318-381.* Reprint of 1988 title. Grand Rapids: Baker Academic, 2005.

———. *Tradition in the Early Church.* Philadelphia: Westminster Press, 1962.

Harnack, Adolf von. *History of Dogma.* 7 vols. Translated by Neil Buchanan. Eugene, OR: Wipf and Stock Publishers, 2000.

Hart, Trevor, ed. *Dictionary of Historical Theology.* Grand Rapids: Eerdmans, 2000.

Hartshorne, Charles. *The Divine Relativity.* New Haven, CT: Yale University Press, 1948.

———. *The Logic of Perfection and Other Essays in Metaphysics.* La Salle, IL: Open Court, 1962.

———. *A Natural Theology for Our Time.* LaSalle, IL: Open Court, 1967.

———. *Man's Vision of God and the Logic of Theism.* Chicago: Willett, Clark and Company, 1941.

———. *Omnipotence and Other Theological Mistakes.* Albany, NY: SUNY, 1984.

Hasker, William. "An Adequate God." In *Searching for an Adequate God: A Dialogue Between Process and Free Will Theists,* edited by John B. Cobb Jr. and Clark H. Pinnock, 215-45. Grand Rapids: Eerdmans, 2000.

———. *God, Time and Knowledge.* Ithaca, NY: Cornell University Press, 1998.

———. "A Philosophical Perspective." In *The Openness of God: A Biblical Challenge to the Traditional Understanding of God,* edited by Clark Pinnock, Richard Rice, et al., 126-54. Downers Grove, IL: InterVarsity Press, 1994.

Helm, Paul. *The Eternal God: A Study of God Without Time.* Oxford: Clarendon Press, 1988.

———. "God and Spacelessness." In *Contemporary Philosophy of Religion,* edited by Steven M. Cahn and David Shatz, 99-110. Oxford: Oxford University Press, 1982.

Heppe, Heinrich. *Reformed Dogmatics: Set Out and Illustrated from the Sources.* Revised and edited by E. Bizer. Translated by G. T. Thomson. Reprint of a 1950 title. London: Wakeman Great Reprints, n.d.

Highfield, Ron. "Divine Self-Limitation in the Theology of Jürgen Moltmann: A Critical Appraisal." *Christian Scholars Review* 32 (2002): 47-71.

———. "Does the World Limit God? Assessing the Case for Open Theism." *Stone-Campbell Journal* 5 (2002): 69-92.

———. "The Function of Divine Self-Limitation in Open Theism: Great Wall or Picket Fence?" *Journal of the Evangelical Theological Society* 45 (2002): 279-99.

———. "The Problem with the 'Problem of Evil': A Response to Gregory Boyd's Open Theist Solution." *Restoration Quarterly* 45 (2003): 165-80.

Hill, William J. "Does God Know the Future? Aquinas and Some Moderns." *Theological Studies* 36 (1975): 3-18.

———. "Does the World Make a Difference to God?" *The Thomist* 38 (1974): 146-64.

Hodgson, Leonard. *The Doctrine of the Trinity: Croall Lectures 1942-1943.* New York: Charles Scribner's Sons, 1944.

Hodgson, Peter C. *Winds of the Spirit: A Constructive Christian Theology.* Louisville: Westminster John Knox, 1994.

Holcomb, Justin S. *Christian Theologies of Scripture: A Comparative Introduction.* New York: New York University Press, 2006.

Holmes, Steven R. "'Something Much Too Plain to Say': Towards a Defense of the Doctrine of Divine Simplicity." In *Listening to the Past: The Place of Tradition in Theology*, 50-67. Grand Rapids: Baker Academic, 2002.

Hughes, Christopher. *On a Complex Theory of a Simple God: An Investigation in Aquinas' Philosophical Theology*. Ithaca, NY: Cornell University Press, 1989.

Hume, David. *An Enquiry Concerning Human Understanding*. Kitchener, Ont.: Batoche Books, 2000.

————. *David Hume On Religion*. Edited by Richard Wollheim. New York: Meridian Books, 1964.

Hunt, David. "The Simple Foreknowledge View." In *Divine Foreknowledge: Four Views*, edited by James K. Beilby and Paul R. Eddy, 65-103. Downers Grove, IL: InterVarsity Press, 2001.

Immink, Frederik. *Divine Simplicity*. Kampen, The Netherlands: Uitgeversmaatschappij J. H. Kok-Kampen, 1987.

Jenson, Robert W. "An Ontology of Freedom in the *De Servo Arbitrio* of Luther." *Modern Theology* 10 (1994): 247-52.

————. "Joining the Eternal Conversation: John's Prologue and the Language of Worship." *Touchstone* 14/9 (November 2001).

————. *Systematic Theology*. 2 vols. Oxford: Oxford University Press, 1997, 1999.

————. *The Triune Identity*. Philadelphia: Fortress Press, 1982.

John Paul II, Pope. "The Loving God Has Revealed Himself as Eternity Itself." General Audience, September 4, 1985.

Kant, Immanuel. *Critique of Practical Reason*. Translated by Lewis White Beck. New York: Macmillan, 1956.

————. *Critique of Pure Reason*. Unified Edition. Translated by Werner S. Pluhar. Indianapolis: Hackett Publishers, 1996.

Kaufman, Gordon. *God-Mystery-Diversity: Christian Theology in a Pluralistic World*. Minneapolis: Fortress, 1996.

————. *In the Beginning Creativity*. Minneapolis: Fortress, 2004.

Kaufmann, Yehezkel. *The Religion of Israel: From Its Beginnings to the Babylonian Exile*. Translated by Moshe Greenberg. New York: Schocken Books, 1960.

Kearsley, Roy. "The Impact of Greek Concepts of God in the Christology of Cyril of Alexandria." *Tyndale Bulletin* 43 (1992): 307-29.

Kelly, J. N. D. *Early Christian Doctrines*. New York: Harper and Row, 1960.

Kirk, Russell. *The Conservative Mind: From Burke to Eliot*. 7th rev. ed. Washington, DC: Regnery, 1985.

Kleinig, John. "What's the Use of Praising God?" *Lutheran Theological Journal* 38 (2004): 76-88.

Kondoleon, Theodore J. "The Immutability of God: Some Recent Challenges." *The New Scholasticism* 58 (1984): 293-315.

Krivocheine, Basil. "Simplicity of the Divine Nature and the Distinctions in God, According to St. Gregory of Nyssa." *St. Vladimir's Theological Quarterly* 21/2 (1977): 76-104.

Küng, Hans. *Does God Exist? An Answer for Today*. Translated by Edward Quinn. New York: Vintage Books, 1981.

————. *Justification: The Doctrine of Karl Barth and a Catholic Reflection*. Translated by

436

Thomas Collins, Edmund E. Tolk, and David Granskou. Reprint of 1964 title. Philadelphia: Westminster Press, n.d.

LaCugna, Catherine Mowry. *God for Us: The Trinity and Christian Life.* San Francisco:
HarperCollins, 1991.

Lapide, Pinchas, and Jürgen Moltmann. *Jewish Monotheism and Christian Trinitarian Doctrine.* Translated by Leonard Swidler. Philadelphia: Fortress Press, 1981.

Leftow, Brian. *Time and Eternity.* Ithaca, NY: Cornell University Press, 1991.

Leibniz, Gottfried, and Samuel Clarke. *The Leibniz-Clarke Correspondence.* Edited by H. G.
Alexander. Manchester, England: Manchester University Press, 1978.

Leigh, Edward. *A Treatise of Divinity.* London, 1647.

————. *System or Body of Divinity.* London, 1654.

Lewis, C. S. *The Four Loves.* New York: Harcourt, 1960.

————. *Surprised By Joy: The Shape of My Early Life.* New York: Harcourt Brace Jovanovich,
1955.

Lindbeck, George A. *The Nature of Doctrine: Religion and Theology in a Postliberal Age.*
Philadelphia: Westminster Press, 1984.

Locke, John. *Essay Concerning Human Understanding.* Edited by Maurice Cranston. London: Collier-Macmillan, 1965.

————. *The Reasonableness of Christianity.* Edited by Ian T. Ramsey. Stanford: Stanford
University Press, 1958.

Lonergan, Bernard. *Insight: A Study of Human Understanding.* New York: Harper and Row,
1978.

Lösel, Steffen. "Murder in the Cathedral: Hans Urs von Balthasar's New Dramatization of
the Doctrine of the Trinity." *Pro Ecclesia* 5 (1996): 427-39.

Lossky, Vladimir. *The Mystical Theology of the Eastern Church.* Crestwood, NY: St. Vladimir's, 1985.

Luther's Works. American Edition. Edited by Jaroslav Pelikan and Helmut Lemann. 55 vols.
Philadelphia and St. Louis: Concordia Publishing House, 1955-1986.

Lyons, William. *Emotions.* Cambridge, UK: Cambridge University Press, 1980.

MacIntyre, Alasdair. *Three Rival Versions of Moral Enquiry: Encyclopedia, Genealogy, and
Tradition.* Notre Dame, IN: University of Notre Dame Press, 1990.

————. *Whose Justice? Which Rationality?* Notre Dame, IN: University of Notre Dame
Press, 1988.

MacDonald, George. *George MacDonald: 365 Readings.* Edited by C. S. Lewis. New York:
Macmillan, 1986.

Mackie, John. *The Miracle of Theism.* Oxford: Oxford University Press, 1982.

Macquarrie, John. *Principles of Christian Theology.* 2nd ed. New York: Scribner's, 1976.

Maddox, Mickey L. "Martin Luther." In *Christian Theologies of Scripture,* edited by Justin S.
Holcomb, 94-113. New York: New York University Press, 2006.

Maddox, Randy L. "The Enriching Role of Experience." In *Wesley and the Quadrilateral:
Renewing the Conversation,* edited by W. Stephen Gunter et al., 107-27. Nashville:
Abingdon Press, 1997.

Martin, Thomas F. *Our Restless Heart: The Augustine Tradition.* Maryknoll, NY: Orbis
Books, 2004.

Mascall, E. L. *He Who Is.* London: Libra Books, 1966.

McDonald, Lee Martin. *The Formation of the Christian Biblical Canon.* Revised and enlarged edition. Peabody, MA: Hendrickson, 1995.

McFague, Sallie. *Models of God: Theology for an Ecological, Nuclear Age.* Philadelphia: Fortress Press, 1987.

McWilliams, Warren. *The Passion of God: Divine Suffering in Contemporary Protestant Theology.* Macon: Mercer University Press, 1985.

———. "Trinitarian Doxology: Jürgen Moltmann on the Relation of the Economic and Immanent Trinity." *Perspectives in Religious Studies* 23 (Spring 1996): 25-38.

Meijering, E. P. "A Discussion in Time and Eternity." In *God, Being, History: Studies in Patristic Philosophy,* 81-88. Amsterdam: North-Holland Publishing Company, 1975.

Melanchthon, Philip. *Melanchthon on Christian Doctrine: Loci communes 1555.* Translated and Edited by Clyde L. Manschreck. Grand Rapids: Baker Books, 1965.

Metzger, Bruce M. *The Canon of the New Testament: Its Origin, Development and Significance.* Oxford: Clarendon, 1987.

Molina, Luis. *On Divine Foreknowledge (Part IV of the Concordia).* Translated by Alfred J. Freddoso. Ithaca, NY: Cornell University Press, 1988.

Molnar, Paul D. *Divine Freedom and the Doctrine of the Immanent Trinity: In Dialogue with Karl Barth and Contemporary Theology.* London: T&T Clark, 2002.

———. "The Function of the Trinity in Moltmann's Ecological Doctrine of Creation." *Theological Studies* 51 (1990): 673-97.

Moltmann, Jürgen. *The Crucified God: The Cross of Christ as the Foundation and Criticism of Christian Theology.* Translated by R. A. Wilson and John Bowden. New York: Harper and Row, 1974.

———. *God in Creation: A New Theology of Creation and the Spirit of God.* Translated by Margaret Kohl. Minneapolis: Fortress Press, 1993.

———. *The Spirit of Life: A Universal Affirmation.* Translated by Margaret Kohl. Minneapolis: Fortress Press, 1992.

———. *The Trinity and the Kingdom.* Translated by Margaret Kohl. Minneapolis: Fortress Press, 1993.

Moonan, Lawrence. *Divine Power: The Medieval Power Distinction Up to Its Adoption by Albert, Bonaventure, and Aquinas.* New York: Oxford University Press, 1994.

———. "On Dispensing with Omnipotence." *Ephemerides Theologicae Lovanienses* 65 (1989): 60-80.

Moore, George Edward. *Principia Ethica.* Cambridge, UK: Cambridge University Press, 1968.

Morris, Thomas V. "Perfection and Creation." In *Reasoned Faith,* edited by Eleonore Stump, 234-47. Ithaca, NY: Cornell University Press, 1993.

Mosley, J. K. *The Impassibility of God: A Survey of Christian Thought.* Cambridge, UK: Cambridge University Press, 1926.

Muers, Rachel. "Silence and the Patience of God." *Modern Theology* 17 (2001): 85-98.

Muller, Richard A. *God, Creation and Providence in the Thought of Jacob Arminius.* Grand Rapids: Baker, 1991.

———. *Post-Reformation Reformed Dogmatics.* 4 vols. Grand Rapids: Baker Academic, 2003.

Murphy, Mark C. "Divine Command, Divine Will, and Moral Obligation." *Faith and Philosophy* 15 (1998): 3-27.

Nellas, Panayiotis. *Deification in Christ: Orthodox Perspectives on the Nature of the Human Person.* Translated by Norman Russell. Crestwood, NY: St. Vladimir's, 1997.

Neville, Robert. *Creativity and God: A Challenge to Process Theology.* Albany, NY: SUNY Press, 1995.

Newman, J. H. *A Grammar of Assent.* Garden City, NY: Doubleday and Company, 1955.

Nielsen, Niels C., ed. *Religions of the World.* New York: St. Martin's Press, 1983.

Nietzsche, Friedrich. *The Complete Works of Friedrich Nietzsche.* 20 vols. Translated by Thomas Common. Edited by Oscar Levy. Edinburgh: T. N. Foulis, 1909.

O'Hanlon, Gerry, S.J. "Does God Change? — H. U. von Balthasar on the Immutability of God." *Irish Theological Quarterly* 53 (1987): 161-83.

————. *The Immutability of God in the Theology of Hans Urs von Balthasar.* New York: Cambridge University Press, 1990.

Oakley, Frances. "The Absolute and Ordained Power of God in Sixteenth and Seventeenth Century Theology." *Journal of the History of Ideas* 59 (1998): 437-61.

————. *Omnipotence, Covenant and Order: An Excursion in the History of Ideas from Abelard to Leibniz.* Ithaca, NY: Cornell University Press, 1984.

Oden, Thomas. *Systematic Theology.* 3 vols. San Francisco: Harper and Row, 1987.

Olson, Roger. "Trinity and Eschatology: The Historical Being of God in Jürgen Moltmann and Wolfhart Pannenberg." *Scottish Journal of Theology* 36 (1983): 213-27.

Owens Joseph. *An Elementary Christian Metaphysics.* Houston: Center for Thomistic Studies, 1985.

Padgett, Alan. "Eternity as Relative Timelessness." In *God and Time: Four Views,* edited by Gregory E. Gannsle, 92-110. Downers Grove, IL: InterVarsity Press, 2001.

————. *God, Eternity and the Nature of Time.* New York: St. Martin's Press, 1992.

Pailin, David A. "The Utterly Absolute and the Totally Related: Change in God." *New Blackfriars* 68 (1987): 243-55.

Pannenberg, Wolfhart. *Anthropology in Theological Perspective.* Translated by Matthew J. O'Connell. Philadelphia: Westminster, 1985.

————. *Metaphysics and the Idea of God.* Translated by Philip Clayton. Edinburgh: T&T Clark, 1988.

————. *Systematic Theology.* 3 vols. Translated by G. W. Bromiley. Grand Rapids: Eerdmans, 1991-1998.

Papanikolaou, Aristotle. "Divine Energies or Divine Personhood: Vladimir Lossky and John Zizioulas on Conceiving the Transcendent and Immanent God." *Modern Theology* 19 (2003): 357-85.

Pascal. *Pensées.* Translated by A. J. Krailscheimer. London: Penguin Books, 1966.

Pasewark, Kyle A. *A Theology of Power: Being Beyond Domination.* Minneapolis: Fortress Press, 1993.

Pelikan, Jaroslav. *Christianity and Classical Culture: The Metamorphosis of Natural Theology in the Christian Encounter with Hellenism.* New Haven, CT: Yale University Press, 1993.

————. *The Christian Tradition: A History of the Development of Doctrine.* 5 vols. Chicago: University of Chicago Press, 1971-1991.

Perkins, William. *The Works of William Perkins*. Edited by Ian Breward. Berkshire, UK: Sutton Courtenay Press, 1970.

Pictet, Benedict. *Christian Theology*. Translated by Frederick Reyroux. London: Seeley and Burnside, 1834.

Pike, Nelson. "Divine Omniscience and Voluntary Action." *The Philosophical Review* 74 (1965): 27-46.

————. "Omnipotence and God's Ability to Sin." *American Philosophical Quarterly* 6 (1969): 208-16.

Pinnock, Clark. H. "Between Classical and Process Theism." In *Process Theology*, edited by Ronald Nash. Grand Rapids: Baker, 1989.

————. *Most Moved Mover: A Theology of God's Openness*. Grand Rapids: Baker Academic, 2001.

————. "From Augustine to Arminius: A Pilgrimage in Theology." In *The Grace of God, The Will of Man*, edited by Clark Pinnock. Minneapolis: Bethany House Publishers, 1989.

————. "God Limits His Knowledge." In *Predestination & Free Will: Four Views of Divine Sovereignty & Human Freedom*, edited by D. Basinger and R. Basinger. Downers Grove, IL: InterVarsity Press, 1986.

————. "Systematic Theology." In *The Openness of God: A Biblical Challenge to the Traditional Understanding of God*, edited by Clark Pinnock, Richard Rice, John Sanders, et al. Downers Grove, IL: InterVarsity Press, 1994.

Plantinga, Alvin. *Does God Have a Nature?* Milwaukee: Marquette University Press, 1980.

————. "Is Belief in God Properly Basic?" In *Contemporary Perspectives on Religious Epistemology*, edited by R. Douglas Geivett and Brendan Sweetman, 133-44. New York: Oxford University Press, 1992.

————. "Reason and Belief in God." In *Faith and Rationality: Reason and Belief in God*, edited by Alvin Plantinga and Nicholas Wolterstorff, 16-93. Notre Dame, IN: University of Notre Dame Press, 1983.

————. *Warranted Christian Belief*. New York: Oxford, 2000.

Plato. *The Dialogues of Plato*. Translated and edited by Benjamin Jowett. Reprint of 1892 title. Bristol, UK: Thoemmes Press, 1997.

Plotinus. *The Enneads*. Translated by Stephen Mackenna. Abridged by John Dillon. London: Penguin Books, 1991.

Pollard, T. E. "The Impassibility of God." *Scottish Journal of Theology* 8 (1955): 353-64.

Prestige, G. L. *God in Patristic Thought*. London: SPCK, 1975.

Preus, Robert D. *The Theology of Post-Reformation Lutheranism*. 2 vols. St. Louis: Concordia, 1970-1972.

Pritchard, James B., ed. *Ancient Near Eastern Texts Relating to the Old Testament*, 3rd ed. Princeton, NJ: Princeton University Press, 1969.

Quinn, John M. "Triune Self-Giving: One Key to the Problem of Suffering." *The Thomist* 44 (1980): 173-218.

Quinn, Philip. *Divine Commands and Moral Requirements*. Oxford: Clarendon Press, 1978.

Rahner, Karl, ed. *Encyclopedia of Theology: The Concise Sacramentum Mundi*. New York: Crossroad, 1975.

————. "Concerning the Relationship Between Nature and Grace." In *Theological Investigations I: God, Christ, and Mary,* 297-317. New York: Crossroad, 1961.

————. *The Trinity.* Translated by Joseph Donceel. London: Burns and Oates, 1970.

Rahner, Karl, and Herbert Vorgrimler, eds. *Dictionary of Theology.* 2nd ed. New York: Crossroad, 1985.

Ray, John. *The Wisdom of God Manifested in the Works of Creation.* London, 1692.

Rice, Richard. "Biblical Support for a New Perspective." In *The Openness of God: A Biblical Challenge to the Traditional Understanding of God,* edited by Clark Pinnock, Richard Rice, John Sanders, et al., 11-58. Downers Grove, IL: InterVarsity Press, 1994.

————. "Process Theism and the Open View of God." In *Searching for an Adequate God: A Dialogue Between Process and Free Will Theists,* edited by John B. Cobb Jr. and Clark H. Pinnock, 163-200. Grand Rapids: Eerdmans, 2000.

Richards, Jay Wesley. *The Untamed God: A Philosophical Exploration of Divine Perfection, Simplicity and Immutability.* Downers Grove, IL: InterVarsity Press, 2003.

Ridgley, Thomas. *Body of Divinity.* Edited by Rev. John M Wilson. New York: Robert Carter and Brothers, 1855.

Rist, John M. *On Inoculating Moral Philosophy Against God.* Milwaukee: Marquette University Press, 1999.

————. *Real Ethics: Reconsidering the Foundations of Morality.* Cambridge, UK: Cambridge University Press, 2002.

Ritschl, Albrecht. "Metaphysics and Theology." In *Albrecht Ritschl: Three Essays.* Translated by Philip Hefner. Philadelphia: Fortress Press, 1972.

Robson, Michael. "Saint Bonaventure." In *The Medieval Theologians,* edited by G. R. Evans, 187-200. Malden, MA: Blackwell, 2001.

Rogers, Katherin A. "Eternity Has No Duration." *Religious Studies* 30 (1994): 1-16.

————. *Perfect Being Theology.* Edinburgh: Edinburgh University Press, 2002.

————. "The Traditional Doctrine of Divine Simplicity." *Religious Studies* 32 (1996): 165-86.

Rooney, Paul. "Divine Commands and Arbitrariness." *Religious Studies* 31 (1995): 149-65.

Rowe, William L. *Can God Be Free?* Oxford: Clarendon Press, 2004.

————. "Clarke and Leibniz on Divine Perfection and Freedom." *Enlightenment and Dissent* 16 (1997): 60-82.

————. "Divine Freedom." *Stanford Encyclopedia of Philosophy.* Available at http://plato.stanford.edu/entries/divine-freedom/#1 (accessed February 10, 2006).

————. "The Problem of Divine Perfection and Freedom." In *Reasoned Faith,* edited by Eleonore Stump, 223-33. Ithaca, NY: Cornell University Press, 1993.

Rowe, W. V. "Adolf von Harnack and the Concept of Hellenization." In *Hellenization Revisited: Shaping a Christian Response within the Greco-Roman World,* 69-99. Edited by Wendy E. Helleman. Lanham, MD: University Press of America, 1994.

Russell, Bertrand. *Why I Am Not a Christian.* New York: Simon and Schuster, 1957.

Sanders, John. *The God Who Risks: A Theology of Providence.* Downers Grove, IL: InterVarsity Press, 1998.

————. "Historical Considerations." In *The Openness of God: A Biblical Challenge to the Traditional Understanding of God,* edited by Clark Pinnock, Richard Rice, John Sanders, et al., 59-100. Downers Grove, IL: InterVarsity Press, 1994.

Sarot, Marcel. "Patripassionism, Theopaschitism and the Suffering of God: Some Historical and Systematic Considerations." *Religious Studies* 26 (1990): 363-75.

Sartre, Jean Paul. "No Exit." In *Four Contemporary French Plays*. Edited and with an introduction by Ruby Cohn. New York: Random House, 1967.

Schaff, Philip. *The Creeds of Christendom, With a History and Critical Notes*. 3 vols. Revised by David S. Schaff. Reprint of 1931 title. Grand Rapids: Baker Book House, 1990.

Schleiermacher, Friedrich. *The Christian Faith*. Translated by H. R. MacKintosh and J. S. Stewart. Philadelphia: Fortress Press, 1976.

Schmid, Heinrich. *The Doctrinal Theology of the Evangelical Lutheran Church*. 3rd ed. Edited and translated by C. A. Hay and H. E. Jacobs. Minneapolis: Augsburg, 1961.

Scholder, Klaus. *The Birth of Modern Critical Theology: The Origins and Problems of Biblical Criticism in the Seventeenth Century*. Translated by John Bowden. Philadelphia: Trinity Press International, 1990.

Scholem, Gershom G. *Major Trends in Jewish Mysticism*. 3rd ed. Reprint of 1954 title. New York: Schocken, 1961.

Schoonenberg, Piet. "God as Person(al)." In *A Personal God?* Edited by Edward Schillebeeckx and Bas van Iersel. New York: Crossroad, 1977.

Seeberg, Reinhold. *Text-Book of the History of Doctrines*. 2 vols. Translated by Charles Hay. Grand Rapids: Baker Book House, 1977.

Shalkowski, Scott A. "Atheological Apologetics." In *Contemporary Perspectives on Religious Epistemology*, edited by R. Douglas Geivett and Brendan Sweetman, 58-77. New York: Oxford University Press, 1992.

Shults, F. LeRon. *Reforming the Doctrine of God*. Grand Rapids: Eerdmans, 2005.

Sia, Santiago. "The Doctrine of God's Immutability: Introducing the Modern Debate." *New Blackfriars* 68 (1987): 220-31.

Smith, Wilfred Cantwell. *Towards a World Theology*. Philadelphia: Westminster Press, 1981.

Sokolowski, Robert. "Creation and Christian Understanding." In *God and Creation: An Ecumenical Symposium*, edited by David B. Burrell and Bernard McGinn, 179-92. Notre Dame, IN: University of Notre Dame Press, 1990.

———. *Eucharistic Presence: A Study in the Theology of Disclosure*. Washington, DC: The Catholic University of America Press, 1994.

———. *The God of Faith and Reason*. Washington, DC: Catholic University Press, 1995.

Sorabji, Richard. *Time, Creation and the Continuum: Theories in Antiquity and the Early Middle Ages*. Ithaca, NY: Cornell University Press, 1983.

Spurgeon, Charles. *The Metropolitan Tabernacle Pulpit*. 57 vols. Pasadena, TX: Pilgrim Publications, 1969-1980.

Staniloae, Dumitru. "The Holy Trinity: Structure of Supreme Love." In *Theology and the Church*, 73-108. Translated by Robert Barringer. Crestwood, NY: St. Vladimir's, 1980.

———. *The Experience of God*. 2 vols. Translated and edited by Ioan Ionita and Robert Barringer. Brookline, MA: Holy Cross Orthodox Press, 1994, 2000.

Stead, Christopher. "Divine Simplicity as a Problem for Orthodoxy." In *The Making of Orthodoxy: Essays in Honor of Henry Chadwick*, edited by Rowan Williams, 255-69. Cambridge, UK: Cambridge University Press, 1989.

Strauss, Leo. *Natural Right and History*. Chicago: University of Chicago Press, 1950.

Stump, Eleonore. "Persons: Identification and Freedom." *Philosophical Topics* 24 (1996): 183-214.

Stump, Eleonore, and Norman Kretzmann. "Eternity." *Journal of Philosophy* 79 (1981): 429-58.

Sudduth, Michael Czapkay. "The Prospects for 'Mediate': Natural Theology in John Calvin." *Religious Studies* 31 (1995): 53-68.

Swinburne, Richard. *The Coherence of Theism.* Oxford: Clarendon Press, 1977.

Tatarkicwicz, Wladyslaw. "The Great Theory of Beauty and Its Decline." *The Journal of Aesthetics and Art Criticism* 31 (1972): 165-80.

Thomas à Kempis. *The Imitation of Christ.* Translated by Aloysius Croft and Harold Bolton. Peabody, MA: Hendrickson Publishers, 2004.

Tillich, Paul. *Systematic Theology.* 3 vols. Chicago: University of Chicago Press, 1967.

Torrance, Alan. "Is Love the Essence of God?" In *Nothing Greater, Nothing Better: Theological Essays on the Love of God,* edited by Kevin J. Vanhoozer, 114-37. Grand Rapids: Eerdmans, 2001.

Torrance, Thomas F. *The Christian Doctrine of God: One Being, Three Persons.* Edinburgh: T&T Clark, 1996.

———. *Transformation and Convergence in the Frame of Knowledge: Explorations in the Interrelations of Scientific and Theological Enterprise.* Grand Rapids: Eerdmans, 1984.

———. *The Trinitarian Faith: The Evangelical Theology of the Ancient Catholic Church.* Edinburgh: T&T Clark, 1998.

Tugwell, Simon. "Spirituality and Negative Theology." *New Blackfriars* 68 (1987): 257-63.

Turcescu, Lucian. "The Concept of Divine Persons in Gregory of Nyssa's *To His Brother Peter, on the Difference Between Ousia and Hypostasis.*" *The Greek Orthodox Theological Journal* 42 (1997): 63-82.

———. *Gregory of Nyssa and the Concept of Divine Persons.* New York: Oxford University Press, 2005.

Turretin, Francis. *Institutes of Elenctic Theology.* 3 vols. Translated by George Musgrave Giger. Phillipsburg, NJ: Presbyterian and Reformed, 1992.

Ursinus, Zacharias. *Commentary on the Heidelberg Catechism.* Translated by Rev. G. W. Willard. Reprint of 1852 title. Phillipsburg, NJ: Presbyterian and Reformed, n.d.

Van den Brink, Gijsbert. "Capable of Anything? The Omnipotence of God." In *Understanding the Attributes of God,* edited by Gijsbert van den Brink and Marcel Sarot, 139-59. New York: Peter Lang, 1999.

Van den Brom, Luco J. "As Thy New Horizons Beckon: God's Presence in the World." In *Understanding the Attributes of God,* edited by Gijsbert van den Brink and Marcel Sarot, 75-97. New York: Peter Lang, 1999.

———. *Divine Presence in the World: A Critical Analysis of the Notion of Divine Omnipresence.* Kampen, The Netherlands: Kok Pharos Publishing, 1993.

Vanstone, W. H. *The Stature of Waiting.* New York: Seabury, 1983.

Von Rad, Gerhard. *Old Testament Theology.* 2 vols. Translated by D. M. G. Stalker. New York: Harper and Row, 1962.

Wainwright, Geoffrey. "The Praise of God in the Theological Reflection of the Church." *Interpretation* 39 (1985): 34-45.

Wallace, James D. "Excellences and Merit." *The Philosophical Review* 83 (1974): 182-99.

Ware, Bruce A. *God's Lesser Glory: The Diminished God of Open Theism.* Wheaton, IL: Crossway Books, 2000.

Weber, Otto. *Foundations of Dogmatics.* 2 vols. Translated by Darrell L. Guder. Grand Rapids: Eerdmans, 1981.

Weinandy, Thomas G. *Does God Change? The Word's Becoming in the Incarnation.* Still River, MA: St. Bede's Publications, 1985.

———. *Does God Suffer?* Notre Dame, IN: University of Notre Dame Press, 2000.

Westphal, Merold. "Not About Me." *Christian Century* (April 5, 2005): 20-25.

Wheelwright, Philip, ed. *The Presocratics.* New York: The Odyssey Press, 1966.

Whitehead, Alfred North. *Process and Reality: An Essay in Cosmology.* New York: Macmillan, 1929.

Wielenberg, Erik J. *Value and Virtue in a Godless Universe.* New York: Cambridge University Press, 2005.

Wierenga, Edward. "A Defensible Divine Command Theory." *Nous* 17 (1983): 387-407.

William of Ockham. *Philosophical Writings: A Selection.* Translated by Philotheus Boehner. New York: Bobbs-Merrill Co., 1964.

Williams, Daniel H. "Reflections on Retrieving the Tradition and Renewing Evangelicalism: A Response." *Scottish Journal of Theology* 55 (2002): 105-12.

———. *Retrieving the Tradition and Renewing Evangelicalism: A Primer for Suspicious Protestants.* Grand Rapids: Eerdmans, 1999.

Wolterstorff, Nicholas. "Divine Simplicity." In *Philosophical Perspectives,* 5 (1991) *Philosophy of Religion,* edited by James Tomberlin, 531-52. Atascadero, CA: Ridgeview Publishing, 1991.

———. "God Everlasting." In *Contemporary Philosophy of Religion,* edited by S. Cahn and D. Shatz, 77-98. Oxford: Oxford University Press, 1982.

———. *John Locke and the Ethics of Belief.* Cambridge, UK: Cambridge University Press, 1996.

———. "Suffering Love." In *Philosophy and the Christian Faith,* edited by Thomas V. Morris. Notre Dame, IN: University of Notre Dame Press, 1988.

———. "Unqualified Divine Temporality." In *Four Views: God and Time,* edited by Gregory E. Ganssle, 186-213. Downers Grove, IL: InterVarsity Press, 2001.

Zizioulas, John. *Being as Communion.* Crestwood, NY.: St. Vladimir's, 1997.

———. "On Being a Person: Toward an Ontology of Personhood." In *Persons, Divine and Human,* edited by Christoph Schwöbel and Colin Gunton, 33-46. Edinburgh: T&T Clark, 1991.

———. "The Teaching of the Second Ecumenical Council on the Holy Spirit in Historical and Ecumenical Perspective." In *Credo in Spiritum Sanctum,* edited by J. S. Martins. Rome: Libreria Editrice Vaticana, 1983.

Index of Names and Subjects

447

Hegel, G. W. F., 289

Heidegger, Johann, 351

Heidelberg Catechism (Reformed), 63, 358

Hellenistic philosophy and divine impassibility, 376, 381-84

Heraclitus, 248

Herrmann, William, 266

Hilary of Poitiers, 278

Hodgson, Peter, 51

Holiness, divine, 177-83; and divine grace, 200-201; and divine jealousy, 178-79; and divine judgment, 178; and divine mercy, 205-6; and divine wisdom, 220; holy love, 180-81; holy mystery, 181-82; holy opposition, 179-80; and human fear response, 179, 181-82; religion and the domestication of the holy, 182-83; in Scripture, 177-79; and separation, 177, 178; theology of, 179-82

Holmes, Steven, 268, 269, 271, 274

Holy Spirit: and God as Spirit, 243-44; personhood of, 118; Protestant Reformers' view of Scripture's authority and, 33, 34; in Scripture, 116-17

Hopkins, Ezekiel, 281

Hopkins, Samuel, 397

Hume, David: and arguments for God's existence, 91; and divine omnipotence, 342-43; and reason, 42, 44

Huxley, Thomas, 83-84

Hyperius, Andreas, 55

Hippolytus, 383

Ignatius Loyola, 63, 383

Immink, Frederik, 269

Immutability, divine, 358-75; and change, 363-66; contemporary objections to doctrine of, 366-69; contemporary objections, responding to, 369-75; and divine changeability, 360-61, 364; and polarity within God, 372-74; process theology's critique of, 367-69, 370-74, 384-85; and question of God's "responsiveness" to our needs, 374-75; in Scripture, 359-61; theology of, 361-66,

370-71; traditional doctrine, 361-63, 366-70. *See also* Impassibility, divine

"The Immutability of God" (Clarke), 367

Impassibility, divine, 375-89; and Christology, 388; contemporary critics of, 380-89; defining, 375; divine love and human suffering, 386-89; function in traditional theology, 377-79; and God's suffering, 384-85; Hellenization theory, 381-84; and pagan religion, 378; and passion, 376-77, 379-80; and the problem of evil, 381, 385; in Scripture, 375-76; and the suffering of Jesus Christ, 381, 386-87, 388-89; traditional doctrine, 376-80. *See also* Immutability, divine

Incarnation: and divine eternity, 310; and divine omnipotence, 343-44; and divine omniscience, 319-20

Incomprehensibility, divine, 143-44

In the Beginning Creativity (Kaufman), 52

Irenaeus, bishop of Lyon: and the Christian canon, 23; and divine freedom, 223; and divine impassibility, 378, 382; and tradition, 35

"Is God Essentially God" (Sennett), 229

Jenson, Robert, 133, 145, 244, 253

Jerome, 347

John of Damascus, 63; and divine immutability, 364; and divine incomprehensibility, 144; and divine omnipotence, 335; and divine omnipresence, 279, 284, 286; and divine omniscience, 321, 322; and divine simplicity, 262, 271, 273; and doctrine of the Trinity, 134, 271, 273; and method of theology, 55

Junius, Franciscus, 5

Justin Martyr, 63, 277, 378

Kabbalah, 121

Kant, Immanuel: and natural revelation, 18; rejection of arguments for God's existence, 91-92, 95-96

Kaufman, Gordon, 51-52

Kaufmann, Yehezkel, 228

Kempis, Thomas à, 411-12

313-15; and self-knowledge, 312-13;
Socinians, 326; sources of God's foreknowledge, 330-31; theological tradition and critics, 321-29; theology of,
315-20; and the Trinity, 318
On Loving God (Bernard of Clairvaux),
164
On the Trinity (Augustine), 130
Open theism: and divine immutability,
367, 370; and divine omniscience, 327-
28, 329, 330; and problem of evil, 328;
and traditional grammar of talking
about God, 151-53
Oration On Holy Baptism (Gregory
Nazianzus), 138
Origen, 360
The Orthodox Faith (John of Damascus),
144
Orthodox theology: and the divine attributes, 143-44, 153-54; and divine incomprehensibility, 143-44; and the in-
communicable attributes, 153-54; and
natural revelation, 12; and reason, 41
Owen, H. P., 232n.29
Owen, John, 154, 185
Owens, Joseph, 90, 142

Padgett, Alan G., 301-2
Paganism: and arbitrariness of divine
command, 406-7; and divine
impassibility, 378; and the existence of
God, 73-74, 86-87; pagan gods/idols in
Scripture, 256-57; and personhood of
God, 246-51; perspective on divine
substance, 229
Palamas, Gregory, 63
Panentheism, 288-89
Pannenberg, Wolfhart, 7, 167, 195, 243
Pantheism, 288-89
Papanikolaou, Aristotle, 251n.71
Parmenides, 247
"Pascal's wager," 97
Paseward, Kyle, 338
Patience of God, 206-12; defining, 207-8;
and divine love, 206; and divine self-
limitation theories, 209-11, 212, 221; and
divine wisdom, 220-21; as freely exer-

cised, 208-11; Jesus Christ as patience
incarnate, 211-12; in Scripture, 206-7;
theology of, 207-12
Paul of Samosata, Bishop of Antioch, 127
Pelikan, Jaroslav, 223-24
Perfection. *See* Immutability, divine;
Impassibility, divine
Perichoresis, 134-35, 290, 308
Perkins, William: definition of theology,
53; and divine omnipotence, 337; and
divine omnipresence, 281; and divine
simplicity, 263-64
Personhood of God, 244-54; and definitions of "person," 251-52; and divine
freedom, 252-54; and divine simplicity,
274; and Greek polytheistic religion,
246-51; personhood of the Father, 117-
18; personhood of the Holy Spirit, 118;
personhood of the Son, 118; in Scripture, 117-18, 245; texts that unify the
persons, 119; theology of, 245-54; tri-
personal love (the Trinity), 117-18, 249-
54. *See also* Trinity, doctrine of
Philosophical theology, 65-66
Physics: and concept of time, 299-300;
divine space and created space, 287
Pictet, Benedict: and divine immutability,
362-63; and divine omnipotence, 336;
and divine omnipresence, 281, 290; and
divine simplicity, 263; and reason, 40
Pike, Nelson, 348n.78
Pinnock, Clark, 267, 268, 326-27
Plantinga, Alvin, 75-76, 80, 267-69
Plato: and atheism, 81; on becoming and
being, 248; concept of beauty, 392; and
God's arbitrary commands, 406-7;
ideal forms of, 243
Plotinus, 4, 5-6, 249, 301
Polanus, Amandus: and the divine attributes, 154n.40; and divine immutabil-
ity, 366; and revelation, 5; and the will
of God, 409
Polanyi, Michael, 56
Polycarp, 63
Post-Reformation Reformed and Lu-
theran theologians: and biblical names
of God, 158; and biblical "proof-

456

Index of Scripture References

CPSIA information can be obtained
at www.ICGtesting.com
Printed in the USA
JSHW020917230723
45108JS00004B/207